Richard Morris is Director of the Council for British
Archaeology. He is the author of *Cathedrals and Abbeys
of England and Wales* and *The Church in British Archaeology*.

CHURCHES
IN THE
LANDSCAPE

Richard Morris

A PHOENIX GIANT PAPERBACK

First published in Great Britain by J. M. Dent & Sons Ltd in 1989
This paperback edition published in 1997
by Phoenix, a division of Orion Books Ltd,
Orion House, 5 Upper St Martin's Lane,
London WC2H 9EA

A CIP catalogue record for this book
is available from the British Library.

ISBN: 0 75380 117 5

Printed and bound in Great Britain by
Butler & Tanner Ltd, Frome and London

CONTENTS

List of figures		vii
List of tables		xi
List of plates		xiii
County abbreviations		xv
Acknowledgements		xvii
Introduction		I
I	Roads from Rome	6
II	A voice from the well	46
III	*Mynster, monasterium*	93
IV	Mushrooms in the night?	140
V	In the towns: c.850–1100	168
VI	Mottes, moats, and manors	227
VII	A sense of style	275
VIII	Time and tide	316
IX	All Christian souls	350
X	Anglicans and arcadians	377
XI	The inward witness	388
	Afterword	451
	Notes on the plates	454
	Bibliography	467
	Index	493

FIGURES

1 Areas of pagan and Christian culture in southern Britain, *c.*600
2 Episcopal sees in seventh- and eighth-century southern Britain
3 Places mentioned in the writings of Bede
4 Seventh-century ecclesiastical geography of Canterbury
5 St Martin, Canterbury: south elevation of chancel
6 St Martin, Canterbury: interior elevation of west wall of nave
7 St Martin, Canterbury: plan
8 Distribution of parish churches dedicated to saints Vincent, Vedast, Medard, Radegund and Maurice
9 Great Chesterford, Essex: location of church against selected features of Romano-British topography
10 Ilchester, Somerset
11 Wells, Somerset: site of sub- or post Roman mausoleum
12 Ecclesiastical geography of St Albans
13 Lullingstone, Kent: chapel superimposed upon Roman mausoleum
14 Distribution of parish churches dedicated to saints Bride and Olave
15 Distribution of parish churches dedicated to St Michael
16 Distribution of dedications to St Michael, generalized by trend surface
17 Old English place-names of possible pagan significance
18 Knowlton, Dorset
19 Old English buildings and enclosures at Malmesbury, Wiltshire, Cowdery's Down, Hampshire, Northampton and Yeavering, Northumberland
20 Sticks laid in eleventh- and twelfth-century graves at Lund, Sweden
21 Outline chronology and travels of some British and Irish churchmen in the fifth and sixth centuries

LIST OF FIGURES

22 Christian memorials of the period c.400–700 and 'martyrium' names
23 Cuthbert's *monasterium* on Farne: a conjectural reconstruction
24 Church Island, Co. Kerry
25 Evidence for religious communities in northern England and North Wales before c.875
26 Parishes along the 'Street' between Malton and Hovingham, North Yorkshire
27 Yorkshire minsters identifiable from literary sources
28 Pocklington and its neighbours
29 Ecclesiastical provision in Yorkshire, c.600–875
30 Structure of recorded growth in ecclesiastical provision, c.600–720
31 Graph of the occurrence of references to churches and priests in Domesday Book
32 Groups of parishes in Yorkshire
33 Ecclesiastical geography of the Tees/Swale interfluve
34 Church and associated graves at Raunds, Northamptonshire
35 Place-names which embody the elements *kirk*, *church*, *stow* and *minster*
36 Place-names which embody names of saints, possible owners, positional and other descriptive terms
37 Estimated growth in ecclesiastical provision: (*a*) flows showing plausible limits c.600–1100; (*b*) 1100–1801
38 Twelfth-century ranges in ecclesiastical provision in towns of pre-Conquest origin
39 Lincoln: local churches present by c.1110
40 Parish churches in Norwich
41 York: site of putative *wic*, and later churches
42 Churches, towns and the rank size rule (arithmetic)
43 *Hamwic* and *Hamtun*
44 Churches, towns and the rank size rule (log)
45 Winchester and its churches
46 Colchester: churches, streets and elements of the underlying Roman layout
47 Exeter and its churches
48 Influences of surroundings upon plans of two urban churches
49 Chichester and its churches
50 Wallingford and its churches
51 Oxford and its churches
52 Parish of St Mary-le-Port, Bristol
53 Bristol and its churches
54 Barton-upon-Humber, Humberside
55 Lichfield and its churches
56 Chard, Somerset: diagram of town layout, showing street-sited buildings
57 Canterbury and its churches
58 York: tentative reconstruction of seventh-century land grant
59 Wareham and its churches

60 Distribution of churches dedicated to St Botolph
61 St Mark's, Lincoln: structural development
62 Raunds, Northamptonshire: topographical development
63 Four groups of parishes on contrasting terrain
64 Parishes on the limestone escarpment north of Lincoln
65 Formation of a cemetery platform around a church on an elevated site
66 Aller, Somerset
67 Four mechanisms for village formation
68 Settlements of regular plan in the Vale of Pickering, Yorkshire
69 Proximity of churches and manorial sites in Essex
70 Churches and mottes in Herefordshire
71 St Peter's, Barton-upon-Humber: structural development
72 Repton, Derbyshire
73 All Saints, Laughton-en-le-Morthen, Yorkshire: plan
74 Sulgrave, Northamptonshire: church and ringwork
75 Old Erringham, Sussex: church within ringwork
76 Church Norton, Sussex: church and ringwork
77 Churches and mottes at Meppershall, Bedfordshire, Ashley, Hampshire and Kilpeck, Herefordshire
78 Pleshey, Essex
79 Richard's Castle, Herefordshire
80 Weaverthorpe, Yorkshire: church and manorial enclosure
81 Goltho, Lincolnshire
82 Goltho: outline evolution of buildings and defences in the ninth–eleventh centuries
83 Caerau, Ely, Glamorgan
84 Marston Trussell, Northamptonshire: church and moat
85 Parish churches in Lincolnshire: (a) distribution of churches with surviving spires; (b) distribution of spires, by type
86 Parish churches with rich twelfth-century embellishment in Yorkshire
87 Nave areas of local churches in use between c.900 and c.1050
88 Nave areas of local churches in use between c.1050 and c.1150
89 Long-term flows in the English medieval population
90 Areal development and use of space in a parish church between 1100 and 1300
91 Stainburn, Yorkshire: south elevation of parochial chapel
92 Stainburn, Yorkshire: plan showing reconstructed scheme of lighting
93 Rivenhall, Essex: plan of church, with reconstructed scheme of natural lighting
94 (a) Distribution of churches with long-and-short quoins, megalithic side-alternate quoins and pilaster strips; (b) Jurassic and Permian stones
95 (a) General distribution of waterleaf capitals (inset: waterleaf capital); (b) general distribution of trumpet scallop capitals
96 Medieval centres of quarrying for building stone

LIST OF FIGURES

97 Schematic representation of (*a*) the progress towards collapse of a neglected building, and (*b*) deferral of collapse by intervention maintenance

98 Distribution of surviving parish churches built wholly or partly of wood

99 Rates of recorded abandonment of parish churches in Norfolk

100 Contraction of ecclesiastical provision between 1300 and 1700 in Canterbury, York, Winchester and Norwich

101 Beverley, Humberside

102 Siltlands and peatlands in the East Anglian fens

103 Adderbury, Oxfordshire: plan of chancel

104 Adderbury: costs of project between 1408 and 1419

105 Adderbury: breakdown of expenditure in 1413–14

106 Graph of exports of wool and cloth, 1350–1510

107 Use of space within Holy Trinity, Coventry, in early sixteenth century

108 Unions of parishes in York in the sixteenth century

109 Holdenby, Northamptonshire: plan of garden remains

110 Growth in ecclesiastical provision and population, 1700–1910

111 Kendal, Cumbria: location of Friends' meeting-house

112 Denbigh: location of Lord Leicester's church

113 Denbigh: plan of Lord Leicester's church

114 Distribution of works of church building, alteration and enlargement, *c*.1540–*c*.1700

115 Distribution of surviving furnishings and fittings introduced into churches in Dorset, *c*.1550–*c*.1700

116 Wren's design for a new London, 1666

117 Plans of four London churches rebuilt by Wren after the Great Fire

118 Liverpool, *c*.1670

119 Birmingham in the later eighteenth century

120 Urban and rural mortality in the first half of the nineteenth century: a comparison of examples

121 Idle, Yorkshire: plan of Commissioners' church built 1828–30

122 Commissioners' churches: rates of building between 1818 and 1856

123 Commissioners' churches: stylistic preferences between 1818 and 1856

124 Cambridge Camden Society's vision of an ideal church layout

125 Leeds, Yorkshire, on the eve of industrial expansion

126 Sources of finance for churchbuilding in nineteenth-century Lancashire

TABLES

1 Dates of origin of local churches, established by archaeological investigations: a sample list
2 Urban populations and church-room in the eleventh century
3 Some resource implications of a late Saxon town
4 The condition of church fabrics and cemeteries in Kent as revealed by the visitations of archbishop Warham and his deputies in 1511 and 1512

LIST OF PLATES

Between pages 236 and 237

*For full captions see **Notes on the Plates**, pages 454–66*

1 Jewry Wall and church of St Nicholas, Leicester
2 Church of St Mary and megalithic remains at Stanton Drew, Somerset
3 St John, Stanwick, North Yorkshire
4 St Paul's church, Jarrow, Tyne & Wear
5 Burry Holms, Glamorgan
6 Llangwyfan, Anglesey
7 St Peter, Bradwell-on-Sea, Essex
8 Breedon-on-the-Hill, Leicestershire
9 St Ninian Ninekirks, Cumbria
10 Llandyfaelog, Dyfed
11 Odda's Chapel, Deerhurst, Gloucestershire
12 Site of church at Itteringham, Norfolk
13 Reepham, Norfolk
14 St Martin, Cwmyoy, Gwent
15 St Michael, Duntisbourne Rous, Gloucestershire
16 Melverley, Shropshire
17 St Michael, Burrow Mump, in the Somerset Levels
18 East Witton, North Yorkshire
19 Church and manor house at Great Chalfield, Wiltshire
20 Church and manor house at Holcombe Rogus, Devon
21 Church, ringwork and mound at Earl's Barton, Northamptonshire

22 Burial mound in churchyard at Taplow, Buckinghamshire
23 Laughton-en-le-Morthen, South Yorkshire: church of All Saints and motte-and-bailey castle
24 Church and ringwork at Culworth, Northamptonshire
25 Kilpeck, Herefordshire: church and site of village within castle enclosure
26 Castle Rising, Norfolk
27 St Catherine's chapel, Abbotsbury, Dorset
28 St Mary, Edlesborough, Buckinghamshire
29 St Mary the Virgin, Up Waltham, Sussex
30 St Edmund, Southwold, Suffolk
31 Settlement in retreat: Birkby, North Yorkshire
32 Eglwys Gymun, Dyfed
33 Argham: a lost village and church on the Yorkshire wolds
34 Ruined church at Little Hautbois, Coltishall, Norfolk
35 Egmere, Norfolk: ruined church and deserted settlement
36 New Winchelsea, Sussex
37 St James, Barton-under-Needwood, Staffordshire
38 Staunton Harold, Leicestershire
39 Fawsley, Northamptonshire: church of St Mary, mansion and park
40 St James, Great Packington, Warwickshire
41 St George-in-the-East, London
42 St Alkmund, Whitchurch, Shropshire
43 Mow Cop, on the Cheshire/Staffordshire border
44 Boyne Hill, Maidenhead, Berkshire
45 Cheltenham, Gloucestershire
46 St Bartholomew, Ann Street, Brighton, Sussex
47 All Souls, Haley Hill, Halifax, West Yorkshire
48 Saltaire, West Yorkshire
49 Llangelynin, Gwynedd

COUNTY ABBREVIATIONS

So many places are mentioned in the text that it seemed worthwhile to save space by abbreviating the names of the counties in which they lie. A key to the contractions used is given below.

The adoption of this system turned out to be a source of some anguish and not a little difficulty. The hardest decision was over whether to use the names and areas of counties as they existed before 1974, or after the reorganization of that year. I have no love for the new county structure, and the older counties make much more sense in relation to a book like this. On the other hand, it seems foolish to pretend that the new counties do not exist, and realistic to acknowledge that there is a coming generation of readers who have never known any others. Hence the general policy has been to indicate the counties of today, but where these differ from counties that existed before reorganization, to give the name of the pre-1974 county in brackets.

Here and there this policy has been varied, chiefly in order to minimize unnecessary duplication of new and old county names that are very similar. Thus a place now in West Yorkshire, formerly in the West Riding, will be followed simply by *WY*. But if the place had previously been in the North Riding, the designation would be *WY* (*YN*). Other counties similarly affected include Cumbria/Cumberland, Herefordshire and Worcestershire. In these latter two cases I have dispensed with the modern county altogether, as it seemed silly to name both Hereford and Worcester and then to have to name one of them again.

Changed boundaries may have caused me to misplace a few sites in relation to modern counties. If this has occurred, I would be glad to have the errors pointed out.

COUNTY ABBREVIATIONS

Abd	Aberdeenshire		La	Lancashire
Angl	Anglesey		Le	Leicestershire
Av	Avon		Li	Lincolnshire
Bd	Bedfordshire		M	Merseyside
Brk	Berkshire		Mon	Monmouthshire
Brcn	Brecknock		Mnt	Montgomery
Bu	Buckinghamshire		Mrn	Merioneth
Crn	Caernarvon		Mx	Middlesex
Ca	Cambridgeshire		Nf	Norfolk
Crg	Cardigan		Np	Northamptonshire
Carm	Carmarthen		Nb	Northumberland
Ch	Cheshire		NY	North Yorkshire
Clv	Cleveland		Nt	Nottinghamshire
Cld	Clwyd		O	Oxfordshire
Co	Cornwall		Pmb	Pembroke
Cu	Cumberland/Cumbria		Pws	Powys
Dnb	Denbigh		Rad	Radnor
Db	Derbyshire		Rx	Roxburgh
D	Devon		Ru	Rutland
Do	Dorset		Sa	Shropshire
Du	Durham		So	Somerset
Dfd	Dyfed		SY	South Yorkshire
Ex	Essex		St	Staffordshire
Fl	Flint		Sf	Suffolk
Glm	Glamorgan		Sr	Surrey
Gl	Gloucestershire		Sx	Sussex/East & West Sussex
GLo	Greater London			
GMa	Greater Manchester		TW	Tyne & Wear
Gnt	Gwent		Wa	Warwickshire
Gwd	Gwynedd		WM	West Midlands
Ha	Hampshire		We	Westmorland
He	Herefordshire		WY	West Yorkshire
Hrt	Hertfordshire		Wi	Wiltshire
Hu	Humberside		Wo	Worcestershire
Hnt	Huntingdonshire		YE	Yorkshire, East Riding
IoW	Isle of Wight		YN	Yorkshire, North Riding
K	Kent		YW	Yorkshire, West Riding

Note on references

References for facts, arguments or quotations are given by the 'Harvard' or author–year system. In this system references are embedded in the body of the text, and consist of the author's name, the year of publication or edition cited, and (if relevant) page number(s). Named references are gathered into a single alphabetical sequence in the Bibliography at the end of the book.

ACKNOWLEDGEMENTS

The author and publisher are indebted for permission to reproduce passages from published works: to Professor Asa Briggs for extracts from *Victorian Cities*; to Cambridge University Press for the extract from Bertram Colgrave's translation of Bede's Life of Cuthbert; to Dr James Stevens Curl and Constable Ltd for quotations from *A celebration of death*; to Oxford University Press for passages from Bede's *Ecclesiastical History*, translated and edited by B.Colgrave and R.A.B.Mynors (1969), Marjory Chibnall's translation of the *Ecclesiastical History* of Orderic Vitalis (1973), Dr P.Godman's translation of Alcuin's poem on the kings, bishops, and saints of York (1982), and M.R.Watts's book *The Dissenters* (1978); to Macmillan London Ltd for the extract from Thomas Hardy's novel *Far from the Madding Crowd*; to A.R.Mowbray Ltd for the extracts from Benedicta Ward and Norman Russell' *Lives of the Desert Fathers*; to Simon Keynes and Michael Lapidge for the passage from *Alfred the Great* published by Penguin Books Ltd; to Professor Michael Port for the quotations from *Fifty New Churches*; and to W.Smith for the extract from *The Register of Richard Clifford*. Extended quotations from essays in journals and collections of papers have been used by kind permission of the following scholars: Dr John Blair, Dr Margaret Gelling, Professor E.P.Hennock, Dr Derek Keene, Rev J.M.Turner, and Dr Patrick Wormald. Extracts from translations of original sources in volumes 1, 2, and 5 of *English Historical Documents* have been used with the consent of Eyre & Spottiswoode. For permission to base figures upon drawings produced by others special gratitude is extended to Fred Aldsworth (76), Mick Aston (10, 56, 79), Brian Ayers (40), Steven Bassett (55), Neil Batcock (99), Professor Martin Biddle (45, 72), Guy Beresford (81, 82), David Butler (111),

ACKNOWLEDGEMENTS

Dr Lawrence Butler (86, 112, 113), Graham Cadman, Andrew Boddington and Northamptonshire County Council (34, 62), Canterbury Archaeological Trust (4, 57), Alan Carter (40), City of Lincoln Archaeological Trust (61), Philip Crummy (46), Dr Margaret Gelling (17), Macmillan Educational Ltd (89), Dr David Hill and Basil Blackwell (102), Eric Holden (75), Laurence Keen (59), Martin Millett (19c), Julian Munby (49), Oxford Archaeological Unit (50, 51), Professor David Palliser (108), Professor Colin Platt (43), Professor Philip Rahtz and Lorna Watts (52), Derek Renn (70), Dr Warwick Rodwell (11, 54, 71, 93), RCAHM Wales (83), RCHME (18, 19a, 74, 84, 101, 109, 117), Peter Ryder (73), David Stocker (85), Tim Tatton-Brown (5, 6, 7), C.C.Taylor (67), Dr Harold Taylor (94), Frances Williams (78), John Williams (19b), and Ann Woodward (66).

TO MY MOTHER AND FATHER

INTRODUCTION

Most people in southern Britain dwell within sight or sound of a church. Church on the corner, church on the hill: there are more than 18,000 of them. Parts of the English countryside are so lavishly provided with churches that a visitor who climbs the tower of one will see a dozen others. There are towns of pre-Conquest origin, like London or Norwich, wherein the pedestrian can pass the sites of fifteen medieval churches in as many minutes.

Richly varied in form, style, size and materials, redolent of so much in our history that makes us what we are, our parish churches belong in the vanguard of the greatest national achievements, not least because many of them were products of local endeavour. There are those utterly simple, like Llanfaglan *Crn*; ancient and numinous, like Deerhurst *Gl*; capacious, like Holy Trinity at Hull *Hu* (*YE*) or St Peter Mancroft in Norwich; lofty, like Boston *Li*; or low and solid, like Tickencote *Le* (*Ru*). Tideswell *Db* is known thereabouts as the 'cathedral of the Peak', and there are other grand buildings which have been similarly designated by local acclaim: Altarnun *Co*, 'the cathedral of the moors'; Newland *Gl*, deep in the Forest of Dean, the 'cathedral of the forest'; Westwell *K*, 'the village cathedral'; or the Edwardian St Andrew's at Roker *Du*, the 'cathedral of the arts and crafts movement'. At the far extreme are pygmy buildings such as Nether Wasdale *Cu*, Culbone *So* or Capel-y-ffin *Brcn* which vie for the status of the smallest church of all.

It comes as no surprise to find that many good books about churches have already been written. So many, in fact, and some so recently, that the author who is about to embark upon another must fall victim to self-doubt. Is there really anything more that needs to be said?

INTRODUCTION

Two reasons argue that there is. First, the notion that historical study can ever be finished is a fallacy. Finding out about the past is not a process of heaping up facts until none are left to be put onto the pile. As time passes, existing methods of investigation are improved and new ones become available. Old data are opened to reinterrogation; former interpretations may be revised in the light of information to which our predecessors did not have access. In practice this cycle of re-evaluation is not smoothly continuous. Rather, it is characterized by periods which alternate, often spasmodically, between movement and arrest. The present condition is one of movement. Archaeology, in particular, has recently emerged as a generous provider of new knowledge about churches (Rodwell 1981). This justifies fresh writing.

Second, there is one aspect of the parish church which up to now has been largely overlooked. This is the subject of the parish church as a place, a component of the pattern of settlement, and churches together as a pattern of places.

Throughout the nineteenth century and for much of our own there has been a tendency to discuss the parish church in detachment from its surroundings. True, location may enter where it is unusually striking, as in the case of St Michael Brentor *D*, which is dizzily perched upon the eroded summit of an extinct volcano; or a matter of exceptional loveliness, like (say) St Mary at Llanbrynmair *Mon*. But where settings have been noticed, as they often were in the deftly written entries to the Collins *Guide* (Betjeman 1958), or in the volumes of the *Buildings of England* series (Pevsner 1951–76), the treatment has generally been a matter of aesthetic appreciation rather than historical analysis.

In fairness, it is proper to record that there have been compelling reasons for this concentration. During the nineteenth century antiquaries were fully occupied, first with laying foundations for the discipline of architectural history, later with establishing an architectural vocabulary for the Gothic Revival, and then with the working out of a philosophy for the care of old buildings. More recently scholars and photographers have devoted themselves to the production of serviceable general studies: books which describe the architectural and artistic development of the parish church; or to particularistic inquiries into such topics as bells, stained glass and wall-paintings. Further, churches have rather lent themselves to disembodied treatment, because most of them are appreciably younger in fabric than they are in site. It is, for instance, possible to enter hundreds of churches mentioned in Domesday Book (1086) and there to see fabric no older than the fourteen or fifteenth century. Many churches erected during the reign of Victoria occupy sites which were turned to ecclesiastical use a thousand years ago. Understandably enough, commentators have preferred to discuss the buildings as they see them, not least because their training has normally been in the realms of art and architectural history rather than in landscape archaeology. In any case, we may suspect that the sheer familiarity of the church as part of the local scene had something of an anaesthetic effect upon scholarly curiosity. To many, the church is simply 'there', and being so its position no more appears to call for comment or explanation than does that of the village pub or primary school.

Finally, we should note that landscape archaeology is itself young. As recently as 1955 Professor W.G.Hoskins could observe that 'there is not one book which deals with the historical evolution of the landscape as we know it'. Today, thirty years on, landscape history has attracted its own practitioners, a philosophy, a dedicated journal, and even its own proselytizing Society for Landscape Studies. While it is true that the landscape itself 'is a palimpsest on to which each generation inscribes its own impressions and removes some of the marks of earlier generations' (Aston and Rowley 1974, 14), the disentanglement and interpretation of that palimpsest calls for co-operation between scholars of many different trainings. Here lies the basic reason for the avoidance of the subject of churches as places: until very recently only a supremely self-confident dilettante or a consortium of authors could ever have entertained such a project. That no one did so is thus neither cause for surprise nor reproach. A specialized study of this sort could not have been conceived in advance of the birth of the genre that is its parent.

Churches *are* places. Although in terms of area the medieval parochial sites of England and Wales do not amount to much – maybe twenty square miles in total, or about 0.039 per cent of the land-surface – quantitatively, as we have seen, these places are far more significant. Most of the *c.* 12,000 ancient sites represent decisions taken before the thirteenth century, sometimes long before, when churches were located in relation to other components of the pattern of settlement – roads, dwellings, cemeteries, fortifications, fields, earlier places of worship – some or all of which may since have been altered or disappeared. Thus it is that a delightful twelfth-century church, complete with apse, is all that survives to remind us of the former rural village of East Ham that was engulfed by London's dockland. On the edge of Billingham *Du*, a place of flaring stacks and chimneys, now much devoted to the manufacture of chemicals, there stands a church with a slender Anglo-Saxon tower. Within, carved stones testify to an ecclesiastical presence at the spot by the first half of the eighth century. At Church Wilne *Db* the church stands alone, 'surrounded by the derelict lagoons and quicksands of the Hoveringham Gravel Company' (Usher 1978, 6). The medieval church of Fawley *Ha* beside Southampton Water is now dominated by an oil refinery. St Bridget and St John at Beckermet *Cu* keep company with the nuclear reprocessing plant at Sellafield. Few motorists who travel along the A1 past the power station at Ferrybridge *WY* realize that the site of a church established more than nine hundred years ago lies at the feet of the cooling towers.

These industrial juxtapositions lead us to think of the parish church as a stable point in a changing landscape. While accepting this as a general principle it would be wrong to underestimate the strength of forces which could lead to change. Not all churches occupy their original sites. Some have been relocated. Others were abandoned, left to fall down and never replaced. If only 1 per cent of churches were so discarded in each century between 1100 and 1900, this would have involved a minimum of eight hundred buildings: the equivalent of all the churches in a very large medieval diocese. Fluidity, as well as immobility, must therefore find a place in our thinking.

A church is a place on the ground. It is also distinguished as a holy place. Historically, the holy place has been conceived as the site of an encounter between the human and the divine:

> Draw not nigh hither: put off thy shoes from off thy feet, for the place whereon thou standest is holy ground.
>
> (Exodus 3:5)

Holy places are meeting-places, points of convergence between the material and the spiritual, temporal and eternal, natural and supernatural, earth and heaven (Cope 1972, 6-8).

Churches are unusual, however, in that they bind together functions which in most other religions have been kept separate. In the Graeco-Roman world a holy site was typically characterized by an enclosure or *temenos* which was accessible to visitors, and a focal shrine or temple which was the abode of a deity. Such arrangements were essentially non-congregational.

Judaism at the time of Christ recognized two types of religious structure: the temple, which was unique, and the synagogue, which was a meeting-house. The eventual contribution of Christianity was to unite these two functions in church buildings which were at once congregational meeting-places and houses of divine residence. On occasion there was a triple fusion which assimilated the site of an ancient, traditional sacred place as well.

Christians discarded the locational preferences of other religions for the further reason that they developed a predilection for superimposing their temples upon graves. The human remains of saints and martyrs were thought to radiate power. It was believed that saints were close to God, yet accessible to humans. In consequence, churches were raised over saints' tombs. And, because human remains are portable, saintly power could be transferred from one place to another.

Saints were not the only people to be buried in or beside churches, although they were the first to be so. In time the privilege was extended, so that from the ninth century to the eighteenth almost everyone in western Europe was interred in consecrated ground. It has been calculated that the remains of upwards of 100 million people lie within British churchyards alone. In Wales and in England the parish church which perches upon a thick platform of burials is a familiar sight. This juxtaposition between the community of the living at prayer and the community of the dead awaiting resurrection has rendered the church-place outstanding in yet one more sense.

If, for reasons outlined above, a study of churches as places is now due, it is far from obvious what such a study should encompass, or how it should be organized. There are no full precedents for this book, and writing it has not been easy. The task has been made harder by a self-imposed decision not to dwell unduly upon freaks and mysteries. Why is there an isolated church inside the Neolithic henge at Knowlton *Do*? What prompted medieval builders to put a church atop Glastonbury Tor *So*? How should we explain the presence of two churches inside one church-yard at Alvingham *Li*? Such curiosities could be multiplied, probably to the extent of providing sufficient material for a complete book. Perhaps someone will write it. Strangeness is not excluded here, but the main aim is to elucidate that which was persistent.

It remains for me to thank my helpers. This book has been long in the making – far too long, according to my family – and the patience of its publishers leaves me much in their debt. The work would have been more protracted still if I had not had the benefit of information, advice or criticism from many friends and colleagues: Ken Adams, Fred Aldsworth, Dr N. Allen, Mick Aston, Professor Richard Bailey, Stephen Bassett, Martin Biddle, Elizabeth Bishop, Elizabeth Briggs, Andrew Boddington, Eric Cambridge, Dr Wendy Childs, Dr James Stevens Curl, David Dawson, Derek Edwards, Dr Margaret Faull, Donald Findlay, Tim Gates, Mrs Margaret Gelling, Dr Richard Gem, Frances Griffith, Michael Hare, Carolyn Heighway, Eric Holden, Nancy Holindrake, John Holmes, Heather James, Dr Jim Lang, Richard Kemp, Harry Kenward, Alan Meredith, Arthur Owen, Professor David Palliser, David Parsons, Professor Philip Rahtz, Dr Warwick Rodwell, Professor Peter Sawyer, John Schofield and Tim Tatton-Brown. Special gratitude is due to Dr Lawrence Butler, David Stocker and Dr Ian Wood. They read parts of the book while it was being written, rescued me from errors and contributed many valuable ideas. Table 3 is the work of Roberta Gilchrist. Lyn Greenwood, Ingrid Laurie and Sue Raines assisted with the final typing. The figures have been drawn by Dick Raines and Malcolm Stroud. Lyn Greenwood produced the index. Christopher Stevens and his colleagues at the Air Photographic Library of the National Monuments Record are to be thanked for their efficient and cheerful help. The sources of the various illustrations are acknowledged separately, but warm thanks are offered here to all those who gave permission for their work to be reused. All photographs, other than those taken from aeroplanes, were taken by Mick Sharp.

Richard Morris

I

ROADS FROM ROME

When St Augustine and his small band of companions landed in Kent in the spring of 597, about one-third of Britain south of the Clyde–Forth isthmus was already inhabited by people who had heard of Christ. Augustine's mission was aimed at the English: heathen *transmarini* who in the space of about 150 years had gained control of the greater part of south-east Britain and who more recently had consolidated their hold upon land and power within a loose confederation of tribal kingdoms. It is a question how this seizure had been accomplished, whether by force of arms, political manoeuvring, or, least likely, by weight of numbers. What can be said is that, outside the zone of English dominion, there was nothing novel about Christianity in sixth-century Britain (Fig. 1). While the English worshipped Woden, Thunor, Tiw and Frig, made offerings to idols of wood and stone, and dispatched their dead into a heathen hereafter, equipped for recreation, work and war, their British neighbours knew a living Church. Pre-Augustinian Britain had her bishops, intellectuals, churches and religious communities. Upon her landscape were holy places. As the late John Morris put it: 'The Christianity of the British Isles is a continuing whole, and the absorption of the English appears as a new starting point only if its earlier history is disregarded' (1973, 389).

We do not know the brief which pope Gregory I gave to Augustine in 596. However, Gregory did send further instructions after the missioners had settled in. New directions were set forth in letters which were written in June and July 601 and conveyed to Kent by Mellitus, the leader of a second group of missioners sent out to reinforce the first. Bede, the Northumbrian monk and scholar, copied several of these documents into his

6

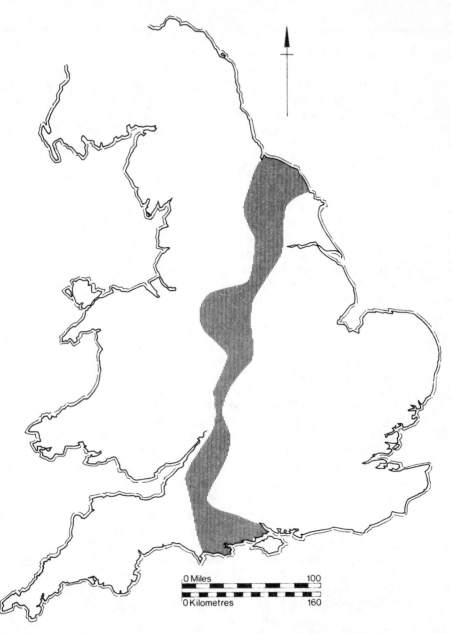

1 Likely areas of pagan and Christian culture in southern Britain around the time of Augustine's arrival at the end of the sixth century. Territory to the east of the shaded area was occupied or controlled by the English, who at that time were pagan; land to the west was in British hands. The shaded area represents the probable frontier area *c.* 600. The map presents a very simplified picture. Large pagan enclaves may have existed in the British sector, or there may have been pagan strata in British society, while pockets of Christian tradition might have survived in parts of eastern England. The map is over-simple also in that it presents the two regions as unified blocs, whereas the reality is likely to have involved numerous small tribal units and kingdoms

Ecclesiastical History of the English People (*HE*) about 130 years later. In one letter Augustine was told to establish himself as metropolitan in London, and to ordain twelve bishops in 'various places' who would be subject to his authority. A similar scheme – a mirror image, in fact – was prescribed for York and the north. British bishops were to be subordinate to the new metropolitans, who would in their turn be answerable to the papacy in Rome (*HE* i.29). In another letter, written at the same time, Gregory urged king Æthelberht of Kent to overthrow the heathen shrines and temples of his people (*HE* i.32). Gregory continued to ponder on this point; within a month he had changed his mind and dispatched yet another message, advising Augustine to do just the opposite: to convert idol temples to Christian use (*HE* i.30; cf. Markus 1970).

Little is recorded about the extent of Augustine's achievements in these matters. Perhaps there was not much to record. When Augustine died, probably in 605, little progress had been made towards the Christianization of the English. The royal family of Kent was receptive, but Gregory's idea of establishing a metropolitan see in London was never realized, and more than a hundred years were to pass before even a modest network of English dioceses was brought into being (Fig. 2).

As for the British, Augustine did manage to attend a colloquium at a place which in Bede's day was called Augustine's Oak, on the borders of the Hwicce and the West Saxons (*HE* ii.2), but the outcome was inconclusive. A second meeting ended in bitter disagreement. Bede placed all the blame for the failure upon the British bishops and teachers, alleging that they refused to keep Easter at what Augustine regarded as the correct time. However, this can hardly be the whole story, since at that date the mode of Easter calculation to which Bede refers had not even been adopted by the papacy itself. At best this is an anachronism; at worst, a Bedan calumny. The British clergy were reported to have engaged in other practices which Bede did not specify, other than to say that he thought they were not in keeping with the unity of the Church. Worst of all, despite Augustine's 'brotherly admonitions', the British declined to co-operate with the missioners in preaching the word of God to their English neighbours. Bede was fiercely critical about this. In an earlier chapter of his *History* he had listed the shortcomings of the British, ending with the accusation that, in addition to other unspeakable crimes, they

> never preached the faith to the Saxons or Angles who inhabited Britain with them. Nevertheless God in His goodness did not reject the people whom He foreknew, but He appointed much worthier heralds of the truth to bring this people to the faith.
>
> (*HE* i.22)

Bede was unable to conceal his glee when he described how, at a later

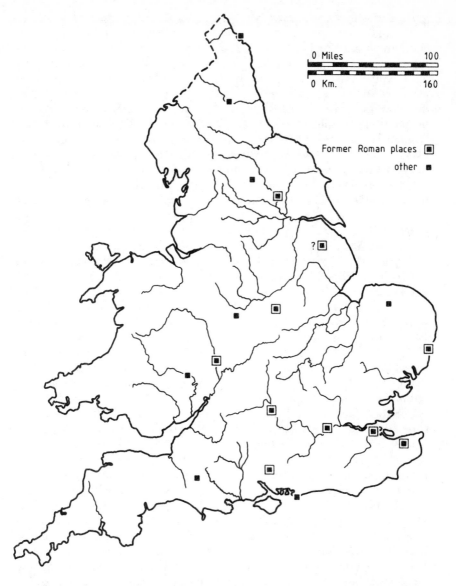

2 Episcopal sees founded in seventh- and eighth-century England. Sees in former Roman places are indicated

date, several hundred Welsh monks had been massacred by English warriors in fulfilment of Augustine's prophecy that

> those heretics would also suffer the vengeance of temporal death because they had despised the offer of everlasting salvation.

> (*HE* ii.2)

We must recognize the risks of relying upon Bede for either an objective or a comprehensive view of these early encounters between British churchmen and foreign missionaries. Bede never travelled outside Northumbria. For his history writing he relied upon a selection of books and texts, and upon data supplied by correspondents. A map showing the places, districts and rivers mentioned by Bede is eloquent of the limited distribution of his pen-friends (Fig. 3). Moreover, since part of Bede's purpose was to affirm the important place of the English in a greater Church which derived its authority directly from the apostolic see, it would be natural for him to downplay or to exclude altogether any materials which did not suit his theme.

The picture of lovelessness in Anglo-British relations which we receive from Bede is to some extent reinforced from other quarters. The Old English word *wealh*, for instance, from whence our word 'Welsh', came to be employed by the English not merely in its basic sense of 'Britisher', but also with a pejorative emphasis in such meanings as 'slave' and 'foreigner' (Faull 1975). Racial antipathy of this kind may help to explain why British Christians were disinclined to carry the faith to their English neighbours. Late in the seventh century the scholar Aldhelm gave details of the disdainful way in which English visitors to south-western Wales were treated. Welsh clergy declined to celebrate the divine offices with Englishmen, and made a point of purifying any vessels they had used for eating or drinking. Catholics who went to live in Wales were expected to spend forty days in penance before the Welsh clergy would associate with them. According to Aldhelm the Welsh clergy liked to call themselves *cathari* 'pure ones' (Lapidge and Herren 1979, 158).

For their part, highly educated English churchmen of the eighth century might not have wished to lay stress upon any British contribution. The Northumbrian intellectual Alcuin described the Britons as a 'slothful race'. The peoples of Germany, by contrast, were 'an ancient race, powerful in war, of splendid physique' (trans. Godman 1982, 7). Felix, the eighth-century biographer of a hermit called Guthlac, tells how his hero was plagued by evil spirits who filled his house with fire, prodded him with the points of spears – and chattered to each other *in British*. In the seventh century, too, the Roman missioners may have been glad to distance themselves from the native Church. If being Christian was a way of being British, it might be prudent for the men from Rome to emphasize that the good news they brought was of a superior and distinctly different kind. On the other hand, it is probable that the British and the English had more in common than might be supposed from a reading of tendentious clerical writings. Aldhelm's remarks about the supercilious behaviour of bishops in Wales occur in a letter addressed to 'the most glorious King Geraint', who was a British magnate who ruled over Devon and Cornwall (Lapidge

3 Places, districts and rivers mentioned by Bede in his *Ecclesiastical History*, completed early in the 730s. Regional names which have dropped from modern use are underlined. Lengths of rivers that were named are shown; continuations under other names have been omitted

R.Tweed

R.Glen

R.Aln

R.Tyne

R.Wear

GILLING

R.Swale

RIPON

R.Derwent

LOIDIS

ELMET

INDERAUUDA

LINDSEY

R.Idle

R.Trent

R.Severn

OUNDLE

ELY

R.Pant

INFEPPINGUM

R.Thames

SURREY

THANET

R.Hamble

I. of
WIGHT

0 Kms   100
0 Miles   100

and Herren 1979, 140–3). Royal genealogies of the English kingdoms contain a number of British names. There was intermarriage between members of some British and English dynasties. English and British leaders formed alliances when it suited them to do so. And Guthlac understood the conversations of the demons who came to annoy him only because he had passed some time living among the British and could speak their language.

Augustine's journey north from Rome had started in the spring of 596. Neither Augustine nor his companions are said to have had much enthusiasm for the trip. It was not that the enterprise was entirely without precedent: Gregory had recently initiated missionary activity in Sardinia, Corsica and Sicily (Markus 1970). But a scheme for taking the Word into the world of Germanic heathendom was something new.

Previously Augustine had been in charge of Gregory's monastery of St Andrew, which was set upon the Coelian Hill at Rome. Bede attributed the idea for the mission to Gregory, and explained it as the product of divine inspiration. Not long after its departure the entire party appears to have been seized with fear. Augustine returned to Rome to plead with Gregory for the abandonment of the trip. Gregory responded by letter, urging Augustine to set forth once again, and giving encouragement to the other members of his faltering expedition:

> My dearly beloved sons, it would have been better not to have undertaken a noble task than to turn back deliberately from what you have begun: so it is right that you should carry out with all diligence this good work which you have begun with the help of the Lord. Therefore do not let the toilsome journey nor the tongues of evil speakers deter you.
>
> (*HE* i.23)

To anyone with an eye for history, the probable route taken by Augustine to England involved a journey through time as well as space. The first stage was by sea, to the island of Lérins: the site of a famous monastic settlement which had been founded shortly before 410 and quickly attained a high reputation as a nursery for religious ascetics, scholars and future bishops. Lérins would be a place where alarming and possibly quite accurate stories could have been told about the pagan ways of the English. It may have been here that the missioners paused in the hope that Gregory would recall them.

From Lérins the mission moved inland via Aix to Arles. At the end of the sixth century Arles was a significant ecclesiastical centre, with a number of important churches and monasteries. Although Bede thought that Augustine later returned to Arles to be consecrated as bishop of the English (*HE* i.27), it is likely that the consecration took place here on the outward journey (Markus 1963). In 314 the city had been the scene of an ecclesiastical Council at which bishops from Roman Britain had been present. Three of them are actually known to us by name: a certain Eborius from York, Restitutus from London and Adelfius from a place styled as *civitate Colonia Londinensium* which can hardly be correct and seems to call for the amendment *Lindensium*, which would point to the *colonia* at Lincoln (Mann 1961; Thomas 1981, 197). There were two other British clerics at Arles in 314, but we do not know where they came from. Later in the fourth century, if not already in 314, the Romano-British episcopate is likely to have been appreciably larger than this. It has been plausibly suggested that the presence of three or possibly four delegations at Arles could have been connected with the administrative reorganization of Britain into four *provinciae* which had taken place not long previously (Hassall 1976). Leaving Arles, the mission now proceeded along the valley of the Rhône to Vienne and Lyon: two rival ecclesiastical centres with which some churchmen from western Britain may have been in intermittent contact. Both cities were places of monastic prominence. Lyon, for example, contained a number of churches, including a building which had been superimposed upon the burial place of St Irinaeus (d. 202), another funerary basilica named after St Justus, a church on the opposite bank of the Saône dedicated to St Nicetius, and several others.

At Lyon, as at Arles and Vienne, there was a marked correspondence between some important ecclesiastical sites and the zones of older cemeteries. The reason for this must now be explained.

In late antiquity the burial places of martyrs and certain other distinguished Christians had come to be held in a special, almost obsessive regard. Saints, it was believed, were close to God; living Christians desired to be close to the remains of saints. This aim could be achieved by building a place of worship over the tomb of an admired martyr. Alternatively, the remains of the saint could be exhumed and installed in a church elsewhere. On the time-scale of classical antiquity this sort of juxtaposition between the living and the dead was something very new. Traditionally, human remains had been excluded from towns. It was the rule that corpses should be buried or cremated outside the limits of the city. Sometimes the funeral was held in an extra-mural cemetery, or amid a straggle of wayside graves adjacent to trunk roads leading away from the town. On other occasions the deceased might be deposited within a mausoleum. All these types of burial place are well represented in England, as for example around the *coloniae* of Gloucester and York (Heighway 1980a; Ramm 1971) and beside the regional capitals of Canterbury and Winchester (Day 1980; G.Clarke 1979). Outside Dorchester *Do* a large fourth-century cemetery of probable Christian character has been excavated (Green 1979). Elsewhere in the later Roman world it was sites of this sort which on occasion later came to accommodate some of the earliest and most famous Christian buildings. In the process, some cities acquired additional or entirely new foci.

When Augustine left it, Rome was surrounded by about forty-five cemeteries ranged along the various *viae* that led out of the city. St Peter lay within a pagan necropolis beside the Via Cornelia. St Paul was buried between the Via Ostiense and the Tiber. Not far off were the resting places of other saints whose names were carried into England during the seventh and eighth centuries: St Pancras, adjacent to the Via Aurelia Antica; and St Lawrence, a short distance outside the Porta Tiburtina, with which it was connected by a covered walkway (Krautheimer 1980, 25). Some of the cemeteries had developed as underground warrens comprising subterranean burial rooms and labyrinthine passageways containing the graves of early Christians who were laid to rest in bunk-like recesses (*arcosolia*) along the walls. (It is possible that the crypts constructed beneath Wilfrid's churches at Ripon *YN* and Hexham *Nb* towards the end of the seventh century were designed in stylized imitation of Roman burial galleries. Wilfrid visited Rome on several occasions.) Later, churches were superimposed upon the tomb sites of some important saints. A few of these churches, notably the basilica of St Peter on the Vatican Hill, provided countervailing foci to the great antique monuments and public places inside the old city.

Rome never moved sideways, but this did happen elsewhere. At a number of towns in Gaul and in the Rhineland centres of devotion became established over the traditional burial places of saints. In later centuries some of these churches seem to have exerted a magnetic effect upon settlement. The dead, previously excluded from the residential area, could now provide its nucleus. These changes in the emphasis of urban geography reflected a fundamental shift in intellectual outlook. The entombed saint was no mere object of pious curiosity. He, or she, was believed to exert a dynamic power: in intercession, in healing, in political affairs and in the reinforcement of the spirituality of those who lived and worshipped in the vicinity. This was in sharp contrast to the circumstances which had prevailed until the third century, when the place of the dead had been strictly circumscribed both in urban topography and in the imagination (Brown 1981).

Such considerations loomed large at Tours, to which the Augustinian group now proceeded, possibly after a courtesy call to Châlon which was the seat of the Merovingian court. Several centuries previously Tours had been a substantial city, with a grid of streets occupying an area of perhaps a square mile. The fourth century seems to have seen a contraction, with a new defensive *enceinte* erected at the east end of the city, incorporating part of the old amphitheatre. The cathedral stood towards the south-west corner of this walled area. Outside, over half a mile to the west, lay cemeteries, one of which contained the funerary church of St Litorius, a bishop who had died *c.* 370.

Exactly how Tours would have looked to Augustine is difficult to determine. The picture painted only a very few years before by Gregory of Tours suggests an active place, somewhat straitened as a result of the attentions of the Merovingian Franks, but with most of its urban functions intact, and a substantial population. Archaeology has yet to confirm this.

The cathedral still existed, together with the bishop's residence and another church nearby (Galinié 1978). Away to the west the view would have been dominated by the basilica of St Martin, begun as a simple oratory in an area of former habitation shortly after Martin's death in 397, remodelled on a grander scale in the fifth century and rebuilt again in the 550s. Several other churches stood nearby. This curious concentration of buildings may have grown up to take advantage of pilgrim traffic to the shrine of St Martin. We shall meet Martin again in a later chapter, but it is appropriate to say something here about his background and achievement.

Martin was born in Pannonia, probably in the second decade of the fourth century. His father was a soldier in the Roman army who went on to become a military tribune. Martin's childhood was passed in Pavia. At the age of ten 'he took himself, against the wish of his parents, to the Church, and asked that he might become a catechumen'. The parallel between Martin's precocious behaviour and that of the boy Jesus, who returned to the temple in order to continue discussion with the elders, is characteristic of the writing of Sulpicius Severus (c. 363–420), upon whose rather tendentious *vita* we must rely for the earliest account of Martin's career (Stancliffe 1983). Martin was subsequently enrolled in the Imperial Guard but, after a number of adventures, he retired from the army and attached himself to the circle of Hilary of Poitiers. After ordination, Martin's aim was to lead the life of a hermit, seeking a perfect state of being through contemplation and asceticism. Martin modelled this lifestyle upon what he had been able to find out about the proto-monks of Egypt and Judaea. His knowledge of this subject was probably quite good. Hilary had actually been out to the Levant, while Athanasius, patriarch of Alexandria (328–73), whose career coincided with the first galvanizing half-century of monastic development, had passed periods in exile at Trier and Rome and had talked with Hilary.

Before long, news of Martin's holiness and abilities began to spread. The citizens of Tours sought him out and had him nominated as their bishop by popular acclaim. For a time, Martin resided in the city. He attempted to reconcile the tasks of maintaining the position of a bishop and of leading the life of a pious ascetic. This proved to be difficult, mainly on account of the large numbers of people who wished to visit him, so he established a secluded 'monastery' for himself about two miles outside Tours. According to Sulpicius this spot

> was so secret and retired that he enjoyed in it the solitude of a hermit . . . on one side it was surrounded by a precipitous rock of a lofty mountain, while the river Loire had shut in the rest of the plain by a bay extending back for a little distance.

Sulpicius hoped that his readers would notice the parallel between Martin's lifestyle and the hardships endured by ascetics in the Levant. St Antony had been pestered by admirers who attempted to invade his solitude. On more than one occasion an Egyptian proto-monk was so determined to maintain his independence of worldly affairs that he actually had to be arrested by the authorities who wished to appoint him as a bishop. The topography, too, is described in terms which recall the remote fastnesses which had been occupied by such men as Antony and John of Lycopolis. Of course, there was no serious comparison to be made between the countryside around Tours and the extreme conditions of, say, the Desert of Scetis. Sulpicius was out to make a point.

Martin's episcopate marked a new departure in the development of the western Church. In conjunction with his life as an ascetic, Martin devoted much energy to evangelization in the hinterland of his diocese. In Italy and Gaul, and probably in Roman Britain, it was normal for episcopal administration to be centred upon towns. In the fourth and fifth centuries, Christian leadership was largely reserved to a narrow section of the urban aristocracy. The administrative framework of the Church usually coincided with that of secular government. The idea of taking the Word to country-dwelling peasants was novel. Martin's ministry consisted mainly of preaching, but a disproportionately large part of Sulpicius's biography is devoted to dramatic episodes: Martin cutting down a pine tree dedicated to a demon; Martin smashing up heathen temples; Martin breaking idols; Martin grappling with demons. A number of Martin's encounters with the forces of darkness led him into extreme personal danger. In the later fourth century, ascetics were coming to replace martyrs in popular esteem. In a Christian empire, opportunities for martyrdom became rare. New challenges were sought. This would explain the detail with which Sulpicius invested his stories of Martin's clashes with aggressive *rustici* who were resentful at the overthrow of their sacred sites. Sulpicius wanted to depict Martin as a man with the mettle of a true confessor.

Martin died in November 397. One of his admirers, Victricius of Rouen, visited Britain at about this time. It is reasonable to suppose that some details of Martin's career were becoming known to active Romano-British Christians. At Tours, Martin's immediate successor, Brictius, erected a simple church over the site of his grave. (Someone, perhaps a follower of the Conqueror, dedicated a church to St Brice at Norton, now Brize Norton *O*.) During the period 466–72, Perpetuus, bishop of Tours (458–88), rebuilt the church and invited Sidonius Apollinaris, a Gallo-Roman nobleman who was enthroned at Clermont as bishop of the Arverni, *c.* 470, to pen a poem for inscription upon the wall of the new building. In a letter to a friend Sidonius expressed the hope that his verse would not 'disfigure the majesty' of the great new church, but nevertheless went on to quote it in full. The poem relates how Perpetuus replaced the former edifice 'of mean style' which had become a source of shame to the citizens of Tours because 'the glory of the man should be so great, and the beauty of the place so small'. Sidonius then explained how Perpetuus

removed the inner shrine that formed the modest chapel and raised a lordly pile by building outside and over it; and so by the favour of its mighty patron the church has grown in size, the builder in merit, and well might it vie with Solomon's temple which was the world's seventh wonder.

(Ep IV, 18; trans. Anderson 1963)

Despite Sidonius's ponderous rhetoric, it is evident that by this time (c. 470) Martin was regarded as a saint. By raising a new church above Martin's burial place, Perpetuus was giving emphasis to the cult not of a martyr but of a great bishop. Other cults of comparable type were soon to flower, such as those of Germanus of Auxerre and Medard at Soissons. They followed in seventh-century England as well: Augustine at Canterbury, Chad at Lichfield, Cuthbert at Lindisfarne. In their turn, these cults and others like them were to furnish dedications for local churches. We shall be meeting some of them in due course.

The church visited by Augustine in 596 was not the building which had been erected by Perpetuus. According to Gregory of Tours (538–94) the church had been rebuilt following a serious fire in 558. We cannot know what thoughts passed through Augustine's mind if he knelt in prayer beside Martin's shrine, but he could hardly have been unaware of the analogy between Martin's career as missionary and pastor to the rustici and his own forthcoming role as apostle to the English. Six months later, Augustine was in Kent.

When Augustine died, probably in 605

his body was buried outside but close to the church of the apostles St Peter and St Paul ... for it was not yet finished or consecrated. But as soon as it was consecrated, the body was carried inside and honourably buried in the porticus on the north side.

(HE ii.3)

The remains of this church can still be seen. They stand within the ruins of the later Benedictine abbey of St Augustine, a short distance to the east of the Roman city wall, in the vicinity of a late Roman inhumation cemetery. We have met this sort of site before: at Lyon, Arles, Tours and, of course, at Rome itself.

As a result of recent archaeological work a certain amount is now known about the condition of the city of Canterbury around the time of Augustine's arrival. There is no sign of any significant resident population that could be called urban. It seems that the city was abandoned before the end of the fifth century. Wherever archaeologists have had the opportunity to look, 'the roofs of the Roman buildings had fallen in and the walls were beginning to collapse. On top of these destruction levels a black soil was beginning to form which must indicate the growth of weeds and wild plants' (Tatton-Brown 1980, 13). In the later sixth or seventh century we catch the first glimpses of a new population. Whether we call these folk English or Anglo-British it appears that there were not many of them living in Canterbury, for only a few of their simple timber-and-wattle huts have been found, scattered about amid the remains of Roman buildings. In effect, this is rural settlement superimposed upon an urban background. To claim this, however, is not to exclude the possibility that some small sector of Canterbury had been kept alive as a *villa regia*: that is, one of a series of administrative villages which served as the residences and judicial centres of peripatetic royalty. During the next two centuries the ancestors of some of the earliest parish churches in England were to be established as components of *villae regales*: a process which will be described in Chapter 3.

Augustine needed a town for his first church. Ecclesiastical convention insisted that bishops' churches should be in towns. Since there were no living towns in sixth-century England, an empty one would have to do:

> After Augustine had ... received his episcopal see in the royal city, he with the help of the king restored a church in it, which as he was informed, had been built in ancient times by the hands of Roman believers.

(*HE* i.33)

The cathedral was positioned inside the walls of the former city, in the north-east corner of the defended area. Hence it was not Canterbury as a whole that was being reoccupied, but merely a small part of it: a new, living settlement within an old, dead one (Fig. 4). It is interesting to hear that Augustine and his colleagues *restored* a church. Whether the building in question actually had been a church before *c.* 450, or merely resembled one, is a question to which, one day, archaeology may supply an answer. Augustine gave his church the dedication *Sancti Salvatoris*: the old name of the papal cathedral St John in the Lateran (Levison 1946, 34–5).

We recall that sixth-century Tours had consisted of two parts: the cathedral and palace within an area bounded by walls in need of maintenance, and the family of churches centred upon the funerary church of St Martin. The picture at Canterbury is similar. Even without Bede's testimony our attention would be drawn to the row of churches which lies beside the Roman road from Canterbury to Richborough: an arrangement reminiscent of the extra-mural ecclesiastical geographies that we have been noticing on the continent.

Nearest to the city was the church of SS Peter and Paul. This church was founded by Augustine and the Kentish king Æthelberht, partly as the church of a *monasterium* and partly as a place for royal and archiepiscopal funerals. In this, Augustine may have respected the traditional Roman prohibition against burial inside city limits. After Augustine's death, a

4 Canterbury in the second quarter of the seventh century. Former Roman defences and selected streets are shown. Hatched areas represent the approximate extent of known Roman cemeteries. 1 Christ Church (cathedral); 2 monastic church of SS Peter and Paul; 3 St Mary; 4 St Pancras; 5 St Martin (*Source*: Canterbury Archaeological Trust 1982)

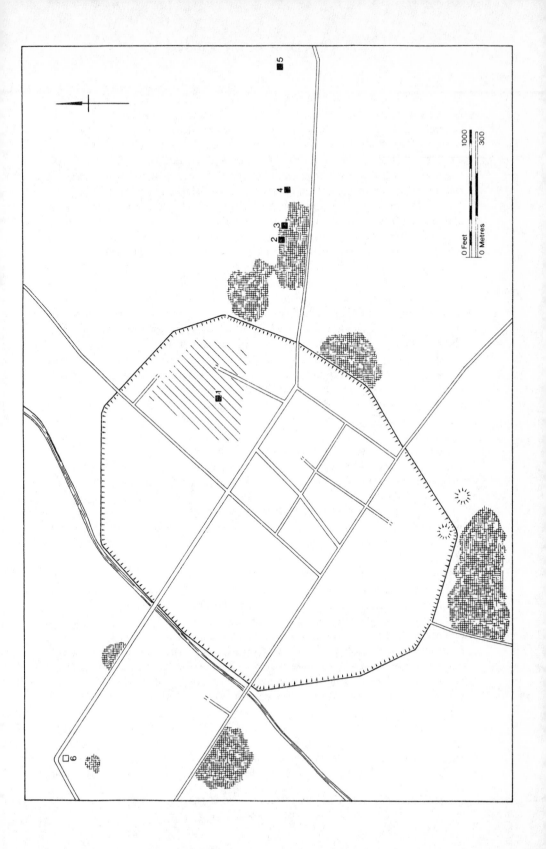

church dedicated to St Mary was constructed a little to the east of SS Peter and Paul. About one minute's walk eastward of St Mary's stand the ruins of the church of St Pancras. No really satisfactory explanation for the presence or function of this church has ever been forthcoming. Bede did not mention it. It had no parish in the later Middle Ages. In the fourteenth century the chronicler William Thorne reported a tradition which connected the church with St Augustine, and stated that before 597 the building had been used by the English as a heathen temple (Bede, ed. Plummer 1896, ii, 58–9; Howorth 1913, 71). Sir Alfred Clapham was in no doubt as to what St Pancras represented in architectural terms: 'Its character . . . so exactly conforms to that of the churches already described' (i.e. SS Peter and Paul, which survives in incomplete outline, and St Mary's, which has been all but obliterated) 'that there can be no doubt as to its date' (1930, 19). This interpretation of St Pancras as being a typical church of the seventh century has recently been questioned (Thomas 1981, 170–4). As first planned it now seems that the building lacked the lateral *porticus* lying astride the junction between nave and chancel which Clapham regarded as being so typical of the 'remarkably homogeneous' group of seventh-century churches in south-east England. The deposits underlying this building may have been no later than Roman. In the seventh century this first building was heavily modified, if not actually rebuilt (Jenkins 1976). St Pancras, moreover, stands close to the edge of a late Roman inhumation cemetery, if not actually within it (Thomas 1981, 174).

Resuming our eastward journey we come last of all to the church of St Martin. Unlike all the previous buildings which have been mentioned, St Martin's is today a straightforwardly parochial church in regular use. The prologue is over. We are crossing the threshold; the study of parish churches begins.

St Martin's is not a big church, but what is lacking in scale is made up for by complexity. The walls teem with Roman bricks and there are ghosts of blocked windows and doors (Figs 5, 6). It is best to begin by considering the plan (Fig. 7).

The earliest visible portion of the church corresponds with what is now the western half of the chancel. Limited excavations made at various times have disclosed traces of walls running westward from this rectangular core, but their significance is not yet understood (Jenkins 1965). Next in sequence comes the present nave, a simple rectangle roughly 40 ft (12.2 m) long internally and 24 ft (7.3 m) broad, with vestiges of flat pilaster buttresses at three of the four external angles. In the thirteenth century the chancel was lengthened to the east, and the tower was added in the fourteenth century. It is the earlier components that concern us here.

The modern visitor to St Martin's will see that the builders of both of the early phases made use of Roman bricks bound by a 'salmon pink hard mortar' (Tatton-Brown 1980, 13). This method of building was employed in Canterbury during the third and fourth centuries, and perhaps again,

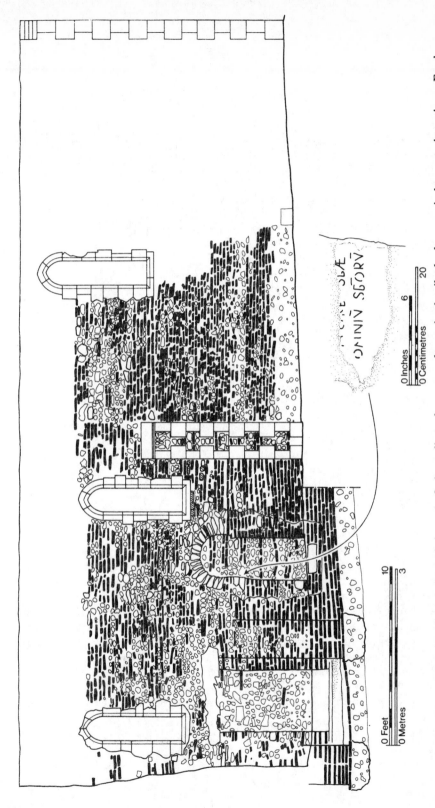

5 St Martin, Canterbury: south elevation of chancel. Only earliest phases are shown in detail; the lancet windows are insertions. For key to conventions see Fig. 6 (*Source:* Tim Tatton-Brown)

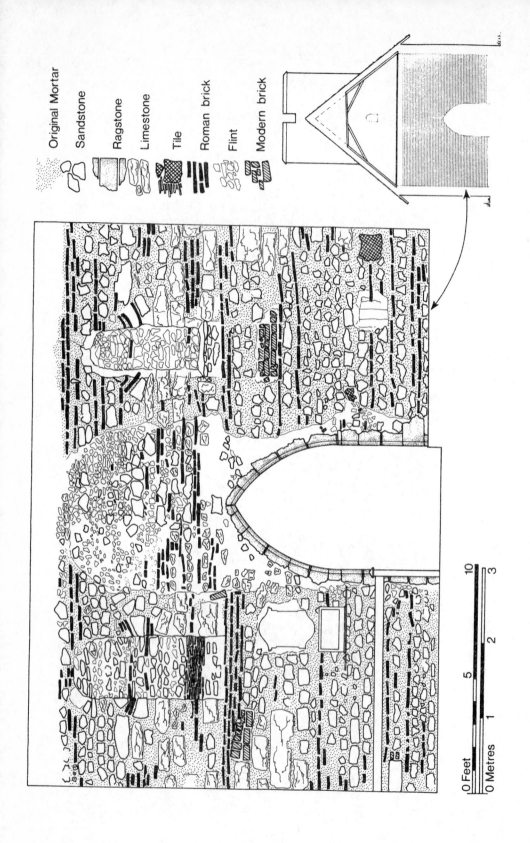

Original Mortar
Sandstone
Ragstone
Limestone
Tile
Roman brick
Flint
Modern brick

0 Feet   5   10
0 Metres   1   2   3

briefly, in the period following the arrival of the missioners in 597. It was never used thereafter. On *prima facie* grounds, then, we might suppose that these parts of the church date at latest from the seventh century. However, it may be possible to glean more than this, because there are differences between the techniques of walling used in the western part of the chancel and in the nave. While we must accept that it is impossible to assign a definite date to any part of this early building without modern scientific investigation, the facts we possess at least permit the idea that the nave belongs to the seventh century, and that the chancel dates either from around 600 or else was inherited from a structure of late Roman date.

There is a further dimension to the site of St Martin's that must be discussed. In the nineteenth century digging in the vicinity of the church disclosed a number of sixth-century Frankish coins, including a medallion bearing the name 'Liudhard' (Grierson 1952–4). Seventeen years or more before Augustine's arrival, Æthelberht had married a Frankish princess, Bertha. Bertha was a Christian. Some knowledge of the Christian religion had already reached Æthelberht, therefore, and he had received Bertha

> from her parents on condition that she should be allowed to practise her faith and religion unhindered, with a bishop named Liudhard whom they had provided for her to support her faith.
>
> (*HE* i.25)

When Augustine and the missioners settled into their new quarters at Canterbury they soon discovered that

> There was near by, on the east of the city, a church built in ancient times in honour of St Martin, while the Romans were still in Britain, in which the queen, who, as has been said, was a Christian, used to pray. In this church they first began to meet to chant the psalms, to pray, to say mass, to preach and to baptize, until, when the king had been converted to the faith, they received greater liberty to preach everywhere and to build or restore churches.
>
> (*HE* i.26)

This tale has caused many writers to suppose that the early portion of the present St Martin's church is to be identified with the church mentioned by Bede. Professor Thomas, on the other hand, has confessed to doubts (1981, 170). First, as we have seen, the only part of the building that could plausibly be claimed as Roman would be the small compartment which forms the western part of the chancel. (Even this may be dubious: D. F. Mackreth has recently argued that the building is unlikely to be Roman 'as it is too insignificant a building to be built completely of brick in the Roman period – a technique best evidenced in imperial projects'

6 St Martin, Canterbury: east-facing (interior) elevation of west wall of nave (*Source*: Tim Tatton-Brown)

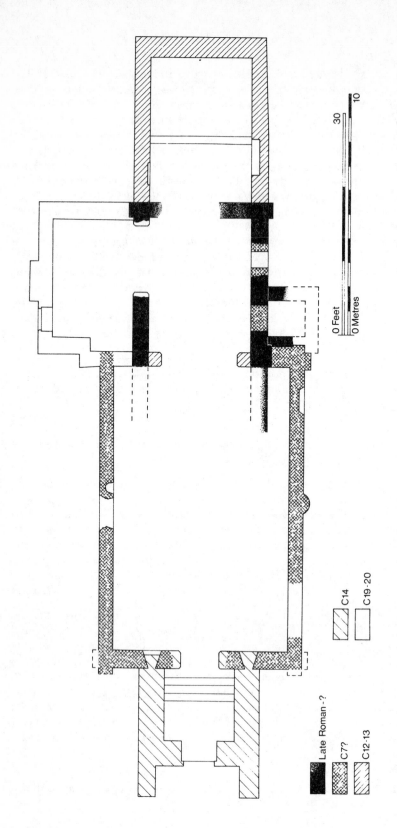

Late Roman - ?

C7?

C12-13

C14

C19-20

0 Feet — 30

0 Metres — 10

7 St Martin, Canterbury: plan. Dating of the earliest phases is conjectural (*Source:* Tim Tatton-Brown, with information from Jenkins 1965)

(1987, 138).) Viewed on its own, this structure could resemble a mausoleum or *cella*; it does not look like a church. Second, since Bede was quite explicit that the church he had heard of was an extra-mural building, and since extra-mural churches are likely to have been located within cemeteries, doubt must arise from the fact that St Martin's does not appear to stand within an appropriate burial ground. Thomas suggests that the church rehabilitated by Bertha and Liudhard, and adopted by Augustine, was the building we now know as St Pancras. Even in its first phase, St Pancras displays an ecclesiastical aspect, it does lie at the edge of a late Roman cemetery, and it would have been large enough to accommodate the missioners and their first converts. A later confusion at Canterbury is invoked to explain the substitution of the dedications.

This is an attractive theory, but it should be noted that most of the objections to an equation between St Martin's and the church in the Bedan statement are removed if it is supposed that the building in which Bertha used to pray was not necessarily, in origin, a church. The assumption that it was rests entirely upon hearsay testimony, noted down perhaps three-and-a-half centuries after the 'church' is supposed to have been built. Moreover, if, as some students have now begun to postulate, and *pace* Mackreth, the first building began as a mausoleum or *cella*, this rather militates against the idea that the site of St Martin's had no connection with burial outside late Roman Canterbury. In any case, would Bertha and Liudhard have required anything more than a building the size of an oratory for their private devotions?

Before taking leave of St Martin's, we must consider the dedication, for it is probably the oldest church dedication in England that we know. Presumably, the dedication to St Martin is attributable to Bertha and Liudhard rather than to the citizens of Roman Canterbury. Even in Tours, so the argument runs, the idea of a church being dedicated to *Saint* Martin is hardly conceivable before the latter years of the fifth century, by which time Canterbury was crumbling into decay. Martin, moreover, would have been especially appropriate for Bertha, because her father, Charibert, had ruled over Tours until her bridal journey to Kent in the period *c.* 672 × 680, and, according to Gregory of Tours, her sister had been a nun at St Martin's. On the other hand, Sulpicius did his best to ensure that Martin became a legend in his own lifetime. And the recent discovery of a Visigothic gold tremissis in a terminal stratum of Roman Canterbury has provided an indication of the sort of date to which life within the town may have continued. The coin points to activity of some sort down to the last quarter of the fifth century (Kent *et al.* 1983). So there might just have been scope for a sub-Roman dedication to St Martin, although an explanation involving Bertha is still to be preferred; and if Bede's interpretation of St Martin's as having been a Romano-British church is set aside, then a sixth- or seventh-century date for the choice of dedication becomes inescapable.

While on the subject of early cults it is interesting to notice that all of the dedications most favoured by Merovingian royalty were applied at one time or another to parish churches in medieval England. Dedications to St Denis were numerous. Much less common are Medard (Soissons), who occurs only at Little Bytham *Li*; Vincent (Châlon and Paris) at Littlebourne *K*, Burton-by-Lincoln and Caythorpe *Li*; Vedast (Arras) at Tathwell *Li*; Radegund (Poitiers) at Grayingham *Li*, Maplebeck *Nt* and Scruton *NY*; and a rather longer list of dedications involving Maurice (Agaune) that includes Briningham *Nf*, Eglingham and Ellingham *Nb*, Winchester and York, where there were two. Nothing certain is known about the beginnings of any of these churches. It has, however, been suggested that the churches dedicated to St Lawrence and St Maurice in Winchester 'may reveal a conscious attempt to associate the city of the kings of Wessex with the splendours of the Ottonian or later *Reich*' (Keene 1985, 9). Dr Keene points out that each of these churches was

> closely associated with a point of entry into the precinct of the New Minster or that part of the royal palace precinct which was taken over from New Minster. Lawrence came to be a common dedication for imperial churches following Otto the Great's victory over the Magyars on that saint's day in 955. In that battle Otto was carrying St Maurice's lance, which continued to be an important item in the imperial regalia throughout the Middle Ages.
>
> (1985,9)

It may be added that at York, also, one of the churches dedicated to St Maurice stood beside an entrance into the city, and that the gate was located close to the edge of the cathedral precinct. Interest in Maurice on the part of tenth-century kings is possible. It was later reputed that king Athelstan (924–39) had been given Maurice's standard as a present by Hugh the Great, *dux* of Paris. Maurice apart, most of the other dedications have usually been regarded as exotic introductions of the eleventh or twelfth centuries, or the consequence of appropriations to foreign religious houses. This is likely, but to assume it everywhere may be to oversimplify. The likely extension of devotion to Martin to sixth-century Kent through royal marriage illustrates one sort of mechanism which could have worked elsewhere. The concentration of these dedications in Lincolnshire, where interest in Martin was also strong, is particularly curious. Most counties have no dedications of this type. A few contain one or two. Lincolnshire has them all (Fig. 8).

Returning now to early Christian Canterbury, we have before us a hieratic row of extra-mural churches, some at least with definite funerary associations, balanced by an episcopal enclave inside the city. The whole ensemble combined features of contemporary continental and residual Romano-British religious topography. This is an intriguing picture, but it is fair to ask if it can be of any real relevance to parochial geography elsewhere in England or Wales. Two factors, in particular, must prompt

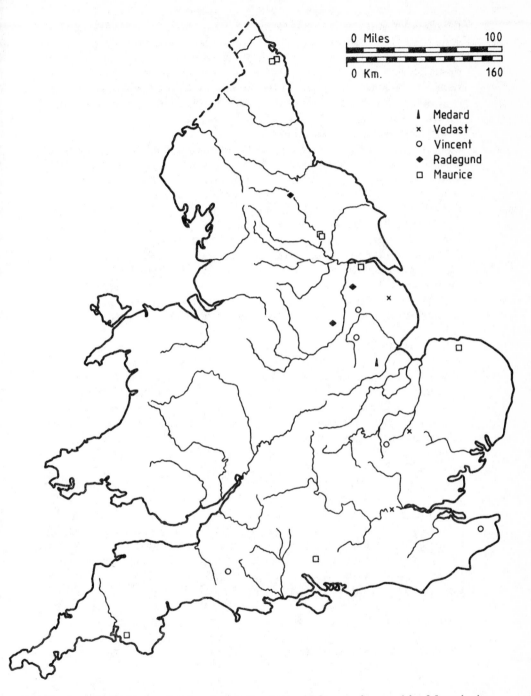

Ι	Medard
×	Vedast
○	Vincent
◆	Radegund
□	Maurice

0 Miles 100
0 Km. 160

8 Distribution of parish churches bearing dedications which were favoured by Merovingian royalty

doubts. The first arises from an allegedly general paucity of evidence for the presence of Christianity in Roman Britain on any extensive basis. The second stems from a view, widely held, which states that the great majority of our parish churches were founded in the tenth and eleventh centuries. Taken together, and exceptional coincidences apart, these assertions would appear to rule out the possibility of there having been any dynamic relationship existing between places frequented by Romano-British Christians and the sites of medieval parish churches.

In reply to the first objection it need only be said that the minimalist view of Romano-British Christianity is no longer tenable. There is a good deal of evidence (Thomas 1981). More emerges year by year. As for the second argument, it is doubtful if the origins of our parish churches are reducible to simple generalizations. They lie, rather, in an amalgam of factors, some of which are only just coming to be perceived. Neighbouring churches which appear to be very similar in structure and status in the later Middle Ages may turn out on detailed scrutiny to have originated in entirely different ways, and far apart in time. In entertaining a Roman dimension to the origins of *some* of our churches we should remember that the concept of the parish church did not really crystallize before the twelfth century. By this time, however, as we shall find in later chapters, most of the church *buildings* were already present, and some of them were very old.

Our first task is to sieve out all those churches which may appear to have some connection with Romanity but where, on closer inspection, the link is found to be unrelated to the choice of site. There is, for example, a long list of churches which contain Roman tombstones built into the fabric, as at Corbridge *Nb*, Wigton *Cu* and Brough-under-Stainmore *We* where a Roman tombstone bearing an inscription in Greek was encountered during restoration of the church. In most cases of this sort we are probably dealing with nothing more than opportunism on the part of medieval builders who looked upon derelict Roman temples, forts, villas and graveyards as ready sources of second-hand building material. This explains the presence of numberless Roman bricks and tiles in the walls of churches in those parts of East Anglia and Essex where good freestone was scarce, and it must be the reason also for the Roman architectural items, dedication stones and altars which can be seen in such churches as Brimpton *Brk*, Atcham *Sa*, Lanchester and Gainford *Du*, Cliburn *We*, Fetcham *Sr*, Tunstall *La* and Kirby Hill (Boroughbridge) *NY*. Finds of this sort of material are still being made. At Godmanstone *Do* alterations to the chancel in 1964 disclosed a limestone altar which had been reused to form the base of the south side of the chancel arch. Excavations at Ilkley *WY* in 1982 yielded a Roman inscription under the threshold of the tower, together with two large altars which had been refashioned to form monolithic window heads for an earlier church.

It is clear that, in some areas, as churches went up, so Roman buildings came down. There is an interesting study to be made of the stages by which Roman architecture disappeared from the countryside as a result of scavenging by masons. At Wroxeter *Sa*, for instance, someone grubbed out stylobate blocks which had formerly carried the colonnade of a basilica in the old Roman city of Viroconium. A scrap of metalwork which was dropped in one of the trenches suggests that the stone diggers were at work no earlier than the ninth century. It has been argued that the blocks 'were being recovered for building one of the early churches in the neighbourhood, probably Atcham or Wroxeter itself, both of which have complete walls of stylobate-sized stones' (Barker 1979, 180). On the whole, these recycled items tell us more about the Roman structures from which they were obtained than about the churches. At Winteringham *Li* Roman architectural sculpture occurs near the foot of the church tower; Dr Warwick Rodwell has suggested that the builders of the west tower went to the trouble of dismantling a Roman monumental structure at the top of Ermine Street in order to provide themselves with stone.

Occasionally, items of Roman worked stone were put to more specialized uses. At Corbridge *Nb* there is an altar which was reused as a water stoup. Wroxeter *Sa* contains a font which was formed by gouging out the middle of a column base. Roman altars were converted into fonts at Chollerton and Hayden Bridge *Cu*, also at Kenchester *He*. At Bowes *NY* an altar was used as a font base.

Presumably most of the foregoing examples involved straightforward expediency, but in instances where the source of supply was either under or very close to the church it may be that other factors played a part. In this class we could place the churches which appear to stand upon the remains of Roman pagan temples, as at Silchester *Ha*, Ancaster *Li* and possibly Haile *Cu* and Staunton-on-Arrow *He*. Then there are the appreciable numbers of churches like Woodchester *Gl*, Widford *O* and Alphamstone *Ex* which occupy the sites of Roman villas. These relationships will be explored later on.

We have now winnowed our way to two very interesting and distinctive, though not necessarily significant, classes of parish church: those that stand within the zones of late or sub-Roman cemeteries, and those that have prominent sites within the *enceintes* of former Roman towns. It should be explained at the outset that in no case is it obvious, or even likely, that we are dealing with instances of 'continuity' of religious activity through the fifth, sixth and seventh centuries; at least, not in the coarse sense with which this word has been employed in recent years. On the other hand, if any of the churches that are about to be discussed were to be translated to, say, the Rhineland, or to Gaul, some sort of religious or cultural link would probably be assumed. At base, this may be a conflict which comes down to differences between historiographical traditions, but these in their turn have tended to influence the outlook of archaeologists, and it is possible that we in Britain have been mistrustful of patterns which do not conform to long-held preconceptions.

Great Chesterford *Ex*. The church of All Saints is a once-mighty building that fell upon hard times. By the thirteenth century the church had been developed to its maximum extent, being a large cruciform building with an aisled nave of some six bays and a substantial western tower. Around 1400 the tower and two bays of the nave were deleted, and there have been many alterations since. The historical significance of cruciform plans is discussed in Chapter 3; our interest now is occasioned by the fact that here is a church of manifest prestige which occupies a site displaying signs of an early origin.

When it has been shorn of modern development, the layout of the village of Great Chesterford consists of four streets projecting from a triangular core (Fig. 9). The site of Manor Farm is some distance east of the church, while the church itself stands towards the western edge of the settlement. The element *ceaster* in the eleventh-century form of the place-name *Ceasterford* must be referred to the Roman settlement which lay to the north-west of the modern village, while the ford would be a crossing-point on the River Cam, which skirts the village along its western flank.

Roman Chesterford was a small town. It seems to have been unusual among other small towns of the region in that it possessed walls. At first sight little of the Roman layout is now reflected in the village plan. However, in July 1719 the antiquary William Stukeley 'had the pleasure to walk round an old Roman city there, upon the walls, which are still visible above ground' (1776, 78). The walls were later levelled by local residents who took the bricks to improve their houses, but this husk of 'an old Roman city' had survived for long enough to imprint itself upon parts of the local road pattern. The length of road that passes the north side of the churchyard follows the track of a Roman predecessor, and the road junction *c.* 150 yd (137 m) to the west is likely to coincide with the position of the south gate of the Roman town.

As was customary, the townsfolk of Roman Chesterford buried their dead outside the walls. Romano-British graves have been discovered at various times, and a fourth-century cemetery is known in the narrow belt of ground which runs between the western wall of the town and the river. However, All Saints, with its extra-mural roadside site, beside the approaches to a principal gate, is also in the sort of position where one would expect to encounter individual graves, if not a cemetery. In fact, there is an old report of a Roman inhumation 'in or near Chesterford churchyard'. This may refer to the discovery in 1854 of four skeletons accompanied by 'Roman objects' which was made in ground adjoining the churchyard. The date of these burials is problematical, as items which would be characteristic of gravegoods in a pagan English cemetery were found at the same time (Neville 1856). This may imply an English cemetery which reused, or continued to use, an earlier burial ground: a tendency which has also been noticed in east Kent. Great Chesterford is one of the few places in Essex where English settlement during

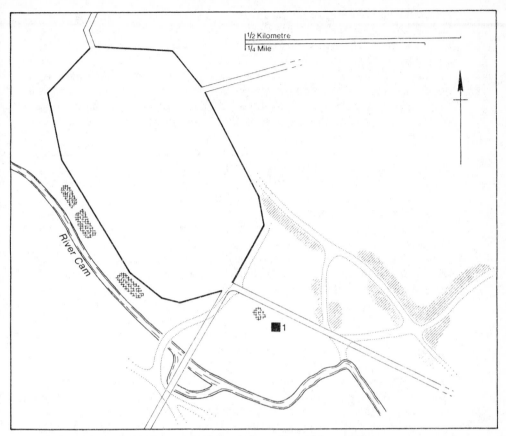

9 Great Chesterford, Essex: diagrammatic outline of former Roman town, showing site of medieval church outside southern gate, where later roads (dotted) converge. The core of the modern village is indicated by open shading. Areas of cross-shading represent places of burial in the Roman period

the fifth and sixth centuries is archaeologically attested on any appreciable scale.

The site of All Saints, the churchyard and its surroundings are clearly of high interest, although a modern archaeological investigation would be required to establish the date of the first church on the site, and to ascertain whether this building was founded within a pre-existing cemetery, or even focused on a particular grave. All that can be said at present is that the topographical framework here is reminiscent of the sort of patterns we have been noticing on the continent.

Ilchester So. At the time of the Norman Conquest Ilchester was a thriving town. It contained a mint, a flourishing trading community and a substantial population. Four intra-mural parish churches are mentioned before the end of the thirteenth century; a fifth, St Mary Minor, stood just outside the walls, and a church dedicated to St Michael was perched over the south gate. There may have been others (Aston and Leech 1977, 69–70; Aston 1984). The fourteenth and fifteenth centuries were a period of decline in Ilchester's fortunes, however, and when John Leland wrote about the place only one parish church remained in use. The survivor, St Mary Major, occupies a central site within the roughly kite-shaped *enceinte* which may owe something to the outline of the underlying Roman town of *Lindinis*.

Domesday singled out but one church at Ilchester in 1068. Maurice, bishop of London, held it, together with three hides of land from the king. Maurice's church was dedicated to St Andrew. It has been suggested that St Andrew's was served by a community of priests rather than a single cleric. This is likely: three hides formed a good endowment for a local church and creates the suspicion that it was or had been a minster (see Chapter 3).

Now, as far as we know, there was no church dedicated to St Andrew within the walls of medieval Ilchester. However, a church with this dedication does stand on high ground beside the Fosse Way about one-fifth of a mile beyond the River Yeo. This is the parish church of Northover (Fig. 10). It was rebuilt late in the Middle Ages, when it was provided with a rather severe west tower, and again in 1821, but the cruciform layout may preserve something of an earlier scheme.

Here, then, is an extra-mural church, in existence before 1066, very probably a royal minster, established beside a Roman trunk road just outside a former town. Moreover, at various times during the last 150 years there have been discoveries of Roman burials at Northover, including several contained in sarcophagi of stone and lead (Leech 1980, 357). In 1982, exploratory excavations located an extensive late Roman cemetery. This cemetery did not extend as far north as St Andrew's, but the possibility of burial plots or individual mausolea spread further north along the Fosse Way has to be considered. Indeed, the detachment of St Andrew's from the inhumation cemetery is reminiscent of the independence of St Martin's from the eastern Roman burial area outside Canterbury.

In a prescient article, published in 1975, Dr R. R. Dunning suggested:

> It is at least possible that this ancient ecclesiastical site was once a Roman shrine, perhaps associated with a Roman cemetery; and that here should be sought the signs of early Christianity, in an extra-mural development away from the confined military and administrative quarters of the town, forming a separate ecclesiastical and residential development beyond the river.
>
> (1975, 46)

In his discussion of St Andrew's credentials as a putative minster, Dunning noted that the earliest documented minster in Somerset was at Wells,

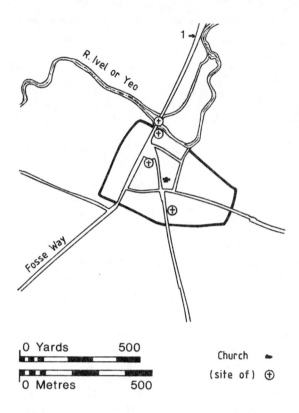

O Yards 500

O Metres 500

Church

(site of)

10 Ilchester, Somerset: Roman defences, selected roads and medieval churches (former and existing). 1 St Andrew, Northover (*Main source*: Aston 1984)

where the church is known from written records to have been in existence before the last quarter of the eighth century. Recent excavations in the cloister area at Wells under the superintendence of Dr Warwick Rodwell have disclosed a fascinating picture. As at Canterbury, there appears to have been a row of churches. The easternmost building embodied a chapel-mausoleum of the tenth century which overlapped the site of a late or sub-Roman mausoleum that had come to act as the focus for a cemetery in the seventh–eighth centuries (Rodwell 1984, 13). The significance of Wells as a cult centre will be mentioned again in the next chapter: here it is only necessary to point out that Rodwell's excavations have at least provided evidence for a succession of funerary structures between the fifth–sixth and later centuries (Fig. 11). Whether this sequence allows us to think in terms of unbroken Christian tradition is a different matter, but the archaeology does allow us to reflect upon this possibility. The implications of the discoveries at Wells for a church like St Andrew at Northover are unknown, but they reinforce interest in the potential of its site.

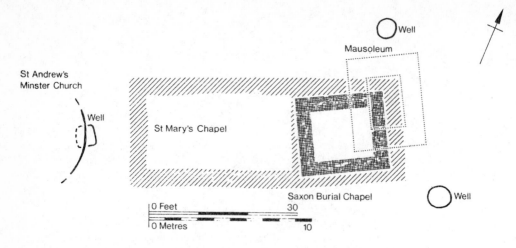

11 Wells, Somerset. Excavation within the cloister of the medieval cathedral disclosed the remains of a pre-Conquest burial chapel which followed upon a late or sub-Roman mausoleum (*Source*: Warwick Rodwell)

St Mary de Lode, Gloucester. St Mary de Lode offers another instance of a medieval parish church which occupies an earlier burial place, conceivably of early post-Roman date. The present church, which is still in regular use, is on a plan that dates from the twelfth and thirteenth centuries, although the tower is older and the nave was rebuilt in 1826, complete with cast iron columns. Following excavations carried out in 1978 and 1979 it is now confirmed that a substantial Roman building lies beneath the nave. Churchbuilders in later centuries respected the alignment of this early structure.

In the fifth century or later, the Roman building having been demolished and its debris levelled off, a timber building was erected on the site. Several graves oriented east–west were found under the floor of this structure. Evidence for other, possibly contemporary funerals was found nearby. The following stage in the development of the site is known only from fragmentary traces; it is difficult to characterize and has not been precisely dated. Later came the remains of a church, built in the tenth or eleventh century, which apparently contained a western gallery made of wood. The eleventh century saw the insertion of a permanent font. Around 1100 the church underwent further remodelling, and gained a tower which intervened between the nave and the chancel (Bryant 1980, 16–17).

Here, in shadowy outline, we have another possible example of development from a post-Roman mausoleum, through successive structures of increasingly ecclesiastical aspect, to a medieval parish church. Of course, we cannot be certain that this development was uninterrupted, any more than we can be sure that the sleepers in the earlier wooden building were Christians and not pagans. On the other hand, local tradition avers that St Mary de Lode was an ancient foundation. This belief is supported by the fact that the original parish seems to have been very large, that it was apparently coincident with a royal hundred, and that it was later dissected (Heighway and Hill 1978, 119; Heighway 1980b, 219; Thacker 1982, 207). This need not imply an origin for the church itself any earlier than around the start of the tenth century. However, the topographical context of the church may also be of relevance and calls for description.

St Mary de Lode stood in the western suburb of medieval Gloucester. The church took its byname from a nearby arm of the River Severn which had become choked with silt. Other names were 'St Mary de Port' and 'St Mary-before-the-Gate'. The gate in question was set in the wall which enclosed the precinct of St Peter's abbey. In the fourth century the site lay close to the waterfront of Roman Gloucester. At this stage the branch of the Severn was still navigable. Substantial buildings stood in the vicinity of the quay. The lines of Gloucester's western defences at this date are not exactly known, but it seems possible that they had been augmented to embrace the waterfront area. No Roman burials have yet been recognized in the immediate vicinity of St Mary's, but excavations on the site of the ruined minster of St Oswald, just over a hundred yards to the north-west, have disclosed a small quota of late Roman graves (Heighway 1980, 207-8). This may suggest that the contemporary city wall or boundary passed between the two sites. If so, St Mary's cannot be strictly described as having been extra-mural. To say this, however, is to define the circumstances of post-Roman Gloucester in fourth-century terms. By the eighth century, when the monastery of St Peter had been established in the north-western corner of the former *colonia*, it is to be supposed that settlement had retracted. There may therefore have been an interval during which St Mary's, or whatever preceded it, was effectively extra-mural, until it was reabsorbed into a suburb of the medieval town. Such a sequence might stand comparison with that which has been described at Tours, where Martin was buried in what had previously been an inhabited area of the city (cf. Bullough 1983, 179). But if at Gloucester a cult had developed around one of the graves inside the wooden building which preceded St Mary's, it did not endure.

St Albans *Hrt*. The example of St Albans has been left until last, partly because it is the most complicated and also because it offers the widest, and most tantalizing, array of evidence.

The modern town of St Albans stands on a hill, apart from the site of the Roman city of Verulamium. The place takes its name from one of only three Romano-British martyrs whose names have come down to us. The other two, Aaron and Julius, are associated by tradition with Caerleon, in south-east Wales. The name Aaron, incidentally, serves to remind us that one of the main mechanisms for the westward spread of Christianity in the first and second centuries involved Jewish communities in cities around the Mediterranean. The first stages of this process are chronicled in the New Testament.

Not much is known about Albanus. Even the date of his death is the subject of dispute. All that we can reasonably suppose is that he was the victim of an outbreak of persecution in the third or fourth century. We are on firmer ground when we turn to consider the development of the cult. In 429 the Gaulish bishop Germanus visited Britain in order to combat the Pelagian heresy. Germanus's biographer informs us that the bishop was told about Albanus, and that he went to look at the *martyrium*. Gildas, writing somewhere in Britain during the first half of the sixth century, adds the important detail that Albanus lay at Verulamium. Later still, Bede stated:

> The blessed Albanus suffered death on 22 June near the city of Verolamium. ... Here when peaceful times returned, a church of wonderful workmanship was built, a worthy memorial to his martyrdom. To this day [c. 731] sick people are helped in this place and the working of frequent miracles continues to bring it renown.
>
> (*HE* i.7)

Bede had access to a *passio* (an account of the death of a saint) that existed in a version that has not survived. There are recensions of the Albanus *passio* which can be dated to the seventh and sixth centuries, but it is evident that the sixth-century recension was based upon an earlier text. Since the sixth-century recension was not the one that Bede saw, we must assume that the *passio* originated in the fifth century. For other reasons, too, this is probable. The *passio* is anti-Pelagian in tone, placing strong emphasis upon the necessity for divine intervention and downplaying good works. For example, when Albanus was led to his execution his path out of the city was barred by a throng of spectators. By an act of God, reminiscent of an earlier episode, the river waters were parted. Albanus walked across, dry shod, to his death. These, and other details seem to reflect some real acquaintance with the topography of Verulamium, and it is likely that the author of the fifth-century *passio* was someone associated with Germanus's circle. During the sixth century the cult of Albanus was taken up abroad; there are early church dedications to him on the continent, especially in the Rhineland.

Modern interest in the ecclesiastical development of St Albans has centred chiefly upon the area around the abbey which lies at the core of the medieval town. The present church, promoted to cathedral in 1878, is virtually all that survives of the great Benedictine layout that was established there shortly after the Conquest (Brooke 1977a). This monastery replaced a pre-Conquest house. According to William of Malmesbury, a religious community had been founded there by the Mercian king Offa c. 793. It is a fair assumption, although no more than that, that the site selected by Offa had to do with the miracle-working centre mentioned by Bede, which in its turn is likely to have had some connection, supposed or real, with the burial place of the hero Albanus himself. Excavations within the abbey precincts under the co-direction of Professor Martin Biddle and Mrs B.Kjølbye-Biddle have produced finds which encourage them to believe that 'the Anglo-Saxon use of the hilltop may have been both complex and long-lived and that a "context for Alban" in the Romano-British use of the hilltop may also be within reach of future work' (1982, 9).

While the metamorphosis from *martyrium* to Benedictine abbey was taking place on the hill, other developments seem to have been in progress in and around the deserted city of Verulamium itself (Fig. 12). First we must notice the site of the parish church of St Michael. St Michael stands close to the forum complex of Verulamium. There are reports of a basilican building lying diagonally under the church which was glimpsed during early excavations through paths in the churchyard. The fact that a parish church and the site of a Roman public building here coincide may be entirely fortuitous, but analogous superimpositions can be observed elsewhere, and in several cases, at least, it is likely that the original association was determined by something more than chance. At Leicester, for instance, the large parish church of St Nicholas embodies pre-Conquest fabric, including several windows which can still be seen above the north arcade. Just outside the west end of the church there stands the famous Jewry Wall; a rugged cliff of Roman masonry which still rises to a height of over thirty feet. In her report on excavations adjacent to the Jewry Wall, Dame Kathleen Kenyon suggested that the survival of this portion of Roman work may have been due to its incorporation within the structure of an Anglo-Saxon predecessor to St Nicholas (Kenyon 1948, 8; cf. Liddle 1982, 4, Fig. 2). Other parish churches in or beside former Roman city centres include St Andrew, Aldborough *NY*, part of which appears to be directly founded upon the remains of a Roman building; St Tathan, Caerwent *Mon*; St Peter Cornhill in the City of London; and St Paul-in-the Bail in Lincoln. In the case of St Paul, excavations by the Lincoln Archaeological Trust have confirmed that the medieval parish church occupied a site which was close to the centre of the forum courtyard of the Roman *colonia*. The results of these excavations have not yet been published in full, but from the preliminary statements that have been released it would appear that the first church on the site was erected no later than the seventh century, and conceivably as early as the fourth (Jones and Wacher 1987, 36, Fig. 19). In other words, the building at the root of the ecclesiastical sequence may actually have been Roman. The site was in use as a cemetery between the fifth and seventh centuries. Burials yielding dates within this period have been found in the near vicinity of medieval churches in several other towns of Roman origin, such as Exeter (Bidwell 1979) and Worcester (Barker *et al.* 1974).

On a military site the corresponding position for a church would be near the *principia*, as at York. A number of parish churches take this posi-

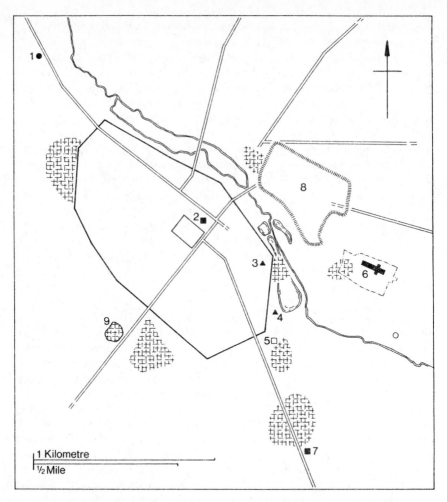

12 St Albans, Hertfordshire: ecclesiastical and funerary geography, Roman to medieval. The irregular polygon represents the defences of the Roman city (*Source*: Frere 1972). **1** St Mary de Pré (Benedictine nuns and leper hospital); **2** St Michael (parish church); **3** St Mary Magdalene (chapel); **4** St German (chapel); **5** possible Roman cemetery church (Anthony 1968); **6** abbey; **7** St Stephen (parish church); **8** Kingsbury; **9** pagan Anglo-Saxon cemetery

tion. St Peter's at Chester lies just above the junction between the *via praetoria* and the *via principalis* of the former legionary fortress, as if the entrance to the *principia* had been adapted to serve as the first church. At Caerleon *Mon* the headquarters building is partly overlain by what is now the parish church of St Cadoc (Nash-Williams 1953, 19). Loughor *Glm* presents a similar picture. For various reasons, therefore, the site of St Michael at Verulamium arouses curiosity.

St Michael was not the only church to stand within the walls of the old city. To the south-east stood a chapel dedicated to St Mary Magdalene. The twelfth-century historian William of Malmesbury thought that this building had been founded by Wulsin, the sixth abbot of St Albans. Not far off stood another chapel. This was dedicated to St Germanus. In the thirteenth century it was believed that the chapel marked the site of the house where Germanus lodged during his visit in 429. The chapel is said to have been in ruins during the time of Eadfrith, the fifth abbot, and it was rumoured to have been re-established as a hermitage by a Dane. This chapel stood *outside* the city wall, apparently within a zone of Roman inhumation burials. Nearby, the remains of what may be a defunct Romano-British extra-mural church were excavated early in the 1960s (Anthony 1968). Further to the south-east is another parish church, St Stephen's. This churchyard has yielded Roman cremation burials.

William of Malmesbury reported that the churches of St Michael and St Stephen, together with another church, St Peter, which stands half a mile north-east of the abbey, had been 'piously built in part' at the instigation of abbot Wulsin, 'both for the adornment and for the use of the neighbourhood, and for the salvation of souls' (*Gesta abbatum* i.22; cited in Salzman 1967, 357). Wulsin's dates are not exactly known, but a period for the construction of the churches around the middle of the tenth century is indicated. It has been proposed that the three churches betoken a plan on Wulsin's part to develop St Albans as a town, but the dispersed pattern of the sites is hardly in accord with this and appears rather to indicate a pre-existing pattern of small settlements – whether secular or religious it is impossible to guess – one of which was centred on the core of the old Roman city. There is in any case some doubt as to whether Wulsin actually began the churches, or whether one or more of them could have been redevelopments of existing sites. Beyond this, we cannot even be sure if the story about Wulsin's involvement rests upon any reliable foundation. Nevertheless, it is interesting to meet the suggestion that the leader of a powerful religious house could create a group of local churches at a single stroke.

The point has been reached at which we must try to take stock. Most of what has been offered by way of example and analogy has been couched in terms of innuendo. The sites of certain parish churches may be 'suggestive' or 'potentially significant'. Early origins are 'presumed' and there has been a good deal of nimble vaulting across wide gaps in the historical and archaeological records. No evidence has been produced which can testify unequivocally to Christian continuity between fifth-century sites and those of later parish churches. On the other hand, the data now available from Wells, Gloucester and possibly Lincoln do certainly offer some promise as stepping stones across the dark waters, even if, as yet, there is no bridge. With these points in mind it may be added that there is quite a large number of parish churches, not so far mentioned, which display the same sort of topographical relationships as have been under

39

consideration here. These include St Mary, Great Dunmow *Ex*; Old Malton *NY*; St Mary, Godmanchester *Hu*; the ancestor of St Botolph's Priory at Colchester, where the site of a *martyrium* has been suggested on the grounds of the position of the church, outside the Roman south-east gate and away from the Anglo-Saxon town centre (Crummy 1980, 274); and St John, Chester (Thacker 1982, 200–1). This list could be lengthened to include such churches in Wales as St Peblig, beside the road running south-east out of Segontium (Caernarvon); or St Cattwg, Gelligaer *Glm*. Just beyond the former limits of Roman Carmarthen there was the medieval Augustinian priory of St John the Evangelist and St Teulyddog. It was not unusual for Augustinian houses to be established as the regular successors of more ancient religious communities.

What factors can be envisaged as having influenced the selection of these church sites? In asking this question it is necessary to be aware that some of the Roman places mentioned above, and others that could have been, were empty before the Roman occupation came to an end. One possibility is that in a proportion of the examples given the church may reflect the presence of a post-Roman secular power which came to be seated in or alongside a former Roman place. Such churches would then be explicable as adjuncts of centres frequented by kings or lords: in effect, originally, as private chapels. Traditions of burial do not have to be invoked.

On the other hand we should remind ourselves that a place of political authority could benefit through association with a source of spiritual force. The entanglement of sacred and secular factors as an aspect of the development of early medieval settlement will be explored later on; here, it is enough to notice that our two tentative explanations – 'cult' and (for the moment) 'non-cult' – need not be mutually exclusive. Indeed, in the case of a recent burial, such as of a prominent leader or venerated ancestor, maybe even a pre-conversion ancestor, it is not difficult to envisage a process of occlusion whereby the features of one process came to be cloaked by those of the other. Theorizing apart, we are on firmer ground in supposing that features of the devotional traditions which developed at the gravesides of martyrs and holy men on the European mainland appeared also in Britain.

Turning to mechanics, a tale recounted by Roger of Wendover in the twelfth century is instructive. A man was visited by St Alban in a dream. The saint showed him some *tumuli* near Redbourn *Hrt*, known as the Hills of the Banners, and singled one out because it contained the remains of St Amphibalus. (In the later Middle Ages Amphibalus was venerated as the missionary who had converted St Alban. However, it would appear that Amphibalus was conjured up out of a misreading of Gildas by Geoffrey of Monmouth *c.* 1135, who confused *amphibalus* 'a woolly cloak' with a personal name (McCulloch 1981).) On the following day a party of monks set out for Redbourn. They excavated the barrow. Sure enough, the bones of the holy man were unearthed, together with those of two companions, the skeleton of a fourth individual lying at a different angle and six others nearby. 'St Amphibalus' was accompanied by two knives, disposed in a fashion which the monks believed to be in accordance with the story of his martyrdom.

Apart from the identification of Amphibalus and the dream, there are details in this story which look acceptable. Multiple inhumations in barrows are common, as are secondary burials on different alignments. Knives often accompanied the heathen (and some Christian) English into the hereafter, although without knowing more it is just as possible that 'Amphibalus' was a Dane. The interest of the story lies in its illustration of the foreshortened historical memory of the medieval historian and an inability to distinguish between antiquities of different periods. Bearing in mind the intense interest in relics throughout the period, it is possible to see this episode as providing a key to a more general mechanism whereby perfectly normal and probably pagan burials could on occasion be promoted as objects of cult attention. To be more specific, two ways can be suggested in which the process might have worked.

First, the minutes of early councils contain admonitions about the impropriety of giving attention to pseudo-cults. In the mid-fourth century, for example, churchfolk in Gaul were being warned not to frequent cemeteries or chapels dedicated to 'so-called martyrs' belonging to heretics, for prayer or divine service. St Martin found an altar that had been dedicated to a criminal in the mistaken belief that some martyrs had been buried there. Being Martin, he cross-examined the shade of the dead man and then broke up the altar. In 517 the council at Epaon issued a prohibition against the keeping of relics in private oratories, ostensibly because there would be no clerk to sing psalms over them, but just as possibly as a means of retaining control over the verification of local cults. The pagan custom of presenting food offerings to the dead on certain days persisted for several centuries, and was sometimes modified so that the offerings were made on the feast days of particular saints.

When it was faced with superstitious practices which it could not eradicate, the Church sometimes attempted to render them respectable by 'discovering' a saintly identity for the dead person. There is no evidence to show that this sort of thing went on in England, but the fabrication of *passiones* and *vitae* was certainly practised in Merovingian Gaul (Wood 1979, 103, 109) and there is no reason to suppose that the arts of deception developed there could not have been applied here. A context for such a process is available. Take, for example, the case of Lullingstone K, where a small church was erected upon the site of a curious Roman structure, allegedly a hybrid between a temple and a mausoleum, at some time before the Conquest (Taylor and Taylor 1965; Meates 1979) (Fig. 13). Not far away at Stone-by-Faversham K, Anglo-Saxon builders took another Roman building of probable religious or funerary function and turned part of it into a church (Fletcher and Meates 1969, 1977; Taylor and Yonge 1981). The presence of the element *stān* in these place-names may signal the

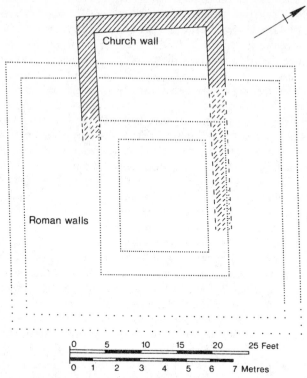

13 Lullingstone, Kent: ruin of church superimposed upon remains of Roman mausoleum adjacent to villa (*Source*: Meates 1979)

existence of some feeling on the part of the English that they were the inheritors of stone and therefore, by definition, *Roman* buildings (Rigold 1972, 38). The church at Cuxton *K* (*Cucolanstan*) might also be placed in this category.

Second, if dreams and visions stretch credulity, we must assume that 'saints' were unearthed first, whether by accident, during treasure hunting, or, possibly, on a hunch, and 'identified' afterwards. In such cases the dream would be a retrospective invention. This requires us to ask why a few burials were treated with respect and the great majority of others were ignored, as by the monks from Ely who, in the seventh century, rummaged through a cemetery outside Roman Cambridge in order to acquire a decent sarcophagus (*HE* iv.9). In fact, one can envisage a wide variety of circumstances which could have given rise to superstitious fantasies, not to mention the extensive scope afforded to religious by old burial grounds for downright fraud. As one illustration of the credulous aspect, there may have been potential latent in the Roman practice, adopted by Christians, of packing certain corpses in gypsum or plaster (Ramm 1971; Green 1977). The plaster was intended to act as a preservative, and this may have led to some 'miraculous' discoveries of incorrupt bodies or the survival of their garments in later centuries. Plaster burials have been found under several parish and monastic churches. There is, for instance, this intriguing account of a discovery made at Brixworth *Np*, published in the *Northampton Herald* on 16 December 1865:

> On excavating the floor of the square tower, I discovered the bases of two circular columns on each side of the original west entrance, with a wall running from one of them towards the nave. . . . These bases had been hacked on the outer side of each, to receive respectively the corpse of a fully-grown person, who from being cramped up would appear to have suffered a violent death; one of them was encased in mortar, and till exposed to the atmosphere, the teeth and bones had an appearance of great comparative freshness.

The phenomenon of rapid decay after exposure to the air is sometimes associated with gypsum or plaster burials. It also recalls the curious legend which appears in the medieval poem *St Erkenwald*. The poem was written towards the end of the fourteenth century, but it was set in London during the episcopate of Eorcenwold, an historical figure who was bishop of London from *c.* 675 to 693. The tale describes how workmen digging beside the foundations of the cathedral disinterred a marvellous tomb, wherein was found a corpse in a perfect state of preservation. Eorcenwold was summoned. The corpse talked to him, explained that in life he had been a good man, a fair judge, but that he had had the misfortune to live in a pre-Christian age. As a result, his soul was in limbo. Eorcenwold was much moved by this. He recited the baptismal formula and shed a tear on the face of the pagan. Almost immediately the man's soul was 'seized in bliss', and the corpse crumbled to dust.

There are several reports which refer to the finding of early burials on the site of St Paul's cathedral; descriptions of the objects found in the graves suggest that some of them could have been late Roman, although elsewhere in the City no *dated* burial has been found within the walls which is later than the end of the second century. A local origin for the tale is in any case unlikely, since early in the eighth century a similar story was told at Whitby which involved the pagan Roman emperor Trajan, who was rescued from hell by Gregory the Great (Colgrave 1968, 127–9). Is it conceivable that discoveries of gypsum or plaster burials may have provided a familiar context or some materials for this class of legend, or reinforced existing beliefs about the significance of incorrupt bodies?

In conclusion it must be asked why, Albanus apart, if Roman or early post-Roman burial places were indeed occasionally singled out and became the nuclei of later churches, this process left no mark in medieval tradition or the pattern of church dedications. Several points may be relevant. The simplest of them lies in the likelihood that in Britain, as in Gaul, there had not been all that many martyrs. Consequently the tombs of genuine martyrs were rather rare. The trend towards bishop–saints which took hold in Gaul during the fifth century was not, as far as we know, accompanied by any corresponding movement in south-east Britain. Further, the 'discovery' of saints in Gaul was chiefly a phenomenon of the sixth century and so in advance of the Roman mission to England, while being later than the point to which the Romano-British Church can be expected to have survived. The finding of Albanus by the visiting bishop Germanus in 429 is actually a very early example of this sort of episode.

Another factor which needs to be considered is that the invented martyrs in Gaul were typically portrayed as evangelist figures. In the seventh century England and Ireland were producing evangelists of their own: men like Aidan, Chad and Cuthbert. The process witnessed in Gaul may thus have been unnecessary here. Put another way, if cults did sometimes centre upon older tombs in Britain, the demands people made of them would have differed from those made on the continent.

It should also be remembered that there were many English and Welsh saints about whom little or nothing could be recalled by the twelfth century. 'Does not the whole island blaze with so many relics that you can scarcely pass a village of any consequence but what you hear the name of some new saint?' wrote William of Malmesbury around 1125. He added: 'And of how many have all records perished?' (trans. in *EHD* 2, 290). To give just one example, Bede wrote at some length about the exemplary career of a lady called Æthelburh who became abbess of a monastery at Barking *Ex* before 675. Bede tells us that he drew upon a *Life* of Æthelburh which had achieved a wide circulation (*HE* iv.7). Yet interest in this cult had declined even before the Conquest, and the text of the *Life* did not survive. By the sixteenth century only one church in England is known to have carried her dedication, and that was in the City of London and may perhaps be connected with the fact that Æthelburh's brother, Eorcenwold, had been a famous bishop there.

When all these points are taken into account, it should come as no surprise if minor and perhaps dubious or makeshift cults based upon a pre-Augustinian stratum of graves found no permanent place in people's thoughts. Indeed, in these circumstances even the three names, one *vita* and the handful of suggestive place-names that have come down to us begin to look positively copious. If there is any other residue of information, it lies encoded in the sites of churches, and in their archaeological deposits, not in documents.

If the foregoing discussion seems to be unduly speculative, we are entitled to assert that Christian holy places, or places which could later be portrayed as such, did exist in Wales and parts of England in the fifth and sixth centuries, and that there may have been some scope for their reclamation or redefinition in after years. Gildas, as we have noted, knew about Albanus. He was also aware of a contemporary belief that there were graves and places of suffering of martyrs in various parts of Britain which 'would now have the greatest effect in instilling the blaze of divine charity in the mind of beholders, were it not that our citizens, thanks to their sins, have been deprived of many of them by the unhappy partition with the barbarians' (Gildas, *De Excidio* 10; trans. Winterbottom 1978, 19). This returns us to the English, and to heathenism, and it is to this darker prelude to the origins of local churches that we must now turn.

II

A VOICE FROM
THE WELL

Between eternity and the numbered days of human experience there is the difficult time we call prehistory. Prehistoric time is 'difficult' because on the scale of, say, rocks or oceans, it scarcely signifies; yet from the standpoint of the individual it borders the unimaginable.

Before the mountains were brought forth, or ever thou hadst formed the earth and the world, even from everlasting to everlasting, thou art God . . . for a thousand years in thy sight are but as yesterday when it is past, and as a watch in the night.

(Psalms 90:2, 4)

Let us try to place prehistory into some sort of comprehensible perspective. Sit still. Watch a clock for one hour. Imagine this to represent the span of human existence upon our planet. If we seek the beginnings of mankind's religious sensibility in *Homo sapiens neanderthalensis*, then relative to those sixty minutes the entire history of the Christian religion up to the present will have been contained in the last two to three minutes. Should we decide to look back to earlier hominids the birth of Christ would occur only a few seconds before the hour.

The sheer novelty of Christianity prompts questions. How, for instance, did early Christians look upon the sacred places of former centuries? Was the map of sanctuaries and shrines wiped clean and religious topography suddenly reinvented? Or do we see Christianity rather as a revaluation of humanity's relationship with the divine: a recent episode in a continuum with beginnings beyond recorded memory?

Our questions will be shaped and coloured by the beliefs we hold today. That aside, the asking of them presupposes a unitary character for the

46

early Church which it did not actually possess. By the end of the fourth century the Christian world was large. The attitudes of churchmen towards paganism, and paganism itself, differed from place to place. And when senior figures travelled to take up appointments in distant parts, opinions which had been moulded in one area could be transferred to another. Seventh-century Canterbury provides examples. One of the abbots of the monastery of SS Peter and Paul was by birth an African; Theodore, archbishop 669–92, came from Asia Minor.

How, then, did the Christian concept of a *place* of worship arise, and how did it evolve? The evangelists who preached their way from city to city around the shores of the Mediterranean during the first century held that the old law and writings of the prophets were a 'shadow of good things to come, and not the very image of those things' (Hebrews 10:1). Blood sacrifices and holy places of the past had been necessary that 'the pattern of things in heaven should be purified with these'. But Christ 'is not entered into holy places made with hands' (Hebrews 9:23–4); rather, 'ye are the temple of the living God' (II Corinthians 6:16).

These teachings remind us that Christianity began as a sect within Judaism. However, as early as the fourth decade of the first century Christians are found preaching to Gentiles:

> they which were scattered abroad upon the persecution that arose about Stephen travelled as far as Phoenicia, and Cyprus, and Antioch, preaching the word to none but unto the Jews only. And some of them were men of Cypruse and Cyrene, which, when they were come to Antioch, spake unto the Greeks, preaching the Lord Jesus.
>
> (Acts 11:19–20)

Now, as Professor Markus has put it, 'was Christianity a way of being a Jew or was it something else?' (1974, 22). Universality prevailed. The question of the relation of the old law to Gentile converts was faced in the declaration, 'Ye are not under the old law, but under grace' (Romans 6:14), and elsewhere (e.g. Acts 15:23–9).

How, if at all, these views might be applicable to the *sites* of Gentile worship was not explained. St Paul regarded the tabernacles and sanctuaries of ancient Israel as 'figures of the true'. But temples, shrines and other sacred places which existed elsewhere, in the Gentile world, could hardly be categorized in the same way.

One reason for the absence of a contemporary ruling on this point is that until *c.* 200 the issue did not really arise at all. At first, those Jews who subscribed to Christian teaching continued to attend their synagogues. In due course Christianity acquired a separate identity. But the Church of the later first and the second century was still small, consisting of cells of initiates who neither needed nor wanted permanent buildings. For them, the act rather than the place of worship was what mattered, an attitude which is witnessed in the primary meaning of *ekklēsia* (whence the Latin *ecclesia* 'the Church', and later, by extension, 'church building'): 'an assembly of those called out'.

The third century saw some relaxation on the part of officialdom towards Christianity, and after episodes of persecution under Decius (250-1) and Valerian (257-9) it acquired the status of an officially approved cult. The fourth century brought rapid change. Following the capture of Rome by Constantine in 312 and the Edict of Toleration in the following year, Christianity began to gain an institutional face, wealth and a public architecture. What had previously been looked upon as an introverted and, at times, subversive cult was now on the way to exploding into a mass movement.

Official interest was directed towards places which were precious to Christians. At Jerusalem excavations were made on the traditional site of the tomb of the Lord, long since engulfed by the construction of Aelia Capitolina and buried beneath the temple of Jupiter Capitolinus. In 326-7 the temple was demolished and a structure interpreted as the Divine Grotto was disinterred (Coüasnon 1974, 11-13). In Rome, the grave of St Peter, in the midst of a pagan necropolis, was covered by a new church which left access only to the cult place of the saint beneath it. Other Constantinian developments took place on the funerary sites of St Sebastian, St Lawrence and St Agnes. The church which was superimposed upon the cemetery containing the grave of St Lawrence stood beside the Tiburtine road, where 'a portico, still preserved in the eighth century, ran all the way to the city gate, protecting the faithful from sun and rain' (Krautheimer 1980, 25, 24-8). Elsewhere in the west, at Trier, Mainz, Lyon and at petty golgothas outside other places, churchbuilders followed suit.

Within the walls, meanwhile, capacious new basilicas were erected for congregational use. In towns which were administratively important space would be sought for the *episcopium*: a complex which could include a cathedral, baptistery, mansion for the bishop, together with residential and secretarial quarters for his staff.

In several respects these developments stood custom upon its head. One novelty lay in the functional character of a church. Pagan temples were the abodes of gods. They could be approached and entered by individuals, but they were not designed to accommodate congregational worship. Churches, on the other hand, were meeting-houses, both in a spiritual and a practical sense. Being so, they exerted new influences upon town life and town planning. As for the cemetery churches, nowhere can the reversal of the values of pagan antiquity be seen more clearly.

At first, but with Rome excepted, the growth in influence of the Church was not matched by any coherent policy on the treatment of pagan monuments. Until the middle years of the fourth century urban Christianity and pagan cults were permitted to co-exist. Thereafter pagans found themselves subject to a series of increasingly intolerant edicts which culminated in an outright ban upon their activities in 395. As the Church grew in power, so some temples, pagan properties and revenues were taken into ecclesiastical control. Many temples were demolished. Others were taken over for use by Christians, or else flattened to make way for churches.

These transitions were not always peaceful. Around the eastern and southern shores of the Mediterranean there were ugly scenes. Gangs of monks and ascetics, a self-appointed *Schutzstaffel* of the Church Militant, stormed temples and synagogues and harassed those who attended them. Religious terrorism was notably brutal in Syria and Egypt, the heartlands of the monastic movement, but disturbances spread to the west. At about the same time as a contingent of ferocious monks tore apart the Serapeum in Alexandria, the bishop Martin was annoying rustics in the Touraine by breaking up their shrines and cutting down sacred trees. Destructions of Mithraea and other fourth-century temples have been recognized in Britain. Usually it would be rash to assume that Christians were responsible (Thomas 1981, 133–5), but excavations at Icklingham *Sf* have produced evidence which at the least is suggestive of the demolition of a pagan building, closely followed by the erection of a small church and baptistery nearby (West and Plouviez 1976).

Temple-wrecking was not universal. There were occasions when pagan buildings were adapted for use by Christians. Famous cases include the temple of Athena at Syracuse and the Hephaiston at Athens. Before the middle of the sixth century a temple, possibly that of Apis, had been transformed into a church at Memphis in Egypt. Damascus provides the celebrated case of the Umayyad mosque, which originated as a temple, was converted into a church in the time of Theodosius I (379–95), and later passed into Islamic hands, to be turned into a mosque by Caliph Walid in 709–15 (Wilkinson 1977, 155). As for Rome, according to Bede, pope Boniface IV (608–15)

> obtained for the Church of Christ from the Emperor Phocas the gift of the temple at Rome anciently known as the Pantheon because it represented all the gods. After he had expelled every abomination from it, he made a church of it dedicated to the Holy Mother of God and all the martyrs of Christ, so that, when the multitudes of devils had been driven out, it might serve as a shrine for the multitude of saints.
>
> (*HE* ii.4)

The dedication ceremony was held on 13 May 609. Eight years before, pope Gregory (590–604) had advised Augustine to convert idol temples in England to Christian use (see p. 70). As far as is known, the Pantheon was the first pagan temple to have been so converted in Rome itself.

On yet other occasions temples were demolished and replaced by churches. Pagans in the Palestinian city of Gaza, for example, were able to use their principal temple, the Marneum, until 406, when it was destroyed and a church built upon the site (Wilkinson 1977, 157). In Gaul,

Roman temples occur under urban churches with some frequency, as at Arles, Angers and Sens. In the countryside, too, pagan sites were sometimes adapted for use by Christians. Mont-Beuvray, Saône-et-Loire, furnishes a sequence of probable Iron Age shrine, Gallo-Roman temple and an early medieval chapel which was built over the temple ruins and dedicated, appropriately, to St Martin (Horne and King 1980, 433–4).

Britain has a small quota of parish churches and chapels which overlie the sites of Romano-Celtic temples. Some examples were mentioned in the previous chapter, and a few will be discussed again in more detail below (p. 59). Our difficulty is to know whether such temple sites had retained any religious significance for people at the time, several centuries later, when the churches were built. In order to tackle this question it is first necessary to examine a dichotomy which existed within paganism itself.

Accounts of the destruction and the takeover of pagan sites by Christians conceal a distinction between the character of religious life in cosmopolitan cities and the indigenous paganism of the countryside. Large Roman towns were centres of institutionalized religion. For several reasons the state gods of late antiquity were under stress. Town communities were becoming less intimate, more shiftless and their members prone to a range of anxieties (Brown 1971, 60–88). Christianity offered a salve to this unease. It bestowed a sense of identity, an expectant mood and the prescription for a clearcut lifestyle. Also, the Roman administrative system, which was based upon towns, provided an institutional framework for the emerging Church. Words familiar to us, like *vicar*, and particularly terms to do with land and jurisdiction, like *parish* and *diocese*, originated in the technical language of the civil government of the late Roman empire.

Out in the countryside, meanwhile, farmers lived as they always had done: by the rhythm of the seasons and the unremitting obligations of agricultural labour. Their religion was essentially propitiatory in its purpose, and their deities were ancient. Propitiation was achieved through the performance of a variety of rituals, the potency of which would depend in large part upon the correctness with which they were enacted. Some rituals were a matter for the individual. With others the family, or a group of neighbours, might be involved. A few were seasonal festivals: large, regional events at which recreation, feasting, trading and religious observances were combined. Each class of ritual would have its own sort of venue, ranging from the simple household shrine through to the ceremonial meeting-place at which many people might gather on important occasions.

Prehistoric societies were not stationary in their beliefs. The externals of their religion evidently underwent change. But between the early Iron Age (if not sooner) and the sixth century AD it would seem that the underlying *aims* of rural religion altered little, even if there were regional and temporal variations in the ways that these aims were expressed. In Gaul and Britain the Romans introduced new cults. However, this was seldom done with the intention of superseding indigenous deities. On the contrary, the personalities of Roman gods and goddesses were often merged with those of local deities, so that each reinforced the other.

Despite its antiquity, rural paganism can never have seemed hoary or worn out, for its central theme turned upon the annual cycle of decay and renewal. It was therefore ever young. It follows that the technical demands of Christian evangelism in cities and in the countryside were different. Whereas social conditions in the greater urban places actually fostered the growth of Christianity during the third century, and provided an institutional framework for its consolidation in the next, in rural regions paganism remained strong. The conversion of country-dwelling populations was thus a continuing process rather than something that could be undertaken once-for-all. Where towns declined, as they did to vanishing point in Britain in the period c. 350–500, paganism may actually have been gaining ground. Britain remained substantially rural until the Industrial Revolution, and we shall find that features of pagan belief and practice co-existed with Christianity down to the nineteenth century. (Obelkevich 1976, 280–99). The word 'pagan' derives ultimately from the Latin *paganus* 'country dweller'.

Although rural paganism was deeply entrenched, there were aspects of Christian teaching and history which could be accentuated in order to impress the rustic mind. Missionaries played upon the belief in an active spirit world. There were miracles and supernatural happenings aplenty both in the scriptures and in more recent Christian tradition. Moreover, churchmen did not deny that heathen deities existed: pagan gods were acknowledged as being both real and dangerous. Inevitably, therefore, monks and missionaries emerged as wonderworkers, for by challenging and vanquishing deities, and destroying their shrines, they were performing miracles. The Celtic attachment to particular landscape features, regarded as the abodes of deities, provided a lattice of points across the landscape, some of which, at least in Gaul, were redefined and incorporated within the new Christian geography. Gregory of Tours gives instances of the emplacement of churches upon pagan sites, and there are both archaeological and literary indications that some of St Martin's churches were so located.

There were other aspects of rural religion which could be turned to advantage by Christians. Churchmen found it helpful to synchronize their festivals with customary turning points in the pagan calendar. As was described in the previous chapter, bishops sometimes contrived to 'discover' the tombs of 'saints' in convenient places. And when ecclesiastical leaders died, the graves and shrines containing their relics provided new points of focus within the landscape. Here was a real asset, for human remains or items that had been placed in contact with them were portable, and saintly power could therefore be transferred from place to place. This later enabled churchmen, Christian kings and aristocrats to exercise a considerable degree of choice as to where holy places should be.

Pagan deities, meanwhile, evicted from their sanctuaries, lingered on in popular thought. Here too the Church may have played some part. Discredited idols provided the Church with material for its demonology. Some of the grim figures that illustrate the techniques and perils of sinful living, as depicted in parochial wall-paintings, windows and corbel tables of the later Middle Ages may be their remote descendants.

Not all heathen god(esse)s were so downgraded. Dr Anne Ross has discerned a pattern 'whereby the attributes, functions and even the names of pagan deities were taken over by the early Irish Church and allocated to saints' (1967, 360). A possible example is Brigid, an Irish goddess who seems to have been merged with the personality of St Brigid of Kildare (1967, 360-1). Presumably there *was* a holy lady, Brigid, and the attributes of the goddess were assimilated to those of the saint (Fig. 14).

The subtleties of such a process are illustrated particularly well in the case of Michael the Archangel. Michael, in common with many pagan deities, is a saint of multiform and to an extent elusive aspect. Alongside his familiar roles as a heavenly warrior, guardian and receiver of souls, Michael was also looked upon as an intercessor for the sick. His enemies, the order of angels that had gone to perdition, present a negative image of his own attributes.

Michael was popular as a dedicatee for parish churches in both England and Wales. Before the era of Victorian parochial expansion roughly 6 per cent of all churches were dedicated to him. He ranked sixth in general popularity as a patron saint. However, enthusiasm for Michael was more intense in some areas than in others. In the dioceses of Hereford and Exeter, for instance, Michael lies near the top of the league table of church dedications, whereas in some other areas he is much less in evidence (Figs 15, 16). The reasons for such unevenness are not immediately apparent. If Michael had actually lived an explanation could be sought in the presence of his relics at certain places, and the influences of such cult centres upon lesser churches in their hinterlands or in their direct possession. But in an age which set great store by the physical remains of saints, Michael stands out as one who had led, and in the medieval mind continued to lead, an excarnate existence. Heavy concentrations of dedications to him cannot therefore be accounted for in ordinary hagiographical terms. Michael's great prestige is additionally interesting for the reason that he appears only once in biblical writing (Revelation 12:7-9).

Michael came to popular attention in a succession of spectacular visions. The first was on Mount Gargano in southern Italy in the 490s. Another occurred in Rome during an epidemic, when pope Gregory I saw the saint sheathing his sword above the mausoleum of Hadrian. Further episodes included the incineration by lightning of a group of Saracens who were attacking Christians, and the dream experienced by bishop Aubert of Avranches *c.* 707 when he fell asleep on the Rocher de la Tombe and

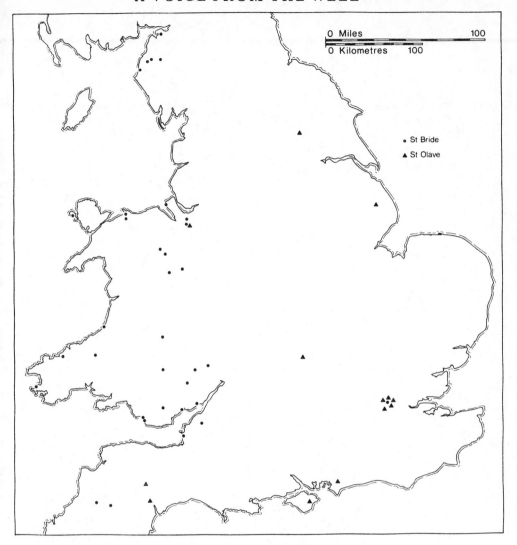

14 Distribution of parish churches bearing dedications to St Bride and St
Olave. All the dedications shown are thought to be older than the nineteenth
century, but note that dedications made at different times are here gathered
into a single distribution

was instructed by the saint to build a church there. A church was duly
constructed and was replaced by the great Benedictine monastery of
Mont-Saint-Michel.

Michael's activities in the heavens, and the elevated sites of the visions,
help to explain why so many churches dedicated to him are found in high
places. John Aubrey remarked how frequently churches of St Michael in
Britain stood on high ground, or else possessed a lofty steeple. There are

53

15 Distribution of parish churches bearing dedications to St Michael. All the dedications are
thought to be older than the nineteenth century, but note that dedications made at different
times are here gathered into a single distribution

16 Dedications to St Michael, generalized by trend surface

churches in the former category, like those on Glastonbury Tor *So* and Bren Tor *D*, which are truly dramatic in their situation. The church of Llanfihangel-yng-Ngwynfa 'St Michael in the Winds' *Pws* (*Mnt*) stands in a curvilinear enclosure a thousand feet up. However, while altitude is undoubtedly a characteristic of the cult of St Michael in Britain, it is so on a relative rather than an absolute basis. Often the site is nothing more than a low hill, as at Lichfield *St*, or a local knoll such as Winwick *Np*, or even above a city gate, as formerly at Canterbury and Winchester.

It has been suggested that in Gaul the cult of St Michael involved a wholesale substitution for the worship of the classical god Mercury. Resemblances between the two render this plausible. Both were active in the heavens. Each played a part as a protector of souls. Mercury was also regarded as a guardian of flocks and herds, and is associated with venery in wooded regions, so that a correspondence with Michael in the uplands and some other areas of Britain where a pastoral economy was practised could help to explain the uneven distribution of Michael dedications. The phenomenon of *interpretatio romana* creates ambiguities, however, as in both Gaul and Britain Mercury was equated with a number of other deities. The Celtic god *Lugos*, for instance, was linked with Mercury in a cult of wide distribution, evidenced both archaeologically and by such place-names as *Lugudunum* (Lyon) in Gaul, and *Luguvalium* (Carlisle) in Britain. At Lyon there is iconographic evidence to connect *Lugos* with Mercury, and a major fifth-century cult of Michael, centred at Ainay, in the Rhône–Saône confluence. (Curiously, the twelfth-century bishops of Carlisle possessed an important outstation at Melbourne *Db* where their church was dedicated to St Michael.)

Equally striking is the case of Moccas *He*. A god named *Moccus* occurs at Langres in Gaul. The name means 'pig', and *Moccus* was equated with Mercury. The Herefordshire Moccas appears in the twelfth-century Liber Llandaff as *Mochros* 'moor for swine', a meaning which is confirmed by its rendering in Latin as *locus porcorum* 'place of pigs'. The church at Moccas is the successor of an important pre-Conquest ecclesiastical centre, which is likely to have existed before *c.* 620 (Davies 1979, nos 163b, 164, 165). It is dedicated to St Michael and All Angels.

Michael has brought us to Britain, and at first glance the pre-Christian religious history of England and Wales appears confusing. Not only were the conversions undertaken fitfully, by several groups of missioners acting in different ways and at different times, but the paganism that they challenged owed many debts: most remotely, perhaps, to aboriginal cults of the Bronze Age; more recently to Celtic religion; to Rome, which as we have seen conflated the *personae* of its own state cults with the identities of indigenous deities; and latterly to Germanic heathendom. Beyond this, in the ninth and tenth centuries there was a revival of rural heathenism in areas which were affected by Scandinavian colonization.

Faced with such a jumble of cults and observances, almost all ill understood, the question of possible relationships between pre-Christian

sacral places and later parish churches becomes bewilderingly complicated. In order to make progress it is helpful to consider two contrasting
hypotheses.

First of all let us assume that the religious practices of each successive
period or culture were carried on in detachment from those that preceded
and followed them: that, for example, all stone circles and henges were
no longer frequented for religious purposes after the early Bronze Age, or
that all Romano-Celtic temples passed out of use before the end of the fifth
century. This, which we may call the *sectional view* of pre-Christian
religion, would insulate churches from anything other than coincidental
contact with all but the most recent pagan sites.

As an alternative to the sectional view let us erect another hypothesis,
which can be described as *regenerative*. This allows that some sites may have
remained in use for cult purposes for extended periods that cut across at
least one of the cultural divisions by which we have become accustomed
to chop up, perhaps a little too arbitrarily, our national history. Sites of
this sort should not be imagined as places where anachronistic rites were
practised doggedly for centuries after they had died out elsewhere.
Rather, we should expect to see signs of adaptation and change, the main
constant being evidence for religious, ceremonial or other gatherings over
a long period of time within a small geographical compass. Uley *Gl* and
Yeavering *Nb* are possible cases in point (Ellison 1980; Hope-Taylor
1977).

These hypotheses are, of course, naive and crude. In order to test them
one would have to identify and take account of a host of variables that
have not so far been mentioned. Sites traditionally regarded as being in
the regenerative class, like Knowlton *Do*, may turn out on closer examination to belong more plausibly in the sectional category, while regenerative
attributes need not signify religious continuity. As will emerge in this and
later chapters, religious sites were not independent of their surroundings,
but generally originated as adjuncts, counterparts or components of places
which were already of significance for other reasons. Moreover, the
likelihood that there were *hierarchies* of heathen site-types increases the
number of indeterminate factors well beyond the point at which one
begins to wonder whether the subject is susceptible to serious study at all.
In particular, there is no reason why sectional and regenerative processes
should not have been in play simultaneously, at different places.

With all this said, the hypotheses may nevertheless be retained as temporary frameworks within which to consider the material that follows.
And since we are beset by uncertainties, it is convenient to begin by ex-
amining paganism in England during the seventh and eighth centuries
AD: the years when conversion was taking place. By reviewing what we
are told about heathen places of worship in this period, we may hope to
gather clues to elucidate the subject in a longer perspective. The aim is
to ascertain whether English heathenism had a geography all of its own,
a sectional pattern of only one or two centuries' standing, or whether

ritual sites of the English were sometimes superimposed upon more ancient sacral places.

Literary references to English heathenism are abundant. They are scattered through Bede's *Ecclesiastical History* and *De Temporum Ratione*; there are several vivid episodes in Stephanus's *Life of Wilfrid*; and there are prohibitions and statements about paganism in penitentials, minutes of councils and correspondence.

Detailed accounts of heathen rites, on the other hand, are few, and descriptions of pagan sites are rare. Among the best known is Bede's relation of Paulinus's mission to the Northumbrians in the 620s. When Edwin, king of Northumbria (616–32), publicly accepted the gospel which was preached by the Roman missionary he turned to Coifi, the chief of the priests, and asked which of them should be the first to 'profane the altars and the shrines of the idols, together with their precincts'. Coifi answered that it would be appropriate for him to take the lead himself. Coifi breached two taboos:

> a high priest of their religion was not allowed to carry arms or to ride except on a mare. So, girded with a sword, he took a spear in his hand and mounting the king's stallion he set off to where the idols were. The common people who saw him thought he was mad. But as soon as he approached the shrine, without any hesitation he profaned it by casting the spear which he held into it; and greatly rejoicing in the knowledge of the worship of the true God, he ordered his companions to destroy and set fire to the shrine and all the enclosures. The place where the idols once stood is still shown, not far from York, to the east, over the River Derwent. Today it is called Godmunddingaham.
>
> (*HE* ii.13)

This is unusually explicit. It may be factual, for otherwise we would have to suppose that Bede invented the two taboos simply in order to enable Coifi to break them. More usually, Bede's references to paganism take the form of vague formulas; his comments about the 'false remedies of idolatry' in times of epidemic (*HE* iv. 27) are typical. So the singularity of the Goodmanham story could be held to reinforce its credibility.

Elsewhere in the *Ecclesiastical History* we are told that idols were fashioned both from wood and stone (iii.22), and that they might be given the likeness of human form (ii.10). There are a number of references to altars, including the account of a small temple patronized by Raedwald, king of the East Angles (late sixth century-*c*. 616 × *c*.626), wherein 'he had one altar for the Christian sacrifice and another small altar on which to offer victims to devils' (*HE* ii.15).

Bede's coyness towards the particulars of paganism exemplifies our basic problem, which is that everything which was recorded about heathen activity was written down in monasteries. Since churchmen found pagan behaviour abhorrent, their scriptoria acted as filter beds which eliminated the explicit and left only a residue of generalities. Late in the eighth century Alcuin, scholar of York, wrote about the subject in terms more reminiscent of Virgil than Teutonic heathendom:

> First banish afar the foul worship of idols,
> on their profane altars let the blood of animals smoke no more,
> nor the soothsayer look for omens in the warm entrails,
> nor the meaningless augur attend to the songs of birds:
> let all the images of gods be smashed to the ground!
> (Alcuin, lines 158–62; trans. Godman 1982, 17)

Alcuin's lines do nothing to allay an anxiety that both he and Bede may have been visualizing Romano-British rather than English pagan remains. Despite the numerous references to idols – including *stone* idols – and altars, it is a puzzle that not a single such item of English manufacture has ever been recognized. Romano-British statues and altars, by contrast, were commonplace, not least around the old military bases along Hadrian's Wall and at York, the heartlands of Bedan and Alcuinian experience. This matter is considered more fully below (p. 71–2).

Alcuin's reference to ornithomancy, by contrast, is congruent with what we know from Welsh and Irish sources to have been an elaborate system of prophecy based upon the calls and flight patterns of different species of bird (Ross 1967, 269–70). Early in the eighth century a monk at the Yorkshire monastery of *Streanaeshalch*, assumed to be Whitby, related how once when king Edwin was going to church to receive religious instruction, watched by a crowd 'of those who were still bound not only to heathenism but also to unlawful wives', a crow 'set up a hoarse croaking from an unpropitious quarter of the sky' as they left the hall. The royal company, said to be *in platea populi* 'in the public square', heard the noise and concluded that the new religion would be useless. Realizing this, the missionary Paulinus turned to one of his young helpers and ordered him to shoot the bird. The crow was duly killed. Paulinus then explained that it was God who had dominion over the fowl of the air, not the foretellers who 'boast that they understand the ways of birds by their own native cunning and so deceive the foolish' (*Earliest Life of Gregory the Great*, 15; trans. Colgrave 1968).

More illuminating than the history books and *vitae* are the details contained in law codes, penitentials and the minutes of synods. Taken individually the statements in these sources are usually laconic and lacking in explanatory information that would set them in context. When viewed collectively, however, a basic homogeneity of attitude can be discerned.

As late as 1075 we find delegates at a council in London ruling that the bones of dead animals ought not to be dug up in order to ward off cattle disease, and issuing prohibitions against the drawing of lots (*sortes*), telling fortunes (*auruspicia*), divining the future or any other *opera diaboli* (Clover and Gibson 1979, 79). Significantly, the terminology used on this occasion bears a close resemblance to lists of unacceptable practices which had been issued several centuries before. The third canon of the council of Clofesho (747), for instance, enjoined bishops to tour their dioceses every year in order to oppose *divinos, auguria, auruspicia, fylacteria* and *incantiones* (Haddan and Stubbs 1869–71, III, 190–1). Similar prohibitions occur not only in laws issued subsequently (e.g. 1 Edmund 6 (941 × 946); so-called 'Canons of Edgar' 16 (1005 × 1008); Northumbrian Priests' Law 48 (1008 × 1023)), but also in continental sources dating from the sixth and seventh centuries.

As with behaviour, so also with types of place. In the twelfth century William of Malmesbury echoed the eighth-century *Penitential of Egbert* (iv.16) when he mentioned the English dread of 'powers which reside at cross-roads' (*Gesta regum* ii.22). A law code promulgated by Cnut *c.* 1020 stated:

> It is heathen practice if one worships idols, namely if one worships heathen gods and the sun or the moon, fire or flood, wells or stones or any kind of forest trees, or if one practises witchcraft or encompasses death by any means, either by sacrifice or divination, or takes part in any such delusions.
>
> (5.1 (Whitelock *et al.* 1981, 489))

The so-called 'Canons of Edgar' (1005 × 1008) exhorted every priest to

> zealously teach the Christian faith and entirely extinguish every heathen practice; and forbid worship of wells, and necromancy, and auguries and incantations, and worship of trees and stones, and that devil's craft which is performed when children are drawn through the earth, and the nonsense which is performed on New Year's day in various kinds of sorcery, and in heathen sanctuaries and elder trees.
>
> (Whitelock *et al.* 1981, 320)

Egbert's *Penitential* forbade the making of offerings to or vows at trees and wells (ii.22).

All of these prohibitions were foreshadowed in continental sources. A council held at Tours in 567 deplored pagan festivities at New Year; we learn elsewhere that this included people dressing up as cows or stags on the first day of January. The same council opposed soothsaying, and referred to illicit practices at rocks, trees and springs. A meeting at Auxerre in the 580s urged the abrogation of vows made beside thorn bushes, holly trees or springs. At Toldeo in 665 the heathen usages of New Year's day were again condemned. William of Malmesbury's remark about cross-roads was pre-echoed in a sermon delivered by Eligius, bishop of Noyon, around 640, in which he pleaded that no Christian should

> place lights at temples, or stones, or springs, or trees, or *ad cellos* [at sanctuaries], or at places where three ways meet.
>
> (cited in Bonser 1934, 52).

Another thread of pagan belief which seems to stretch unbroken between the world of late antiquity and the twelfth century concerns a cult of the dead. Necromancy is hinted at or mentioned directly in a number of Old English sources. The 'Canons of Edgar' warned those attending funerals not to consent to 'any foolishness at the body' (Whitelock *et al.* 1981, 335–6). Ælfric, writing between 993 and *c.* 995, advised priests as follows:

> You shall not be glad about men's decease, nor attend on the corpse unless you are invited to it. When you are invited to it, you are then to forbid the heathen songs of the laymen and their loud laughter. Nor are you yourselves to eat or drink in the place where the corpse lies, lest you are imitators of the heathenism which they practise there.
>
> (Whitelock *et al.* 1981, 218)

Ælfric's statement echoed a homily of pope Leo IV (847–55) which had mentioned the singing of vulgar *carmina diabolica* beside corpses. Earlier, councils held in Gaul and Spain had agreed curious regulations about the treatment of the dead: for example, that the eucharist should not be administered to corpses, or that one corpse ought not to be buried on top of another. The *Penitential of Archbishop Theodore* prescribed a penance of five years for 'Whoever burns grain where there is the corpse of a man, in order to cleanse the house' (xv.3).

The aims of such funeral practices are difficult to interpret, for this is where the prejudices of ecclesiastical writers supervened. In general terms, however, we know from the condemnation in Theodore's Penitential that grain-burning was intended to secure the favour of the dead man's spirit. William of Malmesbury attributed to the English an 'almost congenital credulity', reflected in their belief that corpses could be reanimated by the agency of the devil.

Beliefs of this sort were widely held. Continental sources speak of sorcerers who were able to coax speech from the tongues of dead men and ascertain the future from such utterances (Bonser 1934, 50–1). Confirmation that necromantic practices were real enough comes from the rather surprising source of the gild regulations of the Palmers in Ludlow, made in 1284 but possibly based upon earlier ordinances; the prohibitions are quite close to those given by Ælfric, and may indicate that dark games involving corpses during the night preceding a funeral were still being played in the thirteenth century (T.Smith 1870, 194).

Taken together, these various references to paganism suggest that between the sixth century and the twelfth, or later, churchmen in different parts of north-west Europe attacked the same sorts of magical practices and used a common vocabulary to describe them. In part this must have to do with the way in which authors of penitentials and law codes borrowed freely from previous compilations, piling up each new set of regulations from a store of material which had started to accumulate in the councils of the Gallo-Roman Church. But this cannot be the whole story. Similarities between the categories of pagan site and practice condemned in the seventh century, and by Cnut in the eleventh, are too close to be explained away by repetition alone. Men like Ælfric and Wulfstan, both hostile to heathenism, would hardly have addressed themselves to problems that no longer existed.

A second aspect of the paganism that is revealed by the literary sources is its triviality. Bede's Goodmanham story apart, there is little to suggest that English heathenism amounted to a structured religion. Rather, it seems that we are looking at a cobweb of superstitions, tendencies, customs and relatively simple propitiatory rituals. Not much information has come down to us about the deities of the Germanic pantheon: Thunor, Tiw and Woden. This may be because churchmen suppressed the details. But it may also be because there was not much to suppress. A loose amalgam of taboos, calendrical events (like feasts following the slaughter of cattle) as much social as religious, brutal traditions involving the ritual mutilation of animals, and a pervasive interest in genealogy tracing tribal identity to divine ancestors may be close to the sum of the whole issue. This would explain why undercurrents of heathen belief continued to swirl for so long. Rural paganism subsisted more as a system of relationships than as a system of theology. Until those relationships were broken heathenism would continue. This took time. In the seventh century missionaries sought to reach the rank-and-file population through the example of the king and his circle. But royal influence was limited. In the years between c. 600 and c. 850 Christianity did not so much displace pagan religion as form a kind of crust upon the surface of popular culture. The intellectual shapelessness of paganism helped it to persist. The diffuse practices of natural religion presented the Church with no clear target. This may be why bishops attacked the specifics of superstition rather than paganism as a concept. The onset of urbanism from the late ninth century probably did more to weaken pagan religion than the combined efforts of churchmen in the preceding period. Towns created conditions for the forging of new relationships – economic, institutional, social – and the dissolution of some old ones.

From all that has been said so far it would seem that the archaeology of English heathenism is likely to be elusive. And this is so: not one site or structure which can be incontrovertibly claimed as a pagan shrine, sanctuary or temple has yet been found. This problem apart, the lists of pagan foci offer a framework within which to explore topographical considerations. Cnut's list included springs, stones, and forest trees. Pseudo-Theodore has the addition of *cancellos* 'sanctuaries'. The Northumbrian Priests' Law linked the two, for it specified a penalty

if there is on anyone's land a sanctuary [*friþgeard*] round a stone or a tree or a well [= spring] or any such nonsense.

(54; Whitelock *et al.* 1981, 463)

The Northumbrian Priests' Law is a late source, drafted probably between 1008 and 1023, almost contemporary with the Cnut code, and therefore likely to reflect real conditions. Trees, stones and springs may therefore be taken as heads for discussion, to be introduced by an examination of evidence for the sanctuaries that are said to have surrounded them.

Sanctuaries, enclosures and temples. To begin, let us look at the word *friþgeard* 'sanctuary'. The first element *freoðian* derives from the Old English verb *friðian* 'to protect' (cf. the Old English *friþ* 'peace'). It appears in Christian as well as pagan contexts, as for instance in connection with the famous ceremonial stone chairs, the so-called 'frith stools', which survive from the pre-Conquest monasteries at Hexham *Nb* and Beverley *Hu* (*YE*). The second is the forerunner of our modern 'yard': in Old English the 'g' was sounded as our modern 'y'.

Freoðian occurs in place-names, such as Frinsted *K*, Frinton-on-Sea *Ex*, Fritton *Sf* and Fryton *NY*. In all these the meaning is something like 'enclosed place', and may signify no more than a small settlement or hall girdled by a hedge or fence. There is no hint of any religious connotation. However, it is of interest that the German *Friedhof* 'churchyard' is essentially the same as these English names in its basic meaning of 'enclosed place'. In Germany, therefore, we might posit a link between the use of the word for sanctuary in an older sense, and its continued employment to describe the later Christian enclosures. Old English words for cemetery were *lictun* 'body place' or 'corpse enclosure' (whence the common Middle English word for churchyard *lytton* and today's 'lychgate') and *legerstow*. We may notice that our modern 'churchyard' incorporates the *second* element of the Old English word for sanctuary, just as the German word incorporates the first. Some connection between the two classes of site, whether topographical or analogous, might at least be entertained. Both in Germany and in England many local churches originated in private hands. In Germany this has been traced to a pagan custom involving 'family assembly for religious services and the cult of ancestral graves' (Barlow 1979, 183). The statement in the Northumbrian Priests' Law implies that sites of the *friþgeard* type would be on private land. Since small rural churches of the tenth and eleventh centuries were also founded by individuals, families or groups of neighbours (see Chapter 4), it is tempting to speculate upon a connection between them and those pagan sanctuaries which existed in the same social surroundings. Such a connection might, of course, be a matter of concept rather than of place: this point will be examined below, when the discussion of focal points within sanctuaries is reached.

Two Old English words which denote heathen shrines, *hearg*, and *wih* or *wēoh*, occur in place-names (e.g. Harrow *Mx*, Willey *Ha*). Alongside them one may consider heathen gods like Woden, Tiw and Thunor, whose names appear as elements in such place-names as Wednesbury *St, Tislea Ha* or Thundersley *Ex*. Together these names total over forty. They have

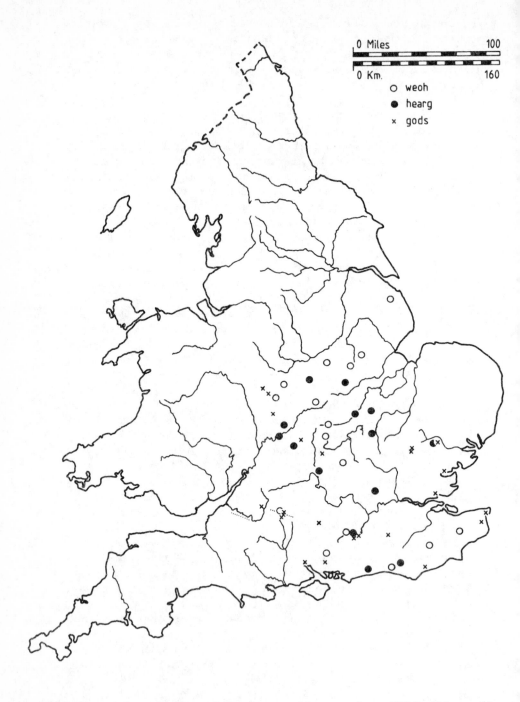

17 Distribution of place-names containing elements that may refer to Old English paganism (*Sources*: Gelling 1961; D. Wilson 1985)

been brought to attention by several scholars (B.Dickens 1934; Ekwall 1966; Stenton 1941, in 1970), and discussed most authoritatively by Mrs Margaret Gelling (1961; 1973; 1978, 158–61), and more recently still by David Wilson (1985). Names in these two categories which have been securely identified are mapped on Fig. 17.

The interpretation of Fig. 17 calls for care. Some areas which saw heavy English settlement from an early date, like East Anglia, are devoid of English place-names which refer to pagan activity. Elsewhere there is sometimes a tendency for names to occur in clusters, but there are also large zones that contain none at all. Possible reasons for these discrepancies have been put forward by Mrs Gelling, who believes that the latter aspect

> can more easily be explained by reference to the course of the conversion than by reference to the original settlement. . . . It is reasonable to assume that pagan sanctuaries had a widespread existence before the coming of Christianity . . . and it may be that the commemoration of such sanctuaries in place-names was more probable if they were at some distance from the centres from which Christianity was dispersed.
>
> (Gelling 1961, 20; cf. 1978, 159, Fig. 11)

Gaps and clusters in westerly counties may have to do with the likelihood that English paganism within them was short-lived. British Christians already lived in these regions, and colonization by the English took place only a few years before the arrival and expansion in influence of the Roman and Irish missions. Individual shrines may, of course, have been retained for use after the era of conversion, while in other cases the former existence of a *wēoh* or *hearg* may have been recollected in a later place-name. In the western zone, it may be added, we find Old Welsh *nimet* 'shrine', 'holy place', occurring in the names of such places as Nympsfield *Gl*, and Nympton and Nymet *D*.

Old English authors employed *hearg* and *wēoh*, *wīh*, in a variety of senses (e.g. idol, shrine, temple), with the result that we have no idea what such sites might actually have looked like. Would a *hearg* be surrounded by a hedge? A ditch? What sort of area did it cover? A few square yards? An acre? Given our inability to answer even such basic questions, how much less likely is it that such a site could be discerned beneath a medieval church and its surrounding jumble of graves. Moreover, the belief that many pagan shrines *were* superseded by churches remains to be tested. Most of the places with names which appear in Fig. 17 did not acquire medieval churches. Even when lost places, like *Cusanweoh*, and names applied to travelling earthworks, like Wansdyke *So* (Woden's ditch), have been discounted, the places with heathen names that lack churches still outnumber those that have them. There are about twenty-seven names of locatable places which incorporate words of the 'heathen sanctuary' type. Eight of them possess medieval churches. Places which incorporate names of Old English gods also total about twenty, only five of which have churches today.

Although they are in a minority, the places bearing pagan names which *do* possess churches present an intriguing picture. Four groups of characteristics can be isolated from among them which may throw light on the status and character of the sites we seek.

First, several churches stand on hilltops. Most famous is St Mary at Harrow-on-the Hill *Mx*. The element *hearg* is recorded in a charter of 767 (Sawyer 1968, no. 106). The oldest fabric that can be discerned in the present church dates from the twelfth century. Mrs Gelling has observed how the hill at Harrow 'is an extremely impressive site, commanding a wide view over the home counties, and it is reasonable to assume that the Christian church which crowns the hill today is the successor of a very early church on the site of the *hearg* from which the name derives' (1961, 9). At Wednesbury *St* the parish church of St Bartholomew occupies an elevated site. The element *burh* could indicate some sort of enclosure. Conceivably, as Mrs Gelling suggested, this was an earlier *enceinte* within which the English established a cult place dedicated to Woden, which was in its turn 'supplanted by, or transformed into, a Christian church in the second half of the seventh century' (1961, 10–11). A third church which occupies a lofty site is St Peter at Thundersley *Ex*. From here, as at Harrow, there are extensive views in different directions. All Saints, Great Harrowden *Np*, stands on a spur of high ground above the valley of the River Ise. Stenton (1970, 288) and Wilson (1985, 181) have observed how often *hearg* names are associated with hills.

Second, at least four of the churches were originally in some sense monastic, or associated with monastic sites. Wye *K* possesses a splendid church which was formerly collegiate. The dedication is to St Gregory and St Martin: saints who were favourites among Kentish churchmen during the seventh and eighth centuries. By itself the dedication is no proof of an early origin for the church. However, an eleventh-century source tells us that Wye had been one of the chief minsters of Kent. The place-name occurs in a charter of 762 (Sawyer 1968, no. 25), when Wye was described as a royal vill. Wye is well worth a visit today, partly in order to savour the atmosphere of the town, and also to view the remarkable chancel and tower of the church. These date from the eighteenth century and replaced medieval portions which were destroyed when the central tower fell in 1685.

Harrowden, just outside Bedford, is adjacent to the site of the Benedictine nunnery of Elstow. The abbey was not founded until *c.* 1072, but burials older than this have been found on the site and point to the presence of a pre-Conquest church. Fifth- and sixth-century pottery has been found in the vicinity of the east end of the abbey church, including a complete vessel containing a cremation (*Medieval Archaeology* 13 (1969), 230).

A monastery founded at Farnham *Sr c.* 685 was endowed with lands which included a property called *Cusanweoh* (Sawyer 1968, no. 235). The transaction was executed at a place called *Besingahearh*. Of this Sir Frank Stenton wrote:

> The name, which means the holy place of the Besingas, is never mentioned again, and there is no real clue as to the position of the site. But this uncertainty does not affect the curious fact that one of the greatest ecclesiastical estates in England was first devoted to religious uses by an unbaptized king (Caedwalla) at what must very recently have been a tribal heathen sanctuary.
>
> (1970, 288–9)

Weedon Bec and Weedon Lois *Np* both possess medieval churches: SS Peter and Paul and SS Peter and Mary, respectively. The places took their 'surnames' from foreign religious houses. Weedon Bec belonged to the abbey of Bec in Normandy. At Weedon Lois a small priory was established as a cell of the Benedictine abbey of St Lucien, in the diocese of Beauvais, early in the twelfth century. Since these arrangements date from after the Norman Conquest they can have no direct bearing upon our present theme. However, a place called Weedon, probably Weedon Bec, occurs in tradition as the site of a monastery founded by St Werburgh in the seventh century. Werburgh was a daughter of Wulfhere, king of Mercia (657–74). She established several religious houses. Most of what is reported about her is legendary, but there seems to be no reason to doubt her association with Weedon.

A tale about Werburgh which circulated in the later Middle Ages related how, while residing at Weedon, she had confronted a flock of wild geese. The geese were grazing on young crops and causing damage. Werburgh commanded the birds to fly away, and it was later believed that wild geese would not alight in order to graze in the locality. The poet Drayton reported in his *Polyolbion* that the River Nene flows past

> Weedon, where 'tis said,
> Saint Werburg princely born, a most religious maid,
> From those peculiar fields, by prayer the wild geese drove.

The Weedon episode is one in a series of Anglo-Saxon miracle tales involving abbesses and wildfowl. It is just possible that some deeper significance may lie behind the fable of Werburgh's declaration of a gooseless zone. An attack on ornithomancy is one possibility. Another could be that the story disguises an account of the ritual cleansing of a pagan enclosure by a Christian abbess. Old English stories of this sort were prefigured in Celtic mythology. There is, for instance, an Irish legend which relates how the

> Ulster aristocracy is afflicted by a flock of destructive birds which lay waste to the plain of Emain. The king and his noblemen decide to hunt

the birds. They get nine chariots ready, and the king's daughter Deichtine acts as the charioteer for Chnochobar her father. There is a long pursuit of the destructive birds, and the text describes their great beauty and the loveliness of their song in flight.

(Ross 1967, 238)

The description leaves little doubt that the birds in question were either swans or geese (cf. Ross 1967, 273). Later, there was the superstitious belief that souls of the unbaptized took the form of wild geese.

The site of Werburgh's monastery is not known. It may have been at Weedon Bec, conceivably in the vicinity of the later parish church. If so, it is not unlikely that the seventh-century monastery was superimposed upon the *wēoh*, because the second element of the place-name *dūn* 'hill' indicates that the sanctuary was on some sort of eminence. The most prominent spot in the parish is Weedon Hill, about one mile south-west of the church. There is, however, an alternative location for Werburgh's community. This is in the adjacent parish of Stowe-Nine-Churches. The church is dedicated to SS Peter and Paul. It contains pre-Conquest fabric (Taylor and Taylor 1965, 594), and although this is unlikely to be older than *c.* 1000 it may be noted that the church occupies a prominent site with extensive views. The epithet 'Nine Churches' is not explained. It has been suggested that a medieval patron of Stowe held the advowsons of nine churches. This is ingenious, but to the best of the writer's knowledge it has not been substantiated. There is the apparently parallel instance of St Ninian Ninekirks *Cu*. Aerial reconnaissance has given indications that a religious settlement existed here, although 'Ninekirks' is most straightforwardly explicable as an eponym. Perhaps a literal interpretation of 'Nine Churches' at Stowe should not be ruled out. The multiplication of small churches in early monasteries is a phenomenon which is well known in England (H.M.Taylor 1978, 1020), and in Ireland, where the legendary number was seven. 'Families' of churches can still be seen at such places as Clonmacnois, Inishcaltra and Inchcleraun (Hughes and Hamlin 1977, 68–9). This apart, the fabric of Stowe church embodies earlier sculpture, and within there are items of architectural sculpture which appear to have been taken from a Roman building of monumental character.

Third, in 1961 Mrs Gelling argued from the information then available that names in *hearg* and *wēoh* were possessed of a 'specifically Anglo-Saxon significance' (10). This remains broadly true. However, evidence has been accumulating slowly which suggests that not all English pagan sanctuaries were established on virgin sites. Great Harrowden *Np* is close to a Roman settlement (RCHME *Northamptonshire* 2, 80–1). Wye *K* has produced evidence of Roman industrial and agricultural activity. Harrow Farm near Hinckley *Le* has yielded a Roman coin hoard. This may be of no religious significance, but it could be 'a votive offering at a rural shrine' (Liddle 1982, 6). In the parish of Woodeaton *O* is a place which was called *Harowdonehull* in the fifteenth century and which is known to have been the site of a Romano-Celtic temple (Gelling 1961, 10).

Finally, attention has already been drawn to the fact that the foundation charter for the *monasterium* at Farnham *Sr* was issued at a place called *Besingahearh*. The names *Besinga* and *Gumeninga* (associated with Harrow-on-the-Hill) are thought to refer to tribal groups. Wilson has suggested that *hearg* sites may fall into a category 'of shrine or temple, one that occupied a prominent position on high land and was a communal place of worship for a specific group of people, a tribe and folk group, perhaps at particular times of the year' (1985, 181). Are we glimpsing a process which involved the substitution of tribal minsters for tribal sanctuaries? At the least, it would appear that some of the places were possessed of a significance which extended beyond the immediate neighbourhood. Mrs Gelling has noticed that three of them were hundredal meeting-places (1978, 161). (So too, it may be remembered, was Knowlton *Do*.) Attention has also been drawn to the frequency with which pagan place-names occur on the boundaries of estates (1978, 161). In part this may be a function of the kind of information that pre-Conquest charters provide. But there is a collateral interpretation to be explored in the tendency for religious gatherings to be exploited as occasions when people could buy and sell. Early medieval fairs and markets were often associated with minsters and other religious communities, hundredal manors and boundaries (Sawyer 1981, 160–4). Boundaries 'were appropriate locations for markets because people could gather from both sides without having to travel through strange territory' (1981, 162). Weyhill *Ha* was the scene of a medieval fair which had its site at a place where the bounds of at least three parishes converged. (This fair is interesting for the additional reason that newcomers to it in the eighteenth and nineteenth centuries were liable to initiation by the wearing of a cap fitted with horns, possibly those of a fallow deer (Heanley 1922, 23). The origin of this custom is unknown, but it is intriguing to find that a radiocarbon determination made upon a set of reindeer antlers used in the horn dance at Abbots Bromley *St* has yielded a date-range centring in the eleventh century (Buckland 1980).)

If these four aspects – locally conspicuous sites, substitutions of Christian communities for pagan sanctuaries, occasional signs of pre-English activity, and indications of district or sub-regional rather than purely local status – are conflated, no definite pattern emerges; few places have more than two of the attributes listed, and most have only one or none at all. They may nevertheless give perspective to further thought. In particular we should look again at the advice given by pope Gregory to the Roman missioners in 601. In this year

Pope Gregory sent more colleagues and ministers of the word together with his messengers. First and foremost among these were Mellitus, Justus, Paulinus, and Rufinianus. ... He also sent a letter in which he announced that he had dispatched the pallium to him [Augustine] and at the same time directed how he should organize the bishops in Britain.

(*HE* i.29)

Gregory's letter was dated 22 June. It was written shortly before the departure of Mellitus, and makes no mention of the purification of heathen shrines. On the contrary, in another letter bearing the same date, addressed to king Æthelberht, Gregory urged the king 'to suppress the worship of idols' and 'overthrow their buildings and shrines' (*HE* i.32).

Mellitus and his companions set off for England. On 18 July Gregory wrote another letter, to Mellitus, and entrusted it to a messenger who caught up with the main party. It is this document which contains the famous passage advising the conversion of heathen temples into churches:

> when Almighty God has brought you to our most reverend brother Bishop Augustine, tell him what I have decided after long deliberation about the English people, namely that the idol temples [*fana idolorum*] of that race should by no means be destroyed, but only the idols in them. Take holy water and sprinkle it in these shrines, build altars and place relics in them. For if the shrines are well built, it is essential that they should be changed from the worship of devils [*cultu daemonum*] to the service of the true God. When this people see that their shrines are not destroyed they will be able to banish error from their hearts and be more ready to come to the places they are familiar with, but now recognizing and worshipping the true God.
>
> (*HE* i.30)

Gregory's earlier letters had been concerned with ecclesiastical organization and etiquette, and with the demolition of pagan structures. What happened between 22 June and 18 July? The answer seems to be that Gregory had received a letter from Augustine (Markus 1970). Such a letter would have detailed English religious customs, and asked for advice about what should be done to overcome them. Gregory reflected, and then replied in specific terms:

> because they [the English] are in the habit of slaughtering much cattle as sacrifices to devils, some solemnity ought to be given in exchange for this. So on the day of the dedication or the festivals of the holy martyrs, whose relics are deposited there, let them make themselves huts from the branches of trees around the churches which have been converted out of shrines, and let them celebrate the solemnity with religious feasts. Do not let them sacrifice animals to the devil, but let them slaughter animals for their own food to the praise of God, and let them give thanks to the Giver of all things for His bountiful provision.
>
> (*HE* i.30)

Our task is to interpret *fana idolorum*. Were these all of English establishment, constructed recently (*c.* 500–600) and on virgin sites? Presumably some of them were, yet it is difficult to believe that the pursuit of English paganism required the systematic avoidance of pre-existing shrines and sacred places. Not only would such a ban have been difficult to enforce, but sites important to the indigenous population are just as likely to have been retained and patronized by English leaders who were concerned to legitimize and strengthen their own positions in British eyes.

Statements about the enslavement of the English to idols reintroduce the question of whether some of these objects were actually of Romano-British origin. No doubt some idols consisted of unworked branches or stones that bore chance resemblances to animals or people. A cloven oak branch, suggestive of the female form, and with the feminine characteristics accentuated by carving, was found in a bog at Foerlev Nymølle, Denmark, in 1961 (Glob 1969, 180, Fig. 71). Such objects may have been common. Wood perishes, and although deposits of wooden cult items have occasionally been found preserved in exceptional conditions, as from marshes at the source of the Seine, close to the Gallo-Roman sanctuary of Sequana, the general absence of wooden images from the archaeological record occasions no surprise. Written sources are, however, firm in reporting that English idols were also made of stone. When Sigeberht, king of the East Saxons (c. 617–53), visited Northumbria it was impressed upon him that 'neither wood nor stone were materials from which gods could be created' (*HE* iii.22).

Such statements must be set against the fact that no stone image that can be regarded as being of English pagan manufacture has ever been found. More perplexing still, until the later seventh century the English have no record as carvers of stone. Indeed, English masoncraft and stone-carving began under ecclesiastical influence: that is, lapidary crafts were first promoted by the very organization that was also dedicated to the overthrow of heathenism.

Unless we reject the testimony of seventh- and eighth-century correspondence and literature, there must be some suspicion that the English sometimes worshipped cult figures of Roman origin. Statues are portable, and may have been transferred from Roman(o-Celtic) to English shrines. Roman cult statues have occasionally been found in curious contexts. Ancaster *Li* provides an example. The medieval church of St Martin stands upon the site of a Roman temple. In 1831 a sexton working in the south-east corner of the churchyard encountered a sculpture of three seated goddesses, a representation of the Romano-Celtic Mother-Goddesses in triple form. When found this sculpture

> was still standing upright, facing south and had been placed on top of a rough stone block at one end of a massive 6 × 4 ft stone slab. At the southern end of the slab was a small, elaborately carved stone altar ... which had been set on a stone disc 9 in. in diameter placed on top of a stone column 1 ft 8 in. high. The column itself stood on a stone block 5 in. × 15 in. (Ambrose 1979, 2)

The discoverers believed that the altar on the column, and the Mother-Goddesses, were in their original positions. However, the whole arrange-ment sounds decidedly odd, not to say architecturally amateurish, and it may be wondered if what we have here is the piecemeal reuse of Roman components at some later date.

Roman altars and chunks of religious sculpture have been found in and around a considerable number of churches. Such occurrences were con-sidered in Chapter 1, together with churches like Silchester *Ha*, Lull-ingstone *K* and Kirkby Underdale *Hu* (*YE*) which stand upon or close to the sites of Roman(o-Celtic) temples. They throw no light on the matter of whether Roman idols were worshipped by English pagans, although they illustrate the ready availability of Roman religious sculpture during the period in question. Later on, ecclesiastical interest in such carvings was not always confined to their usefulness as building material. At Tockenham *Wi*, for instance, the statue of a Roman *genius* is to be seen built into the exterior of the south wall of the church of St John (Toynbee 1978, 330, Pl. 21). Unless this was installed as the result of some eighteenth-century antiquarian fancy, it would appear that the figure was reused in the Middle Ages because of its supposed resemblance to a saint, or con-ceivably to Christ himself.

Before proceeding to examine evidence for the focal points of 'natural' sanctuaries – trees, stones and springs – it is worthwhile to review the chief points which have emerged from what has been said so far.

First, the essentials of rural paganism were ancient, and transcended ethnic divisions. Pagans in Germany, Gaul and England had much in common. Differences between Celtic and English heathenism were prob-ably less notable than the similarities.

Second, such information as we have points to a distinction between sanctuaries of purely local significance, like the family *friþgeard*, and sites of regional or tribal status (cf. Olsen 1986). The latter were places of assembly, but not necessarily centres of continuous occupation. In few in-stances is there evidence for the establishment of churches at or near such centres in the seventh and eighth centuries. However, archaeological work in the Norwegian church of Maere, North Trøndelag, has yielded a series of gold plaquettes which were found in association with what has been in-terpreted as a pagan cult building. Later literary sources indicate that Maere was the religious focus for Inner Trøndelag in pre-Christian times, and that this subsequently became the site of the shire church of the area (Lidén 1969). Corresponding sites in England might include some chur-ches at hundredal meeting-places, like Knowlton *Do* (Fig. 18).

Knowlton is often cited as the *locus classicus* for the depaganization of a heathen monument through the emplacement of a Christian church. In fact, the significance of the site is ambiguous. It is a question whether the Knowlton henge would still have been looked upon as a sacral monument 2–3000 years after its construction. Moreover, the church within it had the status of a chapelry, and this could mean that it was founded *after* most

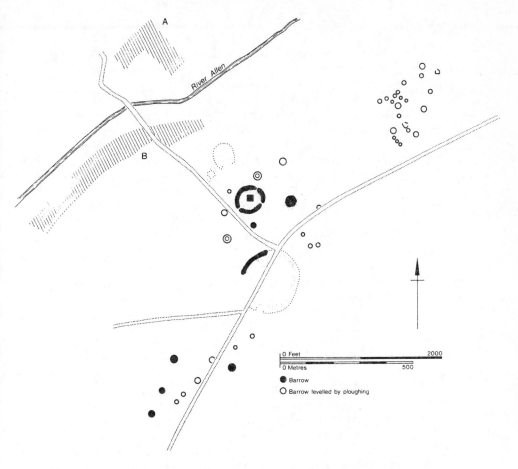

18 Knowlton, Dorset: earthen circles and barrows. The position of the ruined church within the centre circle is indicated by a solid square. The location of the church within these prehistoric earthworks remains unexplained. Traces of a former settlement have been detected beside the River Allen, to the west of the henge, and it is possible that the founders of the church simply made use of a ready-made enclosure. However, in the pre-Conquest period these earthworks served as a hundredal meeting-place (*Source*: based on a plan by the Royal Commission on the Historical Monuments of England)

of the other churches in the vicinity had already been established (see p. 166). Nevertheless, the pre-Conquest use of Knowlton rings as a meeting-place could indicate that the site had retained, or reacquired, some special significance within the locality. There is the further point that not all chapels were of late foundation. Some, like St Peter at Bradwell-on-Sea *Ex*, were churches which had originated before the parish system was laid down and were then marginalized by later developments. St Pancras at Canterbury and the church at Stone-by-Faversham *K* (p. 41) are other examples in this category. So Knowlton's juniority in the parochial hierarchy does not force us to assume that the church was founded after *c*. 1100; it could equally have been established at some point before *c*. 900. Further speculation would not be profitable: new information about Knowlton can only come from excavation.

There is, however, another site which has been excavated in recent years, with intriguing results which have potential for resolving the question of how a church like Knowlton could come into existence. This is Thwing *Hu* (*YE*), where Mr T. G. Manby's investigation of a large Bronze Age ringfort on Paddock Hill has shown that the site was reoccupied after *c*. AD 700. Part of the interior was divided off by a fence, and a hall constructed within. Nearby were found the remains of an oven, together with a midden containing quantities of animal bone, remains of shellfish, pottery and eighth-century coins. On the other side of the fence lay a cemetery comprising about 111 interments. Adjoining the cemetery was a small wooden building, perhaps a chapel, and the setting for a large orthostat. Two graves found inside the 'domestic' sector of the site contained burials of unusual character: 'the graves were too small for the length of the bodies and both had their neck vertebrae severed' (Manby 1986, 2).

The ringfort on Paddock Hill, which enclosed an earlier henge, appears to have suggested the name of the local wapentake: Dickering, i.e. 'ditch ring'. Manby observes that the function of the site in the eighth century 'appears to have been that of an administrative centre for gatherings and meetings, with a large residential hall, but the scarcity of other domestic structures and debris such as loom and weaving equipment suggests it was not of the usual domestic nature' (Manby 1985). On this view the two anomalous burials could be regarded as judicial killings. The large hall and associated oven are features which stand comparison with later sites in Scandinavia and Iceland, where buildings known as *hof* were used for periodic assemblies and common ritual feasts. Professor Olsen suggests that the *hof*

> was not exclusively a sacred building, but a term used for houses in private ownership which besides their normal function as daily living quarters served as meeting-places for organized pagan worship. We may assume that the free population gathered on particular days of the year at certain farms which were *hof*, in order to eat their convivial meal under the direction of the chieftain farmer. No special building was needed for this. The big living room of the farm would suffice.
>
> (1986, 129)

Olsen points to the ruined farm of Hofstaðir in Myvatnssveit, Iceland, as a possible illustration of this arrangement. It is a long house comprising a large single room, with an annex at one end. Nearby lay a large oval pit which was used for cooking. 'Its size and position in the open would make it unsuitable for daily cooking, but it would be ideal for the ritual preparation of sacrificial animals for a convivial meal attended by a large crowd' (Olsen 1986, 130).

Whether Hofstaðir or statements in Icelandic sagas about rooms for idols which were annexed to halls have any relevance for sites in England before the Danish invasions are matters of uncertainty. Nevertheless, it is of interest that both Knowlton and Paddock Hill were associated with sub-regional territories, for which they appear to have been meeting-places. Could the 'chapel' at Paddock Hill be compared with the church at Knowlton, seen in an arrested state of development? During the early stages of conversion, the substitution of a chapel for a roomful of idols might have seemed a reasonable compromise; seasonal gatherings and feasts could have gone on much as before. The presence of a lord presiding over such proceedings could also have assisted in elision between pagan and Christian practices. In later chapters it will be argued that most parish churches were founded by local lords, who often built them next to their places of residence. This in itself might almost be seen as a development out of pagan custom, the family chapel taking the place, though not necessarily the physical position, of what had previously been the idol-room, or an alfresco shrine. Eighth-century prohibitions against laymen ministering in their own churches, though arguably aimed at the correction of monastic abuses, may also have been drafted with this in mind. And there are some intriguing resemblances between the ordinance of some seventh- and eighth-century residential complexes and the position of the church in relation to later manorial enclosures (Fig. 19).

The existence of an earlier, pre-parochial stratum of local church or chapel is for the moment an hypothesis. Such buildings would have been fabricated from timber, and their designs would have been derived from traditions of vernacular rather than ecclesiastical building. If these buildings existed, therefore, a correct interpretation of the archaeological traces that they have left will not be easy. Recognition will be made harder by the likelihood that many such buildings may have lasted for only one or two generations, while others could have been discarded as a result of shifts in power, or changes in the pattern of settlement (see p. 230). These problems aside, the example of Yeavering *Nb* may illustrate the sort of transitional process that has been postulated above. Bede knew the place as *Adgefrin* and defined it as *villa regia*. King Edwin used it, and it was visited by the Roman missionary Paulinus (a colleague of Mellitus) who is said to have spent

> thirty-six days there occupied in the task of catechizing and baptizing. During these days, from morning till evening, he did nothing else but instruct the crowds who flocked to him from every village and district in the teaching of Christ. When they had received instruction he washed them in the waters of regeneration in the River Glen, which was close at hand.
>
> (*HE* ii.14)

Thanks to archaeological work undertaken by Dr Brian Hope-Taylor we can visualize the appearance of Yeavering at the time of Paulinus's visit. Excavation disclosed the imprints of two large timber halls standing in tandem; subsidiary buildings disposed according to geometrical principles which seem to have ruled the whole layout; the settings for several tall orthostats; the wedge of a wooden grandstand; and a building, possibly a temple, next to which was found a stack of ox-skulls, suggestive of periodic feasting. Yeavering was not newly founded by the English: archaeological evidence carries the ritual and funerary history of the site back to the Bronze Age (Hope-Taylor 1977). The place might therefore be characterized as regenerative.

Yeavering was evidently a centre of regional status. This explains why so many people converged upon it within a short space of time. From the point of view of a missionary working *ab initio* such a place would have several advantages. By stationing himself there at the time of a pagan religious festival Paulinus could introduce his message to the population at large. The encounter would take place in traditional surroundings. The king would be present, and his support for the missionary would be manifest.

Bede reports that the *villa regia* at Yeavering 'was left deserted in the time of the kings who followed Edwin' (*HE* ii.14). But there were other *villae regales* which did go on to develop into medieval settlements, and it was normal for churches to be added to them.

With all this in mind, let us now turn from sanctuaries to consider the objects that they enclosed.

Trees loom large in natural religion. Oak, yew and ash were among species that were held in special veneration. Some specimens provided points of assembly or the foci of ritual enclosures (Ross 1967, 33–8). The statement in Gregory's letter to Mellitus that the English were to be encouraged to make huts 'from the branches of trees around the churches which have been converted out of shrines' implies that some pagan temples stood in the midst of groves.

Oak was prized as a building material, and it is not impossible that some sacred trees were ostentatiously felled and used for the fabrication of wooden churches or oratories. Such an episode is recorded in the *Life* of St Boniface, an English missionary who worked in Germany during the

19 Some middle Saxon halls in relation to fences at enclosures at **A** Cowage Farm, Malmesbury, Wiltshire (after Hampton); **B** Northampton (after Williams); **C** Cowdery's Down, Hampshire (after Millett); **D** Yeavering, Northumberland (after Hope-Taylor). The apsidal building in **A** may be a church. It is a question why the annexes of halls in **C** and **D** projected into fenced enclosures. The right-hand building at Yeavering stood amid the graves of a cemetery which in the seventh century was enclosed by a fence (*Source*: Hope-Taylor 1977, 70–85)

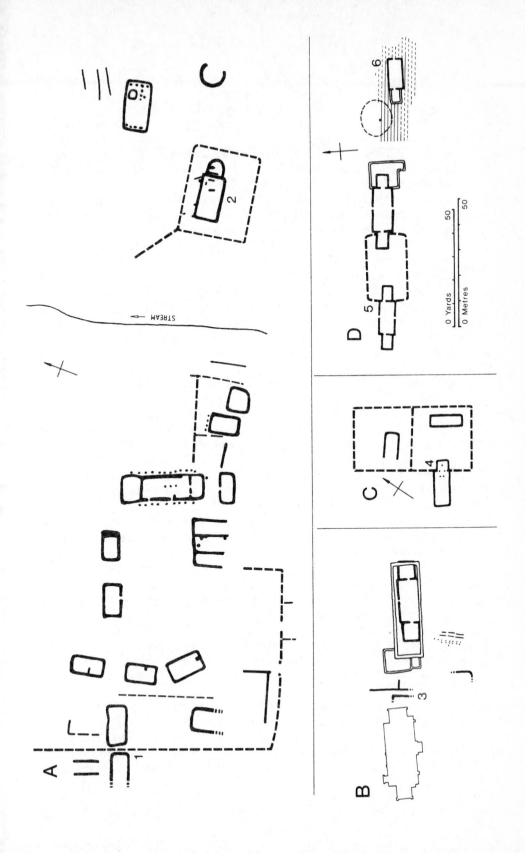

A

STREAM

C

B

C

D

0 Yards   50

0 Metres   50

second quarter of the eighth century. Boniface cut down an oak tree sacred to Thor at a place called Geismar. The wood was used to build a chapel dedicated to St Peter (cf. Parsons 1983, 281-2).

Associations between the sites of churches and sacred trees are usually impossible to demonstrate. In Britain few trees live to any great age. A 500-year-old oak would be very ancient indeed. No oak or ash tree in or beside a medieval churchyard is likely to be anywhere near the age of the church itself. Place-names like Holy Oakes *Le* and Hollytreeholme *Hu* (*YE*), recorded in Domesday Book as *Haliach* 'Holy oak' and a twelfth-century charter as *Halitreholm* 'Island with a holy tree', respectively, are suggestive but cannot now be linked with particular sites.

'Oak' and 'ash' descend from Old English words. 'Yew' derives from the Irish *Éo*. References to sacred yews occur in early Irish and Welsh contexts. Yew trees are particularly common in churchyards. Many of them were planted in the nineteenth century, some no doubt as a result of the influence of J.C.Loudon's treatise *On the laying out, planting and managing of cemeteries* (1843), but there is a significant minority of trees which are a good deal older than this. The yew in the churchyard at Totteridge *Hrt* measured 26 ft (7.9 m) in girth in 1677. At Ashbrittle *So* there is a vast ruined yew that stands upon a low mound, conceivably a barrow, close to the south porch of the church. The outer wood has split apart, and a younger trunk rises within the hollow centre. Yews on mounds occur in churchyards elsewhere, as for example at Kennington *K* and Llangower *Gwd* (*Mrn*). St Michael at Llanfihangel nant Melan *Pws* (*Rad*), rebuilt in the nineteenth century, is ringed by large yews which may delineate the original *llan*. Another circle of ancient yews is to be seen at Llansantffraed-in-Elvel *Pws* (*Rad*), where the trees are arranged concentrically within an even larger curvilinear enclosure. Other notable yews survive beside Welsh churches at Cilycwm *Dfd* (*Carm*), Llandrillo and St Cywair, Llangelynin *Gwd* (*Mrn*). In England a list of the largest, compiled by Mr Alan Meredith (to whom I am indebted for much information on the sizes and locations of yew trees), would include Breamore *Ha* (a pre-Conquest minster), Cusop *He*, Aldworth *Brk*, Loose *K* and several dozen more.

It is not easy to estimate how old these trees may be. Without doubt, many trees of exceptional girth go back at least to the fourteenth or fifteenth centuries, for they are sometimes found at the sites of churches which disappeared at the end of the Middle Ages. The lost church of Capel Aelhairn *Gwd* (*Mrn*), for example, is commemorated by a yew. So, too, is the extinct Capel y Ywen near Llandeilo Fawr *Dfd* (*Carm*). At Capel Tydist, Llandalog, the chapel was turned into a barn and a yew outlived it.

Being long-lived, the yew, like some other evergreen trees, was deployed by classical writers as an image of immortality. The presence of a yew in a churchyard – at once a type of death, of God's enduring presence, and of hope for the resurrection – was thus appropriate. 'My shroud of white, stuck all with yew' sings Feste in *Twelfth Night*, and there are other indications that sprigs of yew were sometimes tucked into shrouds at late medieval funerals. Variants of this custom, involving box, persisted into the nineteenth century. Lancashire cottagers knew box as 'burying box', and an eyewitness account of a funeral at Penynygold *Cld* (*Fl*) described those present after the grave had been filled in 'plucking sprigs of evergreen, and sticking them all over the grave' (Vaux 1894, 169, cf. 170). A cognate custom may have attended medieval Easter ceremonies, presumably involving a symbolic grave of Christ, which took place in churches. In 1086 the church of St Michael in the Castle at Shrewsbury held Lower Poston *Sa*, where 'one man renders thence a bundle of box on Palm Sunday' (DB Shropshire, trans. Drinkwater 1908, 313). Practices of this sort are also reminiscent of an older and essentially pagan habit of placing twigs, wands or boughs upon corpses (Fig. 20).

Few large yews seem to have been dated by scientific methods. Yews with girths in excess of 30 ft (9.1 m) occur in churchyards, as at Linton *He*, Darley Dale *Db* and Crowhurst *Sr*. Many more have circumferences of between 25 and 30 ft (7.6 and 9.1 m). The largest, of which that at Llanerfyl *Pws* (*Mnt*) is an example, have girths of more than 35 ft (10.7 m). Even granted the possibility that some of these giants have attained their size as a result of the slow fusion of multiple boles, it seems clear that among them there are trees which are very old indeed. Although size alone may not be the best criterion for estimating the age of a tree, some of the yews in question were attracting attention by their girth several centuries ago, and must by then have been ancient. Given the fact that as late as the eleventh century it was illegal for anyone to own land whereon stood a sanctuary centred upon a tree, is it conceivable that among the monster yews there are specimens which are the progeny of trees which germinated in pre-Christian centuries on pagan sites? Indeed, can we rule out a possibility that a few churchyard yews might be survivals from pre-ecclesiastical landscapes: natural pegs which join sanctuary and church-yard together through time?

William of Malmesbury's biography of Wulfstan, bishop of Worcester (1060–95), contains a curious tale about a tree. A certain Ailsi, formerly a royal servant, summoned Wulfstan to his village, Longney-on-Severn *Gl*, to consecrate a new church. When Wulfstan arrived he found a large nut tree standing in the churchyard 'with broad, shady foliage which by the extent of its unpruned branches darkened the church'. Wulfstan ordered the tree to be felled. Ailsi objected, ostensibly because he liked to sit beneath it on hot summer days, playing dice and drinking. Ailsi per-sisted in his refusal, saying that he would rather have his church left un-consecrated than see his tree cut down. Wulfstan responded by cursing the tree, and in time it became barren and started to wither. Eventually Ailsi had the tree cut down himself, although formerly he had 'jealously possessed it and loved it dearly' (*Vita Wulfstani* ii.27). This may be no more than a piece of narrative, lightly embroidered to illustrate Wulfstan's saintly power. But it is tempting to discern within it an

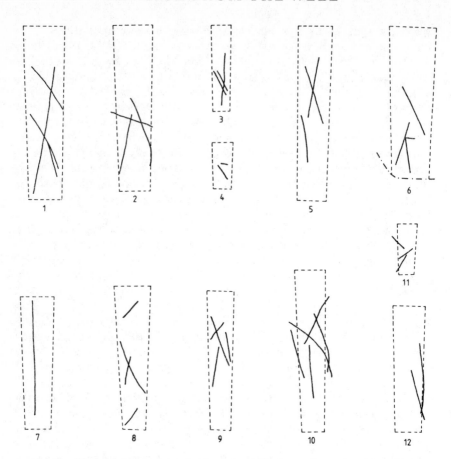

20 Sticks of hazel laid on or under burials of the later eleventh and twelfth centuries at Lund, Sweden. Most were found in the graveyard of a stave church, excavated in 1961. Nos 7 and 12 were excavated at St Drotten. Similar discoveries have been made in a few English churchyards and churches (e.g. Barton-upon-Humber *Hu*, Hickleton *SY*) (*Source*: Blomquist and Mårtensson 1963, Figs 38, 39, 71)

account of the destruction of a sacred tree. This would explain Ailsi's intense affection for it, the fact that it was his personal property, and why Wulfstan regarded the church as being 'darkened' by its presence. From the description given we may guess that the tree was not less than fifty years old, although the church sounds to have been new in the 1060s.

The controversy at Longney-on-Severn was over a nut tree. Nuts, especially hazel, and the boughs from which they hang, had been held in a special regard for several thousand years. Deposits including 'hazel nuts and the twigs of fruit-bearing trees' were noted in the Kennet Avenue at the great prehistoric ritual complex at Avebury *Wi* (Burl 1979, 213). A well shaft at Ashill *Nf*, some 40 ft (12.1 m) deep, was found to contain debris of the Roman period below which were deposits consisting of 'fairly perfect urns placed in layers, and embedded in leaves of hazel and hazel nut' (Ross 1967, 28). Walnuts, hazel nuts and entire hazel boughs have been found in a well close to the high altar in Beverley minster *Hu* (*YE*) (Stephenson 1879). The vegetation was taken into the church, presumably with official acquiescence. At these three sites – Neolithic Avebury, Iron Age Ashill and medieval Beverley – we have a recurrence of pattern in the character of what appear to have been ritual deposits.

Magical properties attributed to nuts had to do with wisdom and knowledge. Nuts were also thought to possess curative powers. A biography of the Cornish 'martyr' Melorus, copied out in the fourteenth century, repeats a legend that Melorus had been a Briton of aristocratic birth who had lived at the time of the origin of the Christian faith. At the age of seven Melorus suffered the loss of his right hand and left foot, which were cut off on the orders of a hostile uncle:

> There were . . . afterwards made for the blessed Melorus a silver hand and a brazen foot, and the pious and innocent child . . . was brought up in a certain monastery of Cornwall, and read divine scriptures until his fourteenth year. For one day in summer the abbot of that place gathered nuts and presented them to the boy as to his lord: who began to collect them with his silver hand, and that silver hand in wondrous fashion became supple as if it were flesh, and he began to stretch out his hand and to draw it in again, as if it were a natural hand with bones, nerves, veins, blood and skin.
>
> (Doble 1964, 21)

In summary, trees worshipped by pagans might have been converted into building material for churches. There may also have been occasions when such trees were tolerated in new churchyards. Some ancient practices and beliefs involving fruit-bearing trees were absorbed into marginal Christian traditions.

Stones. Pre-Conquest sources tell us nothing about the appearance of, or properties attributed to, stones within heathen sanctuaries. We can speculate that some of them were natural boulders, perhaps chosen because of chance resemblances to other things, or even because they contained striking fossils.

Another reason for singling out a stone would be because it had been venerated in the past. This raises the question of whether churches were ever deliberately positioned in close topographical relation to megalithic monuments, or built from the debris of such structures.

Examples of the co-location of megalithic and Christian structures are more often found abroad than at home. They are most numerous in the Iberian peninsula and in Brittany. There are instances of megalithic burial chambers being embodied in churches, as at Alcobertas in Portugal, San Miguel, Arrichinaga, or the Dolmen Chapel of the Seven

Sleepers near Plouaret. Crosses were sometimes incised upon megaliths, as at Brignogan on the north coast of Brittany, or the Dolmen de la Chapelle, Confolens. On other occasions a chapel was built nearby, as at the Tumulus de Saint-Michel at Carnac.

Looking to Britain, the *Life* of St Samson, written possibly at the end of the seventh century and referring probably to events early in the sixth, recounts how the saint came upon a rural temple in Cornwall and cut a cross in the surface of a stone image (*simulacrum*) which stood on a nearby hill (*Vita Samsonis* c. 48, 49). The church of St Michael at Awliscombe *D* stands on a hilltop, and there is a large, reputedly 'pagan' stone at the threshold of the west door. In 1890 the renovators of the church of St Tysilio, at Llandysiliogogo *Dfd* (*Crg*), uncovered a huge stone buried in the nave. The stone was so large that its finders were unable to remove it (Bowen 1971). A similar incident occurred in Guernsey twelve years previously, when a stone of unusual size was discovered beneath the chancel floor at Câtel.

It is often claimed that churches were built upon or beside stone circles in order to depaganize them. On Bernera in the Hebrides there is a pillar in the church which is said to be part of a stone circle (Swire 1966, 205). At Midmer Kirk *Abd* there is a stone circle in the churchyard (Burl 1976, 12). In England the best example of a church and stone circle in close proximity is at Stanton Drew *So*. Two large stones which lie in the churchyard at Bolsterstone *SY* (*YW*) may be the vestiges of a megalithic structure.

Other examples could be mentioned, but it would be surprising if the full list were to run far into double figures. The compilation of such a list might also lead to the discarding of some cases that previously seemed secure. For instance, four large stones in the churchyard boundary at Ysbity Cynfyn *Dfd* (*Crg*) used to be regarded as survivors from a prehistoric stone circle, but this is now contested (C. S. Briggs 1979). Given the very large totals of both prehistoric stone monuments and medieval churches, the lack of correlation between the two seems conclusive.

On the other hand, the very singularity of those cases that are known may invest them with a potential significance. They are unlikely to be accidents, and the fact that churches were seldom superimposed upon megalithic structures does not in itself show that religious or superstitious interest in such objects had been extinguished before the Christian era began. Further, we should examine the part played by the Church in removing prehistoric monuments, not least because this may affect our perception of the mutual distributions.

Rudston *Hu* (*YE*) is a good place from which to begin to explore all three questions. An orthostat, 25 ft 6 in. (7.77 m) tall, presumed to be prehistoric, stands in the churchyard just north of the chancel. The churchyard, in its turn, lies in the midst of an extensive pattern of late Neolithic 'ceremonial' earthworks. At least three cursus, one henge monument and several barrow groups occur in the neighbourhood. The cursus converge in the vicinity of the church. One of them may actually be aligned upon the monolith. Barrows occur near the farther terminals of two of the cursus, and it is possible that the area round the churchyard was also anciently of funerary importance.

The tendency for prehistoric religious monuments, not all of the same period, to occur in clusters has been observed elsewhere. The idea that such neighbourhoods acquired enduring ceremonial personalities cannot be ruled out. The seventh-century *villa regia* at Yeavering was found to overlie traces of a Bronze Age barrow and a Neolithic stone circle (Fig. 19D). The excavator did not regard these correspondences as fortuitous. There was, for example, the setting for a prominent orthostat which had been erected at the centre of the barrow, attracted several unusual graves and was finally incorporated into the boundary of a seventh-century cemetery. The central monolith of the stone circle was found to have been removed to make way for a series of wooden posts that served for the attachment of radial inhumations. 'From first to last', writes Dr Hope-Taylor, 'there was ritual reference to physical datum-points, and the primary points were allowed to beget secondary ones' (1977, 258). The intentions behind these transmutations are unavoidably obscure. Moreover, Hope-Taylor's perception of Yeavering's archaeology as indicating a connected series of restructurings of the ritual landscape, each phase eliding with the next, has recently been questioned (Bradley 1987, 5–7). On the other hand, features of physical prominence and of ritual importance may not always have been the same, thereby rendering archaeologists near blind to the religious landscapes of some periods and clear-sighted in others.

However this debate unfolds, it seems likely that Rudston will be of abiding relevance. The earliest attested form of the place-name *Rodestan* 'Rood-stone' (1086), suggests that either then or before the monolith had been viewed as a type of the cross. The etymology of Radstone *Np* is comparable, although if a large stone ever stood in the churchyard of St Lawrence, it is not there now. It may be observed how few tall prehistoric monoliths have survived in lowland England. Apart from Rudston, the only other stones of comparable size occur in a group known as the Devil's Arrows, near Aldborough *NY*. Here too there are henge monuments in the vicinity. Elsewhere, a systematic attack on such monuments by churchmen, leaving only the largest and least tractable, could be invoked to explain their disappearance. But literary evidence for the overthrow of megaliths on the orders of clergy is scanty, and most of it occurs in writings of the later Middle Ages (Burl 1976, 208), when the risk of pagan revival had gone. A more plausible explanation is that the stones were broken up for building material, perhaps especially in the tenth and eleventh centuries, when thousands of churches were built and rebuilt in stone for the first time and quarrying on an industrial scale had not yet begun.

In some areas the absence of standing stones might also have to do with the activities of craftsmen who carved high crosses in the eighth and ninth centuries. The blanks for monolithic shafts must have been obtained from somewhere. As usual, some suitable stones may have been found in Roman structures. But in size and shape prehistoric orthostats of the Rudston class could have been attractive.

The recycling of such stones for Christian purposes may have been motivated by more than opportunism. No fully convincing explanation for the origins of the high cross has ever been put forward. Continental sources speak of the setting up of crosses in Gaul as early as the fifth century, and Bede mentioned episodes involving crosses at *Hefenfelth*, the site of a battle, and at Cuthbert's residence on Farne (*HE* iii.2; *Vita Cuthberti*, 37) (Wood 1987, 25–30). The specialized high form was invented within the British Isles, probably in Northumbria around the end of the seventh century. During the next 150 years the making of such monuments was practised mainly in northern England and in Ireland. Pagan iconographic material appears on some of the Irish crosses, as at Clonmacnoise where a horned god is to be seen on the shaft of a Christian stone cross. Since evidence has been noted at Yeavering for the existence, and apparent importance, of tall posts, it is tempting to entertain a pagan tradition anterior to the Christian series. Signs of large orthostats have been found elsewhere: at Thwing, for example, or Cadbury Congresbury *So*, where excavation revealed a rock setting for a prominent upright on the edge of a hill (Rahtz and Watts 1979, 199). Samson's dealing with the hilltop *simulacrum* in Cornwall returns to mind.

A Celtic habit of decorating pillars with human heads may also be considered. An example at the temple of Entremont, Bouches-du-Rhône, shows a series of heads arranged vertically (Ross 1967, 64). At Roquepertuse, in the same area, monolithic pillars, apparently from the portico of a temple, were pierced with oval niches to contain human skulls. These monuments were already a thousand years old, distant and forgotten, when the first high crosses were raised. But pillar-mounted heads also occur in Ireland, where the head remained iconographically important long into the Christian era (Ross 1967, 113–15), as for instance at Clonfert, and the theme of the head can be followed through Celtic religious tradition in Britain and Gaul. On high crosses such as those which stood at Otley *WY* and Rothbury *Nb* the heads were now those of evangelists, while toy architectural details, vine-scroll and executive skill derived from the Mediterranean world. The high cross may nevertheless be a product of one of those moments of religio-cultural elision postulated above, between an indigenous tradition of pillar-monuments and the new imagery of the redemptive execution of Christ.

Very few high crosses are known still to be exactly *in situ*. We cannot be sure that they did not originally possess also some positional significance within or near the enclosures of religious communities.

Springs.

From those streams and wells put into agitation after a ritual manner, our forefathers pretended to foretell future events. This mode of divination . . . has been transmitted from age to age in Cornwall; and still exists among the vulgar, who resort to some well of celebrity at particular seasons, and there observe the bubbles that rise, and the state of the water, whether troubled or pure, on their throwing in pins or pebbles, and thence read their future destiny.

Thus wrote the Cornish cleric Richard Polwhele in his *History of Cornwall*, compiled between 1803 and 1808. His observations explain the presence, in particular wells, of curious assemblages of objects. The basic meaning of the Old English *wylla* is 'spring'. More than any other type of feature *waeterwyllas* span the transition from pagan to Christian geography. During the later Middle Ages springs and shaft-wells retained their importance. In certain parts they are venerated still (Rahtz and Watts 1979, 205–8).

Divination, the art of discovering facts about the future, is frequently mentioned as a pagan practice. The modern custom of scrutinizing patterns of tea-leaves would not have been approved by the bishops who gathered for a conference at *Clofesho* in 747 and condemned divination and augury as heathen. The connection with the future explains why so many wells are now remembered as *wishing* wells: as at Stockwell *Dfd (Carm)*, Penylan *Glm*, Ffynnon Angoerion *Pws (Mnt)*, and hundreds of others. The custom of throwing objects, often coins, into wells lingers on, although the original reason (described by Polwhele, above) has been generally forgotten. This is a good example of the way in which a ritual act may become a superstitious reflex.

Many place-names contain the elements 'holy', ostensibly from the Old English *halig*, and 'well', whence Holywell *Hu (YE)*, Holwell *O* or Halliwell *La*. But the Old English word for 'omen' was *hāel*, and it may be asked if some 'Holywell' names, at least in northern England, derive ultimately from this meaning rather than from 'holy' in the Christian sense that is often assumed. This would fit with the predictive functions of wells that have been mentioned above.

Other wells were famed for powers of healing. Polwhele mentioned Cornish wells with reputed therapeutic or medicinal properties, many of them linked with the names of unfamiliar saints such as Madern, Colurian, Gulval and Keyne. At St Levan *Co*, near Land's End, there is a clifftop chapel and a St Levan's well. When the well was inspected about 250 years ago by the antiquary Dr Borlase, he reported: 'The water is reckoned very good for eyes, tooth-ache, and the like.' He added that the beneficial effects of the water would be enhanced if people who had washed in it would sleep upon a large slab of stone that overlay the spring.

Curative powers of wells were often specific to particular diseases or conditions. Water from Pistyll Golen *Dfd (Carm)* was thought to be good for rheumatism; Ffynnon Gynhafal *Cld (Dnb)* cured warts; Barruc, on Barry Island *Glm*, fevers and agues, and so on (Jones 1954). St Nun's well, Altarnun *Co*, was believed to cure mental disorders. According to

Polwhele it was the custom to place a person disordered in mind on the edge of a square pool filled with water from St Nun's well:

> The patient having no intimation of what was intended, was, by a sudden blow into the breast, tumbled into the pool, whence he was tossed up and down by some persons of superior strength, till being quite debilitated, his fury forsook him; was then carried to the church, and certain masses sung over him.

If the therapy did not work, the immersion was repeated. Polwhele also gave information about St Euny's well at Sancred *Co* which used to be regarded as a place where a cure for disease could be obtained on the last day of the year.

One notices the tendency for many wells to take the name of a saint, frequently an *obscure* saint; and also a necessity for performing customary rites either in a particular way or at a specific time of the year, moon or day. Thus at St Teilo's well, Llandeilo *Dfd* (*Carm*), it was the custom to drink water from the cranium of a human skull. Water from Ffynnon Beca *Dfd* (*Carm*) was supposed to be drunk before sunrise; from Ffynnon Seiriol *Angl* at dead of night; from Cefn Bryn Wells *Glm* on Sunday evenings during summer; and the well in the churchyard at Oxwich *Glm* not at all during hours of darkness (Jones 1954).

These requirements and taboos point unmistakably to the origins of well-cults in popular superstition, and hence perhaps to the sites of those parish churches that took their places. Polwhele himself inferred that 'the well had before a spirit: it had now a guardian saint'. Sometimes the name of the saint resembles that of a postulated displaced deity. A proportion of wells dedicated to Helen, for example, may derive not from the saint, but from the rather more disturbing figure of Ellén, a Celtic goddess with three heads who in Irish tradition 'used to emerge periodically from the Cave of Cruachan, believed in Christian times to be a gateway into Hell and traditionally associated with the pagan otherworld' (Ross 1967, 122). In British pagan belief springs were regarded as points of contact with an underworld. Such interpretations are risky, however, unless they have etymological support. A more prosaic, and perhaps more common, derivation for (St) Helen('s) well may be from the Old English *ellern* 'elder tree' (Charles 1938, 165). At Middleham *NY* the church is dedicated to St Alkelda. Nothing is known about this saint. There is but one other Alkelda dedication, at Giggleswick, in the same county. Also found in Yorkshire, however, is the place-name Hallikeld, in which either Old English *halig* 'holy' or *hǣl* 'omen' is yoked with Old Scandinavian *kelda* 'spring'. It is probable that St Alkelda was conjured out of a corrupt version of an Anglo-Scandinavian hybrid word meaning 'holy spring' or 'omen well'.

A point sometimes overlooked by students of well-cults and dedications is that the distribution of springs is determined by geological factors. This gives the primary reason why churchyard wells and well chapels are common in some areas – for example, in western English counties, in Wales and in upland parishes on the flanks of the Pennines – and not in others. The occurrence of wells in concentration would also help to explain the survival of regional customs, such as the well-dressing ceremonies in Derbyshire. Wells are decked with flowers in a number of villages, often on patronal festivals. Well-dressing is still practised at Barlow; at Tissington on Ascension Day; at a well near the church of St John the Baptist, Tideswell; and at Wilne.

Wells in churchyards could, of course, fulfil practical as well as cult or superstitious needs. Water was needed for baptism, for the cleansing of vessels used in the eucharist and for the ritual ablutions of the clergy. Such requirements may lie behind many instances where a church was built close to a well. Jones counted nearly two hundred occurrences in Wales (1954, 24–5, 28), and they are not unusual in England: as for example at Gayton-le-Wold *Li* where a spring rises beside the church. In places where a priest originally had his residence beside the church, the availability of water for domestic purposes would have influenced the decision as to where the church should stand. Wells next to hermits' chapels such as those at Penmon *Gwd (Angl)* and St Govan's Head *Dfd (Pmb)* perhaps originated in domestic contexts (or, rather, the springs played a part in determining where the hermitages should be) and acquired a wider 'sacred' reputation only after the hermitages had fallen into disuse.

Springs or running water are sometimes found *inside* churches. There are many chapels in Wales which were built above a well, as at St Trillo's Chapel *Gwd (Crn)* and Capel Ddeuno *Cld (Dnb)* (Jones 1954, 26–8). Such arrangements are less often observed in England, but do occur. At Aspatria *Cu* there is a well in the church. At Kirkoswald in the same county water from a spring is ducted under the church into a well at the west end. Beneath the chancel of the church of St Kenelm in the Clent Hills *Wo* there may have been a crypt which stood over a spring that was later diverted to a nearby field (W. A. Clark 1937, 37–8). Instances of churches being placed over springs, and underfloor channels for water, are known on the continent, as at Disentis in Holland, the Michaeliskirche in Hildesheim and Schöppingen. This phenomenon has been studied in some detail by Gunther Binding (1975). No comparable survey has been undertaken in Britain, but following an expansion of archaeological research in and around churches which has taken place during the last fifteen years, it seems possible that there were more spring-sited churches in England than was formerly realized. Excavations at Repton *Db* have revealed two stone-built ducts in close proximity to the pre-Conquest crypt (Biddle & Kjølbye-Biddle 1985). Excavations inside the church of St Peter at Barton-upon-Humber *Hu (Li)* disclosed a group of wells under the east end of the medieval nave. These wells were formerly external to a church which was built late in the tenth century, and were absorbed within the building when the church was enlarged (Rodwell and Rodwell

1982). Across the Humber at Beverley a well was enclosed within the eastern transept of the minster in the thirteenth century. Finds from this well included gold pins as well as the vegetation described on p. 81. Wells and associated features are found in other great churches, such as York minster and the cathedral of St Mungo in Glasgow (Gordon 1980). The pre-Conquest religious communities at Bath and at Wells *So* were both established in the immediate vicinity of sacred springs: that at Bath, in the seventh century, beside the great former Roman spa-temple of Sulis Minerva (Cunliffe 1986); and Wells, not later than the 770s, next to a spring 'which seems to have been a focus of interest in the prehistoric and Roman periods ... judging by the scatter of debris in the area' (Rodwell 1984, 13; Rodwell 1980; 1981; 1982).

It has been argued above that medicinal and forecasting wells share a pagan pedigree, traceable not only in customs of timing, but also in assemblages of material which have been recovered from particular sites. A similar background might be expected for church-related springs. To state this as a generalization, however, would be to ignore a substantial body of scriptural writing which places emphasis upon the importance of running water. Jeremiah (2:13) has an image of God as 'the fountain of living waters' (cf. Joel 3:18). Essential to virtually all forms of life, water is necessary for washing and purification, and is therefore naturally possessed of a symbolic significance which would be easily appreciated by people of any rank or background. In Christian teaching, water is also associated with the spiritual rebirth of baptism, prefigured by Christ's own initiation at the hands of John in the River Jordan (Mark 1:4-5). Christian initiation involves a ritual death, an idea which was explored by St Paul:

> And ye are ... buried with him in baptism, wherein also ye are risen with him through the faith of the operation of God, who hath raised him from the dead.
>
> (Colossians 2:10-12)

The parallelism between the rebirth of initiation, and death and resurrection, found its way into iconographic and architectural thinking. Baptisteries were sometimes designed to resemble mausolea. On occasion the two functions were combined, as in the baptistery–mortuary church which Eadmer (*c.* 1060–*c.* 1130) tells us was built at Canterbury by archbishop Cuthbert (740-60) and dedicated to St John the Baptist (Taylor 1969, 102, 126). (Do the stone channels which issued from beneath the (?) eighth-century mausoleum at Repton *Db* hint at a cognate arrangement?) The biography of Dunstan, archbishop of Canterbury (960-88), mentions how the saint called forth water from a rock on the occasion of the consecration of a new church (ed. Stubbs 1874, 109; cf. Exodus 17:6; Ezekiel 47:1). Links between baptism, and hence by extension sometimes also burial and *fons vitae*, must therefore be remembered when springs or wells in churchyards are considered.

In summary, it emerges that springs may have been heathen sites which were retained in use behind a token Christian disguise; or sites at which pagan traditions were more thoroughly assimilated to biblical ideas; or places which were singled out for ecclesiastical use for entirely practical reasons. One asks if it is possible to differentiate between sites in these different categories. More particularly, is it within the power of historical study to give estimates of the relative sizes of the categories; perhaps even to assign sites to broad chronological bands? Even an 'early/middle/late' classification would be an improvement on the present position, where there is a tendency on the part of many commentators to assume an early origin for the devotional use of a majority of sites, and hence to tilt the whole subject towards a generalized expectation involving pagan beginnings.

Some progress towards giving answers to these questions can be achieved through an exploration of the cult of St Ann. An apocryphal source identifies Ann as the mother of the Virgin Mary. The geography of her cult displays five aspects which call for discussion. First, in England, but not in Wales, Ann seems to have been regarded as a senior patron saint of wells, and of churches associated with wells. Second, there seem to be no documented examples of churches having been dedicated to Ann before the twelfth century. Third, out of the eighty or so churches which had been dedicated in honour of Ann before 1899, less than half were of medieval origin. Fourth, the known pre-sixteenth-century dedications display a westerly emphasis in their distribution, and a tendency to congregate in Lancashire and nearby counties. And last, a large proportion of dedications to Ann are found to concern chapelries, or churches, now parochial, which were formerly of chapel status. In the former group one can mention chapelries like Edgeside *La*, Haverthwaite, Knowle and Hugill *Cu*. In Wales there are, or were, chapels dedicated to St Ann at Monkton *Dfd* (*Pmb*), Llandegai and Capel Fleming *Gwd* (*Crn*), but hardly any medieval parish churches seem to have been dedicated to her. A few Welsh wells took her name – that near the church at Llanfihangel *Glm* where the water 'flowed through breasts of a female bust sculptured upon a stone slab' being a notable and possibly more recent example (Jones 1954, 180) – but it is noticeable that most of them occur in areas that were subject to Anglo-Norman colonization.

Several factors combine to explain Ann's suitability as a dedicatee for chapels. We have seen that interest in Ann as a patron saint seems only to have been awakened in the twelfth century. By this time most parish churches were extant. Chapels, by contrast, continued to be founded during the remaining medieval centuries. It was not rare for the dedications of parish churches to be changed, but a new dedication would have to be exceptionally popular to oust old ones in large numbers. Patterns of dedications which crystallized after *c.* 1150 are therefore more easily discerned among chapels-of-ease than among parish churches. This probably explains the apparent preference for Ann in north-west England: in this region parishes were often very large, and many chapels were created within them for the convenience of those who lived far from the mother church. Another factor which may have played a part was the rise in Marian devotion. During the thirteenth and fourteenth centuries this became intense, and led by extension to an interest in the Virgin's relatives, especially her mother.

As for Ann's watery associations, the explanation is found not in Britain, or elsewhere in western Europe, but in Jerusalem. When the Crusaders reached Jerusalem in 1099 they encountered a church dedicated to St Ann adjacent to the Sheep Pool, in the neighbourhood immediately inside St Stephen's Gate, a little to the north of the temple enclosure. The church was rebuilt c. 1140 and still stands. The Sheep Pool is heard of in St John's Gospel:

> Now there is at Jerusalem by the sheep market a pool, which is called in the Hebrew tongue Bethesda, having five porches. In these lay a great multitude of impotent folk, of blind, halt, withered, waiting for the moving of the water.
>
> (5:2-3)

In the third century Origen mentioned the five porches, explaining that four of these ran round the edges of the pool, and that the fifth stretched across the middle: a configuration which has been confirmed archaeologically (Duprez 1970). After the creation of Aelia Capitolina by Hadrian the area continued to be frequented as a place of healing, although now linked probably with the cult of Serapis. By the fifth century there was a church which partly occupied the median causeway, dedicated to My Lady Mary. The connection with Ann is found in a tradition which stated that Mary's childhood home had existed nearby. In the eleventh century the early church was still standing, but in a ruinous condition. The church of St Ann was constructed close to it, to enshrine the reputed site of the dwelling of the Virgin's parents.

Taken together, all these details illuminate the cult of St Ann in Britain. The conjunction of the traditional site of Mary's girlhood home and the Great Pools, for long regarded as being possessed of spiritual or medicinal properties, may be seen as an antetype of the association in this country between chapels dedicated to St Ann and holy wells. The Crusades provide a mechanism for the spread of this information to the west, and after c. 1150 the great church dedicated to St Ann which stood in Jerusalem would have added lustre to the tradition. Other aspects have been demonstrated as products of the interaction between the cult and the development of the English parochial system.

Behind this example there lie lessons of wider application. Dedications to exotic or unusual saints – whether native, biblical or apocryphal – were seldom made in other contexts before the tenth century, and only started to achieve broad popularity from the late eleventh. There is no reason to suppose that well-cults departed from this pattern of development, and it is quite likely that they followed in its wake. Hence, the obscurely named well-cults are unlikely to have attained their recorded forms until after the parochial system had been laid down. More probably they proliferated in the period c. 1200–1500: an age which saw episodes of romantic interest in national origins, and when new outlets for the expression of quasi-devotional superstitions were being sought in reaction to the extension of ecclesiastical officialdom. Wells with genuine claims to association with early hermits and ascetics are particularly likely to have originated in non-devotional circumstances. In a sense they were contact relics. They were the byproducts, not the objects, of cults.

None of this is to say that wells bearing exotic names were not used previously as the foci of heathen sanctuaries. Very probably some were, but the lateness of the processes described above would suggest either that *waeterwyllas* comprised the last class of pagan site to be Christianized, or that the springs so converted were among the least important places within the heathen hierarchy.

Heathen water-cults of real importance were probably captured by the Church in the seventh and eighth centuries, as at Bath, Wells, perhaps Beverley and elsewhere. Their Christian renamings should therefore belong to the older or, more strictly, timeless stratum of dedications, such as Andrew, John the Baptist and Mary.

Our information about paganism is so varied – in quantity, quality and potential relevance – and so vulnerable to distortion when viewed through the prism of twentieth-century experience, that firm conclusions about the relationships between heathen and ecclesiastical geography are probably unattainable. Yet several trends or tendencies seem to stand out.

The time-scale of conversion was long. England in the eighth century was arguably more Christian than pagan, but in many respects rural populations were still possessed of pagan inclinations a thousand years later (Obelkevich 1976, 280–99). Stories about the sacrifice of lambs, the burning of live oxen and even talk of the sacrifice of children are found in nineteenth-century sources (Vaux 1894, 285–7). So the strength of heathen beliefs in the tenth and eleventh centuries, recently reinforced by those of Scandinavian immigrants, must not be underestimated.

Conversion acted upon different sections of society in different ways, and at varying speeds. Missioners addressed themselves first of all to kings, and to people in the immediate circle of kings. Until churches proliferated at neighbourhood level, and there were reliable resident clergy to serve them, contact between churchmen and the rank-and-file population was intermittent. Scope for the maintenance of heathen practices and sites therefore remained extensive at least until the tenth century.

This in its turn affected the way in which the Christian message was perceived. The spiritual values of kings and noblemen were in process of transformation from an early stage. But even here the change was gradual, and for ordinary people the realignment can scarcely have begun to take effect before the eleventh century. Until then, acceptance of Christianity was for many more a matter of adopting one system of magic instead of another. Ælfric, writing at the end of the tenth century, ascribed powers to certain herbs by explaining that their efficacy derived from God rather than from heathen forces. The fact that the herbs were possessed of power was never in question; power was simply traced to a different source. Likewise, the famous *Aecer-bot* spell (Storms 1948, no. 8) illustrates the extent to which members of the Church not only tolerated syncretism but took an active part in it. The spell describes a ceremony aimed at increasing the fruitfulness of land. The language (recorded, one must assume, by a churchman) is an amalgam of heathen and Christian material. The village priest participates in the ritual, and part of it is enacted in the village church.

As regards religious topography, the implications are clear. Pagan sites of regional or tribal status would have been affected first, either because they were abandoned, or because they were superseded by religious communities or royal minsters. The episode at Yeavering, described above, indicates that such sites were, in fact, convenient places from which to preach during the first stages of the conversion process. Mass baptisms recorded elsewhere (for example in the River Swale near Catterick, or in the River Trent (*HE* ii.14, 16)) could betoken the presence of important heathen sanctuaries or customary meeting-places nearby.

Local sanctuaries of the *friþgeard* type persisted in use to within a generation of the Norman Conquest. Aristocrats, though Christian, would not necessarily wield influence over day-to-day religious activity within communities on their estates. If such men and women were wealthy they would hold tracts of land in different places, and they would often be absent. Their remoteness from ordinary affairs would have allowed heathenism to continue. In later chapters we shall see that the founding of local churches seems to have been a phenomenon chiefly of the period *c.* 850–1050. But from what has been said it will be evident that such churches, precisely because they were *local*, arose within a *milieu* wherein paganism was still very much a force to be reckoned with. Whether or not parish churches were commonly built upon the sites of neighbourhood sanctuaries remains an open question.

III

MYNSTER, MONASTERIUM

O n the tenth day of the month [of January] is St Paul's festival;
he was sixteen years old when he first went into the desert, and
he lived there until he was a hundred and thirteen years.
There he never saw nor heard anything else than the roaring of lions
and the howling of wolves, and he ate the apples of the desert and drank
water from the hollow of his hand. At last he was fed sixty years by a
raven who brought him half a loaf every day: a short time before his
death St Antony the hermit came to him, and immediately the raven
brought him a whole loaf. Antony saw Paul's soul ascending to heaven
as white as snow among the hosts of angels; and two lions dug his grave
in the desert's sand; there rests Paul's body covered with filthy dust,
but on Doomsday he will rise up to glory.

This is an entry in an Old English martyrology of the ninth century
(Herzfeld 1900, 17). It refers to Paul of Thebes: an Egyptian who went into
the desert while he was a teenager and remained there until his death
c. 341; and Antony (c. 251–356), who spent most of the last forty years of
his life at a remote hermitage on Mount Kolzim, near the Red Sea.
Antony is regarded as the father of monasticism, but desert-seeking was
not a new practice. Christ had spent time alone in the Judaean wilderness.
He had been baptized by John, a holy wildman, and was prefigured by
Elijah and Elisha.

After Paul and Antony came a vast company of men and women who
were eager to withdraw from the world. Fourth-century Egypt teemed
with them. 'There are so many', wrote a visitor c. 395

that an earthly emperor could not assemble so large an army. For there is no town or village in Egypt and the Thebaid which is not surrounded by hermitages as if by walls. . . . Some of them live in desert caves, others in more remote places. All of them everywhere by trying to outdo each other demonstrate their wonderful ascetic discipline. Those in the remotest places make strenuous efforts for fear that anyone else should surpass them in ascetic practices. Those living near towns or villages make equal efforts, though evil troubles them on every side, in case they should be considered inferior to their remoter brethren.

(*LDF*, 50)

Paul's neighbours in the martyrology were English: Pega, a holy maiden (8 January) and Benedict Biscop, a Northumbrian aristocrat (12 January). Both were credited with lifestyles and a relentless pursuit of values which, albeit in different ways, bear a clear and intended resemblance to the deeds and aspirations of the Desert Fathers.

Pega was the sister of a hermit called Guthlac. At the age of twenty-four Guthlac abandoned a promising career as an aristocratic warrior and entered a monastery at Repton *Db*. For two years he trained in 'canticles, psalms, hymns, prayers, and ecclesiastical customs' (*EHD* 1, 710). But Guthlac sought a life of greater austerity than Repton could provide. Leaving Repton, he travelled to the island of Crowland in the south Lincolnshire fens. Crowland was said to be infested with demons. Guthlac made his abode on the site of an old burial mound, and vanquished the evil spirits. Later, the hermitage was superseded by a larger religious community. This in turn developed into one of the wealthiest monasteries in eastern England. Today, a fragment of the medieval monastic church remains in parochial use. After the death of her brother in 714 Pega founded a religious community of her own. At the end of the tenth century this place was known as Peakirk 'Pega's church' *Np*. Here, too, there is a parish church, still in use, which may stand upon or close to the site of the religious settlement which was established in the eighth century.

Paul's other neighbour in the martyrology was Benedict Biscop. Benedict was born late in the 620s. Like Guthlac he was a nobleman. Unlike Guthlac, he acquired his monastic education abroad. Benedict visited seventeen monasteries in Gaul and Italy, and passed two years in intensive study with the famous religious community on the island of Lérins. He also visited Rome. Eventually Benedict returned to Northumbria. In 673–4 he founded a monastery beside the mouth of the River Wear *TW* (*Du*). Eight years later this settlement was augmented by a second foundation, at Jarrow *TW* (*Du*), where the River Don flows into the Tyne. Benedict made a further journey to Rome, bringing back

a great supply of holy books, some sweet memorial of the relics of the blessed martyrs, paintings, worthy of reverence, of the canonical stories, but also other things, gifts from foreign parts, as he was accustomed; especially teachers to teach in the church he had recently founded the order of chants and services according to the rite of the Roman use.

(EHD 1, 699)

Guthlac and Benedict might each be seen as representing one of two tendencies within the monastic movement. Guthlac chose a path that faded into desolation. Benedict's monasticism was social. When Ceolfrith, Benedict's friend and successor as abbot of Wearmouth-Jarrow, died in 716, his biographer reported that 'he left in the monasteries a company of soldiers of Christ of more than six hundred' *(EHD* 1, 706).

These twin aspects of monasticism, the solitary or *eremitical*, and the collective or *cenobitic*, had been present from the start of desert-seeking as a mass movement in fourth-century Egypt and Syria. At the immediate head of the eremitical tradition we find men like Paul of Thebes, Antony and Euthymius (377–473). Cenobitic monasticism developed in parallel, most conspicuously in the Thebaid, a district of central Egypt. Here a man called Pachomius (*c.* 290–346) organized men into disciplined colonies several hundred strong. The first of them was in a deserted village at a place called Tabennesis *c.* 320. Pachomian colonies existed as components of larger, federal communities, some of them numbering 3000 or more in total membership. Pachomius had once been a soldier, and his communities were organized on somewhat military lines. Late in the fourth century a visitor described life in one of these settlements. The existence was strict:

> they wear sheepskin coats, eat with their faces veiled and their heads bowed so that no one should see his neighbour, and keep such profound silence that you would think you were in the desert. Each one practises his own asceticism in secret: it is only for the sake of appearance that they sit at table, so as to seem to eat, and then they try to avoid being observed by each other.

(LDF 3.1, 65)

Daily life was characterized by incessant prayer and constant reference to scripture. Literacy and learning were encouraged, although art was shunned. At another place in the Thebaid the visitor saw a monastery 'which was fortified with a high brick wall and housed a thousand monks. Within the walls were wells and gardens and all that was necessary to supply the needs of the monks, for none of them ever went out' (*LDF* 17.1, 101). Near Atripe was a site known as the White Monastery (*monasterium candidum*), surrounded by sheer walls and approachable only through two small tunnels.

The distinction between eremitical and cenobitic monasticism was seldom sharp. In practice the two traditions were intertwined, and to some extent interdependent. Some of the most influential figures in the history of social monasticism began as solitaries. Pachomius lived thus until followers invaded his seclusion. In fifth-century Italy, Benedict of Nursia (*c.* 480–550) compiled a written Rule which in later centuries was adopted as the blueprint for cenobitic life, although the early stages of his career were spent alone in a cave at Subiaco. Some of the most determined solitaries were men of great personal warmth. Such charismatic people attracted disciples. So a journey into the wilderness could lead to the formation of a holy city. Conversely, would-be solitaries often underwent a period of preparation in a cenobitic monastery before committing themselves to the desert. Guthlac's career had followed an old pattern. Towards the end of their tour, the fourth-century visitors to Egypt arrived at Nitria, one of the most famous monastic communities, about forty miles south-east of Alexandria. The place was earlier described as containing about fifty 'stations', 'set near together and under one father. In some of them, there are many living together, in others a few and in some there are brothers who live alone. Though they are divided in their dwellings they remain bound together and inseparable in faith and love' (Rufinus; *LDF*, 148). Nitria was a kind of monastic tern colony, where upwards of 3000 devotees lived in loose but spiritually intimate association. Here 'there was no question of being out of earshot of each other. If you stood at the centre about the ninth hour, you would hear psalmody from every station until you thought you were up in Paradise' (Chitty 1966, 31).

About ten miles from Nitria was a district known as The Cells. This was a place of withdrawal for monks who had started to train in Nitria and wished to live 'a more remote life, stripped of external things.... For this is utter desert and the cells are divided from one another by so great a distance that no one can see his neighbour nor can any voice be heard. ... Only on a Saturday and Sunday do they meet in church' (Rufinus; *LDF*, 149).

At first, desert-dwelling monks pushed their minds and bodies to the limits. They mapped the boundaries of human endurance. Antony asked a prospective follower to stand still and pray, and then observed him as he scorched in the sun for a week (*LDF* 24.1–2, 114). Macarius of Alexandria managed to forgo sleep for twenty days. On another occasion, 'Convicting himself of vengefulness in killing a mosquito which had bitten him, he stayed naked for six months by the Marsh of Scetis, "where the mosquitoes pierce through the hides of wild boars", and came back to his cell so swollen and disfigured that he could only be recognized by his voice' (Chitty 1966, 33). Many deprived themselves of food, fasting for days or even weeks at a time. One related how in his early days as a hermit he had taken only one meal a week; more recently he had become accustomed to eat once a day, but extremely lightly, 'so as not to be satisfied' (Arsenius 15; Ward 1981, 23). When Macarius of Alexandria discovered that Pachomian monks did not eat cooked food during Lent, he avoided cooked food for seven years (Chitty 1966, 33). But such feats of asceticism formed a kind of excess. They bred a competitive spirit, which led to pride – which was a sin. In time, moderation prevailed.

When Antony died in 356, Athanasius, patriarch of Alexandria (328–73), set to work on his biography. The *Life of St Antony* quickly became influential. Evagrius of Antioch translated it into Latin, and two versions were circulating in the west before Athanasius's death. Pilgrims from Europe journeyed to visit Jerusalem, the Holy Places and eastern monasteries. Some stayed on, to join religious communities or to found new ones. Others returned and reported upon what they had heard and seen. Hilary of Poitiers studied the monastic movement during a period of exile in the east. As a result of such contacts, experiments in monastic life were taking place in Italy and Gaul from as early as the 350s. Eusebius of Vercellae introduced a monastic regime in his household before 355. Sulpicius Severus tells us that Martin had established a *monasterium* at Milan before Hilary returned from the Levant (*Vita Martini* 6). In the 360s Hilary and Martin set up a monstery at Ligugé, possibly in an adapted villa (James 1977, 437–8). The monastery on the island of Lérins which was later visited by Benedict Biscop originated early in the fifth century. Its founder, Honoratus, was the dedicatee of part of John Cassian's *Confessions*. Cassian, the founder of a monastery at nearby Marseille (St Victor), had previously passed several years in a Palestinian monastery, and seven with the famous colony of ascetics at Nitria.

It is difficult to believe that the espousal of monastic ideas by westerners in the fourth century could have been confined to Italy and Gaul. Victricius, bishop of Rouen, admirer of Martin, visited Britain in the 390s. Wealthy members of Roman society often held interests in different parts of the empire. Enthusiasts for monasticism were among them. Melania the Younger, for instance, a Roman noblewoman, disposed of her huge wealth before 410 and later removed herself to Jerusalem, establishing a monastery for herself on the Mount of Olives, and another nearby for her husband. The properties which Melania sold included estates in Britain.

Some of the first monasteries in Gaul originated in decisions taken by aristocrats to transform their country houses into religious communities. Domestic monasteries, comprising family, retainers and servants, may just as easily have been founded in Britain. We should look for them first among the well-appointed villas, some of which flourished in the later fourth century. Lullingstone *K* is a likely candidate. Excavation disclosed traces of internal decoration bearing Christian iconography, including a series of *orantes*: standing figures with arms outstretched in prayerful attitude (Meates 1955; 1979; Wood 1982).

Lullingstone evokes a pattern that is discernible in fifth-century Gaul: a tendency for holy men to emerge from landed families. We hear of a man called Sequanus 'who began to fast in what appears to have been a deserted villa, close to his parents' home. Later, following the advice of a relative, he settled on an inherited estate.' Romanus, founder of the monastery at Condat, 'broke all family ties by setting off for the forest lands beyond his parental estates. It was often to the marginal land, just within or beyond estate boundaries, that ascetics journeyed: this was their *desertum*' (Wood 1981, 4).

Towards the end of the ninth century a Breton writer called Wrmonoc produced a biography of a sixth-century British churchman called Paul Aurelian. Paul was reared in Wales, but later migrated to Brittany and became bishop of Leon. The *vita* shows knowledge of several sets of Welsh traditions, and probably conflates stories about more than one Paul. This aside, the text also owes a debt to another *vita*, concerning a Welsh holy man called Illtud. Paul trained in a school at Illtud's monastery, at a place known in early sources as Llanilltud Fawr and today as Llantwit Major *Glm*. Eventually Paul decided to adopt a more ascetic lifestyle. After obtaining permission from Illtud – a formality which biographers of saints would often stress, as reflecting the proper observance of monastic discipline – he withdrew to a desert place on land which adjoined his father's possessions. Paul was of high birth. His father was a British chieftain.

This story recalls the margin-seeking behaviour of noblemen in early post-Roman Gaul. And while Wrmonoc's *vita* is too late in date, and was written from too remote a standpoint, to be admissible as evidence for what was actually going on in sixth-century Britain, there are other sources which support an interpretation of British monasticism as having evolved out of late Roman devotional traditions. The indications can be considered under three heads: chronology, learning and topography.

Illtud's dates are not known. However, we do have information about another member of Illtud's circle: Samson, who was educated at Illtud's monastery, later transferred to Brittany, presided over a monastery at Dol and died *c*. 565. Samson is recorded as signing documents as a bishop in Tours during the 540s. Assuming that he was then in his fifties, his birth would have occurred around 490. Entry to Illtud's school could therefore be envisaged in the decade 490–500. Obviously, Illtud's own education must be placed some years before. Illtud could hardly have been younger than thirty in 500. He may have been nearer fifty. Plausible limits for Illtud's birth date may thus be set at *c*. 450–70.

Gildas, who wrote about the condition of Britain in his *De Excidio Britanniae*, might also have obtained advanced schooling somewhere in Britain, or in Gaul, before the end of the fifth century. *De Excidio* has conventionally been assigned to the 540s, but reconsiderations of this work now point to a somewhat earlier period for its production. It has been suggested that at the latest the *De Excidio* was written in the 520s; it may belong to the last fifteen years of the fifth century (Wood 1984, 22–3; but Dumville (1984) prefers a later date). Since Gildas tells us he was forty-three years old when he wrote it, Gildas's education could, on Wood's reckoning, be placed somewhere in the second half of the fifth century.

A third career that affords chronological insights is that of Patrick. Born in Britain, Patrick spent the greater part of his adult life evangelizing in Ireland. Patrick's dates are uncertain, but only to the extent that we cannot be sure whether he was operating in Ireland from 432, the traditional date, or from a starting point some years later (Thomas 1979).

We can combine these careers in a time-chart (Fig. 21). It matters not that exact dates are lacking, because even after generous allowance has been made for the inevitability of error, it is still clear that fifth-century Britain was producing active Christian leaders and thinkers. In about 840, Constantius, the biographer of St Germanus, stated that the Church was flourishing in Britain (Constantius, *Vita Germani*, 27). Although Constantius was writing in Gaul, the lifespans of men like Gildas and Illtud make this credible. Moreover, it is evident from the writings of Patrick and Gildas that they were schooled in monastic ideas.

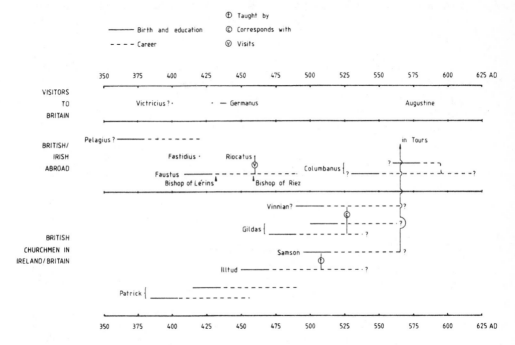

21 Outline chronology and travels of some British and Irish churchmen in the fifth and sixth centuries

The time-chart takes on extra significance when we turn to examine the state of intellectual life in early post-Roman Britain. Patrick's *Confessio* is explicit about the existence of a literary elite in fifth-century Britain. Deficiencies in his own education made him self-conscious:

> I have long had it in mind to write but have in fact hestitated up till now, for I was afraid to expose myself to the criticism of men's tongues, because I have not studied like others, who have successfully imbibed both law and Holy Scripture alike and have never changed their

language from infancy but rather have always been bringing it nearer to perfection.

(*Confessio*, 9; trans. Hood 1978, 42)

Samson's biographer may have lived in the seventh century. He claimed first-hand knowledge of the monastery at Llantwit Major and its traditions. Illtud, or *Eltudus* as the name is written at the start of the *vita*, was remembered as being 'the most learned of all the Britons in the knowledge of Scripture, both the Old Testament and the New Testament, and in every branch of philosophy: poetry and rhetoric, grammar and arithmetic' (*Confessio*, 7). Such accomplishments remind us that out of fourth- and fifth-century Britain had come a number of formidable intellectuals, including Pelagius, a man capable of assimilating and propounding ideas to an extent which prompted papal countermeasures and elicited a refutation from no less a person than Augustine of Hippo; the shadowy Fastidius, and the brilliant Faustus of Riez. All in all, the evidence points to a notable period of British Christianity in the later fifth century.

It has been suggested that British monasticism had roots in the behaviour of late Roman landowners and noblemen. By analogy with Gaul we might therefore expect to find a distribution which includes topographical juxtapositions between centres of early monasticism and late Roman residences of high status. And we do.

Once again, Illtud's *monasterium* at Llantwit Major is the starting point. The position of the monastery is unlocated. But Llantwit is known as the site of a Romano-British villa (RCAHMW *Glamorgan* 1.2, 110–14). Moreover, excavations made at various times show this to be the largest villa that has yet been found in Glamorgan. The mansion was in use at least until the middle years of the fourth century. At a later date, apparently after the residential quarters had been abandoned, part of the building was used as a cemetery. An argument that links these burials with a post-Roman monastic reoccupation of the villa has not found archaeological support. However, the occurrence of the most celebrated monastic centre in early post-Roman southern Wales in the immediate neighbourhood of an impressive villa is at least reminiscent of circumstances in contemporary Gaul, when Gallo-Roman aristocrats abandoned their homes and families in order to establish ascetic communities on their estates nearby. Is Illtud to be imagined as a hairy Welsh *sanctus* who settled near a derelict mansion, or as Eltudus, the cultured son of a wealthy landowner?

Other monastic sites in south-east Wales were located in proximity to former villas. Llancarfen possessed both an early monastery and a villa (RCAHMW *Glamorgan* 1.2, 114: there may have been a second villa here). So did Llandough (W. Davies 1979, no. 101). Further west, at Oystermouth, there appear to be remains of a villa directly under the parish church. Generations of gravediggers have pierced mosaic pavements in the churchyard (RCAHMW *Glamorgan* 1.2, 110–11). No monastery is recorded at Oystermouth. Documents which refer to specific religious communities in the period *c.* 500–700 are few, however, while references to unnamed sites are sufficiently numerous to show that there are monasteries which await identification.

In distributional terms the Roman villas in south Wales are regarded not as an independent group but as an extension of the thick pattern of villas which existed in the Cotswolds and Somerset and extended into Dorset. Many of these villas were flourishing in the fourth century. Occupation in some continued beyond 400 (G. Webster 1969). An intriguing thing about them is that they include a considerable number of the instances were a later parish church is found upon or beside a Roman structure. Frocester (Gracie 1963), King's Stanley and Woodchester (Clarke 1982) are well-known examples in Gloucestershire. In Dorset and Somerset it has been observed that 'more or less substantial Roman buildings, possibly villa establishments' seem to lie behind a series of monastic sites such as Whitchurch Canonicorum, Wimborne, Tarrant Crawford and Halstock (Pearce 1978, 52–3, 97–104).

Conjunctions between villas and monasteries in south Wales might thus be seen as components in a larger pattern which extended on both sides of the Bristol Channel. Behind this pattern we could visualize the espousal of monastic values by members of aristocratic or landowning circles in the fifth century. It is difficult to estimate how far east such a pattern might have extended in the period (say) 450–75, when the English had only just begun to assert themselves. But it may be that sites which lay outside the dominion of the English during the sixth century were available to be absorbed and then reorganized by the English when they advanced into south-west England in the seventh and eighth centuries. It is not suggested that any of these sites retained their original character as villa monasteries until that time. But they may have retained their sites.

All this is hypothesis: a model. But it is a model which is directly paralleled by contemporary happenings in Gaul, and by a topographical pattern in Britain. It is also prompted by a need to explain how monasticism became so firmly established in western Britain by the first half of the sixth century. The idea that Wales was evangelized by missionary monks working out of Gaul no longer seems acceptable. Gaulish monasteries did not send forth missionaries at this time. Nor did they later preserve or lay claim to any tradition which took credit for the Christianization of Wales, still less for the introduction to Britain of monastic ideas. If anything, churchmen journeyed in the other direction. Faustus went to Riez; Samson to Dol; Paul Aurelian to Leon. Patrick longed to go, or return, to Gaul (*Confessio*, 43). Meanwhile, we have to account for the presence of educated men who were acquainted with monastic values in fifth-century Britain and Ireland. Patrick wrote about Irish *monachi et virgines Christi* who were of high birth (*Confessio*, 41). The simple explanation is that monasticism reached Britain at about the same time as it reached Gaul. For a century or so it developed in a similar way, and during that time it was introduced into Ireland from Britain. The receptivity of early post-Roman Iron Age societies to monasticism is intriguing, and deserves more attention than it has received. There are indications that Celtic culture already embodied a tradition which involved holy men and eremitical behaviour, and with which Christian monasticism could be identified. But the context within which monastic ideology was implanted was essentially late Roman. Complementary evidence for the Roman derivation of post-Roman Christianity in Atlantic Britain is provided by the existence and distribution of several hundred inscribed memorial stones which were erected in south-west England, Wales and south-east Scotland in the fifth, sixth and early seventh centuries (Fig. 22).

Returning – finally – to the villas, there are two important points to add. The first concerns the common assertion that local churches and former villas often share the same site because old Roman buildings provided a convenient source of building material. This is doubtful. As this book unfolds it will become obvious that the sites of churches were almost always determined by the interests or aspirations of the individuals, families or groups of neighbours who founded them. Issues of fleeting concern, such as the whereabouts of second-hand bricks or stone, seldom outweighed these larger considerations. Had it been otherwise one would expect to see the emplacement of churches on or beside Roman buildings as a commonplace. In fact, the numbers involved are rather low. By contrast there are hundreds of churches which do *not* stand on Roman structures but which do nevertheless incorporate reused Roman materials. In other words, Roman materials were far more commonly taken to the site of a church than were sites of churches taken to the materials. Quite apart from this, there is the further point that until the tenth century, if not the eleventh, most churches were made of wood. Rivenhall *Ex* is a good example. The church stands upon a villa. But the (?) tenth-century church which preceded it was a timber structure (Rodwell and Rodwell 1986). In this case, the recovery of masonry can scarcely have been a factor which influenced the original decision about the site. In the English kingdoms of the seventh and eighth centuries it now seems clear that stone-built churches were generally restricted to foundations of monastic, episcopal or royal character. But for western Britain we can go further and suppose that virtually *all* ecclesiastical building in the period *c.* 450–700 was executed in wood (Thomas 1986). In western England and Wales the convenience of salvage ought thus to be placed low on the list of factors which may have influenced the selection of monastic sites before *c.* 700.

The second comment concerns the difficulty which has been experienced in locating fifth/sixth-century monasteries on the ground. A possible reason for the invisibility even of such comparatively well-attested sites as Llantwit Major and Llancarfen would be that they were, in physical terms, not significantly different from contemporary secular settlements. Monasticism originated as a system of values. The emergence of types of building and settlement which were felt to provide appropriate surroun-

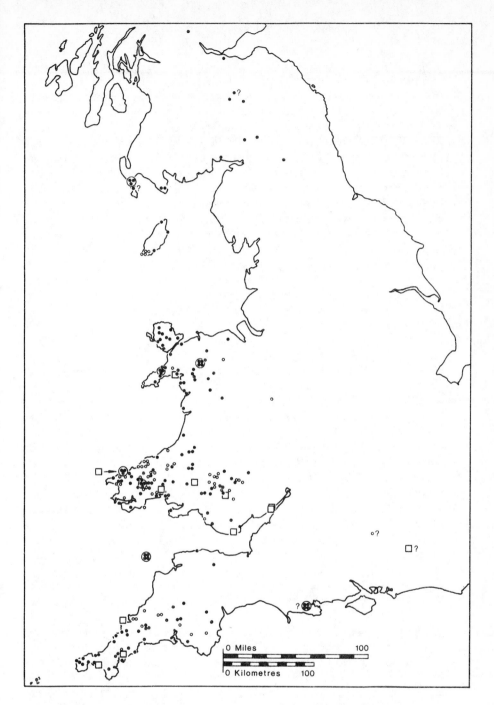

22 Distribution of inscribed memorial stones of the fifth–seventh centuries. Stones bearing inscriptions in Latin and Ogham are denoted by solid and open dots, respectively. Place-names which embody such words as Welsh *merthyr* or Cornish *merther* are shown. Deriving ultimately from Latin *martyrium* 'place with the remains of a martyr', the British term seems to have acquired a meaning such as 'place with the remains of a saint' (*Source*: Thomas 1971, 89)

dings for the pursuit of those values took time. Around 500 a *monasterium* might have been defined by the behaviour of its members, but not by the form or disposition of its structures. Since archaeologists cannot excavate values, we are left with the possibilities either of working backwards in time from the better known to the unknown (cf. Thomas 1981, 157), or of proceeding forwards from the milieu into which monasticism was implanted. Hitherto it has been the technique of backtracking which has been tried most often. Attention is drawn throughout this chapter to places where it is assumed or suspected that a medieval parish church has inherited the position of a former monastery. But the testing of such assumptions may not be easy – for example, because a parish churchyard in continuing use may not lend itself to extensive excavation; or because the archaeologically fugitive and possibly *domestic* character of the primary phase may be difficult to recognize or disguise.

It seems equally logical to try to approach the issue by working forwards, out of a fourth/fifth-century context. By doing this we may also hope to avoid being misled by 'postconceptions'. In 1969 Dr Graham Webster argued that the abandonment of villas in the late fourth and fifth centuries was not necessarily to be equated with a cessation either of occupation in the neighbourhoods of villas or the agricultural use of surrounding land. Webster postulated a process which involved the evacuation of the main mansion, with its increasingly unserviceable amenities like underfloor heating and baths, and the establishment of simpler forms of settlement nearby: for example in outbuildings, or new wooden structures. In result, the former house might itself become a kind of outbuilding relative to the whereabouts of fifth-century occupation. Parts of it could be used for ancillary purposes such as workshops, for storage or the disposal of the dead, or simply left to fall down.

Evidence for fifth- and sixth-century habitation around former villas has been recognized at a number of sites, including Rivenhall *Ex* (Rodwell and Rodwell 1986), Latimer *Bu* (Branigan 1971), and Shakenoak *O* (Brodribb *et al.* 1971). The identities of the people concerned – whether noblemen and their families who went native, or servants and estate-workers who were left to their own devices by departed lords – are obscure. But landowners who abandoned villas in order to lead austere lives elsewhere on their estates could have been among those who moved.

Christian monasticism – for neither eremitical nor cenobitic monasticism is peculiar to Christianity – originated in the kingdom of the scorpion and the hyena: a world of rock and heat. Several centuries later the biographers of holy men in north-west Europe depicted their subjects as seekers after landscapes and environments which were correspondingly forbidding. Men like Columbanus, Samson, Guthlac and Cuthbert found their *desertum* in the interstices of the pattern of settlement: caves, Roman ruins, coastal promontories, islands, marshes. Their realms were shared by the wolf and the owl, the crab and the gull – Cuthbert was once fed by an osprey – and sometimes too by the ghosts which were feared to lurk around the borderlands of ordinary habitation. Prayers mingled with the calls of wildfowl and the thump of surf. Solitude was in the damp desolation of a winter dusk.

These, at any rate, are some of the images which we are invited to turn in our minds. Alongside them we can entertain others. Early penitentials contain some curious entries. The Irish Canons specify a penance of seven-and-a-half years on bread and water for the sins of drinking blood or urine. The Canons of Adamnan warn that a cistern containing water contaminated by the slime of a decomposing carcase, or the corpse of a man, should be drained and cleansed before it used (Bieler 1963, 161, 177). To dispense liquor in which a mouse or weasel was found dead attracted a penalty of three special fasts. It was considered wrong to eat a scab from one's own body.

It is likely that such rules were intended to prevent acts of bravado on the part of ascetics who might otherwise be tempted to engage in such revolting practices in order to punish themselves. But there are other regulations which suggest that the standards of hygiene and behaviour which prevailed within monasteries and society at large were low. Gluttony was a problem. Individuals who vomited the host because they had eaten too much were expected to do penance for twenty days. If a dog happened to consume the vomit this would be increased to one hundred days. Heavy drinking was discouraged. We are told that one of the factors which caused Samson to leave the community at Caldy was the persistent drunkenness of its abbot. The fact that this abbot was regarded as a saint comes as a warning against overestimation of monastic standards in general at this time. Sexual sins occupy much space in the Penitentials. The *Penitential of Cummean* went into minute detail about them. It contains an elaborate tariff of penalties, organized according to the seriousness of the offence. In a society where filth, buggery, incest, sodomy and pederasty seem to have been taken for granted, a monk who kept himself fairly clean, avoided fornication, did not engage in the seduction of small boys, watched his diet and masturbated only occasionally might have the makings of a minor saint.

Lengthy penances could be cut short by commutation, whereby the offender submitted to some brief but highly unpleasant alternative penance. Some of these short, sharp, shocks are described in conversion tables which were drawn up as adjuncts to the penitentials proper. They include such acts as spending the night in freezing water, lying on nettles or nutshells, or even with a corpse. Another commutation was to remain in the posture known as cross-vigil while chanting fifty psalms, or the *Beati* four times, the arms to be stretched out to the horizontal and held there unsupported throughout (Bieler 1963, 281).

The harsh and bestial world into which the penitentials afford glimpses is that of sixth- and seventh-century Wales and Ireland. There is no reason to think that the English in this period were any better mannered.

In the penitentials we see monastic and secular values in tension. Monasticism provided a new source of civilizing influence, but was itself at constant risk from corruption by the secular culture within which it existed and upon which it hoped to act. This uneasy reciprocity is reflected in the wide variety of sites which religious communities chose, or were invited, to occupy. They range from places of marginal character which were shunned by ordinary people for practical or superstitious reasons, to attractive, even comfortable, sites with access to valuable resources. In some cases motives behind the choosing of sites are reported to us, but *vitae* which were written to boost the reputations of individual holy men may not always be the best guides to their original thinking. Certainly, it would be highly unwise to assume that the most inhospitable sites were always occupied by virtuous ascetics, or that the more agreeable places would have been colonized by communities which were lax. Nevertheless, by identifying those categories of site and landscape which seem to have appealed to religious communities, we may hope to gather some clues which could illuminate their mentalities.

It is helpful to begin by looking at an example about which we are unusually well informed: Cuthbert's hermitage on Inner Farne. Like others before him, Cuthbert withdrew from cenobitic life not abruptly but by stages. Each phase of withdrawal can be seen as a preparation for the next. At the outset Cuthbert lived within the community on Lindisfarne. Next, he moved to a cell in the outer precincts. But this did not satisfy his desire for a solitary life, so he sought more complete detachment on the island of Inner Farne. The site of his hermitage was described as being hard and stony. Cuthbert excavated an area within which to live, and used the upcast to surround it with a wall. This structure was

> almost round in plan, measuring about four or five *perticarum* 'poles' from wall to wall; the wall itself on the outside is higher than a man standing upright; but inside he made it much higher by cutting away the living rock, so that the pious inhabitant could see nothing except the sky from his dwelling, thus restraining both the lust of his eyes and of the thoughts by lifting the whole bent of his mind to higher things. He made this same wall, not out of stone nor of bricks and mortar, but just of unworked stone and of turf which he had removed from the excavation of his dwelling.
>
> (Bede's *Life of Cuthbert*, 17; trans. Colgrave 1940)

Cuthbert is said to have erected two buildings inside his sunken enclosure: an oratory and a living hut. Both were roofed with rough timber and straw. Beyond, at the landing place, there was a larger house, and a well, for the use of visitors. Cuthbert cultivated a plot of ground where he attempted to grow wheat and barley. When birds threatened his crops Cuthbert resisted the temptation to harm them, but invited them to leave. In this 'he followed the example of the most reverend and holy father Antony, who with one exhortation restrained the wild asses from injuring the little garden that he himself had planted'.

On Farne, wrote Bede, Cuthbert built a *'civitas* "city" fitted for his rule, and in it houses suited to the city'. Here we see the physical structure of a monastery stripped down to its utter essentials: an enclosure, a dwelling, a place in which to pray, and a place to die (Fig. 23).

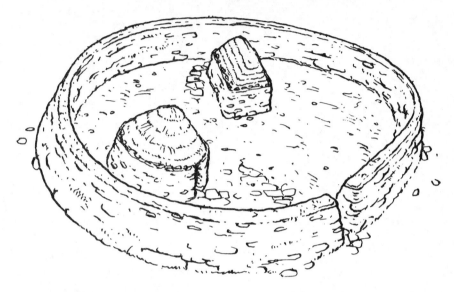

23 Cuthbert's hermitage on Farne: a conjectural sketch, based upon Bede's description of the site in his biography of the saint

Islands were natural sites for hermitages and small colonies of ascetics. An intrepid man named Balthere made his dwelling on Bass Rock, off North Berwick at the mouth of the Firth of Forth. For sheer drama few places can compete with Sceilg Mhichil, which rises over 700 ft (213.4 m) above the sea off Co. Kerry. Sceilg Mhichil supported a group of hardy monks. Considerable remains of their cells and oratory can still be seen clinging to the precipitous site. By comparison, Church Island, near Valencia, is more mundane. It consisted of a simple chapel, dwelling hut, a few outbuildings, a cemetery, all surrounded by a boundary wall which gave shelter to an interior of about an acre (Fig. 24). Worm's Head, a tidal promontory at the south-western extremity of the Gower Peninsula *Glm* is said to have supported a royal infant, Kenyth, who was raised by seabirds. In later life Kenyth is reputed to have established himself on the tidal islet of Burry Holms at the other end of Rhossili Bay.

Near the confluence of the Rivers Severn and Wye there is a small island, visible a few hundred yards to one's left when travelling westwards across the Severn Bridge. A thirteenth-century source mentioned a chapel

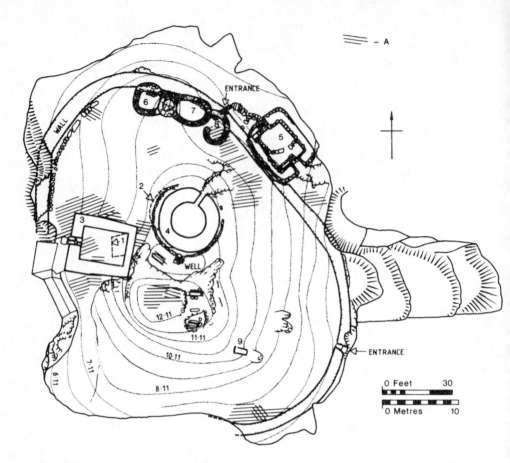

24 Church Island, near Valencia, Co. Kerry, has a surface area at high water of around 0.9 acre (3642 sq. m). About 0.4 acre (1676 sq. m) is suited to habitation. The island is approachable on foot at certain low tides, but is otherwise accessible only by boat across a channel some 328 yd (300 m) wide. A natural landing place is sheltered by a staircase of rock which projects eastwards from the island.

Excavations in 1955 and 1956 (O'Kelly 1958) confirmed that the island had been occupied in the early Middle Ages. The earliest buildings recognized had been made of wood: a tiny oratory (1) (diagnosed as such by the presence of associated graves and the absence of domestic deposits), and a circular structure interpreted as a house (2). At some later stage the oratory and house were rebuilt in stone on a larger scale (3). The occupant(s) of the house (4) cast forth a fan of food refuse from around the doorway. Metalworking was practised. In due course, another house (5) was erected. Next, the inhabited area was surrounded by a stone wall. Burials were made in various parts of the site: their general whereabouts and trends of orientation are indicated on the plan. A cross-incised stone was found in the south-west corner of the site; towards the south-east part was a 'cist-like structure of slabs' (9) which on excavation yielded 298 white quartz pebbles. It is possible that this was some sort of shrine, perhaps intended to contain the bones of a venerated individual or founder (1957, 87–90). After the oratory and houses had fallen into disuse, there was a brief period of reoccupation which led to the construction of new shelters (6, 7, 8), apparently in the late thirteenth or fourteenth centuries.

Although the early occupation is not dated, the excavator's surmise that 'Here surely we have the simple story of the establishment and growth of a small early Irish monastery' (1957, 115) remains attractive (Fig. 23). The size of the cemetery has been attributed to its use by the lay population from nearby places. The surrounding cashel seems to have had no defensive function, but may rather have served to shelter the inhabitants from gales, or to define the strictly monastic part of the island's surface. The archaeology of Church Island provides vivid insights into the actuality of eremitical life in such places: a tiny garden; a diet which included shellfish (winkles, cockles, clams, limpets) and seabirds; a water supply in building 5 which was in part 'filtered through the domestic refuse of the round house and even through a human burial' (1957, 125). Such an existence may seem far removed from the world of scholarship and intellectual pursuits indicated by refined manuscripts, though not from the Penitentials

---

of St Tryak there. In the fifteenth century the antiquary William Worcestre knew it as 'Rok Seynt Tryacle'. Others since have written of a 'St Treacle'. The man at the root of this legend may have been Tecychius, who is reported to have been a follower of the Irishman Tatheus, who in turn has been credited with the foundation of a monastery inside the walls of the old Roman town at Caerwent (Knight 1970). Islands in inland waters might also be suitable for withdrawal. Guthlac's dryspot in the fens at Crowland has been mentioned. Cuthbert was acquainted with a hermit called Herebertus who lived on an island in Derwentwater *Cu.* Wordsworth wrote about it:

> Stranger! Not unmoved
> Wilt thou behold this shapeless heap of stones,
> The desolate ruins of St Herbert's cell.
> Here stood his threshold; here was spread the roof
> That sheltered him, a self-secluded Man,
> After long exercise in social cares
> And offices humane, intent to adore
> The Deity with undistracted mind,
> And meditate on everlasting things,
> In utter solitude.

Tradition holds that Herebertus and Cuthbert died within the same hour. The Mercian ascetic Berthelin, like Kenyth a saint of royal birth, is reported to have lived for a time upon a small island in the marshes of the River Sow *St.* (A similar story was told about St Modwen in connection with St Andrew's Island in the Trent at Burton *St.*) After the death of Berthelin's father the grant of this island was rescinded. Berthelin withdrew into the Peak District, allegedly to a craggy spot near Ilam in Dovedale *Db.* Some larger islands supported communities. In the seventh century there was a small community on Coquet Isle, off the coast at Warkworth *Nb.* According to the *Vita Samsonis* there was a monastery on the island of Caldy in the sixth century. Other Welsh communities existed on Priestholm, off the eastern tip of Anglesey, and Ramsey Island.

Islands which were cut off from the mainland at high tide but accessible at low water seem to have held a special attraction. Lindisfarne *Nb*, which was occupied for monastic purposes in the 630s, is the most celebrated site of this kind. But there were others. In his *Life of Willibrord*, written in the late eighth century, Alcuin relates how Wilgils, the saint's father, had established a hermitage 'in the headlands that are bounded by the North Sea and the River Humber' – apparently a reference to Spurn Head, which at about this time was entering upon one of its periodic phases of destruction and may have been temporarily semi-detached from the mainland, approachable between tides (Talbot 1981, 3). Bede describes how bishop Wilfrid founded a monastery at Selsey *Sx* on land which had been given to him by Æthelwealh, king of the South Saxons (-674 – 680 × 685). 'This place', wrote Bede, 'is surrounded on all sides by sea except on the west where it is approached by a piece of land about a sling's throw in width' (*HE* iv. 3). On a larger scale, Sheppey *K* is analogous and was the home of an important religious community from *c*. 670. A substantial part of the present parish church may date from that time. At the other extreme, there were small sites like Burry Holms and 'Rok Seynt Tryacle', mentioned above, which fall into the overall pattern. So too do places with later churches such as Llangwyfan and Llanddwyn, both on the west coast of Anglesey. At Llangwyfan a small church stands upon a rocky platform and is approachable along a rough causeway at low tide. The remains of a substantial cruciform church are still visible within a circular enclosure on the tidal peninsula at Llanddwyn.

Peninsulas, promontories and headlands offered benefits of natural definition and semi-seclusion which were similar to those of tidal islands. A number of seventh-century monasteries occupied such sites along the coast of Northumbria. Among them were *Coludi urbs*, which lay somewhere on or close to St Abb's Head; Hartlepool, founded in the later 640s (*HE* iv. 23) and recently examined by excavation (Cramp and Daniels 1987); Tynemouth, in existence before 651; and Whitby, founded probably in the 650s (*HE* iii. 24). At least three of these communities – *Coludi urbs*, Hartlepool and Whitby – consisted of companies of women and men who lived under the rule of an abbess. Remote sites and austere living did not always go hand in hand. According to Bede a majority of the community at *Coludi urbs* became preoccupied with 'drinking, feasting, gossip, and other delights'. The women occupied their spare time by 'weaving elaborate garments with which to adorn themselves as if they were brides, so imperilling their virginity'. This monastery was burned down, ostensibly because of carelessness, but in Bede's view as a divine punishment 'for the wickedness of those who dwelt there' (*HE* iv. 25).

Inland, counterparts to coastal promontories could be found in the triangles of ground which were formed where rivers met. Jarrow *TW (Du)* is so positioned. The twelfth-century priory at Leominster *He* inherited the site of a pre-Conquest religious community which was established on ground enclosed to the north and east by the Rivers Kenwater and Lugg;

Mr Joe Hillaby has suggested to me that the substantial bank and ditch which is still visible on the west and south flanks of the precinct could be a monastic *vallum* of early date. The seventh-century monastery at Ripon *NY* lay close to the confluence of the Rivers Ure and Skell. Today the area of land involved seems unduly large to be considered as a monastic precinct, but in the past the point at which the rivers converged seems to have been preceded by low-lying marshy ground and minor watercourses which together would have made an effective barrier. River meanders made excellent enclosures. Sites largely surrounded by the loops of winding rivers were chosen at Melrose *Rx*, Sockburn *Du*, Lancaut *Gl* and elsewhere. Churches which may be the successors of eighth- or ninth-century religious communities, like Kirkham and Little Ouseburn *NY*, are also sometimes found in similar surroundings.

Some Irish hermits established tentative settlements on the tops of hills, as at Slieve Donard in the Mourne Mountains. Malmesbury *Wi* appears to take its name from an Irish holy man named Mailduibh who occupied the hill there in the seventh century. Traces of sixth-century occupation, possibly monastic, have been found on the summit of Glastonbury Tor *So*, which is crowned by the ruin of a later church (Rahtz 1971). In the eighth century an anchorite called Echa is reported to have died at Crayke *NY*. The place-name Crayke is thought to derive from an Old Welsh word *creic* meaning something like 'rock' (Ekwall 1966, 129); the site is an outstanding eminence on the eastern margin of the Vale of York. Like Glastonbury Tor, it commands wide views. Lofty sites were selected also at Hanbury *Wo* (Sawyer 1968, no.190) and Minster-in-Sheppey *K* (no.22), where the present parish church stands on high ground overlooking the Thames estuary. A particularly impressive hilltop site is at Breedon-on-the-Hill *Le*, which is said to have come into monastic possession late in the seventh century. Breedon is discussed further below.

Naturally remote, isolated and yet conspicuous, hilltops may have appealed to monastic settlers for the additional reason that they featured so often and importantly in the topography of the scriptures: Ararat, Sinai, Zion, the Mount of Olives, Golgotha. But summits are often waterless places, and this drawback may have prevented the colonization of some hills by large communities, while at the same time increasing their appeal in the eyes of hard-bitten ascetics.

Most monasteries overlooked running water. Typically, the community was established upon the level ground of a terrace which had been formed by a river or stream. The river might be large, like the Thames at Tilbury (*c.* 653 (*HE* iii.22)) or Barking *Ex* (*c.* 666 (Sawyer 1968, no.1171)), or the Trent at Repton, but just as often it was a lesser stream, as at Tetbury *Gl* or Gilling *NY*. Parish churches which occupy the sites or stand in the neighbourhoods of former monasteries are commonly found in similar positions. Bede refers to the monastery built near the River Dacre *Cu* 'from which it received its name' (*HE* iv.32). Croft, Gainford and Sockburn are next to the Tees. Hexham *Nb* is on a bluff that overlooks the Tyne. The community of St Frideswide at Oxford occupied a terrace beside the Thames. Examples of putative monastic sites, now parochial, are to be seen at Easby and Wensley *NY*, next to the Rivers Swale and Ure, respectively. Narrow water-cut valleys were also sometimes favoured, as at Kirkdale *NY*, where the church is concealed from general view and occupies the last of the level ground before the sides of the valley converge. In the twelfth century the founders of Fountains abbey were given a site which, though on an altogether larger scale, was in other respects very like that at Kirkdale.

In addition to sites fashioned by nature, there were some which had been prepared or modified by the hand of man. Several of those already mentioned, like Breedon and Hanbury, were girdled by prehistoric for-tifications. The walls of old Roman forts and towns offered ready-made enclosures, and quite a number of these were colonized in the seventh and eight centuries by both eremitical and cenobitic communities. To all of these categories we shall return.

Many factors could influence the selection of a site for religious use. The character and size of a community were important. Eremitical groups might need little beyond the land upon which they lived. Peregrine monks might exist on alms. Permanent communities, by contrast, required regular supplies of food and materials. Just how substantial these re-quirements were it is difficult to assess, because information about early monastic populations is sparse. When figures are given they tend to con-cern sites of special celebrity. Thus the combined memberships of Wear-mouth and Jarrow early in the eighth century are said to have exceeded 600. Lérins had about 500 monks at this time. Jumièges is reported to have had 900 inmates by 664. According to Bede there was at early seventh-century Bangor-is-Coed 'so great a number of monks that, when it was divided into seven parts with superiors over each, no division had less than 300 men' (*HE* ii.2). Such an arrangement is reminiscent of the Pachomian communities in the fourth-century Thebaid. Other British and Irish communities are said to have contained upwards of 2000 devotees.

Even if such figures can be relied upon, their typicality is doubtful. Nevertheless, it may be assumed that many monasteries were at least as large as any contemporary secular settlements, and that some were larger. Monasteries therefore needed land in quantities which were at least commensurate with the requirements of their populations. The initial endowments of Wearmouth and Jarrow were 70 hides and 40 hides, respectively. The monastic estate of Pagham *Sx* was 70 hides. Abingdon *O* (*Brk*) held 170 hides. Oswiu, king of Northumbria (654–70) gave twelve estates of ten hides each for the foundation of monasteries. Each estate was deemed sufficient to provide a site 'and means ... for the monks to wage heavenly warfare and to pray with unceasing devotion that the race might win eternal peace' (*HE* iii.24). The fact that these estates were described by Bede as being 'small' may be taken as an indication that many monastic endowments were larger.

Apart from food and building materials, monasteries needed other more specialized items: pigments for the illumination of manuscripts, textiles, hangings, gems. Measured against land, these were expensive. Aldfrith exchanged three hides of land for two silk shawls (Roper 1974, 64). On another occasion he gave eight hides in return for a book on cosmography. The production of a book could itself make considerable demands upon rural resources. Professor Richard Bailey has pointed out that three bibles which were made in the scriptorium at Jarrow around 700 'required the slaughter of nearly 1500 calves to obtain the necessary vellum'. 'Even the Lichfield Gospels, which have a much smaller format, are made from the skins of 120 animals' (1980b, 16). The fact that not all of these beasts may have been required at once does not diminish the scale of the investment. The acreage of grazing land which lay behind these seventh- and eighth-century manuscripts must have been large.

Benefactors were important, for upon them would depend the range of sites and lands that might be made available for monastic use. In return for such gifts the donors hoped for spiritual benefits: the support of prayers in life, intercession for the soul when life ended, and a grave close to the force-field of a saint. Some communities received more land than they could manage from one centre, and it is of interest that in a number of areas there is a tendency for monasteries to occur in clusters. Communities which became too populous may have been divided, the better to take advantage of separated estates. Wearmouth and Jarrow, for instance, were described as one monastery in two places. Links of kinship could also play a part (Cambridge 1984). Constellations of early religious sites are discernible in Yorkshire, most notably around the Vale of Pickering and in the north of the county (Fig. 25), as well as in Durham and Northumberland. Proximity was not the only factor. Fraternity could span great distances. The Community of St Cuthbert, for instance, consisted of a monastic federation, with sites all over northern England and extending into southern Scotland. The linear disposition of some monastic places, and their proximity to old Roman roads and trunk routes, remind us that communication within the federation, and obligations of hospitality, could be further factors which might influence a decision as to where a monastery should stand (Figs. 25, 33).

Convenience, access to economic resources, the changing sympathies and patterns of generosity among magnates take us some way towards an understanding of early monastic geography. But alongside these factors, and to some extent in tension with them, were the more traditional aspirations of the holy men themselves. Some of the more reclusive figures are depicted as going out of their way to court danger by residing in places which were believed to be governed by supernatural forces. Guthlac was pestered by demons. To Cuthbert, part of the appeal of Inner Farne lay in its reputation as a place where 'almost no one could remain alone for

25 Evidence for religious communities in northern England before *c.* 875. 1
land above 200 ft (60 m); 2 Roman roads; 3 marsh or moss. Nos 4–7 indicate
types of evidence which have shaped modern knowledge: 4 sculpture,
architectural remains; 5 written source; 6 place-name; 7 retrospective
indication in later source. Former Roman towns and larger forts (8) and
episcopal sees (9) of the seventh and eighth centuries are shown

any length of time on account of the various illusions caused by devils'
(*Anon Life* 3.1; trans. Colgrave 1940, 97). Balthere experienced similar
challenges on Bass Rock, where according to Alcuin he

> Vanquished time and again the hosts of the air
> That waged war upon him in countless shapes.
>
> (trans. Godman 1982, lines 1328–9)

Pagan burial places were sometimes occupied by ascetics. Guthlac made his dwelling beside a *hlaw* 'burial mound'. St Marnoch is said to have resided from time to time in a Neolithic chambered cairn at Ardmarnoch (Grinsell 1976, 18, 221). Near Brecon there is a chambered cairn known as Tŷ Illtud. Pilgrims in the later Middle Ages imagined this to be a structure which had been associated with the saint, and there are several other prehistoric monuments in the vicinity which bear his name. At one of them, Bedd Gwyl Illtud, a Bronze Age mound, a watch used to be kept during the night before Illtud's feast day (Grinsell 1981, 134–5). Whether Illtud himself was ever associated with these sites we do not know; the point is rather that such places were imagined as appropriate for the activities of a saint. Empty Romano-British villas formed another category of site wherein ghosts and demons could be challenged. Even more appropriate for this sort of bravado would have been former Roman temples. It is interesting that several temples in south-west England, like Lamyatt Beacon *So* and Uley *Gl*, show signs of limited fifth/sixth-century occupation, with small groups of oriented burials nearby. The post-Roman phase at Uley has yielded a small structure which has been tentatively identified as a church (Ellison 1980). Did small groups of *monachi* mount guard over these temples, maybe warding off unregenerate pagan devotees as well as demons? This had been the pattern in North Africa a century or less previously; why not here?

With all this said, it is not easy to decide whether stories of demon-seeking are to be taken literally, or as topoi which were deployed by biographers who were anxious to draw parallels between the lifestyles of their subjects and the deeds of the Desert Fathers. Antony, we recall, had shut himself in a pagan mausoleum in order to grapple with the malevolent spirits who lived there. Macarius the Egyptian once used a mummy as a pillow. Holy men were expected to take risks. The sources must be read with that in mind.

Landscapes could be depicted as being alarming in themselves. During the 650s a Northumbrian cleric called Cedd established a monastery at Lastingham on the edge of the North York Moors. According to Bede this place was situated

> amid some steep and remote hills which seemed better fitted for the haunts of robbers and the dens of wild beasts than for human habitation; so that, as Isaiah says, 'In the habitation where once dragons lay, shall be grass with reeds and rushes'.
>
> (Isaiah 35:7; *HE* iii.23)

Cedd's first task was to 'cleanse the site ... from the stain of former crimes'. To do this he intended to spend the whole of the approaching season of Lent at the site in prayer:

> Every day except Sunday he prolonged his fast until evening ... and then he took nothing but a small quantity of bread, one hen's egg, and

a little milk mixed with water.... This was a custom of those from whom he had learned the discipline of a Rule that, when they had received a site for building a monastery or church, they should first consecrate it to the Lord with prayer and fasting'.

(*HE* iii. 23)

When the work of fasting and prayer was ended Cedd built the monastery 'and established it in the religious observances according to the usage of Lindisfarne where he had been brought up'. Cedd died in an epidemic in 664. He was buried outside the walls, 'but in course of time a stone church was built in the monastery in honour of the blessed Mother of God, and his body was buried in it on the right side of the altar' (*HE* iii.23). Cedd left Lastingham to be governed by his brother Chad, who afterwards became bishop of Lichfield. Two other brothers, Cynebill and Caelin, were also members of this community. All four, reports Bede, were 'famous priests of the Lord, a very rare thing to happen'.

Lastingham is on a natural boundary. Today the church (which was rebuilt late in the eleventh century) lies on the frontier between agricultural land at the edge of the Vale of Pickering and the North York Moors. In the seventh century it is possible that the moor extended further down towards the Vale, and that the monastery stood in surroundings which were genuinely desolate. But Cedd's site cannot have been far from the boundary. By the twelfth century people had found it profitable to establish settlements of regular form at nearby places like Hutton-le-Hole and Appleton-le-Moors. Nor may Cedd's have been the only community in this area. A line of churches with attributes that are suggestive of early origins is found along the edge of the Vale of Pickering. Apart from Lastingham they include Kirkdale, where finely wrought grave-covers of the eighth or ninth centuries point to high-status funerals; Kirkbymoorside and Middleton, both of which have pre-Danish sculpture; and Pickering, which was a royal minster (p.135).

Liminality found expression in monastic topography in various ways. The conception of the religious life itself as a progress, involving staged withdrawal from the world and a corresponding intensification of austerity, can be traced back through the margin-seeking practices of fifth-century Gaulish noblemen to the world of the Desert Fathers in the fourth century. At Nitria, we recall, there were some devotees who underwent long spiritual training for the ultimate rigours of life in The Cells. Cenobitic monasteries provided preparation for individuals who later journeyed into solitude. The careers of men like Guthlac, Cuthbert and Samson followed this pattern. Samson, for instance, began his monastic life in relatively congenial surroundings at Llantwit Major. In due course he moved to the island community on Caldy, and from there with three companions he withdrew to a small abandoned fort near Cardiff. Later, he abandoned the whole area, and moved by stages across to Brittany, founding several further communities en route. Samson did not return.

Samson's spiritual odyssey may be compared to an episode related by Bede concerning a holy man called Fursa. Fursa was a bishop who came to East Anglia from Ireland in the 630s, during the reign of king Sigeberht. Fursa 'was renowned in word and deed and remarkable for his singular virtues. He was anxious to live the life of a pilgrim [*peregrinus*], for the Lord's sake, wherever opportunity offered' (*HH* iii.19). Sigeberht, who himself became a monk, gave Fursa an old *castrum* 'fort' in which to live and to establish the observance of a Rule. Bede described the place as being 'pleasantly situated', close to woods and the sea, at a place which the English called *Cnobheresburg*, 'that is', explains Bede '*Urbs Cnobheri*' (iii. 19). The site is usually identified as Burgh Castle *Sf* (Rigold 1977, 72; but see now Johnson 1983). Fursa busied himself in preaching to the East Angles, but in due course

> he longed to free himself from all worldly affairs, even those of the monastery itself; so leaving his brother Foillán in charge of the monastery and its souls and also the priests Goban and Dicuill and, being free from all worldly cares, he resolved to end his life as a hermit. He had another brother called Ultan, who, after a long time on probation in the monastery, had passed on to the life of a hermit.
>
> (*HE* iii.19)

The preparatory aspect of Ultan's time in the cenobitic monastery is here clearly stated. Fursa sought Ultan out, 'and for a whole year lived with him in austerity and prayer, labouring daily with his hands'. But even this degree of detachment was felt to be insufficient. Fursa forsook England and sailed for Gaul. Clovis, the Frankish king, made him welcome. At a place called Lagny Fursa now established yet another monastery, 'where, not long afterwards, he was taken ill and died'.

Peregrine monks like Fursa in the seventh century, or Samson and Columbanus in the sixth, left trails of monasteries in their wake. Such wanderings may explain the presence of Irishmen who are glimpsed at various places in seventh-century England: Mailduibh at Malmesbury, for instance, or the monk called Dicuill (out of *Cnobheresburg*?) whom Bede informs us 'had a very small monastery in a place called Bosham (*Sx*) surrounded by woods and sea, in which five or six brothers served the Lord in humility and poverty' (*HE* iv.13). The abandonment of homeland, friends, mother monastery and – perhaps above all – kin, was looked upon as an outstanding sacrifice, a kind of social martyrdom: *peregrinatio pro Dei amore, propter nomen Domini, ob amorem, pro amore, pro nomine Christi, pro Christo, pro remedio animae, pro adipiscenda in caelis patria, pro aeterna patria.*

Holy men often became the confidants of kings. Columbanus counselled Childebert; Aidan advised Oswald; Ethelwald was a frequent visitor to Cedd's community at Lastingham. If men of outstanding religiosity remained in one place for any length of time, they could expose themselves to the risk of office. This was not always welcomed. Apart from the distractions of administration, episcopal life threatened to visit status and celebrity upon men whose minds were fixed upon the contrary ideals of humility and obscurity. In the fourth century some monks had avoided office by self-mutilation (*LDF* 20.14, 106–7). Later, figures like Fursa and Columbanus evaded permanent responsibilities by keeping on the move. Others were less successful. Cedd was coaxed out of Lastingham to become bishop to the East Saxons. His brother Chad was appointed to the see of Lichfield in 669. Cuthbert became bishop of Hexham in 684, although shortly afterwards he exchanged his see with Eata for that of Lindisfarne.

Men who were drawn back from the margins of settlement to positions of political and social prominence might nevertheless hope to preserve some degree of physical and devotional privacy. Quite a number of religious communities seem to have been located in the vicinity of royal centres, but at a sufficient distance to maintain monastic detachment from worldly affairs. Lindisfarne and Bamburgh provide a good example of this sort of duality. Catterick and Easby *NY* could offer another. It is interesting that Lichfield lies but two miles north of the former Roman town of *Letocetum St.* A bond between these places seems to be indicated by the fact that in the later Middle Ages the parish of St Michael in Lichfield extended southwards in order to include this ancient site.

Monasteries themselves could be structured so as to provide zones of greater and lesser privacy. During his episcopate at Lichfield Chad is reported to have built a place of retreat for himself *non longe ab ecclesia remotiorem* 'not very far from the church', to which he and seven or eight brothers were accustomed to retire for purposes of prayer and study when other duties allowed (*HE* iv.3). The site is not identified, but could lie under or close to the church of St Michael which stands upon a hill, a little apart from the town, within a large curvilinear churchyard (see Fig. 55). A similar retreat existed at Hexham *Nb*. Bede depicted it as a remote dwelling, *vallo circumdata* 'enclosed by an earthwork', set amid scattered trees about a mile and a half from the main monastery, and separated from it by the River Tyne. The enclosure contained an oratory which was dedicated, as at Lichfield, to St Michael. It was here that John, bishop of Hexham (*c.* 687–705), 'with a few others very often used to devote himself to prayer and reading when a favourable opportunity occurred, and especially during Lent' (*HE* v.2). The site may have been at Warden *Nb*, where a church containing early fabric still survives within an earthwork (Taylor and Taylor 1965, 632–4). Not all retreats were so elaborate. When Columbanus wished to withdraw from his monastery at Annegray in the Vosges he went to a cave. Samson, too, had a cave to which he would go for up to a week at a time for private prayer and contemplation. At Kirkdale there are caves in the side of the valley near the church.

Christ's period of fasting and temptation in the Judaean desert can be seen as an antetype of the use of outlying oratories or caves during Lent.

Each of the sites mentioned above could be looked upon as a stylized wilderness. Such an idea could also help to explain the presence of some other ecclesiastical sites which existed in the vicinity of religious centres. The ruined church atop Glastonbury Tor is one example. St Patrick's Chapel at Heysham *La* is another. The chapel stands on a headland overlooking the Irish Sea. Although ruined, the fabric embodies a number of features which are characteristic of pre-Conquest workmanship (Taylor and Taylor 1965, 312–15). Ten yards to the west are six rock-cut graves. The date of the chapel is uncertain. The Taylors were inclined to place it early in the ninth century. Excavations carried out in 1977 were said at the time to have been inconclusive as regards chronology, although they did show that the chapel had originated as a shorter structure which had later been lengthened. The investigation also produced several pieces of carved stone to which dates in the eighth or ninth century were provisionally assigned (Andrews 1978). One of these was the head of an eagle: a remarkable piece which seems to have had an architectural function, perhaps intended as a decorative projection from the apex or base of the triangular portion of a gable. The chapel, with its associated graves and finds, together make fuller sense if they are considered in conjunction with the nearby parish church of St Peter. St Peter's stands a short distance inland on a lower and more sheltered site. Here too there is some pre-Conquest fabric, and a collection of sculptured stones which date from the ninth–eleventh centuries. St Peter's could be regarded as the parochial successor of an earlier religious community to which the chapel was formerly attached. A juxtaposition such as this might also offer a clue to the original function of some of the small island- and cliff-sited churches and chapels which are found around the coasts of Atlantic Britain. Such churches have sometimes been visualized as the first plantations of missionaries who entered Wales from overseas, established coastal hermitages and gradually carried their ministry inland. A more measured explanation would reverse this view, and interpret the coastal sites as satellite retreats for monasteries which occupied more favourable sites.

Early religious communities were often established within the defences of former forts. The factors which led to the choice of such sites are seldom explained, and it is likely that they varied from place to place. Desires for seclusion, to confront the past, for good communications (Roman forts fitted into a ready-made network) or simple opportunism may all have played a part at one time or another. If there was any general influence it is likely to be found in the fact that many of these sites were in the gift of kings. A late source tells us that in the sixth century a Welsh prince, Maelgwyn Gwynedd, gave the fort at Holyhead *Angl* to a Cornish holy man called Cybi. The fort became known as Caer Gybi. Today the Roman defences are still visible, in places rising to a height of more than twenty feet. The large medieval parish church of Holyhead stands within. Sigeberht's gift of *Cnobheresburg* to Fursa has been mentioned. Another of Sigeberht's grants was to Felix, a bishop who received a site for his East

Anglian see at a place called *Dommoc* in the 630s. *Dommoc* could be Dunwich *Sf*, but a case has been made for identifying it with the Roman coastal fort of Walton Castle that stood close to the church at Felixstowe *Sf* until it was destroyed by the sea in the eighteenth century (Rigold 1961; 1974). During the 650s the Roman coastal fort at *Ythancaestir*, now Bradwell-on-Sea *Ex*, was used by the Northumbrian Cedd as the base for his mission to the population of Essex. Cedd was working with royal encouragement. A laconic entry in the *Anglo-Saxon Chronicle* for the year 669 states: 'In this year Egbert [king of Kent 664–73] gave Reculver to Bassa the priest to build a church there'. A charter of *c.* 767 records a grant of land to Heaberht, abbot, and his *familia* in the minster at Reculver (Sawyer 1968, no.31). Part of the seventh-century church survives. Other royal gifts of forts are recorded, as at Ebchester *Du*, or might be inferred from reports of the presence of religious communities at places, no longer identifiable, with names like *Tunnacaestir* and *Kaelcacaestir* (*HE* iv.22,23) that are characteristic of former Roman sites. *Kaelcacaestir* may be equatable with Tadcaster *NY* (*YW*), the *Calcaria* of the *Antonine Itinerary* (Rodwell 1975, 83), although one wonders if by the seventh century the name had been transferred to the nearby Roman fort at Newton Kyme. This fort, situated on a terrace overlooking the River Wharfe, would be a classic locale for monastic activity at that date. Another place-name that remains to be located is Sidnacester: the site of the see of Lindsey in the eighth century. This might refer to a part of Lincoln, and there has been speculation about Caistor and Horncastle *Li*. The idea that Sidnacester was another Saxon Shore fort that has been claimed by the sea is attractive. There may have been such a fort on the north coast of the Wash, in the vicinity of Skegness (Whitwell 1970, 51–3). The first Lincolnshire bishopric would then fall into the pattern that has already been noted at *Ythancaestir* and *Dommoc*.

We are told quite a lot about monasteries which were founded in England during the period *c.* 630–700. By contrast, little detail is reported about the character of fresh foundations which were made in the first half of the eighth century, or indeed about what was happening to existing communities which had been established only one or two generations previously. Lastingham and Bradwell are cases in point. Bede described their origins in some detail, but said nothing about the lives of their communities in his own day. Yet it is clear that they continued to exist. Lastingham has a series of stone monuments that were carved during the eighth and ninth centuries. The church dedicated to St Peter which survives at Bradwell is likely to have been built after the days of Cedd (Rigold 1977, 72–3).

Sculptural and architectural evidence indicates that more religious communities existed during the eighth century than attracted notice in written records (Fig. 25). Sculpture that would have been appropriate to religious communities is found at places like Dewsbury *WY*, Easby, Masham *NY*, and Bewcastle *Cu*. Whoever prescribed the iconographic programme of the cross-shaft at Otley *WY* which bears images of the four evangelists was well acquainted with the scriptures (Wood 1987). Scenes like those to do with the annunciation that are found on the 'frieze' at Hovingham *NY* belong to a world of theological scholarship as well as artistic excellence. The frieze may have been the side of a shrine. Yet Otley is never heard of before the tenth century, while Hovingham was not recorded as a religious centre at all and we have no clue as to the identity of the saint who was venerated there. Churches which contain fabric of this era include Escomb *Du* (Pocock and Wheeler 1971; Cambridge 1984) and Ledsham *WY* (Bailey 1983); possibly also Seaham *Du*, Corbridge and St Peter's at Bywell *Nb*. At a later date all these buildings were put to parochial use, but it seems likely that they originated as the sites of religious communities.

One reason why some monasteries went undocumented during the eighth century is that the character of the sources underwent change. Monasteries founded in the seventh century are typically recorded in connection with the deeds of holy men and women. The biographies of Cuthbert, Wilfrid, Ceolfrid, Felix and Bede's *Ecclesiastical History* (which embodies a number of abridged *vitae*) account for the large majority of these references. In the eighth and ninth centuries religious communities are more commonly mentioned in correspondence, and in charters for the conveyance of land. Stonegrave *NY*, for instance, was described as a *monasterium* in a letter written by pope Paul I in 757 or 758. The letter was addressed to Eadberht, king of Northumbria (737–58). An abbot named Forthred had complained to the pope that three monasteries which had been granted to him by an abbess had been taken from him by the king, who had given them to his brother. The other monasteries were at Coxwold, about nine miles west of Stonegrave, and a place called *Donaemuthe*, which is unlocated (*EHD* I, 830). Stonegrave is but two miles from Hovingham (Fig. 26). The fact that we hear about the presence of monasteries at Coxwold and Stonegrave in such an incidental way, and that so many religious communities could exist in such close proximity, suggests that unrecorded monastic settlements may have been quite numerous. Other sources should cause us to expect this. Writing at the end of his *Ecclesiastical History*, Bede observed that

> In these favourable times of peace and prosperity, many of the Northumbrian race, both noble and simple, have laid aside their weapons and taken the tonsure, preferring that they and their children should take monastic vows rather than train themselves in the art of war. What the result will be, a later generation will discover.
>
> (*HE* v.23)

Looking to Mercia, an appreciable number of the eighth-century references to monasteries occur not in ecclesiastical contexts but in charters. At Ismere *Wo*, for instance, the Mercian king, Æthelbald,

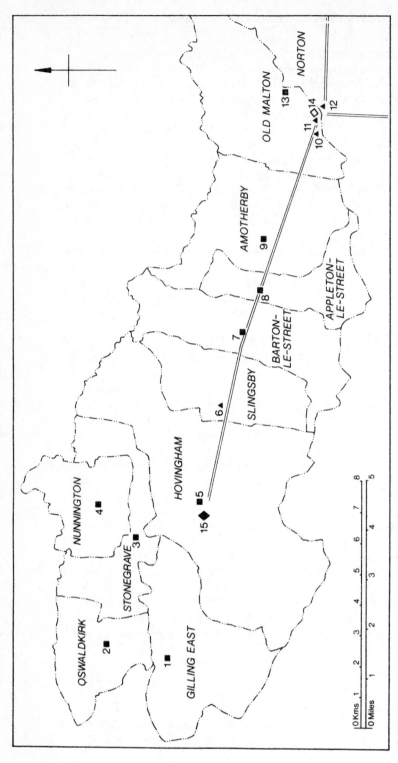

26 Parishes along the 'Street' between Malton and Hovingham, North Yorkshire. *Key*: **1–5, 7–9, 13** sites of parish churches; **6, 10–12** parochial chapels (**10** and **11** in Malton); **14** core of Roman *Derventio*; **15** site of Roman villa. Boundaries correspond with what is known of the parish layout before the nineteenth century. The 'Street' was established by, possibly within, the Roman period; its name could indicate a paved Roman road. The Street ran from *Derventio* to Hovingham, following the edge of the Vale of Pickering (characterized hereabouts by marsh and carr), just below the scarp of the Howardian Hills. Most of the parishes encompass portions of both types of landscape and lie at right-angles to the physical boundary between them. Religious communities existed at Stonegrave and Hovingham by *c.* 800; Stonegrave is attested in a papal letter of the mid-eighth century; Hovingham retains part of a reliquary shrine of *c.* 800. Old Malton may have been another religious centre before the Conquest

granted ten hides of land to his *comes* Cyneberht in 736 for the construction of a monastery (*EHD* i, 492–3). A few years previously Æthelbald had granted land at Acton Beauchamp *He* to his *comes* Buca to be a perpetual dwelling for the servants of God (Sawyer 1968, no.85). Hanbury *Wo* is heard of in 836 when its privileges were extended (*EHD* i, 518). A religious community which worshipped in a church dedicated to St Michael at Bishops Cleeve *Gl* is mentioned in 768 × 779 (Sawyer 1968, no.141). Other places which come to attention in similar fashion include Fladbury *Wo*, Cookham *Brk*, Cheltenham *Gl*, Stratford-upon-Avon *Wa* and Bromyard *He*.

The shift from sources concerned with sanctity towards records of a more administrative nature may to some extent have been paralleled by a change in the types of site that were selected for monastic use. After *c.* 680 monasticism entered a less austere phase. Sites were now almost always of congenial character. Religious communities may have pro-liferated as fast, or faster, in the eighth century than before, but it was the earlier foundations which more often achieved celebrity because they were so often associated with outstanding figures.

Feats of asceticism and the performance of miracles were a function of the process of conversion, or spiritual revaluation, in late antiquity and the early Middle Ages. Holy men and women made their marks upon society less through systematic preaching than by living remarkable lives. It is true that Aidan, Fursa, Cedd and Cuthbert were all preachers. It is equally plain that their ultimate interests lay in the direction of ascetic liv-ing. As preachers, seventh-century religious leaders directed themselves most often to kings, and to people in the immediate circle of kings. The work of conversion which caught the attention of historians thus has the appearance of having been undertaken from sites which for one reason or another would look impressive to the uncommitted: for example, because they were remote, dangerous, unprofitable, exposed to extremes of weather or because people thought they were haunted.

If restlessness, asceticism and sites to match, were depicted as being characteristic of the first stages of conversion, the next phase, inaugurated by archbishop Theodore (668–93) saw emphasis transferred to the building of an ecclesiastical organization, and the introduction of more discipline and consistency into the institutional affairs of the Church. A conference held at Hertford in 672 ruled that bishops should not intrude into the dioceses of their colleagues. Monks were not to wander from one monastery to another without authorization from their own abbot, and they were expected 'to remain under that obedience which they promised at the time of their profession' (*HE* iv.5). Such consolidatory work called less for saints than for administrators and, increasingly, sites which were convenient for priests who were prepared to devote themselves to hum-drum pastoral duties. With the onset of regulation it is no surprise to see that the eighth century was not on the whole depicted as a period of great domestic holiness. This may be one of the reasons why some of the greatest individualists elected to become missionaries in heathen Frisia and Germany. A number of the sites they received for episcopal sees and monasteries are reminiscent of those which had been granted in seventh-century England. At Utrecht the old minster of St Salvator, founded by Willibrord (658–739), stood in the south-west quarter of an old Roman fort. Another church, dedicated to St Martin, was founded in the quarter diagonally opposite by Boniface (c. 675–754). Boniface's first mission-station in Germany was in the reoccupied Iron Age hillfort of Amoneberg 'where he found the local leaders and people practising pagan rites under a thin veneer of Christianity' (Parsons 1983, 281). Other elevated strong-points which were colonized by English missionaries in this period included Buraberg, Fulda and Wurzburg.

If the post-conversion phase of the English Church was not an age productive of new generations of saints at home, it was nevertheless a period of continuing sanctity. New saints were hardly needed because those of the seventh century lived on, ever immanent, their deeds celebrated in *vitae* and their power radiating from tombs and shrines. Significantly, the eighth century was a period when the authorship of *vitae* prospered (Stephanus, Bede, Felix, Alcuin) and the ninth was a time when more crypts started to be built. If the monastic world was now becoming a tamer place, there was scope for vicarious access to the glamour of saintly heroism through the cult of relics.

Human remains are portable, and in time this enabled the map of holy power-sources to be altered (Rollason 1986). Initially, however, there was a strong reluctance to move bodies over long distances, or to dismember them. The first translations were usually no further than from a grave in the monastic cemetery to a place of honour within the church. This disinclination to tamper with bodies may explain why two of the earliest episodes involving fragmentation and distant translation involved the salvaging of remains of kings who had perished in battle. Some time after 685 the community ruled by Hild at *Streanaeshalch* mounted an expedition to retrieve the body of king Edwin from its grave at *Haethfelth* (Colgrave 1968, cap. 18–19). Hild's interest is explained by the fact that she was Edwin's grand-niece. According to Bede, Edwin's head had previously been deposited in the *porticus* of St Gregory which formed part of the cathedral at York, itself on the site of Edwin's baptism (*HE* ii.20). It is likely that Hild entertained a hope that Edwin would come to be regarded as a saint. This did happen to Oswald, who succeeded Edwin as king of Northumbria in 633 (after a brief hiatus) and died in battle, also at the hands of the heathen Mercian king, Penda, in 641. Oswald's body was cut up. Allegedly this was on the orders of Penda, who is said to have instructed that Oswald's head and arms be severed and hung on stakes (*HE* iii.12). A year later the head was retrieved and taken to Lindisfarne, where the religious community had been established only six years previously at Oswald's invitation. The arms were taken to the nearby *villa regia* at Bamburgh. The remains were thus divided between the spiritual and royal foci of the region. The resting-place of Oswald's trunk and legs at this time is not reported, but late in the seventh century the remains were 'discovered' and taken to Bardney *Li*, an important monastery in the kingdom of Lindsey. This came about through the efforts of Osthryth, wife of Æthelred, king of Mercia (674–704). Osthryth was Oswald's niece. Edwin and Oswald belonged to rival branches of the Northumbrian royal family. Feuding between the two branches continued for the greater part of the seventh century. (Despite Oswald's later saintly reputation, when Edwin perished at *Haethfelth* his wife took the precaution of sending his infant son and a small grandson to Gaul where they would be out of Oswald's reach (*HE* ii.20).) This internecine conflict could even lead to the founding of monasteries. Gilling *NY*, for instance, was established by king Oswin (who was Oswald's brother) in expiation for the murder of Oswine (who belonged to Edwin's side of the family). One wonders how many other monasteries could have originated cenotaph-fashion, perhaps as a way of halting the progress of blood-feuds. Certainly, the dynastic tensions within the Northumbrian royal house were mirrored in ecclesiastical patronage, varying affection for religious centres, and the ways in which kings and their relatives aligned themselves upon different saints and cults. The dearth of interesting relics at York in the later Middle Ages may ultimately be explicable in terms of the success of the Bernician branch of the royal family.

It was not only among sovereigns that the demands of kinship found expression in ecclesiastical geography. By the early eighth century the founding of monasteries was escalating in a way which looked to Bede to have got wholly out of hand. A hint of this unease is contained in the passage at the conclusion of the *Ecclesiastical History*, quoted on p. 121. On 5 November 734 Bede completed a letter to Egbert, archbishop of York, in which he set out his misgivings at great length (*EHD* i, 799–810).

After admonishing Egbert on the need for a bishop to conduct himself with due dignity and sobriety, Bede drew attention to the huge size of the diocese of York, and the absence of any effective pastoral provision within it:

> For we have heard … that many villages and hamlets of our people are situated in inaccessible mountains and dense woodlands, where there is never seen for many years at a time a bishop to exhibit any ministry … not one man of which, however, is immune from rendering dues to the bishop.
>
> (*EHD* i, 802)

Bede recalled how pope Gregory had decreed that there ought to be twelve bishops in northern England, among whom the bishop of York should receive the *pallium* and be metropolitan:

> I should now like you, holy father… to endeavour to complete that number of bishops.… But indeed we know that through the

carelessness of preceding kings and through most foolish donations it has come about that it is not easy to find a vacant place where a new episcopal see should be made.

(*EHD* 1, 804)

These 'foolish donations', it seems, were grants of land which had been made to laypeople for the foundation of monasteries. Bede continues:

there are innumerable places, as we all know, allowed the name of monasteries by a most foolish manner of speaking, but having nothing of a monastic way of life; some of which I would wish to be transformed by synodal authority from wanton living to chastity, from vanity to truth, from overindulgence of the belly and from gluttony to continence and piety of heart, and to be taken over in support of the episcopal see which ought newly to be ordained.

(*EHD* 1, 806)

Bede tells us that these pseudo-monasteries were 'many and large'. He regarded them as being 'useful neither to God nor man'. His criticisms of their poor spirituality are set out at length. No regular life was being practised in them. As often as not they were headed by reeves, thegns or royal servants who had simply declared themselves to be abbots. Their monasteries were populated by

whomsoever they may perchance find wandering anywhere, expelled from true monasteries for the fault of disobedience, or whom they can allure out of the monasteries, or, indeed, those of their own followers whom they can persuade to promise them the obedience of a monk and receive the tonsure. With the unseemly companies of these persons they fill the monasteries which they have built, and ... the very same men are now occupied with wives and the procreation of children, now rising from their beds perform with assiduous attention what should be done within the precincts of monasteries. Moreover, with like shamelessness they procure for their wives places for constructing monasteries ... and these with equal foolishness, seeing that they are lay-women, allow themselves to be mistresses of the handmaids of Christ.

(*EHD* 1, 806)

Bede also objected to these monasteries on socio-political grounds. The endowment of monasteries led to the permanent alienation of land which would in normal circumstances revert in due course to the king's hand and so be available for redistribution. Instead, 'those who are totally ignorant of the monastic life have received under their control so many places in the name of monasteries ... that there is a complete lack of places where the sons of nobles or of veteran thegns can receive an estate' (*EHD* 1, 805). Laymen had bribed kings to provide lands 'under the pretext of founding monasteries ... and in addition cause them to be ascribed to them in hereditary rights by royal edicts'. Monastic estates could likewise be exempted from various renders and obligations, not the least of these being the requirement to provide men for military service. Bede was fearful that this would sap the strength of the kingdom, leaving it open to physical attack from without and corruption within.

The justice of these allegations is difficult to assess, not least because of the loftiness of the threshold of Bede's criteria for what constituted 'true' monasticism. The existence of monasteries under secular control is not in doubt. Nor is it in question that monasteries and their estates could pass according to family relationships. After Caedwalla captured the Isle of Wight he gave one-quarter of its 1200 hides to bishop Wilfrid, who promptly entrusted his portion to one of his clergy who was his sister's son (*HE* iv.16). Alcuin tells us that he was in charge of the small community at Spurn because it had passed to him by lawful descent. Yet here lies the problem. Wilgils founded this community because of his 'zeal for the spiritual life'. Must it be assumed that such an aspiration would necessarily have been compromised by the connections of kinship? Alcuin said not, assuring his readers that Wilgils's successors 'still follow the example of his holiness' (Talbot 1981, 3).

In Bede's eyes the family-owned monastery represented a retreat from idealized standards. But, in Patrick Wormald's words:

> The abuses denounced by the Church Fathers may legitimately be seen as evidence, not of Christianity's failure but of one of its greatest triumphs: it had been successfully assimilated by a warrior nobility, which had no intention of abandoning its culture, or seriously changing its ways of life, but which was willing to throw its traditions, customs, tastes and loyalties into the articulation of the new faith, and whose persisting 'secularity' was an important condition of the richness of early English Christian civilization.
>
> (Wormald 1978, 57)

As for the family monasteries, Wormald advises us to accept that the foundations Bede disliked

> were essentially expressions of the understandable sense of kindred in the Anglo-Saxon upper classes. To associate the government of a religious house with the members of the 'Founder's Kin' came naturally to the Anglo-Saxons.... It would probably be wrong, moreover, to regard every such *minster* as a den of vice. No doubt there were abuses ... but several apparently dubious houses seem to have achieved high standards of Christian culture. The early ninth-century *De Abbatibus* of Æthelwulf makes it quite clear that this otherwise unknown Northumbrian *minster* was ruled more than once by members of the founder's family, yet the impression given in the poem is of a serious and sober community. We hear of books illuminated and ornaments made, while the poet's Latin, if not exactly a model of lucidity, is certainly not unlearned. It is likely that it was in the form of such foundations that

Christianity reached most parts of the British countryside, and its best monuments may be the surviving early Anglo-Saxon churches.

(Wormald 1978, 53–4)

The word *mynster* has at last been introduced. In order to explore its meaning it will be helpful to come forward for a moment into the tenth century, and to work backwards from later usage. In its original sense *mynster* was simply the Old English rendering of Latin *monasterium*. But by the tenth and eleventh centuries *mynster* had acquired a versatility in sense which has sometimes acted to tease, if not confuse, modern historians. At this time *mynster* could denote a church of superior status, or a church of any status, or simply a church building. The flexibility of *mynster* is nicely illustrated in a law code of 1008. A monk who has no *mynster* is directed to approach the diocesan bishop and pledge himself to God to observe his vows, while canons are expected to 'hold their *mynster* with right observance and with chastity' (5 Æthelred 6, 7). Monks and canons are carefully differentiated here, whereas *mynster* is used both in the sense of 'regular monastery' and 'church of a community of canons'. Around 1000 the meaning of *mynster* would be ascertainable from the context in which it was used. But although there were occasions when *mynster* signified just 'church', some ultimate distinction between a church and a *mynster* seems to have been perceived. According to the *Leechdoms* the sixteenth day of the moon was propitious for the founding of a *mynster*, whereas the sixth day of the moon was thought best for the founding of a church (Cockayne 1866, 178–81).

The statement in the *Leechdoms* could be explained by the fact that in the tenth and eleventh centuries *mynster* was commonly deployed in the sense of 'superior church'. Minsters were superior because they were often long-established, and it was to them that people paid their dues. Dues which citizens owed to their *ealdan mynstres* are listed in legislation issued by king Edgar (959–75) in 960 × 962: tithe, churchscot, hearthpennies (2 Edgar 1.1–2.1, 2.2, 2.3, 3.1, 4). Similar dues had been itemized by Athelstan (925–39), including tithe, churchscot, soulscot (burial fees) and plough-alms (1 Athelstan 3, 4). In these laws *mynster* is being used with an effective meaning not far removed from that of parish church, although the *parochiae* of minsters were generally much larger than the local parishes which took form in the eleventh and twelfth centuries and which eventually robbed the *ealdan mynstres* of their pre-eminence.

The *ealdan mynstre* of 2 Edgar was certainly territorial. It ruled a parish from within which tithe was to be rendered 'both from the thegn's demesne land and from the land of his tenants, according as it is brought under the plough' (2 Edgar 1). It was not unusual for the parish of an old minster to be co-extensive with an administrative hundred, and for the minster to stand at the hundredal centre, which was often, or once had been, a royal vill. Continuing royal involvement is indicated by the procedure to be followed in the event of a refusal to pay tithe:

the king's reeve is to go there, and the bishop's reeve and the mass-priest of the minster, and they are to seize without his consent the tenth part for the minster to which it belongs, and to assign to him the next tenth; and the [remaining] eight parts are to be divided into two, and the lord of the estate is to succeed to half, and the bishop to half, whether it be a king's man or a thegn's.

(2 Edgar 3.1)

Minsters were called 'old' in the tenth century not because they were necessarily very ancient, although many were, but in order to distinguish them from newer local churches which were now being built by lay lords on their estates. As minsters came to be jostled by new foundations it became necessary to define their entitlements more closely, and to invent a hierarchy whereby different types of church could be classified. Æthelred's code of 1014 mentions three grades of minster: head minsters (cathedrals), *medemran* 'lesser' (= old) minsters, and those that were less significant still (8 Æthelred 5.1). This last category is likely to have consisted largely of churches in private ownership. It would include churches which had their own graveyards on the bookland of thegns ('If ... there is any thegn who has on his bookland a church with which there is a graveyard, he is to pay the third part of his own tithe into his church' (2 Edgar 2)). Possession of a cemetery differentiated churches in this third grade from the *feldcircan* 'field churches' of the fourth. *Feldcircan* lacked burial grounds of their own (2 Edgar 2.1). This may help to explain why 8 Æthelred classified the thegns' churches of 2 Edgar as a minor species of *mynster*; traditionally, possession of a graveyard had been a mark of superior status.

Churches varied also in the level and degree of permanence in their staffing. Churches with groups of priests were *mynstres*. A church with one priest was sometimes called a *mynster*, but was more likely to be referred to as *cirice*. Yet not all churches with graveyards were served by full-time priests. In the eleventh century we hear of churches 'where there is little service and yet there is a graveyard' (1 Cnut 3.2). Perhaps such churches were served by priests who visited from the old minster, or by a priest who was attached to the household of a lord who commuted between his estates and had churches in several places (cf. Blair 1985).

Minsters varied a good deal in size and wealth. Many had no more than a couple of priests; Wroxeter *Sa* had four; at Stafford there were thirteen canons. Endowments of between one and five hides were common. Others were more lavishly provided for. Calne *Wi*, for instance, had six hides in 1086. Crewkerne *So* was rated at ten. Bosham *Sx*, with 147 hides, was exceptionally well provided for.

A record of the dues rendered to a minster illustrates the dependence of such churches upon the produce of land. As minsters went, St Michael at Lambourn *Brk* was very modestly endowed. It had one hide. But beyond this there was the tenth acre in the king's land, and two acres ... at harvest, and the tenth lamb and the tenth young pig, and at Michaelmas a wey of cheese, and at Martinmas two sesters of corn and one pig, and at Easter 15 pence ... and pasture for the priest's ten oxen and two cows along with the king's, and for his ... bullocks ... and for the priest's sheep next after the king's so that they do not mix together, and free pasture for 40 pigs in wood and open country, and every day one horse or two men carrying wood from the king's wood for the priest's fire, and pasture for the priest's two horses along with the reeve's.

From Up Lambourn and in Lambourn itself the minster could expect

1 acre as tithes or 100 sheaves at harvest, and every *geneat* a sester of corn as church dues, and from the thegn-land of the manor 2 acres as tithes and two sesters of corn as church dues, and from Ralph's estate at Bockhampton 2 acres as tithes and 2 sesters of corn as church dues, and from Edward's estate at Bockhampton 2 acres as tithes, and from Eastbury 2 acres as tithes and 1 measure as church dues.

(Robertson 1939, 241)

If the minsters of late Saxon England have the look of a settled pattern, it should not be assumed that they were all of great age, or that their territories were immune from change. Administrative reorganization could involve the transfer of land from one hundred to another, with consequent repercussions for a minster's *parochia*. The outlines of royal, episcopal and aristocratic holdings were seldom static. When estates were broken up or reassigned, minsters could be affected.

Routine modifications and tenth-century reinforcements aside, there is a theory which states that old minsters had existed as a class of church almost from the beginning of English Christianity. The typical old minster, it is said, was established at or near a royal vill in the seventh or eighth century. It is moreover suggested that these minsters were founded as an expression of broad policy, to assist in the process of conversion, and to provide the rudiments of pastoral care. Later, if not from the outset, minsters came to differ from cenobitic monasteries both in their architectural forms and institutional characteristics. Minsters, in short, constituted an independent category of ecclesiastical provision.

There are many minsters for which an explanation along the foregoing lines works rather well. There are, equally, many others for which it is not so satisfactory. A review of some of the sites already mentioned will show a dissimilarity in their origins which makes it hard to conceive of them as products of any coherent campaign. Ripon, with a small community of canons in the eleventh century, had been a house of monks who used the Rule of St Benedict in the seventh century (Stephanus, 14, 47), and who had themselves replaced an earlier colony of monks 'who followed Irish ways' (*HE* iii.25). Around 700 Repton was a royal monastery under the rule of an abbess, and either then or soon afterwards a necropolis for Mercian kings. In 1086 it had two priests. Bosham at Domesday was one of the wealthiest minsters in England, yet in the later seventh century it had been occupied by a small colony of humble Irish monks. Admittedly, these are contrasts of beginning and end. Like subterranean rivers, the intervening institutional histories of places like Bosham or Ripon are hidden, vanishing around 700 only to reappear changed out of all recognition several centuries later. At some places the metamorphosis from monastic community to secular minster may have been gradual. But the swiftness of Wilfrid's reorganization at Ripon in the seventh century shows how change could also be wrought at a stroke by a bishop or king who held strong ideas. Conversely, one wonders if some of the smaller communities of priests met with for the first time in tenth- or eleventh-century sources could represent a form of religious life which was made to seem archaic or 'unmonastic' by the adoption from the tenth century of the Benedictine blueprint. In such cases, perhaps it was monasticism, rather than the communities, which had changed?

However this may be, an equal difficulty attends acceptance of the theory that part of the original *raison d'être* of a minster was that it should form a base for the systematic provision of pastoral care. References to churches at royal *tūn* are common enough, and there is no doubt that in the tenth and eleventh centuries such churches exercised considerable pastoral responsibilities. Such evidence as we have, however, points more to the *initial* purpose of these foundations as private chapels for the use of the king, his family and *comites*. In the eighth and ninth centuries *villae regales* were characteristic locales for ecclesiastical ceremonies involving royalty. Chippenham *Wi* was the scene of king Burgred's marriage in 853. King Æthelwold was married at Catterick in 762. Guthrum was buried at Hadleigh *Sf* in 890; Brihtric at Wareham *Do* in 786; Æthelred and Sigeferth at Wimborne *Do* in 871 and 962; Æthelwulf at Steyning *Sx* in 857.

Institutionally there seems to have been no set pattern. Minsters commonly consisted of small communities of priests, as befitted the needs of a royal household, but there were some of more 'monastic' complexion, or which aspired to it. Some minsters may have passed in and out of monastic phases, according to the whims or inclinations of individual rulers.

The practice of furnishing royal *tūn* with churches began early, and could occur in advance of the establishment of more serious religious communities. Edwin's *villa regia* at *Campodonum* (*WY?*) possessed a church before 632, for instance, and there was a church at Bamburgh *Nb* not long afterwards (*HE* ii.14; iii.6). References to mass baptisms at Catterick and Yeavering (*HE* ii.14) have given rise to speculation that such centres could acquire pastoral functions. However, as was explained in Chapter 2, it is more likely that missionaries attended these places because they were already used for large seasonal or annual gatherings. Their usefulness for conversion purposes would thus have been correspondingly episodic, and there are no references to great alfresco assemblies after the 630s. Missionary work *was* practised from a royal estate near Bamburgh, but the context is revealing. Here the bishop Aidan had 'a church and a cell where he often used to go and stay, travelling about in the neighbourhood to preach. He did the same on other royal estates; for he had no possessions of his own except the church and a small piece of land around it' (*HE* iii.17). The implication is that at this date mission was a function expected of individual personalities rather than of places.

The *locus classicus* for the notion of the monastery as a mission-station is Breedon-on-the-Hill *Le*. 'Here', wrote Sir Frank Stenton, 'there is definite evidence that the monastery ... was founded in order to bring teaching and baptism to the men of the surrounding country' (1970, 149). But this is not quite what the source reports. Some time between 675 and 692 Friduric, the *princeps* of Æthelred, king of Mercia (674–704), made a grant of land at Breedon to the monastery of St Peter at *Medeshamstede* (Peterborough). This grant was made 'so that a *monasterium* and oratory of monks serving God, should be founded ... *and also* a priest of honest life and good reputation instituted, who should bring the grace of baptism and the teaching of the Gospel doctrine to the people committed to his care' (Birch 1887, no.841; Sawyer 1968, no.1803) (my italics). The grant was made in order to start a monastery: and a rather remote monastery at that. There was an intention that pastoral work should take place, but this was to be achieved through the attachment to the community of a priest; it was not necessarily the concern, still less the rationale, of the community as a whole. Indeed, the conjunction between the two aims stated in the grant, *necnon etiam et*, could hardly be more emphatic (Birch 1887, no.841). It is possible that the ministry of Breedon's priest would have been limited to the lay population which lived and worked upon the monastery's estate. The idea that monasteries had a responsibility towards their estate-dwellers is hinted at elsewhere, for example in the Penitential of archbishop Theodore (Haddan and Stubbs 1871, 195), and could lie behind some reports of the founding of churches upon monastic property. A church consecrated by Cuthbert in 686 or 687 at a place in the possession of the monastery of *Streanaeshalch NY*, in a *parochia* 'district' called *Osingadun* may have been such a case (*Vita Cuthberti*, 34). Mr Eric Cambridge has rightly stressed the monastic context of this foundation, and its status as a dependency of *Streanaeshalch* (1984, 74). But that interpretation need not be in conflict with an intention to make provision for laypeople for whom the mother monastery was now, in effect, their lord.

Kings and monasteries were not the only founders of churches. *Comites* – veteran companions of the king who assisted with royal administration – did so too. Among the earliest references to local churches are two which mention foundations made on comital estates in eastern Yorkshire at the beginning of the eighth century (*HE* v.4,5). Several *monasteria* mentioned above, like Ismere *Wo* and Acton Beauchamp *He*, were established by *comites*. As with foundations made by kings, the process could begin early. Around 630 a *praefectus* (reeve? royal official? subking?) called Blaecca and his household were associated with the construction of a church in Lincoln (*HE* ii.16).

Perhaps this closes a circle. Can comital minsters be equated with the *monasteria* headed by 'numberless ... *prefecti* or thegns or servants of the king' which caused Bede so much anguish in his *Letter to Egbert*? Presumably many of them can, although Bede was careful to differentiate between thegns and *comites* who used religious foundations as a means of evading their secular responsibilities, and others who did not (*EHD* i, 804).

When kings and *comites* founded churches on their estates they did so primarily for the use of their own households. But a lord could feel responsibility for the spiritual welfare of his followers, and to this extent his church could have a pastoral function, coincident with his landed interests. The minster of a magnate could be a virtuous and disciplined community, a place of laxity with no real spiritual life or simply a household chapel. At different times it might have been all three. The mistake, perhaps, has been to view such foundations as products of a coherent pastoral strategy. In fact, minsters originated in different ways, out of a variety of motives. Being essentially personal or familial foundations they were not, as a rule, systematically located in order to provide comprehensive coverage of the landscape. That they came to acquire the semblance of a system was due to the men of the tenth and eleventh centuries, who threw an administrative net over a disorderly pattern.

The working through of these processes will obviously have varied from area to area, and there are regional imbalances in the quality and quantity of the evidence that is to hand. An exploration of the contrasts lies beyond the scope of this book. A regional illustration of the processes described or adduced in this chapter is nevertheless required, even if the case-study which forms the coda of this chapter has no claim to be representative.

Yorkshire is an interesting area to examine, partly because of the high incidence of pre-Conquest ecclesiastical sculpture which must point to, even if it seldom institutionally defines, the whereabouts and broad chronology of early provision, and also partly because it is a county wherein most traces of minsters are sometimes said to have been obliterated by the Scandinavian invasions. In fact, even the picture revealed by literary sources is far less featureless than it has sometimes been made to seem (Fig. 27). Admittedly, the majority of these references date from after 1100, when the pattern they describe had begun to dissolve. But they are so numerous as to suggest that the pattern had once been extensive. In addition to important churches revealed by Domesday Book at places like Topcliffe and the Bishophill area of York, twelfth- and thirteenth-century documents are quite rich in references to churches of superior status. Until 1152–3 Easby was being served by a group of clergy called *fratres*, and 'when the abbey of St Agatha, a house of Premonstra-

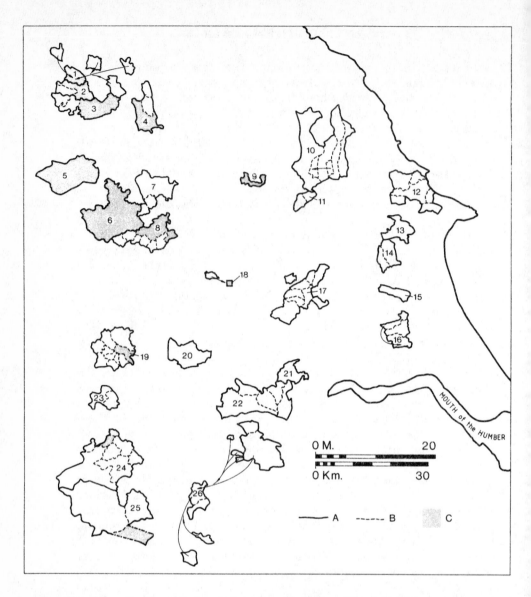

27 *Parochiae* of superior churches in pre-Conquest Yorkshire. The parochial outlines are those of later medieval parishes and do not therefore necessarily correspond with the original *parochiae*. They are depicted in this way in order to give an impression of the amount of coverage that might have been achieved before *c.* 850. Additional coverage, suggested by sculpture and archaeology, is mapped in Fig. 29

A possible core-territory of superior church; **B** boundary of later parish or chapelry; **C** pre-Danish sculpture present within parish.

1 Gilling (C8, Bede); 2 Easby (C12, charter; sculpture); 3 Catterick (C8, Bede; C12, Northumbrian Annals); 4 Northallerton (C12, charters); 5 Masham (C12 and later, status); 6 Ripon (C8, Stephanus, Bede); 7 Topcliffe (1086, DB); 8 Aldborough (C12, charters, later status); 9 Stonegrave (C8, papal letter); 10 Pickering (C12, charters, later status); 11 Old Malton (C12, status); 12 Hunmanby (C12, status); 13 Kilham (C12, charters); 14 Driffield

(royal *tun* 705; C12, charters); **15** Watton (C8, Bede); **16** Beverley (C8, Bede;
C12, Northumbrian Annals); **17** Pocklington (C12, charters; C13, *Reg. Gray*);
18 York, Holy Trinity Micklegate (1086, DB); **19** Leeds (later status);
20 Sherburn-in-Elmet (1086, DB); **21** Howden (C12, Giraldus Cambrensis);
22 Snaith (C12, charters); **23** Dewsbury (marks of status: Faull and
Moorhouse 1981, i, 216-18); **24-6** Silkstone, Ecclesfield, Conisbrough (marks of
status: Hey 1982)

---

tensian canons, was founded on the same site, the church was called a
monasterium or minster' (*EYC* 5, 169, 231, 232).

> From then to the dissolution the vicar was always one of the canons.
> The ordination of the vicarage only involved a financial separation of
> abbey and parish church. The fact that the vicar was one of the canons,
> meant that from early times till 1537 the care of souls at Easby was exer-
> cised by a priest belonging to a community of clerks living round the
> parish church.
>
> (Addleshaw 1987, 16-17)

Other possible communities are glimpsed at Osmotherly and, less certainly, Upper Poppleton. (Other parish churches described in the twelfth century as *monasteria* included Warmfield, Silkstone and Barnburgh *SY*, East
Keal, Hundleby and Withcall *Li*. *Monasterium* at this date could be used
as a synonym for 'church', but in a number of cases (e.g. Stanway *Gl*,
Hitchin *Hrt*, Silkstone *SY*) it appears to have been used as a kind of
courtesy title to denote a former minster.) Ancient parishes of large size
and ancient importance are found at Snaith (*EYC* i, no.472), Dewsbury
(Faull and Moorhouse 1981, i, 216-18, map 15), Ecclesfield and Conisbrough
(Hey 1982, 12-13) and Northallerton. Aldborough, Pocklington, Kilham,
Driffield and Pickering were important crown demesne manors.
Aldborough, Pocklington and Pickering had extensive *parochiae* containing
numerous dependencies, the rights over which Henry i was careful to
safeguard (*EYC* i, nos 426-9). Continuing research into sources of the
later Middle Ages may well disclose further examples.

The *parochiae* of Pocklington and Pickering survived into the later Middle Ages. The register of Walter de Gray, archbishop of York (1215-55),
contains a remarkable entry about Pocklington. In 1252 the *parochia* of
Pocklington included not only Pocklington itself but nine other settlements: Fangfoss, Yapham, Great Givendale, Millington, Burnby,
Hayton, Thornton, Allerthorpe and Barmby Moor. Each of these places
had a church which was subordinate to Pocklington (Fig. 28). De Gray
ordained a vicarage at Pocklington, and amalgamated the nine dependencies into four parochial units. To all intents and purposes these were
parishes, but the ultimate supremacy of Pocklington was maintained (*Reg.
Gray*, 211-13). Most of the surrounding churches contain some architectural
indication that they existed by the twelfth century. Their dedications are
interesting. Two have no dedication at all, perhaps because their identities

were so closely bound up with that of their mother, or the neighbour with which they were paired. Of the others, four concern saints who came to be widely honoured towards the end of the eleventh and during the twelfth century: Catherine, Giles (twice) and Botolph. The fallacy of trying to employ dedications to date churches is understood. The point is simply that these dedications would be appropriate to a context in which Pocklington itself took priority. Pocklington, like Driffield, Kilham and Northallerton, was dedicated to All Saints.

The earlier histories of some of these places are worth attention (Fig. 29). Pocklington's *parochia* was bracketed by two parishes which have pro-

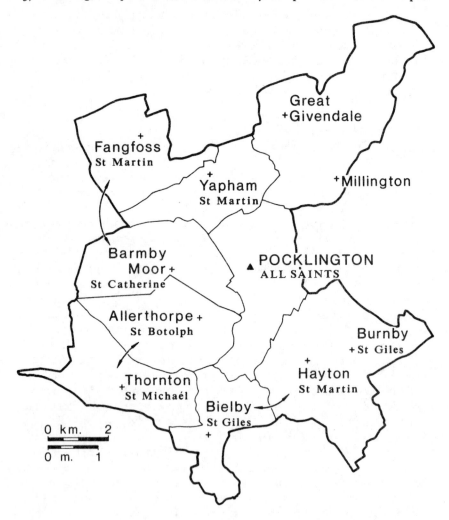

28 Reconstruction of the *parochia* of Pocklington in 1252 (*Source: Reg. Gray*, 211–12)

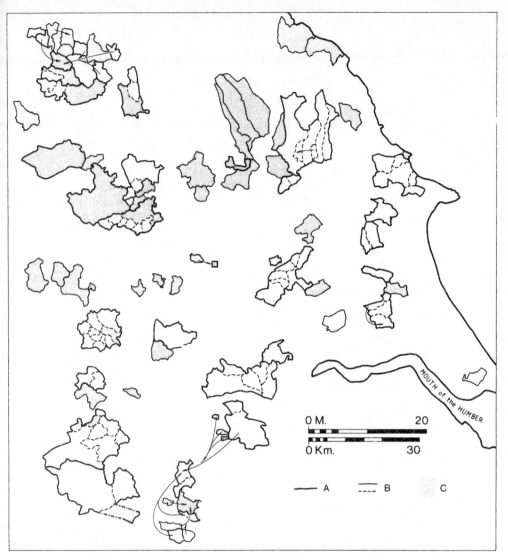

29 *Parochiae* of superior churches in pre-Conquest Yorkshire around centres suggested by literary, sculptural, architectural and archaeological indications. Caveats about the significance of parish outlines, explained in caption to Fig. 27, apply here also. The inclusion of sculptural evidence, which in Fig. 27 was recorded only at centres otherwise indicated by written records, increases the possible extent of provision, but does not help to define its character. Both here and in Fig. 27 only sculpture of the pre-Danish period is shown

duced pre-Viking-age sculpture. Carved stones of the eighth and earlier ninth centuries are relatively uncommon, and it can probably be assumed that where they occur they signal the presence of religious foundations – though whether these stones enable us to differentiate between magnate minsters or virtuous communities is doubtful. Driffield was probably a royal *tūn* by 705, when king Aldfrith died there. Like Kilham, Driffield is of additional interest in that it seems to have been a focus for burial in the pre-Christian period. Easby's claim to an early origin is amply substantiated by the remains of a spectacular high cross of eighth- or ninth-century date. Northallerton, Aldborough, Dewsbury and Otley are among other places mentioned which have yielded carved stones from this period.

The 'afterlives' of the Yorkshire minsters are also significant. Northallerton and Howden passed into the hands of Durham. Otley was the centre of an archiepiscopal estate. Pocklington, Kilham and Pickering were given to the deanery of York by Henry I. They became, in effect, peculiars which were exempt from most aspects of episcopal jurisdiction (Addleshaw 1987, 15). The annexing of valuable churches to the offices of capitular dignitaries, Crown servants or to canonries, as prebends, was a technique practised often after the Conquest. This is why in southern England, where earlier documentation is more plentiful, it is possible to see how churches of superior status so often ended up as churches of prebends, or as royal free chapels (cf. Blair 1985, 125-6). Most of the putative Yorkshire minsters fit snugly into this well-attested pattern.

An interpretation of the various factors is offered in Fig. 30. In several respects this is a fantasy, but it expresses the main lines of development which have been adduced for the seventh and eighth centuries; it suggests ideological or political contexts for the origins of some of the churches concerned, and may give a rough measure of the size of the contribution of this period to later provision. The early existence of a *spectrum* of minsters goes far to explain the ambiguity of later terminology. The idea that all religious communities, royal or comital churches were intended as bases for systematic evangelical action, or that their *parochiae* should give uninterrupted coverage across an entire kingdom, is a modern assumption. Doubtless there were more early minsters than we know, but the impression of unevenness in early provision could well be more than a trick of the sources.

The main points in the chapter must now be drawn together. From *c.* 450 to *c.* 700 holy men loom large. Their monasticism was generally of a personal kind, locationally unstable, exemplary rather than regular, and the toughest of them had topographical preferences for boundaries (of one sort or another) and extremes. Side by side with the saints there developed a Christianity of a more social kind. This found its earliest and readiest expression in the kin-structure and ambitions of royal families and the higher nobility. It quickly produced churches attached to the centres of royal and comital estates: in general, places of convenience, with access to useful resources and good land. Some of these foundations were made with monastic pretensions, or later acquired or rejected them, and others did not. Churches from this primary phase which survived into the tenth century were often classified as *ealdan mynstres*, in contradistinction to newer foundations being made at local level.

a

Estate of comes, praefectus, etc		+																++	
Estate of religious community												+							
Dependency of religious community						+					+			++					
Religious community **B**			+			+	+	+		+	++	++	+++			+	+		
Religious community **A**					+	+ ++	++		+		+		+			+			
Royal tun			++	+												+			

| 620 | 625 | 630 | 635 | 640 | 645 | 650 | 655 | 660 | 665 | 670 | 675 | 680 | 685 | 690 | 695 | 700 | 705 | 710 |

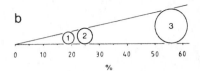

b

$$0 \quad 10 \quad 20 \quad 30 \quad 40 \quad 50 \quad 60$$

%

30 Recorded foundations of churches in seventh-century Northumbria and Lindsey, categorized according to context. Religious communities of type **A** were made with direct royal involvement or participation; communities of type **B**, though often begun with royal support, were depicted in more idealistic terms. Magnate minsters and churches at royal *tun* are few, but it is interesting that both types appear very early. More may have existed; lacking resident saints or other pious 'stars', perhaps lacking also a capacity to generate their own internal records, it could be that they featured only incidentally in the writings of commentators like Bede. The inset diagram takes the sites mapped in Fig. 29 and attempts to characterize them. Group 1 represents places of reportedly serious monastic character; group 2 includes monastic foundations made with close royal participation; group 3 – the largest category – contains sites which cannot at present be characterized. It is suggested that a substantial number of royal and comital minsters may lie within this group

It is to such diverse beginnings that the sites of our most ancient parish churches may be traced. But just as thegns and *comites* followed the example of the king, so lesser lords thought to do likewise. The start of their contribution – numerically, the largest of all – was not to be long delayed.

IV

MUSHROOMS
IN THE NIGHT?

S hortly before 1066 a thegn called Edwin made his will. Edwin's bequests included ten acres of land to each of the churches at Algarsthorpe, Little Melton, Bergh, Apton and Sparham *Nf*. Churches at Holverstone and Blyford *Sf* were assigned four acres apiece. In due course eight acres from an estate at Thorpe were to go to Ashwell church; eight acres from the estate at Wreningham *Nf* to the *elde kirke* 'old church'; two acres to Fundenhall church *Nf*, and two to the church at Neyland *Sf*. Another church, 'which Thurward owned', is mentioned but not located (Whitelock 1930, no. 33).

Other wills drawn up in East Anglia at about this time refer to local churches, although none survives that favoured so many as the twelve which were endowed by Edwin. The bequests of Ketel, Edwin's nephew, included ten acres to the church of Harling *Nf* (1930, no. 34). Ketel's mother, Wulfgyth, had granted to Stisted church '*Eldemes* land and in addition so much that in all there shall be after my death fifty acres of woodland and of open land'. This was in addition to what Wulfgyth had given to the church during her life. Wulfgyth also willed sixteen acres of land 'and one acre of meadow' to the church at Somerleyton.

Another lady, Siflaed, had left instructions later in the tenth century or early in the eleventh that 'my church is to be free and Wulfmaer my priest is to sing in it, he and his issue, so long as they are in holy orders. And free meadow to the church' (1930, no. 37). The *tunkirke* 'village church' at Marlingford *Sf* was to receive from Siflaed 'five acres and one homestead and two acres of meadow and two wagonloads of wood'. Two other village churches, at Wetheringsett *Sf* and Weston *Nf*, appear in the will of an important thegn called Thurstan, drawn up between 1043 and 1045 (no. 31).

Wills suggest that eleventh-century East Anglia was crowded with churches. Domesday Book confirms this. About 416 churches are mentioned in Domesday Book for Suffolk: a figure which represents about 75 per cent of medieval parochial provision in this county. Unfortunately, the Domesday officials did not attempt such full counts of local churches elsewhere. Domesday Book's weakness as a guide to the presence of local churches is well illustrated in Kent. From this county there happen to have survived three lists, compiled for ecclesiastical purposes, which together disclose the presence of more than 400 churches (over 90 per cent of Kentish provision) before 1100 (Ward 1932; 1933). But the Kent Domesday mentions only 186 churches and chapels, while the three independent lists together record 159 churches at vills with names which do not appear in Domesday Book at all.

The extent to which churches were under-represented in Domesday varies from county to county. The will of a lady, Æthelgifu, drawn up between 980 and 990 (Gelling 1979, 18, 85), refers to four churches in Bedfordshire. This is as many as were recorded for the entire county in 1086. Yet in the adjacent county of Huntingdon the Domesday officials recorded 59 churches (67 per cent of medieval provision in this shire).

Genuine regional differences in provision are likely to have existed (Blair 1987, 276), but the main reason for disparities in Domesday itself is to be found in the way in which the compilation of the survey was organized. Counties were grouped into circuits, for which separate teams of commissioners were responsible (Galbraith 1961). Interpretation of the articles of inquiry varied from circuit to circuit. This emerges when the ecclesiastical data are presented graphically (Fig. 31). Most of the counties in each circuit have their own distinctive signatures. The profiles possess characteristics which tend to be consistent within the circuit, but to be in contrast with those of counties in other circuits. Nevertheless, despite its limitations, Domesday Book either records, or allows us to infer, the existence of about 2700 local churches. Given the extensive omissions this figure is high.

Ecclesiastical records which mention local churches do not become available in a continuous series until the thirteenth century. By this time almost all medieval parish churches were in existence. This means that the origins of all but a handful are unrecorded. Other methods can be used to ascertain whether churches existed before they begin to be mentioned in documents, although they point more to presence than to origins. In Yorkshire, out of a medieval total of perhaps 550 churches, about 390 (71 per cent) retain either fabric or a font of the period before 1150, or pre-Conquest sculpture equatable with the presence of an ecclesiastical site, or both. In parts of the county it is possible to find blocks of contiguous parishes wherein there is evidence that *all* the churches existed before 1100 (Fig. 32). Similar blocks can be identified in other areas. Since our knowledge about these groups has been determined mainly by patterns of the *survival* of evidence, they are unlikely to be exceptional. The questions

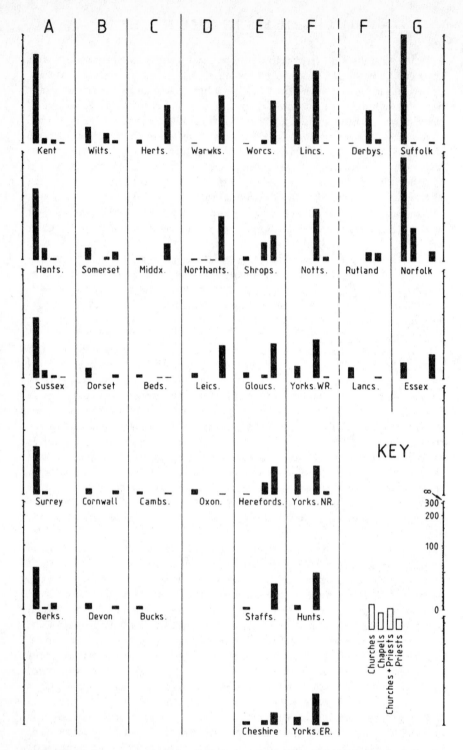

31 Graph of the occurrence of references to churches, chapels and priests in Domesday Book arranged according to the circuits by which the survey is thought to have been compiled

to be considered in this and the following two chapters are when, how and why proliferation occurred.

In Chapter 3 we saw that some local churches originated in the context of religious communities. It was noted that kings founded minsters at royal *tūn* in the seventh and eighth centuries, and that some *gesiths* did likewise on their own estates. By the ninth century such royal and comital churches could have formed an appreciable base from or around which later growth could proceed. The four Bedfordshire churches in Æthelgifu's will, for instance, were all secular minsters. The difficulty lies in estimating what 'appreciable' might mean in actual figures. It may also be asked whether the primary component was added to steadily between the ninth and twelfth centuries, or whether there were some periods when little churchfounding took place and others when the tempo quickened.

Uncertainty is almost as great at the end of the period as at the beginning. It is clear that some churches were new at 1100, but how typical these were is not obvious. William of Malmesbury's biography of Wulfstan, bishop of Worcester (1060–95), lights up the beginnings of several. Wulfstan was much in demand to consecrate new churches. On one occasion he was invited to Gloucester for this purpose, and on another to Ratcliffe *Nt* where a wealthy layman called Sewi had built a church on his estate. Ratcliffe was outside Wulfstan's diocese, and he took care to observe the formalities by obtaining a licence from the archbishop of York. The curious episode involving a new church and an old nut tree at Longney-on-Severn *Gl* was described in Chapter 2. Wulfstan also consecrated a church which had been newly built by Ailric, an archdeacon in his diocese, and on another occasion he was invited to dedicate a church at Wycomb *Bu* which had been built by a certain Swertlin who was 'blessed with great riches' and had built the church at his own expense. The invitations to preside at dedication ceremonies outside his own diocese may reflect Wulfstan's popular prestige as the last Anglo-Saxon bishop within an episcopate now dominated by foreigners, or his ability to preach, in the Old English tongue, a dedication sermon.

Wulfstan's biographer emphasized the enthusiasm of the bishop in building churches on his own estates, and in causing churches to be built upon lands owned by others. Yet it is difficult not to see these efforts as other than a work of completion, the rounding out of an existing pattern. Churches are everywhere. We are told that when Wulfstan travelled he would always go to sing matins in a church, sometimes on foot and in the worst weather, however far the church might be from his lodging. Among Wulfstan's many small preoccupations was his concern to prevent horsemen from riding at random through churchyards, trampling graves. He campaigned for the removal of wooden altars from churches in his diocese and their replacement by others built of stone. At Westbury, the site of a small religious community established by his precursor Oswald in the tenth century, he found an old church in ruins, saw to its rebuilding with cut stone and provided lead for its roof. We hear that Wulfstan cared

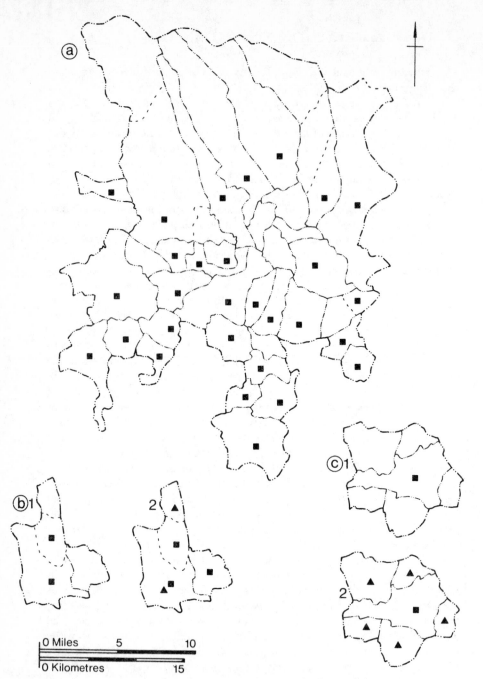

32 Three groups of parishes in Yorkshire. **A** Ryedale *NY*. A block of 35 parishes wherein at least 29 of the churches appear to have existed before the end of the eleventh century (evidence: architecture, sculpture, Domesday Book). **B** Allertonshire *NY*. No churches are mentioned in DB. However, (1) the presence of at least two is signalled by pre-Conquest sculpture, while (2) a more elaborate pattern is revealed by twelfth-century sources which appear to record earlier arrangements. **C** Hunmanby *Hu* (*YE*). Ecclesiastical pattern as revealed by (1) DB, and (2) a source of 1125 recording the gift of the mother church and its dependent chapels to Bardney

little for luxurious living, and that in consequence he never built halls or banqueting chambers in his manors. His disapproval of architectural fussiness extended to churches. He was 'little pleased with laboured or curious work': a precious insight into the aesthetic attitudes of an eleventh-century churchman.

No other single source gives so much incidental detail about church-

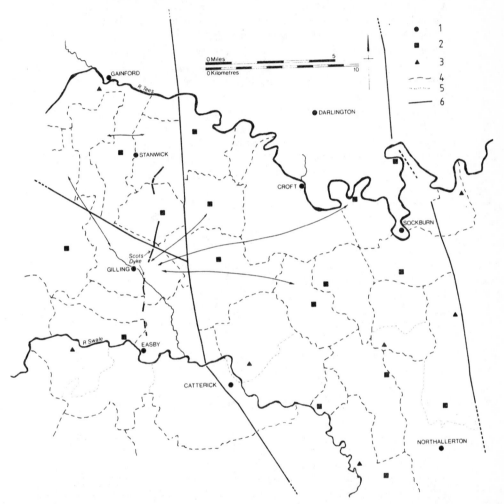

33 Ecclesiastical geography of the Tees/Swale interfluve. 1 religious community or superior church (written source, sculpture); 2 parish church; 3 chapel; 4 boundary of parish; 5 boundary of chapelry; 6 Roman road. Easby, Gilling and Stanwick form a succession of ecclesiastical sites which lie just aside from Dere Street. Gilling was founded as a royal monastery in the 650s; both in terms of morphology and location its site is similar to that of Stanwick. Stanwick and Gilling had connections with Ripon; today, the churches at Easby and Gilling are dedicated to St Agatha. This curious dedication might have to do with (St) Agatho, pope from 678 to 682, to whom Wilfrid appealed for arbitration in a dispute. The sites lie conveniently along a line of travel between Wilfrid's monasteries at Ripon and Hexham

founding at this time. But here and there small windows are opened. The inscription presumed to be from Odda's chapel, Deerhurst *Gl*, speaks directly out of Wulfstan's world. 'Odda, *dux*, ordered this royal hall to be constructed and dedicated in honour of the Holy Trinity for the soul of his brother Ælfric which was carried up from this place' (Okasha 1971, 63-4). The dedication ceremony took place on 12 April 1056. An inscription above the south door of the church at Kirkdale *NY* (1971, 87-8), chiselled in the decade 1055-65, describes how Orm, the son of Gamel, had bought the church of St Gregory as a ruin and ordered its rebuilding. The episode is reminiscent of Wulfstan's renovation at Westbury. In Domesday Book we encounter four brothers at Thorney *Sf* who had built a *capella* beside the parish churchyard because the mother church was too small to accommodate all the villagers.

It may be significant that new churches which are glimpsed abuilding in the decades immediately either side of 1100 are often found to have been created for the convenience of people who lived at some distance from an existing mother church. This was so at Kingston Bagpuize *Brk*, founded 1078 × 1097 (*Chron. Abingdon* ii, 30-1), and apparently also at Whistley in the same county. A writ of king Stephen (1135-47) confirmed a gift of half a hide of land in Quarrendon *Bu* to St Mary at Aylesbury, a former minster, in return for leave to establish a cemetery at Quarrendon (*Reg. Antiq.* I, no. 85, 53). This transaction involved a burial ground attached to an existing chapel which had previously been in subjection to Aylesbury to the extent that residents of Quarrendon had had to travel several miles in order to bury their dead. Desire for greater convenience could even lead to the site of a church being changed. When William son of Ernis gave the church at Sutton in Holland *Li* to Castleacre Priory before 1180, he also contributed

> three acres of land in Sutton, in the field called Heoldefen next the road, to build a parish church there. And my wish is that the earlier wooden church of the same vill, in place of which the new church will be built, shall be taken away and the bodies buried in it shall be taken to the new church.
>
> (cited in Owen 1971, 5 and n. 7)

Outside towns, references to the establishment of entirely new mother churches after *c.* 1130 are not generally common. In part this could be due to the paucity of records. But whereas published twelfth-century episcopal *acta* contain numerous references to parish churches, they do not say a great deal about new foundations. The *acta* of Robert Bloet, bishop of Lincoln (1092-1123), for instance, mention twenty-two local churches by name. Only one, at Thurlby *Li* (D. M. Smith 1980, 201), seems to have been new. One other, at East Carlton *Np*, was promoted from being a chapel subject to Cottingham, two miles away, to the status of mother church (1980, No. 7, 7). Corresponding figures for the episcopate of Bloet's successor,

Alexander (1123-48), are sixty-four and two. One of the two involved role-reversal between an inconveniently located mother church and its chapel which took place at Hanslope *Bu* between *c.* 1131 and 1148 (D.M.Smith 1980, no.131; Mason 1976, 19).

In some counties, such as Surrey, Herefordshire and Shropshire, there is evidence for a more sizeable twelfth-century contribution than seems to have been made in northern and eastern England (Blair 1987). Most of what we see, however, reinforces an impression that the majority of churches around which the parochial system crystallized were in position by the early twelfth century. Here and there there were gaps to be filled, and adjustments to be made, particularly in the raising of some existing chapels to the status of mother church, as happened at Cottingham, and also at Allerton Mauleverer *NY* (*YW*) in 1109-14 (*EYC* I, 729-30). But it is the chapels which actually provide one of the surest indications that most parish churches have pedigrees which extend back at least to the Conqueror's decades. Twelfth-century charters teem with them. They cannot all have been new.

The quantitative implications of this picture must now be examined. No one knows exactly how many churches existed in pre-Reformation England and Wales. The first national list, based upon an earlier survey of 1254, was not compiled until 1289-91. Both surveys were made for taxation purposes, and both are known to contain omissions. The preoccupation with values meant that, for instance, churches of negligible worth were sometimes left out. Moreover, because of ambiguities in the method of recording, the total of churches mentioned in the 1291 survey has never been satisfactorily ascertained. Discussion must therefore be about orders of magnitude rather than actual figures. We can say that thirteenth-century England contained no fewer than 8000 parish churches, nearly 20 per cent of them in East Anglia, and that Wales was divided into approximately 950 parishes at this time.

Since so little evidence has been observed for the foundation of *large* numbers of parish churches after the first quarter of the twelfth century, and as indications have been noted from several counties that at least three-quarters of all local churches were standing before the end of the eleventh century, plausible limits for the English total in 1100 could be of the order 6-7000.

The rarity of new foundations after 1150 makes it conceivable that between *c.* 1075 and 1125 1-2000 parish churches were built in a rush. William of Malmesbury's statement, made around 1125, that in post-Conquest England one might see 'churches rise in every village' should be interpreted with this in mind. Malmesbury's comment – which one must remember occurs in a passage designed to emphasize the Norman achievement in England – was made at a time when the movement of local churchfounding was approaching its end. It has been suggested that the 'Norman settlement failed to check, and may have stimulated, the spate of private church foundations, which continued into Henry I's reign unabated' (Blair 1987, 271). Such a statement need not, however, be in conflict with the view that the new work witnessed by Malmesbury was the final infilling of the parochial map. If the accumulation of 6000 small churches had been spread across several centuries, the addition of 1–2000 more within two generations would have seemed impressive. If there is doubt it must be as to whether the total of new parochial foundations which can be attributed to this concluding episode has here been put too high: recently founded sub-parochial chapels may have been included in Malmesbury's generalization, and he may also have been referring to the reconstruction in stone of existing wooden churches.

The movement of new building spread into Wales. A panegyric on Gruffydd ap Cynan (d. 1137) written within twenty years of his death, tells that

> he increased all manner of good in Gwynedd and the inhabitants began to build churches in every direction therein. . . . Gruffydd, on his part, made great churches for himself in his chief places. . . . Wherefore he also made Gwynedd to glitter with limewashed churches, like the firmament with stars.

> (A. Jones 1910, 154–5)

Given the limits outlined above, we may ask how the late eleventh-century figure of 6–7000 had been attained. Was it a matter of steady accumulation spread across several centuries? Or a series of spasmodic advances? Or even a single phase of furious building?

At first sight the large numbers involved would seem to rule out a single concerted outburst of churchfounding. If (say) 25 per cent of local churches existed before 1000, and another 25 per cent were created in the two generations between the Conquest and the days of William of Malmesbury, this would still require us to think in terms of 3000 foundations in seventy-five years. This averages forty a year. It is not an impossible figure. But the pace of construction is hardly likely to have been steady. Churches would have multiplied faster in some periods and areas than in others (Gem 1975). The period 980–1016 was, for instance, marked by turbulence, with renewed Viking attacks that led to the diversion of much English wealth into military spending, and heavy payments of tribute. The years c. 1066–75 might likewise be regarded as a time when little new local churchbuilding was undertaken. On the other hand, piety sometimes intensifies during times of stress. The likely amplitude of fluctuations in churchbuilding is thus hard to assess.

There is no reason to doubt that the English before the Conquest possessed the technical capability to build large numbers of churches. It is to be noted that the Old English vocabulary of building was almost wholly to do with workmanship in wood. We should assume that before c. 1000 most local churches were built of wood, and therefore with local resources, using skills available within the immediate community. Out of about 200 stone churches which can be assigned in whole or part to the late pre-Conquest era, few are demonstrably much earlier than *c.* 1050. Some of the most complete, like Kirk Hammerton *NY (YW)*, may date from the last quarter of the eleventh century, or even the first years of the twelfth. However, recent excavations of churches have typically disclosed not only an eleventh-century phase when the church was first built in stone, but commonly also an *earlier* phase, characterized by a cemetery (as at Barton Bendish *Nf*), sometimes accompanied by Christian gravestones (e.g. St Mark, Lincoln) and the traces of an earlier church built of wood (e.g. Thetford *Nf*, Wharram Percy *NY*, Rivenhall *Ex*). Only one pre-Conquest wooden church actually survives in use, at Greensted *Ex* (Christie *et al.* 1979). But others are recorded. At Old Byland *NY*, for instance, the compilers of Domesday Book noted an *ecclesia lignea*. The existence of a former timber fabric may also be recollected in a place-name. Bradkirk *La* (first recorded in 1235) refers most probably to a church built of boards. So does Berechurch *Ex* (recorded *c.* 1270). Woodchurch *Ch, K* (both recorded *c.* 1100), remind us of an age when the carpenter was still sovereign. Stokenchurch *Bu, Mx*, has the same first element as our surviving word 'stockade', and could mean 'church built of logs'. A church of this sort was mentioned in a charter of the tenth century (Sawyer 1968, no. 670) where the bounds of an estate on the north side of the Thames between the Tyburn and the Fleet *Mx* included the *ealde stoccene sancte andreas cyricean* 'the old wooden church of St Andrew'. Dunstan, archbishop of Canterbury (960–88), is said to have built wooden churches on his estates. Dunstan's biographer tells how the saint went to dedicate a church at Mayfield *Sx*, found it to be incorrectly oriented and pushed it round to its proper alignment with his shoulder (Stubbs 1874).

Some place-names concerning wooden churches may have originated in the twelfth or thirteenth centuries, when stone churches had become the norm and such names could be used to denote particular settlements without risk of confusion. However, as we have seen, several names of this sort enjoyed currency in the eleventh century, and this could suggest that the rebuilding in stone was already under way.

As regards the origins of the churches, the activities of a figure such as Dunstan carry us back to the second half of the tenth century. And if the 'old wooden church of St Andrew' recorded in the charter was indeed then old, say, by 50–100 years, then we are looking at latest to the period *c.* 850–900 for the time of its building. Excavations at Raunds *Np* have revealed remains of a small one-room church which was founded in the period *c.* 875–925, enlarged, rebuilt and reoriented in the eleventh century, and fell into disuse around 1200 (Cadman 1983) (Fig. 34). By the mid-tenth century the creation of small, local churches had become sufficiently common to demand recognition in law codes, and by the 960s limited but significant concessions were being made in respect of the rights they could enjoy (2 Edgar 1–3). At the end of the tenth century the multiplication of local churches was sufficiently well advanced to occasion rules to govern the conduct of priests. Æthelred's code of 1008 forbade

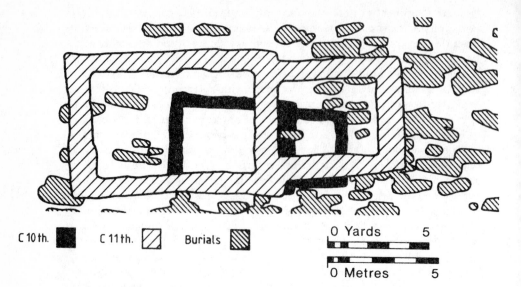

C 10th. ▪   C 11th. ◩   Burials ▧

0 Yards   5

0 Metres   5

34 Pre-Conquest church and associated graves at Raunds, Northamptonshire (*Source*: Boddington 1980)

illegal trafficking in churches (10.2). The use of churches as objects for barter was likewise complained of by Ælfric, who stated around 1000 that men traded with churches as with mills (Ælfric, *Lives of the Saints* I, 430; cf. *Law of the Northumbrian Priests*, 20 (*EHD* I)). A striking illustration of trafficking occurs in the *Clamores* 'Claims' section of Domesday Book for Huntingdonshire. The jurors of Huntingdon stated that

> the church of St Mary of the borough and the land which is annexed to it belonged to the church of Thorney, but the abbot gave it in pledge to the burgesses. . . . King Edward gave it to Vitalis and Bernard, his priests, and they sold it to Hugh, chamberlain to King Edward. . . . Hugh sold it to two priests of Huntingdon. . . . Eustace has it now without livery, without writ, and without seisin.
>
> (*EHD* 2, 862)

Any attempt to plot the dimensions of pre-Conquest ecclesiastical growth must acknowledge that references to local churches in charters and other writings are too few to sustain generalizations. Such references are, moreover, as frequent in the tenth century as in the next, and do not by themselves give support to the idea that there was an acceleration of churchfounding in the eleventh century.

Another factor that needs to be assessed lies in the tendency for references to the foundation of local private churches to occur in the *vitae* of bishops who became saints. Bishops were the consecrators of churches, so it was natural for such events to be mentioned in biographies. Often this was done within the context of a hagiographical tradition, reaching back at least to the days of the Frankish Church (Wood 1986, 77), which looked upon consecration ceremonies as appropriate occasions for the working of miracles. This explains why a comparatively large number of notices of new foundations have come down to us in connection with the era of Æthelwold and Dunstan in the tenth century, and Wulfstan in the later years of the eleventh. Yet in the eighth century Bede described miracles which had coincided with the consecrations by John, bishop of York (705-18), of two churches which had been founded near Beverley *Hu* (*YE*) by *gesiths* (*HE* v. 4, 5). Cuthbert, bishop of Lindisfarne (685-7) was credited with a miracle while on a visit to the place called *Osingadun* in order to dedicate a church on a monastic estate (*Vita Cuthberti*, 34). Taken together, these and other episodes could suggest that the pattern of information about the creation of new churches is likely to have been determined as much by the careers of saints who became the subjects of *vitae* than by actual trends of growth or recession. We cannot assume that bishops who did not achieve special renown were notably less active in encouraging the establishment of new churches. Many consecrations of churches in the ninth century may have gone unrecorded simply because this was not a period of monastic prominence, or one which produced many bishops of saintly potential. (It was, however, said in the twelfth century that Swithun's episcopate at Winchester (852-62) had been marked by his travels around the diocese on foot to consecrate new churches.) Passivity in monastic life may actually have assisted the expansion of local provision: if periods of popular religious fervour usually led to the endowment of monasteries (Barlow 1979, 186), men and women are perhaps particularly likely to have built private churches on their own estates at times when monastic growth was in abeyance; or conversely, would have given already private churches as endowments to monasteries.

While the *vitae* are unreliable as guides to the rate at which local churches were founded, they are important to the extent that they disclose the creation of churches by laymen from 700 onward. There are far too few references for us to guess whether such foundations were common or rare, but it can at least be assumed that *some* expansion took place throughout the period, not just at the end of the era.

To widen our perspective we must now turn to other sources: archaeology, sculpture and place-names. Some archaeological information is summarized in Table 1. Despite difficulties of dating the inaugural phases of churches, it will be seen that there is a good deal of evidence for the designation of ecclesiastical sites locally before 1000, and that in several of the cases presented the site may have been earmarked for religious use before 900. These examples are too few to be of any statistical value, but they may give perspective to what follows.

Turning next to sculpture, what is there to be gleaned from the distribution of pre-Conquest carved stones? Best endowed are the coun-

Table 1 Dates of origin of local churches, established by archaeological excavation: a sample list

Place	First ecclesiastical use		First church to be recognized		Fabric	Reference or source
	Date	Evidence	Date	Form		
Barrow, Humberside (Lincolnshire)	Before 900	Burials	CII	Nave, chancel, eastern apse	Stone substructure	Final report forthcoming (date of first church could be earlier)
All Saints, Barton Bendish, Norfolk	Early CII	Cemetery	c.1100	Nave, chancel, apse	Stone	Rogerson et al. 1984
Lincoln, St Mark	C10ii-iii	Cemetery Gravestones Possible building	mid-C10	Single cell	Wood	Gilmour and Stocker 1986
Norwich 1: dedication unknown	CIII	Cemetery Structure	c.1000 × 1050	Single cell?	Wood	Ayers 1985
Norwich 2: St Benedict	C10iv-C11i	Burials	c.1075 × 1100	Single cell, apse	Stone	Roberts and Atkin 1982
Raunds, Northamptonshire	c.875 × 900	Structure	c.875 × 900	Single cell	Stone substructure	Cadman and Foard 1984 Boddington 1987
Rivenhall, Essex	C7-9?	Cemetery Structure	C10i	Nave, chancel	Wood	Rodwell and Rodwell 1985
St Martin, Wharram Percy, North Yorkshire	C8-9	Sculpture	C10iv	Single cell	Wood	Hurst 1984
York, St Helen	C10iv	Structure	C10iv	Single cell	Stone substructure	Magilton 1980

ties of Lincolnshire, Yorkshire, Durham, Northumberland, Cumbria (Bailey 1980a; Cramp 1984) and parts of Wales (Nash-Williams 1950). It was suggested in the previous chapter that stones carved in the period *c.* 700–850 are likely to signal the presence of religious communities, episcopal, royal or comital minsters. Discussion of this theory is resumed on p. 161. The point to be established here is that in northern and parts of eastern England the practice of deploying carved stones at ecclesiastical sites was greatly extended during the tenth century, to the extent that such items became a commonplace in ordinary village graveyards. The sheer quantity of this material is one of its virtues, for it provides the ecclesiastical geography of northern England with something like the lapidary equivalent of a barium meal. Of course, factors of survival and discovery, acting haphazardly, will affect the pattern of distribution that we see. But the tendency for later medieval masons to reuse old gravestones as building material is often to our benefit; the stones sometimes remain on view whereas the churches that stood beside them have been reconstructed.

It is not quite certain that gravestones of the period 850–1100 can always be equated with the presence of a contemporary church. Some graveyards may have been established in advance of churches. In general, however, this seems unlikely, not least because decisions on the positions of churches were controlled by a variety of factors (see Chapter 6), and it is difficult to see how these could have been anticipated in a pattern of sites selected for funerary reasons alone in a previous era. Further, the vast majority of these stones have been found in, under or beside medieval churches. If the churchless burial ground had been a widespread phenomenon in the ninth or tenth century, one would expect a much larger number of instances where the cemetery failed to evolve from graveyard to churchyard. As it is, there is a church on or near the spot in almost every case. The stones are therefore admissible as evidence in the attempt to give quantitative dimensions to ecclesiastical growth. In the Tees valley (*Du* and *NY*), for instance, a survey has found about 300 items, mostly gravestones, distributed between thirty-seven churches. In all but eleven cases there was no other evidence for an ecclesiastical use of the site before the Conquest (C. Morris 1976).

The publication of the first volume of the British Academy's *Corpus of Anglo-Saxon Stone Sculpture* (Cramp 1984) contains an assessment of the quantities and distribution of the material that is currently known in Northumberland and Co. Durham. Places that have yielded sculpture number at least sixty-seven. Some of the churches concerned were originally monastic, but even when these have been subtracted, the remaining total appears to be around 40 per cent of medieval parish churches in the two counties. In Northumberland modest village churches like Bedlington and Ponteland yield stones of the tenth century. So, too, do some churches in Co. Durham, as at Dalton-le-Dale, where the material could be earlier still (Cramp 1984, 61). Overall, the date ranges of stones in this region suggest that local churches could have existed in appreciable numbers before the end of the tenth century.

In Yorkshire around one-quarter of the eventual total of rural medieval parish churches contain pre-Conquest carved stones. It is to be noted that only 45 of the perhaps 140 places concerned were credited with a church by the Domesday commissioners in 1086: that is, about one church for every three that display sculpture. Up-to-date figures for Lincolnshire are not yet available, but the survey which is being undertaken for the *Corpus* is said already to have resulted in a substantial increase both in the quantity of sculpture that has been recognized and in the number of places that are known to possess it. Here, as in Yorkshire, Durham and Northumberland, there are unexceptional village churches like Glentworth, Marton-by-Stow and Holton-le-Clay, built probably around 1100, which contain carved stones at least a century older. The church at Bakewell *Db* is famous for the massive haul of pre-Conquest stones which were found to have been reused in foundations of its south transept. A similar harvest has recently been obtained from the foundations of St Mark in Lincoln (Gilmour and Stocker 1986). The example of St Mark deserves emphasis, for whereas Bakewell was monastic in background, and a substantial assemblage of funerary sculpture might thus be expected, St Mark was but one small and rather insignificant church among many in Lincoln. Moving south, pre-Norman carved stones become rarer in regions such as East Anglia and south-east England where good freestone is scarce. But they can be found, as at Preston-by-Faversham *K*, or Thetford *Nf*. Whitchurch *Ha* boasts a splendid inscribed gravemarker, probably of the ninth or early tenth century (Okasha 1971, no. 135). Further west, while churches such as Tetbury and Frome had monastic antecedents, others like Bibury *Gl*, Rowberrow and West Camel probably did not. In Wales, too, carved stones are found not only at sites like Meifod *Pws* (*Mnt*) and Llandeilo *Dfd* (*Carm*) with a presumptive claim to early prestige, but also at ordinary local churches such as Llanwnda *Dfd* (*Pmb*) and Llanynis *Pws* (*Brcn*).

These examples, few and taken more or less at random, do not in themselves sustain an argument that local churches were fairly common before the end of the tenth century. What can be said is that a large proportion of the churches which yield tenth-century material seem to have been sufficiently *un*important to allow us to suppose that such sites were rapidly becoming, if they had not already become, a commonplace. Unfortunately, the stones cannot be used to measure the times and rates at which local churches were being founded. They offer only indications of presence, not origins.

Turning next to place-names, it must be said that the evidence they provide is largely impressionistic (Figs 35, 36). Like archaeology, they cannot illuminate more than a small fraction of the total of sites involved; and like carved stones, they usually provide only *termini ante quos* for the existence of churches. Place-names also bristle with hazards for those who, like this author, lack the methodological and linguistic skills which are

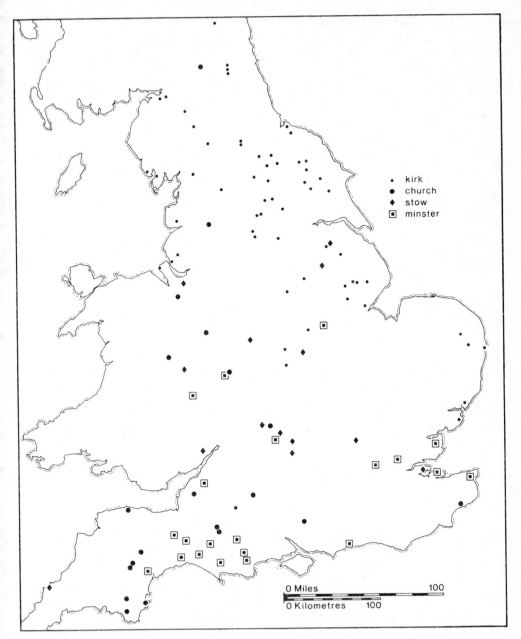

35 Place-names which embody the elements *kirk, church, stow* and *minster*. Some names recorded only from the later Middle Ages have been excluded. 'Stow' was a versatile element, and its mapping here has been limited to places where its use is thought likely to have had an ecclesiastical connotation

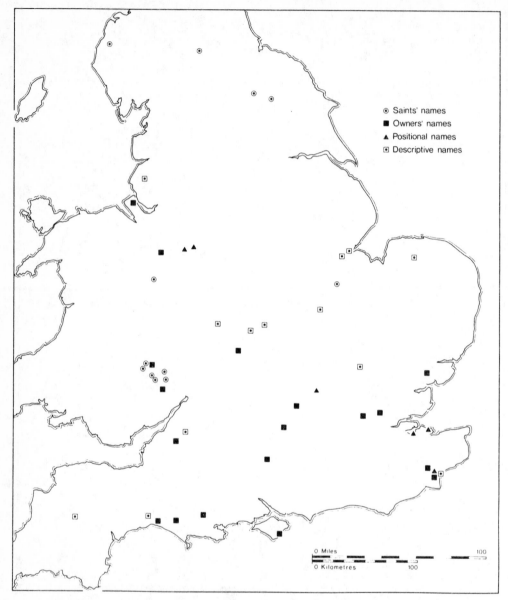

Saints' names
Owners' names
Positional names
Descriptive names

36 Place-names concerning churches which embody the names of saints, laymen (? possible founders or owners), positional and other descriptive terms

essential for their use. For this reason, much of what follows will show a strong dependence upon the works of others, notably Mrs Gelling (1981), who has shown that place-names are of extreme interest, and often afford insights that cannot be derived from other sources.

In the eleventh century proprietary origins are suggested where churches are called after people who were, presumably, their owners. The *Textus Roffensis* mentions Ordmaere's church, Deremanne's church and Siwolde's church, all in Kent. Dodeschurch in the same county may be another such personal name, although it has been noted that *Dudesland* was an area responsible for bridgework at Rochester in the tenth century (Ward 1932, 59). Mertumne's church and Blacemanne's church are today known as Hope All Saints and Blackmanstone *K*, while Aelsi's church is now Eastbridge: three reminders that place-names may change.

Churches bearing the names of individuals were not restricted to Kent. Baschurch *Sa* 'Bassa's church', Colkirk *Nf* 'Cola's church', Offchurch 'Offa's church' and Dunchurch *Wa* 'Dunn's church' were all recorded in 1086. Algakirk *Li* occurs as *Algarescherche* in the Pipe Roll of 1194; could the personal name be referable to the Alfgare who was mentioned here in Domesday Book? Gosberton *Li* was formerly *Goseberdeschirche*, and Layston *Hrt* is previously recorded as Leofstan's church.

It is possible that the individuals whose names occur at these places were the founders of the churches. Usually, however, we lack the information which would be needed to differentiate between the name of a founder and the name of someone who owned the church at a later date. Hawkchurch *D*, perhaps 'Hafoc's church', for instance, is not recorded until 1196. Ormskirk *La* enters the written record in the same year. The fact that it was held by a certain Orm seven years later may signify that the place-name, but not necessarily the church, was then new. As churches changed hands, so may their names sometimes have changed with them. An equation between a particular person and the founder might also be called into question by the recurrence of the same name within a family over several generations.

Most of the place-names in this personal category are not encountered in surviving records older than Domesday Book. Exceptions are Alvechurch *Wa* and Pucklechurch *Gl*, both of which appear in pre-Conquest charters. *Ælfgyþecyrce* 'Ælfgyþ's church' was written into the margin of a charter dated 780 (Sawyer 1968, no. 117) during the first half of the eleventh century. Ælfgyþ was a lady and it is possible that she founded the church in question before 1000. Pucklechurch occurs in a series of charters, not all trustworthy or extant (Sawyer 1968, nos 553, 1724, 1744, 1777), of the mid–late tenth century. Separate testimony for the name is, however, provided by the *Anglo-Saxon Chronicle* (D) for the year 946, when *Puclancyrce* was the scene of the murder of king Edmund, who was stabbed to death on the feast day of St Augustine. It would be interesting to know the dedication of the church at this date. Pucklechurch was a royal *tūn*. Was Edmund visiting a minster on the occasion of its patronal festival? Unfortunately this was one of eighty or so churches which were rededicated to St Thomas Becket (also murdered, also an archbishop of Canterbury), after the twelfth century: a further reminder that names could change.

In the eleventh and twelfth centuries *mynster* was sometimes used as a synonym for 'church', and a number of place-names ending in *-mynster* embody names of individuals. Bedminster *So* 'Beda's minster', Buck-minster *Le* 'Bucca's minster' and Kidderminster *Wo* (?) 'Cydda's minster' are examples which occur in 1086. However, whereas the combination of *cirice* and a personal name seems not to be found in any general way before the eleventh century, combinations involving *mynster* are recorded in a number of ninth- and tenth-century charters. In part this may be due to the predominantly south-western distribution of place-names in this category (see Fig. 35), coupled with the uneven survival of charters (cf. D.H. Hill 1981, map 31). Yet this is unlikely to account for the overall pattern of such occurrences, and one is left with the impression that there were several strata of names in *-mynster*, the latest perhaps being equatable with names of the Alvechurch type, and the earliest referring to religious communities.

In the former category we might place Yetminster *Do*, recorded in 1086; Pitminster *Pipingmynstre*, recorded in 938 (Sawyer 1968, no. 440), perhaps 'Pippa's minster'; Beaminster *Do*, *Bebingmynster*, recorded in a lost charter of the ninth century (no. 1782); and Lyminster *Sx*, recorded in the will of king Alfred, drawn up 873 × 888 (no. 1507). Alfred's will also mentioned Sturminster *Do* and Axminster *D*, which may belong to the earlier group and where Axminster, at least, takes its first element from the name of a river rather than a person. Warminster *Wi* would be 'minster on the River Wear'.

Names embodying *-mynster* occur chiefly in the south-west of England, but there is a clump of very early occurrences, all monastic, in Kent, and several other names of positional character occur in the Home Counties: for example, Southminster *Ex*, Upminster *Mx* and, of course, Westminster *GLo* (*Mx*). Emstrey *Sa* appears in Domesday Book as *Eiminstra* and presumably means 'minster on an island'. This is an interesting case, for the minster in question seems to have stood in a loop of the River Severn and has now gone.

Names arising from position – whether descriptive, as at Hanchurch *St* 'high church', and Overchurch *Ch*, or relative, as at Eastchurch *K*, so recorded in the Domesday Monachorum – occur in a thin distribution in almost all regions, and seem to have been combined with *cirice* and *mynster* alike.

Adjectival names form a further group. Those to do with building in wood, boards or planks have already been considered. Ivychurch *K* and *IoW* speaks for itself, and will strike a chord in the mind of the modern churchwarden who grapples with such growth today. Litchurch *Db* looks self-explanatory, *Litlecherche* 'little church', but it gave its name to Litchurch Hundred and the earliest recording *Ludecerce* (1086) offers scope for a different derivation.

The largest single group of descriptive names concern churches which were called 'white': Whitminster *Gl*, Whitchurch *So* and Whitkirk *WY* are examples. Whitchurch Canonicorum *Do* (recorded in king Alfred's will as *aet Hwitancyrccan* (Sawyer 1968, no. 1507) even acquired its own eponymous St Candida: *candida* being the Latin word for 'white', as in Bede's reference to Nynia's church at Whithorn (*HE* iii. 4) which was known in the eighth century, at latest, as *ad candidam casam* 'the white house'. The tradition of 'white' church names was thus venerable and certainly runs back to the first century of the English Church, if not to the epoch of British Christianity that preceded it. It is not entirely clear what these names signified. A church built of cut (free) stone, perhaps light in colour, standing in contrast to darker structures of wood, is often offered as an explanation. This is plausible, especially if such names originated before stone churches became common. It can hardly have applied at Whithorn, however, where the local stone is dark-toned and difficult to cut into regular blocks. The evidence of excavation, most notably from the eleventh-century cathedral at York, where it has been shown that the whole building was sealed in an envelope of white plaster (Phillips 1985), suggests that 'white' may on occasion have to be taken more literally, as meaning a building which was plastered or limewashed. Raoul Glaber's often-quoted remark about the world of the eleventh century putting on a 'white robe of churches' has been reinterpreted with this in mind (Harvey 1974, 96). 'White church' names like Eglwys Wen occur in Wales, and the description of how twelfth-century Gwynedd was made 'to glitter with limewashed churches' may be remembered here.

Along the Welsh Marches there are names either Welsh in form (e.g. Llancloudy: Lann Loudeu, or Loudeau's church; Llancillo 'Sulbin's church' *He*), or translations from Welsh into English (e.g. Kentchurch *He*, formerly Lan (St) Cein; Dewchurch *He*, formerly Lann Deui Ros Cerion). Names in *lan, llan*, both ultimately from the old British noun *lano* – 'cleared space', whence '(ecclesiastical) enclosure' (Thomas 1971, 85, 87), occur outside Cornwall and Wales, though not widely, and usually in nearby counties, as at Lancaut *Gl*, or Landican *Ch* 'lan of St Tecan'. The Cumbrian Lamplugh, corresponding with Welsh *llan plwg* 'church of the parish' is interesting, although whether this reflects British linguistic survival in the north-west, or the influence of a Breton lord after the Conquest, is not clear.

Simple names based upon Old English *cirice* occur fairly widely: Church *La*, Cheristow *D*, Cheriton *D*, *Ha*, *K* and *So*, Chirton *Wi*, Churton *Ch*. Such names are, however, at their commonest in the south-west, and this may reinforce what was said above about the possible interchangeable usage between 'church' and 'minster' as applied to some types of site, or in certain periods.

Many place-names embody the Old Norse *kirkja*. Names either consisting of or including 'Kir(k)by' are commonest, but there are others, like Felixkirk *NY* and Bridekirk *Cu* where *kirkja* was compounded with the name of a saint (cf. Michaelchurch *He*), and yet others, such as Felkirk *SY* (*YW*) 'church made of planks', where there is a descriptive element.

It will be seen from Fig. 35 that such names are particularly common in northern and eastern England: counties that were affected by Scandinavian colonization and episodes of disruption during the ninth and tenth centuries. Their distribution is, however, not wholly co-extensive with the Danelaw counties, being comparatively sparse in that portion of Mercia that fell within Danish dominion.

In her study of place-names incorporating the word 'church', Mrs Gelling pointed out that *kirkja* occurs rather more often than the corresponding Old English names such as Cheriton and Chirton which were mentioned above. She also explains that it is sometimes difficult to decide on the basis of early spellings whether names with 'kirk' represent a Scandinavianization of an earlier name which included *cirice*, or whether the name was an Old Norse formation, perhaps replacing an older and entirely different English name. Some names appear to be hybrids. Kirkham *NY*, for instance, contains *kirkja* as the first element and Old English *ham* as the second. Presumably here it is safe to postulate the Scandinavianization of an earlier *cirice*. A similar combination occurs at Kirkstead *Nf*, although whether Kirkstead *Li* and Kirkstall *WY*, first recorded in the 1150s, refer to old churches or to the new Cistercian monastic foundations at these places is not clear.

It is a puzzle why names of the Kir(k)by type should be so common in Danelaw England. Mrs Gelling suggests that few, if any, of the settlements concerned are likely to have been newly made in the ninth or tenth century.

> In most instances both the church and the village are likely to have been pre-Viking. Old Norse *kirkjuby* was doubtless an appellative applied by Scandinavians to any village with a church, and sometimes replacing the older, English, name of such a village in the speech of the countryside. The use of this appellative, and its success in displacing so many earlier names, may indicate that village churches were still comparatively rare when the Scandinavian settlers became familiar with the English scene in the late ninth and early tenth centuries. It must have been a term which effectively distinguished some villages from others at that date.
>
> (Gelling 1981, 8)

Village churches may indeed have been *comparatively* rare around 900; we have here a group of some fifty potential examples scattered through Yorkshire, Lincolnshire, the East Midlands and East Anglia. This would suggest that *some* local churches were already extant before the end of the ninth century, and available for incorporation in the revised, post-Viking toponymy. A Kirkby would make particularly good sense within the context of a scatter of hamlets all sharing a generic name (e.g. Misperton), but only one possessing *the* church. Later the other hamlets might get their own names, and some their own churches.

There is a further possible aspect to this matter, namely that *kirkjuby* may have been used to denote a particular type or class of church. Could it be that in a proportion of cases the Vikings were naming pre-existing ecclesiastical settlements – in effect, monasteries, or comital minsters? Some support for this could be looked for in pre-Conquest sculpture. Whereas many churches at northern places with names of Kirk- or Kir(k)by type have yielded carved stones of tenth/eleventh century date, a number have also produced earlier pieces which might be regarded as being of monastic origin. Kirkby Misperton, Kirkby Moorside, Kirkdale and Kirby Hill, all *NY*, are examples. *Monasterium* was rendered as *mynsterham* in the Old English translation of Bede (cf. Kirkham, above) and following the logic behind this one could envisage a Scandinavian re-rendering as *kirkjuby*.

It must, of course, be pointed out that many known monastic sites were not renamed as Kirkby, and that the pre-Viking age sculpture is suscepti-ble to other interpretations. One of these, congruent with what Mrs Gell-ing proposes, is that the churches concerned stood within estates owned by high-ranking noblemen. That is, these were not village churches in the later, hum-drum, sense, or always earnest religious communities, but minsters of the aristocracy. This would help to explain why such churches were not unusual, but yet not numerous, in ninth-century England. It would also help to account for the more restricted distribution of Anglian as opposed to Viking age sculpture, and could further be squared with considerations of dispersed settlement, mentioned above. A yet more subtle definition would allow us to see some of these magnate minsters as the family monasteries which Bede condemned so strongly in his *Letter to Egbert*. The various interpretations could therefore be closer to each other than might at first appear.

Many other place-names reflect Christian interests and concerns. Old English *halig* 'holy' occurs fairly widely, and sometimes quite early, as at Halstock *D Halganstoke* (998), Halliford *Mx Halganforde* (962). Old English *ansetl* 'hermitage' lies behind Ansley *Wa* and Anslow *St*. Old Norse *papi* 'hermit' occurs at Papcastle *Cu*. *Diacon* occurs at Dexbeer *D*, and *eglos* in Cornwall, as at Egloshayle and Lanteglos. Place-names incorporating 'cross' are of particular interest and would be worth independent study; note also Old Norse *kross-by* at Crosby in *La, Cu, NY* and *WY*. The Welsh *bettwys*, from Old English *bedhus* 'prayer house' or 'oratory', is fairly common in Welsh toponymy, and also occurs in the border areas, as at Bettwys-y-Crwyn *Sa*. Old English *bed-man* 'ecclesiastic' is echoed in Bed-monton and Badmonden *K*; 'Christ' at Christhall *Ex* and Cressage *Sa*.

Commonest of all are names which include the Old English *preosta* 'priest'. There are at least thirty-seven names of the 'Preston' type alone, of which at least twenty-five are mentioned in 1086 or before, and a further six in the late eleventh or twelfth centuries. The names vary in sense, according to the elements with which they are coupled, and the manner of their compounding. 'Village with a priest' and 'place belonging to a priest, or priests' are common meanings. Prestbury *Gl* occurs in 899 × 904 and might be rendered 'priests' residence' or, anachronistically, 'priests' manor'. Presteigne *Rad* seems to mean 'household of priests', and although the name is not recorded before the thirteenth century, the church structure possibly contains eleventh-century masonry (Taylor and Taylor 1965, 497). Prestwich *La*, Prestwick *Nb* 'priest's *wic*' can probably be interpreted as 'parsonage', and Prescot *La* would be 'priest's house'. A general difficulty, seldom solvable because of a lack of sufficiently early spellings, centres on whether a few or even many of the Preston and Prestbury names originally contained 'priest' in the plural rather than the singular. If plural, this would allow us to infer the existence of communities of priests, perhaps working a large area from a single centre. Such arrangements are attested in the eleventh and twelfth centuries (Blair 1985), and perhaps afford further insights into the organizational character of monasteries or minsters in the later pre-Conquest period. Prestbury *Ch*, for instance, was a medieval parish of large size that contained many separate townships. This was also the only church in its hundred to be singled out in Domesday Book. It may well have been a centre with minster-like attributes: a *matrix ecclesia* served by a group of priests.

The point has been reached at which we must look at some of the implications of what has been said. The study of place-names reinforces the impression that there had been growth in ecclesiastical provision prior to the late eleventh century, and reminds us also that such growth could have proceeded from an appreciable base which was already established by 900. We have seen that in the eighth and ninth centuries the distinction between a monastery and a layman's church could be fine: so fine, indeed, that in the absence of literary evidence we can seldom distinguish between the two. Taken together, these churches – whether virtuous communities, family monasteries or magnate churches – were not numerous by eleventh-century standards. In eastern England north of the Humber, where a substantial proportion of them can be tracked down through historical writings, sculpture and place-names, they seem likely to account for perhaps 10 per cent of later parish churches. Extrapolated to the country as a whole this would give around eight hundred sites.

It is seldom clear how or why a pre-Viking religious community underwent metamorphosis into a local, secular church. This may have happened organically (see p. 165), but it may also have been occasioned by seizure or purchase by an individual. We have also noted instances where monasteries were abandoned and their sites were restored to use, now parochial, some years later. A continuing use of the graveyard by the local secular population during the intervening period might have provided a basis for such recoveries. In the later ninth century Scandinavian immigrants were interested in land rather than vandalism, so while monastic estates are likely to have passed into secular ownership, monastic churches, and especially church*yards*, may have been retained, to be transformed in the tenth century with new churches in their midst.

Meanwhile, across the country between the eighth and twelfth centuries the initial provision made by kings and *comites* was augmented by thousands of new, local churches. Some commentators have been tempted to explain these foundations as the result of co-operative action by groups of neighbours. Undoubtedly there are some which began in this way, but in Chapter 6 we shall see that there are many reasons for believing that the majority were established by local lords. The process could almost be visualized as a kind of social chain reaction: minor lords and noblemen of lesser status imitated the *comites*, as *comites* had followed the king. In chronological terms the question to be considered is whether this process was smoothly continuous, or whether local initiative was delayed until the tenth or eleventh century.

The absence of written evidence for much local churchfounding before the tenth century is not necessarily significant. As Dr John Blair reminds us:

> The first founders of manorial churches were not necessarily hostile to the minsters, and their foundations were not necessarily contentious. It is too often assumed that every lord who built a church did so as an act of separatist defiance, arrogating to it a 'parish' forcibly detached from the *parochia* of the old minster. The status of local churches in their communities, and their relationships to the minsters in whose *parochiae* they were founded, were various: not all had pretensions to independence, and only those which did need have proved a threat. If a thegn could have a priest in his household, why should he not give him a church?
>
> (Blair 1987, 269)

One possible implication of this view would be that unless or until local churches began to encroach upon the interests of minsters, written records would tend to ignore them, much in the same way as taxation surveys of the later Middle Ages could overlook sub-parochial chapels which lacked separate identities. Local churches *do* begin to make their presence felt in administrative records from the second quarter of the tenth century: 'by the 940s, private churches were tipping the balance of pastoral organization in the countryside' (Blair 1985, 119).

When did these private churches begin to multiply? Were some of the churches which were tipping the scales by the 940s of fifty or a hundred years' standing, but only now beginning to assert themselves? Or had they arisen recently, springing up everywhere at once, 'like mushrooms in the night'? (Cf. Stutz 1938). A sudden upsurge cannot be ruled out. Archaeological excavations of English parish churches only seldom disclose a first structural phase which is older than 900. But tenth-century burials are quite common, while traces of small tenth-century churches of one or two cells are not unusual (see Table 1).

Once again, however, the absence of evidence for long structural sequences originating in the eighth or ninth centuries should not be too hastily interpreted. Between *c.* 700 and 1000 the settlement pattern was highly unstable (C.C.Taylor 1983, 109-50). Can it be assumed that the chapels of minor lords, built of wood (and therefore structurally ephemeral) and lacking institutional independence, would always have clung fast to their original sites in the face of change? If not, then it is to excavations *beyond*, as well as within, parish churches that we should be looking for signs of the first stage in local provision. The difficulty in doing this is that we are not yet sure what such structures would have looked like. But there are some straws in the wind. At Rivenhall *Ex*, for instance, excavations *outside* the present churchyard revealed an earlier cemetery, apparently of the period *c.* 600–900, with traces of a timber building set in its midst (Rodwell 1981, 137). At Wharram Percy *NY* there is ecclesiastical sculpture of *c.* 800, although the first phase of the church appears to be no older than the later tenth century (Hurst 1984, 88–90). Was there an earlier place of worship somewhere else?

Whenever it took place, the proliferation of local churches made new demands and posed fresh problems. One of them was staffing. At the outset there must have been a shortfall in clerical manpower, and it cannot be assumed that every local church would have been served by a member of the lord's household. Wealthier magnates could support several priests, and in places there are signs that members of such communities ministered intermittently at churches built on different parts of the lord's estates (Blair 1985; 1987, 270-1). References in late Old English laws to a class of church at which services were held irregularly reinforce an impression that churches multiplied faster than did clergy to serve them. If a priest was to be based upon his church rather than in the household of his lord, a separate and permanent endowment would be needed. As Blair points out, this may help to explain the flurry of land-grants to churches which are a feature of tenth- and eleventh-century wills (1987, 270-1).

Standards, too, were difficult to maintain. Out in the countryside, or in the towns, ignorance, carelessness, lust, greed and residual paganism presented threats which were difficult to counter. A village priest was seldom better than semi-literate. He might be conversant with some basic portions of scripture, and able to recite the main offices from memory. When Wulfstan visited the church at Blockley *Wo* to say mass he was vexed to find the ornaments of the altar 'unworthy of the feast – guttered candles in common candlesticks, and the linen long unwashed' (*Vita Wulfstani* iii. 11). Often the priest would be married, and he might also maintain a concubine. Wulfstan fought a long-running battle against wedded priests, and commanded them either to 'renounce their fleshly desires or their churches'. Eventually Wulfstan refused to ordain any man who was not sworn to celibacy (iii. 12). Lanfranc, the first Norman archbishop of Canterbury (1070–93), issued similar instructions, while early in the eleventh century the *Law of the Northumbrian Priests* had stated that a priest should not leave one woman for another (35). The ecclesiastical implications of marriage were more than moral, for sometimes the priest actually owned his church, and if he had a male heir his son could inherit it. The Northumbrian priests were a rumbustious lot. The law warned them against drunkenness, singing in taverns and carrying weapons into church. They were not to insult one another, or fight among themselves (30, 37, 41). Their educational attainments were suspect: misdirection of the people regarding the correct day of a festival or feast carried a fine of twelve ores (11). Some priests were more interested in money than the cure of souls. When he could, Wulfstan would stand by the doors of his church at Worcester in order to baptize the children of the poor, because 'the love of money had crept up from the shades below, so that priests refused to administer that sacrament to infants unless the parents would fill their pockets' (*Vita Wulfstani* i. 7).

The effect of Danish settlement upon the proliferation of local churches deserves thought. Scandinavian immigrants, though pagan on arrival, used existing Christian graveyards, as well as the burial mounds of pagan Saxons and prehistoric peoples, and were quick to adopt and develop existing traditions of monumental sculpture. In the Danelaw counties the sequestration of monastic estates in this period may actually have facilitated the creation of more local churches, as some minsters, impoverished and institutionally weakened, lost control of the large *parochiae* that they had formerly dominated. The rapidity with which Scandinavians accepted Christianity – whether outright, or only in matters of externals – testifies to the underlying influence of the Church, whatever its institutional shortcomings. This provides a further reason for believing that there was no absolute hiatus in churchfounding during the ninth century.

Until *c.* 950 only cathedrals and important monasteries were likely to have been built of stone; all others were normally fabricated from wood. Stone entered use for the building of some local churches during the tenth century. But as late as 1020, when Cnut ordered the building of a church at Ashingdon *Ex* for the souls of men who had been slain in battle there in 1016, a chronicler thought it worthwhile to specify that the church was built 'of stone and lime' (*Anglo-Saxon Chronicle* (F), *sub anno* 1017). The years *c.* 1050–1150 witnessed a great rebuilding, when almost all churches were reconstructed in stone. This rebuilding, remarked upon by William of Malmesbury, was conducted with a new sense of style, encouraged by Norman lords and churchmen. Churches like Wharram-le-Street *NY* (*YE*), Glentworth *Li*, or Haddiscoe Thorpe *Nf*, are sometimes depicted as belonging to the last generation of Anglo-Saxon village churches, but they could more reasonably be looked upon as being among the first, slightly hesitant, essays in the new idiom. The Romanesque period should therefore be seen as a time when local churches were being modernized and enlarged, but no longer often founded.

Exactly how many churches existed by 1100, and the rates at which they had come into existence, are matters which obviously remain uncertain. Hence the speculative nature of Fig. 37 hardly needs to be stressed. This

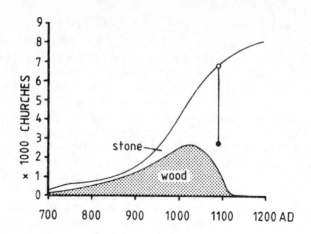

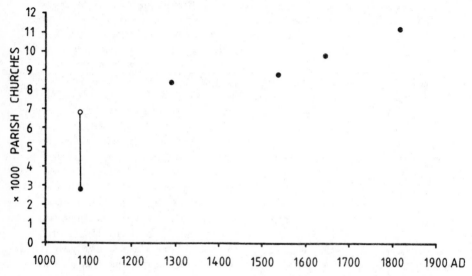

37 Estimated growth in local ecclesiastical provision: (a) flows showing plausible limits c. 600–1100; (b) 1100–1801. The conjectural basis of (a) is emphasized

is no more than an attempt to conjecture quantitative dimensions for an unrecorded process. Apart from the final total – which itself is no more than an estimate – it has no claim to accuracy. But the drawing even of a conjectural graph concentrates the mind, and the extent of the increase which is depicted in the period c. 900–1100 may occasion surprise. Could it have been so explosive? Very possibly it could. In the two chapters that follow we shall find that the pattern of urban and rural settlement was itself undergoing fundamental change at this time, and that many new churches are likely to have been byproducts of a much larger process. One result – or cause? – of this was the transfer of an individual's primary allegiance from kin-group to community. Villages or urban neighbourhoods offered a new kind of social identity, and the change in ecclesiastical geography from a system dominated by minsters to a pattern based upon local parishes may be expressive of a society in transition.

With this said, if local churchbuilding became a volume industry in the tenth and eleventh centuries, the sources we have examined do not contradict the suggestion that the first stirrings of such activity could have occurred sooner. The conception of the church as private property was just as strong in the earlier part of the era as the later, and the scope for individual initiative, whether following the example of the king or of the religious community, was equally great. If there is a difference it may lie in the prospect that a substantial class of local landholder had arisen in the interval. Put another way, membership of the groups which had the capacity to found churches had been expanded. But people with this potential had existed in the eighth and ninth centuries, even if there were fewer of them. Such preliminary growth – whether steady or spasmodic we cannot tell – would render the presence of 6–7000 churches by 1100 more easily explicable, and the gradient of the flows in Fig. 37 that much less precipitous.

V

IN THE TOWNS,
c. 850-1100

'Well?' he said, in a suppressed passion, fixedly looking at her.

'O Frank – I made a mistake! – I thought that church with the spire was All Saints', and I was at the door at half-past eleven to a minute as you said. I waited till a quarter to twelve, and found then that I was in All Souls'. But I wasn't much frightened, for I thought it could be tomorrow as well.'

'You fool, for so fooling me!'

'Shall it be tomorrow, Frank?' she asked blankly.

'Tomorrow!' and he gave vent to a hoarse laugh. 'I don't go through that experience again for some time, I warrant you!'

'But after all,' she expostulated in a trembling voice, 'the mistake was not such a terrible thing! Now, dear Frank, when shall it be?'

'Ah, when? God knows!' he said, with a light irony, and turning from her walked rapidly away.

Thus Fanny Robin and Sergeant Frank Troy, the ill-starred couple in *Far from the Madding Crowd*, the first of Thomas Hardy's novels to be set in Victorian Wessex. It was Hardy who retrieved the name 'Wessex' from pre-Conquest history and restored it to popular use. Fanny could have made an error in any one of above a dozen towns which had existed within the frontiers of the former kingdom. Before 1200 Cricklade *Gl* had two churches, Dorchester *Do* three and Wareham *Do* seven. What confusions might have befallen poor Fanny in twelfth-century Wallingford *O* (*Brk*) where there had been eleven churches? Or in medieval Bristol which had had eighteen parishes, or Oxford with twenty? Exeter – the Exonbury of

Lower Wessex in Hardy's novels – formerly contained at least twenty-nine parochial churches and chapels. Winchester and its suburbs possessed fifty-seven, or more, churches in the twelfth and thirteenth centuries.

Wessex was not unusual in having so many places with more than one church. Out of more than a hundred settlements called *burgi* 'boroughs', *civitates* 'cities', or otherwise singled out as towns in 1086, about 25 per cent are found to have possessed, either then or slightly later, up to five churches (Fig. 38). A further 24 per cent had more. Before the eleventh century was out churches were swarming in Thetford, York, Lincoln, Norwich and London: especially London. The opening of William fitz Stephen's *Life of Thomas Becket*, composed between 1170 and 1183, celebrated the size, wealth and strength of that city, and enumerated the virtues of its citizens. 'As regards the practice of Christian worship', wrote fitz Stephen, 'there are in London and its suburbs thirteen greater conventual churches and, besides these, one hundred and twenty-six lesser parish churches' (*EHD* 2, no. 281).

When, in what circumstances and by whom all these churches were founded are matters which remain obscure. But there are two important generalizations which can be made: places with many churches became urban during the Anglo-Saxon period, and the founders of the churches were usually laypeople.

The first statement is supportable in several ways. Although in the previous chapter it was explained that sources which refer to the plurality of parish churches do not become available until the thirteenth century, it was also noted that there are areas and places for which large minimum totals can be ascertained at earlier dates. Among them are some towns. Ipswich, for instance, contained at least eleven churches in 1086: this is 75 per cent of the later medieval maximum in that town. The Domesday officials troubled to note their dedications: Michael, Botolph, Lawrence, Peter, Stephen, George, Julian and Augustine, together with a Holy Trinity, and two churches which had been dedicated in honour of the Blessed Virgin Mary. Before 1110 Lincoln probably possessed no fewer than thirty-two (65 per cent), and possibly as many as thirty-seven (75 per cent) of its parish churches (Fig. 39). Other useful eleventh-century minima include Leicester with seven (70 per cent) and Norwich, where there were at least forty-six churches and chapels (81 per cent) by 1086 (Fig. 40).

Such figures are in broad accord with the results of archaeological investigation. Since 1955, twenty-five churches, in twelve different towns, have been subjected to systematic archaeological study. No more than five or six of the churches appear to have been founded after 1100 (R. Morris 1987).

Concerning large towns of pre-Conquest origin, therefore, it seems safe to assume that at least three-quarters of parish churches were in position before the end of the eleventh century. One further reason for believing this to be true may be inferred from the development of the conception of what a parish was. From early in the twelfth century canon law, which

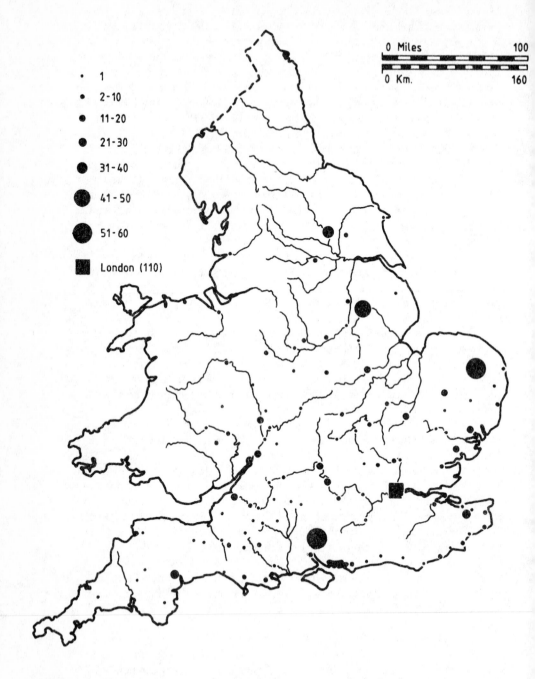

38 Late twelfth-century ranges in ecclesiastical parochial provision in places described as towns or bearing marks of urban status in 1086. London's absolute total is uncertain

regulated the rights and incomes of parish churches, was enforced with increasing rigour (Brooke 1970; Brett 1975). Henceforth it became difficult to prise apart the boundaries of existing parishes in order to create new ones. We must therefore suppose that the great majority of parish churches were already in being before the ecclesiastical administrators took full charge. This explains why after the twelfth century towns of similar size or wealth could display great, or even inverse, differences in the scale of their provision: why, say, Stamford *Li* possessed fourteen churches, while citizens of Boston *Li* worshipped in just one. Stamford was urban before 925. Boston's emergence as a leading port began around 1100.

With regard to the second generalization – that churches in pre-Conquest towns were usually founded by laypeople – we may begin by noticing that in several of the towns concerned (like York and Lincoln) the pre-Conquest religious communities were so few and small that so many local churches could scarcely have been founded by anyone other than members of the secular population. And in some cases there are sources which assure us that this was so. In Winchester the reeve Æthelwine founded the church of St Peter *in macellis* shortly before 1012 (Biddle and Keene 1976, 330). At York an incomplete inscription, now displaced, in St Mary Castlegate records that three men – Grim, Æse and another – erected this minster 'in the name of the holy Lord Christ, and to ... St Mary and St Martin and St C(uthbert(?)) and All Saints' (Okasha 1971, no. 146). The date is uncertain, but on epigraphic grounds it is likely to fall in the period 950–1050. The origins of another church at York are mentioned in the *Anglo-Saxon Chronicle* (D) for the year 1055. 'In this year passed away earl Siward at York, and he was buried in *Galmanho* in the church which he himself had built and consecrated in the name of God and (St) Olaf' (ed. Garmonsway 1972, 184–5). (The C version differs in recording the consecration as having been to 'God and all His Saints'.) St Olave was built close to the edge of a fortified enclosure known as Earlsburgh, which was later said to have been a residence of the late Saxon earls of Northumberland. In the twelfth century this area was absorbed into the precinct of St Mary's abbey. The church of St Olave still stands, although no fabric of Siward's day can now be recognized. At Oxford, according to the Annals of Oseney, the church of St George in the castle was built by Robert d'Oilli in 1074 (Salter 1936, 113–14). Domesday Book describes the beginnings of two churches in Lincoln, where a man called Colsuen had

4 tofts of his *nepos* Cole's land; and outside the city he has 36 houses and two churches to which nothing belongs, which he has built on waste land that the king gave him, and that was never before built upon.

(Foster and Longley 1924, 7)

Colsuen's churches have been plausibly identified with St Peter-at-Wells and St Augustine, which stood in a suburb on the eastern fringe of the

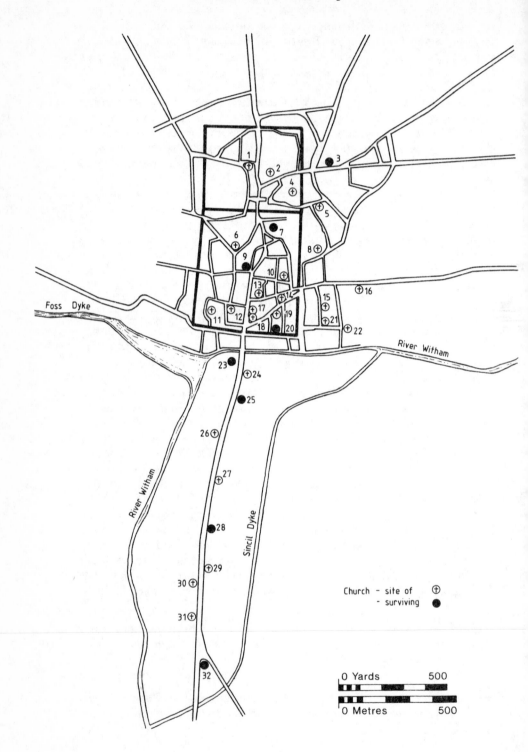

Foss Dyke

River Witham

River Witham

Sincil Dyke

Church – site of   ⊕
       – surviving   ●

0 Yards   500

0 Metres   500

medieval city (J.W.F.Hill 1948, 133-4). At Norwich the Domesday officials recorded another church of recent foundation. This had been built in the 'new borough' – the Norman-French sector – by earl Ralf.

Alongside these examples we may consider others where churches are found passing from lay hands. In 1005 it seems that Æthelmaer, *ealdorman*, gave his church of St Ebbe in Oxford to the religious community which he endowed at Eynsham *O* (Salter 1936, 122; Sawyer 1968, no. 911). At Norwich in 1086 it was recorded that twelve burgesses had held the church of Holy Trinity in the time of king Edward. A certain Eadstan had had two churches, and a small interest in a third. Fifteen other churches in the city were held by burgesses at around the time of the Conquest. Domesday Book records four churches in lay hands at Ipswich. Alwin, a burgess, had St Julian. Another burgess owned one of the churches which was dedicated to the Virgin Mary. A freewoman called Lefflet had held St Lawrence in the time of king Edward. Roger de Ramis held St George. At least three other churches here may have been owned by their priests.

Wrangles over the ownership of urban churches show that they were treated as pieces of property. Churches passed from hand to hand by hereditary descent. They could be bought and sold, or used as collateral in connection with other transactions. Few episodes illustrate these possibilities more graphically than a dispute which was recorded in 1086 at Huntingdon. Here the jurors stated that the church of St Mary in the borough, and land which went with it, had belonged to the monastery of Thorney. The abbot had pledged it to the burgesses, perhaps, as Professor Barlow suggested (1979, 192), as security for a loan. But king Edward gave it to Vitalis and Bernard, his priests. (The reason for the king's intervention is not stated.) The priests then sold St Mary's to Hugh, the king's chamberlain. Two priests of Huntingdon purchased the church from Hugh. Subsequently the church was seized by Eustace, the sheriff.

Another dispute recorded in 1086 points to the emergence of borough customs which were designed to regulate such trafficking. At Lincoln a carucate of land outside the city had belonged to the church of All Saints in the time of king Edward, together with twelve tofts and four crofts. All

39 Lincoln: local churches recorded as present by *c.* 1110. 1 St Paul-in-the-Bail; 2 All Saints-in-the-Bail; 3 St Peter Eastgate; (4 St Mary (cathedral from 1072)); 5 St Margaret Pottergate (possibly also dedicated to St Helen); 6 St Peter Stanthacket; 7 St Michael on the Mount; 8 Holy Trinity Stairfoot; 9 St Martin; 10 St George; 11 St Mary Crackpool; 12 All Saints Hungate; 13 St Lawrence; 14 Holy Trinity Silver Street; 15 St Bavon; 16 St Peter at Wells; 17 St Peter Plees; 18 St Peter Arches; 19 St Edmund; 20 St Swithin; 21 St Rumbold; 22 St Augustine; 23 St Benedict; 24 St John Evangelist; 25 St Mary le Wigford; 26 St Mark; 27 Holy Trinity Wigford; 28 St Peter at Gowts; 29 St Michael at Gowts; 30 Holy Cross Wigford; 31 St Margaret Wigford; 32 St Botolph (*Source*: David Stocker)

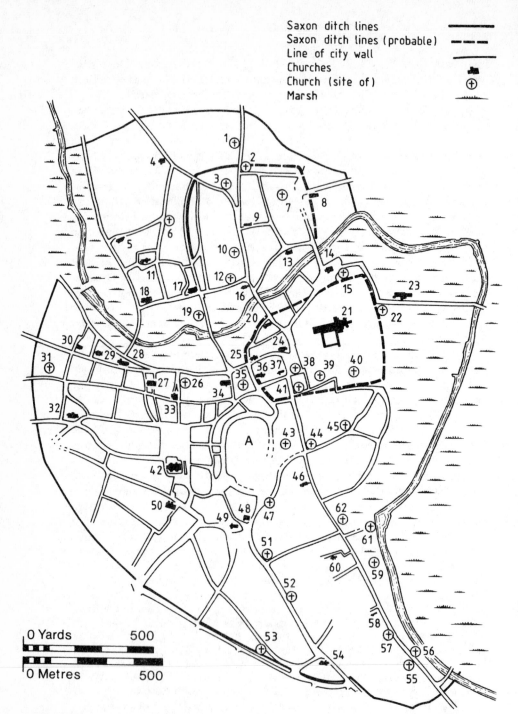

Saxon ditch lines
Saxon ditch lines (probable)
Line of city wall
Churches
Church (site of)
Marsh

0 Yards 500

0 Metres 500

40 Parish churches in Norwich. A castle; 1 St Margaret in Combusto; 2 All Saints
Fyebridge; 3 St Botolph; 4 St Augustine; 5 St Martin at Oak; 6 St Olave Pitt Street;
7 St Paul; 8 St James Pockthorpe; 9 St Saviour; 10 St Mary Unbrent; 11 St Mary Coslany;
12 St John the Baptist; 13 St Edmund; 14 St Martin at Palace; 15 St Matthew;
16 St Clement Fyebridge; 17 St George Colegate; 18 St Michael Coslany; 19 St Margaret at
New Bridge; 20 SS Simon and Jude; 21 cathedral priory; 22 St Helen; 23 St Helen (in

Hospital of St Giles); 24 St George Tombland; 25 St Peter Hungate;
26 St Crucis; 27 St Gregory; 28 St Laurence; 29 St Margaret de Westwick;
30 St Swithin; 31 St Benedict; 32 St Giles; 33 St John Maddermarket;
34 St Andrew; 35 St Christopher; 36 St Michael at Plea; 37 St Mary the
Less; 38 St Michael Tombland; 39 St Ethelbert; 40 St Mary in the Marsh;
41 St Cuthbert; 42 St Peter Mancroft; 43 church excavated in castle bailey,
dedication unknown (Ayers 1985); 44 St John the Evangelist; 45 St Vedast;
46 St Peter Permountergate; 47 St Martin in the Bailey; 48 St John the
Baptist Timberhill; 49 All Saints; 50 St Stephen; 51 St Michael at Thorn;
52 St Bartholomew; 53 St Winwallow or Catherine; 54 St John de Sepulchre;
55 St Peter Southgate; 56 St Olave; 57 St Edward; 58 St Etheldreda;
59 St Clement Conesford; 60 St Julian; 61 St Anne; 62 St Michael Conesford
(*Sources*: Alan Carter; Ayers 1985)

Saints 'and the land of the church, and whatever belonged to it' had been
held by a man called Godric, who acquired it from his mother, Garwine.
Godric became a monk at Peterborough, whereupon the abbot 'obtained'
the church, presumably as the result of the normal gift of personal property which was made on entering a monastery. The burgesses of Lincoln
were concerned about the alienation of such a valuable holding. They
deposed that the abbot had no title to the church 'because neither Garwine
nor her son nor anyone else could give it outside the city or outside their
kindred, except by grant of the king' (Foster and Longley 1924, 4–5).

Further indications of lay interests in, if not foundation of, urban
churches are discernible in the 'surnames' of churches in certain towns.
Usually such names were positional (e.g. All Hallows on the Walls in
Exeter, or St George Tombland in Norwich), less often descriptive (e.g.
Gracechurch in London (see p. 158), or St Peter Stanthacket (= 'thatched'
with stone) in Lincoln). But a few embody the names of people. London
was quite rich in them (Brooke and Keir 1975, 138). St Nicholas Acon
(= Haakon, a Norse name), which was extant by 1085, St Nicholas Aldred
(= Ealdred) and St Mary Woolnoth (Wulfnoth) are examples. It is not
known if such names denote founders, or whether they were added at later
dates in order to differentiate between several churches bearing the same
dedication in one town.

Dedications of urban churches are sometimes suggestive of travel, trade
and international connections. The Flemish St Bavon appears in Lincoln.
St Nicholas occurs very widely. A favourite among early medieval merchants in Lotharingia and Scandinavia, Nicholas was associated with
seafaring and the fish trade (Keene 1985). Another saint with nautical connections was the first-century pope Clement. Legend claimed him as a
martyr, asserting that he had been tied to an anchor and flung into the
sea. Clement was popular in Scandinavia, occurring for example in
twelfth-century Oslo and Århus, and he is found in the Kent ports of
Sandwich, Rochester and Romney, at York, also Worcester, and twice in
Norwich and in London. The surnames of two London churches smack
of commerce: St Clement Eastcheap (*ceap* 'market') and St Clement

Danes, which occupied a site within a market street (see p. 212). At York, Clementhorpe is close to an important trading area. In medieval England almost all the dedications to the Norwegian saint Olave (Olaf: d. 1030) were urban (see Fig. 14). The swiftness with which interest in Olave's cult developed is indicated by his appearance as a dedicatee in Exeter and York before 1066. Churches dedicated to him stood also in Chichester and Chester, and there were two in Norwich. Four London churches bore his name, and a fifth stood across the river in the bridgehead settlement of Southwark.

The economies of nearly all these places were diversified and mercantile. Some of the dedications could reflect the enthusiasms of English merchants with overseas connections. Names like St Nicholas Haakon or St Clement Danes lend themselves to conjecture about the presence of enclaves of foreign traders. Inscriptions bearing non-English names may refer to members of such expatriate communities, or to visitors. *Orate pro anima Costavn* 'Pray for the soul of Costan' reads a makeshift memorial found in York (Okasha 1971, no. 152). The name is difficult to localize, but there appear to be names of similar type in the Isle of Man at a later date. In the tenth century the same Scandinavian dynasty had ruled over Dublin and York together (Smyth 1978, 8); perhaps it was to this Hiberno-Norse world that Costan had belonged. His funeral took place before *c.* 1080, for at around that time builders in Norman employ began to construct a large new cathedral across the cemetery which contained his grave (Phillips 1985). 'Ginna and Toki ordered this stone to be erected' tell the runes which were cut on the edge of a gravestone set up in the cemetery of St Paul's cathedral in London during the eleventh century. Far away in Valleberge, Skåne, in modern Sweden, is a stone inscribed to the memories of Manni and Sveni: 'God help their souls, but they lie in London.'

If we are convinced that laypeople were the usual founders of churches in pre-Conquest towns, it may next be asked how far the numbers in which these churches occur can be relied upon as a guide to the size and wealth of urban populations. At a national level the correlation between numbers of churches and of townspeople seems close. It has been estimated that late in the eleventh century about 10 per cent of the English population lived in towns (Sawyer 1978, 204). In the previous chapter reasons were given for suggesting that the total of churches in England at this time stood somewhere between 6 and 7000. Since about 600 of these churches stood in places which Domesday Book identified as towns, it is possible to believe that around 10 per cent of the churches were urban.

The map of urban churches shows considerable regional variation. In Fig. 38 eleventh-century towns with more than one church have been sorted into numerical bands (2-5, 6-10, etc.). It will be seen that the towns of eastern and south-eastern England together accounted for about 60 per cent of all urban churches. Although the Midlands contained almost as many towns as the eastern counties, they furnish only 22 per cent of town churches. Central-south and south-west England account for the remaining 18 per cent, most of them in just two places: Exeter and Winchester.

Table 2 takes this investigation further, by comparing the estimated late eleventh-century populations of selected towns with their totals of churches. In the five largest towns the correspondence between numbers of people and of churches appears to have been quite close. For such places it is possible to believe that the total of churches might be a good guide to their relative, and possibly even their actual, population sizes.

Towns with populations of around 4000 or less appear to have had proportionately fewer churches than their larger counterparts. Thetford, for instance, which as far as we know possessed about twenty churches, could be expected to have had more than thirty if people and churches there had occurred in the same ratio as obtained in Norwich. This could be because we are overestimating Thetford's population, or because Thetford's decline in the late eleventh century deprived it of the quota of additional foundations which were then being made in more buoyant towns. The pattern, however, appears to be general to the lesser towns, almost all of which display church : people ratios that were appreciably lower than those that are found in the great provincial cities. It may be wondered if these figures disclose a contrast which was not simply one of relative size, but had to do more with such matters as the extent of social diversity, degree of differentiation between urban neighbourhoods, levels of personal wealth, the influence of lords and independence of burgesses. On this view, five or six towns in Domesday England were not only substantially larger than the others, but had also attained states of socio-economic development which placed them in a class of their own. Table 2 may show where the threshold of super-towndom lay (see Figs 42, 44).

After 1100 the value of absolute numbers of churches as an indicator of urban success begins to decrease. One reason for this has already been mentioned: it is that as parishes came to be defined and supervised with greater strictness, so the making of new parishes became more difficult. The usefulness of Fig. 38 as a guide to the ranking of towns is thus largely confined to the eleventh century. Towns such as Bristol and Northampton, which prospered mightily in the twelfth century and outgrew their former limits, probably acquired fewer fully parochial churches than would have been the case if such expansion had taken place only one or two generations previously. This is probably why Bristol and Exeter acquired so many sub-parochial churches. Any conclusions to be drawn from Fig. 38 will therefore have to take account of influences which inhibited the foundation of churches after 1100.

This assessment of the church as a possible measure of urban wealth and population leads us to inquire into the economic conditions which fuelled the growth of pre-Conquest towns, and the social and political influences which gave direction to urban development. As a prelude to discussion of these topics it is useful to review the broad outlines of English urban evolution between the seventh and eleventh centuries.

Towns had existed in Roman Britain, and many English towns occupied the sites of Roman predecessors. Both socially and institutionally,
however, the towns of the English were new creations. Romano-British
urban life had ceased in the fifth century. Roman urban defences, gates
and some types of building were, on the other hand, more durable. Such

Table 2 Churches and urban populations in the later eleventh and twelfth centuries

Town	Estimated DB population (thousands) 1066	1086	Suggested range (thousands)	No. of parish churches (chapels) by c.1200 (c.1300)	Churches (+ chapels): people c.1050 × c.1150?
London			15–25	110	1:136– 1:227
Winchester	6	15	8–12	57	1:140– 1:210
Norwich	6–7	4–5	8–12	57	1:140– 1:210
Lincoln	6+	4–5	6–8	48	1:125– 1:166
York	8+	4–5	6–8	40 (46)	1:150– 1:200 (1:130– 1:174)
Exeter	2	3	3	22 (29)	1:136–(1:103)
Thetford	4–5	4–	4–5	20	1:200– 1:250
Oxford	5+	4–	4–5	20	1:200– 1:250
Wallingford	2		2–3	11	1:182– 1:272
Chester			1.5–2	9 (4)	1:166– 1:222 (1:115– 1:154)
Nottingham			2	3	1:666

Notes:

H.C. Darby, *Domesday England* (1977), was consulted upon estimated DB populations, but
not all the figures are his. Suggested ranges have been compiled from a variety of sources.
In some cases it has seemed reasonable to increase the population figures that are usually
accepted on the basis of the extensive subdivision of urban property which is being disclosed
by archaeological excavation. But all the figures are extremely speculative, and their status
as guesses is emphasized. More confidence attaches to the figures for churches, but London's total is in doubt, and all the figures could be open to some revision. Attention is
drawn to the point that the comparisons in the final column are anachronistic, because the
totals of churches are generally not known before 1200, whereas the population ranges are
those estimated for the end of the eleventh century. The figures would also be affected in
places where basic provision was augmented by the foundation of parochial chapels in significant numbers. However, for reasons explained in the text, not many new churches, effectively parochial, are likely to have been founded in the older towns after the second quarter
of the twelfth century. As orders of magnitude, therefore, the numbers may have some
value. What they seem to show is either that church : people ratios in the larger towns were
more favourable than in less populous urban places, or that there has been significant
miscalculation over the relative sizes of urban populations. The former interpretation is
perhaps to be preferred, and levels of wealth, coupled with the extent of social/neighbour-
hood differentiation, could be among the factors which lie behind it.

constructions would endure for centuries, unless people wished to see them gone, or to recover their materials, and so demolished them. The English therefore inherited much of the hardened infrastructure of former Roman towns, but nothing of their urban life.

The factors which prompted the reoccupation of places like Winchester, Lincoln and York are mostly unrecorded. It is easy to believe that some of them had never been wholly deserted. The presence of royal nuclei is suspected at several. There seems to have been a royal hall in seventh-century London, for instance, and a case has been made for the existence of a royal palace in Winchester, immediately west of the church which was begun by Cenwalh, king of Wessex (643–72) in 648 (*EHD* 1, 631; Biddle 1975, 125, Fig. 3). Early in the eighth century a writer working in the Northumbrian monastery at *Streanaeshalch* described a brief walk which had been taken in York by king Edwin (616–32) from his *aula* 'hall' to the cathedral (Colgrave 1968, 15). *Streanaeshalch* had close contacts with York, and while we have no means of verifying this story, the details of its setting could be correct (R.Morris 1986, 81).

The existence of such royal enclaves elsewhere might help to explain the policy of senior churchmen, who in the period 600–720 established ten episcopal sees within the limits of former Roman places (see Fig. 2). These ecclesiastical centres exerted new influences upon settlement and economy. Unlike royal *aulae*, which were used intermittently, important churches functioned all the year round. They required craftsmen, and resident populations of ancillaries. Intellectual pursuits and the needs of administration generated busy patterns of travel, at home and abroad, involving the bearing of messages, letters, books, diverse goods and gifts. Important churches attracted visitors. Lords and *rustici* alike gathered at *mynsterstowa* for the celebration of major Christian festivals. Episcopal centres could have become temporarily populous in the Paschal season, which was the correct time for Christian initiation. Bishops' churches and certain religious communities may therefore have occasioned fairs and markets, for they were places where people assembled with regularity (Sawyer 1978, 221–2; 1981, 160).

The locales of several episcopal places were known by more than one name. York was called *Eoforwic* and *Eoforwicceaster*. London occurs in a seventh-century source as *Lundenwic*, but is also heard of later as *Lundenburg* and *Lundenceaster*. There is now some reason to think that these variations were used with precision, to denote different portions of York and London. *Eoforwicceaster* is likely to have referred to the area within the former legionary fortress; *Eoforwic* may have been applied initially to an extra-mural trading site beside the confluence of the Rivers Ouse and Foss (Fig. 41). London, likewise, seems to have existed in several parts: the *burg* or *ceaster*, presumably the old Roman walled city; and the *wīc*, plausibly associated with the area west of the City around what is now the Strand and Aldwych, the latter first heard of around 1200 as *vetus vicus*, or *Aldewic*: old *wīc* (Biddle 1984; cf. Vince 1984).

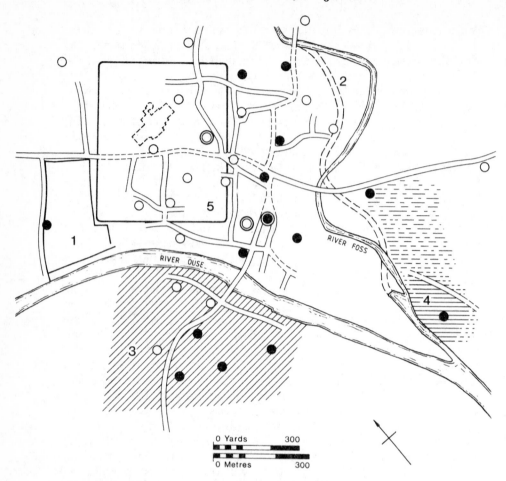

41 York: main topographical elements and selected parish churches.
1 Earlsborough (precinct of St Mary's Abbey from 1080s); 2 assumed former
course of River Foss; 3 area of former Roman *colonia*; 4 area of eighth-/ninth-
century *wīc* (broken shading indicates uncertainty of extent); 5 former Roman
legionary fortress. Churches indicated by solid circles are known to have
existed before 1086; open circles denote churches likely to have existed by this
time. The three churches with concentric rings were held by Durham
cathedral priory at least from the middle of the twelfth century: for the
possible significance of this, compare Fig. 58

The word *wīc* was derived by the English from late Latin *vicus* 'small
town'. *Wīc* occurs often as a place-name element, and commonly indicates
a place with some specialized function, such as the production of salt at
Droitwich *Wo*, or dairy farming at Butterwick *Li*, *Du*, and elsewhere. *Wīc*
was also used to denote important markets, as at Norwich.

Some of the market *wīc* were accessible to seagoing ships. *Eoforwic* lay close to the tidal limit of the River Ouse. Ipswich stood sheltered at the head of the Orwell estuary. *Lundenwic* was on the Thames. *Hamwic*, the precursor of Southampton, faced the River Itchen. Sandwich *K* lay a short distance from Pegwell Bay. Fordwich, virtually a suburb of Canterbury, was nine miles from the coast, but approachable by boat along the Great Stour. All these harbours can be regarded as international markets. London functioned thus before the end of the seventh century, *Hamwic* from *c*. 700. The others are variously attested in the eighth and ninth centuries, but could be older.

Bede referred to London as an *emporium* 'for the many peoples who come to it by land and by sea' (*HE* ii. 3). Regulations concerning London drawn up in 673–85 mention an official with the title *wic-gerefa*: presumably a royal agent who supervised transactions, saw to the protection of strangers, exacted toll and exercised the privilege of pre-emption on the king's behalf. London was probably the largest of the *wīc*, although in physical terms little is yet known about it. The approximate extent of the early trading area can perhaps be dimly perceived in the distribution of seventh- to ninth-century objects found at various times, often by chance, and recently mapped by Professor Biddle (1984) and Mr Alan Vince (1984). If so, *Lundenwic* could have occupied an area of some 220 acres (90 ha).

Hamwic was less than half this size. Archaeologists have found evidence of occupation, trade and industry extending over at least 99 acres (40 ha) (Holdsworth 1976, 30; cf. Hodges 1982, 68). Metalled streets, set out to an orderly pattern, and signs of tenement plots, are suggestive of systematic planning. *Hamwic*'s function as a trading place is indicated by the presence of pottery from northern France, metalwork, glass and quernstones from the Rhine valley, and whetstones from Scandinavia (Holdsworth 1976, 51–7; Hodges 1980; Pay 1987, 9). Other objects witness trading contacts within England. Local crafts flourished. Potting, the carving of bone and antler, the working of metal, glass and leather, and weaving, are attested or implied by diverse residues, waste and offcuts, as well as by some of the products. The general impression 'is of a well-organized artisan community engaged in long-distance trade and small-scale industrial production' (Pay 1987, 16).

Before 800 *Hamwic* was possessed of a number of urban characteristics; by 850 these attributes had begun to melt away. The reasons for *Hamwic*'s decline are still under debate, but political changes abroad which upset the equilibrium of *Hamwic*'s trade and Viking raids may have been contributory factors. The attenuation of *Hamwic* could also be seen as part of a wider domestic process which involved the redefinition and strengthening of some settlements at the expense of others. As *Hamwic* retracted, Winchester, twelve miles to the north, began to expand towards the populous, diversified provincial city that it became in the tenth century (Hodges 1982, 68, 158). This may be coincidence, but possibly cognate developments are observable in other places where the changes were more compressed. At York, for instance, a ribbon of new settlement was un-furled in the second half of the ninth century (Fig. 41). How the *wīc* just downriver fared at this time is not yet known, but by the eleventh century the *wīc* seems to have been regarded as a suburb. A comparable shift seems to have taken place at London, where areas within the ancient walls of Roman *Londinium* were being recolonized from the end of the ninth cen-tury while the *wīc* outside to the west may have undergone a correspond-ing decline (J. Schofield 1984, 25; Biddle 1984).

It is a question whether the unsettled conditions of the ninth century occasioned such changes, or whether they served rather to hasten developments which were already in prospect. There is no doubt that Vik-ing aggression rendered *wīc* and sites of markets insecure. *Hamwic*, for ex-ample, was raided in 840. *Lundenwic* was attacked in 842 and on sub-sequent occasions. Unfortified markets which had hitherto relied for their protection upon customary behaviour and the peace of the king became vulnerable when intruders disregarded the rules. English kings responded by providing defences for selected places. 'The Mercians did this first but it was the West Saxons, above all Alfred, who developed and refined a system of fortified *burhs* that sheltered markets and also served as centres of royal administration' (Sawyer 1978, 194-5). In 893 Asser, the biographer of Alfred (871-99), reflected upon the king's achievements:

> And what of the cities and towns to be rebuilt and of others constructed where previously there were none. . . . And what of the royal halls and chambers marvellously constructed of stone and wood at his command? And what of the royal residences of masonry, moved from their own positions and splendidly reconstructed at more appropriate places by his royal command?
>
> (*Life of King Alfred*, 91; trans. Keynes and Lapidge 1983, 101)

Defence, it seems, was not the only factor in Alfred's mind. The reloca-tion and architectural aggrandisement of *villae regales* also looms large.

Over thirty *burhs* were established or modernized in southern England between 870 and 930 (D.H.Hill 1969). Some, like Chichester and Win-chester, lay within renovated Roman *enceintes*. Others were new. Not all of them were towns, or expected ever to be so. Dr Hill has pointed out that the smallest, generally those of around 15 acres (6 ha) or less, were in-tended only as forts (1981, 143). Nor was Alfred responsible for the concept. Mercian leaders had built *burhs* in the previous century, as at Hereford, and the idea of the defended town was hardly original. Nevertheless, a number of scholars claim to have detected signs of consistency underlying the internal planning of the larger *burhs* inspired by Alfred, Edward (899-925) and Athelstan (925-39) (e.g. Biddle and Hill 1971). It is believed that most of them were furnished with a grid of streets. Often the grid was edged by a perimeter road that ran just inside the defences. However, while the broad anatomy of an urban *burh* may well have been determined at the outset, the manner and chronology of its infilling could be haphazard and spread over a longer period. The internal development of late Saxon towns is considered in more detail below, but the danger of speculation from appearances alone is worth stressing here. At Wareham, for instance, excavation has shown that a street which looks as if it could have formed part of the initial layout was no older than the thirteenth century (Hinton and Hodges 1977, 82).

Nor was urban development during these burghal decades restricted to Wessex, Mercia and Kent. Some of the most thriving towns were in the Danelaw. York and Lincoln were prominent before 900. Norwich was beginning to expand. Thetford *Nf* and Stamford *Li* were significant places before the reconquest of East Anglia and the south-east Midlands by the English in 917–19 (Dunmore and Carr 1976, 9 (but see also Rogerson and Dallas 1984, 197–8); Mahany and Roffe 1982). Less obviously regular in layout than their counterparts in southern England, some of these places nevertheless show signs of corporate organization. In parts of York there are units of property with boundaries that have been traced back into the ninth century. The extension of town life from this period may therefore be regarded as a widespread, though not necessarily homogeneous or unitary phenomenon.

The forces which fuelled urban growth require more attention than can be given here. Fortunately, they have been explored in some depth by others: notably Professors Biddle (1976) and Sawyer (1978, 132–67, 204–33), and Dr Hodges (1982). For present purposes only three aspects will be singled out: the rural conditions within which towns crystallized, the influence of rulers and the impact of the Vikings.

Towns were functions of their surroundings. If markets existed to be threatened or protected in the ninth and early tenth centuries this was because previously there were surplus commodities to be traded, demand for them and people who were able to make regular journeys to particular places in order to buy or sell. Once in being, a town depended upon its hinterland for a proportion of its food, custom and raw materials. Rural affluence and a rising population might therefore be suspected as combining to create demographic conditions which were predisposed to the formation of towns. That the population was growing in certain parts of ninth-century England is likely, although rates of growth almost certainly varied from region to region and are notoriously difficult to estimate. Signs of rural prosperity are more definite. They are to be found not only in interpretations of archaeological and environmental data (Hodges 1982, 130–54), or in the founding of small local churches such as at Raunds *Np* (see Fig. 34), but also in the views of contemporaries. When Asser sought an explanation for the decline of monastic discipline which had taken place in pre-Alfredian days he was unsure whether to place the blame at the door of foreign enemies, or to see it as a slackness born 'of the people's enormous abundance of riches of every kind, as a result of which (I suspect) this kind of monastic life came all the more into disrespect' (*Life of King Alfred*, 93; trans. Keynes and Lapidge 1983, 103). The indications of rural wealth and agricultural surplus are not evenly distributed. It is significant that Wales and large portions of northern England spawned no real towns until after the Norman Conquest. Elsewhere, however, the period *c.* 850–1150 may be regarded as the economic optimum of the Middle Ages, when growth in population, accompanied by an amelioration of climate, enabled the productive application of labour to a landscape that was not yet overcrowded, on soils not yet so exhausted as to be unable to sustain further expansion. The crisis came later.

Kings gave direction to urbanization. To an extent they did so passively, in so far as their administrative *villae* and the royal minsters which were their adjuncts provided nuclei for associated settlement, opportunities for the practice of specialized crafts and occasions for fairs and markets. But the ninth century also saw an active extension of royal claims to a share from the profits of trade. Whereas previously the collection of toll seems to have been confined to *wīc*, rulers now began to levy tolls in urban markets – presumably in response to economic activity which had already begun to increase. This is evidenced first at Worcester in the 890s (Sawyer 1968, no. 223; Sawyer 1981, 158), and slightly later at the fortified *burhs* and *ports* of southern England which were to some extent

under the control of the king and his agents, notably *portgerefan*, port-reeves. In the early tenth century there was an attempt to limit buying and selling to those places. The laws of Edward the Elder include the rule that 'no one shall buy except in a *port*, but he shall have the witness of the port-reeves or of other men of credit who can be trusted'.

(Sawyer 1981, 158; 1 Edward 1)

In the reign of Athelstan (925–39) this clause was relaxed in relation to trifling transactions (2 Athelstan 12). Ostensibly such regulations were designed to ensure that transactions were properly supervised but, as Sawyer argues, 'the king and his agents must also have hoped to profit from tolls and other incidental payments': a desire that was later to be made explicit in the legislation of Æthelred (979–1013) (4 Æthelred 3). Evidently, if the ramparts of *burhs* were intended to exclude enemies, their gates also offered a convenient means of regulating the comings and goings of traders and the movement of the commodities they purveyed.

As towns developed around existing markets, specialization in crafts and trades increased. Beyond the walls, therefore, land was now to be cultivated not only for the benefit of rural communities, but also in order to feed and supply urban citizens who were for the most part agriculturally non-productive. Some of the basic annual requirements of a large late Saxon town are estimated in Table 3. They are considerable.

Interdependence between town and hinterland would have been intensified in a time of rising population, as land acquired a premium, and younger sons gravitated towards towns in search of alternative occupations. It is arguable that such conditions were not approached in any general way until the latter part of the twelfth century (Bridbury 1975, 54). Conceivably, however, the Vikings hastened the onset of these pressures, at least in certain areas. In eastern England the seizure of land by Scandinavians, both from English farmers and from each other, may have caused some of the dispossessed to seek new opportunities for themselves in towns. Late in the ninth century two of the largest and fastest-growing towns, Lincoln and York, stood within regions which were much affected by land-taking.

Viking leaders may have promoted commercial activity in other ways, for they retained links with Scandinavian homelands and developed contacts elsewhere. How far this created scope for a renewal or extension of the overseas trade which earlier had been practised from *wīc* is uncertain. But Thetford's rapid expansion in the tenth century has been attributed in part to trading connections with the continent, achieved via the Little Ouse and the Wash, and witnessed in the importation and imitation of a variety of objects from Germany, Flanders and Norway (Dunmore and Carr 1976, 8–9; for reservations see Rogerson and Dallas 1984, 199). Around 1000 the biographer of St Oswald described York as a place thronged with traders from abroad, especially Danes. Merchants in eleventh-century London journeyed to and from Normandy, the Rhineland, Flanders, Scandinavia and the eastern Baltic. Full records of what was exported are lacking, but commodities glimpsed in transit before the Conquest include grain, cheeses, tin and wool. It has been suggested that the wool trade had already assumed a special importance within the economy before the end of the tenth century (Sawyer 1965). Timber, fish, wine and cloth were among the goods which were imported. Luxuries were brought from afar. Pieces of oriental silk have been recovered from tenth-century levels in Lincoln, and in York. Lincoln has also yielded sherds of early Islamic pottery, and fragments of Chinese stoneware have been found beneath a timber building of the late ninth century (Adams 1980).

At the beginning of this chapter it was suggested that churches can be taken as an index to the populations and wealth of late Saxon towns. Their numbers are a rough measure of the relative importance of towns before 1100, and it might be instructive to set them beside other criteria which have been used for this purpose, such as the productivity of mints, or numbers of moneyers (Petersson 1969) (Fig. 42). Further, the dates and rates at which churches multiplied could provide a basis for comparing the periods and speeds of urban growth in different places. Churches may be especially sensitive as indicators of urban performance in the period *c.* 875–1100. Laypeople were so often their founders, and unless or until urban churches received permanent endowments, their fortunes are likely to have risen or fallen in line with those of their owners. More significant still may have been the death-rate in an expanding medieval

Table 3 Some resource implications of a late Saxon town (*Source*: Roberta Gilchrist)

A Annual consumption and waste in a town of around 10,000 people, *c.*AD 1050: an estimate

Requirement	Commodity or substance	Assumption behind calculation	Estimated annual requirement	Relative composition	Further resource implication
Building materials	Structural timber	2000 households 25-year renewal rate	80 houses	2 mature oaks per house	160 mature trees per annum
Marine resources	Salt herring	5 per person per week	2,600,000		
	Oysters	20 per person per week	10,400,000		
Animal-derived protein	Poultry	0.2 hens per person per week	104,000		
	Eggs	5 per person per week	2,600,000		
	Red meat (beef, pork, mutton)	55 lb (25 kg) per person per annum[1]	550,000 lb (250,000 kg)	1000 pigs 1250 cattle 1750 sheep	Pasturage (sheep only) Flock of 12,500: 12,350–24,700 acres (5–10,000 ha) grazing land
	Cheese	3.5 oz (100 g) per person per day	80,250 lb (36.400 kg)		Ewes' milk: 47,022 gallons (178,000 l)[2]
Grain	Bread	8.8 oz (250 g) per person per day	1,984,126 lb (900,000 kg)	1,984,127 lb (900,000 kg) grain	Arable for culinary grain (c.2 million kg): 494 acres (200 ha)
	Beer	2.2 pints (1 l) per person per day	964,231 gallons (3,650,000 l)	178,571 lb (81,000 kg) grain	(= 1482 acres (600 ha) committed). Allow 50% spoilage from ear to granary: c.29,650 acres (12,000 ha)

Requirement	Commodity or substance	Assumption behind calculation	Estimated annual requirement	Relative composition	Further resource implication
Waste	Human urine	2–3 pints (1–1.5 l) per person per day	961,589 gallons (3,640,000 l[3])		
	Human faeces	0.2–0.4 kg per person per day[4]	720 tonnes		
Clothing	Shoes	2–3 pairs per person per annum	20–30,000 pairs	10–15 pairs per hide	c.2000 tanned cow hides
	Coarse woollen	54 sq ft (5 m²) per person × 2	1,076,426 sq ft (100,000 m²)		

B Essential commodities that cannot be quantified

Requirement	Commodities
Building materials	Coppice wood, roofing material (shingles, reeds, grasses, turf, heather), iron, lead, lime, stone, clay
Heating, cooking	Firewood
Kitchen goods, utensils, tools	Oil/tallow, iron, copper alloy, lead, tin, pottery
Preservative	Salt
Craft/manufacture	Antler, bone, horn, pine resin, beeswax, wood, leather
Luxury goods	Furs, glass, amber, jet, walrus ivory, silver, gold, parchment, linen (flax)
Additional dietary sources[5]	Wine, honey, pulses, vegetables (cabbage, garlic, leek, onion), fruit (grape, bramble, strawberry, sloe, damson, cherry, apple, gooseberry, fig), herbs and spices (saffron, parsley, borage, mint, fennel, rosemary, coriander, ginger, cinnamon, mace, pepper)

Notes:
[1] O'Connor 1983
[2] Trow-Smith 1957, 121–2
[3] Brothwell 1982
[4] ibid.
[5] Steane 1985, 264–70

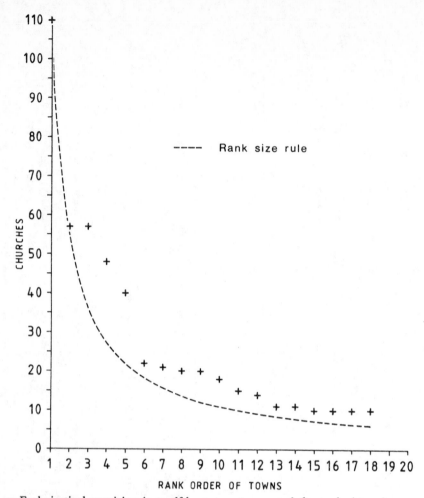

42 Ecclesiastical provision in twelfth-century towns and the rank size rule. Geographers have observed that in some modern countries the population sizes of cities are related. The second largest city will have half the population of the largest, the population of the third city will be a third of the size of the largest, and so on. When plotted as a graph, this inverse relationship between the sizes of urban populations appears in its classical form as a reversed letter J. The population sizes of English towns in the period *c*. 1050–1150 can only be estimated. Estimates vary widely (cf. Table 2). Totals of parish churches, by contrast, can be given with greater accuracy, at least from the thirteenth century. For reasons explained in the text, nearly all of these churches are likely to have been founded by 1150. If there was a broad correlation between the amount of church-room in a town and the size of its population, then totals of parish churches might be expected to behave in the same sort of way as would population data, if these were available. This Fig. examines that possibility. It will be seen that there does appear to be some correlation between the idealized rank size profile and populations of urban churches, although difficulties arise in knowing whether to include some types of chapel for this purpose. The towns concerned were all multi-church places before 1050. Clearly, this approach would be inapplicable to towns which emerged in the twelfth century wherein there were only one or two large churches. (*Source* for rank size rule: Meyer and Huggett 1981)

town. By 950, if not sooner, the need to earmark extra sites for graveyards must have been pressing strongly in places like York and Lincoln. It is of interest that in Lincoln the first users of the tenth-century church of St Mark appear to have invested more heavily in the memorials which stood in the churchyard than in the fabric of the church itself (Gilmour and Stocker 1986, 15–16, 55–82).

Not enough is yet known about the precise chronology of churchfounding for us to be able to take full advantage of its promise. But several useful points stand out. First, it should be noted how few churches stood in *wīc*: or, perhaps more strictly, how few churches in *wīc* achieved permanence. *Hamwic* bequeathed but one church, St Mary, to the later Middle Ages. This was a minster. The superiority of St Mary's was remembered in the thirteenth century, when it was acknowledged to be the mother church of *Hamtun*, where other churches had arisen. At York the church of St Andrew Fishergate is later found in the area of the *wīc*, whereas between seven and twelve churches had accumulated before 1086 along the Micklegate/Ousegate axis of the Anglo-Danish city (see Fig. 41). In the twelfth century intra-mural London was teeming with churches. By contrast only some half-dozen stood out along the Strand/Fleet Street terrace in and around the old *wīc* (from whence Aldwych). Of these, perhaps three (St Andrew Holborn, St Martin-in-the-Fields and St Mary-le-Strand) might be entertained as having originated during the floruit of the *wīc*. Fordwich *K* had one church. Sandwich *K* had three, although two of them, St Mary and St Clement, are regarded as having been established early in the eleventh century. Of known pre-Viking *wīc*, only Ipswich reached double figures before 1086. Here, however, the medieval town was superimposed upon the site of the earlier *wīc*, and at present we have no means of discriminating between churches which might belong to the period *c.* 700–850 and those that were founded later.

For reasons that were given in the previous chapter, it is unlikely that the paucity of churches in *wīc* can be wholly explained by the theory that local churches were not founded in significant numbers before the tenth century. There may, in fact, have been more churches in these settlements than we realize. Excavations at *Hamwic* disclosed at least four cemeteries, one of which contained a wooden building which has been cautiously interpreted as a small church. The cemetery, and presumably the chapel with it, seems to have been abandoned before 800 (Holdsworth 1976, 57; Pay 1987, 27–8). At York traces of a small, clay-floored timber building and associated burials have been found within the area of the *wīc*. This structure, provisionally dated to the ninth or tenth century, is currently visualized as the predecessor of St Andrew which replaced it in the eleventh or twelfth century and stood immediately to the north (Kemp 1986). The evidence from *Hamwic* suggests that ephemeral chapels may have existed in similar circumstances elsewhere, and that, unlike churches founded after *c.* 900, they failed to put down institutional roots and hence were ill equipped to survive. This conjecture aside, the English *wīc* remain conspicuous as having been, by tenth-century standards, comparatively churchless places (Fig. 43).

We must now move on to consider the church-rich towns and cities which developed in England between *c.* 875 and 1100 (Fig. 44). In particular, what factors can be adduced to explain the immensity of urban ecclesiastical provision in eastern England?

One rather striking characteristic of the towns with more than twenty-five churches is that, with the exception of Winchester, all of them were inland ports. This applies also to quite a number of towns with figures in the middle range of ecclesiastical provision. A conclusion which might be drawn is that while different towns attained various sizes according to the nature of the economic landscapes of their hinterlands, additional growth was achieved through participation in trade over longer distances. The extent of such growth was governed by the size and range of the overseas markets to which each town had access. Thus ports on or near western coasts like Chester and Bristol are known to have had active dealings with Ireland and Norway, notably in the import of skins and the export of

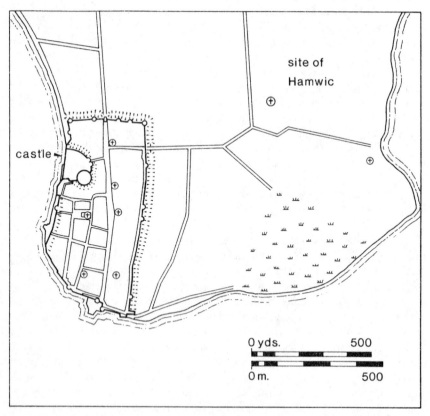

43 *Hamwic* and *Hamtun* (*Source*: Platt and Coleman-Smith 1975, Fig. 1)

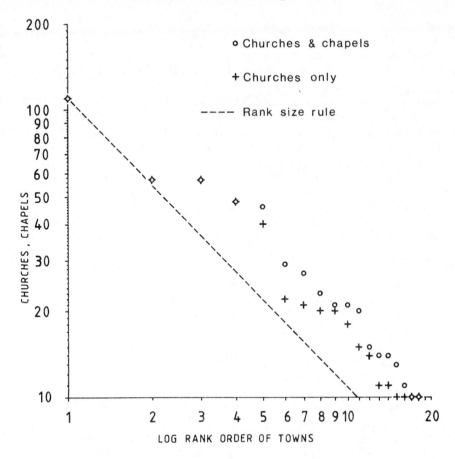

44 This presents the data seen in Fig. 42 in logarithmic form, whereby the idealized rank size profile appears as a straight line. The towns now appear to fall into a series of groups, with something of a staircase effect. This may reflect the presence of four provincial capitals (Winchester, Norwich, Lincoln, York) with sub-regional centres in their hinterlands

slaves. Exeter had diverse trade with north-west France. But towns on rivers that led to the North Sea enjoyed a much wider range of contacts, including the Baltic region, Scandinavia, Frisia, the Rhineland and northern France.

There are resemblances between church-patterns in towns on either side of the North Sea. Towns in the Rhineland and the Low Countries are commonly found in possession only of small groups of large churches. The towns of Denmark and sub-arctic Europe, on the other hand, present an intriguing picture, for in some of them little churches proliferated almost as in England. These places are additionally valuable to us because they grew up in the period *c.* 900–1200 in areas that had had no previous experience of urbanism. Their ecclesiastical geographies thus have a possible value as analogues for their English counterparts.

Between 1050 and 1150 the Danish town of Viborg mustered at least twelve churches, including one dedicated to the East Anglian saint Botolph which was situated in a characteristically peripheral position (see p. 219). Roskilde had thirteen churches within its defences and three more immediately without. The city of Lund, in modern Sweden but formerly in the medieval Danish province of Skåne, contained nineteen intra-mural churches. As at York, there was a church dedicated to St Olaf outside the north gate. No fewer than eight churches stood in the Norwegian port of Bergen. East from the Gulf of Finland the great Russian city of Novgorod lay athwart the River Volkhov, which served as an important link in a trade route that stretched across to the Black and Caspian Seas. The merchants who brought Asian pottery and oriental silk to Lincoln may have obtained them from this direction. Novgorod's connections with Byzantium found expression in the dedication of its cathedral to Holy Wisdom, in imitation of the mighty Hagia Sophia at Constantinople (where there is evocative reflex evidence for communication with the Baltic region in the form of a runic graffito scratched by a Viking visitor). Novgorod's population of small secular churches is difficult to establish, but the sites of at least thirty-two churches have been identified out of a suspected total in excess of fifty (Dejevsky 1977).

Some of these details remind us that in the eleventh century bishops were occasionally consecrated to Scandinavian sees by English metropolitans. There are records of English priests who were appointed to posts in Norway and Denmark (Barlow 1979, 15, n. 4, 233). Aristocrats in the tenth and eleventh centuries might hold estates on both sides of the North Sea, and build churches on them. Cnut (1016–35) ruled over England and Scandinavia together. Family bonds, the mutual interests of trade and the exercise of political power all spun filaments in a web of links which stretched between England and northern Europe.

So far we have seen that the primary factors behind the proliferation of churches in towns before 1100 were population and wealth. It remains to look more closely at the towns themselves, and to see in more detail how, and when, the churches were fitted into them. A convenient way to do this is to consider the churches in relation to other components of urban topography, such as streets, units of property, gates and defences, markets, religious communities and suburbs.

The parcelling-out of urban sites in the late ninth and tenth centuries was not followed by uniform colonization of the regular street-blocks that had been created. Housing was typically at its earliest and most dense along a principal thoroughfare, which commonly served also as a market. Such concentrated growth along a commercial axis within a larger framework of replanning is seen especially well at Winchester (Biddle and Hill 1971; Biddle 1975). Here the east–west High Street already existed when it provided the spine of a planned road system that was set out around 900. Lesser roads ran in parallel attendance to north and south.

These back lanes may have provided rear service access to properties on the main street (Biddle 1975, 27–8).

The distribution of Winchester's intra-mural churches can probably be taken as a rough measure of the density of population in the High Street ribbon. About 50 per cent of the churches occur within this zone, whereas the corridor itself covers only about 25 per cent of the intra-mural area of the town (Fig. 45). It has been pointed out how at least six of the churches along High Street stood towards the rear of the properties with which they were originally associated. This

> remote and enclosed situation might be taken to emphasize the private origin of these churches, but others of apparently similar origin, such as St Mary Tanner Street, were situated directly on the street frontage. The position of the church may rather reflect the intensity of building on the street frontage at the time of its foundation.
>
> (Biddle and Keene 1976, 334)

Three of the churches in question – St Mary Tanner Street, St Pancras and St Peter *in macellis* – have been excavated (Biddle 1975, 312–13, 318–20; Cunliffe 1964, 43–5). St Mary and St Pancras both existed before the middle of the tenth century. St Peter was founded shortly before 1012 (Biddle and Keene 1976, 330, and n. 3). Another of the churches set back from the frontage, St Peter in *Colobrochestret*, is thought to have existed before *c.* 950. If Dr Keene is correct in his suggestion about the intensity of building on the High Street frontages, then this part of Winchester was already becoming well built up in the first half of the tenth century.

Signs of initial linear growth are visible in other towns. At Colchester, where replanning may have taken place in the tenth century, four of the town's nine intra-mural parish churches lined a High Street that embroidered the path of a Roman predecessor (Fig. 46). A contrast between the density, or at least the character, of occupation along the High Street and surrounding areas is also suggested by the pattern of parish boundaries. In the outer zone the boundaries are unswerving for considerable distances; they follow roads (both Roman and later) and primary divisions of property. Nearer to High Street the boundaries become more jagged, and include small salients, reflecting a greater complexity of tenure. This may indicate that the outer areas were rather less built up than the High Street corridor, or had remained in undivided ownership, at the time when the parishes were laid down.

Exeter's churches show a similar tendency to congregate along the main thoroughfare (Fig. 47). Out of twenty parochial churches and chapels within or, in two cases, upon the walls, eight fronted the Fore Street/High Street roadway, and six more were set back to the rear of properties, rather in the fashion already noted at Winchester. Five of the remaining churches were positioned along another main road that ran north-west/south-east through the city. Where the alignments of churches are

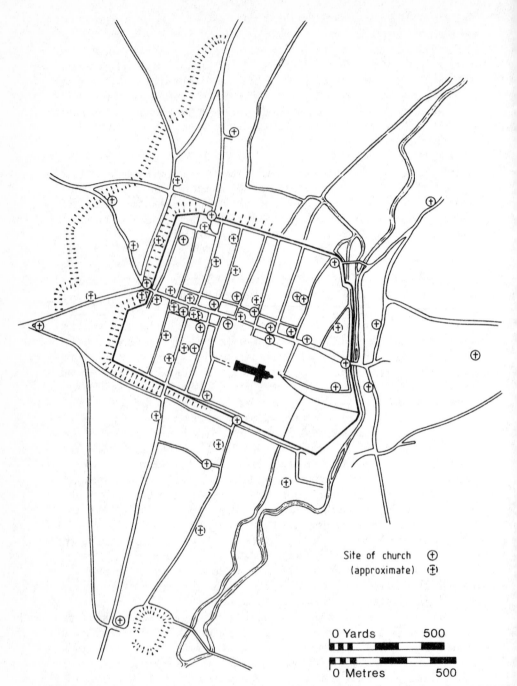

Site of church   ⊕
(approximate)   ⊕

0 Yards   500

0 Metres   500

45 Winchester and its parish churches in the twelfth and thirteenth centuries (*Source*: Biddle and Keene 1976)

known they tend to correspond with those of the street frontages upon which they stood, or to echo the directional trends of surrounding tenements. It is sensible to conclude that most of Exeter's churches were founded after the street pattern had been established. References to Exeter in the *Anglo-Saxon Chronicle* suggest that the defences were strengthened or rebuilt by Alfred in the period c. 880-92. The bone structure of the street plan would have been created at the same time (Biddle 1976, 273; Allan *et al.* 1984, 396, 400-4). However, the dangers of relying too heavily upon suggestive orientations are illustrated by what was seen of the plan of St George's church during excavation in 1945-6 (Fox 1952, 25-9). Even by Anglo-Saxon standards this layout is bizarre (Fig. 48). It would seem to reflect a compromise between the influence exerted by relict Roman topography and the constraints of street-lines and standing properties that existed by the time the church was built.

Chichester is another town where replanning took place within old Roman defences, perhaps by 894, when the town is first heard of in the *Anglo-Saxon Chronicle*. Two chief streets run between the main gates and intersect at a central cross-roads. These streets approximate to the lines of Roman predecessors, but the perimeter road and absence of correlation between Roman and later side roads are marks of the planner (Fig. 49). The layout was certainly established before the Conquest: the Normans disrupted it when they built a castle in the north-east corner of the town.

Chichester possessed eight parish churches within its walls. Five of them stood in the north-east quadrant. The other three were situated south of the main east–west thoroughfare. Nothing is known about the origins of any of these buildings, although the beginning of St Olave's must be placed after Olaf's death in 1030, unless the dedication to St Olave replaced another (which is always possible: it happened, for example, to the nearby ancient minster at Pagham, where the patron saint is now Thomas Becket). As at Colchester, Exeter and elsewhere, the distribution of churches points to a clustering rather than an even spread of population.

Some of the other areas were under special jurisdiction. The neighbourhood known as The Pallants was a liberty of the archbishops of Canterbury. It existed by 1086, when it appeared in Domesday as an appurtenance of Pagham. It may then have been old. The presence of such enclaves – the precinct of the cathedral, which may in part be older than the transfer of the see from Selsey in 1075, is another – may help to explain why the citizens of Chichester congregated in some parts of the town but not in others. But there was ample room for early expansion in the north-west quadrant, and here there seem to have been no churches at all.

Several of Chichester's churches look as if they could have been fitted into tenement plots. Among them were St Mary-in-the-Market, St Olave and St Martin. These 'ecclesiastical burgages' kept their shapes because

Course of Roman road

Conjectured

Parish boundary

0 Yards 300

0 Metres 300

most of Chichester's dead were buried either in the cathedral cemetery, as at Winchester until the fourteenth century, or in a collective town graveyard outside the eastern defences. Parish churchyards within the town were therefore either very small or non-existent (Munby 1984, 327). This perhaps enables us to see the configuration of the original sites with greater clarity than is now possible in towns like Lincoln and York, where graveyards were sometimes extended beyond their first boundaries. The extra-mural cemetery was known as The Litten (ultimately from Old English *lic-tun* 'graveyard' or, perhaps more literally, 'corpse place'). It was watched over by St Michael, who was the dedicatee of a *capella* there. A church dedicated to St Pancras stood nearby.

Next, let us consider Gloucester. Although not specified as a Mercian *burh*, the configuration of streets in the eastern part of the town may indicate that we are again looking at the result of a reorganization. Alfred's daughter Æthelflaed might be credited with this. Before 909 she established a minster in honour of St Oswald just north of the town, and she is known to have been active in the fortification of other Midland *burhs* (Heighway 1984, 40; Radford 1978).

Four of the twelve churches in Gloucester are found in the immediate vicinity of the principal cross-roads. Six others occur beside or, in two cases, actually in the streets that converge upon this intersection. Here, too, the main street frontages seem to have been built up first, and subsidiary roads were colonized more gradually. Residential settlement had reached the south-west quarter by the mid-eleventh century, for sixteen houses are stated to have been sacrificed in the making of the Norman castle *c.* 1070 (C.S. Taylor 1889, 127). Other portions of the outer areas may have remained relatively undeveloped until the thirteenth century, when Dominican and Franciscan friars took them over.

All the foregoing replannings took place within ancient Roman defences. It is instructive to compare them with late Saxon towns that lacked Roman ancestors. Wallingford *O* (*Brk*) and Oxford are good examples in Wessex; so too is Wareham *Do* (see Fig. 59), although this is not discussed in detail here. All three towns appear in a list of fortified places known as the Burghal Hidage, which reached its present form early in the tenth century.

Gardeners in Wallingford are accustomed to find pieces of Roman pottery and coins. It is likely that a Romano-British settlement lay in the vicinity, but it has been established by archaeological excavation that the substantial rampart which still surrounds the town is of Anglo-Saxon date (Durham 1973) (Fig. 50). The configuration of streets recalls the replannings of Chichester and Exeter. Through roads, one of them a broad market street, ran from gate to gate. Lesser side streets were set out at right-angles to the cardinal thoroughfares. The southern area was

46 Colchester: churches, streets, and elements of the underlying layout of the former Roman town. 1 St Helen; 2 St Martin; 3 St Peter; 4 St Runwald (d); 5 St Mary the Virgin (alias St Mary at the Walls); 6 Holy Trinity; 7 St Nicholas (d); 8 St James; 9 St Botolph. Extra-mural churches not shown. Parish boundaries are those recorded in 1848 (*Source*: Crummy 1981)

favoured and settlement seems to have been most full in the south-eastern quarter of the town. Here the street plan shows signs of elaboration, with vestiges of the perimeter road, and the presence of an intermediate street running parallel to the market. Six of Wallingford's eleven churches are found in this part of the town. Three – St Mary the Less, St Peter and St Leonard – stood at corners of the south-west quadrant. St Mary the More and St John flanked the quarter, St Mary central to the market street, and St John on the eastern fringe of the town, overlooking the Thames. Seen together, these five churches give the impression of an orderly distribution. The impression is reinforced by the fact that there was originally another church dedicated to St Peter in the town: it stood not far from the west gate.

It is difficult to believe that five or six churches could have formed part of the primary design of the *burh*. And not all Wallingford's churches were so tidily positioned. St Michael, for instance, occupied a secluded site towards the rear of a property, in fashion similar to examples already noted in Winchester and Exeter. Nevertheless, one might entertain the possibility that certain plots were earmarked at the outset for the future construction of churches. This was sometimes done when planned towns were laid out in the twelfth and thirteenth centuries, as at New Winchelsea *Sx* in the 1290s (Beresford and St Joseph 1979, 238-41). Alternatively, an explanation could be sought in the aftermath of the 'utter destruction' which the *Anglo-Saxon Chronicle* tells us was wrought upon the town by the Danes in 1006. Perhaps an opportunity was found in the general rebuilding to modify the pattern of churches, or to increase their numbers? St Leonard, St John and the two St Peters (cast, appropriately enough, in the role of gatekeepers), standing around the perimeter, could be looked upon as holy protectors. They may even have fulfilled a more direct military role, doubling as lookout platforms or strongpoints. An episode which took place during the Anarchy of Stephen's reign (1135-54) suggests that at least one of these churches was suited to fortification. In 1139-40 Stephen besieged Wallingford castle in order to dislodge men of Brian fitz Count, who had pledged support to Matilda. Stephen is said to have ordered the construction of two siege forts. One of them embodied the church of St Peter at the east gate (*Gesta Stephani*, 61-2; Renn 1973, 338). Perhaps this was no more than opportunism. But churches occur next to gates in other *burhs*: a phenomenon which is discussed at greater length on p. 216. Moreover, the example of St Michael Northgate, in

47 Exeter and its churches. Parish churches: **1** St Lawrence; **2** St Stephen; **3** St Paul; **4** All Hallows; **5** St Martin; **6** St Pancras; **7** St Mary Major (overlying site of earlier minster); **8** St Petroc; **9** St Kerrian; **10** Holy Trinity; **11** St George (*cf.* Fig. 48); **12** St Mary Arches; **13** St Olave; **14** St John; **15** St Mary Steps; **16** St Edmund. Chapels: **17** St Mary in the Castle; **18** St Bartholomew; **19** Holy Trinity (= Christ Church?); **20** St Catherine; **21** St Cuthbert; **22** St Peter Minor; **23** SS Simon and Jude; **24** St James; **25** St Michael; **26** St Edward; **27** St Roche; **28** St Mary; **29** All Hallows on the Walls; **30** cathedral (St Mary and St Peter)

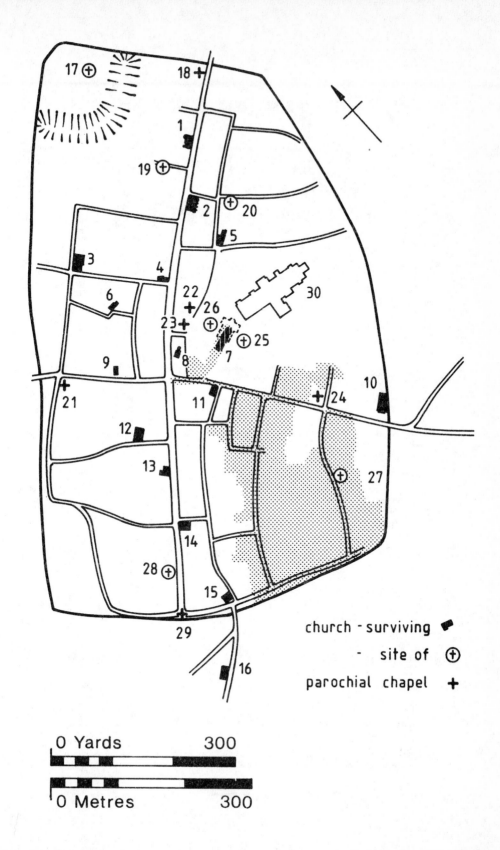

church - surviving ▟

- site of ⊕

parochial chapel ✛

0 Yards 300

0 Metres 300

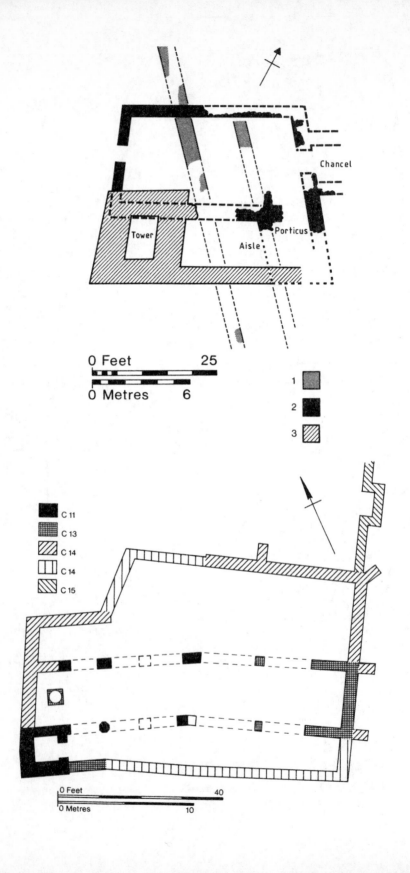

Chancel

Tower

Porticus

Aisle

0 Feet   25

0 Metres   6

1

2

3

C 11
C 13
C 14
C 14
C 15

0 Feet   40

0 Metres   10

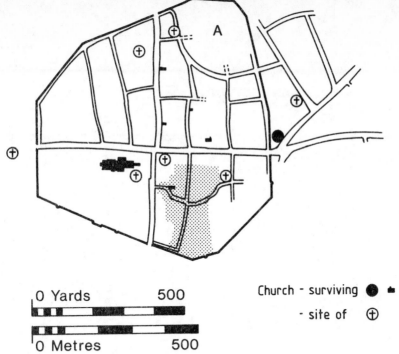

0 Yards 500

0 Metres 500

Church - surviving ● ▲

\- site of ⊕

49 Chichester and its churches. (*Source*: Munby 1984)

Oxford, shows that multi-purpose towers could indeed be integrated with town defences in this area during the eleventh century (Fig. 51).

Wallingford did not permanently outgrow its pre-Conquest defences. After 1250 the town suffered reversals of fortune and began to shrink. The story of Oxford, by contrast, is a tale of growth. The area enclosed by the defences of 912 seems to have been extensively settled before 1000. Early in the eleventh century the *burh* was enlarged to the east. Suburbs grew up outside the principal gates. By *c.* 1050 there was settlement beyond the western defences, witnessed in traces of occupation which have been found beneath the castle that was established shortly after the Conquest.

In 1100 Oxford, as augmented by these various additions, contained at least eight churches and possibly as many as fourteen or fifteen. Two were recent: St George in the castle, built by Robert d'Oilli in 1074, and the suburban St Mary Magdalene, which is plausibly claimed to have been founded in the same year (Salter 1936, 113–14). Domesday provides a *terminus ante quem* for St Michael, St Peter-in-the-East and St Mary. St Martin existed by 1034, when the king gave it to the monks at Abingdon (*Chron. Abingdon* i, 439). St Ebbe was given to the religious community at Eynsham *O* in 1005 (see p. 204). In the previous year king Æthelred confirmed the title of the minster of St Frideswide to estates near Oxford, and at Wichendon *Bu* (Sawyer 1968, no. 909). Æthelred's charter states that the minster had been burned when members of the Danish population

48 Plans of two urban churches, distorted by their sites and surroundings. **A** St George, Exeter (1 Roman walls; 2 outline of (?) pre-Conquest church; 3 later medieval extension) (*Source*: Fox 1952). **B** St Peter, Canterbury

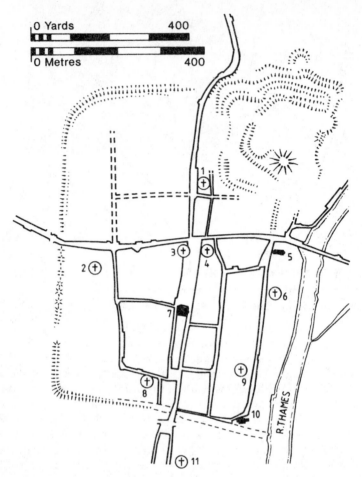

50 Wallingford and its churches. 1 All Hallows; 2 St Peter; 3 St Martin; 4 St Mary the Less; 5 St Peter (ii); 6 St John; 7 St Mary the More; 8 St Rumbold; 9 St Michael; 10 St Leonard. (*Source*: Airs *et al.* 1975)

attempted to take refuge in it during a massacre in 1002, and that the church had since been rebuilt at royal expense.

The minster of St Frideswide may offer a clue to Oxford's origins. The religious community was in being by *c.* 750. It was situated in what was defined in Chapter 3 as a classical position for monasteries of that period: upon a low terrace, overlooking a river, beside an important line of communication. Settlement developed in the vicinity of the minster during the eighth century. The line of what is now High Street was determined before 900 (Ashdown and Hassall 1975, 135). Oxford's secular and ecclesiastical components were bound into a more unified, formal urban framework following the construction of the *burh* defences and the systematic laying out of streets: a programme which has been attributed to Edward the Elder (899–925). As at Wallingford, some of the churches within the tenth-century *burh* are characterized by an orderly distribution. Four churches stood along the principal east–west axis represented today by Queen Street and High Street. The sequence began (again as at Wallingford) with a church of St Peter beside the west gate. Then came St Martin at the central crossroads, followed by All Saints. The procession ended at the east gate, which was marked by St Mary. The main north–south route was similarly punctuated, with churches of St Michael at the north and south gates, St Aldate just inside the south gate and St Martin Carfax common to both 'rows'.

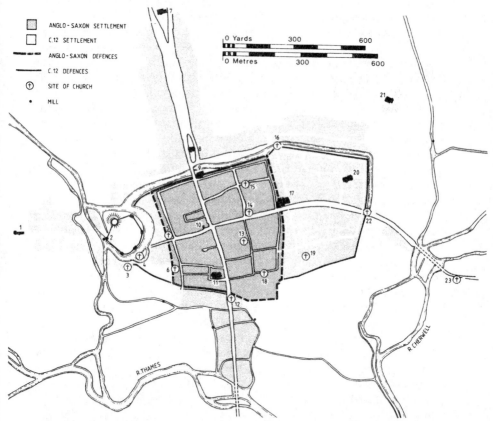

51 Oxford and its churches. 1 St Thomas; 2 castle/St George; 3 St Budoc (removed from 4); 5 St Peter le Bailey; 6 St Ebbe; 7 St Giles; 8 St Mary Magdalene; 9 St Michael Northgate; 10 St Martin; 11 St Aldate; 12 St Michael Southgate; 13 St Edward; 14 All Saints; 15 St Mildred; 16 Lady Chapel; 17 St Mary; 18 St Frideswide (former minster, succeeded by priory in 1122); 19 St John; 20 St Peter in the East; 21 St Cross; 22 Holy Trinity; 23 St Clement. (*Source*: Ashdown and Hassall 1975)

IN THE TOWNS, *c.* 850–1100

St Frideswide occupied a retired position, in a corner of the *burh*. This was a common place for minsters. Members of the Augustinian mission had used it at Canterbury and London early in the seventh century. Later churches had been positioned in the angles of former Roman *enceintes* at Wroxeter *Sa*, Gloucester and elsewhere. The English continued the tradition in *burhs* of their own creation, like Wareham *Do* and Oxford. Presumably in such cases the lines of the defences were manipulated in order to achieve the traditional disposition: a task made easier, and to some extent inevitable, by the tendency for religious communities to occupy sites that overlooked waterways.

It is worth pausing to consider some of the points that have emerged from the survey so far. First, there is little evidence for the presence of *many* small churches before late Saxon street plans were laid down. This is particularly clear at Exeter (Allan *et al.* 1984, 398), and it is the pattern too in Chichester, Wallingford and Gloucester. Second, there are abundant indications that churches multiplied first and fastest in areas where population was at its most concentrated: typically on main thoroughfares, as at Exeter and Oxford, along linear markets, and latterly in outer quarters if settlement continued to expand. The dates of peripheral churches are thus of special interest, as they may be a tentative guide to the periods at or by which towns had begun to grow beyond their 'spinal' phases. At Oxford the church of St Ebbe, in the extreme south-west corner of the tenth-century *burh*, existed before 1005. This may indicate that churches towards the interior of the town were already in place. Simple outward growth, however, and such straightforward chronological implications, cannot always be assumed. Some neighbourhoods within towns seem to have originated as urban estates which were dependencies of rural lordships. Pre-Conquest references to *hagas* 'enclosures' and private *burhs* within towns are not unusual. Some of them were attached to distant places. In 940 a *haga* at Wilton *Wi* was mentioned as pertaining to the rural estate at Wylye (Sawyer 1968, no. 469). In London *Ceolmundingachaga* was given to Worcester cathedral in 857 (Sawyer 1968, no. 208), and the names *Basingahaga* and *Staeningahaga* are recorded in the twelfth century. The names derive from the parent estates at Basing *Ha* and Staines *Mx*. The later London parishes of St Michael Bassishaw and St Mary Staining preserve memories of these names, and may have been co-extensive with the original units (Dyson and Schofield 1984). Urban estates of similar character existed elsewhere, for example in Worcester and in Chichester (see p. 195).

By 1086 *haga* seems to have had a normal meaning of 'tenement plot'. But some of the *hagas* mentioned above had been defined before burghal replanning took place, and these early units may have been appreciably larger than their successors. Tait thought that the first *hagas* were several acres in extent (1936, 7). Moreover, there are signs that early *hagas* in towns of Roman origin were sometimes delineated by relict features such as roads and walls which were still visible in the eighth and ninth cen-

204

turies, but were afterwards (at least in the case of roads) submerged by replanning. It has been suggested that the parish of St Aldate in Gloucester 'represents an early urban estate or *haga* originally laid out on a Roman street' (Heighway 1984, 364). The *hagas* mentioned in London formed a distinct enclave in the north-west corner of the old city; *Staeningahaga* occupied part of the Cripplegate fort. And it was noted above how the lines of several Roman streets in Colchester came to be ghosted in the boundaries of parishes that lay towards the edge of the town.

Once residences of prominent individuals had been established in *hagas* of the eighth and ninth centuries, it was always likely that churches would be erected as adjuncts to their households. Churches which appear in post-Conquest records as dependencies of rural manors, like the 'church in Chichester' that was recorded in the Domesday entry for Pagham *Sx*, no doubt commemorate such arrangements. Urban churches found holding rural property, like St Mary in Oxford (Salter 1936, 113, 120), or with detached out-parishes in the countryside, like several churches in Bishophill, York (R. Morris 1986, 84–6), may also point to the dispersed interests of pre-Conquest lords. It may be significant that many of the churches which have been mentioned in connection with pre-Conquest *hagas* stood slightly apart from what became the built-up town centre in the tenth and eleventh centuries. Some peripheral churches may therefore actually pre-date their downtown neighbours.

This leads us to consider in more detail the relationships which existed between churches and urban property. Already it will be evident that the positions of pre-Conquest urban churches were characterized by great diversity. Churches have been noted on tenement plots, on the frontages of streets, at cross-roads, within streets, against defences and on or near gates. It may be asked if these various locations are imbued with social meanings; and, if so, in what ways may they be expressive. A review of the different categories of location may help us to ascertain how, if at all, these positions reflect the interests and concerns of the people who determined them.

Town churches sometimes grew out of, or were superimposed upon, secular structures or divisions of property. Excavations inside All Saints, Oxford, in 1974, produced information which suggested that the church 'had evolved from a well-constructed domestic stone building which had already been modified' (*Medieval Archaeology* 19 (1975), 238). The same excavation uncovered at least one ninth-century property boundary running underneath the church (Ashdown and Hassall, 1975, 135). The tenth-century church of St Mary in Tanner Street, Winchester, incorporated an earlier, apparently secular building (Biddle 1975, 312–15). In York, excavations immediately north of St Mary Bishophill Junior revealed that the remains of a Roman building had been used to house the processing of fish: apparently herring or sprats (*Medieval Archaeology* 7 (1963), 312). By *c.* 920 the area had been turned into a graveyard. Excavations made at various times in Gloucester have disclosed thick deposits of organic character containing bone, and objects fashioned from wood, and also 'preserving fences and buildings made of wattle' (Heighway 1984, 364). The horizontal separation of these deposits, and the fact that dates derived from them vary from the late seventh to the tenth centuries, may indicate that 'different parts of the town were occupied at different times' (1984, 365). At least one of Gloucester's churches, St Michael, was superimposed upon such deposits (Cra'ster 1961). This is therefore a further case where one sort of settlement gave way to another. Churches were not always built on empty ground. Plots of land were sometimes cleared to receive them, or existing buildings adapted to serve as places of worship.

The tenement or burgage plot was the basic unit of property in most medieval towns. In York modern property boundaries have been traced back to the late ninth century. Such stability is not found everywhere, but the row of narrow, rectangular plots set out at right-angles to the street is still a common component of English townscapes.

The Domesday terms for an urban tenement were *masura* or *mansio* 'meaning a messuage, for which the English word was *haga* that later became *haw*'. What distinguished urban *mansiones* 'was the relatively free terms on which they were held, for they could be bought, sold, bequeathed, and even mortgaged and they rendered money instead of the servile obligations that were commonly exacted from rural tenements' (Sawyer 1978, 205).

Mansiones could be subdivided and sub-let. In Guildford, for instance, Domesday Book recorded 175 men (presumably heads of households) living on 75 *haws*. Subdivision was explicitly attested at Nottingham, where Roger de Busli had three *mansiones* on which stood eleven houses. Holders of *mansiones* paid a special rent called *landgable* to the king. *Landgable* was normally due from urban tenements irrespective of whether houses had been built upon them (Sawyer 1978, 205-6). This explains the recording of vacant units in Domesday Book. For example, in 1086 Evesham Abbey held 28 *masuras* in Worcester, five of which were then unoccupied; 25 plots were empty at Malmesbury *Wi*, while in Lincoln there were 760 inhabited and 240 waste *mansiones*.

A variety of circumstances may lie behind the foundation of churches within urban properties. Churches on single plots could have originated as private household chapels. The first phases of St Mary Tanner Street in Winchester actually communicated with a plot of ground within the curtilage of a substantial residence. In the twelfth century several of Winchester's churches were recorded as still pertaining to individual houses. But 'in a rapidly changing urban situation the town house and its associated land could soon be split up among a number of different tenancies, while the chapel came to be used by all the surrounding householders and so emerged as a parish church' (Biddle and Keene 1976, 333). It follows that churches of this sort are likely to have been founded before subdivision had proceeded far. There must be doubt as to whether all household chapels underwent a metamorphosis from private to public status. Presumably some of them ceased to be used for worship and were converted – or even reverted? – to secular uses. It may therefore be that some towns possessed more of these proto-parochial buildings in the period *c.* 950–1050 than is apparent from their totals of parish churches in the twelfth and thirteenth centuries.

As urban populations grew in size and social complexity during the tenth and eleventh centuries, so distinct neighbourhoods and subsidiary communities formed within them. Groups of citizens, either loosely or closely defined, may have combined for the establishment and upkeep of churches of their own (Brooke and Keir 1975, 132; Brooke 1970). Foundations of this sort are most readily postulated on the basis of the layout of their parishes. In London, for example, the 'variations in shape and size, and irregular outline' of parishes first mapped in the seventeenth century suggest that in origin they were 'related to the boundaries of property; but not to large units of property. For their most conspicuous feature is that in every case a major thoroughfare runs through their midst; sometimes an important cross-roads forms their centre. They are thus natural units, not formed by artificial frontiers' (Brooke and Keir 1975, 133).

Parishes of similar configuration are seen in many towns (Fig. 52), but it is a question how often co-operative action is likely to be signalled by the choice of site for the churches themselves. Burgage space was valuable; unless churches were placed in prominent public positions, such as at the angles of cross-roads or in the midst of streets, as some were (see p. 212), their locations must have been governed by the variable willingness of neighbours to grant or rearrange portions of their holdings. Moreover, a neighbourhood church could no doubt be created through the promotion of a pre-existing household chapel. In such a case the church might stand on a secluded, private site, whereas the shape of the parish would reflect later involvement on the part of surrounding householders. Uncertainty is increased by our lack of knowledge about the motives of founders, whether individuals or groups, who may as often have been inspired by hopes of profit as by thoughts of piety. Some churches were probably built as investments. Hence, a churchyard spanning several tenement plots might be a sign of neighbourly co-operation, but it could also reflect the enterprise of a lord, like Colsuen outside Lincoln, who built houses and provided a church as an amenity for his tenants and a source of income to himself. The church of St Martin in Colchester provides a useful illustration of these ambiguities. The large precinct stretches between two parallel streets and appears to occupy the area of two addorsed *mansiones* (see Fig. 46). Did St Martin's originate as a result of private initiative within a single household (the ample grounds being a consequence of later enlargement), a communal undertaking (former tenements being given up), or seigneurial forethought (the churchyard delimited as part of a general scheme of replanning, tenements subsequently respecting it)? Each possibility, or permutation

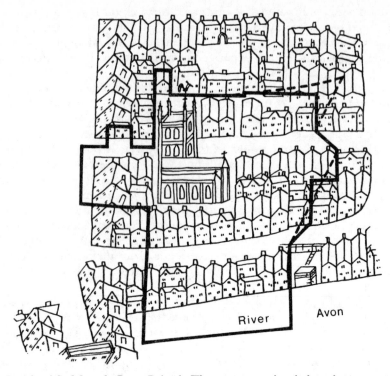

River   Avon

52 Parish of St Mary-le-Port, Bristol. The representation is based upon
Millerd's plan of Bristol (1673) with the outline of the parish as recorded by
Ashmead in 1828 superimposed (*Source*: Watts and Rahtz 1985)

of possibilities, has its own implications for chronology, and significance
for the history of the town.

One other factor which influenced topographical relationships between
churches, *mansiones* and, as we shall shortly see, streets, is that of orientation. In the eleventh and twelfth centuries there are signs of a new concern
with the alignment of churches. This is evident at cathedrals such as
Exeter, Wells and probably York, which were not only rebuilt but also
reoriented after the Conquest. There are signs that similar changes were
made at village level, although whether such realignments were common,
or for that matter were connected with those that affected greater
churches, remains to be seen. The principles which governed ecclesiastical
orientation in early medieval England are not understood. The theory
that churches were commonly aligned towards sunrise on the patronal day
intrigued members of the Cambridge Camden Society in the nineteenth
century and has had its proponents since (Benson 1956; cf. Harvey 1974,
60). Arguably, however, this idea needs to be tested further. It is possible
that a desire for greater strictness in orientation arose out of the Benedictine reforms of the tenth century. Dunstan, an ardent reformer, arch-

bishop of Canterbury (959–88), is said to have corrected the alignment of a new church at Mayfield *Sx* by nudging it with his shoulder. The tale suggests that orientation was a matter upon which the audience of Dunstan's *vita* would expect him to have held firm views. Whatever ideas were then abroad, however, it is clear that builders of small urban churches seldom had sufficient room to put them into practice. Their churches usually had to be fitted into sites that were already circumscribed. In result, urban ecclesiastical alignments were mostly determined by nearby features: property boundaries, buildings and streets. Few town churches looked due east, unless the axes of the town plan as a whole happened to correspond with the cardinal points. Thus in Exeter the majority of medieval churches follow fractional differences in the city layout and face in the region of north-east. At Worcester the chief streets follow curving paths, and the alignments of churches are deflected accordingly. York's churches present an intriguing picture. Some of them, like Holy Trinity Goodramgate, conform to the vector of underlying Roman topography. Others took their cue from nearby streets and properties of the Anglo-Scandinavian city, and are angled this way and that, like so many weather-cocks (see Fig. 41). Similar variation is found elsewhere, so that, in effect, each urban neighbourhood had a ritual east of its own. To a large extent, therefore, the grain of the town plan was a conditioning factor in the matter of whether a church should stand at right-angles or parallel to a street. This in its turn would determine how many *mansiones burgi* were required for the emplacement of a church, and the direction(s) in which an existing site could be enlarged.

Churches had to be accessible to their users. Hence, by their positions in relation to streets, the whereabouts of their doors, subsidiary lines of approach and even the paths taken by processions, churches may provide a commentary upon the topographical and social frameworks of the towns which spawned and accommodated them.

One of the most characteristic positions for an urban church was in the angle of a junction between a major and a minor street. This placed the church in the forefront of neighbourhood life. It gave useful definition to the precinct, allowed access from several directions and did not involve the sacrifice of more lucrative sites at major intersections. St Martin in Micklegate, York, or St George in Stamford are typical examples.

Urban land was valuable, however, and even churches were not exempt from the pressure to maximize the economic potential of property. Apart from the use of churchyards as trading sites (see p. 212), churches themselves were sometimes divided horizontally. St Mary Colechurch in London, for instance, was once at first-floor level and stood over a cellar which later became a tavern. All Hallows Honey Lane was also above a cellar which was occupied separately. St John the Baptist in Bristol is a church of two storeys.

Another convenient place for a church, and perhaps also for trading, was in the triangular space formed between two converging roads. Such sites tended to occur on the edges of towns, typically before a gate, as in the case of St Owen at Hereford. Churches which take this position inside towns, as do All Saints in Northampton or St Swithin in Worcester, may give clues as to the approximate positions of earlier defensive lines.

Churches like St Martin at Carfax in Oxford which stood at important cross-roads were, quite literally, at the hub of local life, and may sometimes reflect co-operation on the part of citizens who founded and maintained them. There may have been an economic motive behind the selection of these sites. In London, where by 1200 some 20 per cent of churches stood at cross-roads, households were assigned to one parish or another on the basis of the distance between their front doors and the door of the church. This method of determination is recorded from the thirteenth century onwards, but it is likely to be older. We know that the same principle was being applied in Gloucester in the 1180s (see p. 226), and it also operated in Winchester (Keene 1985). The procedure by which tithes were assessed gives 'one of the underlying reasons why parish boundaries were established in this way, for tithes in towns were essentially personal payments, paid as a proportion of the rental value of each household and as a charge on wages or commercial profit' (Keene 1985). A cross-roads was thus a favourable position from the point of view of gathering a good number of tithe-paying households. Tithe first appears as a compulsory payment in Athelstan's ordinance on church dues, issued 926 × *c.* 930 (1 Athelstan, Prologue). After *c.* 960 payment of tithe was enforceable by the king's reeve (2 Edgar 3.1).

The economic strength of a cross-roads site could be weakened if other churches were established nearby. Most of the London churches occur singly, but a few stand in pairs. In Gloucester and Bristol there are clumps of churches centred on cross-roads. The members of the Gloucester group may have originated at different times, and only two of them were fully parochial (Heighway 1984, 47–9). In Bristol, on the other hand, the parish churches of All Saints, St Ewan and Christ Church faced each other across the busy intersection of Corn Street and Broad Street. The three therefore stood in the corners of territories which met in the cross-roads itself. Bristol's rise to economic prominence began rather later than most of the towns we have been considering, and it may be that an element of formal parochial apportionment lies behind this arrangement (Fig. 53). It has been suggested that the origins of all three churches may be contemporary with the laying-out of this part of the town, *c.* 1100 (Dawson 1986).

Streets are public places. Churches which actually stood in streets are thus of special interest; their sites are suggestive of corporate rather than private initiative. Two main types can be recognized: churches like St Magnus at the Bridge in London, or St Ruald in Winchester, which projected into busy streets, possibly as a result of encroachment; and those that occupied islands within roadways, with space for passage on all sides.

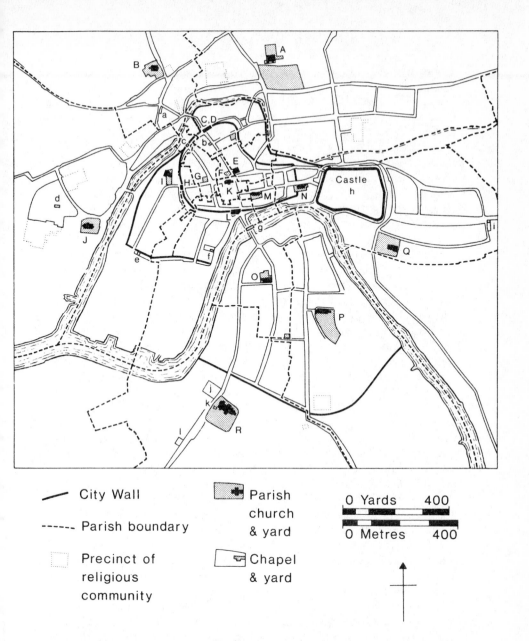

3 Bristol and its churches. **A** St James; **B** St Michael; **C** St Lawrence Bell Lane; **D** St John
he Baptist; **E** Christ Church (alias Holy Trinity); **F** St Ewan Broad Street; **G** St Werburgh;
I St Leonard Corn Street; **I** St Stephen; **J** St Augustine the Less; **K** All Saints (All
Hallows) Corn Street; **L** St Nicholas Nicholas Street; **M** St Mary le Port (*cf.* Fig. 52);
St Peter; **O** St Thomas Martyr; **P** Holy Cross; **Q** SS Philip and Jacob; **R** St Mary
edcliffe. Chapels: **a** Three Kings of Cologne; **b** St George; **c** St Giles; **d** St Jordan;
St Clement; **f** St John the Evangelist; **g** Assumption of the Virgin Mary; **h** St Martin
astle chapel); **i** Holy Trinity; **j** hospital of St John the Baptist; **k** Holy Spirit; **l** hospital of
Mary Magdalene (*Source*: Dawson 1986)

Street-island churches occur widely. They are found, for example, in York (All Saints Pavement), Stamford (All Saints in the Market) and Wallingford (St Mary the More). London offers four: St Michael le Quern, which stood in the Cornmarket, St Audoen in Newgate Street, All Hallows Fenchurch Street and St Clement Danes (see p. 176). At Canterbury a church dedicated to St Andrew was built in the middle row of The Parade before 1086. St Runwald in Colchester reminds us that it is not always self-evident that such churches were originally built out in the open; the position of St Runwald's has been plausibly explained as a result of the part-demolition of properties along a frontage that formerly adjoined it, in order to create a large marketplace (Crummy 1981, 53, 61, Fig. 53).

Island sites seem to have been particularly fashionable in towns of the south-west Midlands. There were at least two in Gloucester, for instance, and two, possibly three, in Hereford. At Gloucester the old minster of St Peter retained control over rights of burial until well after the street churches had been built, and it is possible that the street was considered to be a convenient place to build a church because no burial ground was needed. Some other street churches, such as St Andrew in Canterbury, lacked graveyards, or else acquired land in another part of the town. The funerals of St Runwald's parishioners in Colchester, for example, were held in a detached cemetery some distance from the church. However, while willingness to forgo a graveyard around the church may have played some part, it is not likely to have been a dominant influence, except perhaps in the case of parochial chapels. Some churches on island sites did have their own graveyards, and churches are found in the streets of towns like Stamford and Wallingford where it seems there were no prestigious old minsters with extensive vested interests.

The uniting factor in the great majority of cases is that the streets concerned contained markets. This could be for no other reason than that street-markets tended to be broad and therefore provided room for building. There is, however, a more elaborate theory which states that many markets originated outside church doors and in churchyards, and that some of these sites grew into street-markets, or led to the formation of a proper marketplace nearby.

That some early medieval churchyards were used for trading is not in doubt (Salzman 1931, 124–5). In Lincoln, for instance, there was a skin-market near St Peter Stanthacket, and a cloth-market between Michaelgate and Parchemingate in the parish of St Michael. These markets seem to have been in the churchyards of St Peter and St Michael until an order of 1223 commanded their removal into streets (J.W.F. Hill 1948, 154). In 1285 the Statute of Winchester, 'for the Honour of the Church', prohibited the holding of fairs and markets in churchyards. The precincts of churches provided good opportunities for markets not only because they were open spaces, but also because they attracted regular gatherings of people (Sawyer 1981, 160). Sunday markets were common.

Attempts to ban Sunday trading by Athelstan (925–39) show that the practice was already normal in the first half of the tenth century (2 Athelstan 24; cf. 5 Æthelred 13, 6 Æthelred 22, 44).

Marketplaces are often found next to churchyards in small towns which grew up in the twelfth and thirteenth centuries. At Toddington *Bd*, for instance, a large marketplace adjoined the churchyard and may well have developed out of it. Some churches may have been granted market rights of supervision. Whether churches in cities like York and London assisted in the *formation* of market-streets is, however, doubtful. Street-sited churches do not seem as a rule to have been more important or venerable than their numerous counterparts elsewhere in provincial cities, and it is difficult to see why they alone should have stimulated commercial activity to an extent that necessitated the replanning of their surroundings. In the great towns it is arguable that local churches were normally added to markets rather than the cause of them, although some, like St Mary the More in Wallingford, may have been established at the same time as the marketplace was set out. Dedications to saints such as Clement and Nicholas, or to less familiar figures like Owen, Runwald and Sampson (York) support this view, for these cults became fashionable towards and after the end of the Anglo-Saxon era. Moreover, the building of parochial chapels in marketplaces after 1100, as in the cases of St Mary at Barton-upon-Humber *Hu* (*Li*), St Mary Lichfield *St.* or St Piran at Cardiff, demonstrates that this topographical tradition was very much alive in the twelfth century (Figs 54, 55). Hereford and Gloucester grew strongly in the period c. 1050–1150. Their island churches may bespeak a fashion which was then at its height.

Churches were not the only buildings to be put in streets. Gildhalls and market-houses commonly take this position as well, as for instance in Leeds *WY*, originally at Wigford in Lincoln or Chard *So* (Fig. 56). Since it is possible that some urban churches were founded by gilds, it is tempting to postulate the gild as a common factor. Gilds certainly existed in late Saxon England. They are attested by surviving regulations from Cambridge, Exeter and elsewhere (*EHD* 1, 557). At least three churches in Winchester were associated with gildhalls (Biddle and Keene 1976, 333). Could it be that some street churches originally performed a dual role, being used by gilds both for worship and as places of assembly? Campbell's suggestion that churches 'may indeed in their early days have fulfilled some of the functions of public houses and have been needed as much for general social purposes as for worship' deserves to be taken seriously. As Campbell observes, surviving gild regulations from the late pre-Conquest period suggest that 'the membership of gilds and the supporting of priests, the hearing of masses and the eating of dinners, were things which all went together' (1975, 22, n. 87). This socio-religious aspect will be discussed again, in Chapter 9, in the context of the later Middle Ages. Perhaps some parish churches originated as they later come to seem: as buildings frequented by fraternities which amounted to co-

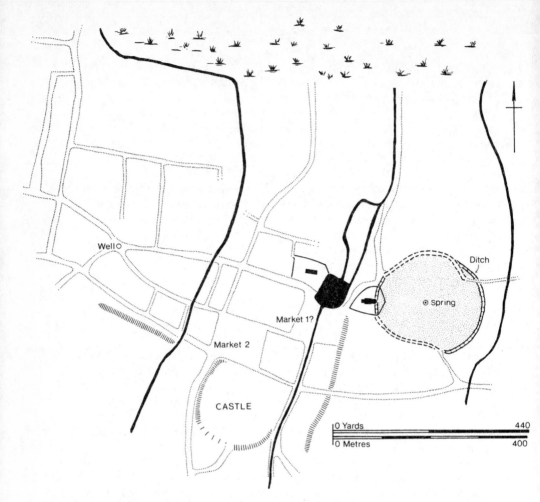

Labels within map: Well ○, Ditch, ⊙ Spring, Market 1?, Market 2, CASTLE, 0 Yards 440, 0 Metres 400

54 Barton-upon-Humber, Humberside (Lincolnshire). Interpretation of historic topography based upon survey of 1796 and Rodwell and Rodwell 1982.

operative chantries as well as social clubs. Is this why places like York and Norwich spawned so many churches – because of their social diversity, which prompted groups of neighbours to unite?

One of the consequences of building a church in the middle of a street was that it set a precedent. It is notable how often other buildings came to be erected nearby, usually in the lee of the church, converting what was formerly a broad street into a middle row of properties with narrow lateral roads to either side. Such infilling is well seen to the west of All Saints in Hereford, All Saints Pavement in York, beside St Mary the More in Wallingford, and Holy Trinity in the marketplace at Richmond *NY*.

Churches were often built upon or beside town gates and walls. Oxford, Wallingford, Wareham and several other *burhs* possessed gate churches. Three of the city gates at Winchester had superincumbent churches. One of them, St Swithin Kingsgate, still exists. Churches also stood at the en-

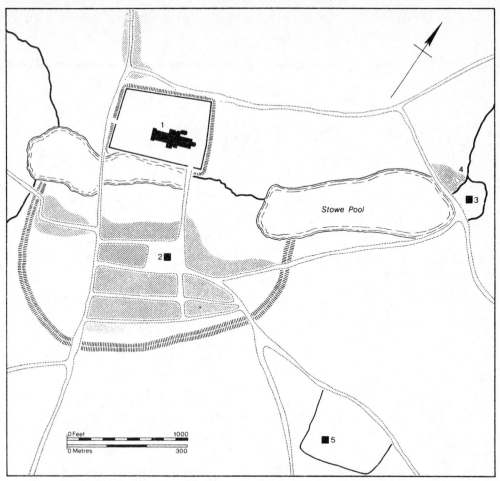

55 Lichfield, Staffordshire. **1** cathedral; **2** St Mary, within marketplace of twelfth-century planned settlement; **3** St Michael; **4** spring; **5** Franciscan friary. (*Source*: Bassett 1980–1)

trances to Winchester's suburbs (Keene 1975, 78; Biddle and Keene 1976, 333; Keene 1985). In twelfth-century Bristol the churches of St Leonard and St Nicholas stood over the west and south gates respectively, while at the north gate there were two churches, St Lawrence and St John the Baptist, arranged in tandem (see Fig. 53). St Lawrence was demolished after 1580. St John the Baptist survives. It is integral with the town wall, and is likely to have been founded when the inner town wall was built *c.* 1100. The church was rebuilt in the fourteenth and fifteenth centuries, and the north gate of the town is actually under the west tower (Dawson 1986). At Exeter the church of St Mary Steps stood beside the south-west gate; a parochial chapel dedicated to St Bartholomew occupied the corresponding site at the north-east gate. Holy Trinity stood a few yards from the south-east entrance to the town (see Fig. 47). St Kyneburgh watched over comings and goings through the south-west gate at Gloucester.

215

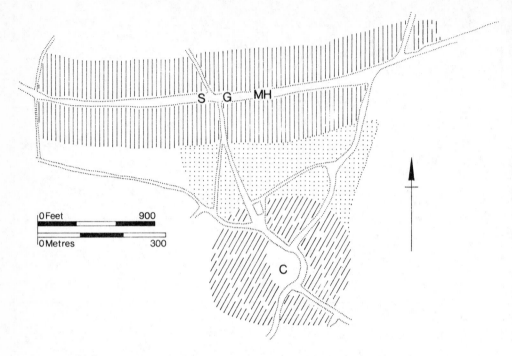

56 Chard, Somerset. Diagram of town layout, showing street-sited buildings and parish church within earlier nucleus. **MH** = market house; **G** = gildhall; **C** = church; **S** = shambles (market stalls) (*Source*: Aston and Leech 1977)

Churches are also found upon or close to gates inside towns, typically near the entrances to precincts of religious communities.

Several different groups of factors may lie behind these choices of site. Gates could be used as convenient reference points for primary sub-divisions of the intra-mural area. Most of the city gates at Canterbury had churches upon or beside them by the twelfth century (Fig. 57). St Edmund Ridingate was probably founded before 1100. St Mary Queningate was ex-tant by 1166. The site of St Michael Burgate has been lost, but may originally have been over the gate itself, as in the case of St Mary North-gate. Holy Cross was above the west gate until its removal to a nearby site in the late 1370s. The gates have been regarded as the pivots of a system of urban wards known as *berthae* (Tatton-Brown 1980). According to the *Historia de Sancto Cuthberto*, king Ecgfrith (670–85) gave Cuthbert an estate in York which comprised 'all the land that lies from the wall of St Peter's church to the great west gate, and from the wall of St Peter's church to the city wall towards the south' (Harrison 1960, 234; Arnold 1885, 199). This early urban estate can be reconstructed in general terms (Fig. 58).

In spiritual terms a gate, as was a bridge, might be the scene of some

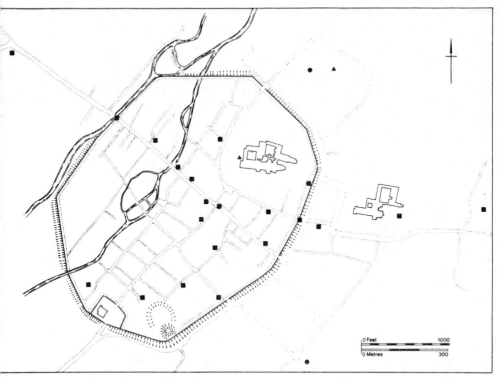

57 Canterbury and its churches (*Source*: Canterbury Archaeological Trust 1982)

rite de passage where a traveller invoked divine protection for a forthcoming journey, or expressed gratitude for one just safely completed. For allied reasons, gates may have been profitable locations for churches. In addition to their ordinary revenues, and any income which may have accrued as a result of their proximity to extra-mural trading sites (cf. Keene 1975, 71, 73), such churches are likely to have attracted offerings from those who were newly arrived or on the point of departure. These aspects could be reinforced by the choice of suitable patron saints. St Michael, being a saint of high places, and a protector, was appropriate for churches which were raised above the ground. Another popular gateside dedicatee was St Martin. Examples include the church which formerly stood over Burgate in Canterbury, Wareham *Do* (Fig. 59) and Ludgate in London. A church dedicated in Winchester between 934 and *c.* 939 stood by the west gate. This has been tentatively identified as St Martin-in-the-Ditch (Biddle and Keene 1976, 329–30). Some of these dedications may recollect an episode in the *Vita Martini*. While still a soldier Martin had divided his cloak for the benefit of a beggar. The gift was made at a city gate.

The presence of so many dedications to St Botolph beside gates, bridges and at the edges of town is not easy to explain. Botolph was an ascetic

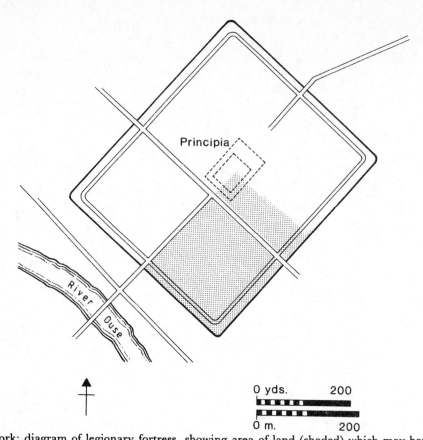

Principia

River Ouse

0 yds. 200

0 m. 200

58 York: diagram of legionary fortress, showing area of land (shaded) which may have been delineated by an alleged grant to Cuthbert by king Ecgfrith of 'all the land that lies from the wall of St Peter's church to the great west gate, and from the wall of St Peter's church to the city wall towards the south' (*Historia de Sancto Cuthberto*, 199; trans. Harrison 1960, 234). Earlier attempts to interpret this grant (which, though possibly not authentic, is recorded in a pre-Conquest source) have assumed that the pre-Conquest cathedral, like its present successor, lay due east-west. Excavations under York minster between 1967 and 1972 did not disclose the pre-Conquest cathedral, but extensive remains of a cemetery were found (Phillips 1985). Burials within this graveyard were oriented south-west/north-east: that is, in accord with the long axis of the remains of the underlying Roman fortress. Since the fortress lies at about 45 degrees to the cardinal points of the compass, there are in principle two 'souths' and two 'wests' to be considered. The 'great west gate' referred to in the grant might therefore have stood either on the north-west flank of the fortress, or in the south-west wall, facing the River Ouse. Being the 'great' gate, the latter position might be preferred, not least because the road running from it led westward. If the early cathedral lay somewhere close to the heart of the fortress, this might also explain the second part of the grant, which refers not to a gate, but to the city wall: it will be seen from the diagram that the fortress was characteristically of rectangular, not square, plan. Although this interpretation would establish one ordinate of the pair described, it does not of course define the north-easterly limit, which could lie anywhere other than along the *via principalis* (the road that runs across the fortress from gate to gate). The limit shown here is therefore a speculation. There is, however, a clue that this is on the right lines. In the twelfth century the Community of St Cuthbert held three churches in York. Their positions are shown in Fig. 41. One lies within the quadrant shown here, the others just outside it, the parish of one of them including a portion of the relevant area. How the church within the fortress (Holy Trinity Goodramgate) came into Durham's possession is unclear

monastic leader who flourished in East Anglia around the third quarter of the seventh century. Later enthusiasm for Botolph's cult was strongest in East Anglia and the hinterland of the fens (Fig. 60). No doubt this reflects some memory of the site of Botolph's monastery at *Icanho*, probably Iken *Sf* (Martin 1978; West *et al.* 1984), and more particularly the later whereabouts of his relics, which had once been at Peterborough, and were later taken by Æthelwold, bishop of Winchester (963-84), who distributed them between Ely, Thorney and king Edgar. Folcard's biography of Botolph, written at Thorney in the late 1060s, gave publicity to a cult that was already popular. This can be said because the name of the saint had found its way into English toponymy. Botolph Bridge, for instance, is a name which occurs twice in the Domesday record of the county of Huntingdon, and similar names are found elsewhere: for example at Bramber *Sx* and *Sandtun*, next to Lympne *K*.

The connection with bridges is significant, for by the end of the eleventh century Botolph seems to have been regarded as a patron saint of boundaries and, by extension, of travel and trade. Three of London's gates were accompanied by churches dedicated to him, and a fourth St Botolph stood next to the waterfront at Billingsgate, where merchants from Flanders, Normandy and the Rhineland were paying tolls around 1000 (Robertson 1925, 71-9). A large church dedicated to Botolph stood at the southern tip of Wigford, Lincoln. Not only did this mark the limit of the city, but it stood on the frontier between Kesteven and the ancient kingdom of Lindsey. Hadstock, where there is a pre-Conquest minster dedicated to Botolph (Rodwell 1976), stands on the boundary between Essex and Cambridgeshire. These liminal associations are intriguing, and it is interesting to see that urban churches which were dedicated to Botolph abroad often occupy similar positions. St Botolph at Viborg in Denmark stood on the edge of the medieval town (Neilsen 1965). At Lund the church is almost central. Lund's origin as a settlement dates to *c.* 990. However, the church was later placed close to the site of the principal meeting-place of the first market settlement (Blomqvist 1951; Blomqvist and Mårtensson 1963). Here, perhaps, is a clue to the combination of liminal and mercantile associations that Botolph sites so often present. Boundaries were appropriate locations for trading, markets and fairs. Botolph's feast day was 17 June: close to midsummer, and the start of the season for great regional fairs. In England few fairs achieved greater renown than that held at Boston *Li* - literally 'Botolph's stone' - which had its origins as an international port around the end of the eleventh century.

Churches which clung to town walls, like All Hallows London Wall, St Alphege and St Augustine Papey in London, or St Clement in Worcester, might be looked upon as saintly bastions, providing a holy shield for citizens within. Around 1195 the monk Lucian wrote in just these terms about the church of Holy Trinity at Chester (Alldridge 1981, 25-8). Lucian's perception was not then new. Writing of Lyon in the sixth cen-

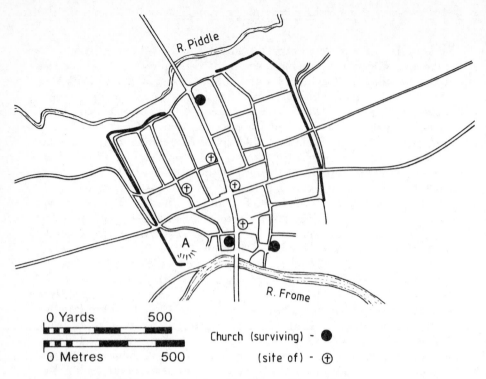

R. Piddle

R. Frome

| 0 Yards | 500 |
| 0 Metres | 500 |

Church (surviving) - ●

(site of) - ⊕

59 Wareham (Dorset) and its churches (*Source*: Keen 1984)

tury, Avitus of Vienne had described it as a city 'protected more by its basilicas than by its bastions' (Avitus, *Hom.* 24). Holy Trinity was one of three churches in Chester which stood atop the sites of former Roman gate towers. The others were St Bride and St Michael, which faced each other across the south gate. A church of St Bride occupies the main gateway of the old Roman fort at Kirkbride *Cu* (Bellhouse and Richardson 1982), and there used to be a church known alternatively as Holy Trinity and Christ Church on or beside the site of the *porta principalis sinistra* of the legionary fortress at York. The origins of the York church, as of the others, are obscure, but a late tradition asserted that the gate-block had once been the site of a residence of the Scandinavian rulers of York. This is possible: when first heard of, in 1268, the church was referred to as being *in curia regis* 'in the king's court' (*Reg. Giffard*, 192).

No doubt there were practical reasons for placing churches on gates or next to walls. Roman gate-blocks were robust, and their upper storeys could be converted to ecclesiastical use. Where a church was built against existing defences, the founders might make use of the town wall as one side of their building. This is illustrated in a remarkable way at St Mary Northgate in Canterbury. Here, a length of city wall was incorporated as part of a nave which was added in the twelfth century to a pre-existing chancel above the Roman north gate. The north wall of the church is thus

60 Distribution of churches dedicated to St Botolph. All the dedications shown are thought to be older than the nineteenth century, but note that dedications made at different times are here gathered into a single distribution

the Roman city wall which has been heightened. Traces of crenellation are yet visible (Tatton-Brown 1978, 80–1).

In towns of Roman background one might expect the dates at which gate churches were founded to reflect the times at which former gates regained their importance as urban locales. When the tempo of urban life quickened, traffic increased, and *portgerefan* became vigilant, conditions for the foundation of gate churches would be created. The consecration ceremony beside the west gate at Winchester in the 930s, mentioned above, may thus have a bearing upon the progress of Winchester's expansion in the tenth century. But there may have been other, even contrary, factors. In London several old interval towers were used intermittently as the abodes of hermits (J. Schofield 1984, 69–70). It may be wondered if similar occupations elsewhere could have prompted the establishment of churches on sites that were remembered as being holy. Religious communities, too, may have provided examples which were subsequently imitated in towns. St Peter-on-the-Wall at Bradwell *Ex* lies across the line of the west wall of a Roman Shore fort. The church is thought to flank, or possibly to override, the site of the west gate (Rigold 1977, 72–3). The original context here was monastic, never urban, although seventh-century Bradwell was the site of an episcopal see and counted as a *civitas* in the terminology of Bede (*HE* iii.22; cf. Campbell 1979). The late Stuart Rigold saw St Peter's not as the principal church of the monastic community, but as a *capella ad portas*, approachable both from within and without, added at a later date. An arrangement like this might be regarded as having been in some way ancestral to the urban tradition. The tradition, at any rate, was venerable. At Le Mans around 624 Bertram, a bishop, willed land to a church (of St Michael) which he had recently built in *dextra parte de posteriola* 'in the dextral part of the gate'.

In this chapter we have seen how the multiplication of small churches created local units of pastoral care. Commonly these units were co-extensive with the secular interests of the people who founded or maintained the churches. The proliferation of private churches was facilitated by the fact that they were not yet in any strict sense *parish* churches. In so far as 'parish' has any meaning for us before the eleventh century it applies to the rights which pertained to the mother churches or old minsters which had grown up on royal, episcopal and comital estates. Sometimes portions of these rights were waived or reassigned in favour of a local church, but as long as the owners of small churches made no sustained effort to divert income away from minsters there was in theory no limit upon the number of new churches that might be built.

As just described the pattern seems static, but of course it was not. Relationships between minsters and lesser churches always had potential for change. Nor did the system exist everywhere in the same way. Some minsters were weak or in decline before 1000; others remained assertive until 1200 or later. In general, however, the eleventh century was the time when old minsters were coming to be displaced by lesser churches in economic power. This created uncertainties. In 1092 Wulfstan, bishop of Worcester, convened a meeting 'of all the wisest persons of the three shires of our diocese, namely Worcestershire, Gloucestershire and Warwickshire' in order to investigate a dispute which had arisen between two priests in Worcester, 'namely Alfnoth, priest of St Helena's and Ala, priest of St Alban's, concerning the parishes and customary rights of their churches'. After three days a committee delegated to examine the matter reported that although there were a number of churches in Worcester 'in the whole city . . . there was no parish which did not pertain to the motherchurch', that is to the cathedral priory of St Mary (*EHD* 2, 624–6). It was a pedantic decision, and one that could hardly have been applied in cities like Lincoln and Norwich, which had already been festooned with small churches by their citizens, and where there had been no reformed monasteries before the Conquest with substantial interests to protect. Archaeology shows us that the small churches of Cambridge, Lincoln, Norwich and York possessed burial grounds from the moment of their establishment, whereas the lesser churches of Winchester, Gloucester and Hereford for the most part did not. The distinction here is perhaps between towns with dominant mother minsters that maintained a paramount right to spiritualities, and towns where the rights of minsters had been seriously curtailed. Lincoln probably had at least one minster before *c.* 925. It is tentatively identified with the church of St Martin, on the grounds that for a fleeting period there was a silver St Martin's coinage, similar to the St Peter's money which was minted in York (Dolley 1978, 27; Stewart 1967). But by 1086 the former importance of this church seems to have been forgotten, although it left its mark in the form of a large, central parish.

The periods and rates at which small churches multiplied must have varied from place to place. In Lincoln and York it is likely that large numbers had come into existence before 1000. Too few churches have been excavated for us to be sure of this, but churches like St Mark in Lincoln and St Helen-on-the-Walls at York were present by the second half of the tenth century. The fact that these churches seem to have been of no more than average importance makes it unlikely that they stood alone. St Mark occupied a place midway down a ladder of parishes in Wigford. It is hard to see how this position could have been reached unless most of the neighbouring units were established at about the same time. St Mark's began as a small wooden building in a cemetery which was enlarged in the eleventh century (Fig. 61).

Proliferation in Winchester may have started sooner than in Lincoln. Three out of the five parish churches which have been excavated existed before 1000; two of them may have originated before 950, and there is written evidence for the consecration of a church in an inner suburb before 940.

Ecclesiastical growth in Norwich is difficult to measure. Only two

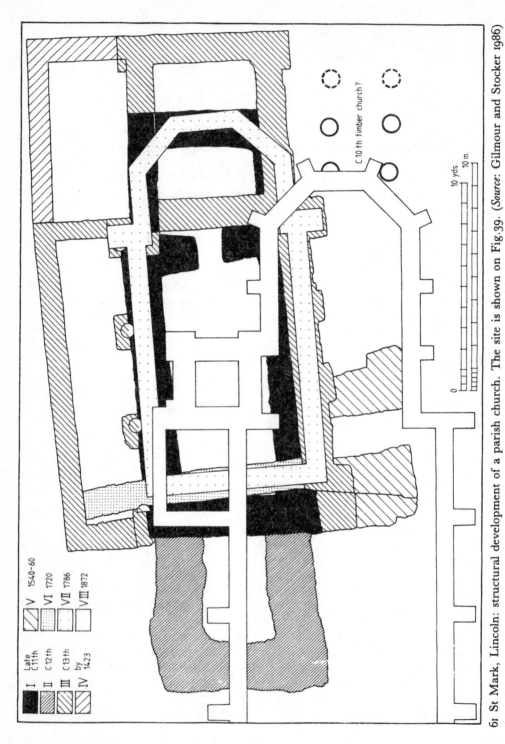

61 St Mark, Lincoln: structural development of a parish church. The site is shown on Fig.39. (*Source:* Gilmour and Stocker 1986)

churches have been fully excavated. St Benedict's was probably built late in the eleventh century, although evidence was noted for the presence of graves that preceded this structure (Roberts and Atkin 1982). The other church is highly significant, for the Normans destroyed it in order to make way for their castle at the end of the eleventh century (Ayers 1985). Similar disappearances of otherwise unrecorded churches are known elsewhere (e.g. from Cambridge) and may mean that we are underestimating rather than exaggerating the scale of pre-Conquest growth. However this may be, it is possible that Norwich acquired the majority of its churches in the eleventh century, perhaps especially in the period *c.* 1050-1100, and that churchfounding was latterly stifled by the imposition of parochial discipline. Thetford, by contrast, was already in decline by 1100: a sure sign that most of its twenty or so churches had originated in earlier decades.

The pattern of ecclesiastical growth in London remains uncertain. Archaeological work of various kinds has taken place at at least eleven of its churches since 1960, but only three or four of these projects were sufficiently extensive to shed light upon the issues which have been discussed here (Grimes 1968, 173-99, 203-9). Full results from the most complete excavation - of St Nicholas Shambles - have not yet been published, but it appears that the church originated in the eleventh century. Given London's pre-eminence one would expect a considerable rate of churchfounding in the tenth century. But this remains to be demonstrated.

Urban growth in the late Saxon period is measurable not only by the multiplication of churches, but also by their enlargement. Between the mid-tenth and late eleventh century the nave floor area of St Mark's in Lincoln increased by about 350 per cent. In Winchester the nave areas of St Mary in Tanner Street and St Pancras grew by 140 per cent and 181 per cent respectively. Expansion of St Michael in Thetford was of the order of 200 per cent. The simple explanation for these enlargements would be that there were more people to cater for. This may also explain why churches which were originally unicellular started to acquire chancels, as at St Helen-on-the-Walls in York: if altar, priest and people were in one room, removal of the altar into a new chancel would be a way of releasing additional space in the nave. However, the strong likelihood that there were more people to be accommodated by 1100 than there had been a century before may not be the only reason why churches were enlarged. It has been suggested that some churches were founded for private or household use and subsequently acquired a more public, neighbourhood function. If this happened, then presumably the buildings concerned would have been extended at the time of transition.

The building of larger, more permanent churches could also reflect an increasing consciousness of, and confidence in, the emerging institution of the parish. Wulfstan's uncertainty as to the precise definition of what a parish was could be taken as a measure of the extent to which local pastoral units had already assumed a practical significance in people's minds. England, and especially her older towns, was now packed with small local churches, and the great majority of them were soon to be accorded the status of *matrix ecclesia* 'mother church'. To each would pertain a series of rights belonging to the living and the dead. Such rights – to baptize, to marry, to bury, to a variety of customary dues and obligations, and to tithe – provided the parish with both a pastoral purpose and the economic basis for its continued presence. Parish boundaries now came to matter greatly, for upon their lines depended the directions in which revenues would go. Whereas early in the eleventh century archbishop Wulfstan (1002–16) had found it necessary to remind priests that it was wrong for them to lure another's parishioner in order to acquire extra income, in the twelfth century boundaries could be disputed down to the last yard. The precision that was now sought is illustrated by a dispute which arose in Gloucester over the parochial allegiance of one Richard Rufus. In the 1180s Rufus bought two adjoining houses which happened to stand either side of the boundary between the parishes of All Saints and St John. Rufus knocked the houses into a single dwelling, which now lay athwart the frontier. After discussion it was agreed that as the front door of the combined house was in the parish of All Saints, and because Rufus had formerly been accustomed to go to All Saints for the sacrament, two-thirds of his oblations were to go to All Saints and the remaining one-third to the priest of St John's, presumably by way of compensation for the revenue that had been lost from the former household (D. Walker 1976, no. 11). The details of this episode are additionally interesting for the way in which they shed light on the concept of the parish as originating in a system of personal allegiances; presumably it was through such affiliations that parishes acquired their tettirorial identity, and boundaries came to be defined.

Charters of the twelfth century start to go into minute detail when they record transactions in towns that were likely to have repercussions for parochial rights. Between 1161 and 1184 the abbot of St Mary's abbey in York made a grant to the hospital of St Peter of rights belonging to the church of St Olave (which had been founded a little over a century before) in a piece of land in *vico Sancti Egidii* 'in St Giles-gate'. (The St Giles in question was a suburban church of more recent foundation; St Giles was a popular dedicatee in the late eleventh and twelfth centuries, and churches bearing his name are consequently often found in extra-mural locations, not infrequently (as at Oxford, and here at York) in close proximity to suburban markets.) The land was to be used for building. Its dimensions were scrupulously described. The grant was contingent upon an annual render of 3 lb of pepper and 1 lb of incense, due on Christmas Eve, and with the condition that the occupants of the land should visit St Olave's as their *matrix ecclesia* 'mother church' on the patronal day (*EYC* 1, no. 276). The years of informality and free-for-all in the founding of local churches were over. An age of regulation had begun.

VI

MOTTES, MOATS,
AND MANORS

On 13 April 1403 Richard Clifford, bishop of Worcester (1401-7), exercised his power to apportion revenues from the parish church of Kidderminster *Wo* for the support of its vicar. Clifford took this action because Kidderminster's church had earlier been appropriated to the priory of Maiden Bradley. The priory was enjoying income from the church, and had appointed a vicar to attend to the cure of souls within the parish. But the financial position of the vicar was insecure. So Clifford stepped in. He ruled that the vicar should have a decent residence

> with barn, stable, dovecote and another small house with a yard lying along another part of the street opposite the manse and a meadow called Smalemead with a croft adjacent and all tithes of hay and sheaves of every sowing between the Stour and Dernford and the tithe of hay of the vill of Nethermitton and a croft annexed to the cemetery of the church called Colvercroft containing two acres, and three crofts which are called Dodlescroft by Whitmarsh. The vicar shall have all kinds of small tithes throughout the parish of calves, milk, cheese, apples, flax, hemp, onions, garlic, doves, pigs, geese, vineyards, fisheries, honey, eggs, hens, bees, grazing of pastures, of barley and of gardens and yards wherever sown and of mills in the parish and every kind of oblation in the church of Kidderminster and elsewhere in the parish and obventions of wax and mortuary offerings where death occurred within the parish together with grass growing in the cemetery and trimmings of the trees, also the offerings in Lent that are customarily entered in the lenten roll from old time. They [i.e. the vicar and his successors] shall have the

tithes of lambs' wool and fallen wood anywhere in the parish except in the woods of the priory of Maiden Bradley.

(Reg. Clifford no. 231; trans. Smith 1976, 133–4)

A parish was a unit of pastoral care. But it was also an area which at the outset was expected to be self-sufficient in providing the resources to maintain its church, care for the poor and support its priest. Hence the emphasis upon tithe. Tithe could be exacted upon virtually anything: crops, livestock, timber, salt, fisheries, minerals; or, in towns, profits, rents and services. The parochial system was sustained by the land. The conception of the parish as a closely definable territory arose not only so that individuals should know which church to attend for the sacraments, but also that they should be sure of the correct destination for their tithes, dues and offerings, and, at the end, their corpses and mortuary fees.

Parishes were formed by the partitioning of earlier areas of jurisdiction, a process which if it were to be traced in reverse would ultimately lead back to the largest unit of all: the *parochia* of the bishop, his diocese. The mechanisms of subdivision were not uniform but varied from place to place. In Chapter 3 we noted the widespread presence of churches which by the tenth century had come to be known as *ealdan mynsters*. We saw that many, though by no means all of these churches were indeed of ancient origin. Old minsters had ruled parishes which by later standards were large, and within which they laid claim to a range of privileges and dues. In Chapter 4 it was argued that from the later ninth century there was an increasing trend towards localism in the structure of ecclesiastical provision. A leading part in this process was taken by local lords who founded churches on their own estates. Some of these men took care to seek the consent of the minster. Others acted unilaterally, and by so doing could occasion argument and confusion. It was not always obvious how the financial and jurisdictional rights of existing churches would be affected by new ones. The compilers of law codes attempted clarification. Tithe, churchscot and soulscot were reserved to the old minster. If, however, a lord had a church with a graveyard on his bookland, one-third of his personal tithes could be paid into his own church (2 Edgar 1, 2). A measure of independence was therefore conceded to local churches which stood on land held by charter, and, for some, burial in the cemeteries of such churches was legitimized.

By no means all of the new churches which were established in the tenth and eleventh centuries were intruders or trespassers. Foundations made with the agreement of the old minster have been mentioned. One way in which co-operation could work was when a new church established by a layman was served by a member of the minster community who was seconded for the purpose. An arrangement of this sort was recorded in the charters of the minster at Christchurch *Ha*.

In *c.* 1110 a priest there recalled how, in 1070 × 98, one Ælfric the Small had obtained leave from Godric dean of Christchurch to found a church within the *parochia*, and how Godric appointed 'a certain priest of Christchurch called Elwi' to serve it periodically.

(Blair 1985, 127–8; citing Hase 1975, 211–16)

On other occasions the minster itself was responsible for the creation of additional churches within its territory: a practice which may have been administratively attractive, as a way of devolving burial and the collection of dues to local centres while safeguarding the minster's title to them.

For as long as established churches continued to be jostled by newcomers the ecclesiastical pattern remained fluid. But after 1100 the founding of new churches was decreasing and arrangements began to stabilize. Anomalies were ironed out, disputes were settled by agreement, or episcopal or royal intervention. This phase of negotiation is better documented than the free-for-all which seems to have prevailed earlier. By the reign of Henry 11 (1154–89) the great majority of medieval parish churches were in place, and by 1200 the great majority of their parishes had been defined.

From a secular standpoint the formation of parishes could involve factors apart from questions to do with ecclesiastical jurisdiction. Parishes were superimposed upon a landscape that was already criss-crossed by political, administrative and tenurial divisions. Some of these boundaries may have been ancient (Bonney 1976). Others were more recent (Cam 1944; Roffe 1984). Whatever their age, there was a natural tendency for parishes to observe those of them that happened to be conveniently placed. One of the simplest ways in which this could happen was when a landlord founded a church, and the area served by the church was regarded as being co-extensive with his estate. It is tempting to suppose that the boundaries of most parishes preserve outlines of pre-Conquest landholding. In a limited sense this is probably true, but it is important to appreciate that landholding was always in a state of transition, and that parishes in their formative stages could be affected by changes of tenure. An incident recorded in Domesday Book for Suffolk is instructive. Nigel, a lord, 'invaded' eleven acres of land belonging to the manor of Stow and attached them to the manor of Combs. In result, twelve sokemen who had formerly attended the church at Stow found themselves transferred into the parish of Combs. This illustrates how in the eleventh century the parochial allegiances of many people could be determined not only by where they lived, but also through the affiliation of their lord. Elsewhere, episodes of encroachment, amalgamation or division of holdings would have continued to exert a distortive influence upon parish areas until the later twelfth century, when parishes were removed from the realm of secular tenure and their boundaries frozen. Even then, the framework was by no means rigid. Although most parish boundaries had been finalized before 1200, this did not preclude later adjustments. The extent to which parishes reflect units of landholding in the eleventh century or earlier is therefore a matter which calls for a cautious approach – not least for the further reason that evidence for the precise positions of parish boundaries is often not forthcoming until the eighteenth or nineteenth century.

While some parishes originated as the ecclesiastical counterparts of single estates, there were others which embraced not one manor but several. Multi-manorial parishes were the norm over much of Lincolnshire and Nottinghamshire, for example, and they were at least as common as single-estate parishes in Northamptonshire (Roffe 1984, 118; C.C.Taylor 1983, 150). The processes whereby several manors were gathered into one parish are usually obscure. In some places the parish may be the ghost of an early estate which was later subdivided. In others the parish could have been formed by co-operation between the lords of adjoining manors. Domesday Book shows that in the late eleventh century many churches were being held jointly. Often the division was a half, but quarters were not unusual, and other fractions were recorded, such as the fifth at Higham or the two-thirds at Saxham *Sf*. It must, of course, be remembered that shares in churches could be created, and that they could be transferred by purchase, exchange, gift or bequest. Domesday references to the multiple ownership of churches are thus not necessarily to be regarded as signs that the churches concerned had more than one founder. Nevertheless, the principle is clear enough.

A third way in which several manors could come to be contained in a single parish is that more communities than we realize may originally have possessed churches, but that some of these churches were closed and their territories amalgamated with those of the churches that survived. Such a process seems to have occurred at Raunds *Np*, where archaeologists have excavated a church that was founded *c.* 875 × *c.* 925 and had ceased to function before 1200. About 250 yards away there is another church, which continues in use. Although it is possible that the remaining church was built to replace the one that was closed, it is equally realistic to visualize the two as having existed together. Two manors were recorded at Raunds in 1086. One may have been centred on a site that adjoins the remaining church. The other appears to have been associated with the church that disappeared. In the fourteenth century the manor house was rebuilt on the site of the church, and incorporated some of its remains (Cadman 1983, 120–2; Cadman and Foard 1984) (Fig. 62). Raunds was not the only place where archaeology has shown that prior to 1200 there was more than one church. Excavations at Barrow *Hu (Li)*, Potterne *Wi*, Winwick *M (La)* and Pontefract *WY* have shown that existing parish churches were either preceded or accompanied by other churches on different sites (Davey 1964; Freke 1982; Wilmot 1986). Aerial photography has contributed further examples. References to multiple provision are sometimes found in written records. Documents of the twelfth and thirteenth centuries mention the presence of a *capella* dedicated to St Bega in the parish of Kirkby Ouseburn *NY(YW)*. The site of this church awaits discovery, but it is clear from the context in which it is mentioned that St Bega's stood quite close to the existing parish church. St Bega's cannot

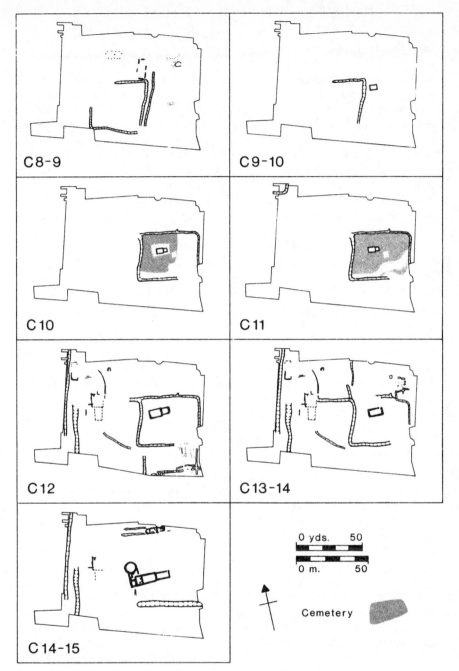

62 Raunds, Northamptonshire. Development of a local church between *c.* 900 and the twelfth century, when it passed out of use. Note how the outline of the cemetery appears to have been influenced by earlier features. Burial began near the church early in the tenth century and was subsequently extended to other parts of the site. The small open area close to the south-east corner of the church marks the site of a grave which was made at an early stage in the development of the church and was respected by later burials (*Sources*: Cadman 1981; Boddington 1987)

therefore be explained as a chapel-of-ease. But several lords and institutions held land in this parish, and it is possible that one of them was responsible for establishing the second church, which did not endure. Place- and field-names may sometimes give clues to the existence or whereabouts of lost churches. However, it is important to differentiate between genuine cases and the many occasions when people bestowed the name 'church' to some locally conspicuous natural feature, or a site containing prehistoric or Roman remains. Ogdenkirk, Halifax *WY*, for instances, is a group of rocks. The 'Sunken church' at Roxby *Hu* (*Li*) is a natural outcrop. The 'Kirk stones' at Gutterby *Cu* are two stone circles; the 'Sunken kirk' at Millom *Cu* is a stone circle; 'Kirk sink' at Gargrave *NY* is the site of a Roman villa; 'Church piece' at Bisley *Gl* contains a Roman structure, and so on.

The theory that in some places there could have been a reduction rather than an increase in ecclesiastical provision during the twelfth century receives support not only from the discovery of the remains of churches that were weeded out, but also from the survival of churches that still stand in close proximity. At Aldwincle *Np*, for instance, there is a church at each end of the village street. Aldwincle was never so large a place as to require two churches. The presence of a pair of churches is explained by the fact that there were two manors. The separate parishes that were born of this division retained their individuality until they were united in 1879 (Beresford and St Joseph 1979, 52, Fig. 16). Places like Eastleach *Gl*, where there are two churches in one village, or Trimley *Sf*, where two churchyards virtually adjoin, are further examples in the genre. Norfolk is quite rich in villages which contain two, sometimes three churches. Some of them stand in a single churchyard, as at South Walsham, Antingham and Reepham. In the Middle Ages this phenomenon was more common than we might suppose, and although the majority of cases that have been identified from written records were in Norfolk, there are surviving examples in nearby counties, as at Swaffham Prior *Ca*, and further afield at Alvingham *Li* and Willingale *Ex*. At Pakefield *Sf* the churches actually adjoined, like Siamese twins, until the naves were united by the removal of the intervening wall in the eighteenth century. Such multiple provision can usually be explained in terms of divided lordship, but there may have been occasions when extra churches arose because parishioners took matters into their own hands. At Thorney *Sf* Domesday Book records that four brothers had built a *capella* alongside the cemetery of the mother church because the existing building was too small to hold everyone in the parish. At a later date such a problem might have been solved by enlarging the church. It is therefore of interest that in eleventh-century Suffolk people could react to overcrowding by enlarging the *number* of churches.

Manorial structure was not the only framework upon which parishes could be draped. In Chapter 3 it was noted how often the parishes of old minsters were coterminous with areas of secular jurisdiction. Conversely, there were other parishes which appear to have been mapped out with little or no regard for existing administrative and tenurial divisions. Over much of northern England it was the township or vill that formed the basic working agricultural unit. In some instances the bounds of a township and parish are found to correspond, but it was more common for a parish to encompass a number of townships, and not unknown for this to happen in a way which cut townships in two, sending people from the same settlement in opposite directions on Sundays. In the Pennines, and some adjacent areas, where parishes were large, the number of townships gathered in a single parish could be very high. The parish of Malpas *Ch*, for instance, held twenty-four townships. Great Budworth *Ch* contained thirty-five.

Unless a church was well endowed with land of its own, the most immediate influence upon the size of a parish was the magnitude of its population. Since tithe was mainly a personal payment, a tax in kind which was levied upon individuals rather than calculated from areas, the economic viability of a parish was initially determined by the size of its tithe-paying population. Parishes in regions that were agriculturally poor and sparsely settled therefore tended to be large, while parishes situated in fruitful districts could be small. It has been estimated that the parishes of central southern England extended on average over approximately 4 sq. miles (10.3 sq. km); those in Wales and Yorkshire about 10 sq. miles (26 sq. km); and in Cheshire, Lancashire, Cumbria, Northumberland and Durham about 18.5 sq. miles (48 sq. km) (Currie *et al.* 1977, 59). Parish sizes were further conditioned by the types of agricultural regime which prevailed in different areas. Regions of great arable wealth both required and, up to a point, had the capacity to support, working populations which were relatively large. Groups of small parishes are often found crowded together in these districts. This may have been for no other reason than that there were more people to cater for, but it could also have related to an expectation that the combination of high agricultural yields and a well-settled landscape would be profitable. In the long run, however, the presence of many parishes in close proximity was not always advantageous. By *c.* 1300 some of these parishes contained too many people; by *c.* 1400, too few. Overpopulation during the thirteenth century increased pressure on rural resources, and assisted landlords who were minded to be ruthless in the exploitation of their estates. Ordinary farm labourers and the lower class of tenants were thereby impoverished and immobilized (Bridbury 1975, 54), with the result that the growth in their numbers was not always proportional to the value of their tithes. (By this time, in any case, the greater tithes of many parishes had been assigned to individuals or institutions elsewhere, and the parishes concerned were often lucky to derive any benefit from them.) Parishes with flexible borders, as at the fen edge, could compensate by bringing new areas into agricultural use. But the great majority were landlocked by their neighbours and suffered accordingly (Fig. 63). The crisis of the fourteenth

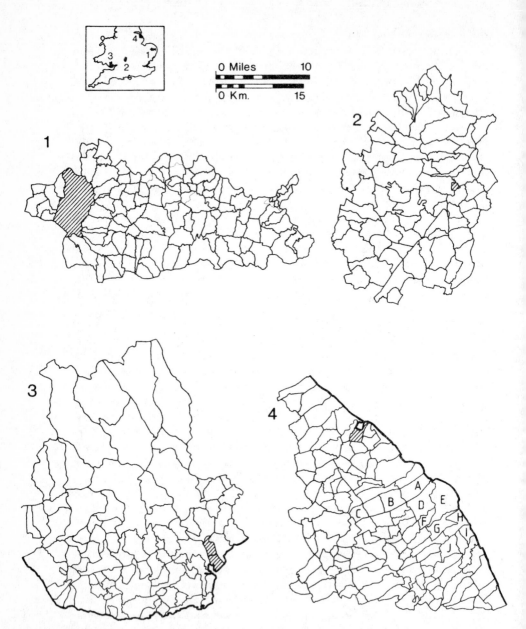

63 Four groups of parishes on terrain of contrasting character. The areas lie around
1 Wymondham, Norfolk; 2 Stow-on-the-Wold, Gloucestershire; 3 Cardiff; 4: Grimsby,
Humberside (Lincolnshire). The boundaries of 1–3 are those of ecclesiastical parishes, as
recorded in the nineteenth century. Boundaries in 4 are those of civil parishes, recorded
1883–7. Key to parishes in 4: **A** Marsh Chapel; **B** Fulstow; **C** Ludborough; **D** Grainthorpe;
E North Somercotes; **F** Conisholme; **G** South Somercotes; **H** Skidbrooke; **I** Saltfleetby St
Clement; **J** Saltfleetby St Peter

and fifteenth centuries was inversely correspondent to that of the thir-teenth. Large numbers of tithe-payers were removed from the scene by famine and pestilence. By 1400 the population seems to have been reduced to a size no larger than that around 1100, and remained hovering around this level for more than a century. Those who remained could take advan-tage of vacant holdings or better land elsewhere. Some settlements, and churches, prospered. Others shrank, or disappeared. These issues are considered at greater length in later chapters (pp. 332–339), but they have relevance here because the destiny of a church after 1400 was often influenced by the economic landscape of its parish, which had been defined three or four centuries before.

The logical shape for territories that are packed together is the hexagon. In actuality, of course, the British landscape is very far from being the isotropic surface that would be required to produce a parochial map which even approximated to this theoretical pattern. Local contrasts in relief, convenience of access to essential resources such as water, building materials and fuel, together with the fertility and extent of land available for cultivation and grazing, all constituted variables which ensured that no two parishes were identical. There are, however, broad resemblances between members of groups of parishes which occupy similar terrain. Parishes in flat or gently undulating areas tend towards compactness. In the uplands parishes may sprawl. Where there is a contrast in relief, as between, say, low and high ground, it is common to find parishes of elongated formation. The examples in Figs 32 and 63 illustrate these varia-tions. In each case the principle is the same: a need to take in centres of population. The North Yorkshire parishes (Fig. 32A) demonstrate this rather well. They rise from the fertile margin of the Vale of Pickering and then proceed across the less hospitable North York Moors for distances of up to twelve miles. Arable, grazing and rough summer grazing were thus included. But the main aim was to capture the residences of farming population, which were for the most part along the flank of the Vale. This explains the largeness of upland parishes, which had to be big in order to take in a tithe-paying population of respectable size. It was not essential that a parish should be agriculturally self-sufficient, and although a desire to secure a good range of tithable resources may be witnessed in parochial morphology, the fact that tithe was ultimately a personal payment, levied from individuals rather than rated upon land, gives one underlying reason why parish shapes and sizes varied.

In areas where a contrast in topography was steadily maintained for a number of miles, parish forms could settle down into a uniform pattern. This is strikingly witnessed by the 'ladder' of parishes north of Lincoln (Fig. 64), which is so remarkably regular as to have suggested to some the influence of a controlling design. This is possible, although it seems likely that the more deterministic process envisaged above would have been just as capable of producing the same result. However this may be, it is in-teresting to seek indications of when the system was formed. For reasons

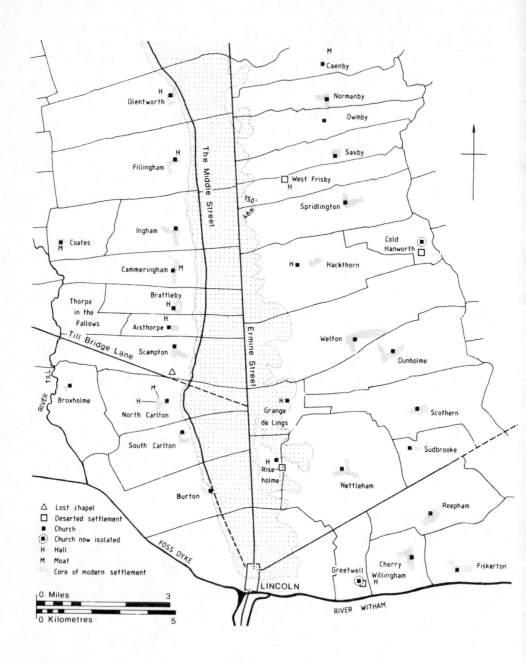

64 Parishes on the limestone escarpment north of Lincoln. Boundaries are those of modern civil parishes which have been edited to correspond with what is known of medieval ecclesiastical arrangements

1 (*Above left*) Jewry Wall and church of St Nicholas, Leicester

2 (*Above*) Church of St Mary and megalithic remains at Stanton Drew, Somerset

3 (*Below*) St John, Stanwick, North Yorkshire (*see pp. 454–5*)

5 (*Above*) Burry Holms, Glamorgan

6 (*Left*) Llangwyfan, Anglesey
(*see pp. 455–6*)

4 (*Below*) St Paul's church, Jarrow,
Tyne & Wear (*see p. 455*)

St Peter, Bradwell-on-Sea, Essex (*see p. 456*)

(*Right*) Breedon-on-the-Hill, Leicestershire

(*Below*) St Ninian Ninekirks, Cumbria (*see pp. 456–7*)

10 (*Above*) Llandyfaelog, Dyfed (*see p. 457*)

11 (*Left*) Odda's Chapel, Deerhurst, Gloucestershire

12 (Below) Site of church at Itteringham, Norfolk (*see pp. 457–8*)

13 (*Above*) Reepham,
Norfolk (*see p. 458*)

14 (*Right*) St Martin,
Cwmyoy, Gwent

15 (*Below*) St Michael,
Duntisbourne Rous,
Gloucestershire
(*see p. 459*)

16 (*Above*) Melverley,
Shropshire

17 (*Left*) St Michael,
Burrow Mump, in the
Somerset Levels
(*see p. 459*)

18 (*Below*) East Witton,
North Yorkshire (*see
p. 459*)

9 (*Above*) Church and
manor house at Great
Chalfield, Wiltshire

10 (*Right*) Church and
manor house at
Holcombe Rogus,
Devon
(*see p. 460*)

11 (*Below*) Church,
ringwork and mound at
Earl's Barton,
Northamptonshire
(*see p. 460*)

22 (*Above*) Burial mound in churchyard at Taplow, Buckinghamshire

23 (*Above left*) Laughton-en-le-Morthen, South Yorkshire: church of All Saints and motte-and-bailey castle (*see pp. 460–1*)

24 (*Below left*) Church and ringwork at Culworth, Northamptonshire

25 (*Below right*) Kilpeck, Herefordshire: church and site of village within castle enclosure (*see pp. 461–2*)

26 (*Above right*) Castle Rising,
Norfolk (*see p. 462*)

27 (*Centre*) St Catherine's
chapel, Abbotsbury, Dorset
(*see p. 462*)

28 (*Below right*) St Mary,
Edlesborough,
Buckinghamshire (*see
p. 462*)

29 (*Above left*) St Mary the Virgin, Up Waltham, Sussex

30 (*Above right*) St Edmund, Southwold, Suffolk (*see p. 462*)

31 (*Below left*) Settlement in retreat: Birkby, North Yorkshire

32 (*Below right*) Eglwys Gymun, Dyfed (*see pp. 462–3*)

3 (*Above right*) Argham: a lost village and church on the Yorkshire wolds

4 (*Centre left*) Ruined church at Little Hautbois, Coltishall, Norfolk

5 (*Centre right*) Egmere, Norfolk: ruined church and deserted settlement

6 (*Below*) New Winchelsea, Sussex (*see pp. 463–4*)

37 (*Above*) St James, Barton-under-Needwood, Staffordshire

38 (*Left*) Staunton Harold, Leicestershire
(*see p. 464*)

39 (*Below*) Fawsley, Northamptonshire: church of St Mary, mansion and park
(*see p. 464*)

(Above) St James, Great Packington, Warwickshire

(Right) St George-in-the-East, London
(see pp. 464–5)

(Below) St Alkmund, Whitchurch, Shropshire (see
p. 465)

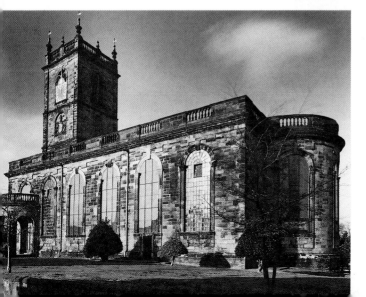

43 (*Above*) Mow Cop, on the Cheshire/
Staffordshire border

44 (*Left*) Boyne Hill, Maidenhead, Berkshire
(*see p. 465*)

45 (*Below*) Cheltenham, Gloucestershire (*see
p. 465*)

6 (*Above*) St Bartholomew, Ann Street, Brighton, Sussex

7 (*Right*) All Souls, Haley Hill, Halifax, West Yorkshire
(*see p. 466*)

8 (*Below*) Saltaire, West Yorkshire (*see p. 466*)

49 Llangelynin, Gwynedd (*see p. 466*)

already given, it may be assumed that this pattern existed in all main essentials by 1200. How much sooner it originated is problematical. There are, however, some grounds for supposing that the system was laid out no later than the tenth century, and that by *c.* 1000 it was already in quite an advanced state of development. Evidence to support these claims is found in the churches. To the west of Ermine Street nearly all of the villages on the spring line at the foot of the scarp have churches. Among them are buildings like Glentworth, which has a tower built around 1100. Gravestones which had been carved a century or more before were incorporated in the fabric of this tower. Many other churches in the Cliff Parishes contain similar material. Hence, while there are no tenth-century church structures surviving in any of the settlements, there are widespread indications of tenth-century church*yards*. Local cemeteries imply local communities, and it seems fair to assume that the main structure of settlement hereabouts had already taken shape by this period. This supposition is reinforced by the fact that it is not only churches in the main villages that offer such evidence, but some of those in subsidiary settlements as well. It will be seen from Fig. 64 that a number of the primary units appear to have been partitioned. Saxby and Firsby, for instance, have parishes of only half the width of their neighbour Spridlington. Signs of fission are particularly obvious at Brattleby and Aisthorpe, where subdivision did not continue for the full length of the 'master parish'. It is tempting to visualize these smaller settlements as latecomers, created perhaps in response to the pressure of a growing population upon rural resources, or divisions of lordship. In some places there are indications that subdivision went too far. At later dates a number of the settlements concerned dwindled to mere farms, like Thorpe in the Fallows, or, like West Firsby and Cold Hanworth, they disappeared. Yet it is clear that a number, and perhaps all, of the 'secondary' settlements had acquired an identity by 1000. Brattleby and Aisthorpe, for instance, have yielded sculpture of the later tenth or early eleventh century. If these components really were the result of subdivision, then the main framework ought to be older.

The extent to which tenth-century graveyards can be equated with communities, which in their turn are regarded as representing later parishes, is of course a matter full of uncertainties. The dangers of such reasoning were emphasized earlier in this chapter. And as the concept of the parish did not acquire full expression until the twelfth century, the boundaries here could be looked upon as a relatively late formalization, albeit one which gave more precise definition to a structure which was older. There are, nevertheless, further aspects of the Cliff Parish system which call for attention, and which offer clues to the chronology of the layout. One obvious feature is the way in which the parishes were set out in relation to ancient roads. This applies not only to the parishes north of Scampton which run perpendicular to Ermine Street, but also to Burton and South Carlton, which lie at right angles to the Middle Street, and to parishes on the east side of Ermine Street which arguably owe their north-easterly deflection to the use of the Lincoln–Horncastle Roman road as their southerly baseline. The exception to this road-related pattern is the road now known as Till Bridge Lane. This originated as a Roman road, and by the third century it had superseded Ermine Street as the important trunk route from Lincoln to York. At first sight the bounds of parishes in the neighbourhood of Till Bridge Lane appear to ignore it. However, it will be noticed that the western bounds of Aisthorpe, Brattleby and Ingham are curiously and, in terms of local natural topography, inexplicably slanted. A possible reason is that they preserve remnants of a rectilinear system of land division which was laid out with reference to Till Bridge Lane (Fig. 64). Such a system might be Roman, or it could be later: we cannot tell. Nevertheless, a Roman origin for something of the overall structure is not out of the question. Fieldwork along the limestone edge north of Lincoln has disclosed the presence of at least six and maybe as many as eleven Roman villas in positions which prefigure the later pattern (Everson 1980, 12). If it can be assumed that these villas possessed estates, it is reasonable to wonder whether the outlines of such holdings could have been ancestral to those of early medieval lords. Of course, given the underlying constants of the terrain and the limited supply of water, any resemblance between the disposition of Roman and medieval settlements could be accounted for in terms of geographical determinism. But this interpretation would not remove, and might strengthen, the possibility that vestiges of a scheme of Roman land allotment could have survived on the ground into the early Middle Ages, and that some of them were sufficiently visible to be incorporated into the bounds of later estates and, eventually, parishes. Such survival would neither imply nor rule out the possibility of territorial continuity.

The uniformity of the Cliff Parishes is remarkable, though not unique. As a rule parish shapes are more amorphous. We have seen that in some areas there was a common tendency for parish boundaries to echo outlines of secular landholding. These in their turn were generally defined with reference to a combination of natural and man-made features. Streams, roads, paths and lines of abutment between field-systems made useful borders; springs, conspicuous trees, boulders, barrows and cross-roads were often taken as turning points. Ease of access to the parish church was considered to be important, and in the absence of a bridge an impassable river was almost invariably used as a boundary. Today it is not unusual to find a length of parish boundary which departs from a river, only to be reunited with it after a distance. The normal explanation for this is that the river has changed its course while the original position of the boundary has been maintained. Where there were no convenient points of reference it was possible for a boundary to be inscribed on the landscape in the form of a ditch. In some places the sinuous wanderings of such local frontiers can still be encountered on the ground, and even those that have been ploughed flat may produce crop-marks which remain visible from the air.

Occasionally there are references to the moments when such features were created. A document of *c.* 1180 records how William de Stuteville was concerned to remove uncertainty over the bounds of Kirkby Ouseburn *NY* (*YW*). In company with a group of villagers who knew the traditional limits of the township he perambulated the bounds and ordered that a *fossa* be dug along the route taken. Lengths of this ditch may still be seen.

The precision with which parish boundaries were first established was by no means uniform. In towns, on land of high value, and wherever there were houses, boundaries were often determined down to the last yard. But where parishes adjoined in marsh, on heath or on moor, the line could be more vague. Exact delineation became necessary only when marginal areas were drained or improved (Roffe 1984, 117). In the fenlands, for instance, the boundaries of parishes which were augmented by medieval and later reclamation are characterized by a much stricter geometry than is found elsewhere.

Within the parish, the selection of a site for the church was influenced by factors of terrain, tradition, the distribution of population and – perhaps above all – tenure.

Sites that were susceptible to flooding were normally ruled out. So too, in general, were places where the bearing capacity of the ground was too weak for building. Although it appears that many churches were located on doubtful ground, it is fair to point out that their sites were chosen for the needs of their own day rather than those of the future. The small stone churches which were mass-produced between *c.* 1050 and *c.* 1150 delivered lighter loads than the enlarged buildings of the Gothic age. Their timber precursors were lighter still. Structural failures in later centuries were thus not uncommon, and there are churches like Surfleet *Li* and Cwmyoy *Gnt* (*Mon*) which display startling distortions. Steeply sloping sites were usually avoided, although there were occasions when falling ground was exploited by the inclusion of a crypt under the chancel. Churches at Whitwick *Le*, Shillington *Bd*, Lastingham *NY* and Duntisbourne Rous *Gl* were among those where this device was employed. If a sloping site could not be avoided, and the church faced up it, the chancel might be substantially raised above the level of the nave, as at Alwinton *Nb*. If the church blocked, or was later extended across a path or road, it was necessary to leave space for a diversion. Occasionally a right of way or a route taken by processions was left unchanged and the church was moulded around it. Roads run through the open arched ground storeys of church towers at Wrotham *K* and St Peter Mancroft, Norwich, for instance. The subways that exist under the lengthened chancels at Walsall *St*, Hythe *K* and Walpole St Peter *Nf* may be connected with processional traditions. A right of way was maintained through the church at Lostwithiel *Co* until 1878.

Other needs included a supply of water, and a churchyard. In the absence of a nearby spring or stream arrangements might be made to collect rainwater from the roof. The ideal churchyard would be roomy enough to accommodate the dead of the community for the foreseeable future. But what, to a tenth-century lord, was 'foreseeable'? Areas that seemed adequate before the Conquest were seldom large enough for later needs. By 1500 even the graveyard of a small village could have received upwards of three thousand burials. At first, it seems, graves were dug in a more or less orderly fashion, with not too much intercutting. When space had been used up overburial began and the pattern became increasingly confused. Some churchyards were enlarged, but if the site was hemmed in by property or a road this was not always possible and the level of the churchyard would rise. It is not uncommon to see churchyards that stand ten or fifteen feet above the level of the village street or a neighbouring garden. At Barwick-in-Elmet *WY*, for instance, the graveyard has risen almost to the eaves against the gable of an adjoining house. It is doubtful if the highest cemetery platforms can be accounted for simply in terms of the volume of human remains. There are signs that some of them originated as natural eminences or artificial mounds which were subsequently cloaked by a surrounding build-up of graves (Fig. 65) (see p. 256). Others may have risen because material was brought in from outside and spread across the surface of the churchyard. There is some evidence for such operations, which may have been carried out in the interests of hygiene. Artificial deepening may also have occurred at sites where the topsoil was thin and gave way to an unyielding material like heavy clay or bedrock, or where the water-table was so high that folk were said to be 'drowned, not buried'.

Drainage, relief and geology were not, of course, the only factors which determined the position of a church. Churches were for the use of people, and it is reasonable to suppose that a church would be located for the convenience of the people who would make up its congregation. But behind this elementary assumption there lies a multitude of uncertainties, most of which can be narrowed to a focus in two questions: which people, and at what dates?

Take the example of Aller *So*. Fig. 66 shows a small village, arranged for the most part along a single street. Although the simplicity of this plan is deceptive – the village is made up of several elements which originated and developed at different times – there is no reason to doubt that the large majority of Aller's medieval inhabitants resided in the area that is occupied by the modern village. Yet the church is situated nearly a third of a mile from the village and keeps company with no more than a single farm. Why?

Aller Court Farm is on the site of a medieval manor house. The farm and church stand on a small patch of Keuper Marl that is surrounded by low-lying moor. The moor was not fully drained until the nineteenth century. It is suggested that the dry island of marl carried the nucleus of pre-Conquest settlement, and that the present village grew up after the site of the church had been determined (Ellison 1983, 13).

The medieval villagers of Aller were not the only ones in Somerset who

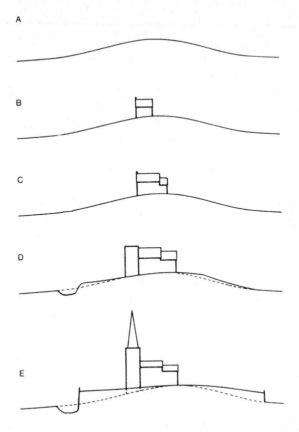

65 Sketch to illustrate possible formation processes for an elevated cemetery platform. Stages **B** and **C** depict the emplacement and first enlargement of a church upon a small eminence. In stage **D** the church has been extended further, burial around the church has caused the ground level to begin to rise, and a trackway passing to the west of the site is beginning to increase the contrast between levels. Phase **E** shows these processes at a more advanced stage. The sketch is not to scale

had to walk for some distance in order to reach their church. In the Somerset Levels there was a natural tendency to seek dry eminences, as in the rather spectacular case of Burrow Mump where the church, now abandoned, occupies a prominent knoll above Earlake Moor. But church and settlement were also separated, often less explicably, at Beercrocombe, Seavington St Mary, Stocklinch, Whitelackington, Broadway, Dundon, Keinton Mandeville, Kingweston, Knowle St Giles, Misterton and elsewhere. From Miss Ann Ellison's survey of 92 surviving medieval villages in south-east Somerset it is possible to see that out of 77 places which possessed churches 14 per cent of the churches were fully removed from the principal centre of population, while a further 57 per cent oc-

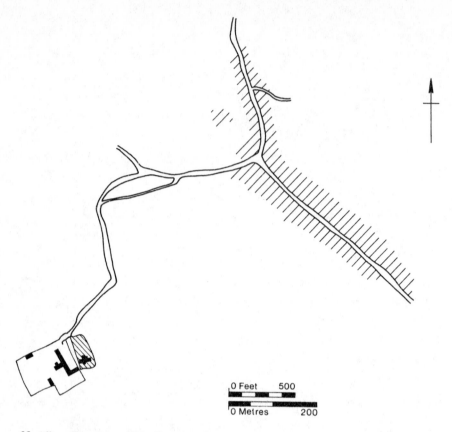

66 Aller, Somerset. The diagram shows the church at a distance from the main settlement, which is itself made up of elements which have developed at different times (*Source*: Ellison 1983)

cupied sites which lay slightly apart from or were peripheral to the village. Churches which stood fully within the medieval settlement were in a minority of 29 per cent. Figures of this order are neither exceptional nor particular to Somerset. In all parts of England there are parish churches which stand apart from the settlements they serve. The frequency and degree of separation vary from region to region, but even in areas where villages were commonly of compact form the church is as often found at, or beyond, the inhabited area as it is at the centre.

One reason why so many churches now seem to be oddly placed is that the pattern of settlement is, and always has been, mutable. Change occurs not only as a result of gain and loss around stable centres, but also through the migrations of the centres themselves. The restlessness of settlement is revealed particularly well in Norfolk, where Dr Peter Wade-Martins's survey of villages in the Launditch Hundred has shown that a number of churches which were established in centres of pre-Conquest occupation were forsaken when communities were rearranged. A classic instance is Longham, where occupation in the immediate vicinity of the church was superseded by a village which developed around South Hall Green. The new village grew fast, and by the fourteenth century there was almost continuous occupation along both sides of the green. Meanwhile the 'area of settlement near the church remained fairly static and afterwards declined quickly' (Wade-Martins 1980, 37). Another case is Mileham, where indications of eighth- or ninth-century settlement have been detected around the church. Subsequently the village moved north from its old site and reformed along the axis of a busy street (1980, 40–7). The church at Stanfield was accompanied by settlement in the tenth or eleventh century, but by c. 1300 the village lay further west, beside a common. 'The study of all these villages', writes Dr Wade-Martins,

> has revealed a lack of stability of settlement sites throughout the whole history of the post-Roman period. Many villages started to shift from their original sites in the twelfth century, and this is probably the explanation for the majority of isolated churches in many parts of East Anglia. . . . By the thirteenth and fourteenth centuries the majority of churches were already lonely monuments in the landscape.
>
> (1980, 87, 88)

Conversely, a church like Burnham *Li*, which seems originally to have stood at the edge of a settlement, could as a result of regrouping (here apparently in the thirteenth century) find itself at the centre (Coppack 1986, 29).

In his valuable book *Village and Farmstead*, Christopher Taylor identifies four ways in which a nucleated village could come into existence. The first is through growth around a stable centre, which at the outset might consist of a hamlet or even a single farm. The second is a process of agglomeration: the knitting together of a number of 'dispersed but closely set farmsteads growing into discrete hamlets which finally coalesce to form a single nucleated settlement' (C.C.Taylor 1983, 131). For settlements which were formed in such a fashion Taylor has coined the term 'polyfocal' (1977). The third process is envisaged as involving the collapse of a pattern of dispersed settlement, followed by the recombination of the people concerned in a single village. From the examples illustrated in Fig. 67 it is easy to see ways in which each of these mechanisms could affect the topographical relationship between a church and its settlement(s): where nucleation has occurred, the site of the church will represent a decision which was taken at some moment before, during or after the process.

The fourth method of village formation to be outlined by Taylor is that of deliberate planning: the blocking-out of an entire settlement at one stroke. Among the leading features of a planned settlement are the overall regularity of its form, uniformity of tenement plots and the presence of a unifying feature such as a straight street or central green (C.C.Taylor

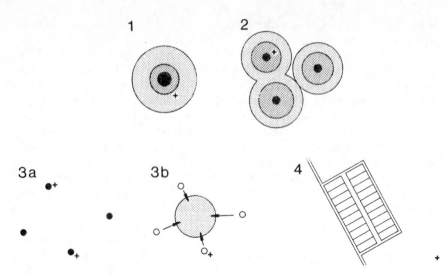

67 Stylized representation of four possible processes for the formation of a nucleated village. 1 steady outward growth from a stable centre; 2 outward growth from several neighbouring foci leading to eventual amalgamation; 3 agglomeration following the relinquishment of an earlier pattern of dispersed units of settlement; 4 co-ordinated planning. In each example a church has been introduced, to show how the relationship between a church and its settlement might be influenced by such developments. In 3a there were originally two churches, one of which is abandoned following the regrouping in 3b. In 4 the church was present before systematic planning took place, and is left standing off to one side (cf. Pl. 23) (*Source*: author's realization after C.C. Taylor 1983, 131)

1983, 133–4). The existence of medieval villages which were systematically planned has been appreciated for some years, particularly in northern England where examples have been identified and analysed in the Vale of Pickering (Allerston 1970), Co. Durham (B.K. Roberts 1972), and in the region as a whole (Sheppard 1976). Taylor's work allows us to see that settlements of this type were even more numerous than was first thought. In the Vale of Pickering, for instance, Pamela Allerston found that out of twenty-nine villages in her chosen district, eighteen had forms which merited the term 'planned' (1970, 95). A new study by Taylor of the eleven villages which were discounted because of their irregular form leads him to claim that at least five and possibly seven of them were also planned, but that their primary forms were disguised by later change (1983, 138).

More important still is the growing realization that formal planning was not confined to northern England. Indeed, two possible examples elsewhere have already been encountered in this chapter: Aller *So*, and the eleventh-century remodelling of Mileham *Nf*. Definite evidence for planning has been noted in Somerset (Aston 1985), Shropshire (Rowley 1978), Oxfordshire (Bond 1985, 115), Cambridgeshire, and elsewhere (Taylor 1983, 146). In Northamptonshire, where the entire county has recently been subjected to detailed study by the Royal Commission on the Historical Monuments of England, Taylor estimates that at least 23 per cent of all the existing villages had planned origins.

It may still be premature to generalize about the chronology of planning. There is some evidence that many, and possibly a majority, of the villages concerned were laid out in the later eleventh or twelfth centuries. In the north it has been suggested that regularity could be 'a product of reorganization following devastations during the late eleventh century' (B.K. Roberts 1972, 54). Attempts to demonstrate a statistically significant degree of correlation between places which suffered from Norman harrying and planning have hitherto been thwarted by lack of necessary information (Sheppard 1976). The idea remains plausible, if unproven. However, if the Conqueror's scorched earth policies are entertained as having provided a context for the laying-out of new villages in the north, then so also must be the numerous occasions in the twelfth century when other regions of England became embroiled in conflict. Settlements in the vicinity of strongholds were commonly wasted in order to deprive the defenders of any means of subsistence. The civil war between Stephen and Matilda (1136–54) was the cause of many such episodes (Aston 1985, 93).

The essential point about planning is that it implies either seigneurial intervention or co-operative action (Dyer 1985, 32). A decision to reorganize may have been prompted by the consequences of warfare, the demands of feudalism, a desire to restructure an estate in pursuit of greater efficiency, or it may simply have been a matter of fashion. In a number of cases, like Old Byland *NY*, Rufford *Nt* and East Witton *NY*, it is either known or likely that a religious community was responsible (Beresford and St Joseph 1979, 159–60, 105–6). Whatever the motive, the abrupt appearance of a new village laid out on preconceived lines must usually signify the action of an individual or institutional landowner, or of a community acting either with the approval of a lord, or on its own behalf in the absence of effective external control.

One reason to think seriously about the twelfth century as a busy time for the creation of new settlements is the relative scarcity of examples where the parish church formed an integral part of the original layout. At first sight this is not obvious. Many planned villages now contain churches, and the positions that the churches occupy often look as if they had been thought of from the outset. But a closer look usually reveals the church either to have been a chapel which was later promoted to parochial status, or as a foundation of the nineteenth century. In other cases there is no church in the village, although there may be one elsewhere in the parish which could be visualized as marking an older centre of settlement. Thus if the eighteen planned villages identified in the Vale of Pickering by Pamela Allerston are examined (Fig. 68), it will be found that twelve of them had no medieval parish church and lay in parishes bearing other names. Of the remaining six, four (Wilton, Thornton, Allerston and Ebberston) were served by chapels dependent upon Pickering (*Reg. Gray*, 213), two of which were well removed from the planned settlements (Ellerburn (Thornton) and Ebberston). Out of eighteen planned villages, therefore, only two had parish churches: Levisham and Middleton. At Levisham the church is remote from the village. Excavations within the church point to an origin for the building on the present site no earlier than the twelfth century, although churchyard monuments of the tenth century imply that a predecessor existed somewhere in the immediate vicinity. The planned village occupies a lofty site about half a mile away (Hall and Lang 1986). There can be little doubt that the position of this church was fixed before the new settlement was mapped out. Only at Middleton is there a pre-Conquest ecclesiastical site within the planned area. This church contains one of the richest assemblages of pre-Conquest sculpture in Yorkshire. Some of this material dates from before *c.* 875, so the site is likely to have been determined by the mid-ninth century, if not sooner. Middleton's tower, on the other hand, dates from the later eleventh century, and it is tempting to wonder if a rebuilding of the church could have formed part of some larger scheme of replanning. This aside, what emerges from our study is a pattern of almost total disengagement between planned settlements and primary parochial centres. Arguments for the comparative youthfulness of the planned villages are therefore reinforced.

A rather similar picture is found further north. In Co. Durham, where village plans have been studied in great detail (B.K. Roberts 1972), many villages of regular form are found either to contain no church (e.g. Ferryhill, Walworth, Carlton, Middleton), or else embody a church at one end of the settlement. In cases of this latter sort the church could be a belated addition, but the possibility that it preceded the phase of planning cannot always be ruled out. At Cockfield, for instance, there was a manorial complex beside the church, and this could have formed an earlier nucleus. Heighington has a church within its green, and this could likewise be a survival from an earlier focus which was absorbed into the new plan. Alternatively – St Michael at Heighington is substantially a twelfth-century building – the church and village might in this instance have arisen together. A number of other green-sited churches are found in northern counties: Trimdon *Du*, for instance, or Elsdon *Nb*.

The alignment of a new village upon a pre-existing focus is sometimes suggested, as at Isle Abbots *So*, or Kirby Hill near Richmond *NY*, where Pevsner noticed the village as lying 'on a sudden hill ... and it has on its hill a perfectly rectangular green with the church alone not following the axial precision of the pattern' (1973, 209). East Witton *NY* presents a similar picture. But here the present church dates only from 1809, and the commanding logic of its position belies the former arrangement whereby a medieval church dedicated to St Martin was situated about a third of

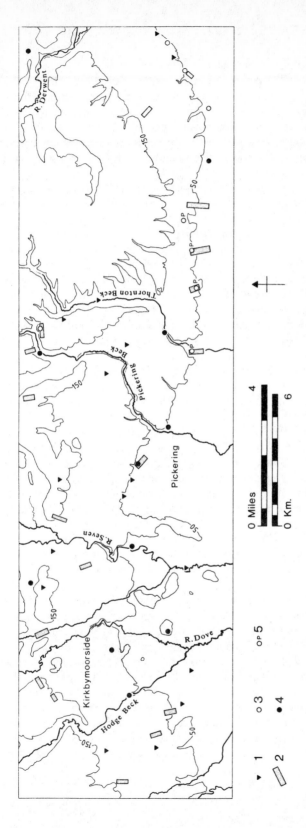

68 Settlements and churches in the Vale of Pickering, North Yorkshire. 1 vills mentioned in 1086 (foci may be unknown); 2 settlements of planned form or showing signs of planning (after Allerston 1970 and C.C. Taylor 1983); 3 parish church; 4 parish church with pre-Conquest sculpture; 5 church, now parochial, formerly subordinate to Pickering. Contours are in metres

a mile to the south-east. Across the valley of the River Ure, within sight of East Witton, is Thornton Steward: another planned village which is estranged from its church. The priority of the church here is indicated both by the presence of pre-Conquest sculpture and signs of pre-Conquest workmanship in the fabric of the building. The Cistercian abbey of Jervaulx was interposed between East Witton and Thornton Steward in 1145. It is likely that the Cistercians were responsible for changing the plans of both villages.

Earlier in this chapter it was suggested that there are four main ways in which a village is likely to have been formed: outward growth, amalgamation, agglomeration and direct planning (C.C.Taylor 1983, 125–50). Other processes, notably those of retraction and migration, have been noted. Hitherto all these factors have been discussed independently, but they could, and often did, work in combination. Moreover, the processes that first gave villages shape acted ceaselessly thereafter, so that at any given moment in the life of a settlement at least one and often several of them would be exerting influence (cf. Taylor 1983, 151–74). The position of the church thus assumes an added interest, as a point of relative stability which could resist the undertow of change to an extent that houses, streets, greens and closes often did not.

But what, at the time of its founding, did a church represent? There is a guarded tendency among some authorities to see it as marking a nucleus of settlement. The pieces of middle and late Saxon pottery which were collected in the near vicinity of Norfolk churches like Mileham, Longham, West Dereham and Tittleshall have been interpreted thus (Wade-Martins 1980, 88). The anomalous positions of churches in Somerset such as Puckington, Long Sutton and Beercrocombe have likewise been entertained as marking places of occupation that existed before the present villages took shape (Ellison 1983). Recent discussions of village development in Oxfordshire, Cambridgeshire and Northamptonshire contain similar observations. Yet the exact nature of the 'settlement' or 'occupation' that is envisaged is seldom clear. Are we speaking of village communities? Hamlets? Single farmsteads? And why should one centre of habitation gain a church when others in the area apparently did not?

The modern traveller through rural England can hardly fail to be impressed by the frequency with which parish churches are found next to buildings or monuments of lordly status. The cluster of church and manor house which can be seen at places like West Ogwell *D*, or Longnor *He*, or Great Chalfield *Wi* is a commonplace. No one has counted these juxtapositions, but an extrapolation from the sample area depicted in Fig. 69 would suggest that they run into thousands. Occasionally the neighbouring hall is a building 'of medieval date. Beside the churches at Warnford *Ha* and Little Wenham *Sf*, for instance, there are houses of the thirteenth century. More usually the house is of Elizabethan, Jacobean or later construction. In many places the church now stands in the parkland of an

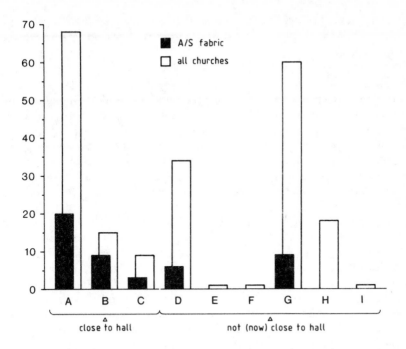

69 Graph showing degree of association between churches and manorial sites in the archdeaconry of Colchester, Essex (*Source*: author's realization of data in Rodwell and Rodwell 1977)

aristocratic mansion: a phenomenon to be discussed in Chapter 10. At the opposite extreme are churches like All Saints at South Elmham *Sf*, More *Sa* or Nately Scures *Ha* which are coupled with a single farm. An approach may have to be made along a private road or farm track. The final stage may be a walk through a garden or farmyard, as at Coberley *Gl* and North Marden *Sx*. In some cases, like Southrop *Gl* or Pixley *He*, it is actually in the farmyard that the church will be found. The visitor to one of these reclusive churches may feel like a trespasser, and as often as not one's arrival is heralded by barking dogs.

It is useful to ask what lies behind these juxtapositions. Do they reflect a variety of separate factors which operated at different times? Or could it be that church and hall have kept company from the outset, with some houses subsequently being rebuilt and enlarged while others dwindled in status or disappeared? There are several reasons for thinking that the latter possibility is the more likely. In some instances this can be confirmed. The farm at Pixley, for instance, which was referred to above, was formerly a manorial centre. At Coberley there was a great mansion that disappeared in the eighteenth century. In Chapter 4 and in the earlier part of this chapter a case was made for local lords as having formed the leading class of churchfounder. The hypothesis now to be examined is that when lords established churches, they put them on sites to suit their own convenience.

To begin, let us consider the regularity with which churches are found in close proximity to mottes. At Eardisley *He*, for example, the church stands next to a motte, which is enclosed by a later moat. The motte could be the *domus defensabilis* 'fortified residence' which was recorded in the neighbourhood in 1086. The conjunction of motte and church is particularly common in Herefordshire, where Downton-on-the-Rock, Llaneillo, Mansell Lacy, Staunton-on-Arrow and St Weonards may be mentioned from among many other examples (Fig. 70). Elsewhere in England such associations occur, with varying degrees of frequency and intimacy, at places as far apart as Rockingham *Np*, Stanton Holgate *Sa*, Somerford *Wi*, Aughton *Hu* (*YE*), Lulworth *Do*, Gilmorton *Le* and Middleton Stoney *O*. The significance of such occurrences will become clearer if we pause to consider what mottes were, and how they functioned.

A motte is an earthen mound which was raised for military purposes. Originally mottes were crowned by defences of wood or stone, or some combination of the two. Often the motte was adjoined by an enclosure consisting of a bank and ditch, known as a bailey. The motte served as a watchtower, a place for the supervision of activities within the bailey, and as a strongpoint in the event of the bailey being overrun.

Mottes were easy and cheap to build. They could be raised out of local resources, if necessary at high speed in response to transient threats. Hence there are far more mottes surviving than were ever in use at any one time. Some were built to control river crossings or routeways. Others were thrown up in the course of brief campaigns or in reaction to sudden scares, and soon abandoned. In a proportion of cases, however, the motte was a seat of local power. A site in this category could be developed into a more permanent castle, or it could be demilitarized, to be replaced by a hall or manor house nearby.

Mottes have survived in considerable numbers from an age which has left only a handful of secular buildings. The heyday of the motte lay in the period 1070–1170, so where mottes exist next to churches the relationship is unlikely to have been formed any later than the twelfth century. Motte-building was at its busiest during the Conqueror's decades, when Norman lords sought to impose their authority upon the shires and hundreds of England, and in the time of the civil wars between 1136 and 1154.

The mottes with which this chapter is particularly concerned are those that had some permanence as centres of seigneurial power. Many of the mottes that are found next to churches are likely to fall into this category. It is nevertheless worth noticing that in a small proportion of cases the reason for the juxtaposition might have been entirely martial. The *Gesta Stephani* record occasions when churches were seized by soldiers and adapted for military use. Mottes could then be built nearby, either for

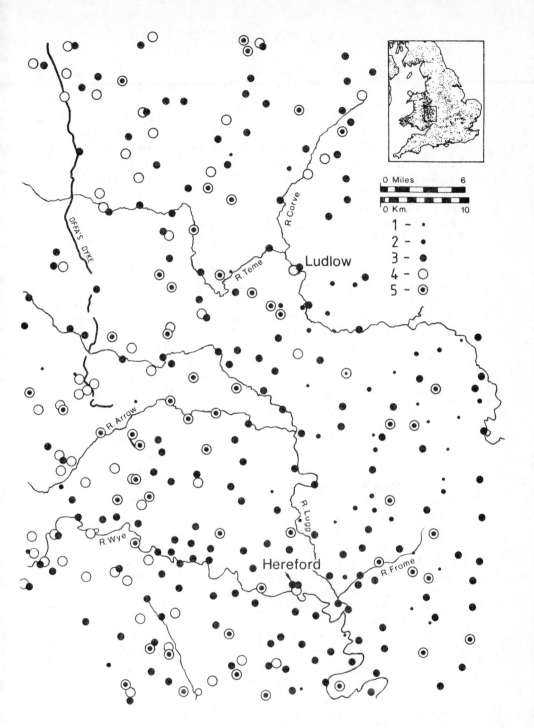

70 Churches and mottes in Herefordshire. 1 isolated church; 2 church and isolated farm or building; 3 church in village; 4 motte, unassociated with church; 5 church and motte in close topographical association ('close' has been taken as *c.* 200 yd (180 m) or less). The inset shows the general distribution of mottes and is after Renn 1973

added strength, or as counterworks by assailing forces, as at Wallingford in 1139 (see p. 198). Matilda's supporters are reported to have constructed a 'fort' of timber on the church tower at Bampton *O* (Renn 1973, 49). There is a motte-and-bailey in the churchyard at Caerinion *Pws (Mnt)*. A ringwork encircled the church at Eaton Socon *Bd*. In 1144 soldiers surrounded the church of St John at Merrington *Du* with a *vallum*. (This church had a large tower which was later thought to have been 'evidently built for defence'. The tower was blown up *c.* 1854 on the pretext that it was dangerous) (Raine 1864, 147). At Meelick in Ireland a motte was formed by filling a church with earth up to the gables (Renn 1973, 49, 69, 101). At Bedford the church of St Paul lay so close to the castle that it appears to have been damaged in the siege of 1224 (Elwes 1874). Usually, one supposes, the misuse of church buildings by soldiers was a matter of opportunism. But there are signs that a few churches were designed with an eye for use in times of disorder. The robust church towers at Brook *K* and Shalfleet *IoW*, for instance, are defensive in character. The westwork of the eleventh-century cathedral at Lincoln contains a number of features which are more commonly associated with castles, including staircases which ascend from doors positioned above ground, observation points and machicolations (Gem 1986b). It would appear that Remigius, the first Norman bishop of this huge diocese, did not feel entirely secure. In border areas that were repeatedly fought over by English and Scottish armies it is possible to find churches like Burgh-by-Sands *Cu* and Ancroft *Nb* with stout, keep-like towers. Such buildings are nevertheless in a minority, even in marcher zones, and for a more general explanation of earlier associations between mottes and churches we must look for other causes. There is reason to think that we shall discover them in circumstances that prevailed not after the Norman Conquest, but before. At Cuckney *Nt*, for instance, it is clear that the site of the church was determined before that of the motte (Barley 1951). This will emerge as a common pattern. But did anything precede the motte?

Although the motte was a Norman innovation, the English were quite practised makers of earthen fortifications. Surviving defences at places like Wallingford and Wareham show this. So might numerous literary references to the existence of *burhs*. *Burh* is an extremely common Old English word with a basic meaning of 'fort' or 'defended place'. The term was applied to a wide variety of sites, including defended places of prehistoric and Roman origin, and the urban *burhs* (from whence our 'borough') that were considered in the previous chapter. *Burh* was also used to denote a place, or perhaps a class of site, that was occupied by a local lord. The frequency of *burh* as an element in the names of places (e.g. Burgh on Bain *Li*, Burpham *Sx*, Burstall *Sf*, Burstow *Sr*), and in particular the ubiquity of the place-name Burton, which in most cases derives from Old English *burh-tūn* 'tūn by a burgh' (Ekwall 1966, 77), suggests that such private *burhs* were extremely common. What they actually consisted of is more difficult to say. In eleventh-century England the possession of a fortified gatehouse was looked upon as one of the attributes of thegnly rank, along with a church, and five hides of land (3 Cnut 60). A gatehouse implies the existence of some sort of *enceinte* within which to place it. It has to be conceded that surviving remains which can be recognized as the enclosures of such sites are extremely rare. Possibly they were defined by hedges, palisades, or simple ditches that have left little trace. Such enclosures would have been sufficient for ordinary day-to-day purposes of controlling access without being designed to withstand sustained attack. If the walls of a local *burh* were meant to emphasize the status of the person who lived within them, rather than to protect him from all military eventualities, this could help to explain why *burhs* in this conjectured category are so fugitive in the field.

So much for speculation. But is there any evidence which can be used to support the theory? It happens that there is, and that much of it relates to churches. In the first place it should be noted that two of the largest and most heavily embellished of all Anglo-Saxon church towers, at Barton-upon-Humber *Hu* (*Li*) and Earl's Barton *Np*, were associated with earthwork enclosures. Towers of this sort are rare, and probably always were so. This renders the topographical parallel all the more striking.

At Barton-upon-Humber a turriform church was erected, probably within the period *c*. 970–1030. The church was situated just to the west of a large curving bank and ditch which appeared to its excavators 'to define an extensive, sub-circular enclosure, much of which can be reconstructed in plan through topographical indicators' (Rodwell and Rodwell 1982, 290). The enclosure surrounded what later became the manorial complex (see Fig. 54). The earthwork was found to have had 'both a long and a complicated history'. Traces of subsidiary ditches and an entrance were discovered, together with indications of a stage when the ditch was augmented by a timber palisade. The date of the ditch is uncertain, but it appears to have been dug before 900. Excavations showed that the church of *c*. 1000 was built within an existing cemetery, and it seems likely that this graveyard belonged to an earlier church which stood elsewhere in the immediate vicinity. The picture is thus of a church and graveyard just beyond the circumference of an enclosure that contained the residence of a lord. The church could hardly have been closer to the enclosure, for when the building was lengthened eastwards in the twelfth century the new nave lay athwart the infilled ditch (Fig. 71).

At Earl's Barton an earthwork is still visible beside the church, although no excavation has taken place and the chronology of what can be seen is uncertain. As at Barton-upon-Humber, the original nucleus of the church was a tower. The tower was placed upon a low spur. On three sides the ground falls away quite sharply. To the north there is the arc of an impressive ditch. The ditch cups a mound which lies half inside the present churchyard. It is not known whether the ditch once continued to complete a circle around or before the tower. Its line is lost as it enters the churchyard.

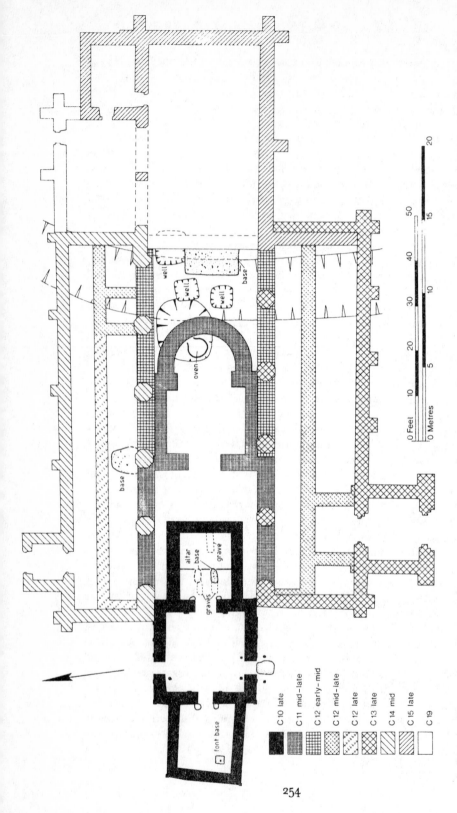

71 St Peter's, Barton-upon-Humber, showing structural development and associated features revealed by archaeological excavation (*Source:* Rodwell and Rodwell 1982)

font base

oven

well

well

well

base

base

base

altar base

grave

graves

grave

C 10 late
C 11 mid–late
C 12 early–mid
C 12 mid–late
C 12 late
C 13 late
C 14 mid
C 15 late
C 19

0 Feet   10   20   30   40   50

0 Metres   5   10   15   20

The presence of this spectacular tower within or immediately adjacent to an enclosure which is at least partly artificial seems unlikely to be a matter of coincidence. Perhaps the tower was a multi-purpose structure, intended to serve both as a chapel and as a strongpoint for a thegn's *burh* (Davison 1967). A private function for the church is in any case suggested by its original form: externally ostentatious, the tower-nave had a floor area which would have been rather small for a village congregation, although it could have accommodated a lord and his family. As to the function of the upper part, the etymological history of the word 'belfry' may be of relevance. In modern speech 'belfry' is associated with bells and bell-ringing. However, the Middle English form *berfrey* points rather to an origin in two Germanic words: **bergan* 'to protect' and **frithuz* 'peace'. In the eleventh century 'belfry' would therefore have meant something like 'strong place', or 'place of security', or simply 'tower'. Bells were certainly hung in early towers, but there seems to be a possibility that these structures could have fulfilled more than one function.

Large numbers of western towers were added to parish churches in the eleventh and early twelfth centuries; many of them had provision for independent access, usually via a west door, and often there is a door at a higher level in the east face. The purpose of these upper doors is a mystery; some of them may simply have been intended to facilitate maintenance, but here and there are signs that they gave access onto balconies or galleries which were later removed (H. M. Taylor 1978, 829, 887, 893–4; cf. Parsons 1979). Towers of this type are normally regarded as forming a category which is functionally distinct from the slightly earlier and more elaborate turriform buildings. But perhaps there is a case for seeing the western tower as a popular derivative of what had previously been a more exclusive and aristocratic form. The sharp increase in tower-building after *c*. 1050 might then be explained as a result of the adoption by local lords of a status symbol which had its beginnings at a higher social level. Did the new churches differ from their predecessors in that 'private' and 'public' functions which had earlier been catered for in different types of buildings were now united in a single all-purpose structure?

One more aspect of the site at Earl's Barton remains to be considered. It is the mound on the north side of the tower. This may be no more than a motte. But conjecture could take us in other directions. Might it clothe a large barrow? Existing mounds, both natural and artificial, were sometimes developed into mottes by Norman lords. At Brinklow *Wa*, for instance, a substantial mound was adapted by the Normans as the nucleus of a large motte-and-bailey. The early origin of this feature is suggested both by the place-name element *hlaw* 'mound' and by the fact that it marks a change of direction in the Roman Fosse Way. The church, formerly a chapelry, 'is set back on the slope of the hill almost touching the bailey earthworks' (Chatwin 1936, 152). Brinklow is also the name of a Hundred, and it may be that the site had the status of a hundredal

meeting-place (cf. Thwing, Knowlton: p. 74 and p. 73). This raises a further question: did some of the mottes that adjoin churchyards originate
as places of burial? Instances of such modification are known, as at St
Weonards *He* where, in the nineteenth century, antiquaries retrieved
human remains from the core of a large mound (Wright 1855). Barrows
were numerous in pre-Conquest England, but most of them were already
ancient. The fact that burial mounds are occasionally found in or beside
churchyards, as at Berwick *Sx*, may therefore reflect no more than the ubiquity of prehistoric and Roman settlement. But there may be some special
cases. Old barrows were sometimes reused by the English, who also raised
new mounds of their own. At Taplow *Bu* there is a large conical barrow
in the old churchyard. Within it was a lavishly furnished burial of the
seventh century. There are some who suppose that the churchyard here
was laid out at a much later date, and that the inclusion of the barrow
within its bounds was fortuitous. But this cannot be assumed. Recent excavations around the church at Repton *Db* (Fig. 72) have disclosed

> not one but two or even more tombs crest-sited along the low cliff of the
> south bank of the Trent. Like the earthen tombs of old, these were sunk
> into the ground, but one at least rose above the surface in monumental
> plinths which recall the mounds, perhaps even the stone pyramids, ap-
> propriate to the burial of princes. Like the mounds of Sutton Hoo above
> the Deben, the tombs at Repton suggest the burying place of a royal
> line; at Repton, however, the context is Christian and the last known
> burial was that of a royal saint.
>
> (Biddle 1986, 22)

If Repton was a necropolis for Mercian royalty it is unlikely that such a
site would have been unique. Others may await recognition. Moreover,
behind Professor Biddle's appeal to the precedent of Sutton Hoo there
must lie a prospect that there were occasions when the metamorphosis
from burial in a 'pagan' to a 'Christian' context could have taken place
within the confines of a single site. Taplow could be reassessed in these
terms.

Also called for is a reassessment of the notion that automatically equates
the seventh- or eighth-century use of barrows with paganism. The equation may lie less in the realm of belief than in that of rank. The importance
of kinship in pre-Conquest society has been discussed (p. 127). The bonds
of kinship extended not only between the living members of a family, but
also to their dead. Ostentatious burial, whether under a mound or in a
church, was a proclamation of status. The presence and accumulation of
such burials also helped to validate hereditary claims to land and
resources. The 'family monasteries' which were considered in Chapter 3
have been visualized as forming an extension of this tradition, albeit in
modified guise (Bullough 1983, 193-7, esp. 196). When taken together,
these elements offer the essentials of a process whereby the genealogical
and future interests of a landed family in the seventh or eighth century

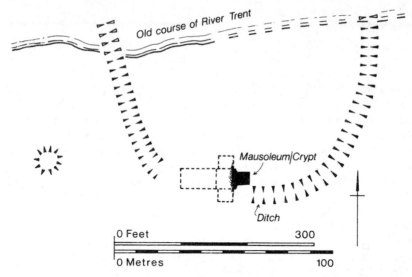

Old course of River Trent

Mausoleum/Crypt

Ditch

0 Feet 300

0 Metres 100

72 Repton, Derbyshire. Geophysical survey and archaeological excavation
have shown that the church was incorporated within a defensive line formed
by the cutting of a deep ditch which enclosed a D-shaped area of some
3.5 acres (1.46 ha) beside the former course of the River Trent. The enclosure
has been associated with the defences of the camp of the Viking army which
is reported to have wintered at Repton in 873-4. The square chancel at the
east end of the church stands upon an earlier mausoleum which was
remodelled as a crypt to cater for visitors attracted by the relics of Wystan, a
royal saint who was buried at Repton in 849 (*Source*: Martin Biddle; caption
based upon Biddle 1986, 16, 22)

might have been gathered to a topographical focus which included a
graveyard, perhaps with mounds, and could ultimately achieve more enduring expression in a church. Usually, it seems, the church was on a
different site, but its removal from the scene of earlier memories was not
invariable, and may have had more to do with changes of tenure and
dynastic fragmentation than with any hostility towards the principle of
superimposition. Nor did the sequence always begin with a barrow and
move to a churchyard. In the ninth and tenth centuries Scandinavian immigrants to parts of north Britain and the Isle of Man buried some of their
dead in mounds which were situated within or close to the limits of
Christian graveyards. Such burials have sometimes been interpreted as
representing a return to paganism under Scandinavian influence. So, too,
have the graves containing Viking weaponry which have been found in
a dozen or more churchyards in various parts of England (Graham-
Campbell 1980, 381). This view may be correct, although the carved stones
and literary sources of the period seem to tell a more complicated story,
first of syncretism and then of an acceptance, at least in nominal terms,
of Christian conventions by Scandinavian leaders. Again, therefore,

mounds and weapons may be of as much, or more, significance in relation to matters of rank and status than to questions of religious belief.

There is no reason to think that many churches were deliberately positioned upon or next to mounds containing ancestral burials. If the hypothesis sketched above has any substance at all, the numbers involved must always have been small (cf. Blair 1987, 268, n. 12). Minsters of supposed 'tribal' origin (pp. 66–7) and churches with traditions of royal burial, like Steyning *Sx*, are perhaps the places where signs of the phenomenon should be looked for first. It is to be expected that the physical signs will normally be inconspicuous or ambiguous. The tendency for mounds to be plundered in antiquity, the effects of erosion and episodes of deliberate reduction will all have conspired to minimize the evidence to an extent that potential cases may lie unnoticed. As for ambiguity, the Earl's Barton mound could be a barrow, or it could be a motte: but might it be both?

Whether or not there are some mounds close to churches for which a sepulchral background should be entertained, we have begun to identify a class of site whereat a church and an earthwork betoken the presence of a lord, and where the genesis of the group pre-dates the Norman Conquest. More examples must now be examined.

At Laughton-en-le-Morthen *SY* (*YW*) the parish church of All Saints dates mainly from the fourteenth century. It has a splendid steeple which is given extra prominence by the position of the church at the top of a hill. Although the church has been much rebuilt, a substantial fragment of early fabric survives at the west end of the north nave aisle. What we seem to have here are the remains of a *porticus*: the west and north walls, together with the stump of an east wall which appears internally as a scar and is confirmed outside by burly quoins at the north-east angle. Central to the north wall is a tall doorway, surmounted by a semi-circular head and flanked by heavy vertical strips rising to impost blocks of square section. These features suggest a date in the eleventh century.

Until an opportunity arises to excavate at Laughton the plan of the church to which the *porticus* belonged will remain unknown. There are, however, several layouts that can be put forward as logical possibilities. If the *porticus* was answered by a similar chamber to the south, then it may be that we are in the vicinity of a former central crossing. This would mean that the ritual focus of the church was later moved eastwards (Fig. 73) (Ryder 1982, 74). Alternatively, the church may have been planned around a central space. An arrangement of the latter sort could indicate a building which was designed for private rather than congregational use. A possible context for this idea is provided by Domesday Book, which tells us that earl Edwin, an English magnate, had his *aula* 'hall' at Laughton. The church might therefore be considered as a component of an aristocratic residential complex.

We do not know where Edwin's *aula* was. However, immediately west of the church is a motte-and-bailey castle. The location of the motte, and

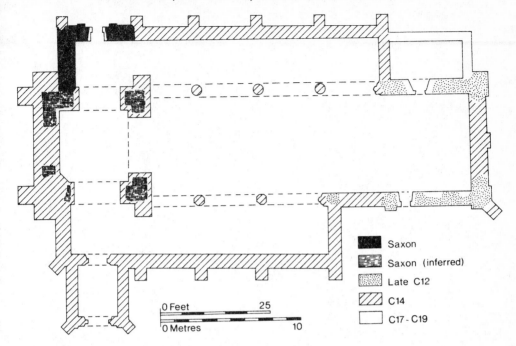

Saxon
Saxon (inferred)
Late C12
C14
C17 - C19

0 Feet   25
0 Metres   10

73 All Saints, Laughton-en-le-Morthen, South Yorkshire (*YW*). Interpretation of the development of the plan, which shows early emphasis upon the western part of the building, is after Ryder 1982

its axial relationship with the church, are likely to have been governed by local topography. The church is on a plateau. To the west the ground falls away steeply. The motte was therefore placed on the crest of the scarp. If Edwin's *aula* stood hereabouts, then it too may have occupied this defensible position, to be superseded by the motte towards the end of the eleventh century.

East of the motte-and-bailey there are traces of a larger enclosure which appears to have surrounded the church. The swelling of what must originally have been a substantial earthen bank is easily visible in the northern part of the churchyard. Churches are often found within baileys which were added to existing castles. English Bicknor *Gl*, Lidgate *Sf*, Owston Ferry *Li* and Pirton *Hrt* are among the many places where churches were so enclosed. Perhaps Laughton should be added to the list. However, there is no reason here to regard the earthwork in the churchyard as an outer bailey which was secondary to the motte. On present evidence this feature could just as well have preceded the motte.

The development which has been proposed for Laughton-en-le-Morthen is conjectural, but there are other places where sequences of possibly similar character have been elucidated by excavation. Sulgrave *Np* has a ringwork which adjoins the west side of the churchyard (Fig. 74).

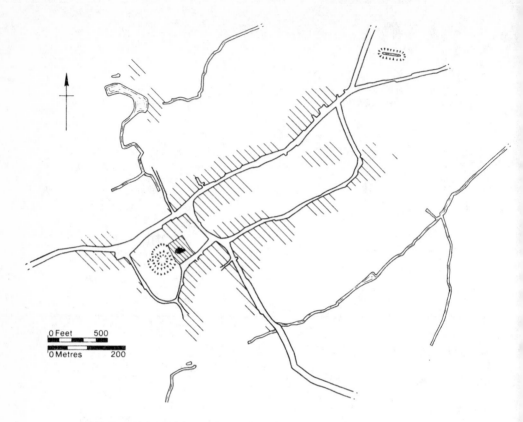

74 Sulgrave, Northamptonshire, showing association between church and ringwork (*Source*: based on a plan by the Royal Commission on the Historical Monuments of England)

Archaeological investigation of the northern part of the ringwork revealed it to have been established on the site of earlier buildings. The earliest of the buildings dated from the end of the tenth century: they were 'a timber hall-like building and a detached building, possibly a kitchen, represented by post-holes and slots cut into the ground surface and by upstanding stone walls' (Davison 1977, 109). Around 1000 the hall was modified, and at some point during the first half of the eleventh century an attempt was made to fortify the site by surrounding it with an earthwork (1977, 111). The Norman ringwork 'enclosed a stone hall and attendant buildings, some of which were those of the earlier Saxon manor centre, retained in use' (1977, 104). The excavator has drawn attention to the fact that the west door of the church is on the same axis as the tenth-century hall (1977, 113). This doorway is of Anglo-Saxon character and may be in its original position (Richmond 1986, 181). Linear relationships are an intriguing feature of Anglo-Saxon planning. They occur in both secular and religious contexts, and some of them incorporated graves and tombs as well as buildings (Figs 19(d), 72).

The example of Sulgrave shows that conjecture about Norman lords fortifying the residential sites of their English antecessors may not be unreasonable. Ringworks also adjoin churches in the nearby parishes of Culworth and Weeden Lois. Elsewhere, some chapels and churches are found inside ringworks. At Old Erringham *Sx* excavation has revealed the plan of a church within a ringwork of probable early eleventh-century date (Fig. 75). At the time of excavation it was not clear whether the church preceded this enclosure or was placed within it (Holden 1980). However, a recent study to be published by Mr John Holmes has led to the suggestion that the church existed before the ringwork. Church Norton, Selsey *Sx*, has the remains of a church which was similarly located; in this case the origin of the church may lie before the Conquest, the ringwork after it (Aldsworth 1979a; Aldsworth and Garnett 1981) (Fig. 76).

When Norman lords dug themselves in, the church was commonly left just outside the primary enclosure. However, it was not unusual for a church, and sometimes an entire village, to be enclosed within an outer bailey. Apart from the examples already mentioned, churches can be seen inside augmented defences at Bramber *Sx*, Loughor *Glm*, Saunderton *Bu* and Ashley *Ha*. Settlements which were taken into the embrace of a castle's outer defences include Pleshey *Ex*, Richard's Castle and Kilpeck *He*, Castle Camps *Ca*, Meppershall *Bd* and Therfield *Hrt* (Figs 77–9). In the last four cases the villages were later abandoned. Meppershall is a reminder that the age of mottes coincided with the period when parishes were crystallizing: two sides of the settlement enclosure are followed by the parish boundary (Renn 1973, 242). Pleshey was founded in 1174. The new settlement lay within an existing parish and therefore came too late to qualify for a parish church of its own. Consent was, however, given for the establishment of a chapel, and in 1339 this was replaced by a collegiate church which was given a position just outside the defences. There is no doubt that the church at Kilpeck preceded the earthworks that surround it: literary sources refer to a church here long before the Conquest, and the church contains some fabric which is of earlier date than the main twelfth-century structure. The origins of the church at Castle Camps are less clear. The church overlies the line of the ditch of the inner bailey. The ditch became obsolete when the defences were extended in the twelfth century, and from this it has been argued that the church was added to the complex after the castle had been enlarged (Taylor 1974, 65). Yet it is not impossible that the church was present beforehand. Apart from the risk of building a new church across a ditch that had only just been filled – a danger to which twelfth-century masons would surely have been alert – it is possible that the church was incorporated in the original defences as a gate-block or ready-made stronghold. It may be recalled that this happened at Repton in the ninth century, and something like it happened also at Thetford *Nf* in the 1070s when the church of St Martin was embodied

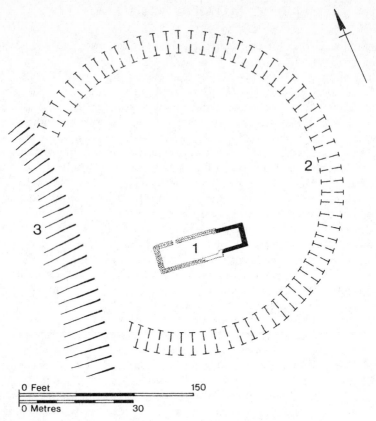

75 Old Erringham, Sussex. Church within ringwork. 1 chapel; 2 enclosing ditch (*Source*: Holden 1980)

in a Norman ringwork (Knocker 1967).

An issue which arises from some of these cases is the extent to which churches found in castle baileys may have originated as castle chapels which were later broadened to wider use. At Doncaster *SY* (*YW*), for instance, the east end of Sir George Gilbert Scott's rebuilding of the parish church of St George overlies the site of the Norman motte. It has been suggested that the parish church originated as the castle chapel (Buckland *et al.* 1981, 30–1). Castles, however, were guarded places, and if a castle chapel was to evolve into a parish church it was usually necessary for the castle to cease to be of any military significance or that part of it which contained the church to be relinquished. It is a telling point that when the castle at Doncaster was in use, the people who lived beyond its defences attended a church dedicated to St Mary Magdalene which stood in the marketplace. Chapel-sharing arrangements between townspeople and castle-dwellers are known of, but they were seldom satisfactory and in the long run they were usually brought to an end by the building of a new church in the civilian quarter. Thus at Launceston *Co* the burgesses built themselves a church late in the fourteenth century. At New Buckenham

Nf a chapel which served both the castle and borough was superseded by a church in the town. Rising *Nf* has within the middle bailey a church which was abandoned, apparently in favour of a new church of St Lawrence which stands in the village. Important castles which achieved permanence almost invariably had chapels of their own, and some of them, like the circular chapel at Ludlow, were buildings of considerable distinction. But these buildings were not regularly accessible to ordinary

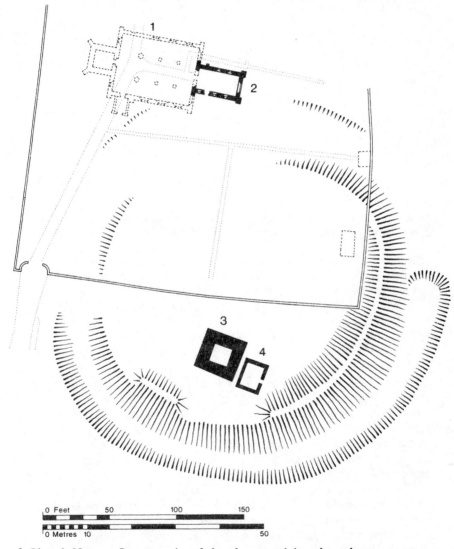

76 Church Norton, Sussex. 1 site of church; 2 surviving chancel; 3, 4 tower and associated building within early post-Conquest ringwork (*Sources*: Aldsworth 1979a; Aldsworth and Garnett 1981)

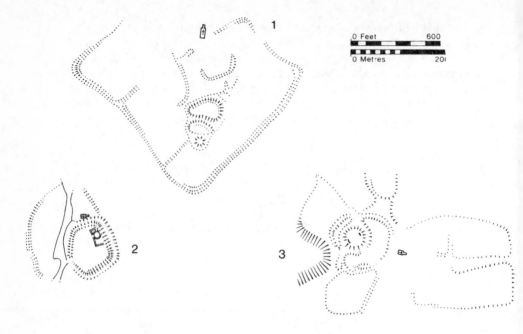

0 Feet 600

0 Metres 200

77 Churches and mottes at 1 Meppershall, Bedfordshire; 2 Ashley, Hampshire; 3 Kilpeck, Herefordshire (cf. Pl. 31) (*Source*: Renn 1973)

citizens, and in such cases it is normal to find a parish church standing in attendance outside the stronghold: a pattern exemplified at Corfe *Do*, Totnes *D*, Eye *Sf* and elsewhere. The communal importance of a parish church was such that urban parishioners liked both to see it and to have it in their midst.

Even the chapels which lay deep inside castles were not always on virgin sites. Recent excavations in the castle at Pontefract *WY* have clarified the layout of the twelfth-century chapel, which was of typical Norman design. Beneath it, however, lay traces of an earlier cemetery: a discovery which points to the presence of a pre-Conquest place of worship nearby, and which could indicate that the hilltop had been occupied before Ilbert de Lacy fortified it some time before 1086 (Thorp 1983). Possibly cognate results were obtained at Mitford *Nb*, where excavations inside the bailey in 1938 revealed a chapel of mid-twelfth-century date which covered an earlier burial ground (Renn 1973, 247).

The foregoing discussion of private *burhs* and Norman defences offers an important clue as to why it should be that so many parish churches stand on hilltops, knolls and eminences. Churches in lofty positions are found all over the country. A few, like Crayke *NY*, Breedon *Le* and Hanbury *Wo* have already been explained in monastic terms (p. iii). But for the large majority there is usually no rational explanation other than in a possibility of the founder's desire to bear witness to God, or that the church was originally coupled with something that is not there now.

Although the part played by purely religious motivation was probably limited, there seems to be little doubt that the position of a parish church could be invested with an iconographic significance. Outside Winchester, for instance, there were four churches on the tops of hills. These buildings have recently been discussed by Dr Derek Keene, who points out that whenever they originated individually 'it seems likely that by the twelfth century they had acquired a special significance as a group. Each was visible from the others, and travellers approaching the city would have seen them from a distance. Each of them played a part in the city's processional liturgy' (Keene 1985, 8). Three of the churches bore dedications that evoked pilgrimages: Giles, James and Catherine. St Catherine occupied the highest of the hills: an arrangement that may have been intended to remind the onlooker of Mount Sinai, whereto Catherine's relics had been miraculously translated in the ninth century. 'Other outlying churches', continues Dr Keene,

> seem to ram the message home: there was St Faith at the limit of the
> southern suburb, and a little further out along the road to Southampton

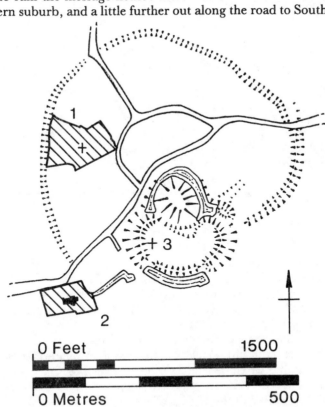

78 Pleshey, Essex. I = possible site of parish church; 2 = College of Holy Trinity, founded 1394; 3 = castle (*Source*: F. Williams 1977)

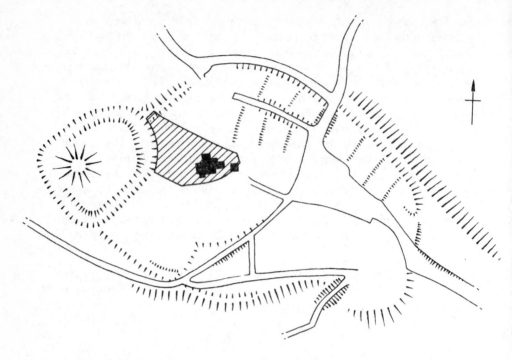

79 Richard's Castle, Herefordshire (*Source*: Aston and Rowley 1974)

and overseas, the Hospital of St Cross, founded by the Hospitallers. . . . the church of St Anastasius in the west suburbs may be in the same category, for, rather than Anastasia or one of the numerous Anastasiuses, it may well have commemorated the Resurrection (*anastasis*) in a verbal form appropriate for those whose minds turned on Jerusalem; it was suited to a suburb which played a major part in the liturgical celebration of Easter.

(Keene 1985, 8)

St Catherine's association with Mount Sinai explains her popularity as a saint suited to high places, and to beacons. The name 'St Catherine's Hill' occurs quite widely, especially in southern England. A number of hills bearing this name are found near monasteries: Christchurch *Ha*, for instance, or Milton Abbas and Abbotsbury *Do*. At Abbotsbury there is an impressive stone-vaulted chapel on the summit of the hill. This was a dual-purpose building which served also as a lighthouse. On Chale Down *IoW* stands St Catherine's Oratory, a purpose-built lighthouse of the fourteenth century with a profile suggestive of medieval rocketry. These were later buildings of specialized function, however, and to explain the presence of the huge number of ordinary churches that occupy lofty sites it is necessary to return to the theme which has recurred throughout this chapter: the church as a witness to the residential preferences of pre-Conquest lords.

There are parts of the country where almost every church stands in an elevated position. This is so in the Vale of York between the Rivers Wharfe and Nidd. Churches at Wighill, Healaugh, Walton and Kirk Deighton occupy prominent sites; so does Hunsingore; Kirk Hammerton is on a knoll. Few break the pattern, save in parishes which are unremittingly flat, and nearly all of the churches which conform to it are known to have originated before the Conquest. Motorists who journey along the M1 will notice many examples of the phenomenon in Derbyshire, Nottinghamshire and South Yorkshire: Sandiacre *Db*, for instance, or High Hoyland *SY* (*YW*). Moving around the country cases are found in practically all areas where there is uneven terrain. At Bishopstone *Sx* the church is on a hillock, set apart from the hamlet. Oldbury *Gl* has a church which is spectacularly situated upon a rocky mound which protrudes from the floor of the Vale of Severn. At Old Sodbury *Gl* the church was placed upon a ledge on the side of the Cotswold escarpment. The church at Pontesbury *Sa* occupies a high spot, with traces of a defensive earthwork. Tichbourne *Ha* lies high on a hillside, with the village below. The church of St Oswald at Malpas *Ch* occupies the highest point in the village. Wakerley, Whiston and Rockingham *Np* are likewise elevated; so too East Horndon *Ex*, Godshill *IoW*, Rivington *La*, Burwell *Li* – and hundreds of others. Why?

The most likely explanation is simply that some pre-Conquest lords lived in prominent positions. In due course they provided their eyries with churches, and the churches have survived whereas the homes of their founders have not. Several of the places mentioned above have names which contain the element *burh*. Oldbury *Gl* was already known thus in 972 when it appears in a charter as *Ealdanbyri*. Sodbury occurs as *Soppa's burg* in *c.* 903 (Sawyer 1968, nos 786, 1446). Such names, and the sites of the churches, are suggestive of the strongholds of local magnates. A particularly good example of a church in this sort of superior location is to be seen at Edlesborough *Bu*. The church is dramatically positioned at the summit of a small hill which is an outlier of the Chilterns. The place-name was recorded in 1163 as *Eduluesberga* 'Eadwulf's beorg'. The element *beorg* may point to a barrow, but it could just as well have referred to the hill itself. Around the church are signs of terracing and an enclosing earthwork. Such a site could have afforded prestige and a measure of security to a pre-Conquest lord. Rather similar circumstances are found at Holme-on-Spalding-Moor *Hu* (*YE*). The modern village lies at the foot of an isolated hill which rises steeply from the surrounding plain. The church stands at the summit. Sculpture visible within the tower suggests that this site was in ecclesiastical use by the ninth century. Level ground to the south would have offered space for a small settlement. Church Pulverbatch *Sa* is another example of a church that occupies a mounded and possibly defensive site.

Minor citadels like Oldbury and Edlesborough are extreme examples of what has here been argued to have been a much more widespread phenomenon. Of course, not all lords sought to put their halls in high places. And when they did do so the reasons may have ranged from fashion and considerations of status to a more basic concern for security. The motives which caused lords either to colonize or ignore high spots must therefore have varied a good deal according to time and circumstance, as well as place. Moreover, some of the mounds upon which churches stand seem too small to have been viable as residential sites. Cheriton *Ha*, Winwick *Np* and Maxey *Ca* (*Li*) are among many churches in this category. At Cheriton *Ha* – *Cherinton* 'church tun' in 1167 – the hump upon which the church was placed is so small as to have caused considerable extra work for the masons who lengthened the building in the later Middle Ages. In such a case we cannot be sure that the advantages which were originally perceived in the site did not include a simple wish to lift the building above the scene of everyday life, or a response to the symbolism of Calvary. In later centuries such feelings might be expressed by increasing the profile of the building, in particular through the raising of great steeples: in effect, making the church itself into a kind of artificial hill. Before 1100, when churches were generally small, perhaps high ground provided the necessary boost.

On the whole, however, it is seigneurial considerations which seem likely to have been most prevalent. Quite a number of the churches which have been mentioned, like Winwick *Np*, and many others that could have been (e.g. Brill *O*, Dethick *Db*) are later found in close conjunction with manorial buildings. Such groups are common almost everywhere from the twelfth century. Those on hills should not, therefore, be seen as forming a separate category, although the factors which first put them there may have operated with more force at certain times, or in certain conditions, than in others.

The topographical relationships which existed between churches and manors in the later Middle Ages are too diverse to receive much attention here. They range from loose patterns where the various buildings stand in open order to the more clustered patterns that are found in some marcher areas, as at Stokesay *Sa* and Croft *He* where fortified houses stand protectively next to their churches. One common tendency which can be noted is for the church to stand either on or very close to the boundary of the manorial enclosure. This is exemplified at Raunds, where the first church of *c.*875 × 900 lay just outside an enclosure which contained buildings that are regarded as ancestral to those of an eleventh-century manor (Cadman and Foard 1984). But a church could stand fully within the enclosure, as at Helmdon *Np*, and there were also occasions when the church appears to have been placed athwart the boundary. This is well illustrated at Weaverthorpe *Hu* (*YE*) where the chancel may once have projected into the compound while the nave lay outside it (Fig. 80). The church was built early in the twelfth century, and the manorial layout may

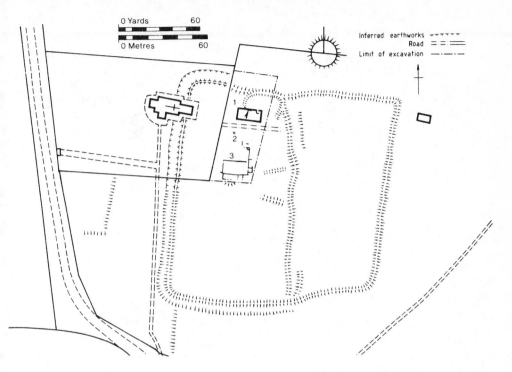

80 Weaverthorpe, North Yorkshire, showing relationship between church and manorial enclosure and buildings. **1** hall I (twelfth century); **2** Stamford ware sherds from hollow; **3** hall II (thirteenth–fourteenth-century) (*Source*: Brewster 1972)

also date from this time (Brewster 1972). Were such arrangements intended to facilitate dual access: the lord coming from within, his villagers from without?

We have seen that the physical appearance of seigneurial complexes before the end of the eleventh century is still a matter of the greatest uncertainty. There are a few intriguing literary references, notably a charter of 1004 which mentions land at Upper Winchendon *Bu* which was defined by bounds that included a *biris dic* 'burh ditch' at a point which is later found occupied by a complex of manor house and church (Gelling 1979, 182–3). But how such statements are to be translated into actual plans remains to be seen. Apart from Sulgrave and Raunds, however, archaeology has delivered the interesting example of Goltho *Li*. Goltho is the site of a medieval village which entered upon hard times in the fourteenth century and was later abandoned (Fig. 81). Today, even in summer, it remains an eerie place. Until the 1970s the sites of Goltho's manor, houses and streets survived as earthworks. Now they have been erased by modern agriculture. But in compensation we have the preliminary results of excavations which were carried out between 1970 and 1974 by Mr Guy

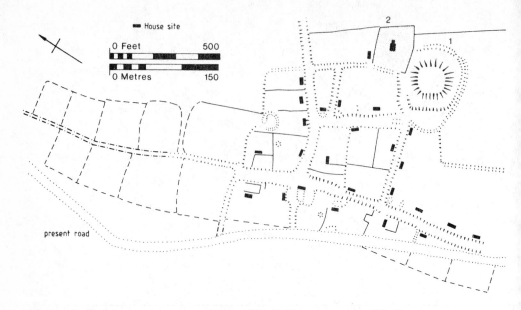

81 Settlement remains at Goltho, Lincolnshire. 1 motte-and-bailey; 2 churchyard (*Source*: G. Beresford 1975)

Beresford. Beresford disinterred a sequence of pre-Conquest halls beneath the twelfth-century manor house. And sandwiched between the two were the remains of a late eleventh-century motte-and-bailey.

The earliest hall at Goltho was erected around 850. It was accompanied by domestic and economic buildings, all set within a fortified enclosure that occupied the highest ground in the neighbourhood. Repairs and alterations were made on several occasions in the tenth and eleventh centuries. The date at which the church was added is not known, but it was recorded in 1086 and could have been there before the motte-and-bailey was superimposed on the site. It seems likely that the church was an adjunct of the late Saxon 'manorial' group (G. Beresford 1981) (Figs 81 and 82). Goltho is unusual perhaps only to the extent that it has been subjected to archaeological investigation on a large scale. So while we are not yet in the position to assess Goltho's typicality, it would be wrong to lay stress upon the singularity of results from this site simply on the grounds of our lack of comparative knowledge. Sites like Laughton, Edlesborough and others discussed earlier in this chapter may harbour cognate sequences. They await the spade.

Essentially, what has been proposed in this chapter is the widespread existence of a class – or classes – of pre-Conquest seigneurial settlement. These settlements seem to have left little in the way of upstanding remains, unless they involved the reuse of more ancient earthworks, and in consequence there has not been much discussion of their physical

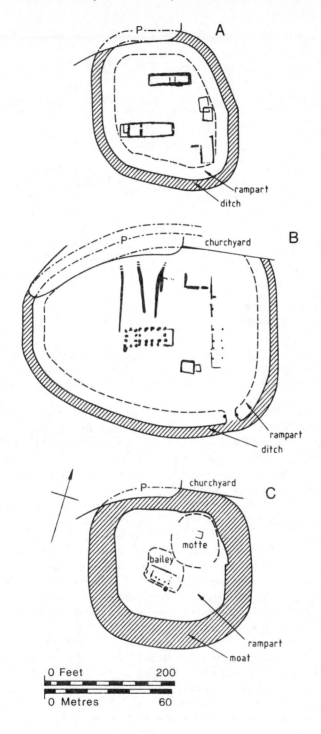

82 Goltho: outline evolution of buildings and defences between the ninth and eleventh centuries. **P** post-medieval pond (*Source*: G. Beresford 1981)

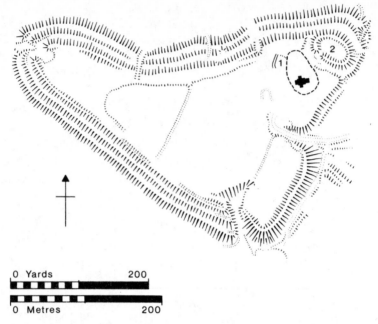

0 Yards 200

0 Metres 200

83 Caerau, Ely, Glamorgan. Medieval church and ringwork set within defences of an Iron Age fort. 1 pond; 2 ringwork. (*Source*: based on a plan by the Royal Commission on the Ancient and Historical Monuments of Wales)

characteristics. Churches, it is suggested, may be among the best indicators of their former whereabouts. This may also explain the presence of churches within or beside some earthwork enclosures of prehistoric or Roman date, as at Burgh *Sf*, Cholesbury *Bu*, Wadenhoe *Np* or Caerau, Ely *Glm*: the churches could testify to the reoccupation of these sites by medieval lords. Another example is Aylesbury *Bu*, where recent excavations have disclosed the former presence of an Iron Age hillfort which surrounded the ridge whereon the parish church of St Mary now stands. St Mary's was a pre-Conquest minster (Farley 1979; Blair 1985). It appears that the ditch of the hillfort was recut before *c.* 710 (*Current Archaeology*, 101 (1986), 189). The reuse of ancient enclosures was not always of sufficient duration for the accompanying church to acquire an independent identity. At Cadbury *So*, for instance, a temporary *burh* was established within a hillfort, probably in the period 1009–19, and this led to the building, or at least the beginning, of a small cruciform church (Alcock 1972, 198–200). But the *burh* was short-lived, and the church did not endure.

Although the *aulae* of pre-Conquest lords have disappeared, it has been argued that some of them were replaced by Norman defences, and that in many cases they were superseded by manor houses. When moats became popular as marks of status for lords and gentry, these too could be added to the sequence, as at Marston Trussell *Np* (Fig. 84), Norwell

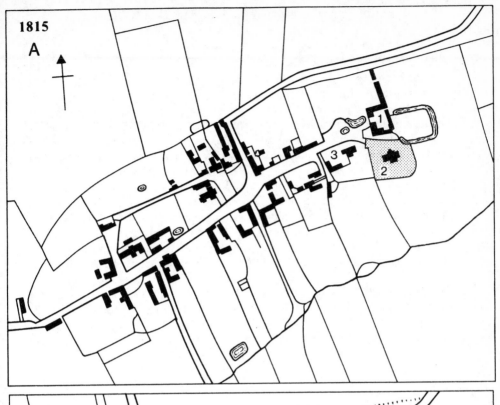

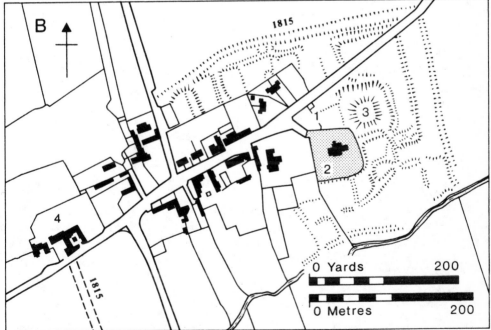

84 Marston Trussell, Northamptonshire: church and moat. **A** village plan as mapped in 1815 (**1** manor house; **2** churchyard; **3** rectory). **B** as mapped in the late 1970s (**1** site of manor house; **2** churchyard; **3** moat) (*Source*: Royal Commission on the Ancient and Historical Monuments of England)

Nt, Roos *Hu* (*YE*), Quarrendon *Bu*, Burton Pedwardine *Li*, and hundreds of other places. In later centuries some manor houses underwent aggrandisement and were developed into country mansions. Others dwindled in importance, declining to the status of farms, or disappearing altogether. The homes of lords could, of course, be transferred to new sites at any stage, and the potential for the process to divide among several possible lines of development at different moments in the sequence leaves the church as the one building which is likely to have kept its ground from the start. Even churches could be moved but, once established, most of them seem to be characterized by constancy. Burton Pedwardine, for example, contains sculpture of the tenth or eleventh centuries, and offers a fixed point in the chronology and topography of the area. Isolated churches may represent settlements which have vanished – a matter to be explored in Chapter 8 – but some of them testify rather to the geography of pre-Conquest lordship. Out of fifty-two isolated churches in the western part of Suffolk, for instance, at least thirty-six stand beside existing halls or moated sites (Dymond 1968, 29). To claim all of these as the successors of pre-Conquest halls would be unjustified. But most of the churches in this area were in position by 1086, and the possibility that many of them then adjoined the homes of local power-holders is an hypothesis that goes further than any other to explain the positions of most medieval churches in the landscape.

VII

A SENSE OF STYLE

By 1400 many cathedrals were so large that their importance was something that thousands of country-dwelling people could see for themselves. Weather permitting, a person could stand upon a saltern mound beside the Wash and view the mother church of St Mary on its hill at Lincoln, fifty miles away. York minster dominated the floor of the Vale of York; visible from many parishes in each of the three Ridings, the massive outline and creamy-white limestone walls of this building combined to catch the eye from as far away as the Pennine foothills or the western flank of the Wolds. Ely cathedral was, and is, the greatest construction in the Cambridgeshire fens. Salisbury's soaring central spire, and the steeples at Chichester, Lichfield and Norwich, were hardly less conspicuous. Not all cathedrals or bishops' minsters were meant to impress from afar – one thinks of St David's, reclusive in its hollow, or peaceful Southwell – but most were reared skywards, jabbed the horizons of ordinary people, and in their prominence proclaimed the temporal power, as well as the spirituality, of the medieval Church.

Kings and noblemen gave estates and materials to endow and erect these buildings. Lesser folk gave as they could. Cathedral administrators were ever ingenious in devising schemes to promote the flow of offerings. In the thirteenth century Lincoln had a chantry which offered unceasing prayers for the souls of those who contributed to the cathedral, as well as a fabric fund, and a plan for regular giving. Donations to the building fund often took the form of plots of land and would secure membership of a special gild (D. Owen 1971, 41–3). Large and small, such gifts mounted up. By 1300 religious communities controlled about 30 per cent of land in England and Wales. Moreover, in the twelfth century the ownership of parish churches by laypeople had come to be frowned upon, with the result that many local churches and their greater tithes were granted into monastic possession. In various ways, therefore, religious houses and cathedrals exerted centripetal influences upon the economies and parishes of their hinterlands and dioceses.

If cathedrals and abbeys are impressive for their structural magnificence and wealth, the parish churches cannot do less than amaze by their huge numbers and artistic diversity. No one knows exactly how many parish churches existed before the Reformation. The record is incomplete, and there were fluctuations, with losses and gains. However, England contained no fewer than 8000 parish churches, probably more, and in what follows 8500 will be taken as a working estimate. Medieval Wales was divided into c. 950 parishes. A combined total of the order 9–10,000 is thus indicated. But even this understates the full extent of provision. In parts of Wales, the Marches and the northern counties, especially in the Pennines and Cumbria, it was the chapelry rather than the parish which formed the working pastoral unit. Parochial chapels were not exclusive to the uplands, although it was in such areas where communications were extended and the population was dispersed that they attained greatest individuality. Lincolnshire's parish churches, of which there seem to have been c. 630, were augmented by at least 125 chapels of parochial or quasi-parochial character (D. Owen 1975), while in thirteenth-century Leicestershire there were 'in a little over 200 parishes more than 100 dependent chapels' (A. H. Thompson 1947, 123). Overall, there can hardly have been fewer than 12,000 parochial churches and chapels in England and Wales by 1500.

The figures are worth some reflection. In earlier chapters it has been argued that all but a few parish churches existed by the second quarter of the twelfth century, and that most of them were in place before 1100. Since local churches seem only rarely to have been built of stone before the eleventh century, it follows that masoncraft was rapidly transformed from its former position as a minority or occasional pursuit among builders to the status of an independent trade. The Great Rebuilding of c. 1050–1150 was a movement of almost seismic character, involving the commitment of craftsmen and resources on an unprecedented scale. The fact that campaigns of monastic, cathedral and castle building were taking place at the same time only serves to emphasize the degree of parochial achievement. It was a feat unsurpassed even by Victorian efforts to enlarge parochial provision. For qualitatively, arguably, and quantitatively, certainly, the work of the nineteenth century was no more than an after-shock to the medieval earthquake: and this despite the greater resources of transport, technology and finance that the Victorians could command. In this chapter, and in the two that follow, there will be an examination of some of the factors which fed or affected this desire to build.

The construction of a church was seldom a once-for-all operation. Episodes of enlargement and modernization usually followed. Here and there can be found churches of the eleventh and twelfth centuries, like Kirk Hammerton *NY* (*YW*) or Up Waltham *Sx*, which remained largely undisturbed. But the period 1150–1500, the Gothic age, presents itself more generally as an era when change was actively valued.

Several issues arise from this. On the one hand it may be asked why the preoccupation with renewal ran so wide and deep, how stylistic preferences evolved, and by what means they were transmitted. On the other, we must examine the extent to which rural resources were exploited for the rebuilding, alteration and maintenance of churches. Underlying both groups of themes, and roping them together, are considerations of patronage, piety and wealth.

Time-lapse photography of the churches dotted upon two hundred square miles of English countryside would capture something of the pattern and chronology of architectural change between 1050 and 1550. As the sequence begins, most churches are already present. They are a motley lot, some new, others ageing, variously built of wood and stone. Nearly all of them are small, and consist of an unaisled nave and square-ended chancel. Fewer than a quarter possess a western tower. The years 1050–1150 bustle with rebuilding, much of it still rather rough-and-ready, but always now in stone. We see more towers, and notice a predilection for apsidal east ends. Aisles remain uncommon. Towards the end of the twelfth century there begins a trend involving outward growth. The tempo quickens, and during the next hundred years few naves do not put forth at least one aisle; apses disappear as chancels are prolonged and sometimes widened. New towers are built and existing ones are heightened. The first lofty spires appear. Porches and chapels begin to bud from the main structural envelope.

By the second quarter of the fourteenth century most churches are approaching their maximum areal extent, and some have reached it. Yet building continues. Chapels and sacristies now multiply. Porches become more substantial, and may be of two storeys. Much effort is now directed upwards: into clerestories, pinnacled roofscapes and steeples. Change is usually accomplished by the grafting of new work onto older fabric. But sometimes whole naves or chancels are taken down and replaced. In a few cases the entire church is demolished to make way for a brand new building. Curiously, while all this is happening some churches are being abandoned and left to fall down.

This is, of course, a very generalized and simplified picture, at once anywhere and nowhere, conflating aspects of design that are found in different areas and omitting many regional types. Were the sequence to be filmed in Buckinghamshire the viewer would see hardly any stone spires; in Northamptonshire, many. Clerestories would rise by the dozen in Suffolk, but there would be few in Kent, and none in Cornwall. In fifteenth-century Yorkshire the theme would be modification and refenestration; in Somerset, towers; in Devon, remodelling or rebuilding.

Stylistic and formal variations can be followed down to a very local level. Even an area so small as our twenty-mile square is likely to contain idiosyncrasies of design or combinations of features that are characteristic of, if not exclusive to, that district. Between Wetherby and York, for instance, there is a group of churches which have been purged of their chancel arches. Just under the limestone escarpment north of Sleaford *Li* there is a family of churches with spires that replicate a single design (Fig. 85). In and around Bristol the clerestories of naves were sometimes limited to a single pair of windows, to illuminate the rood. Comparable traits of kinship, some concerning small details, others more pervasive, are encountered everywhere. The unifying factor varies. It can be to do with communications, like a valley or road; it may be found in a centre of quarrying; it can reflect a phase of economic prosperity; or it may derive from the preferences of a particular social group, a family or an institution.

Influences of the latter kind are exemplified in some of the more remarkable buildings of the Romanesque era. Parish churches which were built immediately before and after the Norman Conquest are usually rather plain. Where a powerful lord was based nearby, as at Kippax *WY*, such churches could be large, but architectural sculpture is seldom other than elementary and sparse (Zarnecki 1951, 10–15). As time went on, builders began to conjure up a broader range of ornamental motifs. The devices of twelfth-century architectural sculpture – zig-zag, beak-head, cable and so forth – were used mainly for the enrichment of mouldings, capitals and the orders of arches and doorways. They have often been surveyed, illustrated and discussed (e.g. Clapham 1934, 128–36; Zarnecki 1951, 1953; Henry and Zarnecki 1957). However, within the widespread and generally standardized distribution of twelfth-century embellishment, there are several geographical areas that stand out as containing groups of churches that are characterized by an exceptionally lavish degree of enrichment. One of these groups is in Yorkshire. The churches of this so-called 'Yorkshire School' are worth attention because they illustrate aspects of patronage, cultural and intellectual stimuli that give perspective to wider questions about style.

Most of Yorkshire's village churches in the twelfth century were simple buildings, typically with two compartments and sometimes a west tower. Few of them bear much sculptural decoration. There are, however, about a dozen which possess elaborate schemes of decoration.

> The themes are essentially literary and draw upon the calendar scenes of the Labours of the Months and the associated symbols of the Zodiac; these are often accompanied by fabulous animals, dragons and hunters. Occasionally there is a choice of biblical narrative scenes, and more rarely still opposed Virtues and Vices, and the clearly identifiable animals of the Bestiary.
>
> (Butler 1982, 81)

Many of these themes can be traced to sources in manuscripts. In itself this occasions no surprise; interplay between the medieval arts was extensive. More striking is the rapidity with which a literary idea could be taken up. The south doorway at Alne *NY*, for instance, displays scenes which draw upon versions of the Bestiary that had only just appeared (Butler 1982, 87–8). Here the interval between literary and lapidary can scarcely have been longer than twenty years and may have been as short as ten.

A possible explanation for this swiftness of transmission is to be found in the person of John of Canterbury, who was treasurer of York minster from 1154 to 1162. Alne was among the possessions of the treasureship at that time. John was a cultured man. He had travelled abroad, and went on to become archbishop of Lyon (Clay 1939–43, 11–19). There is, of course, a big difference between suggesting that John of Canterbury *could* have played a part in dictating the iconographic programme at Alne and arguing that he *did* do so. Today, eight centuries on, when all other information about the people who were connected with this church in the 1150s and 1160s has perished, it may seem astonishing that the one person who can be linked with the building should also happen to have been the begetter of the scheme. Such scepticism would be justified if the example of Alne was isolated. But this was not the case. If we examine the other churches where skills of the Yorkshire carvers are represented, it emerges that they too were mostly in the hands of members of the cathedral chapter, the archbishop, or else were possessions of prominent religious communities. These relationships are mapped in Fig. 86.

Literary inspiration, canalized by patronage, thus emerges as a plausible context for the Yorkshire School. Is it possible to go further, and to identify the milieu within which the ideas behind the carvings were formed and transmitted? The role of the archbishop (perhaps especially Roger de Pont L'Evêque, whose pontificate (1154–81) spanned the years when most of the carvings were executed), and of the capitular dignitaries at York has been mentioned. This falls into a wider pattern. During the eleventh and twelfth centuries there was a tendency for the rural monasteries of northern France and England to subside in importance as intellectual centres. As they did so, the communities of urban cathedrals emerged as new foci of academic learning. This transfer of emphasis is best observed in France, most notably at Chartres, Orleans, Rheims and Laon; but it can also be detected in England, where Canterbury, and to a lesser extent London, Winchester, Lincoln and York, rose in importance as places of educational and scholarly activity.

The significance of this is that urban prelates and cathedral chapters were not limited by the provincialism which often affected rural monasteries. The men who held these posts followed varied careers. They consorted with kings and princes, travelled widely, and moved in circles engaged upon the study of theology, philosophy, the classics and the rediscovery of Greek scientific knowledge. On appointment to ecclesiastical posts in England they maintained contacts and friendships through correspondence and continued travel. It is against this background of high

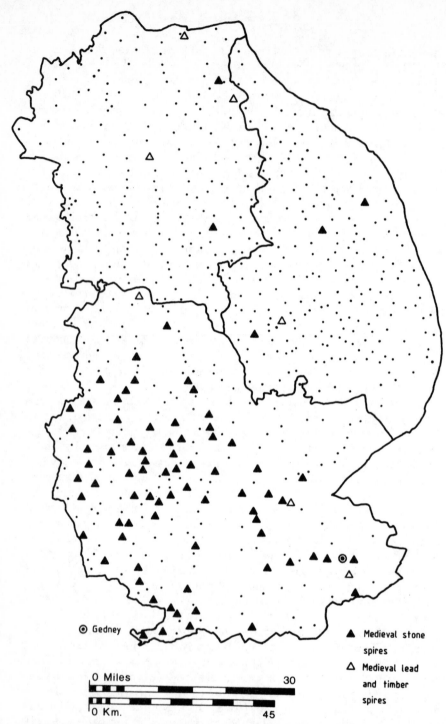

85 Medieval parish churches in Lincolnshire showing (*a*) distribution of
churches with surviving spires; (*b*) distributions of spires, by type (*Source*:
David Stocker)

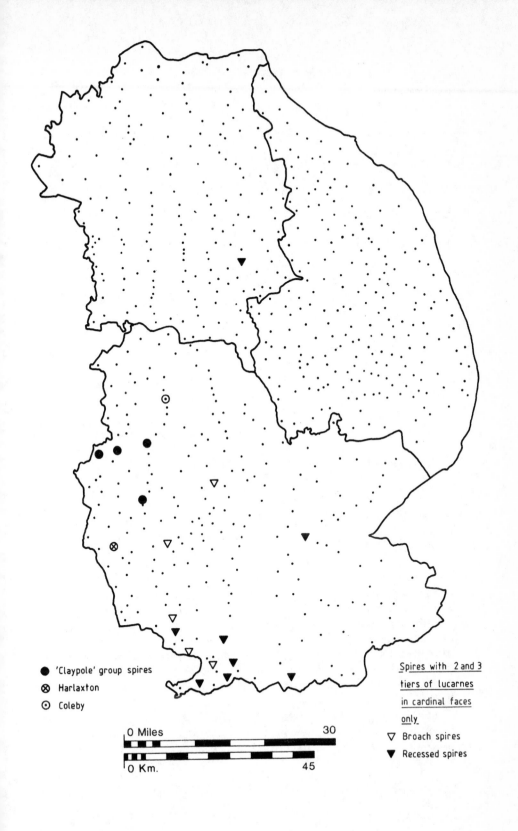

● 'Claypole' group spires

⊗ Harlaxton

☉ Coleby

Spires with 2 and 3 tiers of lucarnes in cardinal faces only

▽ Broach spires

▼ Recessed spires

0 Miles   30

0 Km.   45

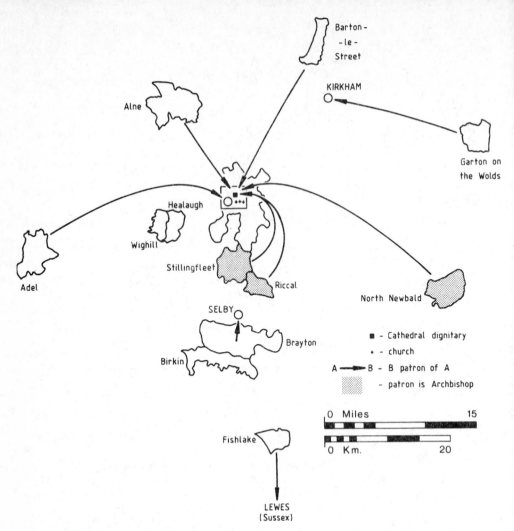

Barton-
-le-
Street

KIRKHAM

Garton on
the Wolds

Alne

Healaugh

Wighill

Stillingfleet

Adel

Riccal

North Newbald

SELBY

Brayton

Birkin

■ – Cathedral dignitary

✦ – church

A ━━▶ B – B patron of A

░░ – patron is Archbishop

0	Miles	15

0	Km.	20

Fishlake

LEWES
(Sussex)

86 Some parish churches with rich twelfth-century embellishment in
Yorkshire, showing possible influences of patronage (*Source*: L.A.S. Butler 1982)

learning and international connections that the sculpture of the Yorkshire
School must be considered. In a sense, minor northern villages like
Fishlake, Riccall and Adel can be regarded as suburbs of Paris or Chartres. By comparison, the influence of St Mary's abbey, York's greatest
monastic community, upon the parish churches in its possession seems to
have been small (Butler 1982, 91). Again, this accords with the broader picture, for while Benedictine monasticism prospered materially under Norman government, the contribution that it made to intellectual life was
limited (Haskins 1971, 39–40).

The example of the Yorkshire School can be translated into a wider
generalization: namely, that in the period *c.* 1100–1300 the patronage of a
magnate, ecclesiastic or an institution is commonly found to lie behind

a parish church of outstanding character. Thus the grandeur of St Mary-le-Bow *GLo*, with its unusual undercroft, is possibly explained by the status of the church as an embassy of Canterbury cathedral priory in the City of London. North Newbald *Hu (YE)* possesses a magnificent cruciform church, built around 1140 and more akin to a miniature cathedral than a parochial buiding. The resemblance may be significant, for Newbald was a prebend of York and a possible former minster. A number of York's other prebends, like Knaresborough and Church Fenton, display signs of cruciformity, as if they were erected in the image of their cathedral mother. Another twelfth-century church of unusual size and elaboration is at Melbourne *Db*. Melbourne was an outpost of the bishops of Carlisle. The curious chapel at Hereford which was built for Robert, bishop of Hereford (1079–95), illustrates how the roles of patron and of builder could be synthesized. The concept for the building derived from Germany, whereas its technical realization was in the terms of Anglo-Norman Romanesque (Gem 1986c).

In the thirteenth century splendid rebuildings of parish churches took place at Potterne and Bishops Canning *Wi* on estates which were held by the bishops of Salisbury. Dunsfold *Sr*, rebuilt comprehensively around 1270, was a possession of the Crown. These examples are significant because full 'end-to-end' reconstructions of parish churches in the Early English style appear to have been unusual. The main reason, one suspects, was financial. In most parishes fundraising was a slow or fitful process. Few could manage the sudden outlay that was required for a complete rebuilding. So the usual pattern was one of enlargement or modernization by stages. There could have been a practical benefit in this, as stylistic development in the period 1200–1340 was so rapid that any work which took longer than about twenty-five years could be out of date before it was finished. Artistic unity in a church is thus very often expressive of an exceptional level of patronage, for where we meet it large resources must have been channelled into the building within a short space of time. St Giles at Skelton, just outside York, is a case in point. When the church was rebuilt in the 1240s it was in the hands of Robert Haget, who was treasurer of the cathedral. Acton Burnell *Sa* owes its purity of idiom to the favour of Robert Burnell, bishop of Bath and Wells, who financed the rebuilding towards the end of the thirteenth century.

This said, the connection between magnates and thoroughgoing architectural renewal in the thirteenth century was not universal. There are some remarkable churches which cannot be attributed to affluent patrons, or where the identities of those responsible are unknown. 'What', wondered Pevsner, 'can the reason have been for Felmersham [*Bd*] receiving the noblest parish church in the county during the noblest age of medieval churches?' (Pevsner 1968, 89). Felmersham was rebuilt during the second quarter of the thirteenth century. The church is aisled, cruciform, has a crossing crowned by a central tower and is distinguished overall by 'a classicity and harmony which ... includes even the west front' (Pevsner 1968, 89). Another thirteenth-century church of superior design is West Walton, in Norfolk marshland. Built at the same time as Felmersham, West Walton has a spacious nave of six bays. Elegantly moulded arches are carried upon circular columns bedecked with Purbeck shafts and stiff-leaf sculpture of the highest quality. The windows of the clerestory alternate between blind panels which carry traces of contemporary painted decoration. Outside, a mighty free-standing bell tower dominates the flatness of the surrounding fenland. A third notable building of the period is Warmington *Np*. Construction here was spread over a longer period than at Felmersham and Walton. Work began around 1200 and there was further enlargement in the mid-thirteenth century. No other parish church in the area was treated to such a comprehensive or lavish rebuilding at this time.

The uniting factor in these examples is that each of the churches was unusually wealthy. Felmersham and Warmington were well endowed. Felmersham was a mother church, with at least two dependent chapels, at Pavenham and Radwell. This helps to explain the value of the living, for although the soils of Felmersham were not especially productive the church was assessed at £26 13s 4d in the *Taxatio* of 1291. Warmington's assessment was £36 13s 4d, whereas the average figure for churches in its vicinity was £11 8s 5d (RCHME *Northants* 6, lxxxiv, 157). West Walton's valuation in 1291 was £28 13s 4d: nowhere near the phenomenal £94 16s 8d which was achieved by nearby Terrington, but still in excess of most parishes elsewhere in Norfolk. The economic strength of Walton lay partly in diversity – livestock, arable, salt-making – but more especially in the scope which still existed for the exploitation of unreclaimed land (Silvester 1985). The advowsons of all three churches were in monastic hands at the time of rebuilding. Felmersham was a possession of Lenton Priory *Nt*. Warmington was held by Peterborough. Walton was shared by the bishop of Ely and Lewes Priory *Sx*. The fact that two of the religious houses, Lenton and Lewes, were Cluniac is probably incidental; the significance of monastic involvement is rather to be seen in relation to the value of the livings.

Since full rebuildings of parish churches in the thirteenth century were out of the ordinary, it is natural to look for exceptional circumstances in order to explain them. Patronage of a high order answers this need. And it is easy to think of ways in which magnates, higher clergy or institutions could have facilitated parish projects: for example, by the secondment of craftsmen, the donation of timber, grants of access to quarries, or by the temporary remission of dues and services which were owed to them in order to release local resources to the work. But such benevolence cannot always be assumed. Indeed, the very singularity of buildings like Skelton and Felmersham could be taken as a sign that the prevailing concern of proprietors lay not with what could be put into a parish so much as what could be exacted from it. The role of the parishioners themselves must therefore be considered.

In earlier chapters it was argued that lay lords and groups of citizens led the field in the founding of local churches before 1100. During the fourteenth and fifteenth centuries large numbers of parish churches were rebuilt or remodelled, often as a result of parochial endeavour (see Chapter 9). What happened in between? The status of the parishioner must be considered. One view is that parishioners were quite influential at the outset, that is before 1100, and became so again in the late Middle Ages, but underwent a decline in status during the interim. Formalization of the parish system in the twelfth century is supposed to have extinguished much of the informality which seems previously to have existed between churchmen and churchgoers. Moreover, after reforms introduced by pope Gregory VII (1073–85) lay ownership of churches and secular entitlement to the disposal of ecclesiastical revenues came to be discouraged, and many parish churches were granted into the possession of religious communities or higher clergy (Kemp 1980). In some cases this led to determined exploitation of parochial revenues by monastic houses. The pastoral interests of the parishes concerned were not always adequately secured. Some of the problems that this could cause are discussed in the next chapter; the point to weigh here is simply the suggestion that in the period c. 1150–1300 parishioners were possibly less influential than at any other time in the Middle Ages. The capacity of rural communities to inaugurate programmes of new building was further limited by the demands of demesne farming, which was then at its height. Add to this the obligations which were placed upon parishioners in respect of maintaining their churches and contributing to repairs, and the scope for new projects begins to look very small.

With all this said, the contributions which were made by parishioners to churchbuilding during the thirteenth century may have been greater than we imagine. If there is truth in the picture of a subordinate laity, the extent of their demotion is open to exaggeration because the primary sources that would help us to gauge it do not exist. The written records of the thirteenth century are chiefly those of diocesan and monastic administrators, while wills which can testify to the level of parochial generosity do not become at all numerous before 1400. There is thus a risk that the survival pattern of available records will cause us to minimize the achievements of thirteenth-century parishioners.

That such an underestimation is possible becomes clear if we return to consider the fabrics of buildings. Hitherto, attention has been directed to the few churches which underwent complete reconstruction. But the thoroughbred Early English church is unlikely to be a good measure of parochial commitment. For reasons already given, full rebuildings were rare and usually depended upon prominent patrons, or perhaps, exceptionally, combinations of layfolk in the richest parishes. Where wealthy benefactors were absent, or people were disinclined or unable to engage in large and abrupt outlay, churches were enlarged or modernized piecemeal. This is one reason why so many medieval churches are anthologies of styles of different periods. If we survey parish churches which stand in the neighbourhoods of the three unusual buildings which have been cited as examples, it emerges that the thirteenth century was a time of great architectural energy. Taking first twenty medieval churches in the area surrounding West Walton, there are five thirteenth-century chancels, eight nave aisles or pairs of aisles, eight towers and two works of other kinds. Figures for the neighbourhood of Felmersham are three, eleven, four and seven, respectively. Those for Warmington district are nine, fourteen, two and three. Altogether, 49 out of the 60 churches examined (81.6 per cent) contain evidence for substantial projects of building in the period *c.* 1190–1300. Of these, 48 (80 per cent) either included or consisted of work west of the chancel and therefore likely to be in the parishioners' domain. These figures do not prove a heavy involvement on the part of ordinary people, but they could point towards it.

The idea that there was a regression in the influence of parishioners during the twelfth and thirteenth centuries hinges on the supposition that groups of rank-and-file laypeople had earlier made an important contribution to the churchfounding movement of the tenth and eleventh centuries. In previous chapters it has been argued that this contribution was not, in fact, particularly significant, and that it was local lords who were for the most part responsible for the origination of local churches. It has also been suggested that the churches themselves show signs of a broadening of function, from private to public use: an aspect which will be discussed again below. The period *c.* 1100–1300 might therefore equally be regarded as a period when parishioners were gaining responsibilities which they did not previously have. And this is rather what the written records show. The first allusion to parochial liability for the maintenance of the nave of a parish church occurs in statutes of 1222–8. References to laypeople who were fulfilling the office of churchwarden, or a role ancestral to that office, are recorded at All Saints, Bristol, in 1261, and in Oxford at St Peter-le-Bailey and St Mary's in 1270 and 1275, respectively. The duties of churchwarden seem to have been laid down first in a statute of a synod held in Exeter in 1287 (Drew 1954, 6–8). It may also be significant that some of the best examples of citizens' churches date not from the tenth or eleventh centuries, but from the twelfth. Hedon *Hu* (*YE*) is a good case. Founded around 1115 within the existing parish of Preston, Hedon possessed at least two churches by 1162 and in due course was to have three (English 1979, 214–15). By 1476 the port was in decline and two of the churches, St Nicholas and St James (appropriate dedications for a nautical town and fishermen) were falling into decay. 'Since the community had built them, the sites were regarded as common property and the corporation disposed of them; during the life of these churches the unique proprietary relationship of the burgesses had been demonstrated by the election of the churchwardens at burgess meetings' (Beresford and St Joseph 1979, 220).

The growth of lay involvement is also witnessed in the architectural development of church buildings. At over half of the churches in the

neighbourhoods of Felmersham, West Walton, and Warmington, considered above, enlargement during the thirteenth century included the addition of one or more aisles. Exactly how many churches received aisles
in this period we do not know, because so many aisles were rebuilt in the
fourteenth and fifteenth centuries. However, of the churches around Warmington it seems that only two had failed to gain an aisle by 1300. We
know from excavation and architectural evidence that aisles were hardly
ever attached to pre-Conquest churches which were of less than minster
status. It is also observable that aisles did not begin to multiply at
parochial level much before the second quarter of the twelfth century. In
view of the questions which have been raised about the role of the laity
in relation to the extension of churches, it is worthwhile to inquire why
this was.

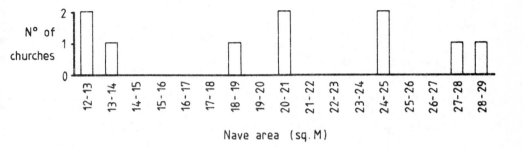

87 Graph showing range in nave areas of eleven local churches in use between
c. 900 and c. 1050. Measurements were taken from plans revealed and dated by
archaeological excavation

Our word 'nave' comes from Latin *navis* 'a ship'. It refers to the main
body of the church. Since this was the portion assigned to the use of the
laity, it is reasonable to suppose that an enlargement of the nave could
reflect a need to accommodate more people, or a diversification of function, or a display of pride. In Chapter 4 it was noted that naves of
churches built or in use during the tenth century were small. It is difficult
to generalize about the actual areas, because of the fewness of excavated
examples, but from the cases known typical figures seem to lie in the range
215–320 sq. ft (20–30 sq. m) (Fig. 87). After c. 1050 × 1100 the naves of local
churches tend to be much larger. Analysis of 60 plans of churches built
in the period c. 1050–1150 suggests that almost 50 of the naves (83 per cent)
had areas in the range 645–860 sq. ft (60–80 sq. m) (Fig. 88). Increases in
nave area between the tenth and twelfth centuries may thus have been of
the order of 300 per cent. Large in itself, this increase is all the more
remarkable when it is remembered that accommodation was also being
agumented by the building of additional churches.
What prompted such expansion? Possibilities which come to mind are

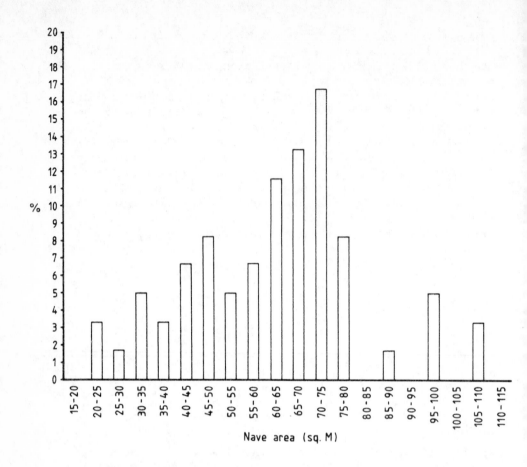

Nave area (sq. M)

88 Graph showing range in nave areas of 60 local churches in use between *c.* 1050 and *c.* 1150.
Measurements were taken from plans both of surviving buildings dated by architectural-
historical methods and of buildings revealed by excavation. The columns are expressed as a
percentage of the total sample. Some of the smaller naves may of course have been inherited
unaltered from the preceding period (Fig. 87). This Fig. offers a basis for cautious
speculation on what proportion of the English population might have been accommodated by
local churches in the first half of the twelfth century. One of the many difficulties in doing
this is our lack of knowledge about how the churches were used. The excavators of the
eleventh-century church at Raunds, for instance, have postulated a congregation of 30–40
people: an allocation of about 8.6–11.8 sq. ft (0.8 to 1.1 sq. m) per person. (Evidence from the
cemetery is said to indicate (in the broadest terms) a contributing population of around 40,
about half of whom would be adults (Boddington 1987). This is a tantalizing figure, being
large enough to be drawn from a small hamlet, yet sufficiently small not to exclude the
possibility that it reflects the household of a lord: his family, associates, and servants.)
However, it would be feasible to achieve a greater density than this, with a unit of area per
person as low as (say) 3.98 sq. ft (0.37 sq. m), with the congregation standing. On that basis a
tightly packed congregation might have been as large as 90. Such a calculation, however,
makes no allowance for items such as a font, or nave altars, which occupied space.
Contrarywise, if, as is likely, some churches were furnished with wooden galleries at this
period, it may be that we are underestimating their capacities.

When these various uncertainties have been allowed for, and assuming a total of *c.* 6750
local churches by 1100, national church-room might be entertained as having been somewhere

in the range of 0.5 million to 1.1 million people. Depending upon the size of the population, estimated then to lie within the range of 1.5 to 2.5 million (Hatcher 1977, 71), the former figure would allow accommodation of between about 20 and 33 per cent of the population, while the latter would enable between about 44 and 73 per cent of people to go to church at once. Since not all members of the population would attend church at the same time, and some (like young children) can be excluded from the reckoning, a figure in the range 35–45 per cent begins to look plausible. In the nineteenth century church-room to *seat* 45 per cent of the population was being aimed at, so provision early in the twelfth century may have been adequate. All the figures mentioned above are necessarily speculative, but may have value as orders of magnitude, to assist thought and discussion

---

that there were more people to be catered for, or that the expectations of congregations had risen. Both beg further questions. The theory of larger congregations, in particular, requires us to ask whether this was because the population had risen, or because congregations were being enlarged following a widening of access to churches which had originated in private hands. It may be that both factors were in operation simultaneously. This might help to account for the largeness of the areal increases, although their relative suddenness could be taken to favour the placing of equal or greater weight upon a social explanation.

However this may be, the dangers of uncritical faith in demographic arguments will become very clear when we examine the next stage of church enlargement. In many places the nave area which had been achieved by the end of the twelfth century remained stable for the remainder of the Middle Ages. Henceforth, enlargement, if it took place, was normally achieved by the addition of aisles: from Latin *ala* 'a wing'. Given that the population continued to rise until the early fourteenth century (Fig. 89), it might seem logical to assume that the main reason for the addition of aisles was to provide extra accommodation. This is the interpretation which has been put forward by L.J.Proudfoot in a paper which surveys the chronology of enlargement of medieval churches in Warwickshire. Proudfoot has drawn attention to the 'pronounced space-time coincidence between periods of maximum floor area extension and maximum population growth, suggesting that population pressure may have been a major determinant of church size' (1983, 231). By tabulating the dimensions of floor areas Proudfoot is able to show that growth accelerated up to *c.* 1340 and slackened thereafter, so that 'the fastest average growth in the size of lay accommodation occurred during the period of early medieval population expansion, particularly between *c.* 1250 and 1340' (1983, 235). Data about parish sizes and the exploitation of wealth within parishes are produced to reinforce this hypothesis.

Convincing as it looks, the idea that aisle-building was normally undertaken in response to an expanding population calls for extensive qualification. Churches in adjoining parishes of similar area and economic potential not infrequently differ quite sharply in the extent of their architectural

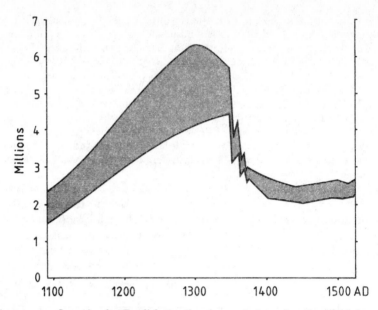

89 Long-term flows in the English medieval population, showing range between plausible limits (*Source*: Hatcher 1977)

developments. There are also marked regional contrasts, so that generalizations about the chronology and character of enlargement which hold good in one district may be inappropriate for another. Another point to be considered is that in some areas, like Devon, or parts of Gloucestershire and Suffolk, there were numerous programmes involving the rebuilding and extension of aisles between 1350 and 1500: that is, in the aftermath of the epidemics which haunted the countryside during the second half of the fourteenth century, when the population had been reduced. Finally, it is noticeable that many of the churches which put forth aisles soonest belonged to bishops, important religious communities or influential lay patrons. Sherburn-in-Elmet *NY* (*YW*), for instance, was one of the chief residences of the archbishops of York. Norham *Nb* was a possession of Durham cathedral priory. Melbourne's connections with the bishops of Carlisle have been mentioned. The powerful de Vere family was responsible for the capacious aisled church at Castle Hedingham *Ex*, where contemporary ironwork may still be seen on the south door. The outstanding quality of St Peter's at Northampton has been tentatively attributed to the earl of Northampton, or even the Crown (RCHME *Northants* 5, 59). When the church of St Michael at Compton Martin *So* was rebuilt in the twelfth century it was furnished with aisles; clerestory windows of the period remain, as do settings for rafters of the aisle roofs. Compton Martin is further distinguished by a vaulted chancel, and one screw-cut column at the east end of the north arcade which seems to derive from the milieu of faraway Durham. Was this the product of some special gift? Just possibly it was; before 1135 Wulfric of Haselbury worked for some years at Compton as the village priest (Bell 1933). It seems that William FitzWalter, the lord of Compton, was inclined to pamper him, and in due course Wulfric relinquished his post and went into retreat as an anchorite in a cell beside the church at Haselbury. Wulfric acquired a national reputation as a holy man. Henry I and Stephen were among his visitors. A *vita* was written after his death in 1155. The rebuilding of Compton Martin took place at around this time. Since Wulfric had the makings of a saint, perhaps the sophisticated features of this scheme could have had to do with the celebrity of Compton as a place associated with a nascent cult.

To summarize, in the earlier part of the Norman period aisled parish churches were rare. When aisles did begin to appear, there was a tendency for them to be bestowed first upon parish churches which were in the hands of powerful men or religious institutions, or where for one reason or another a parish church attracted wealth. So we cannot exclude the possibility that, at parish level, aisles originated as an architectural form, a manifestation of prestige, rather than in response to any simple requirement for congregational space. Such aggrandizement might, however, have had something to do with the character of the services which were held in the churches concerned, for the wealthiest patrons may have been sponsors of ritual which was unusually lavish.

A general rationale for aisles was set forth seventy-five years ago by Alexander Hamilton Thompson. It is worth repeating:

> The usefulness of aisles is at once apparent. They afford greater space for the distribution of the congregation. The aisleless church may be inconveniently crowded from wall to wall: on the other hand, where spaces are left between the nave and side walls, the congregation will mass itself in the nave, but the aisles will be left free until the nave is filled, and thus there will be free access through the side doorways for as long a time as possible. Aisles also afford a clear space for processions, and allow them to turn inside the church at a certain point and without difficulty. In addition to this, aisles form a convenient situation for the smaller altars of a church, and, from an early date, were added with this view.
>
> (1911a, 66)

Comfort and practicality thus emerge as relevant considerations. Aisles helped to service the use of the central space. And any subsidiary altars which had previously been located on either side of the chancel entrance (as we indicated, for example, at Ashley *Ha*) could be removed into the aisles, thereby making the nave a roomier place. There is abundant evidence to show that the east ends of nave aisles normally contained altars. The former positions of such altars are indicated by piscinas, aumbries, corbels or niches for associated images, and sometimes too by the squints which were later bored through chancel walls or tower piers in order to render the chancel and lateral altars intervisible, as at Saxton *NY* or Great Hasely *O*. Most of the architectural evidence for altars in aisles dates from after 1200, but there is no reason to think that the people who added aisles to parish churches in the twelfth century were motivated by desires which differed sharply from those that are known to have existed only two or three generations later. Examples of twelfth-century piscinas in aisles, as at Great Easton *Le*, support this view. The fact that more piscinas of this date are not found in twelfth-century aisles is possibly explained by the likelihood that they were mounted on free-standing pillars which were later superseded by basins of the wall-niche type (Parsons 1986, 110–11).

In the later Middle Ages aisles were used, and sometimes built, to house chantry chapels, the tombs of merchants and dynasties of local gentry, and altars frequented by gilds and fraternities (see Chapter 9). Burial, and a desire for commemorative prayer, family or communal interests, are themes which thread these various aspects together. So it is interesting to ask whether there could have been a conceptual link between the funerary functions of the *porticus* which were sometimes attached to pre-Conquest churches, and the post-Conquest growth of aisles as places deemed appropriate for intercession and the support through prayer of departed souls. Until the twelfth century the burial of laity inside churches was forbidden. There were many occasions when this prohibition was relaxed or ignored, but archaeological excavation is tending to confirm that internal burial was sparse. However, it appears that *porticus* were in some sense felt to be outside the liturgical envelope of a church, and hence that burial within such adjuncts was more readily permissible than within the nave or chancel. By the later Middle Ages this distinction had been dissolved, but in the first half of the twelfth century, when the interment of laypeople inside churches was still officially frowned upon, it is conceivable that ancient custom counted for more. Whether or not this is correct, aisles certainly enlarged the capacity of a church for burial, while the proliferation of altars and their guardian saints increased the number of devotional foci near to which burial was thought to be especially desirable.

Another factor here is the frequency with which aisles seem to have been added first to the *north* sides of naves. Practical considerations are usually invoked to explain this: for example, a reluctance to disturb the south door (itself a numinous place, with important ritual and judicial functions), or to encroach upon burials which tended to cluster outside the south wall. Relevant though these points are, it may also be noted that the north flank of a church seems to have been held in a special regard in relation to death and commemoration. Arcane ceremonies which involved the ritual burial and resurrection of the eucharistic elements at Eastertide made use of the north sides of great churches, as witnessed in the St Sepulchre chapels at Winchester and York (Park 1983, 50; Phillips 1985, 51–3). In a parish church the north wall of the chancel was the conventional place for an Easter sepulchre which was built into the fabric, as at Hawton *Nt* and Heckington *Li*. This tradition may have developed simply because the south wall of the chancel was already cluttered with such features as sedilia, piscina and aumbry. However, northern *porticus* or transeptal adjuncts had long been regarded as places appropriate for important tombs and relics (Biddle 1986, 11). Continuations of this custom into the later Middle Ages are sometimes encountered in parish churches, as at Whitchurch Canonicorum *Do* or Bampton *O* (Blair 1984), while excavations at Hadstock *Ex* disclosed a large grave at the centre of the north transept. If, as suggested above, parish churches started to gain aisles partly in emulation of the architectural precedents which had recently been set by the builders of monastic and cathedral churches, it may also be that ideas about the symbolic or ritual topography of these great buildings subsequently found their way into local thinking. For example: if portable Easter sepulchres preceded, and were always more numerous than, the built-in type, where were they kept? Perhaps a north aisle answered this need, in addition to other functions which have been identified: sites for subsidiary altars, room for more intra-mural burials, space for circulation and an overspill area for the nave (Fig. 90). Hence, while pressure on space may have been one of the factors which prompted the building of aisles, other stimuli could be looked for in the increase of variety and complexity in parochial devotion which took place from the twelfth century.

Although it is unlikely that aisles were built primarily in order to increase lay accommodation, the growth in population which occurred between 1100 and 1300 must have had some considerable impact upon the way in which churches were used. In 1300 the population of England probably stood somewhere between 4 and 6 million. For every one churchgoer in 1100, therefore, there may have been as many as three by 1300. How was this increase absorbed? Four factors may be mentioned. In the first place, there were more churches. Although the foundation of new parish churches slowed down during the first half of the twelfth century, and had virtually ceased by its end, the national total of such 'late' buildings was appreciable. If the eleventh-century figures which were discussed in Chapter 4 are subtracted from the total which is indicated by the *Taxatio* of 1291, the difference is of the order of 1500. Second, the fact that the formation of new parishes had come to a standstill before 1200 did not prevent the foundation of many new churches after this date. Outlying communities and small villages continued to acquire churches: but these buildings had the status of chapels, and were in subjection to the mother churches of the parishes in which they stood. This institutional inferiority meant that many chapels escaped enumeration in the general surveys. In later centuries a lot of them disappeared. It is thus very difficult to count them. But they are certainly to be numbered in thousands. Third, the nave areas which are analysed in Fig. 87, and arguably some of the smaller areas in Fig. 88, were determined in the tenth and eleventh centuries. They were selected precisely because they have been little altered. But the

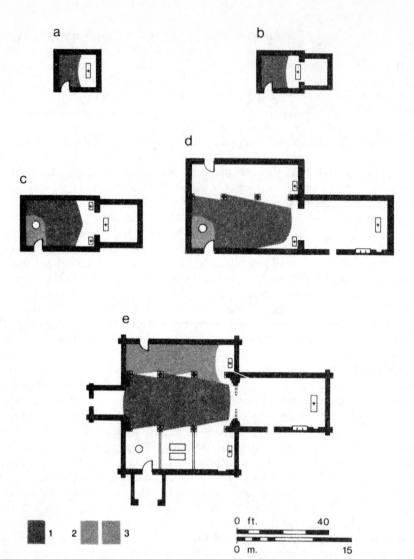

90 Areal development and use of space in a parish church between *c.* 1000 and *c.* 1400. **A** around 1000; **B** mid-eleventh century; **C** first half of twelfth century; **D** first half of thirteenth century; **E** fourteenth century; 1 area most convenient for congregational use at moment of elevation of the host; 2 space compromised by font, doors, etc.; 3 space dependent upon subsidiary altar and possibly available for congregational use. The contrast in use of space between the north and south aisles in **E** may hold lessons which are applicable in earlier periods. Most of the space in the south aisle has been 'privatized' for the tombs and chantry of a local family of gentry. This reminds us that social, as well as demographic, trends should be considered in relation to the growth of church areas. One reason why churches were enlarged may be that the expectations of individuals or particular social groups increased, so that they laid claim to more space than they were earlier accustomed to dominate

large majority of churches *were* altered, and their naves enlarged at least into the 650–850 sq. ft (60–80 sq. m) range. Church-room in the later twelfth century was therefore considerably greater than it had been only three or four generations previously. Fourth, although aisles were not added simply in order to accommodate more parishioners, their presence did help to maximize the use of existing floorspace within the nave and gave some extra room between piers and columns (see Fig. 90). And some naves were widened, or lengthened, or both. When they are taken together, these various factors suggest that churches and chapels were able to absorb the increase in population which took place before 1300.

The extension of naves has been mentioned, and it is useful to look more closely at how this was achieved. There were three main methods. The first was simply to demolish the old structure and to erect a new and larger one in its place. This solution was expensive, and after the early twelfth century occurrences of total rebuilding are found chiefly at churches which had a place in the sympathies of wealthy individuals, or lay in districts of high general prosperity. A second technique was to elongate the nave by adding one or more extra bays. In constructional terms this was straightforward, but expansion westward was often blocked by the presence of a tower, while lengthening to the east would require demolition and rebuilding of the chancel. The third method was to pierce the walls of the existing church with arcades. This had the advantage of being less disruptive than root-and-branch rebuilding. Parishioners might even continue to use the nave while an aisle was being grafted on from without.

Extension by stages had an economic appeal, for it required less immediate outlay than the alternative of full rebuilding. Perhaps this is why aisles were often added one at a time, so that costs were spread. One result of this modular approach to church enlargement is that the spandrels of nave arcades are commonly more ancient than the columns or piers that support them. They may contain fossil features which have been inherited from an earlier, aisleless, phase. Redundant windows, usually blocked or truncated, occur widely. Those at Gretton *Np*, Carlton-in-Lindrick *Nt*, Ledsham *WY* and Avebury *Wi* may be cited from among hundreds of examples. Likewise, when clerestories came into fashion the fabric of the existing nave envelope was normally taken as the starting point. It is thus not at all unusual to encounter nave walls of pre-Conquest or Norman origin supported from below by later arcades, and bearing a clerestory of yet more recent date.

The fact that parish churches were often extended upwards, as well as outwards, introduces a new dimension to this discussion. Functionalist interpretations involving the needs of the liturgy, the provision of accommodation for the living and the dead, and the concerns and ambitions of patrons all take us some good way towards an understanding of the factors which occasioned and fashioned the structural development of the parish church. But a building is something more than a sheltered space in which things may happen. By its ordinance, proportions, adornment, and in its likeness to other buildings, a church may be expressive of the values and aspirations of those who viewed it from without and worshipped within (Krautheimer 1942; Gem 1983). This holds as true for a Quaker meeting-house or a Kingdom Hall as for a medieval cathedral. The iconography of parochial architecture calls for more extended examination than can be given here. But one aspect will be explored: the response of medieval builders to light.

In the beginning, Genesis tells us, God created the heaven and the earth.

> And the earth was without form, and void; and darkness was upon the face of the deep. And the Spirit of God moved upon the face of the waters. And God said, Let there be light: and there was light.
>
> (1:2-3)

Buildings constructed of stone exclude light. We might therefore search for significance in those points in the fabric of a church at which builders chose to admit it: 'And God saw the light, that it was good: and God divided the light from the darkness' (Genesis 1:4).

Windows in the walls of churches built in the eleventh and earlier twelfth centuries were generally few, and small. Thereafter the trend was towards more and larger windows. The quest for size was greatly assisted after *c.* 1250 by the introduction of bar tracery, which enabled the formation of extensive multi-light windows and led to a corresponding reduction in the areas of masonry that intervened. The culmination of this process is to be experienced in airy fifteenth-century buildings, like Southwold *Sf*, which seem almost to have been erected by glaziers.

The development of medieval fenestration might very well be accounted for by a theory of technical determinism. It could be argued that windows before 1100 were small because builders lacked the skills to make them larger: for example, because of the limitations in size which were imposed by the use of monolithic window heads; or what could be achieved with the basketwork hoods that were sometimes used for turning arches of rubble and mortar; or the difficulty of glazing large openings. The use of glass in pre-Conquest churches was by no means so rare as used to be imagined. Nevertheless, it may be wondered how many rural tenth/eleventh-century communities had access to the required expertise, while the methods in use at this date for mounting quarries were practical only for the glazing of narrow apertures. The use of substitutes, like horn, was subject to similar limitations. Fretted slabs meant draughts. Oiled linen or shutters required regular attention, which was tedious, and if neglected could easily be circumvented by birds. So windows were small.

The technical argument has force, but perhaps only to the extent that its significance can be reversed: if builders in the tenth and eleventh centuries were unaccustomed to making large windows, should we not suppose that they lacked the incentive to alter their practices? The glimmer of an answer to this question is suggested by the fact that it is not unusual to find contemporary windows of *different* sizes in a single building of this period. The towers of Skipwith *Hu* (*YE*), Hovingham *NY* and Little Ouseburn *NY* (*YW*), for example, all possess sizeable windows in their elevations, in addition to other openings of smaller aperture. Comparable variation was being practised sixty or seventy years later, as for instance in the parochial chapel of St Mary, Stainburn *NY* (*YW*), which dates from around 1160 (Fig. 91). Why is the window at the south-east corner of the nave larger than its companions? The positions of the other original windows suggest a solution. Externally, their placing looks unsystematic. However, each window appears to have been located in order to shed light upon an area of special significance *within* the building: the altar, the rood or altars either side of the chancel arch, the vicinity of the entrance and the font (Fig. 92). Here, exterior effect was subordinated, or even disregarded, in favour of selective internal requirements. The builders of the little eleventh-century church at Greetwell, which stands beside the earthworks of a shrunken village outside Lincoln, seem to have been similarly preoccupied. The nave retains but one original window. It is narrow, shaped rather like a tall keyhole, and is placed high in the south wall. This window may have had a few companions elsewhere in the building, now smothered or removed, but it is reasonable to conclude that too much light was not wanted. The slender shaft of sunshine that did reach into the church on bright days was intended not as a source of general illumination, but rather as a natural spotlight, angled perhaps upon the altar or rood. At later dates Greetwell's walls were pierced with much larger openings, and today the church has a bright interior that cancels the original effect.

The precision with which window splays were angled by tenth- and eleventh-century builders is sometimes suggestive of great subtlety. At Rivenhall *Ex*, for instance, close archaeological study (Fig. 93) has disclosed a

marked and clearly intentional skew in the south-east chancel window. This could not have increased the volume of light transmitted, but it would have controlled the spot at which the shaft of light fell within the chancel ... when the sun was in the south-east, a shaft *c.* 0.2 m would have passed diagonally across the chancel to the north-west corner. This directional control implies that the light shaft was meant to fall upon something significant at a given time. Most plausibly this was the altar.
(Rodwell and Rodwell 1986, 133, Figs 94, 95, 97)

Small windows were tolerable in these early buildings because the churches were themselves usually small. Limited, selective lighting, as at Old Bewick *Nb*, reinforced the sense of intimacy. Between *c.* 1150 and 1250 we see a trend not only towards more and larger windows, but also towards a greater regard for balance and symmetry in their placing. Outward appearance and inner effect were co-ordinated with notable success

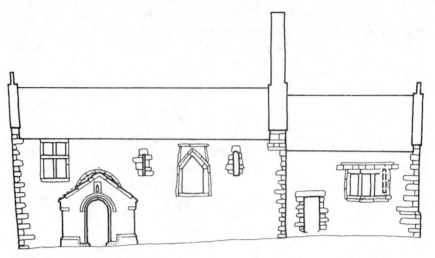

91 St Mary, Stainburn, North Yorkshire: south elevation of twelfth-century parochial chapel

in buildings of the thirteenth century: Haltwhistle *Nb*, for instance, or Uffington *Bk*. Early English poise was soon to be upset by the appearance of much bigger windows, sometimes rather arbitrarily introduced, made possible by the invention of tracery. With the addition of clerestories, churches could now be flooded with light. Indeed, by the end of the fourteenth century it was not unknown for parishioners who worshipped in unmodernized churches to complain that their building was too dark, as happened at Dixton *Mon* in 1397 (Bannister 1929, 445).

This returns us to the original question: did parochial preferences in churchbuilding follow in the wake of technical innovation, or vice versa? And did technical and stylistic advances take place wholly within the realm of great churches, Crown and aristocratic patronage, later to be taken up in parishes by a kind of artistic capillary action, or was there some degree of reciprocity?

In order to begin to address these issues it is relevant to notice that between the extremes of early and late, dark and light, small and large, there is a *general* shift of sensibility, from conditions in which worship involved strong feelings for intimacy towards a state in which acts of worship were observed or heard in greater detachment. A Romanesque church was in a sense part of the ceremonies that it housed, whereas from the later twelfth century church fabrics came increasingly to contain the liturgical action rather than to be so directly implicated in it. Significantly, the gradual disengagement of the building from the events that it sheltered was accompanied by an elaboration of the events themselves. The definition of eucharistic doctrine at the Fourth Lateran Council (1215), and a widespread lengthening of chancels that placed the priest at a greater

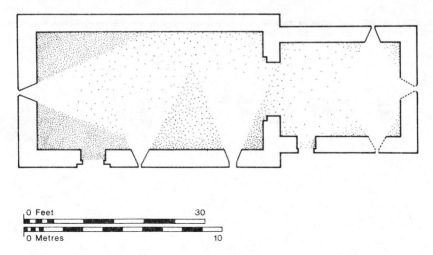

0 Feet 30

0 Metres 10

92 St Mary, Stainburn, North Yorkshire: reconstruction of original scheme of natural lighting, disposed so as to play upon key points in the ritual topography of the interior

distance from the congregation, contributed to the concept of the priesthood as a separate caste. Concurrently, there was an intensification of concern for embellishment of the fabric, and for the *outward* appearance of the church building. Steeples, so characteristic of the later phase, are remarkable not least for their lack of presence within the churches they adorn. Outwardly conspicuous, they are essentially landscape features.

By a paradox, too, the earlier buildings, though highly charged with dramatic potential, were mainly simple and utilitarian. Today, these churches may move us by their plainness. Their bare surfaces and un-complicated volumes define an emptiness within which anything may be imagined. Earthen-floored Sutterby *Li*, or Heath *Sa*, or Odda's Chapel at Deerhurst *Gl* offer spiritual experiences of surpassing power. And if the survival of a twelfth-century painted interior such as survives at St Mary, Kempley *Gl* should jolt us into remembering that parish church interiors were not always thus, the images of the apostles on Kempley's walls and the celestial microcosm upon its chancel vault serve also to emphasize the artistic impassivity of the building itself.

It would be interesting to know what names contemporaries bestowed upon the styles that we now call Early English and Decorated. And what was the relationship between these styles and the evolving structure of English society? What is the significance of a national consensus in taste? Something approaching such a consensus had been reached by 1300. It is reflected not simply in buildings, but in the interplay between different branches of the creative and applied arts. When, for instance, expert masons became preoccupied with botanical realism in the carving of leaves and plants, as at Lawford *Ex*, craftsmen who produced small metal

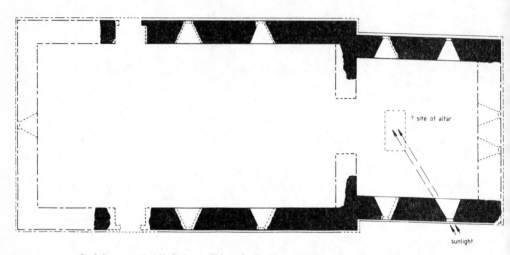

? site of altar

sunlight

93 St Mary and All Saints, Rivenhall, Essex: plan showing reconstructed scheme of natural lighting in chancel (*Source*: Rodwell and Rodwell 1986)

spoons employed the same kind of ornament. Integration was taken further in the uniquely English style that we call Perpendicular: an architecture of unity wherein adornment, form and necessities of engineering became manifestations of each other (Harvey 1978). The economic context of Perpendicular will be considered in Chapter 9. Here it is relevant only to observe how the widespread adoption of this style coincided with a period when English writers, like Geoffrey Chaucer (*c.* 1343–1400), William Langland (*c.* 1330–1400), John Gower (d. 1408) and the *Gawain* poet, thinkers like John Wyclif (d. 1384) and even, latterly, composers such as John Dunstable (d. 1453), were all in their ways erecting the first storey of the edifice of English national culture (Harvey 1947). At some point we must contend with the concept of style as an expression not simply of individual, courtly or other sectional interests and preferences, but of society as a whole. The agreed vocabulary of, say, Georgian house-building, or the eclecticism of late Victorian design, may both be seen as functions not simply of moods or taste, but as organic manifestations of social and political structure. Nearer to us in time, better documented, their significances are so much easier to discern. But the struggle to decipher the sociological 'meaning' of the sinuous, nature-oriented phase of the Decorated style, or the classical reticence of Early English, should not be given up. The fact that each stylistic phase grew out of, but was at the same time in strong contrast to, its predecessor, is also to be noted.

Exploration and conservatism, and the tensions between them, emerge as powerful impulses in medieval life. The Renaissance might be looked upon as the outcome of what happened when this dualism could no longer be sustained.

By now it will be clear that the areal and stylistic development of the medieval parish church was no simple process. It depended rather upon a web of factors, involving public and private wealth, differing degrees of patronage, concern for the soul, changing patterns of ritual, as well as technical traditions that existed in local, regional and national contexts, and which could evolve at different rates. We might visualize these, albeit crudely, as a series of interpenetrating areal, intellectual and temporal contexts. And there are other contexts that have not so far been mentioned: the changing moods and perceptions of individual communities; ideologies; even – as we shall see in the next chapter – climate. Important as they are, however, all these influences would count for little in the absence of a population of craftsmen who were equal to the task of building, enlarging and maintaining up to 12,000 churches. The early development of this capability is a topic of great interest, and it is to aspects of it that the remaining part of this chapter will be devoted.

In Chapters 3 and 4 it was argued that surviving stone churches of the seventh, eighth and early ninth centuries are likely to have been built for religious communities. It was also suggested that although local churches founded for the use of lay families and communities existed before 900, they multiplied fastest in the tenth and eleventh centuries, and that until the eleventh century local churchbuilding was commonly executed in wood.

If these generalizations come anywhere near to the truth, then there must be doubt as to whether churches in the 'monastic' class were sufficiently numerous to have generated an Anglo-Saxon stone building industry before the tenth century. 'Industry' is here taken to mean a continuous craft activity, with its own specialists, tradesmen, terminologies and jargon, internal organization and technical traditions. This statement is not, of course, meant to downplay the achievements of builders in the period *c.* 600–900. On the contrary, the churches erected during these years, far from being the products of inexperienced craftsmen who were feeling their way in an unfamiliar medium, may actually have been rather sophisticated. For as long as stone buildings were few in number – hundreds rather than the thousands which have to be accounted for by the end of the eleventh century – expertise could be concentrated upon them. Masons existed, both native and foreign, but in insufficient numbers, and with insufficient opportunity, for their careers to overlap and multiply in such a way as to braid together into a strong indigenous industry. In the absence of such an industry, every new stone building was something of an adventure. The emergence of a general vocabulary of architectural style could be linked to the start of an expansion of masoncraft from the status of an occasional pursuit to a more general occupation. Two features

301

that are characteristic of Anglo-Saxon workmanship, pilaster strips and long-and-short quoins, turn out when mapped to occur in certain areas but not in others (Fig. 94). The distribution of pilaster strips is in broad correspondence with the presence of Jurassic and Eocene rocks, with known pre-Conquest centres of supply at Barnack *Np* and Quarr *IoW*. The map of long-and-short quoins likewise corresponds with these geological formations, although in this case there is evidence for the export of stone into East Anglia, and the pattern reaches up into Lincolnshire in a way that the pilaster strip did not. What we see here, it is suggested, are the first fruits of an English quarry industry. And since the walls of most of the churches concerned were constructed out of local materials, often rubble, it would appear possible that the industry was initially of limited character, devoted to the production of strips and quoins.

Complementary evidence comes from northern England, where neither pilaster strips nor long-and-short quoins found favour. The pre-Conquest churches that survive in this region display extensive dependence upon stone derived from ancient Roman buildings. This is true not only of churches like Corbridge *Nb* and Escomb *Du*, early and presumptively monastic, but also of village churches like Kirk Hammerton *NY (YW)* and Crambe *NY* which show that reliance upon second-hand materials continued until the end of the eleventh century. In contrast, the fabrics of churches built during the second and third decades of the twelfth century, like Weaverthorpe, Wharram-le-Street *NY (YE)* and Monk Fryston *NY (YW)*, show increasing use of freshly quarried stone.

Let us recapitulate. Some quarrying did take place in England before *c*. 850, but it was not a common process and may well have been tied to a few specific projects. In northern England there was little quarrying for building purposes: such materials as were needed were usually taken from Roman structures. In the tenth century we can discern the emergence of more frequent quarrying, although at first this was on a limited scale, confined principally to Jurassic stones, and producing a limited range of components. North of the Humber, dependence upon salvaged materials continued beyond the Norman Conquest.

Both chronologically and geographically the church of St Peter at Barton-upon-Humber *Hu (Li)* stands on the frontier between these two patterns. In terms of design, the turriform nave, with its gawky stripwork and triangular-headed panels, finds its closest companions in the Soke of Peterborough, where strip- and quoin-producing quarries have already been postulated. At Barton, however, the long-and-short quoining, plinths, stripwork and components of doors and arches are all of millstone grit. The gritstone is reused, having been derived from Roman buildings (Rodwell and Rodwell 1982, 294). It may be significant that the quoins and stripwork were modelled *in situ* (1982, 298). This contrasts with the tendency of masons in later centuries to prefabricate components in the quarry or at the bench, so that carving *in situ* would often be restricted to such adjustments as were necessary to settle the stone in. Another point of interest is that the builders of Barton-upon-Humber appear to have been carpenters at heart. The idea that the general appearance of the church derived from a tradition of building in wood has circulated for many years. Recently this notion has been much strengthened by close study of the stripwork and gable-headed features, which shows that the techniques of carpenters were applied (Rodwell 1986, 172-4). Moreover, the stone shell was heavily embellished with wood. There is excavated evidence for substantial wooden doorcases, conceivably of ornamental character (Rodwell and Rodwell 1982, 298). Even the plan might be visualized as proceeding from the world of wooden halls with axial annexes (compare Figs 19 and 71). Technically and artistically, therefore, Barton emerges as a building of janiform personality, looking backwards into a wooden past and forwards into the age of stone. Radiocarbon determinations made upon structural timbers from the church give some idea of the period within which these currents of building tradition were swirling together: the years between c. 920 and c. 1060 (Rodwell and Rodwell 1982, 297).

The significance of wood in relation to churchbuilding in the tenth and eleventh centuries was not limited to matters of skeuomorphism. As Warwick Rodwell has stressed:

there was considerably more structural and other functional timber-work in the early churches than has perhaps hitherto been appreciated. Add to this the requirements of scaffolding, formwork, centring, and wall shuttering, and it is self-evident that the number of carpenters employed in church construction can hardly have been smaller than the number of masons.

(Rodwell 1986, 171)

The vocabulary of building drives this home. The Old English verb 'to build' was *timbrian*. 'Buildings' were *getimbro*. Our word 'mason' is of French ancestry.

Although the replacement of wooden churches by stone was already in progress before the Conquest, it can hardly be doubted that the expansion of masoncraft was mightily accelerated by Norman demands. Over 200 monastic churches were founded or rebuilt between 1070 and 1130. There were extensive castle-works in this period as well. Add to these the parochial rebuildings, within a population of local churches already assessed as greater than 6000, and a figure somewhere between 500 and 1000 projects per decade begins to look conceivable.

Yet the number of master craftsmen who were required for this work need not have been all that great. In fourteenth-century Oxford, the Poll Tax of 1380 discloses only 23 resident masons out of a craftworking population of 456 (Knoop and Jones 1932, 347). At York the register of Freemen of the city shows that 146 masons were admitted between 1301 and 1500. Three hundred and twelve carpenters were admitted during the same period. The proportion of free craftsmen to the total is unclear, but in

94 Distribution of churches with long-and-short quoins, megalithic side-alternate quoins, and pilaster strips (*Source*: H.M. Taylor 1978)

Great & Inferior Oolitic Limestone

Permian

Gault & Greensand

94(b) Outcrops of stone for which there is evidence of exploitation by churchbuilders in the tenth and eleventh centuries (oolitic limestones) and in the twelfth (Permian)

York the proportion of free masons has been assessed at about 25 per cent, and that of carpenters at around 66 per cent (Swanson 1983, 38, n. 168). The population of York late in the fourteenth century is not known, but it is unlikely to have exceeded 6000. In a given decade masons and carpenters together might therefore have accounted for no more than 0.8 per cent of the urban population. Even this may be rather high. Masons would congregate in places which offered work, like cathedral cities. Out in the countryside the ratio may have been smaller.

These later estimates have some broad relevance for the twelfth century, because building in the Norman period was less demanding of specialized skills than was the case later on. Castles, and most parish churches, did not require teams of master craftsmen. They called for cadres of obedient semi-skilled labour, working under firm, competent supervision. Initially, the number of experienced master masons who were active in post-Conquest England may have been quite small. A cathedral like that begun in York *c*. 1080 (Phillips 1985), or castles such as those at Rochester *K* or Richmond *NY* were not designed by sensitive artists. There are many parish churches, like Kippax *WY*, or Wyham *Li*, or Averham *Nt*, or Wigmore *He*, which were cut from similarly rough-and-ready fabric. In some places, such as Hauxwell *NY*, which is close to Richmond, there is a likelihood that castlebuilders were actually involved. The sparseness of early Norman architectural decoration has been mentioned. The simple forms and limited repertoire of motifs suggest a reliance upon copying rather than invention. One reason why the sculptural 'schools' which began to flourish in twelfth-century Kent, Yorkshire and the west Midlands look so outstanding is that they appeared against a background of building which was, although prolific, still fairly elementary in its attainments.

Plagiarism continued to be an important means by which stylistic ideas were transmitted from one place to another. It was normal for a patron to deliver his commission in the form of a request to imitate an existing building. (Atkinson (1947, 159–61) gives thirty-five examples, including houses, bridges, furnishings and fittings, as well as churches.) Sometimes one can see this in action. In 1433 a contract was made between William Troutbeck, esquire, and Thomas Bates, mason, for the building of a chapel on the south side of the chancel at St Mary-on-the-Hill, Chester. The document specified that the chapel should be embattled 'like to the little closet withinne the castell of Chester, with a corbyl table longing thereto' (Salzman 1967, 503; Harvey 1984, 16). In 1449 Roger Growden was appointed by the corporation of Totnes *D* to add a belfry to the parish church. In the following year Growden and his overseers inspected steeples at Callington *Co*, Buckland, Tavistock and Ashburton *D* in order to make a selection of features that they liked best (Harvey 1984, 126). An agreement between the dean of the cathedral of St Paul, London, and John Taverner, a carpenter, specified that the new roof to be made over the chancel at Halstead *Ex* should resemble the chancel roof at Romford

Ex (Salzman 1967, 490). Two masons undertook to build a tower at Walberswick *Sf* in 1425. The 'wallyng the tabellying and the orbyng [panelling]' were to be modelled on the tower of Tunstall; the west door was to be 'as good as the dore in the Stepel of Halesworth', and various windows were to be 'after Halesworth' (1967, 500). An indenture dated 1487 records an undertaking by Thomas Aldrych, mason, to build a tower at the west end of the church of Helmingham *Sf*, with as many storeys as the steeple of Framsden, and the disposition of the west door and nearby windows to be 'after the facion of the stepyll of Bramston' (1967, 548). Orby *Li* was to be provided with a tower after the 'facion and proporcion of the chirche steple in ... Est'erkele [East Keal]' (1967, 575). Attention has been drawn to the family resemblances which exist between the steeples of a number of churches in parts of Kesteven and Holland *Li*. There were steeples of sophisticated design at Spalding, Sleaford and Heydour, which were the subject of much local imitation. Around Claypole there is a small knot of churches whereat a complete suite of design features has been replicated (see Fig. 85). The conclusion drawn is that the designers were usually local men, and that the building of many churches was something that could have been undertaken out of local resources, without resort to the master masons who moved in royal and higher ecclesiastical circles, and commanded high fees.

Of course, there were occasions when artists of regional or national celebrity were drawn into the process of enlarging or modernizing parish churches. This is one of the ways in which advanced stylistic ideas gained currency in surrounding areas. Although comparatively few parish churches can be attributed to prominent medieval architects whose names are known, there are exceptions. In 1381 a mason called Nicholas Typerton undertook to build a south aisle and porch at the church of St Dunstan in London (Salzman 1967, 462–3). Typerton was not an outstanding figure; but then, neither was he the designer. The contract states that the plans for the work had been drawn up by Henry Yevele: one of the greatest architects of the age (Harvey 1944; 1984). Churches which benefited from this sort of attention were normally in the hands of magnates, or stood at principal local centres. Recent research into the careers of two members of the Raughton family, apparently father and son, who have been credited with important contributions to the cathedrals at Carlisle, York and Lincoln between *c.* 1320 and 1339, leads also to a number of parish churches. They include the important prebendal centre at North Newbald, and wealthy civic churches at Beverley, Hull *Hu* (*YE*) and Nantwich *Ch* (Petch 1986). Very probably there were a number of these 'personal' schools operating in different regions at various times. In Oxfordshire, for instance, the fifteenth-century architect Richard Winchcombe is thought to have been behind works at Broughton, Deddington, Bloxham and the Wilcote chapel at Northleigh, in addition to proven contributions at Adderbury and the Schools in Oxford (Harvey 1984, 336). Linked designs, suggestive of the guiding hand of an individual artist or family dynasty, have been postulated elsewhere (e.g. Fawcett 1982; W.D.Wilson 1980).

Wealthy patrons or associations of individuals with affluent members had access to the skills of outsiders. The systematic study of mouldings in the churches of Hertfordshire has led Dr Eileen Roberts to observe that 'the humblest and least interesting' churches are most characteristic of divisions in local style, whereas 'the finest churches could not be confined within these local styles' (1972, 9). A similar point emerges from David Stocker's survey of Lincolnshire steeples. One of the greatest of them, St Wulfram at Grantham, 'appears to have had no real followers locally either in terms of its overall design or of its more unusual details'. In the pre-Conquest period Grantham was the site of an important royal minster. Later it grew into a market town that was sufficiently populous to attract a house of Franciscans. Grantham, like Beverley, became a place of social diversification, with civic identity and a class of prosperous merchants. Also, St Wulfram's was a prebend of Salisbury. This is just the sort of context where a design of exceptional or regionally intrusive character could be expected.

Two factors have now emerged as important determinants of architectural style. One is the interplay between the sensibilities of patrons and the creativity of individual artists. Originality and innovation, access to new ideas from afar (necessary not only as models, but also as the external stimuli that many artists require to liberate their own ideas), and opportunities to practise, meant that the growing edge of architectural fashion would be in the vicinity of individuals and institutions of advanced taste. The other factor was the means to exercise taste. In the eleventh and twelfth centuries this was restricted mainly to major landholders: the king and his immediate supporters, great religious institutions and, increasingly, bishops and the dignitaries of cathedrals. In the thirteenth century the sources of patronage became more diversified, as higher clergy, local lords and groups of citizens in the wealthier parishes began to realize their wishes. Parishes which were not in the vanguard – the great majority – might nevertheless benefit through imitation of the advances which were made in those that were; and as medieval landholding was not consolidated but dispersed, the buildings which resulted from high patronage were widely, though not everywhere evenly, distributed. This scattering of models facilitated the spread of ideas through copying by observant local craftsmen. In agriculturally poorer areas where landholders of national eminence were fewer or absent, local traditions survived longer, style itself was often more conservative and the buildings less distinguished.

Important as it is, this theory of taste and wealth does not account for all the influences which played upon stylistic development at parish level. One obvious factor is that the nature, characteristics and degree of availability of raw materials would to a large extent determine how the medieval builder went about his work. Some stones are more suitable for fine carving than others. There are strong stones and weak stones; stones that resist decay in buildings and stones that do not; stones that occur in abundance close to the surface and are easily won, and stones that are less accessible (Davey 1976). These variables exerted influence upon the manner of medieval building and set limits upon technical and stylistic possibility. To take an example, Cornwall's churches differ in many respects from those in Gloucestershire partly because the geologies of the two counties are unalike. Gloucestershire builders had access to Jurassic oolitic limestones, with valued sources at Campden, Painswick, Farmington and Guiting. This material could be worked freely, and was shipped as far afield as Arundel, Westminster and York (Davey 1976, 18–19). Cornish stones were more problematical. Granite does not carve easily, and Devonian rocks are not much more responsive. Such intractable stones can be piled up to make impressive towers – Linkinhorne and Lanlivery are noble examples – but they do not lend themselves to architectural sculpture or tracery. In the south-west one can find churches with arcades formed on monolithic columns, as at Clovelly *D* or Kilkhampton *Co*. Devonshire gritstone, Cornish and Lundy granite are strong in tension and hence would not snap in transit from the quarry. There was little point in cutting up cylinders of such stone into small pieces only to have to reassemble them at the church. Besides, lime was scarce in Cornwall and monolithic construction was a way to cut down on the mortar needed for joints and wall-cores.

In a very literal sense, therefore, parish churches *are* the landscape. The interplay between regional geologies and architectural method and style has been well explored in recent years, most notably by the late Dr Alec Clifton-Taylor in his celebrated book *The Pattern of English Building*. Only the wealthiest patrons were able to break this pattern, by importing materials and craftsmen from outside a region. In the fifteenth century, for instance, magnesian limestone from the Yorkshire quarries of Thevesdale and Huddleston was supplied to King's College, Cambridge, and to Westminster. Huddleston stone was also taken to Eton College, while the quarry at Stapleton *SY* (*YW*) had earlier provided stone for Westminster Hall, Westminster Abbey, the Tower of London and St George's Chapel, Windsor (Gee 1981). Stone from Beer *D* was shipped to London, while quarries at Portland *Do* and Painswick *Gl* were among a number which supplied prestige projects outside their own regions. Such long-distance provision was made feasible by water transport.

A large part of the cost of a masonry building lay in the carriage of stone. When Salzman examined the economics of quarrying he concluded that costs of carriage would begin to exceed the expense of winning the stone beyond a distance of about twelve miles (1967, 119). Wherever possible, therefore, builders of local churches would try to make use of sources which were close to hand. Masons at Bodmin *Co* used a local quarry for the rebuilding of the church of St Petrock which began in 1469. In 1429 the parishioners of Warfield *Sr* were given permission to dig stone in the adjoining Forest of Windsor. This consent had a time-limit of two years (Salzman 1967, 119). There was a quarry productive of good stone in the parish of Northleach *Gl*. Documents which specify the sources of stone that were used for building parish churches are rare, but fieldwork and aerial photography will often disclose small quarries or infilled diggings in the vicinity of churches, as at Spofforth *NY* (*YW*). Stone which was of insufficient quality for fair-faced work and carving might nevertheless be adequate for foundations and wall-cores. Hence it was not uncommon for a single project to be supplied from more than one source. This is what happened at Adderbury *O* when the chancel was rebuilt early in the fifteenth century. In 1413–14 Master Richard Winchcombe visited the quarries at Taynton, near Burford, to select stone for the work. Burford is about twenty miles from Adderbury. But stone was also being extracted in Adderbury itself, from a small quarry which had been opened in the rectory garden. When the chancel was finished the hole was filled in.

The relationship between quarrying and building was close. Although stone could be bought from quarries which were run as independent commercial concerns, records of the medieval construction industry indicate that it was common for the processes of acquiring stone and of building to fall under unified control. Accountants' records contain many references to the expenses of master masons who, like Richard Winchcombe, made visits to quarries. When Thomas Mason was working on the steeple at Leverton *Li* in 1498, for instance, he was to be reimbursed for the cost of journeys to and from the quarry (Harvey 1984, 198–9). William Netilton's duties as a mason in charge of work at Louth between 1500 and 1506 included trips to the quarry (Harvey 1984, 213). Netilton's excursions were for the purpose of choosing stone. But the link between quarry and project could be more intimate than this. Squared stones and some carved components like plinths and mouldings were often supplied from quarries ready worked (Salzman 1967, 123). If the quarriers formed an independent concern this could be achieved by sending measurements and templates prepared by the designer to the quarry: a practice attested as early as the twelfth century (Salzman 1967, 370). Where the quarry was close to hand, the builders could extract and prepare the stone themselves, all under the supervision of the designer. Local quarries could be loaned or leased to a parish for the duration of a project, but it is interesting to notice that some of the more celebrated architects came from families which had connections with both quarrying and building. The Winchcombes, for instance, were thus involved, and among other examples one can mention John Beckley, builder of the north transept at Thame *O*, begun in 1442, who may have been related to a quarry master of the same name (Harvey 1984, 16). Such links are significant because, as Dr Harvey has pointed out, 'there is a good deal of evidence that areas of stone quarrying were one of the main sources of the more highly trained types of mason' (1972, 24).

Fig. 95 makes this plain. It is a map of the occurrence of waterleaf capitals in English parish churches. Before considering what the map may signify it is necessary to explain why the waterleaf capital has been selected for this sort of treatment. There are three reasons. The first of them is that the waterleaf is sufficiently distinctive to avoid the risk of sweeping up too many cognate, but separate, sculptural forms which might cloud the pattern. Second, the heyday of the waterleaf was short: it lasted for about twenty years, from 1170–90. Since one of the most intriguing aspects of the subject of medieval architectural style is how specific artistic forms gained currency, it is worthwhile to set the brevity of the *floruit* of the waterleaf against the pattern of its distribution. A third point that favours the waterleaf is its position on the artistic and chronological frontier between late Romanesque and early Gothic. Sometimes it occurs in buildings which embody features of both, as at Bossall *NY*, or Algarkirk *Li*, where waterleaf and stiffleaf forms exist side by side. The waterleaf thus suggests itself as a possible indicator of broad tendencies in the pattern of parish church embellishment late in the twelfth century, when we are only three or four generations forward from the period when quarrying was graduating from its earlier position as an occasional pursuit to the status of a more regular activity. Can we, for instance, discern patterns which would support the idea that schools of design grew up in the vicinity of cathedrals or important religious houses?

In fact, the distribution of waterleaf shows only a scant correlation with the whereabouts of great churches. It corresponds much more closely with some of the areas which were productive of good building stone. For example, the clusters of waterleaf in Rutland, Northamptonshire and southwest Lincolnshire occur along the Jurassic limestone belt, often in the vicinity of quarries. Other examples are to be seen along the outcrop of magnesian limestone north of Nottingham. Conversely, there are counties like Bedfordshire and Buckinghamshire, lacking in first-class freestone, which are largely devoid of waterleaf. Yet not all of the areas which show an absence of waterleaf were poor in stone. Dorset and Somerset, for instance, were productive of good limestones. Why is there so little waterleaf in Dorset? The answer seems to be that there were *other* forms of capital which were contemporary with the waterleaf, and which have a distribution that corresponds with certain quarry zones but not others. When these are taken into account, there are complementary distributions.

The significance of these patterns is surely not simply that masons pursued their craft to best effect in districts where good stone was plentiful, or even that waterleaf capitals or trumpet scallops could be cut to order in quarries for projects elsewhere, with the frequency of each type diminishing as distance, and therefore carriage costs, increased, leaving only those campaigns supported by wealthy patrons or close to waterways to break the pattern. The map might be seen rather as the manifestation of a more basic truth: that quarrying and masoncraft in the later twelfth century had become not only interdependent, but also integrated to the extent that each was substantially assimilated to the other. That would

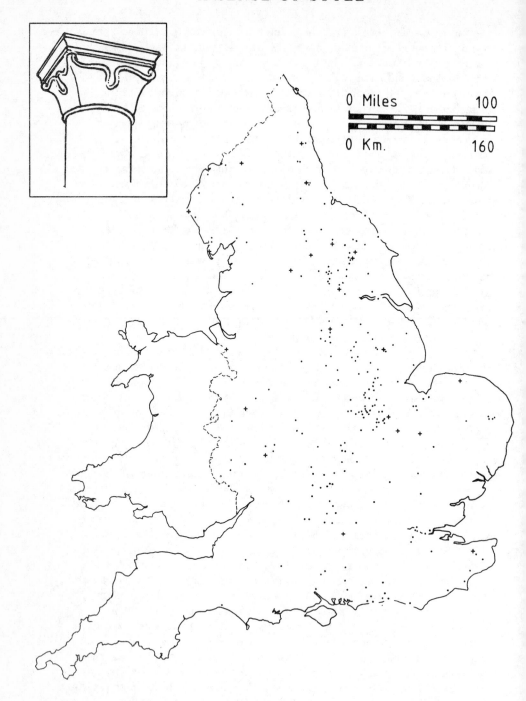

95 General distribution of (*a*) waterleaf capitals (type illustrated by inset); and (*b*) trumpet scallop capitals. Greater churches which feature in these patterns are indicated by a cross

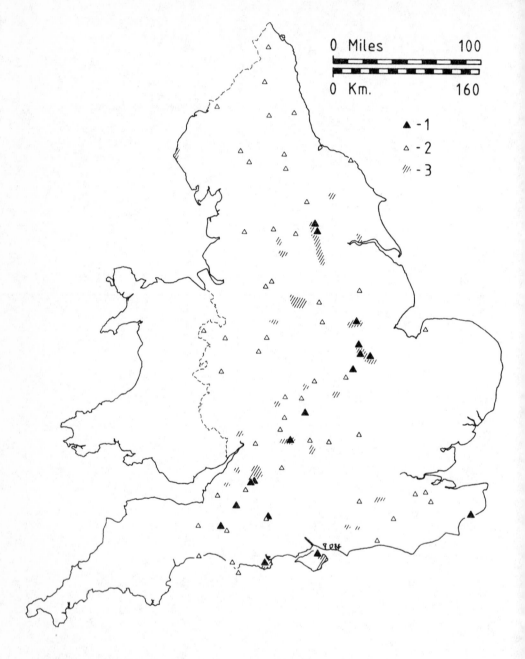

96 Centres of medieval quarrying for building stone: **1** recorded medieval quarries; **2** other quarries thought to have been active during the Middle Ages; **3** districts noted for stone-winning activity

explain the rapidity with which the waterleaf gained currency after its invention in *c.* 1170, its widespread appearances, and non-appearances, and the suddenness with which it was then dropped. The process is too abrupt to be simply accounted for by the theory that stylistic advances originated only in cathedrals, great abbeys and palaces, to be copied into parish church architecture in following decades. Great patrons may have encouraged or funded technical innovation, but areas of stone quarrying acted as conductors for new ideas. The waterleaf map makes manifest the probability that the processes of extracting, carving and building with stone were allied crafts, and that different motifs were developed in different quarry regions. Quarries, in short, were nurseries of medieval masoncraft.

With all this said, there were other aspects of style in medieval building that lay more completely within the realms of aesthetics or intellectual thought, and hence were directly susceptible to promotion by acts of patronage. The waterleaf capital is a minor item. It has little to do with questions of building design or construction. It cannot be discussed in the terms that would be applied to, say, the pointed arch, or the high degree of artistic integration that was achieved in the best Perpendicular buildings. Perhaps the main point that emerges is that a parish church is a kind of cultural alloy, in which the proportions of local, regional and national elements will differ according to circumstance. Every parish church is unique, and the relative importance of parts played by patrons, parishioners, craftsmen and artists is subject to infinite variation. Looking back, searching the distance of history for explanations, it is not always possible to distinguish between the products of function and fancy. Humankind is moved to action by both. Important patrons catch the eye, but may do so because, historically, they are more conspicuous. The role of the parishioner must not be underestimated. In Chapter 9 we shall find that during the fourteenth and fifteenth centuries ordinary people assumed considerable control over their churches. They may have done so sooner. Lords and villeins alike, however, got wet when it rained, and one fundamental aspect of the development of the medieval parish church that has hitherto been ignored must now be introduced: the requirements of maintenance and repair, and their great adversary – the weather.

VIII

TIME AND TIDE

All buildings tend towards collapse. If a new building were to be abandoned at the moment of its completion the initial stages of decay would be gradual. A common way for the process to start is when gutters and downpipes become clogged and water is diverted into the fabric. Within, plaster flakes from the walls, while joists and floor-boards become damp and increasingly vulnerable to outbreaks of rot. Pointing begins to crumble. After a time leaks develop in the covering of the roof, and rot takes hold in the frame beneath. By now saplings have established themselves in various cracks and crevices; their roots disturb and loosen surrounding masonry. When portions of the roof fall in the interior becomes exposed to weather. From this point on deterioration is swift. Sooner or later there is a savage winter, when water which has seeped into the masonry is turned to ice, causing portions of the fabric to crumble and collapse. One or two more winters of this sort will usually be sufficient to deliver the *coup de grâce*. It is by such processes that a roofed building may be reduced to ruin.

The uninterrupted decay of a building could be represented as a curve: flattish at first, then steepening. In most instances the profile would be stepped, with abrupt plunges (episodes of collapse or rapid decay) interspersed between periods of more gentle decline. However, if the first signs of deterioration are regularly looked for, and remedied as soon as they are detected, more serious problems are never given an opportunity to develop and the point of rapid fall-off on the curve is never reached (Fig. 97). Buildings so cared for can be kept sound for centuries. Conversely, a failure to undertake simple repairs or carry out routine maintenance will lead inexorably to an accelerating decline which can be arrested only

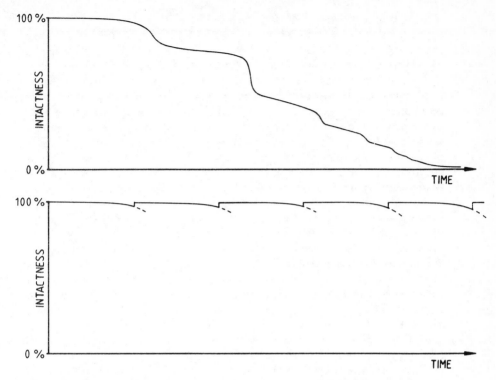

97 Schematic representations of (a) the progress towards collapse of a neglected building, and (b) deferral of collapse by intervention maintenance

through drastic repair, or even rebuilding. This is why the history of parish church architecture is as much a history of maintenance as it is of fashion. Minor lapses of care in one period could occasion considerable new work in another.

Wood, stone and lime mortar were the principal load-bearing constituents of a parish church fabric. Wood went into the upper floors of towers, ceilings and the frames of roofs. Stone was used for the main shell and supports. Lime mortar separated the stone blocks or rubble that formed the skins of walls and more specialized assemblies like arches. Mortar was also important as a binding agent for rubble in the cores of walls. In some types of structure mortar might account for as much as 30 per cent of the volume of masonry.

These materials lose quality at different rates. Under favourable conditions structural timber can survive for hundreds of years. A few twelfth-century churches, such as Chipping Ongar *Ex*, Little Hormead *Hrt* or Wistanstow *Sa*, may still possess their original roofs, or portions of them (Hewett 1980, 35; Cranage 1894, 169). Tenth-century timbers have been found in the Anglo-Saxon church of St Peter, Barton-upon-Humber *Hu* (*Li*) (Rodwell and Rodwell 1982). Odda's Chapel at Deerhurst *Gl*, dedicated in 1056, was until 1965 sheltered beneath a structure which may have included the remains of its original roof (Currie 1983). In some areas churches, and particularly towers and belfries, continued to be made of wood throughout the later Middle Ages. Many have survived (Fig. 98).

The chief enemy of a building is not time, but water. Ingress of water into a fabric can be harmful to timber and masonry. Wood which becomes permanently sodden or damp will fall victim to rot. Wet rots attack timbers where the moisture content is high. Their attacks accordingly tend to be localized, being specific to those portions of wood which are particularly wet. Dry rot may pose a threat which is more extensive. It is caused by a fungus, *Serpula lacrimans*. The spores of *Serpula* are reported to germinate most readily on damp timber in unventilated conditions. In a church a classic locale for an outbreak would be immediately under a blocked valley gutter where there is standing water that regularly spills into the fabric, with little circulation of air, and a suitable temperature. (*Serpula* is said to grow within a temperature band between *c.* 40 and 80 degrees Fahrenheit (*c.* 4–26 degrees Celsius) and to prosper best at around 73 degrees Fahrenheit (23 degrees Celsius).) The growths of dry rot have the capacity to travel through the mortar joints of masonry, and hence to spread to new timber beyond the site of the original attack. However, if the fungus is deprived of the conditions that it requires for growth, its ability to journey, or even to continue living, may be curtailed (Ridout 1986, 27–8). Dry rot prefers softwood to hardwood timbers, and its environmental demands may mean that it did not pose so serious a threat to medieval oaken roofs as did the larvae of deathwatch beetle.

Stone will generally outlast any structure that is built of it, since by the measure of geological time the lifespan of a building is less than the twinkling of an eye. Rapid decay may nevertheless occur, for example if the stone selected is soft and vulnerable to erosion, or if it is laid without regard for its geological characteristics. Sedimentary stones are normally laid in such a way that their planes of bedding correspond with the natural bed. Departures from this practice may reduce the resistance to weathering, while any damp rising through the wall may induce salts to migrate to the surface, causing the stone to spall. Protective roughcast coats or layers of limewash or rendering were often applied to shelter fabrics. Again, if these were not maintained and renewed, walls could suffer.

The walls of many medieval churches consisted of ashlar skins which were separated by cores of rubble and mortar. Wall-cores can remain sound for long periods, provided that there is no serious deformation of the structure to an extent which causes cracking and consequent ingress of water. If water enters in such volume that the core becomes sodden, the lime is dissolved out and mortar failure may ensue. A wall-core so affected loses its solidity and may eventually disintegrate. The failure of a wet wall-core can be hastened by freezing, when the matrix is ruptured by the expansion of ice.

The implications of these hazards for the history of ecclesiastical

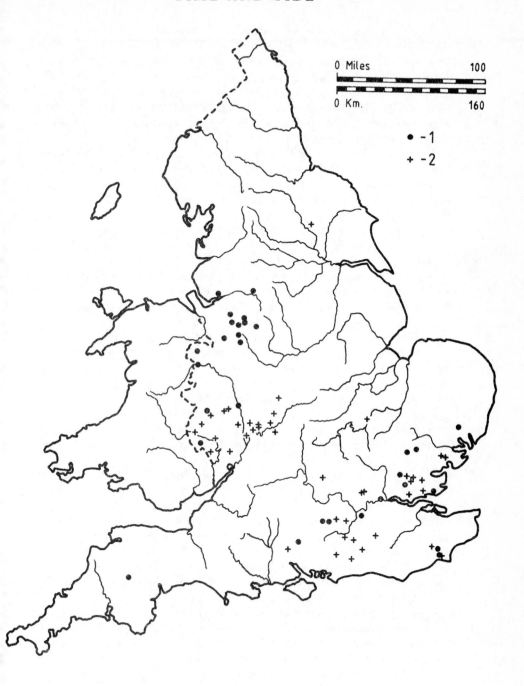

8 Distribution of surviving parish churches 1 built wholly or partly of wood (roofs are excluded), and 2 with wooden towers or belfries

building may be summarized as follows. Stone-built parish churches of the eleventh and twelfth centuries were mostly uncomplicated and robust. They were also relatively new, so that chronic dilapidation is unlikely to have been a widespread problem. Thereafter the picture becomes more variable. Many churches were remodelled, enlarged or rebuilt. Some of these works were undertaken for reasons of pride or piety: factors which were mentioned in the previous chapter, and will be examined again in the next. Others replaced buildings which had simply worn out.

In theory, alteration and renewal gave the fabric of a church an extended lease of life. But there could be negative aspects to such changes. As buildings became more complicated the requirements for maintenance increased and the risks of neglect were correspondingly magnified. Buildings, like garments, tend to fail soonest along their seams: typically at lines of junction between work of different periods. Additions and repairs multiplied these zones of potential weakness. The addition of aisles and chapels gave roof profiles of greater complexity, with attendant threats when valleys and parapet walks became clogged and filled with water, or lying snow. The growth in use of sheet lead for covering roofs brought benefits of durability and efficiency as a weathertight outer skin. But where ponding occurs, for example in a blocked valley, chronic dampness may result which will be harmful to the roof structure within.

Pinnacles, turrets, ornamental parapets and other forms of architectural embellishment which became popular in the fourteenth and fifteenth centuries could present risks. Being remote from the ground, the condition of such features was sometimes difficult to monitor. Defective parapets provided access for water into the main fabric, while stones dislodged by gales might puncture roofs. Spires, particularly those built of wood, sometimes developed faults, and in time many were removed. Lofty steeples attracted lightning.

Another problem which is likely to have increased during the later Middle Ages was rising damp. By the beginning of the fourteenth century many churchyards were becoming crowded. Some, like that of St Michael, Gloucester, were already full (Walker 1976, 17–18). Ideally a crowded cemetery would be enlarged, but it often happened that this was not possible and new graves were dug through old ones. When over-burial was practised the level of the ground around the church would rise, and moist earth pressed ever higher against the exterior walls (see Fig. 65).

Unless churches were properly maintained, therefore, a period of neglect could lead to structural malady. An episode of carelessness need only have been of a few seasons' duration for the processes of decay to be activated, though the full consequences might not become manifest for decades. Chancels in the hands of negligent rectors, or naves and towers left unrepaired or incomplete because of parochial indifference or disorganization were at high risk. But famine or epidemic could interrupt the cycle of maintenance even in the most efficient parishes. And while there is no reason to think that many parishes were remiss in their duties at any one time, the cumulative totals were a good deal more significant.

Institutional shortcomings within the parochial system had repercussions for church fabrics. Chancels were weak points. From the early thirteenth century responsibility for the care of a parish church became divided. Parishioners took charge of the nave. The rector looked after the chancel. Often this apportionment is witnessed in an unequal development as between the chancel and the nave. At Yarwell *Np*, for instance, the thirteenth-century chancel was unusually small, whereas the nave was on a more ample scale until its curtailment in 1782. When the nave at Yatton *So* was treated to a mighty rebuilding in the fifteenth century, the chancel was left unaltered. Such disparities could also occur in reverse. Cotterstock *Np* has a chancel equal to the lengths of the nave and tower combined. Spofforth *NY* boasted one of the largest chancels in Yorkshire until 1854, when the building fell victim to unauthorized alterations. Lavish chancels elsewhere, as at Sandiacre *Db*, Orwell *Ca* or Adderbury *O*, testify to rectorial munificence. It is not unusual for chancels to stand askew from their naves, as at Doddington *Ca* where the bishops of Ely were responsible for a splendid rebuilding in the thirteenth century. Setting-out errors were common on such occasions, and may highlight the chancel as being under separate control.

Disputes could arise along the frontier between the portion of the church which was in the charge of the parish and that of the rector. Twelfth-century chancel arches sandwiched between chancels and naves of differing date may owe their survival to the fact that both parties disclaimed responsibility for them. Crumbling chancel arches were singled out for criticism at several places in the diocese of Hereford during a visitation which was made in 1397 (Bannister 1929; 1930). Cruciform churches posed a related problem: did the crossing fall within the purview of the parishioners or the proprietor? The parishioners of Silkstone *SY* (*YW*) argued with the prior and convent of Pontefract priory about this, on and off, for two centuries. Eventually the matter was resolved when the central tower was dismantled and a new tower was erected in 1479 at the west end of the church (A. H. Thompson 1947, 129–30).

Many rectors were reluctant to do more than the minimum necessary to keep their chancels in repair. A significant minority did less. Rectors were often absent, for purposes of study or in pursuit of preferment. Many were pluralists, residing in one parish and neglecting the others while drawing the incomes they provided, or residing in none and ignoring them all. The rector could be a layman who looked upon the living simply as a financial asset and delegated the cure of souls to a hired chaplain. The rector could also be an institution. By *c.* 1300 over half the parish churches in England had been appropriated to religious communities. Such bodies varied in their diligence. Some were conscientious. Others viewed their pastoral responsibilities in a more perfunctory way, taking the greater tithes of their churches and leaving parish work to a vicar, or to a stipendiary chaplain who was poorly paid and untenured.

It was not unusual for absentee rectors to 'farm' their livings, giving a franchise for the collection of income to a local person who passed on a proportion of what was raised to the rector and kept the rest for himself. Thus at Haydon *Do* a check on the condition of the church in 1405 revealed that the 'Chancel is defective through the fault of the abbot of Sherbourn because he farms his portion of Haydon, Southenay, and Prinnesley' (*Reg. Chandler*, no. 46; Timmins 1984, 24).

References to chancels in poor repair are commonly found in the records of inspections which were made by bishops or their representatives. When Lancaut *Gl* was visited at the end of the fourteenth century the roof, walls and windows of the chancel were said to be in bad condition. Elsewhere in the diocese of Hereford at this time the visitor found things to criticize in the chancels of about 17 per cent of churches. Problems ranged from the crumbling chancel arch at Dixton, just outside Monmouth, to the roof at Yarkhill *He* which was in such a terrible state that the chaplain was unable to celebrate mass when it rained (Bannister 1929, 445; 1930, 96). Yarkhill's leaking roof was not unique. At Stelling *K* in 1511-12 the chancel was described as being 'not repaired insomuch that it falleth in great decay and raineth on the sacrament' (Wood-Legh 1984, 181). In 1336 it was noted that rain fell upon the altar at Scredington *Li*, where the dean and chapter of Lincoln were the rectors, and that drizzle and wind made services impossible during bad weather (D. Owen 1971, 113). Records of visitations made in the diocese of Canterbury late in the thirteenth century reveal the neglected chancel as a commonplace. In 1292 the chancel at Burmarsh *K* was badly covered. Chancel roofs at Goodnestone, St Martin's at Old Romney and Fleet were in poor repair. Defective roofs were also noted at Bilsington, Nonington, Dymchurch and Brookland, where some of the timbers were rotting away. One of the walls at Wingham was *ruinosus*. Fairfield was in a sorry state: the altars were made of wood, the church was made *de ligno et plastura terra* 'of wood and daub', and accordingly had not been dedicated. The chaplain was reported to have pastured lambs in the churchyard. Perhaps poverty had driven him to do this. His portion was said to be meagre, while the rector was 'doing no good in the parish' and had that year sold all fruits of the living to a layman (Woodruffe 1917, 161-2). The routine character of such complaints seems to be confirmed by the fact that a generation later many churches in this area were still dilapidated. Ickham, Eastry and Deal were among a number where glass in chancel windows had been broken and left unrepaired. At Staple, Eastry and Loose the chancel ceilings were *fracta*. Two columns in the church at Eastry were *ruinosae*. The roof at Detling was giving cause for concern.

Records of the fifteenth and sixteenth centuries suggest that whatever improvements had been brought about through the establishment of the vicarage system, which provided security of tenure and a minimum wage for the priest on the spot, rectors could be as neglectful as ever. In 1405 the visitor in the diocese of Salisbury noted defective chancels at Beer,

Fordington, Stratton, Stockwood and elsewhere. Indeed, of the chancels of larger churches and chapels which were reported on at this time only 27 per cent were free from dilapidation. Seven years later the position was not greatly improved (Timmins 1984, xxvi–xxvii). At Willesdon *Mx* in the fourteenth or fifteenth century parishioners complained of their chancel that a boy 'might easily overthrow the walls. Robbers have entered and carried off goods. Mass cannot be celebrated at the High Altar. Owls and crows fly in by day and by night and pollute the church' (Simpson 1895, xxiii).

Visitations carried out in Kent in 1511–12 (Table 4) and in Yorkshire in 1557 provide larger samples from which a general picture may be obtained. Out of 481 Yorkshire parish churches which were visited, 131 (27 per cent) were noted as having decayed chancels. But the pattern of neglect was not uniform. In the deaneries of Doncaster and Ryedale, for instance, dilapidations were restricted to 7.5 per cent and 11.75 per cent of chancels, respectively. By contrast, in Holderness and Dickering the figures were 52 per cent and 53 per cent. These deaneries covered areas wherein many settlements shrank or disappeared during the fifteenth and sixteenth centuries. Although few parish churches were completely abandoned at this stage, the figures indicate that sub-regional variations in prosperity and population could have an impact upon the condition of church fabrics, at least to the extent of diminishing the quality of their maintenance.

Parishioners, too, could be neglectful, though seldom on such a scale as rectors (Table 4). The visitation of 1397 in the diocese of Hereford disclosed 48 cases of neglect by rectors (about 17 per cent of churches), whereas defects in naves and towers which were blamed upon parishioners numbered only 14 (about 5 per cent). One of these cases concerned the inhabitants of Ashford, Ludford and Syde *Sa*, who were declining to contribute towards the upkeep of their *matrix ecclesia* at Bromfield, by then a royal free chapel, formerly a minster (Blair 1985, 128–31): a late continuation of the centripetal influence which had once been exerted by hundreds of superior churches of this type.

Local people usually had a practical and sentimental concern for their church: feelings which a rector did not always share. Even so, there were some displays of parochial shirking. In 1290 Oliver Sutton, bishop of Lincoln (1280–99) urged the dean of Horncastle to galvanize the parishioners of Hagworthingham *Li* into completing their bell tower. A year later this work was unfinished. In a further mandate, issued in 1293, Sutton did not disguise his exasperation at the slowness of the dean in complying with his earlier requests, and the indifference of the parishioners (*Reg. Sutton* iii, 25, 153; iv, 75). Was it by coincidence that this tower collapsed in 1976? Or were the seeds of destruction sown seven centuries ago? Dilatory parishioners are found elsewhere in Lincolnshire at this time, as at Burton Stather and Stapleford, where bell towers stood incomplete. Perhaps churchgoers in these villages were content to hang their bells in frames at ground level, or even in trees. In 1297 the inhabitants

Table 4 The condition of church fabrics and cemeteries in Kent as revealed by the visitations of archbishop Warham and his deputies in 1511 and 1512

Deanery / Problem concerning	Canterbury	Westbere	Sandwich	Dover	Elham	Lyminge	Bridge	Charing	Ospringe	Sittingbourne	Sutton	Total churches reported upon	% of churches with defect
Number of churches	21	12	26	21	15	38	28	25	24	24	26	260	
												Total churches with problem	
Chancel	4	3	8	7	3	16	9	4	7	7	15	83	32
Nave	1	–	–	3	–	2	3	3	3	1	3	19	7
Tower	2	–	2	2	–	–	2	–	1	1	–	10	4
Bellframe	1	–	1	–	–	–	3	–	–	–	–	5	2
Threat of collapse	–	–	–	–	–	1	–	1	1	1	–	4	1.5
Gutters	–	–	1	1	–	2	1	–	–	1	1	7	3
Other defects	–	2	4	1	2	3	1	2	3	1	–	19	7
Enclosure of churchyard	3	1	3	3	4	7	5	5	4	4	8	47	18
Decayed parsonage	2	4	1	3	–	10	1	3	1	3	1	29	11
Other problems over parsonage	1	1	1	1	–	–	1	1	1	1	–	8	3
Complaint of non-residence	5	2	3	7	2	6	2	3	1	6	2	39	15

of Twyford *Mx* were called to church by two bells dangling from church-yard elms. Barfreston *K* had a bell which was suspended from a yew. Where churches lacked towers, trees may quite often have been used in this way. But when a tree became old and unsteady it could pose a threat to the church if it grew too close. The parishioners of Adisham *K* were warned of this in 1327. In 1511 parishioners at Buckland *K* complained that 'the trees nigh the church walls hurteth the church with dripping to our cost, and the profits of the same trees the prior of Dover our pro-prietaries have'. At Basham *K* in 1511–12 it was noted that 'the trees in the churchyard are an impediment for them that bear the cross in pro-cession insomuch it cannot be borne upright for the boughs' (Wood-Legh 1984, nos 74, 158).

It is often difficult to ascertain whether neglect by parishioners was the result of poverty or inefficiency. In 1297 the bell tower at Wickham *Ex* was *ruinosum et sine tecto* 'ruinous and without a roof'. Pelham Arsa's tower was *debile* and uncovered. Over a century later the tower at Wambrook was thought defective. The church at Stockwood was exceptionally unlucky, for here the rector was accused of neglecting the chancel while the parishioners had failed to maintain the nave and tower. Similarly, when the chapel of Winterbourne Dauntsey *Do* was visited on 9 September 1405 it was found that the 'Chancel roof and windows are defective through the Rector's fault. Nave roof is defective through fault of parish.' Other prob-lems noted on this visit included the frequent drunkenness of the chaplain, and allegations of his adultery with one Agnes Thecher. The visitor had a keen eye for detail. When he came to perambulate the churchyard he objected to the encroachment upon it of a new house by a distance of one foot (*Reg. Chandler*, no. 52; Timmins 1984, 27). In 1296 the rural dean and chapter of Ewyas *He* actually ordered the demolition of two houses which had been intruded across the boundary of the church of St Michael (D. Walker 1976, no. 149).

Visitations elsewhere were often equally searching. For this reason, perhaps, they exaggerate the pervasiveness of neglect, giving equal weight to both chronic and evanescent problems. Nevertheless, complaints about clerical misbehaviour which are interspersed between the humdrum details of dilapidated fences, mildewed missals and leaky roofs provide a context in which lay cynicism towards things ecclesiastical would come as no surprise. Breaches of celibacy were fairly common. At Chandler's visitation of 1405 'accusations of sexual misconduct were levelled against 16 per cent of all parish clergy' (Timmins 1984, xix). There were some outstanding episodes of clergy expending their energies other than in the service of the Church. The vicar of Baydon, it was said, 'commits adultery with Agnes Webbe, Katherine atte Hegges, Ellen Benet, and Joan, formerly John Glovere's servant'. Thomas Bourton, the chaplain at Baydon, denied a charge of adultery. Bourton was described as 'an habitual gossip and causes quarrels between parishioners and constantly threatens to beat up Nicholas Raynolde, his parishioner, without cause.

. . . He attacked Nicholas in Margery Hykeman's house intending to beat him up' *(Reg. Chandler*, no. 71; Timmins 1984, 35). At Burbage in 1412 five parishioners assured the visiting dean that the vicar, Alexander Champion, 'committed adultery with Alice, William Burton's wife, for two years and also with Walter Luyde's wife, old John Forst's wife who was caught in his room whom he had for seven years both at Chippenham and Burbage, John Shifford's wife, and a concubine at Salisbury by whom he had many children'. In Lent he solicited wives and servant girls, apparently at confession *(Reg. Chandler*, no. 353: Timmins 1984, 119). Reports of sexual exploits on such an epic scale are exceptional. Yet the fact that parishioners seem to a large extent to have been resigned to such behaviour could signify that lesser or more discreet offenders were actually more numerous than the official records show. Just occasionally we hear of a parishioner who was provoked beyond endurance. In 1405 dean Chandler was told that the chaplain of Netheravon *Wi* had raped Joan Souter of Chisenbury. This chaplain was expected to take services in the chapel of Chisenbury, where he seems additionally to have courted unpopularity among parishioners by stabling his horse in their church and tethering it to the font. One of the Chisenbury men promised to kill the chaplain, who became so frightened as to refuse to administer the sacraments there *(Reg. Chandler*, nos 58, 59).

Other failings, indicative of wider problems, lay behind the Chisenbury episode. The vicar of Netheravon was responsible for services at Chisenbury. But the vicar had resided at Netheravon for only four weeks out of the previous fifty-two, while his boorish chaplain was now unwilling to say mass at Chisenbury for fear of being murdered. Meanwhile the living of Netheravon was being farmed, and the chancel was in disrepair. This was not a lucky church: the Domesday commissioners had found it uncared for in 1086.

Reports of agricultural activity in churchyards are not unusual. In 1292, for instance, the rector of Deal *K* was using the churchyard for winnowing his corn. Although the pasturing of animals in churchyards was not permitted, the practice was quite widespread. If the owner of the animals was the incumbent or parochial chaplain this could lead to a dispute with the churchwardens, who were charged with caring for the churchyard and securing its boundaries. Grass and timber in churchyards were sometimes regarded as part of the glebe, but the line was drawn at horses stabled in church porches, or grazing sheep. Very often, however, it was the parishioners themselves who were at fault by failing to maintain a stockproof enclosure around the cemetery which would exclude their own animals. The early sixteenth-century Kentish visitation contains a number of entries which make this clear. At Kenardington the churchyard was 'haunted with hogs and uncleanly kept'. Aldington's churchyard was 'evil kept from hogs and other beasts'. The unlawful presence of animals was noted in churchyards at Alkham, Barham and Smeeth. At Mersham it was observed that 'hogs dig up the graves in the churchyard' (Wood-

Legh 1984, nos 108, III, 120, 133, 158). In all five cases the churchyard boundary was defective, and the churchwardens were instructed to repair it, although at Smeeth the wardens argued that the parish priest had let the churchyard to farm, and that it was therefore the farmer's duty to keep it clean.

Such grievances were, however, comparatively trivial in comparison with the complaints about clergy who failed to turn up to take services, left chapelries unserved, charged sick people for the sacrament, denied last rites to the dying, were habitually drunk, and insulted or bullied their parishioners. It is difficult to judge how widespread shortcomings of this sort were. Clerical misconduct always makes good reading. Like the derelict church, reports of it have probably been repeated too often, with insufficient emphasis upon the majority of parishes where the visitor found that all was well. Chandler heard material criticisms of clergy at 16 per cent of the places he visited in 1405 (Timmins 1984, xix). In contrast can be placed the visitation of 1519 in Lincolnshire which disclosed fewer than half-a-dozen cases of gross inefficiency (A.H.Thompson 1947). A visitation which took place twenty years previously in the Suffolk deaneries of the diocese of Norwich produced only eleven instances of serious neglect of chancel or rectory in 478 parishes. Two out of the five allegations of clerical immorality went to substance, and three priests were found to be unfitted for the cure of souls because of their illiteracy. A less creditable aspect of parochial conditions in Suffolk which emerged from this visitation of 1499 was the large number of churches which lacked provision for proper pastoral supervision. Superficially the figures look not at all bad: non-residence was noted at 40 churches (about 8 per cent), but of these only 6 (around 1 per cent) were not being served by other clergy. However, a high proportion of churches (34 per cent) had been appropriated to religious houses, and in 40 per cent of these parishes no vicarage had been established (Harper-Bill 1977, 42, 44).

Such figures remind us that since the twelfth century bishops had been labouring to extend their authority over a parochial system which had originated largely outside their control. Poverty, rather than illiteracy, materialism or greed, did most to undermine the ministry of parish priests. The system whereby rectors delegated pastoral responsibility to vicars who might or might not be resident and who in their turn often relied upon hired representatives – the parochial chaplains – meant that in too many parishes the cure of souls was left to men of the slenderest accomplishments. The parish priesthood of the thirteenth century, as it had been in the eleventh, was in large part an ecclesiastical peasantry. Lucrative livings were not necessarily better served than those of low value because income could be siphoned away from the parish by a rector with principal interests elsewhere. Poor livings were susceptible to chronic neglect. Even if they tried, rectors found it difficult to attract priests of good calibre to serve them. Benefices of small worth might thus be served by a long succession of hopeless hirelings.

Mindful of these problems, bishops had campaigned for ordained vicarages, to provide a permanent parish ministry and a minimum income for those within it. Bishops insisted that candidates for the parish priesthood be presented to them, to ensure that such men had been properly ordained, and to establish their competence (Cheney 1941, 34–6). Nevertheless, in an age when facilities for advanced education were concentrated in a handful of places, clerical ignorance was extensive and literacy low. Most parish priests had received no more than an elementary schooling in the elements of the Christian faith. Acquaintance with the Bible was limited; few parishes could afford one, and in those that could it was less than likely that the priest would be able to read it. The words of services were commonly learned by rote. When the religious writer John Myrc compiled his versified manual of instructions for parish priests *c.* 1400 he assured his audience that the mispronunciation of Latin would not invalidate baptism, provided that the first syllable of each word was correctly enunciated. Literary tests set by bishops examined feats of memory as much as knowledge. For instance, in 1291 Oliver Sutton, bishop of Lincoln, is found writing to the dean of Grantham, advising him that one Thomas Isaac had been lawfully ordained. However, in a recent interview Isaac had shown himself to be uncertain about the words of the masses of the Holy Trinity, the Holy Ghost, the Blessed Virgin and the requiem. The bishop had directed the candidate to study these masses further. When he was word perfect it would be permissible for him to celebrate the masses in question. But Isaac was not to be granted the cure of souls (*Reg. Sutton* iv, 73).

Considerations such as these could help to explain some of the contrasts in parochial building: why neighbouring churches could sometimes develop in entirely different ways. Patronage and wealth have been suggested as the most important influences, and with good reason. But if these are set aside, the attitude of the rector, parochial morale and organization remain as underlying constants. And whereas a new chancel or nave could result from the enthusiasm of a single benefactor or generation of churchgoers, the future of the structure would depend upon a less glamorous commitment to countless acts of humdrum maintenance. Moreover, it is a paradox that while conscientious communities could husband increasingly ancient fabrics, handing them on in good order, episodes of incompetence could reduce a church to a point at which rebuilding became easier than repair. Conceivably this is a reason why so many of our minor parish churches were substantially remodelled in the later fourteenth and fifteenth centuries, and intact churches of twelfth- and thirteenth-century date are less numerous. In many cases there was a positive wish to rebuild, for reasons which will be examined in the next chapter. But the likelihood that a good many churches *had* to be rebuilt is an aspect which deserves more attention than it has received.

One factor over which parishioners had no control was the weather. From all that was said at the outset it will be clear that buildings and weather are in a state of perpetual contest. No building can ever win this contest outright. However, fabrics which are properly cherished may endure for many centuries, whereas buildings in neglectful hands will succumb.

The effects of past weather and climate upon parish church fabrics are here considered under two heads: *weather events*, such as thunderstorms or gales; and *climatic trends*, as for example toward wetter and cooler conditions in the late Middle Ages.

Weather events, by their nature, were dramatic, and hence often earned references in written records. Between 1200 and 1450 there are reports of at least thirty-three storms which were the cause of very extensive structural damage. Among them was the hurricane of 15 January 1362, a contender for the worst gale in recorded history. Ten years earlier a storm on or about 1 November 'uncovered houses and churches, overturned mills, uprooted trees', and in 1354 another tempest inflicted similar damage (*Chron. Knighton* ii, 73, 76). On 14 September 1311 Thomas Walsingham recorded 'a very violent wind' which 'threw down innumerable trees with their fruit and the bell towers of Modeford and Gevelton were likewise thrown to the ground' (*Hist. Anglicana* i, 126). Roger of Wendover recalled serious storms in the Midlands on 30 November 1222 which had caused destruction to 'churches and church towers, houses, and other buildings, walls and ramparts of castles'. Twelve days later a cyclone 'threw down buildings as if they were shaken by the breath of the devil, levelled churches and their towers to the ground, tore up by the roots the trees of the forest' (Roger of Wendover ii, 441-2). It is a loss to architectural history that the records of monastic chroniclers seldom specify *which* churches were so badly harmed by these gales. Such details as are given usually concern cathedrals or greater monasteries, like the towers of Chichester, Bury St Edmunds and Evesham, all of which are said to have sustained damage in 1210 or 1211. Information about parish churches is occasionally forthcoming from local sources, however, as in the case of Cawston *Nf*, where in 1412 a 'great wind' blew down the bell tower. Donations towards the costs of repair and improvement were made for some years after, 10 marks to the making of a new bell being willed as late as 1483 (Cattermole and Cotton 1983, 243). The gale that damaged Cawston does not feature in any of the general chronicles, although it was said that in the same year (1412) the belfry of St Giles at Winchelsea *Sx* was struck by lightning which converted 'the whole church and the bells to ashes and by no human help could it be delivered' (*Eulogium Historiarum*, 421).

Churches were among the tallest structures in the medieval landscape. Being so, they were especially vulnerable to lightning. Matthew Paris related how on 14 August 1254, at

> about the hour of prime [i.e. 6.00 am] ... There was a single clap of
> thunder with lightning, which fell on the tower of the church of St Peter

in the town of St Albans, and which penetrated into the upper part of it with a horrible crash, twisted the oaken material like a net, and what was marvellous, ground it into fine shreds. The lightning also left a smoke in the whole tower and an intolerable stench.

(Matthew Paris v, 455).

Paris was describing a process which involves the instantaneous dissipation of energy at a level of around a million joules per yard of fabric. The force of the impact may be compared to that delivered by a car colliding with the structure at a speed of about 60 mph. Since the conductivity of stone is poor, the charge may find its way to earth via routes which are marginally more favourable: along mortar joints, for instance, or damp timbers. The shockwave can cause considerable structural damage. There is release of intense heat, which may lead to a fire such as consumed the church at Winchelsea in 1412. According to Roger of Wendover, when the church of St Wulfram at Grantham *Li* was struck by lightning and set afire on 8 February 1222 'there proceeded such a stench that many who were in the church being unable to endure it, took to flight: at length, however, by lighting the holy taper, and sprinkling holy water, the fire was after some trouble extinguished' (Roger of Wendover ii, 441). In 1511 it was noted that the chancel of Ospringe *K* had been 'burnt by tempest of thunder and remaineth unrepaired' (Wood-Legh 1984, no. 190).

Although weather events caused most of the damage to churches which was reported in medieval chronicles, climatic trends touched buildings in ways which were at once more general and subtle. Storms damaged some churches. Climate affected them all.

To a large extent climatic trends lay outside the perception of medieval observers, who lacked the instruments with which to measure them. But estimates of the temperatures and rainfall which prevailed between 1000 and 1600 can be derived from written records and palaeoenvironmental evidence. They show that between the ninth and twelfth centuries there was a time of warming, with the climate reaching a state of maximum geniality in the period before 1200. The phase of warmth continued through the thirteenth century, though now with interruptions which presaged a downturn as the European climate began to sink towards the Little Ice Age of the sixteenth and seventeenth centuries. Climatic deterioration in the fourteenth and fifteenth centuries seems to have been erratic, with episodes of wet and cold interspersed between spells of amelioration.

Climatic trends affected church fabrics in three main ways. Most obviously, successions of dismal summers or severe winters would have a deleterious impact upon buildings which were not being efficiently maintained. Modern experience teaches that defects which may in themselves be quite trivial, such as the loss of a few roof slates or the accumulation of water in a blocked valley, can have destructive consequences if they are ignored for any length of time. Of course, neither bad weather nor sloppy maintenance were exclusive to medieval England. But a succession of very wet summers such as occurred between 1313 or 1314 and 1317, or a run of savage winters as from 1433/4 to 1437/8 would bring forth the consequences of negligence in the past, and sow seeds of future decay in buildings which were not being adequately cared for at the time. An analysis of John Chandler's register has shown that the need for repairs rose appreciably after the extreme weather of 1407-8, when there was lying snow for twelve weeks and the following summer was exceptionally wet (Timmins 1984, xxvi). Our legacy of visitation records is insufficient for the purpose of making a systematic correlation between meteorology and maintenance in the later Middle Ages. Even so, within the climatic record a number of episodes stand out as being likely to have occasioned widespread structural damage. Savage winters were particularly damaging. Freezing weather shatters wet wall-cores and causes collapses.

Another way in which climate influenced architecture was through the diversion of resources away from building or repair in times of stress. The great famine of 1315 is a case in point. A contemporary wrote:

> Now in this past year there was such abundance of rain that men hardly gathered any crops for sale or stored it safely in the barn ... the inundation of rain consumed nearly all the seed, so that now was seen the fulfilment of the prophecy of Isaiah, and in several places hay was so hidden under water that it could neither be cut nor gathered. Sheep also perished in flocks and the animals died of a sudden murrain.
>
> (*Chron. Edward II*, 214)

Medieval people lived close to the land, and to the weather. When crops failed on such a scale there were no grain mountains to cushion the population against shortages or to steady prices. Environmental disasters dealt a multiple blow to church fabrics. Projects in hand could be interrupted or curtailed. Rectors and lords, their wider interests harmed, might be more than usually ruthless in their exactions, while any reluctance to fulfil obligations towards chancels would be increased. Inflated food prices would claim cash that might otherwise have gone to the church in offerings. Urgent repairs might have to be deferred.

While individual catastrophes such as the great famine could have an immediate effect on some buildings and could interrupt the cycle of maintenance in many, climatic and economic changes had other, more extensive, consequences for churches in the longer term. During the fourteenth and fifteenth centuries many settlements display signs of shrinkage. Some places disappeared altogether. It is not easy to generalize about the reasons for such retraction, except to say that shrinkage was usually gradual rather than abrupt, that its causes are more often to be found in an amalgam of factors rather than in any single explanation such as plague or enclosure, and that many of the places affected seem to have been predisposed towards eventual failure (C.C. Taylor 1983, 165-72).

The twelfth and thirteenth centuries had been a time of rising population. This placed pressure on rural resources. Fields which had been cultivated for several centuries from villages on fixed sites may have been losing their fertility. Extra land had been brought under the plough in the period *c.* 1100–1300, chiefly, it is said, to feed an expanding population, but perhaps also with the aim of augmenting crops grown on soils which were already beginning to show signs of exhaustion. These recent intakes were often of marginal quality, lying on the poorer soils, in places or at altitudes where cultivation had been made feasible by the exceptionally benign conditions which prevailed until the thirteenth century. Such lands were among the first to become unproductive in bad summers, or to be abandoned in the fifteenth century when scarcity of wage labour and shrunken markets rendered them uneconomical. Of course, decline was by no means uniform, and the contributory processes varied in their working and effects from region to region. In the clay plains of the Midlands, for example, a case has been made for the possibility that heavy soils were more readily cultivable in the warmer, drier conditions which developed between the ninth and thirteenth centuries. When rainfall increased (and spring soil temperatures fell?) such lands became less suitable for cereal production and reverted to pasture (G. Beresford 1975).

By 1360 the population of England may have been reduced by as much as a third by famine and pestilence. Some villages, like Tusmore *O*, were wiped out. However, complete and abrupt disappearances were rare. Plague, famine and environmental change were more often catalysts in the process of abandonment than a direct cause. When settlements on marginal land became attenuated the inhabitants who remained could reinforce the trend by gravitating towards villages which were more favourably located. The reduced populations of strong settlements might thus to some extent be replenished, while weaker communities could dwindle into hamlets, single farms or vanish altogether. Enfeebled settlements were especially vulnerable to depopulation engineered by landlords who turned to pastoral farming when demand for cereals fell and labour costs rose.

The combined effects of these changes upon churches were considerable, though not always immediate. Some churches, it is true, dropped out of use almost at once. But at others decline was protracted, while in a third category are churches which survive, in solitude, to this day.

Losses before 1400 seem to have been fairly rare. In Norfolk fewer than a dozen churches are known to have fallen into complete disuse during the fourteenth century: a small number considering the immensity of Norfolk's provision. Elsewhere a thin sprinkling of closures can be found in most counties: at Hutton Wandesley *NY* (*YW*), for instance, where depopulation led to the abandonment of the church *c.* 1400, or West Wykeham *Li* where the parish of St Lawrence was absorbed by Ludford Magna in 1396, or Little Salkeld *Cu* where the church had gone by 1360.

The parishes of Great and Little Collington *He* were united by 1352, and of Whyle and Pudlestone by 1364. The site of Great Collington's church is lost, and there is now no church at Whyle. But these were exceptions; it was in the fifteenth century that redundancy figures began to climb.

The immediate causes of abandonment in the fifteenth century were normally financial. In parishes where the population had been reduced to a mere handful of tithe-paying households, the rector's expenses of maintenance and stipends could come to exceed income from the living. When this point was reached a rector might well try to cut his losses. This was the position at Dunsthorpe *Li* where in 1437 the rector and patrons of the church at Hameringham and the patrons of the church at Dunsthorpe petitioned the bishop of Lincoln saying that

> the church of Dunsthorpe, which was wont to be ruled by a secular rector, is so decreased on account of the lack of parishioners, the few-ness of peasants, their low wages, the bareness of lands, the lack of cul-tivation, pestilences, and epidemics with which the Lord afflicts his people for their sins, that it is hardly sufficient for the eighth part of the salary of a stipendiary chaplain, much less of a rector who has to bear the necessary charges; and that there is no likelihood of its sufficing in the future since the world is going from bad to worse, and that the church of Dunsthorpe has no parishioners, and praying that the two churches may be united.
>
> (Foster and Longley 1924, liv-lv)

The village of Hale *Np* was abandoned as early as 1356, because of 'the pestilence', but its church of St Nicholas struggled on until 1448, when the last rector was instituted (*VCH Northants* 2, 547). Churches which were prone to this sort of malaise often served settlements, like Hale, which had always been small. Their sites are to be found in such areas as the acid, sandy Norfolk breckland, or the thin-soiled chalk country of the Sussex Downs and the Yorkshire and Lincolnshire Wolds. Initially it was parochial chapels, less often parish churches, which were at greatest risk. In the parish of West Dean *Sx*, for example, several chapelries which had developed in the eleventh or twelfth centuries, during a time of agricultural expansion, were approaching closure by 1600 as the settle-ments they served became attenuated. In 1602 the chancel of the Norman church at Chilgrove was said to be 'at fault both in walls and roof like to fall down. The church wanteth paving and glass.' By 1636 the church had been dismantled. The nearby settlement of Monkton was abandoned at around this time, while the church at Binderton, which seems to have been of quasi-parochial status, was taken down *c.* 1670 following a period of decay (Aldsworth 1979b, 110, 121). In eastern Yorkshire there are sites of at least two dozen settlements which were abandoned sooner, mainly in the period *c.* 1400–1600 and which are known to have possessed churches: Argham *Hu* (*YE*), for instance, Barthorpe, or Towthorpe, where the remains of a large chapel were embodied in a later farm. Across the Humber in Lincolnshire there were losses. In some places, as at Calcethorpe, the church was in ruins before the end of the fifteenth century. Other churches serving weakened communities lingered on, only to succumb in the sixteenth or seventeenth centuries. Dunsby, for instance, had been reduced to fewer than ten households by 1428 but kept its church for another century before the living was amalgamated with Brauncewell (Beresford and St Joseph 1979, 127–8). The retreat did not end there. Brauncewell also shrank. Today it is represented by a single farm, earthworks of the former village, and a church. There is doubt as to whether this church occupies its medieval position. It was rebuilt in the nineteenth century and may have been relocated. This church has in its turn been closed.

Similar tales can be told of some dozens of other churches in Lincolnshire, where parishioners in the seventeenth and eighteenth centuries grappled with the consequences of chronic neglect. In some places the churches were abandoned or demolished. Walmsgate, Ludford Parva and Skinnand were among such victims. Other fabrics, adjudged too wretched for repair, were pulled down and replaced by smaller buildings. At Goltho, where the nave was fashioned out of the former chancel in the fifteenth century, contraction began early. Elsewhere, late and early post-medieval decay helps to explain the extraordinarily large numbers of minor Georgian churches in Lincolnshire. Eighteenth-century rebuildings were numerous in Lindsey, where about forty-five survive from a total that was once larger, although in part such survivals could result from a comparatively low level of 'corrective' rebuilding in the nineteenth century.

Closure was sometimes foreshadowed by a period when a weakening living was held in plurality with that of a neighbouring church. Such amalgamations could occur considerably in advance of the time when abandonment came to be seen as inevitable. In 1310 a single perpetual vicarage was established for the parochial chapelries of St Nicholas-at-Wade and All Saints, Shuart in the Isle of Thanet *K*. When fully grown, *c*. 1250, All Saints was a large church. Yet by 1450 it seems to have been in ruins. Rebuilding took place on a much smaller scale, but by 1600 the building was again in decay and was closed for good soon afterwards (Jenkins 1981). Here the long-term, processual nature of parochial shrinkage is indicated. A quarter of Thanet's parish churches were decayed by *c*. 1540. A church at Irthlingborough *Np*, one of two, was pulled down in the seventeenth century. In 1562 it had been described as 'devastated and in utter ruin', and there were only eight parishioners in 1428 (RCHME *Northants*, I, 27).

The neglected church was not a phenomenon confined to areas that suffered from the over-exploitation of poor soils. Casualties also occurred in districts where late Saxon affluence or manorial individuality had led to the building of too many churches in close proximity. Overcrowding meant a thin spread of tithes, offerings and bequests. In times of economic growth or rising population such disadvantages might not be apparent, but in an age of decline they could become fatal. This is one reason why East Anglia, a rich area which as we have seen was thick with churches by 1100, sustained considerable losses. In Norfolk over thirty churches were abandoned before the end of the fifteenth century, and nearly ninety went in the next. By 1600 Norfolk had lost about 16 per cent of its parish churches. The trend continued and today the losses stand close to 25 per cent (Fig. 99). Some of the late medieval redundancies were caused by simple depopulation, which could be natural or enforced, as at Hawkinge *K* where in 1511 it was complained that 'the prior of Folkestone withdraweth certain householders from the parish ... by which the said church is likely to decay' (Wood-Legh 1984, no. 71). But the problem was often more complicated than this, involving the migration of parishioners to vacant holdings on more promising sites, or the cross-feeding of population between settlements. Such movements could unbalance parochial finances, simultaneously depriving some churches of income while enriching others. There are many examples of churches which were left stranded as a result of local migration and rearrangement of settlement – processes which have acted at all periods. Occasionally the church itself was dismantled and a new one erected on a different site. This is what happened at Cowthorpe *NY (YW)*, where the old church was demolished in 1455 and a new one built half a mile away for the convenience of villagers who had complained about the inconvenience of struggling through winter mud and mire. An earlier case is Combe *O*, which by 1350 had practically ceased to exist, apparently because of the plague. 'Yet within fifty years it had been re-established, not on its original site, but on the hilltop above. The new village was apparently planned because it now has a rectangular green and its adjacent church, dated to 1395, also appears to be a new addition' (C. C. Taylor 1983, 171). In the nineteenth century considerable numbers of churches were resited in response to shifts of settlement which had occurred centuries before.

Ecclesiastical overcrowding was a particular problem in towns which had flourished in the tenth and eleventh centuries, when they acquired more churches than were to be needed later. York, Lincoln and Norwich had all shed some churches before 1500, the size of their losses being roughly proportional to the varying economic performance of these places in the later Middle Ages (Fig. 100). In Winchester the process had started before 1300, by which time three of the city's 57 churches had disappeared and a number of others were being held in plurality. In 1400 the number was down to 33, falling to 26 by 1500, 15 by 1550 and 12 by 1600. Today just six of the original 57 churches remain, and only three are still used for worship (Keene 1985, 2). Other places which experienced early decline included Thetford, where only five of the town's twelfth-century complement of about 20 parish churches were of sufficient value to earn entries in the *Taxatio* of 1291; and Wallingford *O (Brk)* where by 1439 all but four of the

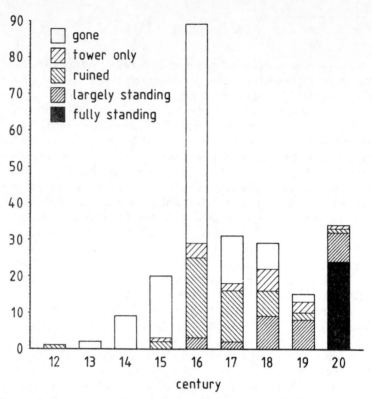

90 ─
80 ─ □ gone
70 ─ ▨ tower only
      ▧ ruined
      ▨ largely standing
60 ─ ■ fully standing
50 ─
40 ─
30 ─
20 ─
10 ─
0 ─
    12 13 14 15 16 17 18 19 20

century

99 Rates of recorded abandonment of parish churches in Norfolk, where some 230 churches and parochial chapels are known to have fallen into disuse or disappeared. The low figures for losses in the twelfth to fourteenth centuries probably give a correct impression, but the possibility of unrecorded redundancies at this and in earlier periods should be remembered (*Source*: Neil Batcock/Norfolk Archaeological Unit)

town's eleven parish churches had been closed. John Leland noted a report that as a 'matter of record' there had been twelve parish churches in Wallingford as recently as the time of Richard II (1377–99). When Leland roamed England and Wales in the sixteenth century the ruined urban church was a common sight, and in some places people were no longer sure how many churches had once existed. Leland found Ilchester *So* 'in wonderful decay'; of the four parish churches known, only one was occupied. The 'tokens' of two were still standing, while the fourth was 'clean in ruin' (L. T. Smith 1907, 3, 156). At Barnstaple *D* Leland noted 'one chapel down', while at Sherborne *Do* 'there was of old time a parish church *titulo S. Emerentianae* now fallen clean down. It stood on the north side of the town where now is a close.' In the same town had been a chapel of St Michael 'now clean down' and another dedicated to Thomas Becket which stood on the green but was 'incelebrated' (3, 153–4). At Malmesbury *Wi* the townspeople had bought the church of the recently dissolved abbey for use as their parish church. The former parish church had been partly dismantled, though the east end had been retained as a civic meeting-place. South of the abbey stood another church, wherein weavers now had their looms (3, 131–2).

There could be a positive side to urban closures. Townsfolk were able to concentrate their resources upon fewer churches. This might be to the benefit of the survivors. Vacant properties gave space for the creation of roomier cemeteries, as happened with the church of St Petroc, Winchester, in the fifteenth century, and later in Canterbury. St Petroc had been derelict and was revived: a reminder that the processes of decline were sometimes fitful in their effects, and could be reversed (Keene 1985). In Canterbury, where amalgamations of parishes proceeded steadily at the rate of two or three a century after *c.* 1350, the graveyard of

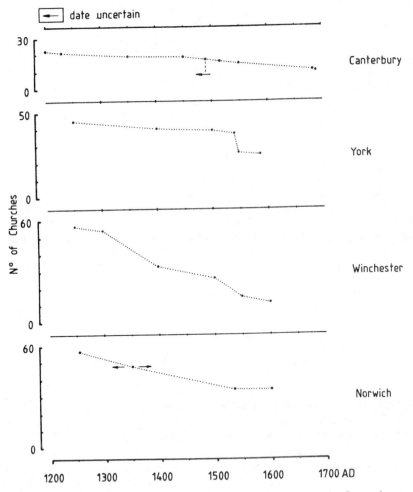

100 Contraction of parochial provision between 1300 and 1700 in Canterbury, York, Winchester and Norwich

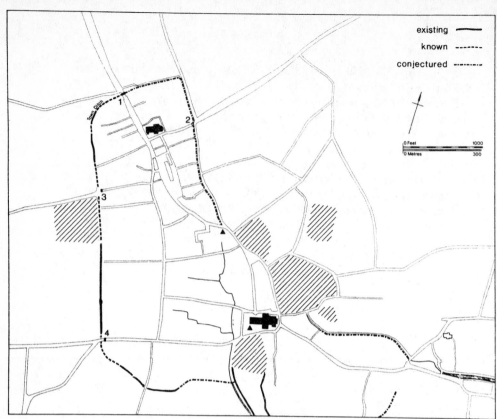

101 Beverley, Humberside (*YE*). Towns which grew strongly after the parochial system was laid down generally acquired only one or two churches, upon which the citizens could concentrate their wealth. The people's church of Beverley was St Mary, which is seen towards the north end of the town, in the vicinity of a marketplace. Its orientation shows deflection from the trend of surrounding streets and burgage plots. Contributions from individuals and groups towards the rebuilding of the nave early in the sixteenth century are recorded upon its piers. The large church on the southern edge of the town is the collegiate minster of St John, which is likely to have been a monastic focus before the end of the seventh century. The suburban church of St Nicholas has gone. 1 North Bar; 2 Norwood Bar; 3 Newbegin Bar; 4 South (Keldgate) Bar. The precincts of religious communities are indicated by diagonal hatching. The whereabouts of chapels are shown by solid triangles (*Source*: based on a plan by the Royal Commission on the Historical Monuments of England (Miller *et al.* 1982))

St Mary de Castro continued in use long after the last of the church disappeared in the seventeenth century. It was used as a burying place by other parishes: St Andrew, St Mary Magdalene and St Mary Bredman. The advantage that lay in a lessening of inter-parochial competition can be most clearly understood from places where it had always been largely absent: typically in towns which had emerged after 1100, where citizens were able to devote the bulk of their offerings and bequests to one or two churches. Hence churches in places like Yarmouth, Boston, Hull, the

338

Redcliffe suburb of Bristol, Ludlow and Market Harborough were treated to mighty enlargements in the later Middle Ages while many churches in a city such as York were approaching or had passed the point of closure. Beverley and Nottingham had several churches apiece (Fig. 101), but they were too few to stifle each other as happened in towns like Lincoln or Winchester. This assisted late medieval growth.

The consequences for churches of weather events and climatic trends have so far been depicted as being primarily indirect in their effects. Environmental change influenced economic and demographic trends, and it was these latter vicissitudes rather than the climate itself which caused some churches to close. Churches which suffered neglect were not necessarily those which were most vulnerable to redundancy. An accumulation of structural problems could hasten the day of closure, but churches did not normally succumb unless the parish as a whole was financially weak and predisposed to eventual failure. Churches which had their own endowments or enjoyed the support of landed families might continue in use for centuries after the desertion or shrinkage of the settlements they once served. At Landwade *Ca*, for instance, the church was rebuilt in the 1440s at the expense of Walter Cotton, a wealthy mercer, although by this time the village itself was virtually extinct.

There were, however, occasions when churches became the direct victims of environmental disaster. The example of Dunwich *Sf* is well known. In 1086 Dunwich had at least three churches. By 1200 it boasted nine. Thirteenth-century Dunwich was a prosperous port. Thereafter the town died a lingering death, inaugurated by economic strangulation and completed by physical destruction, both as a result of marine transgression. Around 1300 the parish church of St Leonard was submerged. In 1328 a severe storm clogged up the harbour. Several hundred houses fell into the sea during the decades that followed. By 1370 the churches of St Martin, St Nicholas, St Michael and St Bartholomew had all perished. The church of St John survived into the sixteenth century, to be dismantled for the sake of its materials. St Peter's was likewise taken down, around the turn of the eighteenth century. All Saints has collapsed within living memory. Today, the only vestige of Dunwich is a small village, once a suburb on the western outskirts of the medieval town.

Medieval builders were on the whole adroit in locating their churches above the reach of flood or tide. Since the worst transgressions might occur less than once or twice in a century this sure touch reflects a long-standing acquaintance with the pattern of natural phenomena in given localities. At Stillingfleet *Hu* (*YE*) worshippers go to church dry shod even in the worst of floods. When the Severn breaks its banks below Tewkesbury *Gl* the peaceful Anglo-Saxon church at Deerhurst is sometimes lapped by water but not overwhelmed.

But there were exceptions, and for convenience they may be divided into three groups. First, churches have sometimes been engulfed by wind-blown sand. Second, rivers, especially in their middle and lower stages, meander from side to side, and there have been occasions when churches have been undercut by these movements. Third, there are lengths of the English coast which are vulnerable to marine transgression or steady erosion. Dozens of parish churches have disappeared as a result of such processes. Conversely, there are other neighbourhoods where land is being gained rather than lost, and as a pendant to the matter of casualties it is appropriate to conclude by considering churches which were established at the growing edges of settled terrain.

Wind-blown sand was the enemy of quite a number of coastal settlements in south-west England and especially in south Wales. A celebrated case is that of St Piran *Co* where a pre-Conquest chapel is said to have been abandoned before the end of the eleventh century, to be superseded by a new church which was in its turn overwhelmed in the Penhale sands. In 1804 a church was erected on a third site, at Lamborne. Another three-stage progression occurred at Kenfig *Glm*, where the first church was replaced in 1262 and another was built further inland towards the end of the fifteenth century. There is a ruined church in Penmaen burrows which seems to have been engulfed early in the fourteenth century. The influx may have been sudden. Antiquaries who excavated the site in 1861 found the stone altar intact and a thurible lying on the floor (Davidson and Davidson 1979–80, 23). In the fifteenth and sixteenth centuries the parishioners at Pennard were troubled by drifting sand. At Rhossili the parish church was abandoned around the middle of the fourteenth century, and a new church and settlement established upon a nearby hill. Part of the earlier church at Rhossili has been disinterred from the dune which buried it, with results which give a glimpse of an interior at around the time of the Black Death. The floor consisted of beaten clay. A portion of the wall which divided the chancel from the nave bore traces of counterfeit masonry joints painted in black and red, with cinquefoil and tendril decoration. Limited seating was provided by stone wall-benches at either side of the nave (Davidson and Davidson 1979–80, 27). Another case is Ebb's Nook *Nb*, where in 1853 the remains of a church were uncovered on a spit of land beside Beadwell harbour. Sand has since recovered the site (Taylor and Taylor 1965, 226–7).

Inland, rivers have sometimes dislodged churches from their original sites. In 1703 the church of St Kentigern at Grindale *Cu* was said to be in ruins and in danger of falling into the River Eden. Parishioners struggled to prevent human remains from being washed out of the churchyard. Part of the church of SS Peter and Paul at Whitney *He* was swept away by the River Wye in 1720. Here a new building was erected which incorporated remains of the old. The parish church of Ripley *NY (YW)* formerly stood beside the Thornton Beck. Following damage inflicted by a landslide at the end of the fourteenth century a new church was erected on a different site. There are surviving churches which occupy positions that from time to time give cause for anxiety. Melverley, for instance, has one of the few remaining timber-framed churches in Shropshire. The site lies adjacent to the River Vyrnwy. When the river is in spate the church seems to be on the point of floating away. During the present century there has been a small quota of losses arising from the flooding of valleys to create reservoirs. A photograph album belonging to my wife's family contains an evocative snapshot of the steeple of the Victorian church at Thruscross *NY* (*YW*) lapped by the rising waters of a new reservoir. In 1975 the Georgian church of St Matthew at Normanton *Le* escaped a similar fate when money was found to create a protective platform around it within Rutland Water.

Another type of locale where a church could fall victim to the consequences of environmental change was at the river mouth. A number of churches lost their *raison d'être* when the settlements they served were adversely affected by the silting or diversion of a waterway. At Alnmouth *Nb* the cruciform church of St Waleric is now a ruin marooned amid sand dunes. When it was founded, possibly around 1100, St Waleric's was an integral part of the town; but the river changed its course, and the church was severed from its users. At West Lynn *Nf* flooding from the tidal River Ouse caused the abandonment of the church of St Peter which was rebuilt on a drier site in the 1270s. Another case is Seasalter *K*, where an isolated church may indicate the former whereabouts of a small pre-Conquest town which later perished as a result of coastal change. In the eleventh and twelfth centuries Romney *K* was a port beside the mouth of the River Rother. The town was prosperous enough to support three churches. A violent storm in 1287 diverted the Rother to a new outlet near Rye. The old estuary rapidly became clogged with silt, and the sea, in Camden's words, 'began by little and little to foresake the town' (cited in Cunliffe 1980, 50-1). Two of the churches were abandoned. Visitors to St Nicholas, the survivor, may reflect that the great storm of 1287 overwhelmed the town to an extent that four feet of silt had to be cleared from the interior. Sarre *K* prospered greatly in the pre-Conquest period from movements of shipping along the Wantsum Channel. Some time after 1100 the Wantsum became choked with silt, Sarre was abandoned, and its church with it. Sarre's parish was added to that of St Nicholas-at-Wade, a dependency of Reculver, which was later to be amalgamated with Shuart (p. 354). Reculver had originated in 669 as a minster. The church stood in the midst of an old Roman fort, conveniently placed to monitor the comings and goings of shipping through the north mouth of the Wantsum. (Is it conceivable that the minster was intended to serve some practical purpose in relation to this traffic? The community was established by royal grant, and the immediate surroundings of the church are exceptionally rich in finds of eighth-century coins.) By the twelfth century Reculver had subsided towards the status of a parish church. When John Leland inspected it *c*. 1540 the sea was at least a quarter of a mile distant. Maps drawn in the seventeenth and eighteenth centuries show that the sea was making inroads towards the village, and by 1785 the north wall of the fort had disappeared. Expecting the worst, in 1802 the vicar sought permission to erect a new church at Hillborough, about a mile inland. This was done, and in 1805 most of the church was demolished. That the rest of it was saved is due to the Trinity Board, which stepped in in 1809 to acquire and preserve the ruins as a sea-mark. The Board took measures to arrest erosion of the cliff, and the ruin still stands.

Other churches were even less fortunate than Reculver. Between the end of the Roman period and the present day parts of the coastline have changed greatly. In the Roman period the coast of Yorkshire between Flamborough Head and Spurn Point lay several miles to the east of its modern position. Lengths of the shoreline of Lincolnshire, Norfolk and Suffolk have also been shaved off. As already described, some coastal districts of Kent and Sussex have passed through metamorphoses of bewildering complexity, involving the disappearance of entire ports and towns, and the emergence of new ones. Other areas which have been intermittently refashioned by flood, tide and reclamation include the Levels of central Somerset and the Severnside region of Glamorgan and Gwent.

The sea has been uncommonly greedy along the shores of Holderness *Hu* (*YE*), where clays and shales have been denuded by the action of currents and storms. Since the twelfth century at least thirty townships have disappeared. At the same time, quite large areas have been claimed from the sea along the north bank of the Humber. Places like Patrington and Keyingham, once virtually coastal, are now well inland. Medieval Patrington was a port and town. The church at Patrington, a possession of the archbishops of York, is among the finest in the region; a monument to fourteenth-century taste, its soaring spire is conspicuous across miles of surrounding flatness. Residents of Ravenser would have seen it on their horizon. But not for long. Ravenser was a port which grew up on a sandbank on the western side of Spurn Head. The place flourished in the thirteenth century, subsequently returned two members of Parliament, held two markets a week and hosted an annual fair of a month's duration. Yet by 1400 Ravenser had gone, just as Wilgils's monastery had been taken by the sea 600 years before. Spurn Head undergoes a cycle of growth, destruction and rebirth. In 1355 corpses were being washed out of their graves in the chapel cemetery, and six years later many of the town merchants removed themselves to the safety of Grimsby or Hull.

Coastal erosion is continuous, and while some medieval churches of Holderness disappeared barely after they were first mentioned in written records, the drownings of others have been recent. The church at Kilnsea, for instance, was depicted in a drawing of 1829 as a ruin perched precariously on the cliff edge. Collapse had been rapid, for another drawing made only three years previously shows the building as being substantially complete. The church of Withernsea was inundated soon after 1400, but by 1488 a new church had been built and consecrated on a safer site. Yet this too was in ruins by the 1830s, and seems to have fallen into decay soon after its completion. Other churches were built to replace doomed predecessors at Skeffling (1469) and Hollym (1488). The cliff edge had arrived at the boundary of Owthorne's churchyard before the end of the eighteenth century. According to records which were transferred to the church at Rimswell, there were fifteen days' attendance at the old church-yard in 1800 'leading' bones to Rimswell (Sheppard 1912, 146). In 1828 a visitor observed human bones falling out of the cliff. Stories told of the last days of Owthorne include how 'during the washing away of the chancel of the old church, the coffin of a former rector was exposed, and the rector and clerk of that time fought for the ownership of the lead'. Writing in 1858, a tourist recalled how 'in some places bones still clad in naval attire, with bright-coloured silk kerchiefs round the neck, were unearthed, as if the sea were eager to reclaim the shipwrecked sailors whom it had in former time flung dead upon the shore' (W. White 1858, 30). Another witness noticed a robin nesting in a skull which projected from the cliff (cited in Sheppard 1912, 148).

A loss to be especially lamented is the former church of Aldbrough. All that remains of it is a sun-dial which was transferred into the existing church of St Bartholomew. The sun-dial bears an inscription in Old English. In translation it reads: 'Ulf commanded this church to be built for the soul of himself and of Gunware.' Now Ulf's church has gone. Possibly his bones and those of Gunware also lie beneath the waves.

Further south, churches were submerged at a number of places along the east coast. In Lincolnshire there were losses at Chapel St Leonards, Trusthorpe and Sutton-on-Sea; also at Skegness before 1540, and Mablethorpe in 1286/7 and again during the reign of Elizabeth I (1558–1603) (A. E. B. Owen 1986). The shores of Norfolk have been subject to both gain and loss. In the north, between Hunstanton and Sheringham, the coastline of the Roman period now lies several miles inland. Between Sheringham and Winterton, on the other hand, the coast is in retreat. Churches at Snitterley, Whimpwell and Keswick have gone. Others were taken down and rebuilt further inland, as at Overstrand at the end of the fourteenth century. At Eccles the antiquary Ladbrooke visited the church in 1823 and sketched what then remained of it: a round tower with an octagonal upper stage standing within the hollow of a sand dune. Today all that is visible is a small shard of the masonry cylinder of the tower, tumbled upon the beach and scoured smooth twice daily by the tide.

Moving clockwise around the coast, recalling the disaster at Dunwich and noting the disappearance of other churches at places like Walton-on-the-Naze Ex, we arrive at the south-east corner of England. To losses already mentioned may be added churches at Folkestone, Broomhill and the former Channel port of Old Winchelsea. Old Winchelsea and its several churches were swallowed by the sea in successive storms during the thirteenth century. Edward I founded New Winchelsea to replace the port that had been lost. As at Salisbury sixty years before, advantage was taken of the opportunity to design a town from scratch. The gridded layout contained spaces for churches. Yet New Winchelsea flourished only briefly. Silting of the River Brede, and the retreat of the sea, robbed the place of its livelihood. Reports of vacant holdings are recorded before the middle of the fourteenth century. By 1575 fewer than sixty houses were inhabited. Two of Winchelsea's three churches fell out of use.

The sea preyed upon churches and settlements chiefly along the coasts of east and south-east England. The geology of Wales is for the most part more resilient. Nevertheless, problems have arisen locally, as at Aberdaron *Gwd* (*Crn*) where the church was abandoned in 1841 in the face of erosion by the sea. The church of Goldcliff *Gnt* (*Mon*) was being undercut by storm and tide in the fourteenth century. Parishioners removed to a new site further inland, although in 1860 the parish went back to the old church when the new proved too expensive to maintain. A plaque in the present church records how in 1606 (*recte* 1607): 'On the XX day of Ianvary even as it came to pas it pleased God the flvd did flow to the edge of this same bras; and in this parish theare was lost 5000 and od pownds besides XXII people was in this parrish drownd.' If the position of the plaque is authentic, floodwaters in excess of 23 ft (7.0 m) above Ordnance Datum are indicated. Similar tablets exist in other churches which stood in vulnerable positions within the Levels of Caldicot, Gwent, and across the Severn estuary in Somerset. At Kingston Seymour *So*, for instance, the flood of 1607 attained a height of 25.4 ft (7.7 m) above Ordnance Datum. The church was flooded to a depth of 5 ft (1.5 m), and water remained for ten days (M. Williams 1970, 87–8; Boon 1980, 30).

Kingston Seymour was flooded at a time when the tempo of works to reclaim low-lying areas around the coast was beginning to increase. The first half of the seventeenth century saw the start of important programmes of drainage in the Humberhead region, the Somerset Levels and the fenlands of eastern England. What distinguished these schemes from earlier efforts was their scale and strategic character. Roman engineers had reclaimed considerable tracts of fenland, but with the ending of Roman involvement in British affairs early in the fifth century the maintenance of canals and flood defences had lapsed. Medieval reclamation had been extensive, but it was usually undertaken piecemeal, as a result of local initiative. The distribution of medieval churches is a guide to how things stood before the great undertakings which began after 1600.

The fenland covers some 1300 sq. miles. Within this area lay more than 130 medieval parishes. Most of the churches were in existence before the end of the twelfth century, and the pattern of their sites reveals a division between two areas of contrasting character: the siltlands and the peatlands (Fig. 102). The siltlands were fertile, and were exploited both as arable and pasture. In 1086 the Wash was fringed with vills, indicating that settlement had taken hold before the Conquest. During the next two centuries the economy of the siltlands flourished. Further reclamations were made to extend it, both seawards and inland towards the zone of peat.

The peaty fenlands were largely devoid of pre-Conquest settlement. They consisted of tracts of marsh and bog interspersed between stagnant pools and streams winding slowly towards the coast. Here and there stood

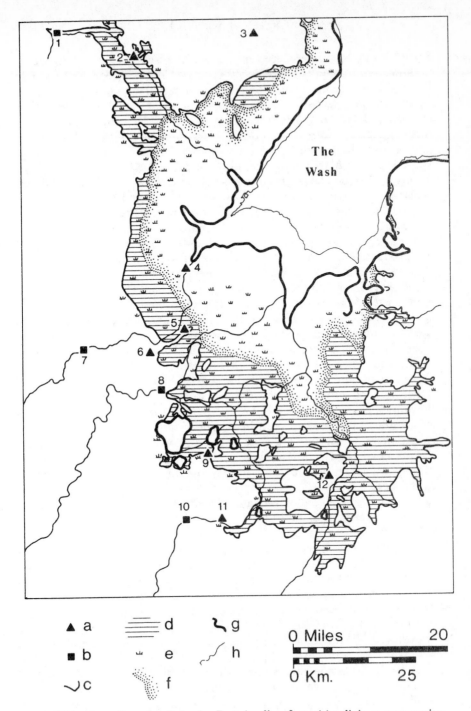

The Wash

102 Siltlands and peatlands in the East Anglian fens: (*a*) religious community;
(*b*) town; (*c*) edge of fenland; (*d*) peatland; (*e*) marsh; (*f*) edge of siltland;
(*g*) eleventh-century coastline (estimated); (*h*) modern coastline. **1** Lincoln;
2 Bardney; **3** Partney; **4** Spalding; **5** Crowland; **6** Peakirk; **7** Stamford;
8 Peterborough; **9** Ramsey; **10** Huntingdon; **11** St Ives; **12** Ely (*Sources*: Darby
1983; D.H.Hill 1981)

dry spots of clay, remembered in modern place-names such as Thorney, Welney, Whittlesey, Gedney and Ely, where the suffix derives from Old English *ēg, īeg* 'island'. The islands had been popular among monastic settlers of the later seventh and eighth centuries, like Æthelthryth at Ely, or the intrepid Guthlac, whose exploits of Crowland were mentioned in earlier chapters. Ely, Crowland and Peterborough re-emerged as important centres of religious life in the monastic revival of the tenth century, and there were new foundations in the area at this time at Ramsey and Thorney. The peatlands, though sparsely settled, were rich in resources. Streams and meres offered an abundance of fish and fowl. Reeds were available for thatching and peat was cut for fuel. Around the margins of the islands there was limited scope for cultivation.

The agricultural economy of the siltlands was augmented by fishing and the production of salt. The significance of salt-making as a prelude to reclamation and the extension of settlement has recently been explored by Mr Arthur Owen in an essay entitled 'Salt, sea banks and medieval settlement on the Lindsey coast' (1984). Mr Owen reminds us that the coastal economy of Lindsey and the fenland was seasonal. Marsh pastures were used for the summer grazing of sheep and cattle. The pastoralists who looked after these beasts also engaged in the extraction of salt. Since prehistoric times salt had been derived from seawater and from salt-impregnated mud. Water collected in pans at high tide was evaporated off either by wind and sun or with the help of heat which was applied by the burning of charcoal and turves around the salt pans. Waste from the process resulted in spoilheaps known as saltern mounds or Red Hills. Since salters were obliged to work close to the high water mark of spring tides, the presence of saltern mounds inland is a reliable guide to the position of former shorelines, or the limits to which tidal water could be channelled.

When salterns fell out of use and were superseded by new working areas farther seawards, they provided elevated platforms which could be used for agriculture and habitation. The village of Newton in South Holland stands upon old salterns, for example, and it has been argued that King's Lynn is similarly situated (D. Owen 1979). Obsolete salterns may sometimes have been used as sites for medieval churches. Mr Owen has collected examples of this phenomenon in Norfolk marshland, at Terrington St Clement and Clenchwarton, in Holland, at Gedney, and in Lindsey. In north-east Lindsey almost every church between North Coates and Theddlethorpe All Saints is reported to be perched upon a saltern.

These observations have an important bearing upon the chronology of reclamation. The incorporation of saltern mounds within the banks of medieval sea defences, as at West Walton *Nf*, suggests that salt-making as a seasonal activity preceded the emergence of settled communities. Salt-making assisted colonization and reclamation. The construction of sea banks came later, when the need was felt to consolidate previous gains.

The process whereby settlement edged seaward has left marks in toponymy and the morphology of parishes. The seasonal activities of grazier–salters, and the secondary character of the permanent communities to which they gave rise, are recollected in place-names like Somercotes, Saltfleetby and Marsh Chapel *Li*. A phase of transhumance may also explain the linear pattern of many parishes in districts where coastal reclamation took place. Seasonal movement of people and animals to and from the coast was along causeways and tracks which led from mother settlements further inland. It was common for these parent communities to have their own lengths of coastal frontage. New vills formed when settlements became established on dead salterns at the coastal ends of the corridors. In some areas this process may have been repeated more than once (see Fig. 63).

Links between parent settlements and their dependencies are witnessed in families of place-names, as around Holbeach and Gedney *Li*, or the Walpoles and Terringtons of Norfolk marshland. Occasionally the coastal frontages of adjacent vills were amalgamated, to give one new unit with two to its rear. Saltfleetby *Li* is a case in point: Mr Owen regards it as a colony planted on the combined marsh of the villages of Grimoldby and Manby. Nearby, the vills of Theddlethorpe and Sutton-le-Marsh appear to have originated in a similar fashion. Whether such unions took place as a result of co-operation between the inhabitants of adjacent vills, or breakaway action by neighbouring groups of marsh dwellers who made common cause, cannot now be discovered. What is clear, however, is that the settlements concerned had crystallized before the end of the eleventh century. Not only do their names appear in Domesday Book, but some of their churches, like Theddlethorpe and Conisholme, contain fragments of Anglo-Saxon sculpture.

Salt, the rich pastures of half-drained marshes and the productive arable of siltland gave areas of coastal reclamation a strong economic base. This is often reflected in the churches. Many of them are large, not a few, like Walpole St Peter, Walsoken and Gedney, outstanding. The line of churches which stand upon saltern mounds between North Coates and Mablethorpe *Li* contains some notable buildings. Marsh Chapel, for instance, has a grandeur which belies its name. The church was completely rebuilt around 1400 and has a lofty west tower. A sizeable Perpendicular tower is also to be seen at Grainthorpe, where substantial fourteenth-century additions surround a core of the late twelfth century. There were substantial campaigns of building further down the coast: at Saltfleetby All Saints in the Norman period and in the thirteenth century; at Conisholm; and especially at Theddlethorpe All Saints, where the main contributions came at the end of the fourteenth century. Several churches in this group were dedicated in honour of saints who were especially appropriate to a setting which was coastal or otherwise remote: Clement at Grainthorpe and Saltfleetby, for instance; Botolph at Skidbrooke. The decline of coastal salt-making and partial replacement by woad growing after the sixteenth century is likely to explain the contraction of some churches, as parishioners struggled with the upkeep of buildings which were now too large for their diminished finances. Conisholme has been much reduced. Skidbrooke's church is smaller than it was at the end of the Middle Ages. Retreat continues: Saltfleetby All Saints, Skidbrooke and Theddlethorpe All Saints have all been declared redundant. Happily, these buildings have been vested in the Redundant Churches Fund and continue to be cared for.

The application of wealth to buildings founded on doubtful ground is reflected in some of the features of marshland churches. Detached towers such as are found at Tydd St Giles *Ca*, West Walton *Nf*, Long Sutton and Fleet *Li*, and at some places in Romney Marsh, may indicate caution on the part of builders who wished to avoid the risks of differential settlement. At Terrington St Clement, for instance, tower and church were but a few inches apart. Instability was a related problem, with consequences visible today in leaning towers at Leverton, Saltfleetby All Saints and Surfleet *Li*. Where churches were erected on marshy ground a substructure of timber piles or brushwood raft may have been provided.

Residence in the fens was always risky. From time to time there were storm surges, and the sea broke in. The Chronicle of Matthew Paris tells of an inundation which occurred in 1236, with tragic consequences. Following an unusually dry summer, when 'deep pools and ponds were dried up, water mills stood useless ... and the earth gaped into cracks', there were sea floods on 12 November which 'forced ships from all their harbours ... drowned a multitude of men, destroyed flocks of sheep and herds of cattle, tore trees up by the roots, overturned houses, and ravaged the coasts'. The water is said to have 'ascended' the shores for two days, 'and did not flow or ebb in the usual way but was prevented ... by the very great violence of opposing winds. The corpses of the drowned were seen unburied near the shores ... so that at Wisbech and the neighbouring villages ... a great number of men perished,' (Matthew Paris iii, 379).

The disaster of 1236 was nearly equalled by bad floods in 1607 and 1613. There used to be a plaque in the church at Wisbech which described the flooding of the town and loss of life. Dugdale gave a vivid description of what happened to the people of Terrington in 1613. Some took refuge in the church. Others perched themselves on haystacks or roofs, while 'Mr Browne the minister did fetch divers to the church upon his back.' In addition to the dangers of sea floods there was the threat of freshwater flooding from the interior, when streams and rivers swollen by heavy rain, or melting snow, or both, broke their banks. Flood defences were thus erected on both sides of the siltland. In some areas, as in the wapentake of Elloe *Li*, there are sequences of earthworks marking successive stages of reclamation, like the growth rings of a tree (Hallam 1965; Darby 1983, Fig. 13).

All these efforts notwithstanding, most of the churches in Norfolk marshland were encroached upon by floods at one time or another.

Perhaps it was anxiety, as well as wealth, which fuelled the compulsion of medieval fenlanders to provide themselves with such splendid churches and to spear each others' horizons with lofty steeples. If the prospect of disaster could never be entirely dismissed, did this place some extra weight upon minds already burdened with concern about the fate of souls?

IX

ALL CHRISTIAN
SOULS

'What do the perpendicular churches prove?' Professor Postan's question echoes still. He posed it in an essay which depicted the fifteenth century as a time of economic recession, marked by a diminution of buying and selling in the countryside, regression towards self-sufficiency on the part of peasants, and a contraction in overseas trade. Decline in the wool trade after *c.* 1350 was in part compensated by an increase in the manufacture and export of cloth. Cloth exports rose rapidly in the second half of the fourteenth century. But, having risen, 'the cloth exports and presumably the cloth production then remained stationary throughout most of the fifteenth century and, if anything, declined in the middle decades' (1973, 44, 45). The purpose of this chapter is not to challenge Postan's bleak characterization of the fifteenth-century economy. Others have done that (e.g. Bridbury 1975; Brenner 1985). Rather, the aim in what follows is to explore aspects of the relationship between wealth and churchbuilding, and beyond that to probe the mentalities and motivations of those who made building possible. But some discussion of Postan's question will provide an avenue of approach to both groups of themes.

What *do* the Perpendicular churches prove? Postan gave three reasons for thinking that they had nothing to do with 'either the growth or the decline of English industry, agriculture or trade' (1973, 46). In the first place, he argued, the possession of wealth and of artistic sensibility do not automatically go hand in hand: 'As if the generations which make the money also know how to spend it best; and as if the abundance of material means leads inevitably and directly to a corresponding rise in the arts of life.' In itself this is a fair observation. But it is hardly to the point. For the argument is not about the excellence of fifteenth-century building. It is about its volume. Discounting, as we must, the countless new windows, tower tops and chapels that were added to parish churches after 1400, the fact remains that this was a period which produced a large number of partial, and a considerable number of total, rebuildings. Whether these campaigns constitute any sort of economic index is a separate question; but to disallow them from discussion on qualitative grounds is fallacious. It may be wondered if, when in 1413-14 expenditure on the new chancel at Adderbury O for the first time exceeded income from this manor, the bursars of New College Oxford would have agreed that churchbuilding was unrelated to economic processes. New College was the rector. Then, and in the next two years, the bursars subsidized the work with money from college funds. Yet the greater part of the project was paid for out of the annual *firma*, so that for four years the college received nothing from Adderbury, and in a further six its income was reduced. This tells us nothing about the economic buoyancy of north Oxfordshire early in the fifteenth century, but it does testify to a willingness on the proprietor's part to forgo income otherwise due – and income that was derived from the profits of land.

Postan reinforced his first argument by questioning whether the commitment of material resources to churchbuilding in the fifteenth century was any larger, 'or even as large as, the stone and mortar that went into the building of the costly parish churches of the twelfth century, the abbeys and cathedrals of the thirteenth and the fourteenth?' (1973, 46). The answer is that it probably was not. But the greatest expenses of medieval building did not lie in the value of basic materials. The example of Adderbury is again instructive (Figs 103-105). Between 1414 and 1416, when work was at its busiest, stone came to only 13 per cent of costs, carriage of stone and timber about 8 per cent, lime (inclusive of carriage) 1.6 per cent, and ferramenta about 7 per cent. During the same period fees for Richard Winchcombe, the master mason, and his apprentice, came to 16.5 per cent, while wages for other masons, and labourers, totalled 40 per cent. In the peak year of activity labour and management costs together accounted for 71 per cent of all expenditure. In each of the three years that followed these costs amounted to 65 per cent. An extrapolation from these figures to building costs in general would be reckless. But the broad picture is clear enough: fees and wages might easily account for more than 50 per cent of outlay on the rebuilding of a parish church.

The expense of glazing also calls for comment. At Adderbury work and materials connected with glazing amounted to about 7.5 per cent of all expenditure on the entire chancel. This figure has implications for Perpendicular generally. In the fifteenth century builders strove to create transparent structures. Windows were enlarged to the limits of technical possibility. Clerestories were added.

All in all, therefore, Perpendicular churches of quality did not come cheaply. How the total costs of building in the fifteenth century would

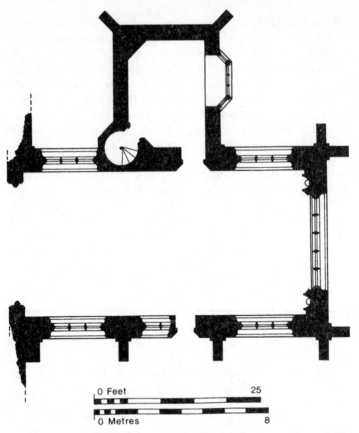

103 Adderbury, Oxfordshire. Plan of early fifteenth-century chancel (*Source*: Hobson 1926)

compare with those of foregoing ages we do not know. The data are not available. In certain areas, however, expenditure in the fifteenth century can hardly have been less than it was previously, and may have been more. Later in the chapter this point will assume extra significance, for whereas the principal rebuilders of parish churches in the twelfth and thirteenth centuries have been identified as religious institutions, wealthier clergy and some magnates, it will be argued that after 1300 much of the new work was increasingly financed out of the pockets of the rank-and-file population.

Postan rounded off his case by asking us to remember 'that many of the so-called fifteenth-century buildings were in fact structures, which like King's College Chapel, were commenced at the beginning of the century but not resumed until the coming of the Tudors, or else structures built either before 1425 or after 1475'. Hence, 'we shall perhaps be doubly careful in regarding either the cloth villages or their perpendicular churches as evidence of the great commercial efflorescence of the fifteenth century' (1973, 46). These cautions read strangely in the context of their author's aim. If architectural achievement was not linked with economic success, what could an absence of such achievement have to do with economic decline? That aside, it must be doubted whether *many* fifteenth-century churches were begun soon after 1400, discontinued, and then resumed after 1485. In this respect the example of King's College Chapel – an exceptional building, unrepresentative of much outside its class of royal religious works like Eton and Eltham – was unwisely chosen. If there are any proofs to be had from Perpendicular churches, they will be derived from a quantification of activity in the generality of parishes, not singular campaigns under Crown patronage and afflicted by the uncertainties of political power.

The building dates of churches in areas which during the fifteenth century were productive of cloth or wool do anything but support the notion

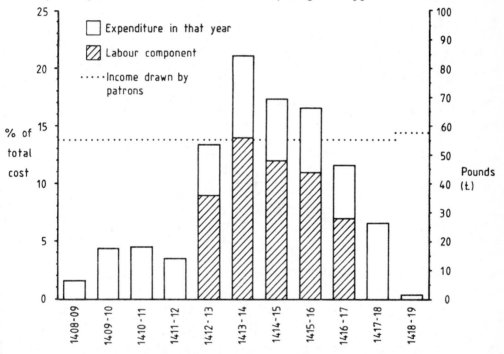

104 Adderbury, Oxfordshire. Costs of project between 1408 and 1419 (*Source*: Adderbury *Rectoria* (Hobson 1926))

of a lull between 1425 and 1475. Taking the Cotswolds, we find the main transformation of Chipping Camden begun probably around 1450 and continuing until the end of the century. Work at Northleach was already well advanced by 1458, and the great tower there belongs to this decade. The parish church at Winchcombe was being rebuilt in the 1460s. Of the grandest Cotswold enterprises, only Fairford and Cirencester post-date Bosworth Field. Fairford was abuilding during the

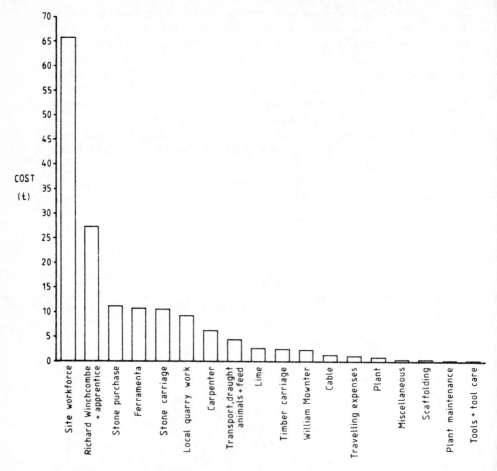

105 Adderbury, Oxfordshire. Breakdown of expenditure in 1413–14 (*Source*: Adderbury *Rectoria* (Hobson 1926))

last quarter of the century. The epic work of Cirencester's nave was undertaken *c.* 1515–30. Yet this was only the latest in a series of considerable additions, among them the huge tower begun *c.* 1400 and proceeding until the middle of the century, the Lady Chapel, thought to be not much later than 1458, and the three-storey porch of *c.* 1490. Meanwhile, remodellings of lesser degree took place at Bibury (mid-fifteenth century?), Chedworth, possibly in the 1480s, Sudeley *c.* 1460, Dursley *c.* 1450, Marshfield *c.* 1470, and elsewhere. In Oxfordshire there were notable rebuildings at Eynsham *c.* 1450, Chipping Norton around 1485 and Church Hanborough (Verey 1976a, 132–9). Work on some of these programmes may have been spread over many decades. Nevertheless, 'the most concentrated period of building in Oxfordshire and the Cotswolds was *c.* 1440–80' (Verey 1976b, 141).

Suffolk furnishes a similar picture. Architectural evidence coupled with what can be gleaned from some thousands of wills, the majority written after 1375, suggest that

> although a certain amount of building was going on in the last quarter of the fourteenth century and the first of the fifteenth, including a handful of towers, the great increase in building took place in the second quarter of the fifteenth century, accelerating through the middle years but declining towards the end.
>
> (Northeast 1980, 24)

Comparable escalations of building are found in some other areas at this time: in parts of Norfolk and the Home Counties, for instance, but notably also in the south-west: in Somerset, where great towers were a fifteenth-century speciality; Devon, where remodelling was widespread; and in Cornwall. The concentrations of rebuilding display a configuration which seems to correspond to areas of long-standing prosperity, and to counties which substantially increased in wealth between the fourteenth and sixteenth centuries (R.S.Schofield 1965). By contrast, lesser alterations – refenestration, the heightening of towers, the addition of chapels – were far more common. Such changes were visited upon perhaps as many as 50 per cent of all parish churches between 1380 and 1530, and tend towards a greater evenness in their spread. The artistic development of Perpendicular architecture has been surveyed by Dr Harvey (1978).

It remains a question whether the Perpendicular churches of Suffolk, or the Cotswolds, or Devon, can be regarded as simple manifestations of contemporary economic success. These structures often took decades to build, so that campaigns of construction spanned medium-term fluctuations of growth and recession. Protracted campaigns may, on the other hand, have been partly caused by such fluctuations.

As far as we can tell, building was financed by a combination of donations from local gentry and merchants, offerings made by parishioners and proceeds from fundraising events. In some places gilds played a part. The relative importance of these different kinds of provision would have varied from parish to parish and is seldom ascertainable. Large contributions made by rich wool-masters and clothiers – men like John Fortey at Northleach, William Bradway at Chipping Camden or the Spring family at Lavenham – were probably valuable in three respects: they launched new campaigns, they could revive an existing programme which was ailing for lack of money and they could ensure continuity of work for several years. Important as they undoubtedly were, we shall be wise not to exaggerate the part played by munificent merchants. Generosity that led to complete rebuilding, as at Fairford, was exceptional. Elsewhere the names of leading donors survive in records, and their effigies in the churches that they helped to pay for, precisely because they *were* generous. But dynasties of rich businessmen were by no means the only or, often, the principal financiers of new building. Much of the outlay on a church like North-leach was met from a multiplicity of donations, a few considerable, many small, by parishioners of every rank. The tower of Eye *Sf*, completed in 1470, was said to have been paid for 'chiefly of the frank and devowte hartes of the people' (Northeast 1980, 24).

Within a parish, money was raised in various ways. Collections, gifts in kind and church ales all played a part. Bequests were especially impor-tant. Medieval wills abound with clauses assigning money to church fabrics. The sums involved range from very modest amounts of a few pence, through more numerous conventional figures of a quarter or half a mark, as in Thomas Rombun's bequest of 3s 4d *ad campanile* at Bill-ingshurst *Sx* in 1424 or the 6s 8d left by Adam Bradwell to the porch fabric at Whittlington *So* in 1407, to more considerable figures like John Cable's provision of £10 to the fabric of the nave at Frome *So* in 1408 (Weaver 1901, 24, 33). Such contributions were important not least because most people made them. A bequest to the church in which you had been baptized was customary. Analysis of late medieval wills made in Norwich shows that 'more testators gave to parish churches than anything else. Only bequests for masses and prayers averaged per testator more in value. 85 per cent of the clergy and 95 per cent of the laity gave to at least one parish church' (Tanner 1984, 126). A fair number of these legacies were large, and were assigned to particular schemes of building (1984, 128).

Donations and small bequests were sufficient for the funding of minor works. Larger projects which ran for years were more difficult to sustain. Charitable income was unpredictable, and in the absence of loans it was not always possible to match cashflow to the fluctuating costs of building (see Fig. 104). This may be why so many parochial enterprises were pro-longed, and why episcopal approval was sometimes sought to send 'beg-ging' proctors round. The threat of interruption is reflected in wills. Testators sometimes directed that the payment of their bequests should be conditional upon the work being carried out promptly, or within a specified period, or when it was finished. It was thus, for instance, at Foulsham *Nf* in 1493, when Thomas Collys contributed 10s to making the steeple in two years, or at Lingwood *Nf* where William Rising promised 5 marks to the new tower with the proviso that it should be finished within four years from the date of his death (i.e. by 1491). In 1460 John Barker gave the large sum of 20 marks for the building of a tower at Heydon 'if parishioners put their hands to it with a will' (Cattermole and Cotton 1983, 247, 254, 251). The tower at Framlingham *Sf* was under construction, on and off, for over fifty years. First heard of in 1483, a bequest made in 1500 was to be paid 'at such time as they next begin work'. Money was being willed for the battlements between 1521 and 1534 (Northeast 1980, 24). Leisurely progress could have advantages. Lime mortar took time to harden to its maximum compressive strength. Towers built at speed were sometimes prone to collapse. A gradualistic approach to tower building was particularly called for in areas like Suffolk which were devoid of good freestone and where in consequence much use was made of flint. Flint is impervious and exerts no suction upon damp mortar (Rodwell 1986). The large towers of the fifteenth century were also heavy, and on occasion a new steeple was left to settle for a time before it was united with the main fabric of the church. In general, however, the fitful character of parochial building extended beyond anything that might be attributable to technical prudence. Even ordinary repairs could be spread across decades, as at St Mary Bishophill Junior, York, where a restoration begun before 1421 was not finished until *c*. 1500. Some parishes were unequal to the task of bringing their projects to completion. At East Bergholt *Sf*, for instance, a great tower was begun soon after 1500 but never finished. Towers at Little Oakley *Ex*, Toftrees and Felmingham *Nf* stand incomplete.

The dependence upon offerings and bequests makes it highly likely that there *was* a connection between parochial building activity and episodes of economic growth or decline, but that this would be manifested less in the size of a project or the date of its inception than in the time which was taken to accomplish the work. Recession might not diminish the flow of contributions, but it could reduce their size. There may be significance in the fact that some of the larger bequests were payable by instalments, principally, one supposes, so as not to remove the immediate incentive for others to give, but perhaps also with an intention to even out the contribution across any lean years that lay ahead.

The great Perpendicular churches in Suffolk and on the Cotswolds are often called wool churches. Strictly speaking, few, if any, of these buildings were financed exclusively from the proceeds of trade in cloth or wool. Nor was wool the only product of husbandry in regions where the sheep population was high. In the fifteenth century arable farming on the Cotswolds was extensive. But crops such as wheat, pulse, drage and oats were grown less for revenue than for local consumption, brewing or animals (Hilton 1957, 107–8). Wool yielded a cash income, and there is no doubt that this enabled successful sheep-farmers and wool merchants to make sizeable contributions towards the rebuilding of certain churches. It is worthwhile to reflect upon the basis of such munificence. When John Fortey, a wool merchant, gave £300 to the rebuilding of the nave at Northleach *Gl* in 1458, this could be represented as about 91 sacks of wool at prices then current, or fleeces from about 19,000 sheep, all ultimately derived from the grazing of over 24,000 acres (9713 ha) of pasture. Demand for wool also enhanced the giving-power of peasants and smallholders, many of whom kept a few sheep and could earn ready money by selling fleeces to middlemen. The 'giving public' in an area productive of wool may therefore have been more broadly and solidly based than in some other types of rural community. Notwithstanding this, there were some areas, like the Lincolnshire Wolds, which were very productive of wool but have poor churches. In Lincolnshire the late medieval increase in the sheep population coincided with a *decline* in churchbuilding.

Cloth was worth roughly three times the value of the wool that it contained, and in times of prosperity clothiers were strongly placed as benefactors. Clothiers fared well between *c.* 1410 and 1440, and outstandingly well in the later fifteenth century. That a slump intervened is not in doubt. But two points about this may be noted. First, while exports of wool and of wool products fell sharply in the middle decades of the fifteenth century, the decline was more pronounced in volume than it was in terms of value (Fig. 106). Second, the medieval economy was extremely regional in its behaviour. Some areas performed considerably better than figures averaged out for the country as a whole would suggest; within those areas were localities which did better still.

The matching of cashflow to the varying expenses of construction has emerged as a critical aspect of parochial building. It may be asked where responsibility for financial supervision lay, and how it was discharged. A few pre-Reformation parish accounts have survived. It is seldom clear who kept them. At St Mary, Grimsby *Hu* (*Li*) in the 1420s the accountant was a chaplain. In 1376 a member of the clerical staff at Moulton *Li* was designated as the 'proctor', an office ancestral to that of churchwarden (D. Owen 1971, 115–17). At Adderbury details of income and expenditure were at first recorded by the vicar, but in 1412–13, when the pace of work quickened, the incumbent was assisted by William Mownter, a member of New College who was drafted in for the purpose. Monastic and collegiate rectors were particularly well placed to provide such expertise. Otherwise, as Mrs Owen suggests, book-keeping must often have been undertaken by chantry priests or clerks in minor orders. Some chantry priests acquired accounting skills while in the service of magnates. Many of them were in any case already involved in part-time teaching, as at Towcester *Np* where one of the objects of a chantry founded by the executors of William Sponne in 1448 included the duty to keep a free school (A. H. Thompson 1947, 151). Churchwardens' accounts which cover rebuilding at Louth *Li* early in the sixteenth century were written out by John Cawood, who was one of the ministers in divine office at the church. He was also an organist and a composer of masses. Cawood seems to have obtained a grounding in accountancy elsewhere, for his accounts contain arithmetic by dots: a technique used in the Exchequer (Dudding 1941, xvi–xvii).

By *c.* 1475 parish accounts were coming to be kept by laymen as well as by clerks. This raises the question of whether building campaigns which were supported by rich merchants were sometimes at an additional advantage: is it conceivable that successful businessmen could contribute financial expertise as well as money? Exactly how such advice might have helped to forward building it is at first sight difficult to suggest. Where accounts survive, as for example at Tilney All Saints *Nf* (Stallard 1922), they are invariably of elementary character, consisting of lists of receipts and expenditure. Cash accounts of this sort are not a basis for cashflow forecasting,

106 Exports of wool and cloth, 1350–1510 (*Source*: Childs 1978, 223, n.l)

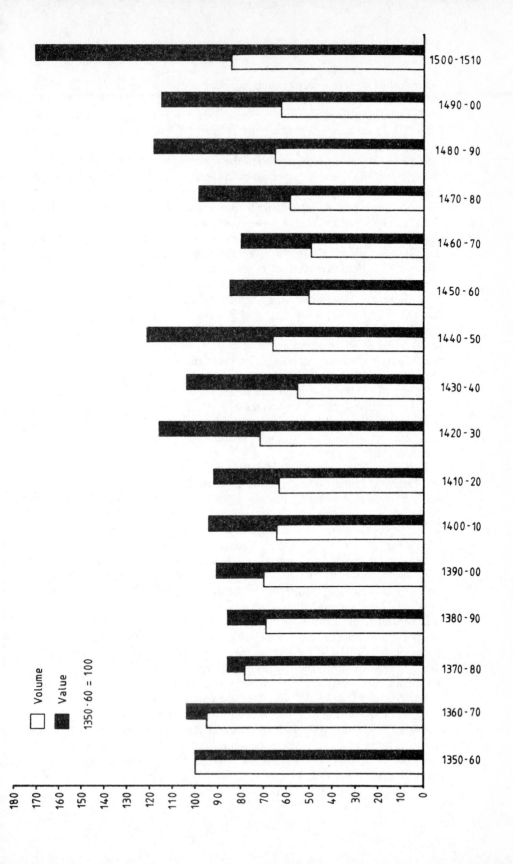

or any other kind of analysis such as a managerial person might have been able to provide. The introduction into England from Italy of book-keeping by double entry using Arabic numerals is supposed not to have taken place on any scale until the second half of the sixteenth century (Jenkinson 1926). There are, however, some straws in the wind. Italian wool buyers were moving about on the Cotswolds in the fifteenth century. A corbel in the Lady Chapel at Northleach *Gl* bears the date 1489 – in Arabic numerals (Verey 1970/Pevsner 1951–76). Improved accounting methods were becoming known to merchants with overseas contacts, in certain ports, sooner than elsewhere. Book-keeping by double entry made its debut in Bristol soon after 1500, and was known there as accounting in the 'Spanish manner'. In the 1460s Exchequer auditors working on port accounts in Hull are found making marginal calculations in Arabic numerals, even though the main framework remained stolidly Roman. The signs are, therefore, that advanced methods of accounting were becoming known in various parts of England before the Reformation, and that these techniques were being practised informally perhaps 50–75 years in advance of their adoption as a matter of convention. It is therefore possible that go-ahead merchants had something to offer their parish churches in the field of financial planning, although if this happened their services ran in parallel to official parish accounts and may not even have been based upon them. However this may be, the numerous conditional clauses in late medieval wills give no support to the theory that parishioners were fatalistic or indifferent in their attitudes towards building work that suffered interruption.

Perhaps the least penetrable aspect of the relationship between wealth and building in the fifteenth century lies in the realm of motivation: what was it that caused so many parishioners to give to their churches? In considering this question it is necessary to recognize the dangers of taking scale or expense as measures of generosity. We cannot be sure that a costly rebuilding in one place involved the assignment of a greater proportion of personal disposable income than some comparatively modest alteration in another. Still less are we able to judge the degree of enthusiasm which lay behind personal giving. Some of the plainest Perpendicular churches, of which there are many, may represent a depth of piety which exceeded the commitment behind more celebrated buildings. The difficulty is, we do not know; we cannot look into the minds of the dead. We can, however, read their wills and contracts, examine their tombs and look at the patterns of their benefactions. From these sources, several themes stand out. One concerns the anxiety of individuals for the fate of their souls. Another has to do with the intensification of communal identity.

In the fourteenth and fifteenth centuries, to die unshriven was to be worse than dead. And since 'nothing is more certain than death and nothing more uncertain than the hour of death', men and women took due precautions. When William de Loriaco, a canon of Lichfield and rector of Bredon *Wo*, made his will in January 1310 he left his soul to almighty

God, the blessed Mary and all the saints. He directed that his body be buried in the church of Bredon 'before the image of B. Mary if it happen that I die in England within one day's journey of the said church'. If he died further afield his funeral was to take place in the nearest church of Friars Minor. Any outstanding debts or forfeits were to be paid and restored from his movable goods. William left 20s to the fabric of the church in which he was buried, and 40s to the friars if his corpse were to go to them. On the day of his obit 100s was to be spent on bread for distribution to the poor in the town in which he was buried. Twenty marks were allocated for the finding of four chaplains to celebrate soul masses for a year in the churches of Bredon, Haliwell, Merston and of the Friars Minor at Loriac in France. Eight pounds' worth of bread was to be distributed to the poor of these places. Smaller sums were earmarked for the fabrics of the four churches, and for chaplains and clerks associated with them. Friaries at London, Reading and Northampton received bequests. So did the leper house at Loriac, the 'poorer hospital' in London and the poor of Windsor. At Windsor the vicar of the church was to receive 4s 'for commemoration of my soul'.

William's bequests of personal property reveal a lavish lifestyle, but also a care for his relatives, friends, acquaintances, and the servants of himself and others. John Manasser, his clerk, was to receive 100s, a mare worth 20s, 'and one of my furred vests'. His two valets were to have 60s and 50s, respectively, together with various items of property. Even Roger and Hanecok, two ordinary servants, were to have 20s each, plus 'the saddles and cloths of my horses in equal portions'. Others were to have candlesticks, silken purses, blankets, cloths, silver cups, 'and to Adam my nephew £20, for his schooling' (*Reg. Reynolds*, 23–4).

The structure of William de Loriaco's will reflects beliefs about purgatory: the place or state of souls between death and the general judgment. Behind the allocation of 420s to good works of various kinds lies the teaching, recently expounded by Thomas Aquinas and reasserted at the Council of Lyon (1274), that the guilt of venial sin is expiated immediately after death by an act of perfect charity. Thus forgiven, William would still have to undergo the suffering of punishment, but he would be helped by the prayers of the faithful, and especially by the offering of masses on his behalf. William set aside 290s for soul masses. He could expect further intercessionary support as a result of his eight benefactions to the friars, amounting to 83s. Bequests for the care of church fabrics came to 90s and would also count in his favour. In all, William earmarked over £44 for purposes directly to do with the securing of his soul. Apart from the legacy to his 'dearest mother', to whom he left £50 and some silver, this was the largest component of William's will.

William de Loriaco's terminal priorities were shared by most people in later medieval England. Only the manifestations differed, being scaled up or down, according to means and station. Magnates and the wealthiest gentry endowed colleges, perpetual chantries and charitable institutions.

Merchants founded chantries, or hired priests to celebrate soul masses for a term of years. Tradesmen and their wives purchased masses. Many found support in the chantries which were collectively endowed by gilds and fraternities. A poor man like William Simeon of Reculver *K* who died on the Sunday after Christmas 1396 might manage 6d

> to the image of St Mary in the church . . . Dom Robert de Langton, vicar of the church, to say a trental for my soul. Henry Corniwaile, clerk of the same church, have 4d. Residue of goods to my wife Isabelle, my executor.
>
> (Hussey 1917, 138)

There were many in late medieval England who were a good deal worse off than William Simeon. The mildest pains of purgatory were held to be infinitely more excruciating than the greatest that could be endured on earth. Poverty magnified this prospect.

The idea of purgation was not, of course, a formulation of the thirteenth century. Nor was there anything new in the concept of the charitable gesture or the intercessionary mass. A comprehensive awareness of all these things appears in Bede's remarkable relation of the vision of Dryhthelm in book five of the *Ecclesiastical History*. There are signs that others were similarly aware. A grant by ealdorman Oswulf to Christ Church, Canterbury, in *c.* 810 provided for the annual distribution of 1120 loaves on the day of his obit (Harmer 1914, 1–2, 39–40). In 833 a priest called Wergard made provision for the feeding of 1200 poor people on the anniversary of his death (Sawyer 1968, no. 1414). Similar benefactions were made in this and later centuries (Campbell 1979, 122). Gilds of laypeople that cared for the exequies of their members existed in late Saxon England (*EHD* 1, 557). The alarming vision of Herlequin's hunt, witnessed by Walchelin, priest of Bonneval, in 1091 and recounted by Orderic Vitalis *c.* 1133 × 1135, contains several episodes that testify to a contemporary belief in the efficacy of the mass for the curtailment of torment. Robert, Walchelin's dead brother, tells him:

> The arms which we bear are red-hot, and offend us with an appalling stench, weighing us down with an intolerable weight, and burning with everlasting fire. Up to now I have suffered unspeakable torture from these punishments. But when you were ordained in England and sang your first Mass for the faithful departed your father Ralph escaped from his punishments and my shield, which caused me great pain, fell from me. As you see I still carry this sword, but I look in faith for release from this burden within the year.
>
> (Orderic, viii; trans. Chibnall 1973, 249)

Compilations such as the *Liber Vitae* of Durham, and the bede-rolls which circulated among religious communities, are reminders that the idea of intercession for the departed lay embedded in the rationale for pious foundations long before the doctrine of purgatory was discussed by thirteenth-century theologians.

The multiplication of chantries and soul masses in the later Middle Ages may suggest that more people thought about their destinies more often, or that the nature of their perceptions underwent some change. Most probably the latter, for the separation of purgatory from hell was not always complete in earlier sources, and in popular belief it was even less so. But by 1240 a bishop of Worcester could think it worthwhile to insist upon the exclusion of animals from churchyards, for reasons of cleanliness, because these places 'contain the bodies of those who shall be saved, many of them now purged of their sins and waiting for the new garment of their glorification' (cited in Brooke and Brooke 1984, 107–8). The remission of penalties would be hastened by masses for the departed. In essence the chantry was just this: a service endowed to celebrate mass for the soul(s) of its founder(s). Its rationale lay in a belief in purgatory as a place or state of temporal punishment, and in the mass as a unit of merit. Generally, the number of masses requested would be proportional to the means of the testator (Tanner 1984, 105).

Although social and demographic, as well as religious, factors have been adduced in connection with the increase in demand for masses and prayers, they do not explain its source. Historians have noted a close relationship between the expansion of the chantry system and the emergence of a middle class. The Black Death of 1348–9, and subsequent virulent epidemics which stalked through town and country in the late Middle Ages, have often been regarded as the promoters of a heightened sense of mutability. Yet the beginnings of the chantry system lay well back in the thirteenth century. Special masses for the dead were increasing before either a middle class began to yearn for them or pandemic ushered in an age of anxiety. It may, indeed, be possible to think of the pre-Conquest minsters as precursors of chantry colleges. With their several priests and altars, paramount rights to corpses, facilities for burial of the privileged within their walls and, quite often, a (later) dedication to All Saints, they were well equipped for such a role. A century or less separates their general demise from the rise of the chantries. But that time had been busy with churchfounding and the endowment of monasteries – actions which may have met the need in the interim?

The desire for more masses was perhaps accentuated by a deepening of reverence towards the sacrament of the altar. This was encouraged, if not occasioned, by the definition of eucharistic doctrine at the Fourth Lateran Council in 1215, and found further expression in the formal institution of the Feast of Corpus Christi in 1264. Purgatory, meanwhile, not only came to be invested with terrifying realism, but in peasant as well as magnate minds it was also differentiated from hell. From purgatory, unlike hell, there was a possibility of eventual release. Both doctrines were brought to the attention of lay audiences, perhaps not least through the preaching of the new orders of friars. Thomas Aquinas, to whom the office for Corpus Christi is attributed, and who wrote at length on the subject of purgatory, was himself a member of the Dominican order. In the eleventh and twelfth centuries there is evidence of popular ignorance as to what the mass, and purgatory, meant. Efforts to dispel this ignorance led to a widening of concern for the fate of the soul.

Colleges of priests were powerful amplifiers of intercessionary prayer. But they were costly to endow, and few outside magnate circles could afford them. Many members of the population were nevertheless in a position to purchase some form of commemoration. Towards the upper end of the scale was the chantry for which land and property were assigned in perpetuity. The expense of endowing and licensing a perpetual chantry meant that such foundations were restricted to those with wealth: typically, the nobility, Crown officials, some knights and their ladies, rich merchants, abbots and higher clergy. People of more slender means might nevertheless form or join a syndicate which endowed a chantry collectively. Otherwise, or in addition, it was possible to fund temporary arrangements involving masses spread over a period which could range from a few days to several years.

Each of these levels of provision had an architectural context. The assimilation of colleges and perpetual chantries to existing parish churches stimulated notable works of extension and renewal. At Cotterstock *Np*, for example, the chancel of the parish church was rebuilt upon an enlarged scale in order to accommodate a college of priests founded by John Gifford in 1338. Gifford was a former rector of Cotterstock who later entered the service of Edward III. The staff of the college consisted of twelve chaplains and a provost. The object of the foundation was to pray for the king, 'queen Isabella, queen Philippa and the king's children, and John Gifford, and for the soul of Edward II' (RCHME *Northants* 6, 38). Collegiate foundations led to the enlargement of chancels elsewhere, as for instance at Wingfield *Sf*, or North Cadbury *So*, rebuilt *c.* 1415–23. Sometimes the old parish church was taken down and a new one built. This happened at Kirby Bellars *Le*, for instance, or Maidstone *K*, where the broad three-aisled church was erected to the commission of William Courtney, archbishop of Canterbury (1381–97). A few such reconstructions were on the most substantial scale. Howden *Hu* (*YE*), an outpost of the empire of Durham cathedral priory, is a pocket cathedral. Edington *Wi* owes its grandeur to the patronage of William Edington, a royal clerk who combined the office of bishop of Winchester (1346–66) with various state appointments, including the chancellorship (1356–63). The church was completely rebuilt between 1352 and 1361 and housed canons of the quasi-Augustinian order of Bonshommes. At Fotheringhay *Np*, a centre of Yorkist power, the parish church was replaced by a magnificent new collegiate building, erected 1414–42. Ralph Lord Cromwell initiated the construction of Tattershall *Li* around 1460. Battlefield *Sa* was started in 1406 as a memorial to the battle between Harry Hotspur and Henry IV which had taken place three years before. There was a similar battlefield chapel at Towton *NY* (*YW*), also by royal foundation. The tradition, like so much else connected with death and commemoration, was ancient. Cnut had built a minster at *Asandun* after the battle in 1016. Oswald's victory over Caedwalla in the 630s was marked by a cross, which was replaced by a church (*HE* iii,2).

Chantries varied in their permanence, according to the size of the resources with which they were endowed. At its simplest the chantry mass required no more than a priest, and room for an altar within a consecrated building at which he could celebrate. Most chantries functioned thus, often at existing altars. Some have left exiguous marks upon the churches that housed them - a piscina in the wall of an aisle or chapel is a common sign of a former altar, if not of a chantry - but large numbers have disappeared without obvious trace. Only affluent founders could afford to place their chantries in a more lasting context. There were two main ways of doing this. One was to enclose an area within the existing building. The other was to enlarge the church. Both solutions conferred a degree of privacy. More important, however, was the scope for ostentatious display. Tomb chapels were status symbols.

Enlargement could be achieved through the erection of an adjunct, like the chapel of St Kathryn founded by Thomas Hall, a wool merchant, at Grantham *Li* in 1496. If they could afford it, extensions to parish churches were favoured by local lords, as at Coberley *Gl*, where the south chapel was added to accommodate the chantry of Thomas de Berkeley, founded in 1337 and augmented ten years later (Haines 1965, 238-9). Tormarton *Gl* received a new aisle for the chantry college endowed by John de la Rivière in the 1340s. The Wilcote chapel at Northleigh *O* was created by extending the north aisle of the nave eastward so as to clasp the chancel. A position flanking the chancel was popular, as at Mere *Wi*, Sawley *Db* or the famous Clopton aisle at Long Melford *Sf*. Such extensions commonly developed as mortuary chapels for local dynasties of gentry, like the Meyrings of Sutton-on-Trent *Nt*, or the Bradestons at Winterbourne *Gl*. Merchants vied with gentry and minor nobility in the creation of outstanding new aisles and chapels. In 1517 John Greenway provided a sumptuous new porch and chapel at the parish church of St Peter, Tiverton *D*. At Cullompton *D* John Lane (d. 1528) was responsible for the building of an outer aisle. This was unusually lavish, and overspread by a fan-vault. Symbols that include clothier's shears and the teasels used for raising cloth are carved upon the buttresses of the Lane aisle: reminders that the building was financed out of proceeds from the worsted trade. But rarely was an adjunct so substantial as the chapel built to house the tomb of Richard Beauchamp, earl of Warwick, which was attached to the collegiate church of St Mary at Warwick in the 1440s. The cost was close to £2480: about six times more than the expense of the entire new chancel at Adderbury.

The work of enlarging a church took time, and the initial outlay was high. A more rapid and economical solution was to create an enclosure within the church as it stood. Often this was achieved by screening off all or part of an existing aisle, as did the Hartington family at Porlock *So*, or the Copplestones at Colebrook *D*. Alternatively, if space permitted, the founder could establish a free-standing structure: a church in miniature, conspicuous within the church. After *c*. 1350 there appeared firms of crafts-men working in freestone, alabaster, wood or metal, which specialized in the production of such chapels to order. Most of these cage-like creations were removed from parish churches following the enactment in 1545 and 1547 of legislation for the suppression of chantries. But some remain. The church of St Mary Magdalene at Newark *Nt*, for instance, retains the stone tomb-chapels of Thomas Meyring and Robert Markham, con-structed *c*. 1500 and 1508, respectively. Chapels of this sort in parish churches were unusual, as the founders who could afford them were generally magnates and prelates who would tend to be buried in the more prestigious surroundings of a cathedral or monastic church. Cage-chapels in parish churches were normally made of wood. A typical example is to be seen at Burford *O*, where the wooden chapel stands between two piers of the north arcade of the nave. At Cirencester the chapel of the Garstang family is tucked into the eastern bay of the south nave aisle, while at Shelsley Walsh *Wo* a parclose chapel adjoins the west side of the rood screen. Sites of the latter sort were popular, presumably because they combined advantages of prominence, proximity to the rood and inter-visibility with the main altar.

The activities of individuals who founded chantries were complemented by, and perhaps to some extent prompted a reaction from, those who were personally unable to afford a permanent flow of masses and prayers. The second half of the fourteenth century saw an upsurge in the formation of gilds and lay fraternities. Fraternities were associations of laypeople who combined under the patronage of a saint or cult to assist each other in life and to care for the exequies of their members when they died. Thus a per-son who belonged to the Fraternity of St Katherine which had its altar in the church of St Botolph Aldersgate, London, could expect to be brought in for burial if (s)he died anywhere within ten miles of the parish. An an-nual subscription to the Gild of the Resurrection of Our Lord in Lincoln secured the benefit of full services if the member died out of the city, or even on or beyond the sea (T. Smith 1870, 6, 177). Fraternities varied in their size, wealth and range of aims (for which see T. Smith 1870; Westlake 1919; Scarisbrick 1984, 20–4), but the provision of a decent funeral and in-tercessionary support were functions common to them all. They were, in effect, co-operative chantries.

Fraternities and gilds influenced the development of parish churches in several ways. Some of them were sufficiently wealthy to enlarge a church, as did the Clothworkers at Tavistock *D* in the 1440s, or even to rebuild it altogether, as at Ludlow where in the fifteenth century the Palmers financ-ed a lavish reconstruction and flattened a twelfth-century motte in the pro-cess. Operations on this scale were exceptional, however, and it was more usual for a fraternity to contribute to the upkeep and adornment of a church. In places this concern extended to the entire building, as at

Cavenham *Sf.* More commonly it focused on a part of the church for which the fraternity had developed a special affection. Often this was an aisle. Every fraternity had its own altar whereat an annual mass would be celebrated for the well-being of members past and present. Such altars were usually located in an aisle of the parish church (Fig. 107). It was natural for the members of a fraternity to come to regard this part of the building as 'theirs'. If the fraternity had sufficient funds to employ a chaplain, so that the chapel was in regular use, the tendency towards proprietory feeling could be strengthened.

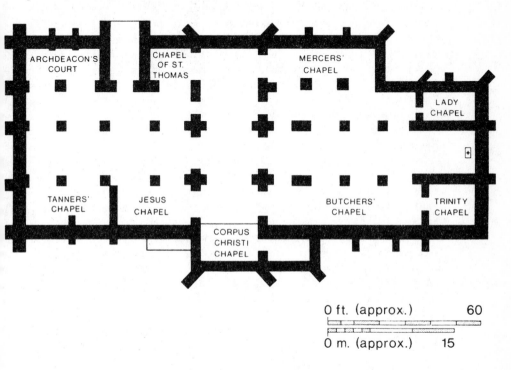

0 ft. (approx.)   60

0 m. (approx.)   15

107 Holy Trinity, Coventry. Diagram to show occupation of space by gilds and fraternities by early sixteenth century (*Source*: A.H. Thompson 1911a)

The wealthier fraternities performed a wide range of charitable, religious and educational functions. A number made themselves responsible for the care of roads, causeways and bridges, or public utilities like a water supply. Quasi-municipal involvements of this sort could lead to the emplacement of a chapel upon or near the feature which had been adopted. Roadside and bridge-chapels combined practical with spiritual advantages, being lucrative places for the collection of offerings from travellers in return for the support of prayers. The toll-house chapel at Kessingland *Sf* is a reminder that the distinction between this form of fundraising and the charging of toll may often have been small.

Associations between churches and liminal installations such as gates and bridges were being formed before the Conquest: a process which was observed in Chapter 5. But the heyday of the bridge-chapel lay in the later Middle Ages. The growth of internal travel and trade which occurred in the twelfth and thirteenth centuries provided a context for this phenomenon, for it led both to an increase in the clientele for specialized religious institutions, and to the enlargement and rebuilding in stone of important bridges. Thus in 1196 a *capellanus* of the bridge is heard of in Exeter. The bridge in question was still in process of construction across the River Exe. The parochial chapel in which the *capellanus* ministered must have been built at about the same time, for a church of St Edmund is recorded in the suburb of Exe Island by 1216. The south wall of St Edmund's rested on the bridge, while the west and east walls stood upon cutwaters. Other cases include the chapel of St Thomas which occupied the High Bridge in Lincoln before the end of the thirteenth century, and a chapel of All Saints which was founded near the north end of the thirteenth-century bridge at Morpeth *Nb*.

The vogue for bridge-chapels came to an abrupt end in 1547, when chantries were suppressed and fraternities were dissolved. Deprived of their rationale and incomes the chapels fell into disuse, and would eventually disappear either as a result of neglect or because the medieval bridges which bore them were rebuilt. A few were saved. The fourteenth-century chapel of St Mary on the Bridge at Derby was transferred into the keeping of the town and still exists. Other survivors can be seen at Rotherham *SY* (*YW*) and St Ives *Ca*. The best of them is at Wakefield *WY*, where the survey of 1546 found a chantry of two priests, 'both unleardend', upon 'the myddes of Wakefield bridges' over the River Calder (Page 1895, 417). The chapel was built *c*. 1350 and licensed in 1357. Offerings made there were used to assist in the upkeep of the bridge. A drastic nineteenth-century restoration notwithstanding, the Wakefield chapel is a precious survival which must today stand for a class of religious building that was once widespread.

Since most bridge-chapels have perished, it is to written records that we must turn for knowledge of their former existence, whereabouts and functions. Sometimes the presence of a chapel is indicated by a will, as in the instance of the 'chapel on the bridge' at Bramber *Sx* which was mentioned in 1466/7. A few chapels lasted long enough to catch the attention of antiquaries or to be recorded in illustrations. The Bristol bridge-chantry of the Assumption of the Virgin Mary, founded after 1247, survived into the eighteenth century but was demolished by 1765. The seventeenth-century antiquary Dr Robert Plot knew of a chapel which had existed on the Swarkestone Bridge over the Trent in Derbyshire. The foundations are still visible. At Droitwich *Wo* John Leland noted 'a bridge of 4 archis of stone over the broke that runneth by the Wiche, and at the hither end of this bridge was a fayre new chaple of tymber' (L.T.Smith 1907, 5, 94). Later, a quirky arrangement was remembered whereby the carriageway on the bridge had passed through the chapel, between priest and people. Chapels which housed important chantries could generate detailed documentation. Next to the bridge over the Medway at Rochester *K*, for example, there existed a chapel called All Souls wherein John de Cobham, knight, founded a chantry of three chaplains in honour of the Trinity, St Mary and All Saints. The objects of this foundation were to say matins and all canonical hours; one chaplain was to celebrate daily the mass of the day, and the other two would assist the devotions of travellers or nobles when on journeys. In each of their masses the chaplains were to pray for benefactors living and dead, of the bridge, chapel and place, and also for the souls of Sir John de Cobham and others (A. Hussey 1936, 234-5). In York a chapel dedicated to St William was standing at one end of Ouse Bridge before 1223. At least four perpetual chantries were founded here.

The popularity of St William's chapel among the citizenry of York could be seen as deriving from a miracle which was credited to the saint. It was said that when William entered the city following his reinstatement as archbishop of York in 1154, the previous Ouse Bridge had collapsed, throwing onlookers into the river. As a result of William's prayers all the victims were spared from drowning. This was a singular incident, however, whereas enthusiasm for chantries on bridges was widespread. The economic advantages of such sites no doubt contributed to the desire to promote them, but these aspects in their turn are likely to have been enhanced by the universal symbolism of the bridge as a place of crossing. For a preoccupation with transition emerges as a leading theme within late medieval spirituality.

A conspicuous feature of provision for soul masses was the attention devoted to their timing. In Norwich, for instance, Tanner's analysis of a large number of wills has shown that most testators 'wanted a combination of a large number of masses and prayers immediately after death together with smaller numbers continuing at regular intervals for a long time. But the former was usually preferred when a choice was made between the two' (Tanner 1984, 106). Precautions of this sort were taken everywhere. They suggest that the moment of death, the going forth of the soul upon its journey, and the shock of the first days of sojourn in purgatory, together formed the period when the soul was at its most vulnerable and in need of intercessionary support. It was not unknown for people to request that their first masses be celebrated before they had actually expired. Fears depicted in fifteenth-century art explain why. Deathbed scenes of a man commending his spirit to God while the archangel Michael and Satan wrestle in a celestial dogfight for possession of his soul stem from an anxiety which was widely and deeply felt.

Related themes were explored in funerary sculpture. In the south chapel of the church at Long Wittenham *Brk* there is a piscina within a niche, the miniature effigy of a knight below, two angels lofting his soul away above. This probably represents a heart burial. After *c.* 1430 there appeared in England a type of two-tier monument which combined an effigy dressed as if in life with an underlying representation of his cadaver. The emaciated corpse is commonly seen in the interval between death and funeral: a state which may be indicated by its partial attire in a winding-sheet. Such monuments were most often made for bishops, like Richard Fleming at Lincoln (d. 1431), or higher clergy such as William Sylke, precentor of Exeter (d. 1485). A cleric may be represented at Heming-borough *Hu* (*YE*). But the tombs of laymen could also take this form, as in St Mary at Bury St Edmunds, or in the instance of John Barton (d. 1491) at Holme-by-Newark *Nt*, or the effigy beneath the brass of Richard Willoughby (d. 1471) at Wollaton *Nt*. Brasses showing cadavers, or simply trussed in a shroud as at Norbury *Db*, are an extension of the theme.

Cadaver tombs were not common. They are nevertheless worth attention as extreme manifestations of a more general engrossment with mutability. Currents of morbidity and desire for mortification eddy through fifteenth-century thought and art (Aston 1968, 172–3). In monuments of the *vermis* type, where the corpse is shown corrupting, contempt for the body may be shockingly explicit. But behind this grisly asceticism there was a more simple point – that we make our exit from the world as we enter: naked, defenceless and wholly dependent upon external power. Birth and death are the ultimate liminal experiences. Maybe bridges recalled that?

Popular concern for the time of disengagement between body and soul found expression in other ways. The passing-bell was, and in a few places still is, rung through the closing minutes of a life, announcing the imminence of a death to neighbours in their homes or out in the fields. The heightened tower of the fifteenth century, with its larger, more sonorous bells, was better equipped than ever before to solicit prayers from parishioners (p. 406).

In some churches the living and the dead alike were watched over by hosts of angels, either carved in stone, as in the chancel at Hillesden *Bu*, or in wood, upon roofs, as at St John's in Stamford *Li*, or March *Ca*, or Blythburgh *Sf*, or Cullompton *D*. At Woolpit *Sf* on a summer evening the solitary visitor might hope to hear the whirr of wings outspread above. Here angels float even above the aisles, where they are carved in silvery relief upon oaken ceilings. Needham Market *Sf* has a clerestory that clasps the roof, flooding light down upon the celestial company. The hammer-beam was ideally suited to such displays, and it may be wondered how far the spread of this form of roof construction was the stimulus for, or the product of, the symbolism of divine messengers. An angel roof reminded churchgoers of paradise, a higher plane of being above and beyond the world of cares below. And in their ultimate rigidity and silence, the angels promise a sinfonia and divine dancing at the general judgment. They often hold instruments, and are poised to play.

From top to bottom late medieval society was pervaded by a longing for commemoration. The places in which this desire found expression, however, reflect allegiances that divided along lines of rank. Thus while the religious sympathies of magnates continued to focus chiefly upon monastic, collegiate and mendicant communities, those of the gentry, merchants and lay fraternities rested more with their parish churches. In Gloucestershire, for instance, it has been calculated that out of the

> 97 known burials of knights, esquires or their ladies between 1200 and 1500 no fewer than 77 were in parish churches. It is hard to say if this preference was becoming more or less strong as the Middle Ages progressed; though in view of the growing identity between the lord of the manor and his local church, evidenced by testamentary bequests, it is very likely that the preference became stronger as time went on.
>
> (Saul 1980, 103)

There were comparable patterns of loyalty in towns. In York, for example, hardly any members of the city's ruling elite sought to be buried in the minster. Instead, when craftsmen and merchants founded perpetual chantries 'the great majority preferred to express their aspirations through the medium of their parish churches' (Dobson 1967, 25). Much the same can be said of Norwich (Tanner 1984, 97), and of London, where over 186 chantries were distributed between 65 of the City churches.

There are signs of a connection between the level of investment in commemorative arrangements and the degree of support which was given to new building. That such a link may have existed is suggested by a comparison between York and Norwich. Some thirty-nine perpetual chantries were founded in York in the first half of the fourteenth century. Thereafter the figures show a steady decline, and were approaching vanishing point after 1500. Few of York's churches were rebuilt in the fifteenth century, and between 1547 and 1586 one-third of the parish churches in the city were closed (Fig. 108). Most of the redundant churches were demolished. A number had been neglected for some time (Palliser 1974, 87). In Norwich, by contrast, foundations of new perpetual chantries did not fall away during the fifteenth century. Indeed, the total of those established in the years 1500–35 actually exceeded the number of foundations in York in the period 1450–1500. Practically every one of the forty-six surviving parish churches in Norwich was rebuilt and enlarged between c. 1350 and 1550.

The involvement of merchants, craftsmen, civic leaders and gentry with the rebuilding of their parish churches is sometimes made explicit by inscriptions upon the fabrics that they helped to finance. When the chancel of St Thomas, Salisbury, fell down in 1450, rebuilding was undertaken in partnership by the dean and chapter of the cathedral, and merchants and citizens of the parish. The names and merchants' marks of parishioners concerned were carved on the capitals of the south arcade. At Stratford St Mary *Sf* gifts from the Moss family are recorded below the windows. The arms of Anthony Ellis, a merchant of the Staple of Calais, are visible upon the massive tower that he paid for at Great Ponton *Li* in 1519. The nave of St Mary, Beverley *Hu* (*YE*), was substantially rebuilt early in the

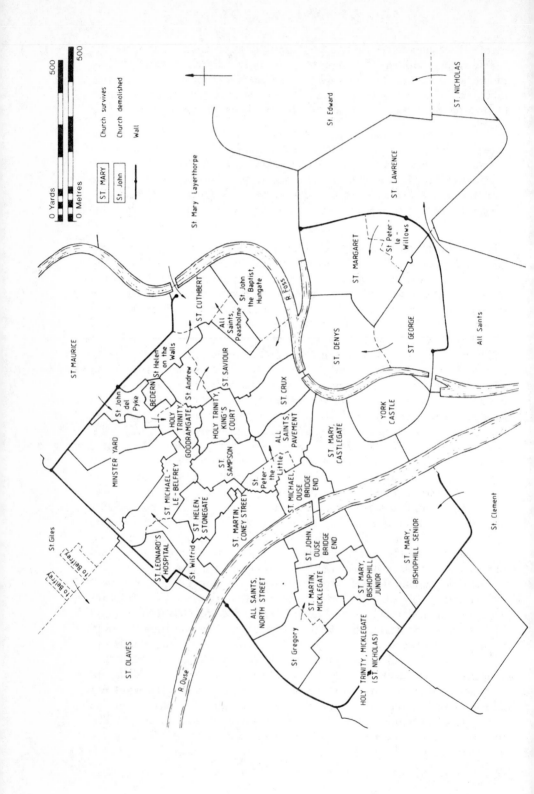

1520s. Carvings above the piers of the north arcade depict benefactors, one of whom gave sufficient funds for two-and-a-half pillars. Many other churches rebuilt in the fifteenth and early sixteenth centuries were similarly annotated.

It may be true that the Perpendicular churches 'prove' little, at least in relation to the rather crude economic demands which were made of them by Professor Postan. But they testify in ample measure to the vitality of parish life in the later Middle Ages, and above all to the growth and consolidation of communal identities. Local lords, merchants, civic leaders and lay fraternities all played parts in this process. Gentry and merchants contributed funds and rallied local endeavour. Their tombs and chapels added lustre to parish churches, and reinforced the allegiances of local dynasties in shire and town. Fraternities gave ordinary people a special stake in their parish churches. They also assisted the trend towards parishioners taking a greater degree of administrative responsibility for the care and running of their churches. It is in this period, the fourteenth and fifteenth centuries, that references to churchwardens start to become more common.

Significantly, enthusiasm for building seems to have been as strong among poor parishioners as among the rich. The church counted as a charitable work. It would endure long after some slim bequest for a trental of masses had been expended. The reconstructed church of the fifteenth century may have been in some degree a monument to spiritual anxiety, but it was also expressive of material pride in the combined efforts of a community: an enterprise from which no one was excluded, and for which everyone could take some credit.

The broadening of responsibility on the part of the laity and the growth of their involvement in parish affairs were trends that continued through the Reformation. And while some types of religious bequest did decline after c. 1515, this was not necessarily accompanied by any significant reduction in gifts to parish churches. In some areas new building was actually on the increase at this time. The years c. 1490–1540 formed a period of great churchbuilding activity in Gwynedd, with rebuildings at Clynnog, Dolwyddelan, Llanengan, Llangwunadl, Llaneilian and Holyhead, with many lesser works besides (Butler 1966, 98). Suffolk contains many sixteenth-century porches. Parts of Cheshire contain numbers of Tudor rebuildings. The tower at Little Budworth dates to the 1520s. Additions were made to Mobberley and Rostherne in the 1530s. St Chad's at Winsford was substantially remodelled c. 1543. Some of this activity may have been in compensation for earlier poverty, or a desire to replace in masonry churches which had previously been framed in wood. A few of these half-timbered churches survive in the north-west Midlands, as at Melverley *Sa*, Marton *Ch* or Lower Peover *Ch* – whereunto a tower was added in 1582

108 Unions of parishes in York during the sixteenth century (*Source*: Palliser 1974)

(see Fig. 98). The cycle of maintenance and renewal of fabric often follow-ed a calendar of its own, independent of ideas about reform.

Reform, in any case, came by stages. Even such a figure as Robert Burgoyne, a leading official in the Court of Augmentations, thought it worthwhile to establish a chantry for his soul in 1545, on the very eve of the passage of legislation for the abolition of such institutions (Scarisbrick 1984, 9). Evidently there was no general precognition. Paradoxically, moreover, the dissolution of monasteries, chantries, fraternities, even the denial of purgatory and of the intercession of saints, all in various ways helped to strengthen the place of the parish church in local devotional life. Rumours that the Crown would in due course suppress superfluous parish churches were among the grievances which sparked the Lincolnshire rising in October 1536 (Dickens 1967, 51). The dissolution of chantries, begun with some stealth in 1545 and pressed home in 1547, was accom-panied by the first real purge from parish churches of furnishings, fittings and possessions. But even this had consequences which could be beneficial to the churches. One was to raise ready money through the sale of plate and ornaments. Another was to concentrate sentiment and bequests upon the fabric. Both assisted repair, and in some places helped to finance new building. At Cheadle *St*, for example, the construction of a new church occupied the middle decades of the sixteenth century, the chancel of 1556-8 being financed by Lady Catherine Buckley – a former abbess.

Churchwardens' accounts and other sources suggest on the whole a stoical compliance with, rather than popular enthusiasm for, the new Pro-testantism. All over the country workmen were hired to dismantle rood screens, remove statues and pull apart altars. Producers of limewash did well in the late 1540s and early 1550s, when their product was applied to conceal the scenes of Doom, the Dance of Death, the Three Living and the Three Dead, the Weighing of Souls, and other eschatological images with which churchgoers had become familiar. But this was hardly ram-pant iconoclasm. Fittings, images, even items of plate, were sometimes held in informal trust by their buyers, to reappear quietly during the reign of Mary (1554-8). It seems to have been not unusual for the *mensa* slab of an altar to be buried on its site. There is literary evidence for this practice, which took place in the hope of a time to come when the hallowed stones could be retrieved and reinstated. Occasionally such slabs are still dug up, as at Carlton-in-Lindrick *Nt* and Royston *SY* (*YW*). Parishioners at Morebath *D* were not acting exceptionally when, in 1549, four sets of vestments in different liturgical colours, a streamer, banner, altar cloth and a 'black pall of satyn' were not sold but distributed among farmers in outlying parts of the parish in order to conceal them from the eyes of Edward VI's commissioners (Binney 1904, 165). Morebath was particu-larly unlucky, for only eighteen months previously there had been heavy outlay on a new 'sute of black vestmentis', towards which the vicar had contributed his tithes of wool and lambs. The total cost of these garments, including a trip to Exeter and back for the blessing of them, had amounted to £6 5s: a considerable sum (1904, 153-5). Similar dispersals are recorded elsewhere (Scarisbrick 1984, 101-2). Apart from the brief reunion with Rome during the reign of Mary – which saw some new introductions in the old vein, such as the rood loft of 1558 at Hubberholme *NY (YW)* – the black, the white, red and blue of such copes and vestments would not be seen again in English parish churches for three hundred years. In many churches they remain absent still.

The contradictions, expectations and mood of the closing years of pre-Reformation England may be well sensed at Barton-under-Needwood *St.* Here a man called John Taylor built an entirely new church, starting it in 1517 and seeing it finished in 1533, a year before his death. Legend has it that Taylor was the eldest of triplets, and on this account was plucked from his rustic background by Henry VII, educated at royal expense and entered into the service of the Crown. He ended his career as Master of the Rolls to Henry VIII. Taylor did not forget his humble origins, and provided his home village with a substantial church which replaced an obscure chapel-of-ease which had existed nearby. It is said that Taylor's church was built upon the site of his parents' cottage and own birthplace. Possibly he hoped to be buried there, intending the church as some form of chantry, uniting the two ultimate liminal experiences? If so, it was not to be. Taylor died in London, apparently out of favour, and he was probably buried there. Architecturally his church looks back to the fifteenth century, but also in some respects onward to the age of Renaissance culture. Tablets fixed on both sides of the nave tell of Taylor's career. Some original glass survives in the windows of the polygonal east end. 'The east window was his gift and represents the Twelve Apostles, Moses, Elijah, and Taylor's patron saint, St John the Baptist' (Wood 1981). Near Taylor's coat of arms, below the crucifixion, is the date of completion and dedication – 1533 – in Arabic numerals.

Two years after Taylor died the principles of prayer in masses, exequies and the giving of alms were all upheld in the Ten Articles of 1536. But the definition of purgatory was by now held to be doubtful:

> forasmuch as the place where they be, the name thereof, and the kind of pains there, also be to us uncertain by Scripture; therefore this with all other things we remit to Almighty God ... to whom is known their estate and condition.
>
> (*EHD* 5, 805)

Eleven years later, and purgatory was wholly denied. One of the motor forces behind lay involvement with local churchbuilding had been removed. In many places there were compensations, already described. But the disbandment of lay fraternities could have fatal consequences for parochial chapels where the position of the chaplain was insecure and no other form of income existed. In some parts of England and Wales chapelries of this sort were common, and a good many of them now started to fall into decay. Parish churches could also suffer. Deleted aisles and blocked arcades are commonly interpreted by historians of settlement as symptoms of a declining population, the contraction or desertion of villages. Often this must be correct. But could some of the derelict aisles convey a more subtle message: the abolition of the fraternities and removal of altars which had latterly given them meaning, and funds for their care? The chantry certificate for the 'service or stipend of Our Lady in the parish church of Kirkburton' *WY* is typical of hundreds in its portrayal of the reliance upon offerings and small gifts:

> Christopher Carter, incumbent. There is no foundation, but that well disposed persons of the parish there hath given certain lands and tend to the supplement of the livings of the incumbent thereof. To the intent to pray for the good estate of the parishioners living, and the souls of them departed, and all Christian souls.

(Page 1895, 304)

Concern for commemoration provided the deepest pedal-point for medieval society. Medieval religion was well adapted to the imminence of death. Archaeology shows us just how close death was. Study of the skeletal remains of the people interred in the small country churchyard at Raunds *Np* between the tenth and twelfth centuries reveals that infant mortality was massive. For those who survived it, it appears that 43 per cent of the females who reached the age of seventeen could expect to be dead before they were twenty-five. For every woman who lived through the age-range 25–35, another would die. The outlook for males who reached adolescence was marginally better, although the odds for a Raunds male in his early teens reaching early middle age were appreciably worse than those for an infantryman in the trenches during the First World War (Boddington and Cadman 1981). In York, the excavation of the cemetery of St Helen-on-the-Walls produced results which suggest that at least 27 per cent and possibly as many as 50 per cent of the population of that parish died as children. Only 9 per cent lived beyond the age of sixty (Dawes and Magilton 1980, 63).

Belief in purgatory and the efficacy of intercessionary prayer had helped to sustain the human spirit in a tragic world. When Protestantism smothered the rich mythology of the medieval Church, this comfort was withdrawn. But the tragedy went on. In cultured circles, the poem became a substitute for the prayer. Elizabethan verses are full of meditations upon tombs, brasses, effigies and graves. Former concern for masses now gave way to an intense preoccupation with mutability. Time has a leading role in most of Shakespeare's plays, and virtually all of his sonnets. It is no coincidence that the artistic upsurge of the later Tudor age should have followed directly upon the heels of the English Reformation, and perhaps no coincidence either that Shakespeare's birth should have occurred just eighteen years after the suppression of the chantries.

X

ANGLICANS AND
ARCADIANS

The sixteenth and seventeenth centuries saw the beginning of a new phenomenon in the English landscape: the creation of formal landscapes by design. Tudor government brought stability and an economy which favoured the moneymaking classes. Aristocrats in court, urban entrepreneurs, the larger farmers and able royal servants were among those who did best. They built capacious houses, and liked to set their mansions in formal gardens which might in their turn come to be surrounded by noble parks.

Neither gardens nor parks, of course, were new. Game parks had existed since the twelfth century. Medieval parks were managed for a variety of purposes. Commonly they were used as vaccaries and stud farms, as well as for the chase. From around 1550, however, parks began to present a new aspect. Unlike the medieval deer reserves, which tended to be on poorer soils, these new parks were conceived as arcadian enclaves, designed for their looks and ambience as well as for economic purposes, and often located in productive terrain.

The dissolution of the monasteries released valuable estates into private hands. This stimulated the land market, and it gave impetus to the formation of parks and the building of new houses. Some houses were actually superimposed upon monastic remains. A Tudor mansion was planted over the site of the Gilbertine priory at Sempringham *Li*. The house, in its turn, has long since disappeared, although something of the two layouts, much entangled, used to be visible from the air (Knowles and St Joseph 1952, 242–5). The church of the Carmelite friars of Aylesford *K* was demolished and two cloister ranges were converted into a house. Houses at Newstead *Nt*, Forde *Do* and Sir William Sharington's conversion of

377

Lacock *Wi* took the monastic cloister as their starting point. At Neath *Glm* it was the abbot's house, and at St Osyth *Ex* the gatehouse. Another venture of this sort involved the remains of the great Cluniac foundation at Bermondsey *Sr*, where a mansion raised out of the ruins by Sir Thomas Pope was existing before *c.* 1568, when it appears in a painting by Hoefnagel. Today, a street runs down the middle of the nave. In London, the choir aisles and eastern chapels of Holy Trinity priory, Aldgate, were turned into tenements which looked in upon a courtyard formed by the unroofing of the presbytery (J. Schofield 1984, 145–8). Elsewhere, there was a tendency for monastic ruins on private estates to be treated at first as quarries, subsequently to pass through a period of neglect, and then to be prized as ready-made picturesque features.

English arcady before the Civil War was eclectic in mood. The Renaissance contributed a preoccupation with classical forms and a desire for calculated effects. Advances in surveying, assisted by the invention of more accurate instruments, made it feasible to set out large sites with a confidence not previously approached. But by later standards, emparking in the Elizabethan era stood at a fairly elementary stage. The main preoccupation lay with the immediate surroundings of the house. 'God Almighty first planted a garden,' wrote Francis Bacon, 'and, indeed, it is the purest of human pleasures.' To Bacon, for gardens to be 'princelike', the contents 'ought not well to be under thirty acres of ground; and to be divided into three parts: a green in the entrance, a heath or desert in the going forth, and the main garden in the midst, besides alleys on both sides'. Bacon liked lawns and great hedges, but frowned upon topiary as being 'too busy'. He regarded fountains as 'a great beauty and refreshment', but warned against the creation of pools, which 'mar all, and make the garden unwholesome and full of flies and frogs' (*Essays* XLVI, 97–8).

Bacon had nothing to say on the matter of what to do with medieval churches, although where a Tudor or Jacobean hall was erected this was often an issue that had to be faced. In the case of the palace at Nonsuch *Sr*, begun in 1538 by Henry VIII and completed after the king's death by the earl of Arundel, an entire village and its church were erased from the map in order to make way for the new work. Excavation in 1959 disclosed remains of the church within the inner courtyard, and a Tudor fountain in the middle of the former chancel (*Medieval Archaeology* 4 (1960), 143, 151–2).

Elsewhere, at first, the solution was usually less drastic, and the handling uncertain. At Holdenby *Np* the church of All Saints came to be incorporated within the terraced formal gardens that were attached to Holdenby Hall. This remarkable building was commissioned by Sir Christopher Hatton, who was appointed Lord Chancellor in 1547 and became a leading favourite of Elizabeth I. Holdenby was laid out on an imperial scale which presumably reflected the size of Gloriana's court on progress rather than the population of Sir Christopher Hatton's household. A village was cleared away in the process. Hatton's 'prodigy house' was destroyed during the Civil War. Some screenwork said to have belonged to it is now to be seen in the church (Pevsner and Cherry 1973, 261). Terraces and a rosary, set out in 1579–87, overlooked the old hall, and the church lay on the edge of these, quite at odds with their alignment (Fig. 109). A little later at Barnwell *Np* the parish church was similarly absorbed into the grounds of a great house, although here the outline of the churchyard was more tactfully assimilated to the new design.

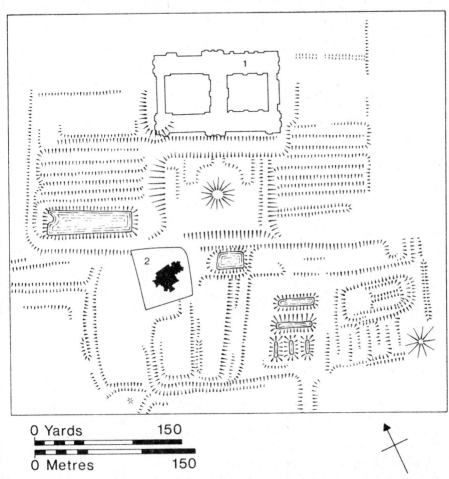

0 Yards 150

0 Metres 150

109 Garden remains at Holdenby, Northamptonshire. The mansion (**1**) was begun by Sir Christopher Hatton in the 1570s. Gardens and terraces were laid out around it, replacing a former village and manor house which stood close to the church (**2**). Hatton's great house passed to the Crown in 1607 and was demolished during the Commonwealth. A later house was built nearby, but this is not shown (*Source*: Royal Commission on the Historical Monuments of England)

Landscapes found a prominent place in the luxuriant writings of sixteenth-century poets. Spenser and Shakespeare invented neighbour-hoods of mixed substance. Rosalind and Orlando played their love game in a Forest of Arden which was part real Warwickshire and part fabulous realm where collective memories could be summoned up:

> They say he is already in the forest of Arden, and many a merry man with him; and there they live like the old Robin Hood of England: they say many young gentlemen flock to him every day, and fleet the time carelessly, as they did in the golden world.
>
> (*As You Like It* I.i)

Arden was a utopian kingdom:

> And this our life, exempt from public haunt,
> Finds tongues in trees, books in the running brooks,
> Sermons in stones, and good in every thing:
> I would not change it.
>
> (II.i)

After the war, utopia changed. Some patrons explored the possibilities of geometrical formalism in the manner of Le Nôtre. Later came the onset of a taste for more 'natural' landscapes, while after about 1750 we en-counter a deepening craving for exotica and dramatic effects. As Britons travelled, traded, collected and fought in different parts of the world, so temples, grottos, obelisks, pyramids, even pagodas began to appear in English parks.

The optimism born of scientific rationalism encouraged pedigreed aristocracy and *nouveau riche* alike to believe that Nature herself was within their grasp. Thus at Rievaulx NY the noble shell of the Cistercian abbey came to be overlooked by a sweeping landscaped lawn in the grounds of Duncombe Park. Later, narrow gaps were left in the planted woodland on the hillside to admit sudden views of the ruins from different angles. 'Nothing can be more truly beautiful than the bird's eye assemblage of objects, which are seen from hence' wrote Arthur Young on a visit in 1768. The scene aroused in him a sense of 'exquisite enjoyment', enhanced by the presence of two temples that faced each other on the terraced escarp-ment, one Doric and the other Ionic. Beyond the 'woody valley' lay an 'old tower' (Helmsley Castle), 'Helmsley church, and the town scattered with clumps of trees', all disposed 'at those points of taste which make one almost think them the effects of design'.

Arthur Young lived in an age which already had some considerable record of achievement in moulding large tracts of landscape to the point at which they could indeed be looked upon as 'effects of design'. Remarkable feats of earthmoving, hydraulic engineering and tree-planting had been performed under the direction of men like William Kent, Bridgeman and Lancelot 'Capability' Brown (1716–83) (Stroud 1975). Brown remodelled some 150 estates during his career. Humphrey

Repton was sixteen years old at the time of Young's visit to Duncombe, and he too was to modify the face of many a parish before his death in 1818. Meanwhile, after *c.* 1725 Georgian men and women of sensibility began to acquire Gothick tastes.

Brown and his contemporaries concentrated upon the creation of idealized natural landscapes. Brown liked to surround the park with a belt of woodland that would exclude the agricultural hinterland but could be interrupted 'to admit any distant prospect or object of pictorial interest' (Hussey 1975, 17). This approach had been tried earlier at Cirencester, and at Holkham *Nf*, where a tall obelisk designed by William Kent in 1729 stood in the grounds from which a number of 'vistas' opened out, one of which led the eye towards the parish church situated on a hill (Cook 1984, 175). Elsewhere lines of sight out of parks led to churches at Trowse *Nf*, and also at Saffron Walden *Ex*, where the steeple makes an effective visual pivot, when viewed across the park from Audley End. Repton's *Red Book* of 1797 for Atcham *Sa* shows a distant spire (Stroud 1962, 107). Wroxeter parish church has no spire today, and it has been wondered if Repton recommended that one be added (Rowley 1972). Views from seats positioned in the grounds of William Shenstone's house The Leasowes *Wo*, near Birmingham, were contrived to include a ruined priory and Halesowen church. At Stowhead House *Wi* the parish church is seen across a lake. A landowner at Tattingstone *Sf* even went so far as to commission a group of labourers' cottages to *resemble* a church (Cook 1984, 183).

A church or monastic ruin as a distant prospect was one thing, but a parish church within the park itself was quite another. Very often the church was close to hand, for reasons that were anticipated in Chapter 6. This could pose problems or offer opportunities. Would the architectural idiom of the church clash with that of the new house? Would it spoil the view? Perhaps it would *improve* the view? If the church was to be retained near the house, would this be inconvenient for the villagers who lived outside the park? And would the hall dwellers welcome villagers walking through their grounds?

In most cases such considerations could be reduced to two areas of decision: where to put the church, and what it should look like. The question of site tended to be answered in one of four ways. The church could be retained close to the house, and perhaps be assimilated to it architecturally. A second solution was to treat the church as something like a piece of ancillary apparatus, grouping it along with stables, dovecot and other subordinate buildings at a respectful distance from the mansion. The third option was to make the church a *point de vue* within the park. The fourth was to remove the church from the vicinity of the house entirely, and to place it towards, on or just beyond the park-edge, thereby rendering it accessible from both private and public directions.

Such manipulations did not always, or even often, involve the physical removal and re-erection of the church. Transfers did take place, as we shall see, but designers of parks would generally take the site of a church as they found it and lay out the grounds with its position in mind.

Mansion and church kept close company most often where the church had originated or was still in some sense regarded as a private chapel. Occasionally, as at Ribston Hall *NY*, the church was completely absorbed into the main façade. At Llanarth *Mon*, where the hall is of *c*. 1820, an earlier church was drawn into close relation with a wing of the new house. More usually, however, the church is to be found detached, but standing in near attendance. Withcote *Le*, where the small and simple church dates from the first half of the sixteenth century, illustrates the type. A panoramic view of Dyrham Park *Gl* by Kip, published in 1712, shows the church tucked in tight beside the house. At Sydmonton *Ha* the church stands on the lawn. Other examples include the medieval grouping of St Stephen and Lympne Castle *K*, and St Brandon and Brancepeth Castle *Du*. At Lilford *Np* there was a church of St Peter that stood next to the hall of 1711, but the church was removed in 1778. Normanton *Ru* possessed a hall and church, but here it was the house that disappeared, after 1945. The setting of the church has been altered again, for the churchyard is now lapped by the waters of a reservoir.

One of the most famous churches in this category is at Staunton Harold *Le*, where the church stands close to Staunton Harold Hall and overlooks an ornamental lake. Here the church of Holy Trinity was built *de novo* to a commission by Sir Robert Shirley in 1653–65. The idiom of the building recollected Gothic achievements, and thereby maintained Anglican values, 'ye best things in ye worst times' as the inscription above the entrance advises, in the face of Commonwealth government.

There is perhaps an intermediate stage between the church that stood adjacent to a great house, and the church that took a position more typical of an ancillary building. In this sub-category we might place the remarkable Palladian church that stands close to Gunton Hall *Nf*. Designed by Robert Adam, built between 1765 and 1769, it looks for all the world like the small Greek temple that it was evidently intended to resemble.

Moving on to consider the second class of site, we find that it was quite common for the church to be located somewhere in the frontier area that intervened between household gardens and park. At Boarstall *Bu* the church is encountered to the east of the mansion, just outside the walled garden. In the same county the chapel at Biddlesden was attached to the stable block. Lullingstone Castle *K* posseses a small church within its immediate grounds; an illustration of the 1670s depicts this building between orchards and formal gardens. At Aspenden Hall *Hrt* the church was on the edge of the garden, with an avenue leading off to the west and an orchard to the south. An engraving of 1721 shows the church of Lulworth *Do* set beside the castle beyond extensive gardens in a churchyard of trapezoidal plan. Fields arranged in four concentric arcs to the south hint at the survival of more ancient arrangements. Cognate relationships can be viewed at Sudbury *Db* and Newton Kyme *NY*. In the latter instance residents of the hall provided themselves with their own entrance to the church, from an enclosed garden, while ordinary parishioners approached along a field path from the south. Castle Ashby *Np* provides one of the best examples in this genre: 'Rarely', wrote Pevsner, 'is a church made so much of the private garden furnishings of a mansion' (1961, 135). Techniques of landscape gardening could affect churches in other ways: at Titchmarsh *Np* the churchyard is enclosed by a ha-ha.

The church as *point de vue* forms what is probably the smallest of the four categories. For sheer effect, few examples can vie with Fawsley *Np*. The church, a former minster, occupies a solitary and prominent position within the parkland of the Jacobean mansion of the Knightley family. The churchyard is enclosed by a ha-ha and overlooks a pair of ornamental lakes. Remains of the village, which was removed to make way for the park, are visible as slight undulations near the church. Inside, the Knightley monuments are of interest not least for the way in which they exemplify the transition from medieval to post-Reformation attitudes towards death and the hereafter. The Knightleys were staunch Puritans. At Patshull *St* the church of St Mary built by James Gibbs in 1743 likewise enjoys a lakeside site. An artificial lake, created in the eighteenth century by the damming of a stream, used to lap the eastern edge of the church-yard at Little Ouseburn *NY* (*YW*). St Margaret in the grounds of Well Hall *Li* was built *de novo* in 1733, and was apparently conceived as part of the overall landscape layout. The church in Euston Park *Sf* was prominent upon a large mound until the building was demolished in the 1920s. At Croome D'Abitot *Wo* the church was repositioned, and rebuilt to an advanced taste in 1763 as part of the sixth earl of Coventry's complex, the work being handled jointly by Robert Adam and Capability Brown. A shift of site was also engineered at Shobdon *He*, although here it was parts of the former Romanesque church that were reassembled as an eyecatcher when the new building was erected in the 1750s. By contrast, the remarkable twelfth-century church of St Michael at Moccas, in the same county (p. 56), was left unmolested when it was absorbed into the park that surrounds Moccas Court.

Nineteenth-century architects and aristocrats rejoiced in parks as much as did their Georgian predecessors. Deane *Ha* and Sherborne *Wa* are cases in point. Parishioners at Privett *Ha*, who until 1876 were accustomed to worship in a small rural church, suddenly found themselves provided with a mighty rebuilding, paid for by Sir William Nicholson. Studley Royal and Skelton-on-Ure, both *NY*, and both built during the 1870s by the architect Burges, are other lavish examples of the later development of the genre. At Skelton, in addition, we encounter a rare case of the church being shifted from a village *into* a park, from the edge of the village of Skelton a short distance into the grounds of Newby Hall. The result is a building of exceptionally ornamental aspect, commissioned by Lady Mary Vyner as a memorial to her luckless son who was killed by Greek brigands.

Lastly, we come to the widespread phenomenon of the park-edge church. Perimeter sites suited parishioners, and they helped to secure the privacy of the park. There were two ways of achieving this solution. The first was to move the church and, if necessary, the village, to a new site. Such relocations took place at Colwick *Nt*, Colston Bassett *Nt*, Madresfield *Wo* and elsewhere. Often there is a ruined church in the grounds of the house to tell the tale, as at Ettington *Wa* and Woodchester *Gl*, or Birdsall *NY* (*YE*) where the remains of the old church stand close to the house. The second method was to plot out the limits of the park so that they fell just short of the village, and the church with it. Wollaton Hall *Nt*, for instance, possessed a great garden, a zone of pasture all enclosed by a brick wall some seven miles in circumference, and then came the church and other houses beyond trees. The village and church occupy a hill. It was unnecessary to disturb them, not least because the village housed the colliers who provided the wealth that built the hall and sustained its residents. Another sequence of gardens, outer ring of pasture and church was contrived at Bifrons *K*, where much of the church (of Patrixbourne) dates from the seventeenth century. An engraving of the 1720s shows the church at Tankersley *WY* exactly on the edge of the park, the pale forming the western boundary of the churchyard. Avington *Ha*, Wistow *Le* and Forcett *NY* are further examples. A full list would be very long.

As to appearance, it will already have been noted that the proximity of a great house could place a church in the way of men and women possessed of fashionable taste, and wealth with which to exercise it. The church of St Peter, Broughton *St*, stands opposite the Elizabethan hall, and was rebuilt in 1630. The church at Ingestre *St* originated as the chapel to the hall, being built to design by Sir Christopher Wren in 1676. On the fringe of Allerton Park *NY* there is the church of St Martin, which was rebuilt in a cool, Italianate–Romanesque idiom in 1745. (Beneath it have been found remains of a predecessor dating from around 1100 (L. Butler 1978).) Slightly later in date is the sumptuous baroque church of St Michael, Great Witley *Wo*, once attached to the house, inside the park created by the Foley family, gardens hard by, the whole essentially Mediterranean in mood. Of the churches mentioned in this chapter, more than three-quarters of them were either built, rebuilt or substantially remodelled in the period *c.* 1650–1850. A distinction was sometimes kept between the external appearance of a church and the furnishing and fittings of the interior. In 1662 Sir Francis Burdett commissioned a church inside the park of Foremark Hall. Gothic without, it was fitted out in Renaissance style. Most of his original furnishings can still be seen. West Ogwell *D* is still essentially medieval in fabric, although box pews, benches and a plaster vault were installed early in the nineteenth century, following the rebuilding of the Manor House in 1790.

It was natural enough for churches in parks to acquire, or perpetuate, a further role, as burial places for the families that lived nearby. Many

English churches, by no means all in parks, contain galleries of memorials to members of these local dynasties. One thinks of the de Pols at Snarford *Li*, or those members of the Fettiplace family who lounge in their niches at Swinbrook *O*. Edenham *Li* has a chancel lined with plaques and monuments to the Berties, some of them represented in effigy wearing senatorial garb. The church at Little Gaddesden *Hrt* had to be enlarged in order to accommodate monuments of the Bridgewater family.

It was open to park-owners to go a stage beyond the use of the parish church by commissioning new mausolea. Sometimes these structures were built in the churchyard, as at Buckminster *Le* and Hovingham *NY*, but many were placed in the park, often on a knoll or the crest of a scarp. There were practical as well as aesthetic reasons for this. A new mausoleum could be capacious in a way which the parish church and its cemetery, both now choked with the bones of a millennium, were not.

Examples are legion, and types diverse. Undoubtedly one of the most remarkable is in the grounds at Castle Howard *NY*. This takes the form of a giant rotunda placed upon an extended platform. Nicholas Hawksmoor designed it, and it was eleven years abuilding. The rotunda form was also chosen at Brocklesby Park *Li*, and there is a small but elegant Palladian specimen in the corner of the churchyard at Little Ouseburn *NY*. The church at Gibside *Du* originated as a mausoleum of 1760 in the park of Gibside House. Great Packington *Wa* originated in a similar way in 1790. Ayot St Lawrence *Hrt* saw the erection of a completely new church in 1778–9. The body of this building is on the lines of a Greek temple, with slender porticus-like adjuncts towards the east end, but it is flanked by two detached mausolea and linked to them by colonnaded wings. All this was conceived within the context of the park, and could be seen from Ayot House (Curl 1980, 181–2).

The great parks were the ultimate form of enclosure: total, self-absorbed. Even today the visitor to a parkland church such as Scrofton *Nt*, Prestwold *Le* or Gate Burton *Li* may feel like an intruder who trespasses onto private property. Part of the original price of such privacy was sometimes the destruction of a village. Apart from examples given, typical displacements of villages for park-making purposes took place at Chillington *St* in the 1760s, and at Shugborough, in the same county, where a start was made on the demolition of houses from 1737 in order to improve the view of Thomas Anson (Palliser 1976, 136). Such clearances could leave the church stranded in the new park, far from the dwellings of parishioners. This is what happened at Edenhall *Cu*. The making of Vanbrugh's great mansion at Castle Howard *NY* involved the destruction of the village *and* church of Hinderskelfe in the first years of the eighteenth century (Barley 1978).

Harewood *WY* provides a well-documented episode. The present village is a replanning of 1760 and occupies the site of the decayed medieval borough. The church was left behind, close to the edge of the park which covered some 2000 acres (809 ha). The medieval village was in the vicinity of the church, and had grown to some importance in the early 1700s on account of the turnpike roads that intersected nearby. The first earl Lascelles commissioned the park. Capability Brown dealt with the landscaping. John Carr designed the new village. The Lascelles were thrifty in their treatment of the church: the east end and west façade that faced the lines of approach were modernized, but the sides were left untouched. Harewood church has yielded pre-Conquest sculpture and represents a still point in a landscape otherwise changed out of all recognition.

Nuneham Courteney *O* provides another instance of enforced depopulation, accompanied by the building of a new planned settlement. Here the model village dates from 1760, and 'Athenian' Stuart contributed a church of 'garden temple' type within Nuneham Park. The partial or total erasure of villages in the cause of park-making was widespread in the later eighteenth and nineteenth centuries. In one county alone (Northamptonshire) it has been estimated that eight villages were completely removed, and at least twenty-five villages underwent significant alteration as a result of emparking (C.C.Taylor 1983, 211). Oliver Goldsmith's (1728–74) poem *The Deserted Village* dealt with such an episode:

> Ye friends to truth, ye statesmen who survey
> The rich man's joy increase, the poor's decay,
> 'Tis yours to judge, how wide the limits stand
> Between a splendid and an happy land.

Goldsmith lamented the destruction of a way of life, the unbalancing of the dynamics of a rural community when 'One only master grasps the whole domain'. Nevertheless, big houses with their gardens and estates provided some jobs. It was not unusual for peripheral settlements to be established for the housing of those who worked on the estate. Coneysthorpe near Castle Howard *NY* is such a place. It is an example of total planning. There is a pleasant sloping rectangular green, with ordered rows of cottages on three sides and a small church at the head. The church looks like a product of the Georgian era, but in fact dates from the 1830s. As one leaves Coneysthorpe the great house looms along the ridge to the south. The class structure of the neighbourhood is embodied in the relative distribution of settlement. Could an awareness of class have played some part in the slight distancing of church from mansion that sometimes occurs, perhaps especially in those instances where the church is grouped with buildings used by servants? Parish priests of the eighteenth century belonged for the most part to the lower strata of the Establishment, and chaplains on country estates were commonly looked upon as menials.

Country clergy in this period were also renowned for pluralism and its concomitant, absenteeism. It would be wrong to seek to explain pluralism simply in terms of clerical self-interest. Variability of income forced some members of the clergy to seek additional livings, and residence within a parish could be difficult if there was no parsonage house in which to live. But whatever the reasons, the problem was large. In 1812 it was discovered that approaching 60 per cent of rural incumbents were not resident in their parishes. Of those who were, not all had been attending to their duties:

> loose in morals, and in manners vain,
> In conversation frivolous, in dress
> Extreme, at once rapacious and profuse;
> Frequent in park with lady at his side,
> Ambling and prattling scandal as he goes;
> But rare at home, and never at his books
> Or with his pen, save when he scrawls a card

wrote Cowper of an un-named cleric. Of course, diligent parsons did labour in their parishes, and no doubt attracted less attention than those who neglected them. But the period of Whig ascendancy can scarcely be characterized as a time of pastoral dynamism or theological achievement as far as the Church of England was concerned. Full members of the establishment may have been less worried by the social inferiority of the parish clergy who served them than by the tedium of their book-bound sermons.

Yet all of this is a narrow picture. While lords and squires tended their estates, snoozed in their pews, and Anglican clergy engaged in worldly pursuits, wrote novels, studied botany, investigated antiquities or simply got on with their parochial duties, different strains of dissent were gathering strength among the poor that would soon threaten to pull down from below much of the structure of established religion. Not for the first time, spiritual life was to be galvanized by those with little, or less: farm labourers, pedlars, miners, workers in the new factories and mills of the Industrial Revolution, and the unemployed. In the eighteenth century, wealth, and inertia, dominated a parochial geography which was still essentially medieval in its configuration. In what follows, much may be traced to the actions of those who lived beyond the pale.

XI

THE INWARD
WITNESS

In 1801 the population of England and Wales stood at 9.06 million. And it was rising fast. The population had all but doubled during the eighteenth century, and such was the rate of acceleration that its increase in just the first two decades of the nineteenth century would exceed the total number of inhabitants who had been living early in the twelfth century when the parochial system was being laid down. Yet in spite of this growth the number of places of worship which belonged to the established Church had hardly risen at all. In some areas there were actually fewer parish churches in 1800 than had been standing five or six hundred years before.

At the start of the nineteenth century churchmen were therefore beset by a crisis. That this was so was not entirely due to lethargy on the part of their predecessors. The problem of underprovision had been recognized in London a century before, and efforts to build more churches had been made. The results fell short of what was hoped for, but the issue had at least been addressed (p. 411). Away from the capital the eighteenth century was fairly well advanced before the need for a substantial increase in provision was perceived. In most areas the stock of medieval parish churches was still sufficient, and in many it was to remain so. Early in the fourteenth century the parish churches of England and Wales had for the most part been sufficient in number and in size to serve a population in excess of four and perhaps approaching six million. The latter figure was not reached again until after 1700. Even then, for a time, the position did not look too bad. But by the 1760s the increasing pace of industrialization and of population growth were beginning to place stresses on the parochial system that had never been foreseen.

To depict the crisis of the early nineteenth century purely as the consequence of a rising population would be too simple. Its causes were more
various than that. Nevertheless, the figures were alarming enough, and
they helped to bring questions of social attitude and spirituality to a sharp
focus. In this respect the basic difficulty lay less in the gross increase of
population than in the alterations which were taking place in its distribution and social composition. The pattern of parish churches had not been
much altered since the late twelfth century, when about 90 per cent of the
population lived in the countryside and laboured in an economy which
was largely agrarian. The average ratio of churches to parishioners is then
likely to have been of the order 1 : 300 × 400. By 1801 the national average
ratio was close upon 1 : 800. Thirty per cent of the population now lived
in towns, and 11 per cent resided in smoky cities of more than 100,000
people, most of whom were employed in manufacturing. Urbanism was
changing in emphasis. Places like Liverpool, Birmingham and Manchester, which had scarcely been more than large villages at the end of the
Middle Ages, were now large cities growing larger. By contrast, most of
the provincial cities which had flourished before the Conquest had not
grown to anything like the same extent. But it was in such ancient towns
as Exeter, Norwich and York that most of the urban churches were still
to be found. York entered the nineteenth century with a population of
fewer than 30,000 and twenty-three churches. Liverpool, with over a
quarter of a million inhabitants, had eight churches. Or to take another
case, thirteenth-century Winchester had accumulated more parish
churches than any other English city apart from Norwich and London. In
1851 Winchester was not even among the sixty-five most populous towns
which were identified by the census for that year. Yet nine of Winchester's
churches remained in use. Meanwhile, eight out of the sixty-five large
towns had more than 8000 inhabitants to every Anglican place of worship.
Wigan *La* had one church for 10,657 people (Coleman 1980, 28–9, 41). Even
in fashionable Brighton the Anglican churches could accommodate only
20.6 per cent of the population (Hennock 1981, 1973).

In the Middle Ages the parochial boat had been loaded with reasonable
evenness. By 1800 not only was the cargo three times as heavy, and becoming more leaden by the year, but it had also shifted to an extent which
threatened to cause the vessel to capsize. Linked with this were problems
that arose from inequalities in the size and staffing of parishes. In southern
counties parish areas averaged 2500 acres (1012 ha) or less. In parts of the
west and north, and especially in upland regions, areas in excess of 10,000
acres (4047 ha) were not unusual (Coleman 1980, 10–11; cf. Currie *et al.*
1977, 59). The parish of Kendal sprawled across half of the Lake District.
In the 1740s the vicar of Halifax *WY* was attempting to minister to a
population of nearly 28,000 in a parish of 124 square miles. These are extreme cases, but the poor value of many northern livings, the practical
difficulties of exercising pastoral care within them, and their remoteness
from centres of social life and intellectual activity, all combined to render

them unattractive to educated churchmen with their minds set on preferment (Coleman 1980, 11). The Industrial Revolution made a poor situation
worse because most of the new cities that it spawned lay in the very outlying dioceses where the parish system was weak.

Parishes were also resistant to change. Until the Church Building Act
of 1818 it mattered not whether parochial coverage was good or ineffectual:
a parish could only be divided by statute, and for the construction of a new
church it was normally necessary to obtain an Act of Parliament. This
obstacle was not entirely cleared away until the mid-nineteenth century.
Apart from the expense and tedium of such formalities, and the labour of
raising funds with which to build, there were also long-term financial implications. New churches required clergy, and incomes which would be
adequate to secure the future of the livings. In an age when non-residence
and pluralism were widespread these aims were often difficult to achieve
in the face of vested interests. A questionnaire which was circulated in the
diocese of Norwich in 1784 disclosed that only 128 of the responding incumbents were resident in their benefices. In 285 of the remaining cases
the cure was served by a curate, although 78 per cent of these men served
more than one parish (Jacob 1979, 322). Since pluralism was rife, and the
poverty of many livings was one of its causes, the creation of new parishes
called for additional resources and might harm the finances of parishes
that already existed. Pew-rents made matters worse. It was common for
most or even all of the seats in a church to be rented. Where this system
was practised its beneficiaries might hasten to oppose any scheme for a
new church which threatened to encroach upon their revenues (Port
1961, 5).

While demographic change and inertia acted to handicap the Established Church, nonconformist denominations were gaining ground. Until the
1730s the Dissenters' challenge had seemed to be containable. The Toleration Act of 1689 and further measures of relaxation that followed had not
led to any sudden upsurge of nonconformity. This was the age of the Old
Dissent: congregations of Independents, Baptists and Quakers, active
since the later sixteenth and seventeenth centuries, and the Presbyterians
who had their background in the Puritan wing of the Church of England,
from which they were excluded by the Act of Uniformity in 1662. Exact
figures for the membership of these groups are not available, but a survey
carried out between 1715 and 1718 reveals the approximate number of
dissenting congregations in England and Wales to have been 1934, and
their supporters as around 6.18 per cent of the total population. By 1800
this had changed. Dissenters' places of meeting now numbered 3701, and
those who attended them were becoming increasingly numerous (Fig. 110).

Much of the increase was due to the impact of the New Dissent. This
derived from the spread and interaction of evangelical ideas which
emanated from sources as widely separated as New Brunswick and
Massachusetts in America, the Herrnhut community in Saxony and

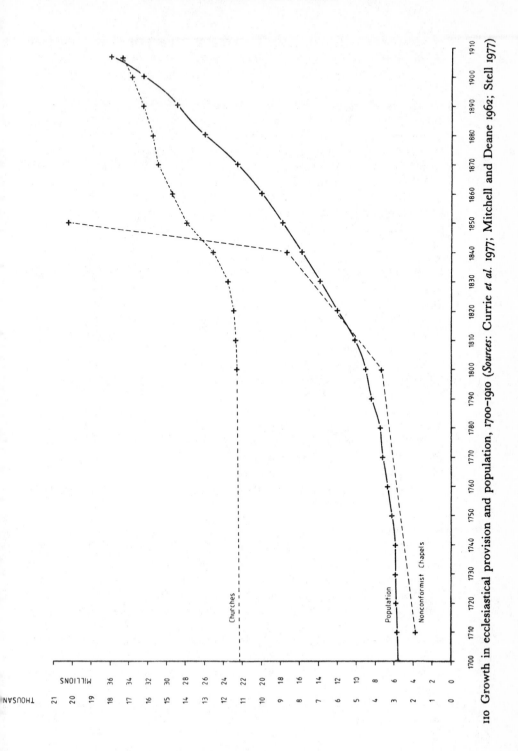

110 Growth in ecclesiastical provision and population, 1700–1910 (*Sources*: Currie *et al.* 1977; Mitchell and Deane 1962; Stell 1977)

revivalism in Wales (Watts 1978, 395-7). Preachers like Howell Harris (1714-73), and clergymen such as George Whitefield (1714-70) and John Wesley (1703-91), embarked upon energetic itinerant ministries which not only attracted members of the Anglican Church, but also helped to reactivate and transform some of the older traditions, and in due course to release the energies of Primitive Methodism.

Denominations born of the New Dissent soon began to acquire buildings of their own, but itinerancy was a lasting and renewable strength which made for success in just the area where the Church of England was most vulnerable. Dissenters were not fettered by the immobility of the parish system. Meeting-houses could be opened and, if necessary, discarded, more or less at will. Methodist preachers ranged freely across the landscape. Houses, halls or churches could be borrowed to proclaim the word. If these were denied, or were too small to contain the hearers, preaching and devotion took place in the open air. 'The world is my parish,' said Wesley, and the total distance of the preaching journeys he made between 1739 and 1791 could have taken him close on five times around it. Whitefield's ministry lasted for more than thirty years, during which time he roamed widely through England, Scotland and Wales, and made thirteen crossings of the Atlantic. In 1747 Harris noted in his journal that he had just covered 600 miles in thirty-three days, visiting parts of five counties in Wales and travelling the west of England 'through Bristol, Bath, Exeter, Plymouth Dock, and Cornwall, and came home at two in the morning last Sunday after travelling last week about 250 miles' (cited in Watts 1978, 397). Senior churchmen viewed such performances with suspicion, for in cultivated Georgian circles 'enthusiasm' was thought of as a form of character-defect.

This, then, was the position which had been reached on the threshold of the Victorian age: strengthening nonconformity and an Established Church which was awakening to the need for reform. Great changes in ecclesiastical geography were about to occur. In order to place these developments in context, however, it is necessary to examine some of the events of the seventeenth and eighteenth centuries in more detail.

The Old Dissent had no single tap-root, and no individual stem. It was rather a kind of bulb, a store or gathering of ideas, attitudes and precepts, accumulated from home and abroad over several centuries, that put forth its first recognizable shoots in the Elizabethan age and bushed out after the Restoration. The Elizabethan Church contained 'a religious subculture of committed rather than merely formal and conventional protestantism which, if not separated, was distinct and, in the language of the age, "singular"' (Collinson 1984, 19). Before this there had been the Kentish conventiclers who preached predestinarian views; figures like the Essex curate Richard Fox who in the 1520s was teaching that 'the sacrament of the altar is not the body of Christ, but done for a remembrance of Christ's passion'; or Thomas Bilney, the Cambridge evangelist who was described by John Foxe as being 'greatly inflamed with the love of true religion' and animated by a desire 'to allure others to the same' (Watts 1978, 9–11; Collinson 1984, 12). And back in the later fourteenth century there had been John Wyclif, testing the ice of eucharistic doctrine and papal authority (Kenny 1985). Hence, while most of the food in the English separatist bulb was derived from continental Calvinism, there were crucial trace-elements which came from native soil.

Among Dissenters the potential for ideological fission was present from the outset – whenever we take that to have been – but the inclusiveness of the Elizabethan Church, events of the Jacobean decades and the Civil War helped to delay the emergence of self-conscious denominational identities. After 1662 four main groupings can be recognized: the Baptists, Quakers, Congregationalists and Presbyterians.

There were two groups of Baptists, the Particular and the General. Although united by a belief in the need for freedom of conscience, religious liberty and the exercise of choice through adult baptism, they were divided by theological differences and had their origins in different movements. The Particular Baptists were strongly Calvinist. Their beginnings are found in Jacobite Presbyterianism. Their main enclaves lay in Montgomeryshire, Monmouthshire and Bedfordshire, with slightly lesser support in some adjoining counties. The General Baptists were thinly spread, with a negligible following west of a meridian that can be imagined from the Isle of Wight to Sheffield. Most of their support lay in Lincolnshire, Cambridgeshire, Buckinghamshire, Kent and Sussex: a pattern which reinforces the thesis that they were heirs to a continuing radical tradition which reached back to fifteenth-century Lollardy (Watts 1978, 283).

The ministry of George Fox, begun in 1647, was to take him 'five times round England, to Wales, Scotland, Ireland, the Netherlands, Germany, and America, and to nine different prisons' (Watts 1978, 194). Quakers, so called for the trembling, fits, 'groans, sighs, and tears' which attended their early meetings, were never numerous. Such heartlands as they had lay in and around the Lake District (where Fox encountered groups of cognate type known as Seekers), London and a penumbra of counties to its north, and Bristol. However, what the Quakers lacked in numerical strength they made up for in organizational skill and enthusiasm. By 1700 'they had more particular meetings and were more evenly distributed over the country than any of the other Dissenting denominations. Of the five major Groups of Dissenters only the Quakers had meetings in every English county' (Watts 1978, 285).

Areas where radical Puritanism had been strong in the Elizabethan period and during the Civil War fostered Congregationalism and Presbyterianism. The former laid stress upon the sovereignty of individual congregations. Being democratic they also came to be regarded as potentially subversive. Their main strength lay in mid- and south Wales, Northamptonshire, Hertfordshire and Essex. Strongest by far were the Presbyterians. At the start of the eighteenth century

393

Presbyterianism flourished most in the south-west (Somerset, Dorset and Devon), Carmarthenshire, the north-west (Cheshire, Lancashire and Cumberland), and in Northumberland. Support was also good in and around the southern Pennines, Berkshire and in Essex. Watts suggests that this pattern can usually be explained

> by one or more of four factors, which themselves were often inter-related: a Puritan tradition going back well before the Civil War; the presence either of a large number, or of particularly energetic, ejected ministers after 1662; deficiencies in the parochial organization of the Church of England; and the existence of a large population which earned its living by trade or by manufacture, especially of textiles.
>
> (1978, 271)

The Presbyterian enclaves in Devon and the north-west derived strength from Puritan groups which had been given tacit encouragement during the reign of Elizabeth in order to counteract the continuing in-fluence of Roman Catholicism. After the expulsion of the 2000 ministers in 1662, a number took sections of their Anglican congregations with them. Others exploited voids and weaknesses in the parish system, either by gravitating to expanding towns like Liverpool and Manchester where Anglican provision was becoming increasingly inadequate, or by laying claim to the territories, and not infrequently the buildings, of chapelries which were either moribund or so seldom served as to be beyond the effec-tive control of Anglican clergy. Thus at Charlesworth *Db* the medieval chapel of St Mary Magdalene which had fallen into ruin by *c.* 1625 was oc-cupied by a Presbyterian congregation in the later seventeenth century. Between 1660 and 1690 more than twenty former chapels in Lancashire and the West Riding of Yorkshire were kept in use by Presbyterian ministers. In 1679 a dispute arose at Idle *WY* between those users of its chapel who wished to secede to Presbyterianism and others who chose to remain as Anglicans. The Anglicans retained possession, but the episode illustrates the ease with which a chapel might enter upon a crisis of iden-tity in the later seventeenth century. Uncertainties of a similar kind some-times surrounded manorial chapels of medieval origin which survived on estates later held by Puritan lords. Such chapels could be transformed into the meeting-places of Dissenters. This happened at Dukinfield *La*. Some magnates continued the tradition of building manorial chapels. At Chow-bent *La* an estate chapel was built in the parish of Lergh in 1645. After the Act of Uniformity in 1662 the chapel remained in Presbyterian hands until 1721, when it was repossessed by the Established Church (Stell 1987). At Bramhope *WY* Robert Dyneley commissioned a chapel in the grounds of his manor house in 1649. It is still there, a precious survival, furnishings intact, although in place of the Dyneley mansion there now stands a hotel. Other chapels which were built at around the same time include Guyhirn *Ca* and Great Houghton *WY*.

The greatest numerical strength of the Old Dissent lay in towns. Figures compiled in 1715-18 indicate that more than 50 per cent of the recorded Presbyterian, Independent and Baptist congregations met in cities, boroughs or market towns (Watts 1978, 285). For comparison, townspeople as a whole are unlikely to have made up more than 20 per cent of the population at this time. Country-dwelling Dissenters had to contend with problems beyond those which faced their urban co-religionists. In areas where Dissenters were few or thinly spread, lack of concentration created practical and economic obstacles to the building of meeting-houses. Fundraising was difficult. Trained ministers were scarce. Village meetings which did become established were vulnerable to demoralization or collapse when prominent members departed or died. Loyalties were tested when Anglican gentry who controlled jobs and tied housing tried to force their employees to conform (Spufford 1974, 304). Communities which were controlled by or relied upon a single landlord could find it harder to found a chapel than those who lived in villages where there was a diversity of employers. Until the mid-nineteenth century there may indeed be a correlation between the presence or absence of chapels and patterns of unconsolidated or consolidated landholding. In 1851 the Religious Census found that 70 per cent of parishes in Kent with subdivided property contained at least one nonconformist chapel, but only 18 per cent of close parishes did so. In Lindsey the figures were 86 per cent and 18 per cent, respectively (Everitt 1972, Table 3; Obelkevich 1976, 10-14). Not all landowners had Anglican sympathies, however, and in some places this influence worked in reverse. The stable block at Raithby Hall *Li*, for instance, has a chapel above. It was built in 1779 by the squire, Robert Brackenby, who was himself an itinerant preacher for a time. At Freeby *Le* a nonconformist meeting existed from the late seventeenth century, 'apparently with the support of Sir John Hartopp of Stoke Newington who possessed an estate at Freeby' (Stell 1986, 120-1). At a slightly later date this group shared a minister with Melton Mowbray, and it may be that villages within travelling distance of towns were sooner able to sustain chapels than their more isolated counterparts.

Rural meetings which did not lose heart or succumb to hostile pressures sometimes developed into district or even sub-regional centres which served many surrounding townships. This can be seen at Rothwell *Np*, where a Congregationalist nucleus which originated c. 1655 built a chapel in 1676 that drew members from more than sixteen places. A new chapel, later extended, was opened in 1735 (Watts 1978, 287; Stell 1986, 146-7). The generous layout of this building may be a reflection of the need to cater for people who came in from far afield. The Baptist chapel at Arnesby *Le* fulfilled a similar function. The first building on this site was erected in 1702 and drew a congregation from at least thirty-five townships (Stell 1986, 118; Watts 1978, 287-8). Fenstanton *Ca* (*Hnt*) was another of these 'dissenting minsters'. Together with the itinerant ministers who worked out of nonconformist centres in cities and market towns they are reminiscent of the pastoral structure of eighth-century England.

Sites for buildings were acquired in various ways: by gift, bequest, like the land which Samuel Lucas left to the Friends at Ettington *Wa* in 1681 (Stell 1986, 233), or through purchase. Purchase seems to have been common and could concern an empty plot or an existing property. Congregations of the Old Dissent often bought domestic or agricultural buildings and modified them for religious use. The Independent chapel at Walpole *Sf* was formed from the amalgamation of two houses in 1647. Towards the end of the seventeenth century the Baptists in Tewkesbury took over a timber-framed building of *c.* 1500 and turned it into a chapel. A new house was registered for use as a Congregationalist meeting-house at Kingswood *Gl* in 1702. Many of the earliest surviving meeting-houses of the Friends either resemble domestic buildings (e.g. Come to Good *Co* (1710), Rawdon *WY* (1697)) or actually began as such. Examples in the second category include Broad Camden *Gl*, where a group of Friends purchased 'two bays of housing' and an orchard in 1663; Amersham *Bu*, the result of a bequest; Almley *He*, a half-timbered structure which was bought *c.* 1672; Woburn Sands *Bu*, acquired in 1672; The Blue Idol, Thakeham *Sx*, which was converted from a farmhouse of *c.* 1560; Stourbridge *Wo* (1680), and a number of others (Southall 1974).

There was a close correspondence between local traditions of domestic building and the layout of meeting-houses. In his study of Quaker meeting-houses in the Lake District, David Butler observes that

> In their internal plan size over half of the rural meeting-houses of before 1800 fall within the customary two bays of traditional building, sixteen feet by thirty or thereabouts. Of the remainder some are the same width but longer, up to fifty-six feet, whilst others are anything up to twenty-four feet wide. There is a clear geographical basis for these two tendencies: length is found in the north, width in the south. This observation agrees with the typical form taken by farm building in the corresponding districts. The long narrow meeting-houses of Cumberland are found where the traditional 'long-house' plan predominated with house, barn and outbuildings in line under one straight roof. In north Lancashire there is evidence of the more complex 'double-pile' plans and wider buildings from the early seventeenth century, giving buildings of the same proportions as we find in the meeting-houses there.
>
> (Butler 1978, viii)

Almost from the outset the Friends insisted upon having their own burial grounds. These could also be used as places of meeting. At Colthouse and Ulpha Bridge *Cu* the enclosing walls had inwardly projecting stones for use as seats (Butler 1978, iii). There is a similar arrangement at Idle *WY*. In 1676 a Baptist congregation in Amersham *Bu*, then accustomed to meet in a private house, bought land for use as a cemetery. When the use of the house was lost a meeting-house was erected on the burial ground. The meeting-house opened at Settle *NY* (*YW*) in 1678 was in a burial ground, formerly a pig yard.

Chapels and meeting-houses that were built from scratch often occupied secluded sites (Fig. III). Plots in the rearward parts of burgages, orchards or adjoining yards behind larger buildings were typical positions. Burgage plots, though narrow, were usually deep, and this could lead to the placing of a chapel at some distance from the street. Keach's meeting-house in Winslow *Bu*, a General Baptist building of 1695, is found behind other property near the cattle market. In 1696-7 the Friends of Chesterfield *Db* erected a meeting-house at Saltergate which occupied the end of a croft behind a house. The Friends' meeting-house at Monyash *Db* is similarly retiring. Ancillary buildings often stood within the curtilages of houses, and these too were sometimes put to use. Thus in 1674 John Halford, who resided in the manor house at Armscote *Wa*, made over a barn for use by the Friends (Stell 1986). Other examples of reclusive siting are the Baptist chapel at Upton-on-Severn *Wo*, the Old Street Congregational Chapel at Ludlow *Sa* and the Friends' meeting-house at Crawshawbooth *La*.

Anxiety, property values and generosity are among the factors which have been considered as influences upon these choices. Until the Riot Act of 1715, which made the wrecking of meeting-houses a felony, attacks on buildings used by Dissenters constituted a real risk. Where violence had been experienced or was expected there may have been an incentive to transfer meetings from private houses into purpose-built chapels. Persecution varied in its intensity. Many places escaped it. But in some areas, particularly in cities like London, Bristol, York and Norwich, organized attacks on Dissenters' property were common. In December 1681, for instance, an attorney named John Hellier led a mob which damaged four meeting-houses and obliged most of those who attended them to hold secret meetings in the surrounding countryside. Even here they were not safe, and one pursuit ended in two deaths. During the following year there were systematic efforts to search out conventicles in London, and by December 1682 so many of the Quakers of Norwich were in prison that their monthly meeting was held in Norwich gaol (Watts 1978, 254-5). In 1702 a meeting-house in Newcastle-under-J ꞏꞏ *St* was ransacked by a Tory mob, and in 1710 chapels were being put to the torch in places as far apart as London, Bristol, Gainsborough and Walsall. 'Further riots followed the accession of George III when, in 1715, Jacobite mobs marked the Pretender's birthday by wrecking some thirty Dissenting meeting-houses, eleven of them in Staffordshire and six in Lancashire' (Watts 1978, 264). After 1715 compensation was available from the state for the repair of meeting-houses which had been damaged by rioters, as at Halesowen *Wo* where the chapel which was destroyed in 1715 was rebuilt with government help in the following year (Stell 1986, 249). After 1690 the frequency of chapel-wrecking declined. Nevertheless, there were sporadic outbreaks of

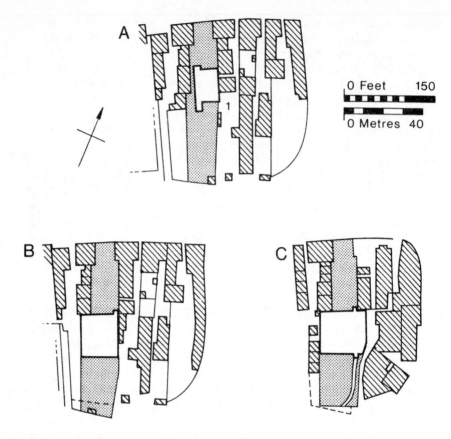

III Siting of Quaker meeting-house at Kendal, Cumbria: **A** 1787; **B** 1833; **C** 1967; **1** tan-yard (*Source*: D.M.Butler 1978)

violence directed at Dissenters' property, and sometimes the Dissenters themselves, until the end of the eighteenth century.

Although a wish to avoid self-advertisement may have been one of the factors which encouraged Dissenters to build on secluded sites, it does not seem likely that it played a decisive part. Regular meetings in private houses soon became common knowledge to neighbours, and the whereabouts of chapels could scarcely have been concealed. Meeting-houses which resembled domestic buildings may have done so primarily not because they were camouflaged, but because they were built by local tradesmen who worked to descriptive commissions that mentioned other buildings in the area. If there was a practical advantage in privacy it probably lay in the reduction of scope for casual acts of vandalism, such as stone-throwing.

Much stronger influences on the positioning of chapels were financial constraints, the limited availability of prime land, and the presence or absence of benefactors. Frontage sites were valuable and hence already likely to be built up. If available, they would be expensive. Back land was cheaper and less encumbered. The location of chapels could also be governed by the willingness of supporters to sell, lease or donate portions of their own holdings as sites. A good illustration of this is provided by the early evolution of the Quaker meeting in York. By 1659 the Friends were gathering in the private house of a prominent tradesman called Edward Nightingale. In 1670-1 Nightingale and eighteen other Friends were heavily fined, and his house on High Ousegate was repeatedly raided during meetings. Despite, or perhaps because of, such harassment, in 1674 several tenements in Far Water Lane that were owned by Nightingale were converted into a meeting-house. In 1688 this building was enlarged, and a nearby mill and stable were modified for use by the Yorkshire Quarterly Meeting. Nightingale also provided land for the first Quaker burial ground in the city. In 1718 a new building, large enough to hold 800-1000 people, was built beside the earlier meeting-house. Around the turn of the nineteenth century the small meeting-house of 1674 was again extended, and in 1816 the large meeting-house of 1718 was demolished and replaced by an even more capacious structure. Further changes followed, so that the meeting-house of 1674 is no longer extant (Willis n.d., 8–9).

What, meanwhile, of the Church of England? The century after the Reformation has often been depicted as a time of architectural lassitude. In their survey of the evolution of parish churches between the seventh and nineteenth centuries, Cox and Ford stated 'There was probably less church building and maintenance carried out during the reign of Elizabeth than for any other half-century.... For the first half of the seventeenth century conditions were much the same' (1941, 63). Today this view seems less than fair. Experiments like Lord Leicester's hilltop church at Denbigh *Pws* (*Dnb*) were rare (Butler 1974) (Figs 112, 113). But few new churches other than chapels and colleges had been founded at any stage since the twelfth century, and in this period of agrarian retrenchment, shrinking villages and underpopulated towns, there was no reason to embark upon a programme of new foundations.

As for repair and rebuilding, there are signs that the amount of work has been underestimated. A recent survey of the churches of south-east Wiltshire concluded that the Reformation 'had little effect on the fabric of the churches' in this area, and found that in the seventeenth century 'enthusiasm for rebuilding and refurbishing churches increased again to such a degree that, as regards fittings at least, it rivalled the generous patronage of the later Middle Ages' (RCHME 1987, 44, 46). Fig. 114 is an attempt to map the main campaigns of English ecclesiastical reconstruction that are known to have taken place in the period *c.* 1540–1699. Quite evidently, a good deal went on. Equally obvious is the impression that it gives of regional variation. There are several possible reasons for this unevenness. First, and most tentatively, there may be correspondence between some of the areas where Congregationalism and

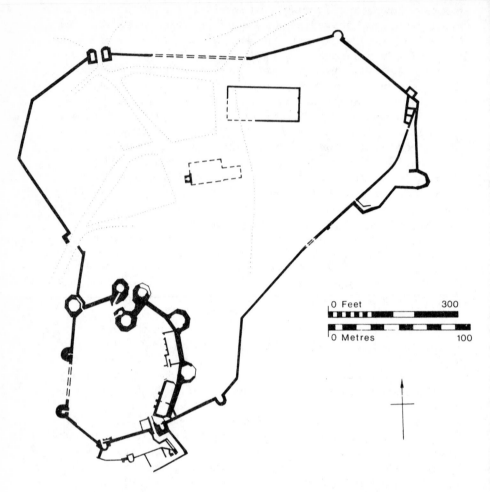

112 Denbigh: location of Lord Leicester's church (*Source*: L.A.S.Butler 1974)

Presbyterianism were later strong, and some of the regions where the level of building activity in the immediately preceding period seems to have been below the average: Northumberland, for instance, or Somerset and Devon. Conversely, there seem to be other areas where the reverse was the case: for example in parts of Cumberland and Lancashire. That might appear to run counter to the idea that Dissent flourished well in districts where the parish system was on its knees. But it should be remembered that until the Restoration Puritanism had hoped to find its expression within the national Church. Until *c.* 1660, therefore, this line of thought is probably best left disregarded. A second factor to be weighed is the extent to which the architectural contributions of the seventeenth century, as of the eighteenth, were purged by further rebuilding at a later date.

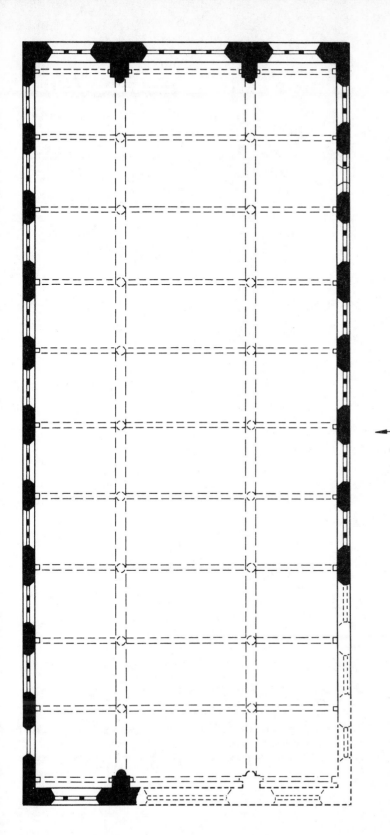

113 Plan of Lord Leicester's church, Denbigh (*Source*: L.A.S.Butler 1974)

0 Feet   30

0 Metres   10

114 Works of churchbuilding, alteration and enlargement, *c.* 1540–1700. Only substantial campaigns (new aisles, naves, towers (indicated by crosses), etc.) are shown; lesser works such as porches, refenestrations, etc. have not been included. Roofs, too, are omitted. The difficulties of dating some work of this period, and of collecting the necessary data, make this map an incomplete statement. It may nevertheless have value as a general impression of the extensiveness of work in a period which has generally been regarded as a time of architectural inactivity

Fig. 114 may be less of a true reflection of Elizabethan and Jacobean enterprise than it is a measure of the success of Victorian efforts to eliminate its traces (p. 435). This applies also to the survival rate of furnishings and fittings (Fig. 115).

The foregoing processes were overlaid upon others that have been mentioned in Chapters 7–9. New building may have been stimulated by a need to remedy earlier neglect, the reduction of buildings which were now too large to be cared for, or the perennial tendency for one parish to imitate the achievements of its neighbour. Conversely, areas like Devon and East Anglia which had seen a high level of building activity in the fifteenth century may have been content to rest on their laurels. Many of their naves (the parts that now mattered most) and towers were reasonably modern, their roofs were new and covered with fresh lead. This cyclical aspect of churchbuilding is an aspect to be stressed. Each region, and many subregions, had cycles of their own. The frequency and amplitude of a cycle would vary according to economic conditions, demographic trends, traditions of building, and the quality and durability of local materials.

Maintenance remained a challenge. The need to keep up with regular programmes of care did not lessen after 1540. The customary division of responsibility for the repair of nave and chancel continued after the Reformation. So did rectorial negligence. Exasperated parishioners pleaded for funds for the repair of chancels from reluctant rectors, or lay impropriators who could be magnates, businessmen, Oxbridge colleges or the Crown itself. At Huddersfield in 1575 the chancel of the parish church was said to be 'out of reparation' so that 'the rain raineth into the church'. The problem here seems to have been more than a leaky roof. Seven years previously the chancel had collapsed, killing the parish clerk. It was asserted that the need for repair had been 'very often presented yet the sworn men say they can never get any amends any way'. The defaulter was Elizabeth I (Purvis 1948, 181). In places where responsibility for the upkeep of a chancel was shared, or kept changing, it could be difficult for the churchwardens to keep track of where the liability lay. This was the problem at Hampton *Wo* in 1668, and also at Great Comberton *Wo* in 1674 and following years. A number of other parishes in the Vale of Evesham experienced related difficulties (Braby 1975, 69–70). Churchwardens' presentments which survive from the seventeenth century in other parts of the country tell of similar episodes, and there has been a tendency to interpret them as symptoms of a general malaise. But were the problems any more widespread than those reported in the records of bishops' visitations in earlier centuries?

The fabrics of naves and towers were maintained with income from church lands, if there were any, and an annual levy which later came to be known as the church rate (Braby 1975, 67–8; Tate 1969, 93–5). Persuading householders to pay the levy was often difficult, and some Dissenters refused on principle. Moreover, the fact that the level of the rate was agreed at the Easter vestry meant that there was a direct link

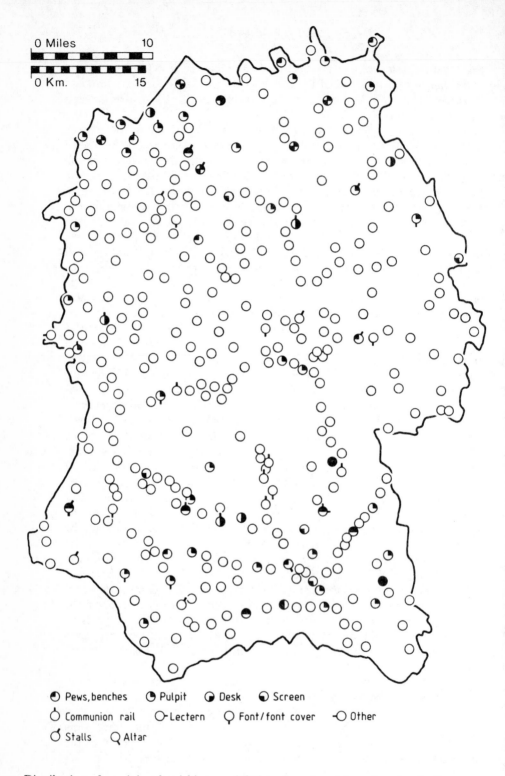

0 Miles 10
0 Km. 15

● Pews, benches ◐ Pulpit ◑ Desk ◐ Screen
◐ Communion rail ○–Lectern ♀ Font/font cover –○ Other
♂ Stalls ♀ Altar

115 Distribution of surviving furnishings and fittings introduced into churches in Dorset
c. 1550–1700 (*Source*: Pevsner)

between the finances of parishioners and the amount of maintenance that could be done. The temptation to defer seemingly trivial works in order to keep the levy down must often have been strong, and many churches slid into decay. In 1702 bishop Nicholson, on tour in his diocese of Carlisle, found the church of St Martin, Brampton *Cu (We)* 'in a slovenly pickle: dark, black, and ill-seated. The Quire is yet more nasty. My Lord Carlile's seats take up more than half of the area' (Cox 1913, 53). When Nicholson visited the church of St Bega at Bassenthwaite *Cu* in the following year he wrote that 'the altar floor is bare [as commonly among these mountains], very uneven and uncomely, cover'd only with a few loose blue slates' (1913, 45). While it is possible that such complaints centred upon what a cultivated man regarded as 'uncomelyness' rather than genuine neglect, other cases leave no doubt that real dereliction affected a significant number of buildings. St Michael at Longtown *Cu* had to be rebuilt in 1609. The church at Bewcastle *Cu (We)* was rebuilt in 1792–3. Kirkoswald *Cu* was semi-ruinous by the early eighteenth century, although here there were special problems because the church had inherited an unusually large chancel after a fleeting existence as a collegiate foundation between 1525 and 1547. St Peter's at Castle Carrock *Cu* was rebuilt in 1888–9 after lengthy neglect and decline into ruin. Rebuilding can, of course, be a sign of parochial vigour, but the fact that some Cumbrian churches had to be reconstructed twice within a relatively short space of time suggests otherwise. Camerton, for instance, was rebuilt in 1694 and again in 1796. The chapel at Raughton Head was reconstructed in 1761, following a previous rebuild in 1678 which had been intended to remedy dereliction. At Thwaite *La* the incumbent reported the roof of his chapel to be in a 'very shaken condition', as indeed was he, having narrowly escaped a blow on the head from a falling slate while officiating at a funeral (Addy 1983, 28).

Carlisle was a poor diocese, and the proportion of its churches which suffered neglect may have been unusually large: though perhaps no more than in parts of dioceses like York, Durham and Chester which covered similar terrain. Yet we have seen that even in prosperous areas the decayed church was no rarity. The condition of a fabric depended as much upon parochial morale, the calibre of churchwardens, the diligence of the incumbent, and the attitude of an impropriator, as upon levels of wealth or the performance of the regional economy. The fifteenth century had been a time of contrasts, an age when some churches were rebuilt and others decayed. There is every reason to think that in many areas this pattern continued through the sixteenth century and into the next. And because, away from court circles, methods and styles of building did not undergo any radical alteration after 1540, it is possible that we have underestimated the extent to which new building went on.

Post-Reformation building is particularly evident in towers (see Fig. 114). The reason may have been functional. Recent study of bell-frames confirms that a technological change in bell-ringing was in progress during the later Middle Ages. In the thirteenth century there was experimentation with methods of swinging, rather than merely tolling or striking, bells. By the fifteenth century more sophisticated bell-frames had been introduced which permitted bells to be rotated through 180 degrees. Half-wheel systems generated more stresses, and where they were adopted steps were often taken to strengthen or rebuild the towers that held them. These developments have been discussed in detail by Andrew Woodger. His survey of medieval parish churches in Huntingdonshire discloses that over *half* of the county's church towers were strengthened, improved or rebuilt in the period *c.* 1500–1700 (Woodger 1984).

An important aspect of Woodger's work lies in his recognition of a stylistic tendency in post-Reformation church architecture which hitherto seems not to have been so clearly perceived. Briefly stated, this involved the revival of motifs and forms which had been popular in the thirteenth and earlier fourteenth centuries. Woodger draws a distinction between this and the more familiar phenomenon of Gothic survival. Gothic survival is taken to be the continued use of late Perpendicular through the Elizabethan and into the Stuart period (cf. Clapham 1953). Examples of churches which are said to contain 'survivalistic' features include Clere *Sf* (the chancel of 1618); Llanfyllin *Pws* (tower, 1706); Dalham and Gislingham *Sf* (towers of 1625 and 1639, respectively); Dursley *Gl* (tower, 1709); Bawtry *SY* (tower, 1712–13); Steane *Np* (1620); Staunton Harold *Le* (1653–65); St John, Briggate, Leeds *WY* (1631); or Broughton *St* (early 1630s). Sometimes Gothic and Renaissance or classicizing features are combined, as at Brightwell *Sf* (restored 1656), or the tower of Leighton Bromswold *Ca* (*Hnt*) (1641), or the earlier case of Risley *Db*, begun in the 1590s. What has been less well appreciated is that builders in the period *c.* 1540–1640 did not always persist with variations on the Perpendicular theme, but looked back to stylistic ideas of earlier centuries as well. Woodger points to churches like Easton, Brington *Hnt* and Tilbrook *Bd* (*Hnt*) where moulding profiles, arches and types of embellishment which had been current in the thirteenth and fourteenth centuries were now revived (1984, 273–5). Woodger coins the name 'Mixed Gothic' for this period of architectural reminiscence. It is 'not of sufficient importance, nor sufficiently readily identifiable, to qualify for the title of a "style" of its own . . . it is more of a method, during a period of uncertainty, when masons were groping for novelty or improvement without seeing clearly the way forward' (1984, 274). And here lies the need for caution. As Woodger reminds us

the masons of the Mixed Gothic period were . . . using exactly the same tools and methods as their medieval predecessors and so, if it is accepted that they were prepared to employ the Decorated and Perpendicular styles (or at least their details) . . . it becomes immediately apparent that it will be extremely difficult to distinguish between work done in the seventeenth century and that of, say, the fifteenth or fourteenth.

(1984, 275)

How many church towers, or porches, or other elements, which hitherto have been assigned to the period *c.* 1300–1500 on the strength of Decorated or Perpendicular detail may in fact have been erected or substantially reworked after 1600?

While it is possible that there has been an underestimation of the extent of rebuilding in the later sixteenth and seventeenth centuries, there can be no doubt that the founding of new churches was at a virtual standstill. It is probable that more old churches were pulled down in this period than new ones established. In some areas this tendency towards net loss was to continue into the eighteenth century. Exceptions were places where the church was repositioned, in some of the coming towns, and London.

London was one place where a serious attempt was made to break away from the medieval pattern and reorganize. The incentive came from two sources. One of them was the dramatic increase in the population of London's suburbs. The other was the Great Fire.

The Great Fire of London burned between 2 and 6 September 1666. Catastrophic as it was, the Fire answered a need. London had become dangerously insanitary. The City was overpopulated, its area crammed with buildings made of inflammable materials that lined streets which were now too narrow to permit the adequate movement of goods. London was fast becoming poisoned by its own filth, and choked by its own density. The Fire provided the opportunity for a fresh start.

At first serious thought was given to a ground plan for the City which would be entirely new. On 8 September spokesmen for the City requested a fresh layout. By 11 September Christopher Wren had produced one, and by 13 September John Evelyn had drawn up another. Further schemes were produced by Robert Hooke, Peter Mills, the City surveyor, and others. But this early enthusiasm did not come to fruition. The task of surveying and valuing all of the *c.* 13,000 holdings which had been destroyed in order to enable an equitable redistribution on a new plan proved to be too much, not least because of the blanket of debris which masked the remains (Reddaway 1940, 62–7). Although steps were taken to widen and improve the surfacing of streets, and to set new standards of construction, the new London was to a large extent an upgraded version of the old.

Wren's projected scheme is nevertheless of the greatest interest. Not only is it one of the most remarkable and tantalizing might-have-beens in the history of city planning, but it gives us a clear insight into the way in which churches could now feature in the imaginings of a designer who was liberated from the constraints imposed by the past. The Wren plan combined gridded and radial elements (Fig. 116). Monotony and rootlessness were avoided by varying the widths of streets, the incorporation of piazzas

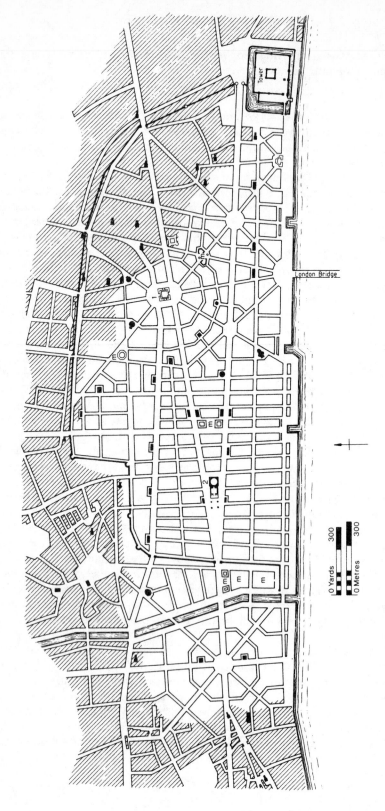

116 Wren's design for a new London, following the fire of 1666. The area affected by the fire is shown free of shading. 1 principal square; 2 cathedral; m = monument (*Source: Parentalia*)

and open areas at points of intersection, and the retention of much of the outline of the old City as a frame (Downes 1982, 50–1). Wren's intentions for London's parish churches display much subtlety. In the first place he proposed to reduce their number, from the eighty-seven which had been burned to around twenty-five. Next, he argued for extra-mural cemeteries, so that the space saved by dispensing with churchyards would enable him to locate the buildings on compact sites adjacent to streets or in the open at points of focus. Just under half of the new churches were to be placed in recesses along the frontages of the two principal trunk roads that he intended to run through the City from east to west. Most of the churches situated on south-facing frontages he envisaged as standing opposite a north–south street: presumably so that the south door of the church would close a minor vista. (This was an effect Wren actually achieved with St James, Piccadilly, where the south door was originally visible from the centre of St James's Square.) Other devices included porticos to be seen at a distance, framed by the sides of buildings which lined the approach; churches visible from two directions along converging streets; and the set-piece location of St Paul's.

None of this was put into effect. Instead, about fifty of the original churches were rebuilt, piecemeal, on their former sites. Rather than grub out old substructures and plan anew, Wren often made use of the old outlines and adapted his designs to fit the sites as he found them (Fig. 117). In this he was to an extent influenced by the wishes of individual parishes: as always, the need for economy loomed large. We therefore find plans wherein medieval irregularities and Wren's preoccupation with geometry occur side by side. Some of the layouts, like the decagonal St Benet Fink, were entirely new, but most of the plan-forms betray a medieval ancestry. Wren's ingenuity in fitting late seventeenth-century superstructures – domes, polygons, ovals, even the curious coffin-shaped St Olave, Old Jewry – onto predetermined outlines is surpassed only by his treatment of the steeples. The main phase of ecclesiastical rebuilding lasted from c. 1670 to c. 1690, with some work continuing through the last decade of the century. But a number of the finest steeples were still to come. Each one is unique. They range from simple early structures like All Hallows the Great (d), through pinnacled towers of greater elaboration like St Mary Aldermary and St Mary Somerset, through to the extraordinary achievements of St Dunstan-in-the-East, St Mary-le-Bow or the sculpted St Vedast. Until the nineteenth century London's skyline was dominated by St Paul's, and lightly afforested with the pinnacles, spikes and spires of Wren's creation.

Post-Fire reconstruction did not answer the need for provision in London's inner suburbs. By 1710 the suburban population of the capital was in the region of 0.4 million, and London as a whole accounted for about 11 per cent of the entire population of England and Wales. Yet London had perhaps 0.6 per cent of the nation's parish churches. In 1709 Jonathan Swift noted that the recent growth of many towns had not been accom-

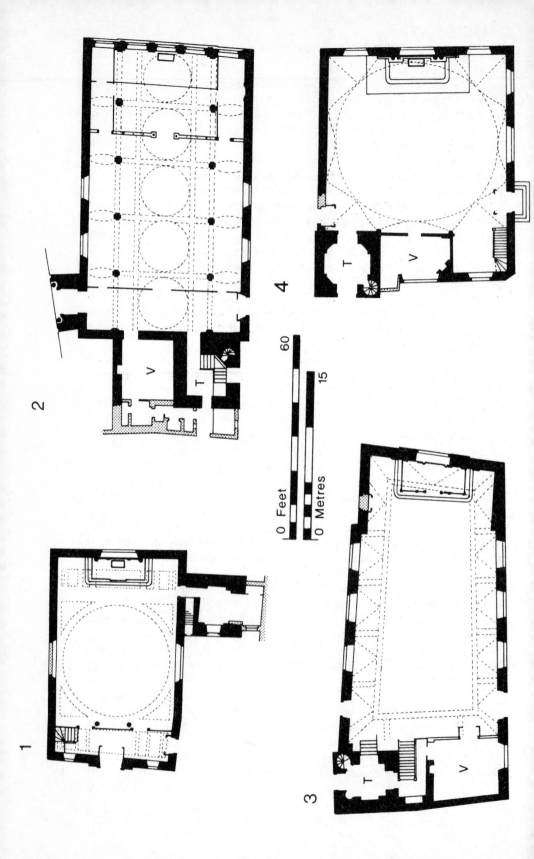

2

1

4

3

0 Feet   60

0 Metres   15

panied by any corresponding increase in the number of churches. In such places he estimated that as many as five people in six were prevented from attending divine service. 'Particularly here in London', he wrote, 'where a single minister, with one or two sorry curates, hath the care sometimes of about twenty thousand souls incumbent on him' (cited in Port 1986, x). Such underprovision aroused fears that the inhabitants of churchless suburbs would be at serious risk from proselytizing by Dissenting ministers and papists. And whereas the Church of England was fettered by the fixedness and vested interest of the parochial system, Dissenters were now at liberty to open chapels and meeting-houses wherever they wished.

Action was called for, and in 1711 Parliament took a hand. A Commission for Building Fifty New Churches was established. The work was to be funded from an additional duty on coals brought into the Port of London.

> The Commissioners received powers to contract for sites for churches, churchyards and parsonage house; to erect churches, and to make chapels into parish churches; ... to treat with patrons of existing parishes; to appoint select vestries for the new churches; and make a perpetual division of parish rates.
>
> (Port 1986, xiv)

The Commissioners were active from 1711 to 1734. By 1715 seven buildings were in hand, of which one, Greenwich, was nearly finished. But by this time the programme was becoming bogged down by financial difficulties. It became clear that the figure of fifty new churches would not be attained. In 1726 it was admitted that

> Expense of building with stone, and purchasing sites is so great, and so far exceeds calculations formerly made, that it will be utterly impracticable to build half the churches first purposed, even employing the whole sum as it now stands. Necessity of having many additional churches about London still continues: several parishes containing 30,000 or 40,000 souls, many at too great a distance from the parish church and having no place to attend divine service, as appears by their repeated applications.
>
> (Port 1986, 135, no. 436)

The achievement of the Commissioners thus fell far short of the ambitions which had been expressed in 1711. By 1733, when the surveyors were discharged, the total of projects stood at nineteen. Of these, one, St Mary Woolnoth, was a rebuilding; two were pre-existing chapels which had been bought; five churches were subsidized from the Commissioners'

117 Plans of four London churches rebuilt by Wren after the fire of 1666: 1 St Mildred Bread Street; 2 St Peter Cornhill; 3 St Stephen Coleman Street; 4 St Mary Abchurch (*Source*: based on plans by the Royal Commission on the Historical Monuments of England)

funds; and eleven were new churches on new sites, built by the Commissioners.

Sir Christopher Wren and Sir John Vanbrugh were elder statesmen of the first Queen Anne Commission. They attended early meetings and urged that due attention should be given to the choosing of appropriate sites. It is interesting to compare their ideas. Wren wanted the new churches to stand in the midst of main thoroughfares. This arrangement had been adopted in some English towns in the eleventh and twelfth centuries (p. 212), and there were precedents like St Clement Danes in London itself. Wren recommended street-sited churches for several reasons. They were convenient for those who wished to arrive and depart by carriage. The frontages of principal streets were valuable, and this would ensure that the church would be surrounded by 'better Inhabitants'. Churches in insular locations would be removed from the reach of fire. Economy, too, was in his mind. A street-island site would mean that the ends, rather than the sides, of the building would be conspicuous. There would thus be no call for extravagant display on the long elevations. The main emphasis would be on the western portico, and there ought to be a steeple 'rising in good Proportion above the neighbouring houses' (Wren 1750, 318-21). Wren realized that his proposals would mean the abandonment of two long-held traditions: east-west orientation, and a churchyard for burials. In the event, the Commissioners remained conservative on both points.

Vanbrugh's ideas were more ambitious. He argued that the new churches should be monuments of national status. They should not be hemmed in by other buildings, but stand free in dignified positions which would ennoble the City. Each church should have a prominent steeple. Central to Vanbrugh's thinking was the theory that the religious feelings of ordinary people are increased by 'the contemplation of ... magnificence' (Port 1986, xxi). The notion that great architecture has an improving effect upon its spectators remained current throughout the eighteenth century and was to play a part in some of the theorizing that accompanied the Gothic Revival. Vanbrugh may have been influenced in his views by Nicholas Hawksmoor (Downes 1977, 257-8). At all events, as the Commissioners' longest-serving surveyor (1711-33) Hawksmoor was directly responsible for the building of five new churches, together with two modified, four built in collaboration with others (three with John James, one with Thomas Archer), and the completion of St Michael Cornhill. Hawksmoor's own projects – Christ Church Spitalfields, St Alphege Greenwich, St Anne Limehouse, St George Bloomsbury and St George-in-the-East – come close to Vanbrugh's ideal of buildings with an inspirational presence.

The criteria and policies which the Commissioners applied to the selection of sites for their new churches were formulated at an early stage. Neighbourhoods which could qualify for a new church were identified according to an ingenious rule of thumb. Henry Godolphin, dean of St

Paul's, noted that in the City, where one church might serve two or even three former parishes, burials seldom exceeded 200 per annum. In some of the suburbs figures of 350 or even 400 were being reached. A formula was adopted which allocated one new church for every 250–300 funerals.

Sites for churches were to be agreed upon before new parishes were formed. Where possible, the situations of the churches should be insular. The Commissioners were strict about orientation. They agreed that 'No site to be pitched upon for erecting a new church, where it will not admit the church being planned east and west, without special reasons, to be particularly approved of by the Commissioners' (Port 1986, 6, no. 8; 12, no. 19). All sites had to be viewed by a delegation of Commissioners before any final decision was taken. Local factors, such as industrial nuisance, convenience of access and the strength of Dissent, were taken into account. Areas of around 2 acres (0.8 ha) were allowed for each churchyard, 'when so much can be obtained on reasonable terms' (Port 1986, 6, no. 9). Land values were an important determinant, and they varied a good deal. Sites in east London like Limehouse could be had for around £400, whereas £1000 was paid for a site in Bloomsbury, and the plot that was acquired for Christ Church Spitalfields was purchased for £1260. The Commissioners acquired up-to-date maps of the areas in which they were interested, and employed legal staff to investigate title and attend to the formalities of transactions. More sites were purchased than were eventually built upon. A few sites were donated. In 1711, for instance, the dean and chapter of Westminster offered a site in Tothill Fields or any other waste ground belonging to them for a new church in the parish of St Margaret (Port 1986, 148, no. 484). Ground was offered gratis in Lambeth by Sir John Thornicroft (1986, 7, no. 9). Some owners of property approached the Commission with sites that they wished to sell. A Mr Willmers offered a site for a church called the Mermaid Brewhouse, in Whitehouse Street in the parish of St Giles Cripplegate, at £550 (1986, 8, no. 11). In December 1711 it was minuted that the earl of Rochester was to speak with the earl of Salisbury, 'to persuade him to set a moderate price on his ground, proposed for the site of a church ... in Bermondsey' (1986, 8, no. 10).

The previous use of land is sometimes reported. Two-and-a-half acres (1 ha) in Deptford were carrying a crop at the time of purchase. The crop had to be valued, which it eventually was at £70 (1986, 15, no. 25; 17, no. 34). At Hatton Garden there were houses, some recently demolished (8, no. 13), others still standing and occupied (63, no. 189). At Shadwell a dispute arose over the ownership of some fruit trees (64, no. 193). At Holborn the old Three Cups Inn was thought to be 'a proper site for a new church within the parish of St Andrew Holborn' (6, no. 9). Britain's expanding influence abroad meant that some of the negotiations extended overseas. In 1717, for example, it was recorded that 'Johnson, of whom site in Lower Wapping was purchased, reported death of Mrs Caley alias Bodelow in Jamaica; to bring certificate from minister and churchwardens of Kingston in Jamaica attested by a public notary, in order to obtain his securities' (63, no. 190).

Hawksmoor and his colleagues are remembered as great architects, but in addition to their responsibilities for the designs and the supervision of contracts, the surveyors spent a great deal of their time attending to mundane tasks like fencing, paving the surrounds of churches and drainage. At Westminster trial holes were dug in 1713 to ascertain the nature of the subsoil, and from 1714 it was decided that test borings should be taken on all sites, 'Hawksmoor to provide an auger'. Excavations for foundations could disturb existing watercourses and drainage, and the surveyors often had to deal with complaints from the residents of houses that adjoined the new buildings. In 1716 one Philip Clement reported that his watercourse had been damaged by the building of Christ Church Spitalfields. The matter was referred to Hawksmoor, who agreed that some damage might have been sustained. Twenty pounds was allocated to make it good (Port 1986, 52–4, nos 154–59). In 1717 John James reported that 'Hollins's house had suffered inconvenience by the turning of a watercourse belonging to Strand new church' (67, no. 201). In 1727 the Commissioners read a representation from one Dr Warren 'complaining of damage to his cellars in his new house at Bow by water from roads' (139, no. 452). Problems arose from pilfering and vandalism. In 1727 damage was being inflicted upon the churches at Limehouse and Wapping by the theft of building materials (139, nos 449–50). Seven years before the surveyors had submitted a memorandum which detailed the need to surround the sites at Limehouse, Wapping, Spitalfields and Westminster with brick walls 'to prevent the harm continually done by the mob to the buildings and works'. Hawksmoor and James also argued the need to barricade the entrances and windows of the buildings 'to hinder idle people and boys from getting in, and finding ways to get upon the roofs of such churches as they are finished, where they are doing continual mischief' (84, no. 253). Disorders of a different kind were reported on 12 September 1717, when the Commissioners heard that the workmen at St Mary-le-Strand had run riot 'upon finishing of tower': evidently a topping-out party which had got out of hand. The master mason and other master craftsmen were summoned to the next meeting, where they were asked to explain themselves 'and charged to try to prevent such disorders in future' (62–3, nos 188–9).

London was the only place in this period which saw a systematic attempt to increase provision on a large scale. In other towns there were some piecemeal additions, and a certain amount of rebuilding. Among the rebuildings there were some stunning additions to townscapes. Harmful fires in Northampton (1675) and Warwick (1694) created opportunities for grand new schemes: All Saints Northampton (1676–80) with its Ionic colonnaded portico, an addition of 1701; St Mary's Warwick, where a kind of classicized Gothic was 'consciously adopted to harmonize with the surviving medieval chancel and to put the citizens of

Warwick in mind of the ancient dignity of their town' (Whiffen 1948, 19). In Oxford, Henry Aldrich, dean of Christchurch, commissioned a rebuilding of All Saints (1707–10), adding a new emphasis to the High Street and a new spire to the skyline. Hawksmoor offered plans for a systematic redevelopment of central Oxford north of the High Street, complete with ceremonial gateways, solemn processions of public buildings and a forum at Carfax – but this came to little, although his influence upon James Gibbs in the form and positioning of the Radcliffe Camera has been pointed out (Downes 1969, 94). Hawksmoor also entertained ideas for a 'reformed' scheme in Cambridge. This would have 'retained the town's Y-shaped street plan, making comparatively minor widenings and realignments and co-ordinating buildings and vistas' (Downes 1969, 90). But this vision also remained on paper. Vistas and designed townscapes were in the air, yet remained elusive, unfulfilled. In towns of lesser celebrity a rebuilt or an extra church was the best that could be hoped for. Places like Leeds and Colchester *Ex* acquired them; St Alkmund in Whitchurch *Sa* was rebuilt because its medieval predecessor was falling down. Four of Worcester's churches were substantially rebuilt in the eighteenth century. At provincial level some of the architecture was of 'reach-down' quality. St Modwen's, Burton-on-Trent *St*, for example, is a near facsimile of Whitchurch. St George at Great Yarmouth is of interest not only for its curvaceous outline and classic auditory interior, but also because it was built on a new site. Even here, however, the ancient parish system refused to budge. St George was a chapel, subordinate to St Nicholas.

Although new provision in this period was commonly made in the form of chapels-of-ease, a limited number of new parishes were created in places where growth was exceptionally rapid. This was so in Liverpool, where until the end of the seventeenth century there was but one church, a parochial chapel of medieval origin (Fig. 118). Its site adjoined the River Mersey, and a fish house. The dedication to St Nicholas was therefore appropriate. In 1694 Liverpool was made into an independent parish. A new church, St Peter's, was founded. In 1714 George I granted the site of the castle, demolished during the reign of Charles II, to the mayor and corporation as the site for a third church. The necessity for this was said to be 'the increase in buildings, and great number of inhabitants employed in trade and commerce', so that within a mere fifteen years Liverpool had become much more populous than when the previous Act of Parliament had been made and the two existing churches 'cannot contain the inhabitants who would resort thither to attend divine service' (Baines 1852, 397). In 1725 the corporation began to consider estimates and designs for the third church, St George's, which was to be erected 'in the late castle upon the ground where the old large square stone tower and the stone buildings adjoining ... now stand'. In 1726 approval was given for a design which seems to have been a conflation of ideas put forward by several members of the committee which had been set up to supervise the

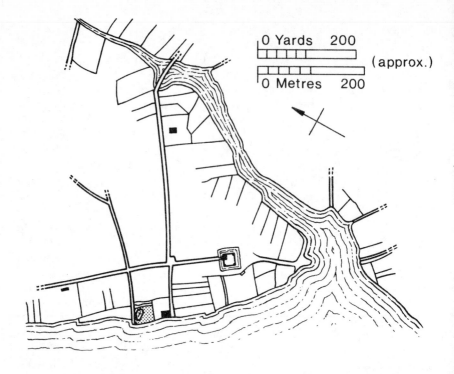

118 Distribution of property in Liverpool about 1670. The parochial chapel of
Our Lady and St Nicholas lies diagonally across a square churchyard beside
the River Mersey. The site of the castle is seen to its north-east, on the
peninsula formed by the Mersey and the Pool (*Source*: Baines 1852)

project. It was slow work. St George's was not opened until 1734, and the
city was growing. Liverpool's expansion in the eighteenth century was
phenomenal, and in 1748 a fourth church, St Thomas's, was begun. The
site was donated to the corporation by a merchant. Two more churches
were built in the 1770s: the only decade in the eighteenth century when
Liverpool did not increase in population. By 1780 the population stood at
c. 34,000, and the ratio of Anglican churches to people was *c.* 1:6000.
More churches were built between 1790 and 1830, but in this period the
population soared, so that by 1830 the ratio was 1:12,000. In terms of
church-room the position was infinitely worse, there being approximately
one place for every 164 people. Liverpool's status as a port was reflected
in the cosmopolitan and plural character of its religion. Dissenters did well
there. Roman Catholicism was strong. The Welsh population was sufficiently large to justify the opening in 1826 of the church of St David, where
services were held in the Welsh language.

A contrasting case is Birmingham (Fig. 119). Of the few new churches
on new sites, St Philip's, Birmingham, was one of the most impressive.
The Act of Parliament under which St Philip's was built was passed in

119 Birmingham in the later eighteenth century (*Source:* Thomas Hanson's map of 1781)

1708. Thomas Archer (who was also employed by the Anne and George Commissions on St Paul, Deptford, 1713–30) was appointed architect in the following year. Records which chronicle the planning and building of the church survive. Archer came from nearby Tamworth-in-Arden. The contractor who supplied the stone, appropriately enough for this part of England, was a William Shakespear. Consecration of the church took place in 1715, although work on the tower continued for another decade. Thomas Archer was a travelled man. Unlike many other builders of his day he had first-hand knowledge of Italian baroque. St Philip's is a remarkable, in some respects daring, building, impressive not least for its tower which has concave sides and is surmounted by a dome. The church quickly gained a place in the affections of the town's citizenry. Later in the century the Birmingham paper merchant and author William Hutton remarked that St Philip's 'does honour to the age that raised it, and to the place that contains it'. Looked at today one might credit Archer with an attempt to place the church within a Midland piazza. In fact, the site was formerly part of a farm, known as Barley Close, and in the early eighteenth century it was still open. 'This well chosen spot', wrote Hutton in 1780, 'is the summit of the highest eminence in Birmingham, with a descent every way; and, when the church was erected, there were not any buildings nearer than those in Bull Street.' The land for the church was given.

St Philip's was only the second parish church to be built in Birmingham. A medieval church, St Martin's, stood on a characteristically funnel-shaped market site. It was remodelled in 1690, and again in the eighteenth century, so that externally only the steeple is of medieval aspect. The spire was partly rebuilt in 1781. Hutton pondered the nature of the site of St Martin, thinking the precinct to have 'undergone a mutilation' as a result of encroachments, and noting the profile of the churchyard 'which, through a long course of interment . . . is augmented into a considerable hill, chiefly composed of the refuse of life'. Hutton could not resist adding the cheerful pun: 'In this place, the dead are raised up.'

By 1780 Birmingham was a town of some 50,000 souls, with a lively and varied economy involving metalwork – brass, nails, buttons, jewellery, cartridges, pails – thread, leather, guns, markets, and benefiting from good communications. Already the town had often to be 'viewed through the medium of smoke', and within sixty years the stone supplied for St Philip's by William Shakespear was noted to be 'not proof against time'. Although late eighteenth-century Birmingham possessed only two parish churches, there were in all fourteen places of worship: four Anglican chapels-of-ease, meeting-houses of Presbyterians, Quakers and Methodists, a 'Romish chapel', and a synagogue. The sites of some of these buildings are of interest, as illustrating the physical growth of the town and the changing aspirations of those who lived in it.

Three of the Anglican chapels were of recent foundation: St Bartholomew (1749), St Mary (1774) and St Paul (1779). The sites of St Mary and St Paul were procured in 1772 under a single Act. In each case the land was donated. The fourth chapel, St John, stood in Deritend, an inner suburb, though in the parish of Aston. St John's seems to have been founded towards the end of the fourteenth century on a site which looks as if it could have been formed from the amalgamation of the residential portions of several burgage plots. The other, recent, sites were more formal. Each chapel had an insula to itself. St Mary and St Paul stood within generous rectangles bounded by streets. St Bartholomew occupied a wedge-shaped plot. Thomas Hanson's map of 1781 shows the area round St Mary's to have been partly built up, but settlement in the vicinity of St Paul's had not yet developed. The chapels thus seem to have been founded at, or a little beyond, the growing edge of the city. Hutton commented about this, remarking that 'wherever a chapel is erected, the houses immediately, as if touched by the wand of magic, spring into existence'. Orderly planning and symmetry were valued. The street grid in the newer part of the town obliged a northerly deflection in the alignments of St Paul and St Bartholomew; in the case of St Mary this was not so obvious because the building, which has gone, was in the form of an octagon. Hutton pondered the propriety of such 'incorrect' orientation, but compared the situation at Deritend where the architect who rebuilt the church in 1735, presumably maintaining the medieval axis, was so 'anxious to catch the East point' that he 'lost the line of the street'.

Anglican expansion had been foreshadowed by the Dissenters. By 1780 the original Old Meeting of the Presbyterians which stood at the bottom of Digbeth had been turned into a workshop and superseded by another, 'large and much attended'. Confusingly, this retained the name of its predecessor, which according to Hutton had been erected in 1730. Then there was the New Meeting. Like the two Old Meetings this has since disappeared, but Pickering's drawing depicts it as a simple box-shaped structure of four bays, not greatly dissimilar from St Paul's though lacking the tower and pediment, and with laterally placed doorways. Other meetings were at Carr's Lane (a scion from the Old Meeting, transplanted in 1748), the Baptist Meeting in Cannon Street, founded in 1738, and the Quakers' Meeting in Bull Street: 'a large convenient place, and not withstanding the plainness of the profession rather elegant', where the congregation was described as 'very flourishing, rich, and peaceable'. The site at Carr's Lane, by contrast, was portrayed as being 'totally eclipsed, by being surrounded with about forty families of paupers' who were crowded within a small area and amply furnished the congregation with 'noise, smoke, dirt and dispute'. In 1745 there was schism within the Baptist congregation which led to the founding of a new cell in Freeman Street. This did not last, and in 1752 the deserters returned to Cannon Street and their little chapel of seven years' standing was turned into a house. Methodists had been active in the city since 1738, first meeting outdoors, then occupying a place in Steelhouse Lane, 'where wags of the age observed, "they were eat out by bugs"', and later making use of a redundant theatre in Moor Street. In 1782, 'quitting the stage', they built what Hutton described as a 'superb' meeting-house in Cherry Street. The Roman Catholics did not enjoy much support. Hutton thought there were fewer than 300 believers. Their chapel in Masshouse Lane had been destroyed in a riot. Roman Catholics now trekked two miles to a chapel in Edgbaston.

This, then, was the ecclesiastical geography of a commercial and industrial town on the eve of a population explosion. Seventy years later Birmingham's population had rocketed to 232,841: an increase of more than 460 per cent. But until the later eighteenth century the picture is one of more gradual growth. The Anglicans were beginning to react to change, though perhaps too slowly. They liked to place their buildings on prominent, formal sites. The Dissenters had been accustomed to make do with such property as they could obtain. Within the space of a century the four principal nonconformist denominations had occupied at least ten sites. But by the later eighteenth century we see a trend towards increasing permanence and more architectural display as their numbers and wealth increased. Even at this date, however, Dissenters were not wholly secure. Industrialization, reasoned thinking, and the extrapolation of some dissenting values into the political arena, contributed to political radicalism. On 14 July 1791 a dinner was held in the Birmingham Hotel to celebrate the anniversary of the French Revolution. Some of those present, including Hutton, were members of a committee which had been formed to lobby for the repeal of the Test and Corporation Acts. A mob gathered, broke up the dinner, and went on to attack the Old and New Meetings, together with the homes of a number of those who were regarded as Dissenters and radicals. The New Meeting was destroyed. Hutton was among those who were attacked. He lost two houses in the riot, and much of his stock (Elrington 1976, xiii–xiv).

It was not only new churches that were coming to be needed during the eighteenth century. Accommodation for the dead was also running out. The need for additional gravespace increased sharply towards the end of the century as the graph of population began to climb. Towns had the worst of this problem, for as urban populations multiplied the proportion that had to be buried rose rapidly. Low standards of hygiene, overcrowding and poor nutrition all took their toll. Diseases spread rapidly. Epidemics were common. Child mortality in some cities was astronomic. In 1844 it was discovered that of 100,000 people born in Liverpool only 48,211 had reached the age of ten. Longevity in country communities could be appreciably better. In rural Surrey, for instance, over 75,000 attained their tenth birthday, and nearly 71,000 went on to enjoy a twentieth. In Liverpool fewer than 45,000 passed the age of twenty (Baines 1852, 670–1) (Fig. 120).

Not only did urban populations expand far more rapidly than their rural counterparts, but the sites of urban churchyards were often hemmed in by buildings or roads which prevented extension. In such circum-

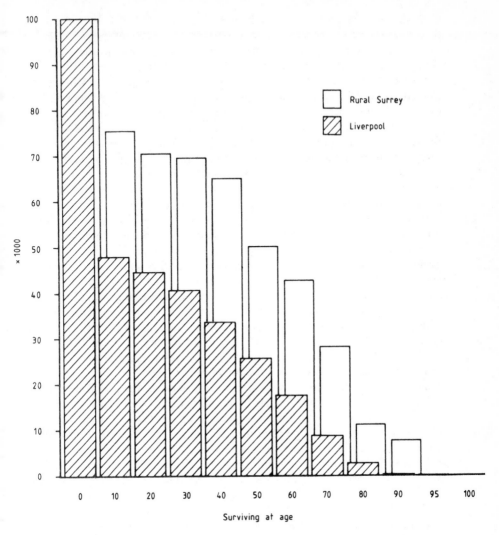

120 Urban and rural mortality in the first half of the nineteenth century: a comparison of examples (*Source*: Baines 1852)

stances the only direction in which a churchyard could grow was upwards. By 1800 many urban churches were quite literally becoming buried by their own cemeteries. As late as 1892 soil in the churchyard at Conway *Gwd* (*Crn*) could be observed pressing against the glass of the windows, having risen above the level of their sills.

The large churchyards surrounding the new chapels in Birmingham were thus very necessary. 'Here is a spacious area for interment,' wrote Hutton, 'amply furnished by death.' Builders of new churches elsewhere knew the problem and tried to circumvent it. We have seen that Wren had argued the case for a ban on burial in London, not least because it restricted the choice of sites. But the churchyard, like the steeple, was felt to be a traditional component of an Anglican site, and people were not yet ready for their church and cemetery to be parted.

For new sites, therefore, a large precinct was important. Within the church some additional space could be gained by raising the building upon a platform and using the underfloor volume for burial. The steps which rise up to the western entrances of Christ Church Spitalfields remind us that Hawksmoor's church is really a two-tier structure, with an extensive underworld of chambers and tunnels. Similar arrangements were adopted in a number of other churches built or rebuilt in the eighteenth and early nineteenth centuries. St Nicholas, Worcester, for instance, was rebuilt c. 1730 over a crypt that occupies the same area as the church above. It must be said that the motivation behind such designs is not always clear. The Commissioners of 1711, for instance, had ruled that burial inside their new London churches was not to be permitted. The underspace indicated in the preliminary designs for St George-in-the-East was specifically allocated for use as a charity school. Yet we know that burial in the vaults at Spitalfields had begun within three days of the date of consecration. Perhaps popular demand, and the financial benefits which accrued to the church, were irresistible. In any case, the extra capacity gained by raising the church upon a crypt was small by comparison with the total numbers involved. Between 1729 and 1859 c. 68,000 individuals are recorded as having been buried at Christ Church Spitalfields; fewer than 3000 were in the vaults (Adams and Reeve 1987).

The need to terminate burial in cramful urban churchyards was eventually answered by the establishment of large new cemeteries in open spaces or at the town edge. Models for such a civilized solution existed abroad: in Italy, Sweden and France. Since the seventeenth century men of education had been pondering the idea of cemeteries of formal layout, and in some cases designs for them had been produced. Precedents were also available in some of Britain's colonies: in India, for instance, at sites such as the South Park Street Cemetery in Calcutta. Nearer to home the Clifton Graveyard had been established in Belfast in 1774, and there was the eighteenth-century cemetery on Calton Hill in Edinburgh (Curl 1980, 135-67).

Père-Lachaise in Paris was widely admired. Here the arts of landscape architecture and monumental design had been combined to produce a romantic city of the dead, with winding tomb-lined streets, avenues and well-contrived vistas (Curl 1980, 156-62). In England, the idea that a cemetery could be pleasant, that it could be designed, and that it need not be wedded to a parish church, took time to win acceptance. Some clergy opposed it, no doubt because they feared some loss or reduction in their fees. The first attempt was the Liverpool Necropolis, opened in 1825. By continental standards this was a very modest affair, covering slightly less than 5 acres (2 ha). The principle of the development was welcomed, however, and four years later a second cemetery was opened. This was the St James's Cemetery. It was formed within a redundant quarry. The architect was John Foster

> who created a setting of great magnificence for the interment of the dead by constructing processional ramps in order that funeral-carriages might travel down to the floor of the old quarry. Chambers were cut out of the sides of the quarry to provide catacombs, tunnels were driven through the rock to provide vistas and Piranesian enclosures. The cemetery was landscaped by Shepherd, a gardener who had worked with Foster on other projects.
>
> (Curl 1980, 208–9)

Interest in the Liverpool developments was strong. In 1830 the landscape gardener John Claudius Loudon published an article which advocated the establishment of several garden cemeteries around London. Two years later Parliament approved a Bill 'for establishing a General Cemetery for the Interment of the Dead in the Neighbourhood of the Metropolis'. The site chosen was at Kensal Green, beyond the area then built up, where 79 acres (32 ha) of land were purchased. A competition was held for the design of the cemetery buildings, and by 1832 the grounds were being laid out and planted with trees (Curl 1980, 213–16). Among the buildings were two chapels: one for Anglicans, the other for Dissenters. Kensal Green opened in 1833. The venture was a success. It inspired imitators: Norwood (1837), Highgate (1839), Nunhead (1840), Abney Park at Stoke Newington (1840) and Tower Hamlets (1841). All of these were to a greater or lesser extent landscaped, with systems of roads and avenues, focal chapels and catacombs. In some cases, like Abney Park, the planting was of a high order of imagination and magnificence, with luxurious shrubberies and eyecatching trees.

Garden cemeteries were a new component of urban landscapes. Until the middle of the nineteenth century they were generally established and run as commercial ventures. Thereafter municipal authority took an increasing hand. Legislation was enacted in the 1850s and 1860s to oblige the closure of urban churchyards. Public cemeteries became the rule.

Loudon's views on the design of cemeteries were influential. In 1843 his published ideas on the subject were collected and reissued in a book: *On the laying out, planting, and managing of Cemeteries*. The ideas in this work achieved a currency which affected churchyards, as well as the new garden cemeteries. Regarding the appearance and upkeep of churchyards, the eighteenth and early nineteenth centuries had been a time of mixed achievements. Records of inspections made by archdeacons are full of complaints concerning rank growths of nettle and bramble, and fences or walls in disrepair which permitted animals to intrude, trample, dig and defecate. Conversely, the rise of interest in landscape design had created a climate of taste in higher social circles which favoured calculated planting, as at Painswick *Gl* where files of yews, now clipped, were planted in 1792. And there were occasions when churchyards benefited from association with wider schemes. One of these was Rivenhall *Ex*, where it seems that Humphrey Repton established a large number of elms in the churchyard while he was engaged upon the landscaping of the park in 1791. In 1838-9 Repton's son returned to contribute a co-ordinated arrangement of cedars, cypresses, yews and holm oaks (Rodwell 1986). The solemnity of such planting would no doubt have appealed to Loudon, who advocated trees of symmetrical shape, like the cypress, and evergreen species such as pines, firs, yew, juniper and cedar. Apart from their symbolic associations such trees made for convenience in maintenance. Large deciduous types, though majestic, produced canopies that excluded light and inhibited undergrowth in summer, and turned into large piles of rotting leaves in winter (Curl 1980, 250).

Many churchyards bear witness to Loudon's influence, although few were redesigned so comprehensively as he might have liked. Loudon's idealized scheme for a churchyard which would be suitable for an agricultural parish is dauntingly formalistic, although his scheme for the improvement of an older churchyard where burial had ceased is more relaxed. Loudon showed how this could be done without disturbing existing memorials (Curl 1980, 258-61). In practice, reluctance to interfere with monuments and graves, and expense, may have tended to deter wholesale remodelling. Hence, alongside the new paths and the introduction of fastigiate yews, cypresses and junipers, indigenous woodland species like lime and elm remained in favour. It is this amalgam of native and invited species, informality and order, that contributes to the special personality of the English churchyard (Greenoak 1985). In some places the church is kept company by one or two magnificent trees: the great Lebanon cedars at Marholm *Np* or Edenham *Li*, for instance, or the weeping beech that stands outside the west front of Nun Monkton *NY* (*YW*), where every May the church is veiled off by a green mist of unfurling leaves. There are dramatic avenues, like the limes that flank the approaches to Acton *Sf* and Crondall *Ha*, or the yew-sided canyon that leads to the west door of Roos *Hu* (*YE*). There are, too, some charming conceits. At Warnham *Sx* the boughs of a group of yews at the entrance to the churchyard have been knitted and clipped into the shape of a lych-gate. Here and there are elegant hedges: Down Ampney *Gl*, for instance, with its *enceinte* of yew, or Rendcomb *Gl*. In the end, however, it is the more naturalistic settings that linger in the mind. Who can forget St Botolph, Skidbrooke *Li*, alone with a clump of trees in a desolate marshscape, or the beeches beside All Saints, Kirk Deighton *NY* (*YW*), when they are thronged with rooks. Such scenes belong in the melancholy of a winter's afternoon.

From gardens, back to grime: the nineteenth century, and the last great epoch of churchfounding. During the first years of the century it was the Dissenters who set the pace. In 1801 there were some 3700 places of worship occupied by the main nonconformist denominations. By 1839 the number had risen beyond 8700 (see Fig. 110). The stronger denominations were now building grand, capacious chapels in conspicuous downtown locations. Viewed from the side these were generally simple box-like structures, but they often presented a more elaborate face to the street. Until the middle of the century Grecian forms predominated. A colonnaded portico and pediment were common, and the intervention of a vestibule between the façade and the body of the interior could help to shut out noise from the street. For the streets concerned were no longer the back lanes and alleys that had once been resorted to. Nonconformity now paraded itself along main thoroughfares and beside city squares.

Methodism and the Greek Revival went hand-in-hand on Bridge Street, Bolton *La* in 1803, Carver Street, Sheffield *SY* (*YW*) (1804), Queen Street, Huddersfield *WY* (1819), and Oxford Place in Leeds (1835). Also in Leeds was Brunswick chapel, which was built to seat 1500 people. Brunswick was one of a number of substantial Greek Revival public buildings 'which reflected the growing wealth and sophistication of contemporary Leeds society' (Powell 1980). The Congregational chapel on East Parade (1839–41) was another. In Hull there were two mighty Congregational chapels, Albion Street and Great Thornton Street, both of the 1840s. Greater prominence could be achieved when a chapel was positioned in the angle between two important streets, as was the Great George Street chapel in Liverpool (1840–1). Smaller editions of such chapels were built on comparably central sites in lesser towns: the Wesleyan chapel on High Street in Uttoxeter *St* (1812), for instance; Barnby Gate, Newark *Nt* (1846); or the Congregational chapel, Bedford Street, in Stroud *Gl* (1835–7) (Stell 1986).

The Grecian grandeur of early nineteenth-century chapels in northern city centres was a departure from the spirit of the first generation of Methodist meeting-rooms, many of which were influenced by the same mixture of thrift and opportunism as had determined the choice of sites by congregations of the Old Dissent a century before. At the outset, frugality in building was considered a virtue. In 1787 John Wesley wrote to a colleague expressing himself 'thoroughly satisfied with your economy in the building of the house. It is exceeding cheap' (Wesley, *Letters* 8, 113; ed. Telford 1931). Wesleyan Methodists converted all sorts of buildings. At Great Gonerby *Li* a sympathizer bought and fitted out a small stone barn; at Newport *IoW* a former auction room was taken over; at Silver Hill, Winchester, a member bought some ruined buildings and restored them. A congregation in Musselburgh, however, was advised to abandon its scheme for occupying the ground floor of a dovecot. The birds were still in residence, and Wesley warned that this would be an 'insupportable nuisance, as it would fill the whole place with flies' (Wesley, *Letters* 8, 30). A few large purpose-built chapels, like that at City Road in London, or the New Room in Bristol, were constructed, but on the whole it was not until the end of the century that a category of specialized Methodist chapel began to emerge.

One reason for this may have been the delayed emergence of a confidence in what Methodism actually was. Wesley himself was an ordained minister of the Church of England, from which he did not wish to separate. Writing on this subject to a friend in 1786, Wesley recalled that

> in the year 1758 it was full considered in the Leeds Conference 'whether we should separate from the Church or no'. After weighing the whole matter calmly, we determined upon the negative. . . . We all agreed (1) to exhort all our people constantly to attend the church and sacrament; and (2), still to preach on Sundays, morning and evening, not in the church hours.
>
> *(Letters* 7, 332–3)

Until the end of the eighteenth century many were uncertain as to whether Methodism was a way of being an Anglican, or whether it was something else. From 1795 each local society was allowed to have the sacrament celebrated by authorized persons (Chadwick 1966, 370). Methodism thus acquired the identity of a separate denomination. But ambiguity remained, and for decades afterwards there were many who were accustomed to attend both church and chapel. Some do so still. Nevertheless, after 1795 it became increasingly natural and logical for Methodists to affirm their independence through buildings of their own.

Wesleyan Methodism was also coming to be associated with bourgeois values. Its membership lay chiefly in cities and provincial towns, to the neglect of some remoter rural areas. And while its more massive inner city temples were not far from the urban poor, their growing respectability could be a deterrent to those who felt themselves to be unfashionable or disadvantaged. Hence it is no surprise that around the turn of the century some Dissenters sought a return to roots and first principles. Back they went to revivalism, itinerancy and the open air.

As before, an igniting spark was struck overseas, this time in the United States. In England, too, the atmosphere of the 1790s was an inflammable vapour, heavy with millenarian fervour (Werner 1984, 30–1). J. M. Turner catches the mood of the time:

> The second revival found a ready soil in the Cheshire Plain and the Potteries where the parish system was weak. There were pockets of undenominational revivalism which crystallized out in the Quaker or independent Methodists of Warrington and Macclesfield, the Band Room Methodists of Manchester, the revivalists of Leeds. . . . Then there were the 'Magic Methodists' of Delamere Forest who specialized in trance-like states led by James Crawfoot, 'the old man of the forest', and revivalism shades off into all sorts of pre-millenarian groups like the followers of Joanna Southcott, which Dr Harrison has recently analysed in his book *The Second Coming.* The links here are with Quakerism and left-wing relics of Puritanism.
>
> (Turner 1982, 1)

The revival flared up in the north-west Midlands, where camp meetings started to be held on Mow Cop in 1807: 'Mow Cop – that outcrop of the Pennines dominating the Cheshire Plain where Anglican parishes were large and ineffective, and where itinerant preachers were common' (Turner 1982, 2). One of the preachers in the area at that time was an American, Lorenzo Dow: 'crazy Dow – asthmatic and epileptic, he cut an odd figure with hair down to his waist, flashing eyes, stooped shoulders, harsh voice, crude gestures' (Turner 1982, 2). Early growth was gradual, but with the ending of the Napoleonic War there followed a phenomenon akin to sideflash in the behaviour of lightning. Revivalism spread, traversing the less conductive areas, but earthing itself to communities of millworkers and labourers in the Trent valley, Lincolnshire and Yorkshire; then the Black Country, onward and outward. By 1819 there were 7842 members. Four years later there were over 33,000. By 1842 membership had risen to 85,565. The Connexion was known as Primitive Methodism. The popular name for them was Ranters.

Primitive Methodism made its impact among the poor. Unlike the Wesleyans or Anglicans there was a virtual absence of any paternalistic or establishment element. Many of the preachers were themselves labourers, millworkers or weavers. Like friars in the thirteenth century they preached their way from place to place, lodging with sympathizers or sleeping in barns or under hedges. Meetings were held as opportunity offered, not infrequently in the face of ridicule, rotten vegetables or bruising stones. The work was advanced by women as well as men. In time Primitive Methodism had an important effect on the organization of secular education among the working class (Bradshaw 1982). In time, too, many chapels were erected. 'Usually the chapels started as cart-shed, joiner's shop, forge, hayloft, converted house or shed' (Chadwick 1966, 387). Such frugality assisted the spread of Primitive Methodist infrastructure into agricultural villages, mining settlements and industrial towns. When purpose-built chapels were erected no money was wasted on superfluous ornament or architectural display. They made their mark in other ways, not least in toponymy: 'Many of their chapels were called by the address of the street, like the chapels of Wesleyan Methodists; but they were also Bethel, Ebenezer, Providence, Zion, Rehoboth, Moriah, Canaan' (Chadwick 1966, 387). In the second quarter of the nineteenth century the Connexion was fuelled by a prodigious energy. Josiah Stamp, a minister based at Louth between 1836 and 1839, recounted: 'We have built 16 chapels, enlarged one, bought another and fitted up a large room and have had an increase of 25 local preachers and 416 members. ... I have walked more than 10,000 miles and have preached upwards of 1,500 sermons and visited 6,000 families' (cited in Turner 1982, 5). Elementary arithmetic argues that Stamp was averaging over nine miles, one sermon and six visits a day.

Industrialization, population growth and the conquests being made by the New Dissent all now backlit the shortcomings of the Established

Church with a brilliance that registered itself even upon the weak eye of Anglican complacency. Most people now saw the necessity for a restructuring of the parish system. There were progressive men, High Churchmen and Evangelicals, who were anxious to bring it about. By 1810 the need for extra parish churches had become a subject for public discussion: in the press, at court, and in Parliament. When the war with France came to an end in 1815 the subject moved higher up the national agenda. The Church Building Act of 1818 established a Commission for 'building and promoting the building of additional churches in populous parishes', and made a million pounds available for this purpose. By 1820 some 85 new churches had been provided for, and in 1821 and 1822 there were further Acts which extended the financial powers of the Commission, assisted it to acquire sites, dismember over-large parishes and combat vested interests. Many projects were aided by funds from subscriptions and parish rates, so that by 1856, when the work of the Commission came to an end, 612 churches had been built at a cost of more than three million pounds. Expenditure from all sources on churchbuilding and enlargement during this period (1818–56) exceeded eight million pounds, and led to the construction in the 1830s and 1840s of more than 2000 new churches.

The greatest number of Commissioners' churches are found in the industrial conurbations of Yorkshire, Lancashire and the Midlands, and in the London suburbs. The Commission had powers to obtain sites for churches and burial grounds. About 1200 plots were earmarked for churches, and a further 800 for cemeteries. Various factors influenced their selection. As in 1711, the need to divide a parish was to be considered before any site was chosen. The Commissioners studied the census returns of 1811 and various reports on church-room and population which had been produced since 1810. They also made a list of the areas where underprovision was at its worst. But beyond this it seems that they did not have any overall strategy for the distribution of their fund: 'instead, they made piecemeal grants, which were often secured by an assiduous minister making an early application, by the promise of a large subscription ... or by a Commissioner's personal knowledge of particular parishes' (Port 1961, 33, 30–32). The state of progress with enclosure could make a difference. Land in private hands could be bought or given, but where the enclosure of open fields and common land had not yet taken place scope might be more restricted.

The Commissioners' broad aim was to build churches which provided the greatest accommodation at the least expense. At the outset they favoured no particular style. Debate about the relative merits of classical and Gothic was initially focused on questions of cost, and seems to have been fairly evenly balanced. 'During the Million era the battle was one affecting merely the trimmings: there was little dispute over the plan of a church, which was primarily an auditorium' (Port 1961, 61) (Fig. 121). The Commissioners did nevertheless show some concern for appearances. A Grecian church could be mistaken for a meeting-house. The remedy lay

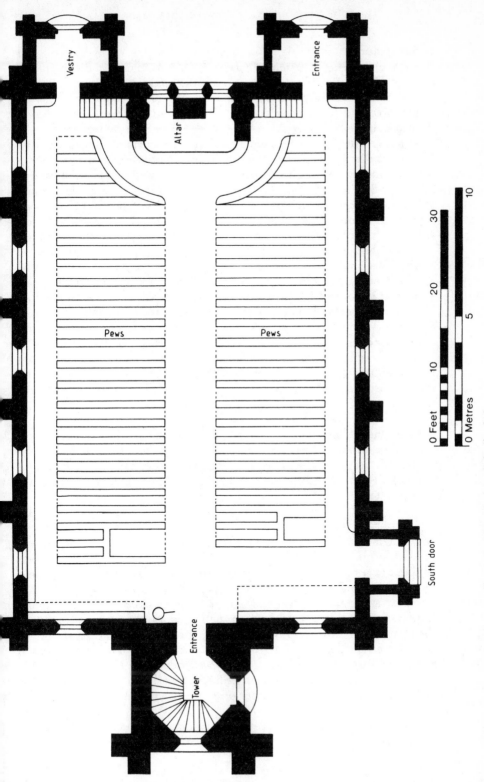

121 Idle, West Yorkshire: plan of Commissioners' church built 1828-30

in the addition of a steeple. This was in any case felt to be desirable, for reasons of practicality, sentiment or tradition. Steeples distinguished churches from afar. They were also useful for the hanging of bells. Sir Robert Smirke thought that the steeple had 'become by long usage the indispensable and proper characteristic of our national churches' (cited in Port 1961, 61).

Although the Commissioners eschewed unnecessary elaboration, the fact that their churches were large, built for capacity, often invested them with a strongly marked presence. Once seen, buildings like All Saints, Stand, or St Philip, Salford *GMa (La)*, are not forgotten. In Leeds, a city of hills and valleys, the church of St Mary, Quarry Hill, was placed in an elevated position and made all the more conspicuous by a dramatic tower. A few of the early churches were built by the Crown Architects – Smirke, Nash and Soane – and among them are several which were positioned in careful relation to their surroundings: a continuation of the Georgian feeling for the church as a pivot in town planning, as for instance in St John's Square at Wakefield *WY* where the church was placed in the midst of an elegant housing development of the 1790s. In London, Smirke's church of St Mary, Wyndham Place, was located at the centre of a small square, 'with its portico and principal entrance to the south, facing the road leading to fashionable Bryanston Square' (Port 1961, 44). In 1820 Nash was invited to design a church which would stand at the entrance to Langham Place. Nash responded with drawings and a letter in which he explained that

> From the nature of the bend of the street the portico and spire will together form an object terminating the vista from the circus in Oxford Street. The spire (I submit) is the most beautiful of all forms, is peculiarly calculated for the termination of a vista and particularly appropriate for a church.
>
> (cited in Port 1961, 47)

Nash's concern to achieve an overall co-ordination of effect was also expressed in his unfulfilled plan for St Mary Haggerston. The church was to stand in a square plot. Nash therefore wondered if the building could be centrally planned: an octagon, perhaps, or a domed circle? He favoured ashlar-faced elevations 'as this church will be seen all round and from a considerable distance'. Nash made suggestions about the layout of the churchyard (with graves in straight parallel lines 'to arrest the attention of the spectator, and produce in his mind that sensation of awe and respect which so solemn a record is so well-calculated to effect'), the curtilage boundary (ornamental iron railings rather than a 'dead' wall), the width and disposition of surrounding roadways, and the houses that would front onto them (Port 1961, 48-9). The Commissioners were unimpressed by this scheme for a designed neighbourhood, and Nash was obliged to build something that was less ambitious.

A graph of·the churches which were built with the aid of the two parliamentary grants shows that progress was fitful (Fig. 122). Starts of churches funded from the first grant reached a peak in 1822, and then subsided only to rise again in the later 1820s as the second grant became available. Between 1832 and 1836 there was little activity. From 1837 to 1841 the tempo quickened. There were only eight starts in 1842 – a year of economic and social crisis – but thereafter the figures pick up again, and between 1844 and 1854 the start-rate averaged over twenty-five and never fell below eighteen. The peak year was 1849 when thirty-seven new churches were begun.

The lifetime of the Church Building Commission saw a radical change in attitudes to style. Until the mid-1820s classical styles remained in favour, though also in a minority. The architects who used them worked chiefly in and around London and in some of the provincial towns and cities. The later 1820s and 1830s saw an attenuation of Anglican interest in classicism. This left the field clear for the Dissenters, some of whom continued to employ it for their powerful chapels in northern cities for another 25-30 years, and in Wales until the end of the century. Simultaneously there arose a willingness on the part of architects employed by the Established Church to experiment with the revival of medieval styles other than Gothic: Lombard, Anglo-Norman and Italianate Romanesque (Fig. 123). These explorations apart, the great majority of the Commissioners' churches were Gothic. Gothic of the 1820s and 1830s was, however, more of a veneer than a style. It was not always applied with much assurance or understanding. Part of the reason was that until the later 1830s *all* styles were looked upon as so many different coloured cloths, to be draped over the standardized skeleton of an auditory interior.

During the 1830s attitudes towards style and form began to be rethought. Antiquary–architects like Thomas Rickman had already been studying large numbers of medieval buildings at close quarters, and publishing their observations. By 1835 Rickman's seminal *Attempt to Discriminate the Styles of English Architecture*, first issued in 1817, had reached its fourth edition. Other architects studied, and learned. Gothic also came to be explored in ideological terms. In 1836 A.W.N.Pugin published his famous *Contrasts*. Seven years later he was castigating styles that 'are now *adopted* instead of *generated*, and ornament and design *adapted to*, instead of *originated by* the edifices themselves' (1843, 2). For Pugin believed Gothic to have been an invention of Christian culture, and saw in its re-employment a proper embodiment of Christian belief.

Pugin's role in the theorizing behind the Gothic Revival was at once central and marginal. Central, because of his buildings, and because he 'laid the two foundation stones of that strange system which dominates nineteenth-century art criticism, and is immortalized in *The Seven Lamps of Architecture*: the value of a building depends upon the moral worth of its creator; and a building has a moral value of, and more important than,

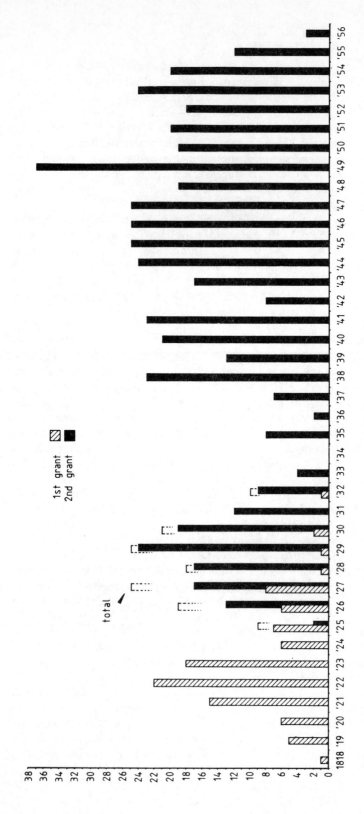

122 Commissioners' churches: rates of building between 1818 and 1856 (*Source*: Port 1961)

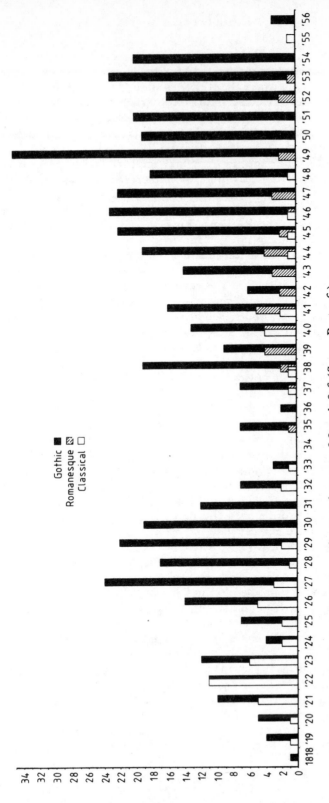

123 Commissioners' churches: stylistic preferences between 1818 and 1856 (*Source:* Port 1961)

Gothic ■ Romanesque ▨ Classical □

its esthetic value' (K.Clark 1950, 202). Marginal, because Pugin's theories led him back into a fantasy world of medievalism. His mind inhabited a temporal region where the Reformation had not yet occurred. And in his theorizing he was being outflanked. When his *Apology for the Revival of Christian* - i.e. Gothic - *Architecture in England* appeared in 1843 the Cambridge Camden Society was already in its fourth year, and all ninety of the *Tracts for the Times* had appeared.

Oxford Tractarianism was initially cerebral. It was concerned with doctrine and ecclesiastical authority. That Tractarianism soon came to be regarded as the inspiration and obverse of Anglican ritualism was actually a worry to a number of its progenitors. In 1866 Dr Pusey averred 'It is well known that I was never a ritualist.' Pusey recalled that 'In our early days we were anxious on the subject of ritual; and we privately discouraged it, lest the whole movement should become superficial . . . we felt it was much easier to change a dress than to change a heart, and that externals might be gained at the cost of the doctrines themselves' (cited in J.F.White 1962, 21). Nevertheless, as ritualism began to catch the imagination of some young Anglicans in the 1840s, there were those at the time who saw ritualism as the practical embodiment of Tractarian theory.

If the Oxford Movement began with the head, the Cambridge Camden Society originated in the heart. The early Camdenians were romantics. Paradoxically, this placed them further from Pugin than they may have realized. In 1844 John Mason Neale is found writing to Benjamin Webb, co-founder of the Society, complaining that 'the Tract writers missed one great principle, namely the influence of Aesthetics'. Neale's argument continued thus: men of immoral character could create beauty; beauty was a manifestation of Godliness; therefore aesthetics could be considered as a force to act upon, but yet be independent of, religious sensibility. Pugin did not subscribe to this. Neither did Pusey (J.F.White 1962, 20). But the mapping of lines and fissures of divergence between the Cambridge and Oxford movements may not be very profitable. Many contemporaries saw them as being complementary. 'Romanism', wrote one critic, 'is taught *Analytically* at Oxford . . . it is taught *Artistically* at Cambridge - that it is inculcated theoretically, in tracts, at one university, and it is *sculptured, painted,* and *graven* at the other' (cited in J.F.White 1962, 142). Ritualism appealed to the followers of both, who found themselves united by a wish to embark upon the renovation of Anglican faith and life.

Ritualism meant colour, music, candles, vestments, a restructuring of the ritual geography of the church and, ideally, surroundings that would be appropriate as the setting for Anglo-Catholic ceremonial. Allied to this went a more determined concern for social responsibility: for education, for orphans, the aged, the hungry, the imprisoned. Tractarian sympathizers built not only churches, but schools, meeting-rooms, orphanages and social centres as well. Sometimes they massed their facilities on a single site, as at Boyne Hill, Maidenhead *Brk* (1854–7, 1865) or, in some ways more remarkable, All Saints, Margaret Street *GLo*, where William Butterfield packed a church, ancillary structures and accommodation within the confines of a restricted site (P. Thompson 1971, 321–2).

Like Pugin, the Camdenians saw the Middle Ages as suffused by a romantic glow. Like Milton, they had hopes that time would run back and fetch the age of gold. Yet their teachings were eminently, perhaps even too, practical. The titles of their publications are littered with *Hints on . . .* and *A few words to . . .* and *Advice to . . . .* From the study of medieval churches they formulated an architectural code to guide modern design, and to indicate how older churches which deviated from their true principles should be corrected. Camdenians placed special emphasis upon interiors. They detested the galleries, pews and other traits of pulpit-centred Protestant worship, and appealed for their removal. Many obliged, and churches with interior layouts that pre-date the 1840s are now rare and correspondingly precious (Chatfield 1979). Chancels were no longer to be shallow alcoves, but of decent depth and proportion, with floors elevated above the level of the nave and altars that were higher still. Intervisibility between priest and people was considered to be important (Fig. 124). Camdenians liked stained glass, screens, chapels, organs that did not bulge into the main spaces, piscinae, sedilia, aumbries, choir stalls. Above all, they liked Gothic. In 1842 it was asked if there had been 'some period in the history of the Church . . . at which the architectural and ritual provision for Christian worship should have reached its point of perfection' (J. F. White 1962, 29). By 1844 the question was answered. Norman was unacceptable, because during this era 'the Catholick Church was forming her architectural language'. Tudor was unacceptable because in this period 'she was unlearning it'. Early English was a possibility, but should be used 'very sparingly'. The Society ruled that the architecture most truly correlative to Christian doctrine was the 'Decorated or Edwardian style, that employed, we mean, between the years 1260 and 1360' (J. F. White 1962, 87).

Thus inoculated with true principles, members of the Cambridge Camden Society roamed England and Wales, inspecting new churches and reporting upon restorations of old ones. Such works were reviewed, rather like new novels or symphonies, in the Society's journal, *The Ecclesiologist*. Camdenian authors praised some buildings and derided others. Acerbity and pomposity were their stock-in-trade. Many architects fell foul of *The Ecclesiologist*, for in practice the task of building or restoring a church could seldom approach the Camdenians' ideal. This was just as well. Hundreds of medieval churches were destroyed or practically rebuilt in the name of ecclesiology; thousands were tampered with. Village communities which possessed modest, adequate twelfth-century churches that would now be treasured could suddenly find themselves equipped with over-large Gothic fantasies which they were unable either to fill or to maintain. Ecclesiology made its contribution to the landscape. Like elms, if the nineteenth-century spires of churches like South Dalton

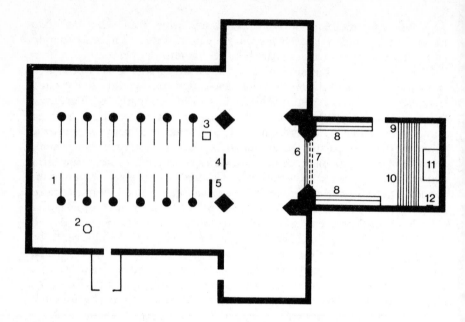

124 Idealized 'Catholick arrangement' of a church, put forward by the
Cambridge Camden Society in *A Few Words to Church Builders* (1841).
1 wooden seats; **2** font; **3** pulpit; **4** faldstool; **5** eagle desk; **6** steps to chancel;
7 roodscreen; **8** misereres; **9** founder's tomb; **10** three flights of three steps; **11**
altar; **12** sedilia. The plan, though not the interior layout, appears to have
been based upon the church at Pagham, Sussex

and Scorborough *Hu* (*YE*) were now to be removed we should miss them
badly. But it is a paradox that in their pursuit of a medieval vision that
was narrowly defined, the Camdenians fostered the destruction of much
medieval fabric.

    The architectural McCarthyism of the Cambridge Camden Society left
many people unmoved. One of them was Francis Close, perpetual curate
of Cheltenham. Close regarded the restoration of churches as a dangerous
practice that would lead to popery (Yates 1983, 16). Close's services were
low-church marathons. A visitor to St Mary's, Cheltenham, in 1842 con-
fided to his diary:

    Mr Close preached extempore with much of his known fluency, self-
possession, impressiveness, and ability. . . . The body of his sermon was
argumentative, against the Millenarians. Great numbers of com-
municants of every class . . . attended, and although the words of administration were not pronounced individually the service was of very
long continuance: begun at 11 a.m. it was not concluded till a quarter
to 3 p.m.

(ed. Verey 1978, 15)

Conflict between low-church and ritualist values could be externalized in buildings, and in their sites. Seventeenth-century Puritans had dismissed the concept of the holy place as idolatrous. 'Reverence for the church building and its furnishings had been thoroughly leached out of Anglicanism by the 1830s' (J.F.White 1962, 4). And the greater shrines of English Protestantism were historical rather than holy. Tourists sought their *virtus* at such sites as John Bunyan's birthplace, John Hampden's grave, Gainsborough's studio, William Caxton's printing office or Thomas More's garden. Ecclesiologists and ritualists explored ways of reinstating a religious sense of place. One aspect of this was the need to invest a church with presence. The Camdenians' affection for country churches caused them some difficulty in towns. In 1850 George Edmund Street produced a treatise *On the Proper Characteristics of a Town Church* in which he diagnosed the problem as being that 'men have taken ancient country churches as their models and have failed to discover that between them and churches in towns there ought to be a distinct and marked difference'. The remedy lay in Perpendicular, a style characteristic of many medieval urban churches 'which essentially fits it for the neighbourhood of houses' (cited in J.F.White 1962, 186). Fourteen years later William Burges reiterated the point, but offered a modified solution.

As to putting a little village church in London it is simply absurd. London has increased enormously: we are rebuilding it as rapidly as we can, and getting houses five or six storeys high. We might get churches quite as high, and also get great masses, so as to distinguish them from private houses.

Three years later he added:

We should not be building little copies of thirteenth-century village churches with Kentish rag and rubble walls in the heart of the nineteenth-century metropolis. On the contrary, we should build thick and high walls . . . so thick that they should bear vaulting or domes, and so high that they should over-top the huge warehouses which surround them.

(cited in Crook 1981, 209–11)

This much, then, was theory: ritualism required churches not simply as containers of people on handy sites, but as sacramental places. Ritualists sought medieval roots; Tractarians traced a continuity of Church authority; Camdenians saw 'true' architecture as the indispensable analogue of true religion. For the building itself, and especially in towns, prominence and scale were further aspects.

In practice it was not always so straightforward. A concomitant of a large church was a large parish, whether in terms of area, or population, or both, and not everyone was agreed that this was desirable. 'The parochial system never meant the kind of arrangement which prevails in our great cities, of leaving a large population under the care of one man', said the Rev W.D.Maclagan, vicar of Newington Sr, in 1872. In the 1840s W.F.Hook, vicar of Leeds, had deliberately embarked upon a process of partitioning the monster parish which he had inherited from the minster era of the eighth century, and which now happened to coincide with a large conurbation. New churches which were founded to give practical expression to Hook's policy of localization were on the whole smaller than their predecessors, usually with accommodation in the range 500–800. Another reason that was put forward for thinking small arose from the fear that members of the disadvantaged Victorian industrial underclass were too ill-educated to benefit from the intellectual content of Christian teaching. 'The rich', said the Rev James Taylor at a conference in 1872

> and those who are accustomed to discourses upon things of an abstract character, can supply a few words of a sentence which they don't happen to hear, but the poor cannot. They can appreciate anything about hard and soft, wet and dry, long and short ... anything affecting the senses ... but when we begin to speak to them about the attributes of God ... it is a difficult matter for them to understand.

Accordingly, Taylor called for intimate buildings: 'We want to get the people close to us if they are to understand us. What we want is not large magnificent churches ... we want small churches.'

G.Gilbert Scott Jnr argued exactly the contrary. He attacked the policy of building small, local churches in great cities.

> Certainly if the object be to provide places in which, what are called respectable people, may pay their Sunday tribute to propriety, what we do is well enough. The district church matches excellently well enough the semi-detached villa. But if our object is to act upon people at large, upon the artisans and mechanics, the labourers and the poor, who constitute the bulk of the nation, then we need quite another kind of building. It is quite certain that men and women of different classes in society will never be brought to meet in the same church, unless there is, to put it plainly, plenty of elbow room.

Scott pointed to the contrast between churches in England and the large churches found in France and Belgium where

> you may see the beggar, the strolling musician, the working man ... and the fine lady, all ... at the same mass ... simply because the church is large enough to give everyone plenty of room. It is only in large buildings that persons of all ranks can be brought together with mutual satisfaction. Small churches will always be ... the monopoly of the respectable classes. Into these the people at large are at once too proud and too shy to intrude themselves.

Like Street, like Burges, Scott advocated fewer, larger, churches 'on the scale of our own factories, our town halls, our railway stations'. Although rich embellishments would have to be forgone, for reasons of expense, the exterior, however plain 'is sure to have a certain dignity from its dimensions'. A corollary of Scott's proposal was the need to place churches at right-angles to the street, to take up as little of the frontage as possible where land values were high. Such adornment as might be afforded could then be concentrated on the west front. 'The façade serves, as it were, to advertise the church. In other cases, acting on the same principle, the tower alone may stand upon the street front, the church standing completely behind, and the principal entrance being through the tower' (Church Congress 1872, 84–5).

Scott and Taylor were in agreement on one point: the essential problem that confronted the Church was one of social class. In the background, too, can be detected the theory which had circulated at least from the time of Vanbrugh, that fine churches could exert an ennobling, even moral influence upon the poor. Admittedly, the theory was difficult to test, as for much of the nineteenth century most churches were kept locked when they were not in use for services. 'If our church doors were not shut out of service time,' said the architect J.P.Seddon, 'what valuable aids to education might not their walls be made? We blame the poor for dullness of apprehension, but do little to enlighten them. Our own houses are closed to them, and the art provided for their cottages are but pot dogs and bad lithographs' (Church Congress 1872, 94). Others were less convinced. The architect, C.Hodgson Fowler, had experience of building and restoring churches in mining communities, where robustness of fabric and furnishings came before beauty. In some of these places 'the young fellows would take up the stones and throw them at your new church doors for a little Sunday amusement; there chairs would not do, because they would kick them to pieces'. Class was the underlying issue. As Disraeli remarked: 'How are manners to influence men if they are divided into classes – if the population of a country becomes a body of sections, a group of hostile garrisons?' (cited in Briggs 1963, 45).

Class differences were manifested in arrangements for seating. In rural areas where there was only one parish church all people had to sit together. But they did so in customary positions, according to rank and wealth. The seating plan of a country church could be a microcosm of the social structure of its parish (Obelkevich 1976, 109–10). In towns the pattern was more complicated. In the older churches many sittings were 'appropriated' – i.e. pre-booked, either by rent or by custom – and in these the poor could feel unwelcome. In some churches private interests became so strong that they acquired structural expression. The squire's pew or family chapel was a commonplace, but at Bisley *Gl* where mill-owners from nearby Stroud became accustomed to worship, their personal galleries proliferated to an extent that demanded eleven separate entrances (Verey 1976a, 169). Churchmen tried to counter such problems by building new churches in working-class areas in the hope that the poor would gravitate to them. But even these efforts did not always achieve their intended effect. They could be thwarted if the churches concerned became fashionable, with the result that local parishioners were displaced by wealthier people who came in from outside. In others the clergy made little impact and their churches remained empty.

The obstacles to churchgoing that were sown by class distinctions are found as much in places of fashionable elegance as in gritty industrial cities. Take Cheltenham. In the sixteenth century John Leland had found Cheltenham to be 'a long town having a market'. There was one parish church, St Mary's, which had once been a minster. Between 1720 and 1780 there were modest developments which focused upon the mineral-laden waters which were pumped from a spring. In 1740 Dr Short, a connoisseur of spa waters, opined that Cheltenham's were superior to those of Bath – which was expanding mightily at this time (Cunliffe 1986, 112). But it was not until 1786 that serious measures were taken for upgrading the facilities at Cheltenham, and not until 1788 that a visit by George III and Queen Charlotte brought Cheltenham to the forefront of social attention. Rapid growth followed. In 1801 Cheltenham contained just over 3000 residents; not many more than in 1713. By 1826 the population had risen to c. 20,000.

As usual such expansion brought a demand for extra churches. Permission had earlier been sought for the installation of a gallery over the north aisle of the parish church 'otherwise our families and lodgers cannot be accommodated with the convenience of hearing the word of God' (cited in Hart 1965, 133). The Dissenters were active, building chapels in the High Street in 1808–9 (for services 'conducted on the plan of Lady Huntingdon's chapels'), North Place in 1816 (reopened three years later under the control of the Countess of Huntingdon's trustees), Grosvenor Street in 1817–18 (Strict Baptist), King Street in 1812–13 (Wesleyan Methodists, replacing a succession of earlier chapels on other sites), and Knapp Road in 1820 (Baptist) (Stell 1986, 75–7). Cheltenham had a large and fluctuating population of visitors. The strength of Dissent in general, and the presence of the Countess of Huntingdon's Connexion, is likely to reflect this. But the Anglicans did not begin to increase their provision until the 1820s. Then they built three churches: Holy Trinity, Portland Street; St James, Suffolk Square, on the new Montpelier estate; and St John, which was erected for 'the use of inhabitants of the new houses in and around the upper High Street'.

Cheltenham's class differences were exposed by the three new churches. It was observed that the churches had been built 'at the expense of private individuals, or as joint stock speculations'. They therefore 'partook of an exclusiveness scarcely perhaps recognized by the Gospel. While every facility was there afforded to the wealthy and affluent' (those who had subscribed had guaranteed places; visitors bought tickets at the door) 'comparatively little care had hitherto been manifested to provide for the spiritual instruction of the poor' (cited in Hart 1965, 184). Accomodation in the parish church was now 'totally inadequate'; there too most of the sittings were earmarked. 'To remedy this evil, the Rev Francis Close proposed the erection of a Free Church, where the poor might be accommodated as well as the rich' (cited in Hart 1965, 184). A citizen gave land for the site, which lay in the midst of workers' housing. The Commissioners made a grant of £3626 towards the total cost of £6871 (Port 1961, 144–5). Residents of Cheltenham raised the balance. The new church was opened in 1831. It was dedicated, appropriately enough, to St Paul.

Cheltenham was by no means all tree-lined avenues, terraces of agreeable Regency housing and fashionable churches like the elegant Christ Church (1838–40). There were poor areas, and sharp social contrasts. Another church which was located in an area of deprivation was St Peter's, completed in 1849. Its district was one 'where life and property are not safe'. Robberies were quite common, and there were occasional murders. The new church was staffed by two clergymen. But during the 1850s they seem to have made little impression. St Peter's was 'nearly empty of a Sunday morning' (cited in Hart 1965, 236).

Individual members of the clergy could have a decisive influence upon the parochial development of a town. In Leeds, W. F. Hook succeeded in breaking up his huge, unwieldy parish, which on the eve of its dismemberment in 1844 contained 152,054 people, 21 churches or chapels of which 18 were curacies without the cure of souls and 3 were private property from which the poor were excluded, and where the township of Leeds alone had just 13,000 sittings, of which only 5500 were free, for a population of close on 89,000 (Stephens 1879, 164–6) (Fig. 125). In Brighton there were in 1870 17 churches and 5 chapels serving c. 80,000 people – but still only one parish.

In the 1820s Brighton grew more swiftly than any other town in Britain. It has been fairly said that in Brighton the nineteenth-century contribution to church architecture and townscape can be studied in microcosm. Some of the most eminent Victorian architects worked there: Blomfield, Bodley, Carpenter, Somers Clarke; and there are contributions by William Morris and by artists such as Rossetti and Ford Madox Brown. And yet the Religious Census of 1851 found Brighton to be unusually deficient in church accommodation (p. 389). On the map things did not look too bad. Apart from the parish church of St Nicholas, inherited from the Middle Ages, and the Chapel Royal (1795), there were numerous churches and chapels of various kinds. But here lay the snag. Five of the churches were proprietary: they were controlled by groups of investors and lay outside the parish system, where they functioned to the exclusion of the poor. Chapels-of-ease had been built, but several of them attracted fashionable congregations. A different approach was to locate churches within the poorer areas of the town. This was tried in the 1830s and 1840s, with All Souls, Upper Edward Street, St John's, Carlton Hill, and St Paul's, West Street.

The vicar of Brighton himself paid most of the £14,000 that was needed

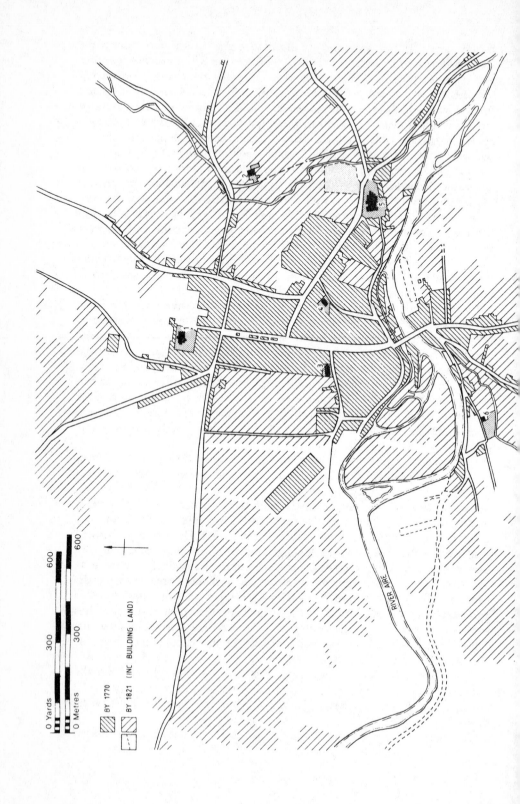

O Yards   300   600

O Metres   300   600

BY 1770

BY 1821 (INC BUILDING LAND)

RIVER AIRE

to build St Paul's. In 1850 his son, Arthur Wagner, became its priest-in-charge. Arthur Wagner was interested in Tractarianism, and St Paul's became well known as a centre of ritualist worship. However, like St Peter's and Christ Church, Montpelier Road, it also became fashionable. Wagner devoted much of its resources and his own considerable fortune to pastoral and charitable work within the district. If the poor did not actually come to church, they might nevertheless send their children to its school, orphans to its nursery or their aged to its infirmary.

From 1862 Wagner began to increase the scope of this work by planting a series of mission churches. The first was St Mary Magdalene in Bread Street. Next came the Church of the Annunciation (1864). In the 1880s this achieved considerable success under the effective ministry of George Chapman. Like St Mary Magdalene it was a simple building, and it is interesting that when in 1881 the structure required enlargement, Chapman resisted Wagner's wish to build something new and dramatic. 'Instead, the enlargement was achieved modestly, keeping the low roof and mission-church intimacy' (Hennock 1981, 181). But by now Wagner was determined to build something out of the ordinary: a church which would be massive without and numinous within; a church which would at once proclaim and embody his twin ideals of mission and ritualism. So he built St Bartholomew. It was designed by a local architect called Edmund Scott, and it was located on waste ground in an area of workers' housing. St Bartholomew was conceived on an epic scale. The aisleless interior measures 58 ft (17.67 m) across, and thus exceeds by a wide margin even the largest of the clear spans of medieval English cathedrals. The cost, again met mostly out of Wagner's pocket, was such that little could be spared for embellishment. But in its plainness St Bartholomew's rather proved Scott's point, that a church on the scale of a factory or a town hall would be 'sure to have a certain dignity from its dimensions'. And it contained no pews. All the sittings were free.

'From the very first', points out Hennock, 'St Bartholomew's was meant for more than the immediate district in which it stood. Placed alongside the London–Brighton railway line just where the trains slowed down to pull into the station, its vast height and bulk beckoned to the visitors, towering above the roof line of houses, as cathedrals do' (Hennock 1981, 182). The success of this effect can be judged from the barrage of anti-ritualist criticism that it attracted (183–4). For low churchmen St Bartholomew's was not out of sight, and what it represented was not out of mind. Wagner's third mission church, St Martin's, was more tactfully contrived. Rather than reach again for the sky – a plan which in any case

125 Leeds, West Yorkshire, on the eve of industrial expansion. 1 St John, Briggate; 2 Methodist meeting; 3 Presbyterian meeting; 4 Independent meeting; 5 St Peter (parish church); 6 Quaker meeting (*Sources*: T.Jeffreys' map of 1770 and C.Fowler's map of 1821)

was ruled out by the municipal authorities – 'something of the same sense of vast internal space was achieved by digging the foundations deep and laying the floor below ground level' (Hennock 1981, 185).

Despite their size and celebrity, St Bartholomew's and St Martin's were still mission churches. The Wagner dynasty ruled Brighton as a single parish, a kind of parochial palatinate within the diocese of Chichester. Another face of Tractarian social concern could be paternalism, and a reluctance to relinquish centralized authority.

It was not unusual for men like Arthur Wagner to sink their own money into schemes for church extension or projects of related type. In 1848 Francis Witts noted the generosity of J. H. Monk, bishop of Gloucester, following his announcement of a plan 'to devote a large sum, over which he has entire control, and which he might without blame appropriate to his private purposes, above £9000, to the erection of parsonages in small benefices in the diocese' (ed. Verey 1978, 172). Witts noted that the money came partly from the bishop's private savings, and partly from

> the sale of his interest as Bishop in the manor of Horfield, near Bristol, to the Ecclesiastical Commissioners. This was a very valuable property, said to be then worth £200,000, all of which he intended to give to the Church Commissioners, for the advantage of the Church generally, except a comparatively small sum to go towards his parsonage house fund.
>
> (ed. Verey 1978, 172).

But clerical wealth was insufficient and too uneven in its availability to counteract the socially divisive problem of appropriated pews. Public subscription remained indispensable as an adjunct to institutional sources in fundraising for new churches. It was possible for the Commissioners to contribute 70 per cent of the cost of a new church, as at Oldbury *Wo* in 1840–1, but for fewer than 50 per cent of the sittings to be free. An Act of 1851 enabled the Commissioners 'to extinguish pew-rents where a satisfactory endowment had been provided: a significant move . . . and a reflection of the growing agitation against such distinctions in church' (Port 1961, 121). In the forefront of the agitators were the Camdenians. They hated pew-rents and played a large part in the campaign for their abolition.

Another force which was disruptive of traditional class-values behind churchbuilding comprised businessmen and industrialists: the coming elite of Victorian England. They can be detected in Leeds during the 1840s, helping W. F. Hook towards his goal of parochial devolution. The site of St Philip's, Wellington Street, was contributed by Messrs Gott. St Thomas, Melbourne Street, was built in the midst of back-to-back housing at the expense of M. J. Rhodes. St John the Evangelist at Holbeck was built by Marshalls, the flax tycoons.

Individual industrialists channelled wealth towards causes for which they had special sympathy: schools, mechanics' institutes, libraries, mission societies – churches. Regional or national academies which trained

Dissenting ministers relied heavily upon such support. Many factory masters were of nonconformist persuasion, and their impact upon local politics was often allied to denominational attachments. In a number of towns and cities the Unitarians exerted an influence on civic affairs which was out of all proportion to their numerical strength. This was so not only in smaller communities which were dominated by a single mill-owning dynasty, but also in provincial towns, like Leicester, and in some industrial cities such as Manchester, Liverpool and Birmingham. The substantial Gothic Revival Church of the Messiah built in Broad Street, Birmingham, in 1860–1, 'was more than the centre of a small sect: it was a cultural and intellectual centre of a whole society, a place where ideas about society were openly and critically discussed' (A. Briggs 1963, 204). Quakerism, too, was strong in Birmingham, and nonconformist influence upon the social and political development of the city 'was strengthened by the fact that the prestige – and wealth – of the majority of Birmingham's most respected families were moving forces behind local dissent' (A. Briggs 1963, 206).

In the north textile masters contributed the lion's share of the costs of church- and chapel-building and repair in the middle years of the nineteenth century (Fig. 126). Apart from financial alliance with the Anglicans there were dramatic new chapels, some now in the Gothic style. The industrialist John Kay paid for the Methodist chapel at Summerseat La in 1847. Peter Whitehead built a meeting-house in Rawtenstall La. The Pilkingtons built chapels around Blackburn La. In Todmorden WY the Fieldens spent £36,000 on a magnificent Unitarian church, opened in 1869. The grandeur of this building, aglow within with polished stone, is reinforced by its position on the side of a hill. When built, this church proclaimed a present confidence; it could be seen from the Fielden mansion at Dobroyd, but it also pointed back towards Todmorden's industrial origins. The building overlooks their mill at Waterside which by 1846 was processing more poundage of cotton per week than any other plant in the world. It also overlooks the cottages where the Fieldens' grandfather had toiled in the founding of their business two generations before. It was here, too, that John Fielden MP, Lord Shaftesbury's ally and parliamentary associate in the campaign for the Ten Hours Act, had been born.

Most Victorian cities were not large undifferentiated conurbations but assemblages of districts, each of which had its own sense of identity and social character. To a large extent Birmingham was governed

by a small knot of Nonconformist families, who knew each other well ... and continued until the middle of the twentieth century to dominate local social life. Many of them lived in Birmingham's most distinctive 'suburb', Edgbaston, a carefully-planned residential estate belonging to the Calthorpe family, and situated only one mile from the centre of the city.

(A. Briggs 1963, 206)

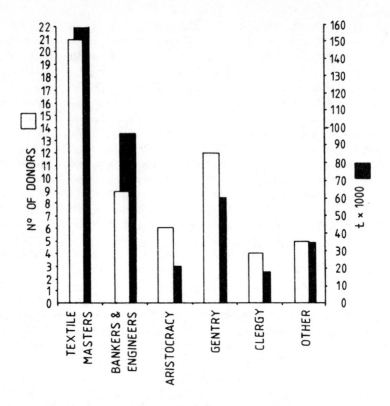

126 Sources of finance for churchbuilding in Lancashire between 1840 and 1875 (*Source*: Howe 1984, 284)

There were comparable enclaves in other cities. In Leeds, for instance, a number of the distinguished families lived on Headingly Hill, removed from the hurly-burly of the city centre and the noise and smells of mills and leatherworking in nearby valleys. Among their number were wealthy Congregationalists who combined to pay for a large chapel which was built in 1864–6. The status of this enterprise is reflected in the choice of architect: Cuthbert Brodrick, the designer of Leeds Town Hall (1853–8). The church was located at right-angles to the main road, amid the prosperous villas and ample terraces then inhabited by the elite of Leeds. In common with other large chapels of the later nineteenth century, a Sunday School and meeting-room were incorporated in a basement storey beneath the church: an arrangement facilitated here by the sloping site. In nearby northern resorts like Ilkley and Harrogate the influence of Dissent is equally pronounced. The grassy Strays of Harrogate are fringed by large houses, hotels, churches – and chapels. The Victoria Road development of 1861 finds its end-stop not in an Anglican parish church, but a prominent Congregationalist building with a competitive steeple. Harrogate's development as a spa continued up to the First World War, and what is arguably its greatest church, St Wilfrid, Duchy Road, was not begun until 1905. St Wilfrid's stands in the sumptuous surroundings of an affluent Edwardian suburb; it is well seen in May, when the nearby gardens are adazzle with laburnum and flowering cherry. The Early English idiom of the church has a cool restraint. Concern for a correct alignment set it askew from the road.

The structure of commerce could have an effect upon how churches were founded, and where they were put. Towns with economies based on many small businesses would have to rely upon co-operative action in church extension, whereas places which were effectively in the hands of a small number of employers offered scope for unilateral action. It was common for industrialists to erect dwellings close to their factories to accommodate the workforce. Standards varied, but some of the housing commissioned by benevolent figures, like John Fielden at Lydgate outside Todmorden *WY*, was of advanced character. Occasionally such men went further and created entire settlements. In Wales there were experiments with planned towns late in the eighteenth century: at Milford, for example, effectively begun *c.* 1797 on a simple grid plan which included a Gothick church. Other schemes were undertaken at Tremadoc *Gwd* (*Crn*), conceived in the early 1800s, and Morriston *Glm*, which was founded by Sir John Morris *c.* 1768 to house employees at his copper works. The main development began in 1790, and had its focus at a church which occupied an island site within a cross-roads (Hilling 1976, 149–52). Elsewhere in south Wales iron companies provided churches or chapels for their workers at Glyntaf (1838), Tredegar (1836) and Dowlais (1827). In the countryside of England and Wales there were many estate villages such as Milton Abbas *Do*, Acton Reynold *Sa*, Merthyr Mawr *Glm* or Easton Neston *Np* which were established at various times in the eighteenth and nineteenth centuries by improving landlords, and which may have contributed to the thinking which lay behind some of the more advanced industrial developments. At Copley *WY* the Halifax mill-owner Colonel Edward Akroyd financed the building of a mill estate in 1849. Akroyd later added a school, library and a church (1863–5). In 1861 Akroyd embarked upon another model village, at Boothtown on the northern edge of Halifax. He called it Akroyden. Akroyden's church, All Souls Haley Hill, was begun in 1856 to designs by Sir George Gilbert Scott. All Souls therefore preceded the village. It has been observed how in 1855 the Crossleys, another family of Halifax industrialists, had begun to build a large church in the centre of the town. The Crossleys were Congregationalists. They provided their church with a mighty steeple some 235 ft (71.6 m) tall. In 1863 the Crossleys built an estate village of their own at West Hill Park. The original conception, not realized, called for a central focus comprising a large church and school, flanked by symmetrical rows of housing. Perhaps the alternating achievements of the houses of Crossley and Akroyd teach a lesson which could be considered in relation to the multiplication of so many local churches in the tenth and eleventh centuries, and indeed to their later outward and upward enlargement?

Arguably the greatest example of High Victorian total integrated planning is Saltaire, which was established in open countryside on the edge of Bradford in the 1850s. The founder was Titus Salt, who made his money through the processing of alpaca and mohair. His brand-new mill, designed by the great engineer William Fairbairn, opened in 1853, formed a colossal centrepiece. Beside it stood a large grid-plan village, eventually of more than 800 dwellings. Salt's employees were furnished not only with decent housing, but also a school, library, institute and a park. Like Crossley, Salt was a Congregationalist, and his community was duly furnished with a large and rather impressive baroque church. It stands on the periphery of the village, aligned upon the mill: Mammon and God duly balanced, Anglicans excluded.

In the nineteenth century it was not only places that changed, but also the nature of communications between them. 'Delightful weather', wrote Francis Witts in his diary on 4 May 1839. On that day he left his rectory at Upper Slaughter *Gl* a little before 8.00 a.m., drove to Northleach in an open carriage, and there transferred to the Magnet coach which took him to Oxford (in time for lunch), and on to the station of the Great Western Railway near Maidenhead. He arrived at the station just before 5.00 p.m. Fifty minutes later he was in London.

It is hard to exaggerate the range of changes – in mentalities, patterns of life, the economy, the landscape – that railways wrought. Nine years before Witt's journey the passenger network had scarcely existed. Eleven years after it ran to 8000 miles. Remote rural places were now linked to cities. Journeys that had taken days could now be accomplished in hours. Information, ideas and rumour could be exchanged at speed. For ecclesiologists the railway was a Godsend. John Mason Neale thought railways unromantic and regretted their coming. But by 1860 there were not many parish churches that stood so far from a railway station as to be beyond the range of an ardent ecclesiologist. The direct acquaintance of scholars and architects with large numbers of individual buildings was correspondingly increased.

Even the building of railways had an effect on churches and churchgoing. For the construction of the Bramhope tunnel on the Leeds–Thirsk line in 1845–9 the contractor had nearly 2000 men. They erected a shanty town of 350 wooden shacks. Their children crowded into the local school. 'The Methodist chapels at Pool and Bramhope were filled on Sundays and in use every week-night' (Seals 1967). The tunnel was long, and the work of driving it was hazardous. Many workmen died. In the churchyard at Otley stands a memorial which was erected to the memory of those who lost their lives. It is in the shape of a tunnel portal.

The social impact of railway-building was experienced in many places. It was, of course, short-lived. But when the army of workmen had departed, life had changed. Agricultural villages in the vicinity of large towns could acquire a new function as dormitory suburbs. This could be a further stimulus to churchbuilding. With the coming of the railway, Brighton and neighbouring coastal towns like Worthing and Bognor became readily accessible from London. By the end of the nineteenth century many wealthy financiers had discovered the merits of residing on the south coast and commuting to the City. Brighton, Hastings and Eastbourne were bracketed together as 'isolated suburbs of London' (Sala 1895, 13).

Railways did much to promote the growth and formation of seaside towns. Like spas, seaside resorts had existed as places for the health and pleasure of the select since the early eighteenth century. Some of them, like Eastbourne *Sx*, Weymouth *Do* and Scarborough *NY* were flourishing and expanding before 1800. Railways broadened public access to such places. Seaside towns situated on flat coastal plains were not always planned out with much originality. Typically there is a monotonous rectilinear grid, as at Worthing *Sx* and Southport *La*; occasionally the grid is crosswoven, as at Clacton-on-Sea *Ex*. All three places inherited medieval churches, although others were added. Here and there planners looked to churches for effect. At Skegness, for instance, the grid of broad tree-lined streets which was blocked out in 1873-5 incorporates a central circus within which stands the large church of St Matthew, begun in 1879. Butterfield's scheme for a new seaside town at Hunstanton *Nf* reflects his interest in the possibility of a town church as a focal feature (P. Thompson 1971, 319-20). Resorts on hilly coastal sites, like the rather unsuccessful Saltburn *Clv* (*YN*), offered more scope: churches could be perched on terraces, or related to sinuous roads which wound around the sides of valleys. Bournemouth and Scarborough are among the resorts which are rewarding from this point of view.

Railway England of the mid-nineteenth century was still rural England. A visitation made at Stainburn *NY* (*YW*) in 1743 found a curate who read 'publick service' twice every Sunday, catechized after the second lesson at Evening Prayer in the summer, and administered the Sacrament in the chapel 'three times Yearly'. There 'is only a School-House in Stainburne without any Endowment, to which Parents, who are all small farmers, send their children at the most vacant times of the Year, where they are taught to read English and instructed in the Church-Catechism'. In many places a century later circumstances had not greatly changed. After the Religious Census of church attendance on 30 March 1851, the Rev Richard Moore, vicar of Horkstow *Li*, attributed the below-average size of his congregation to the fact that it was 'the time of year when many persons are engaged with lambs and other outdoor necessary duties' (ed. Ambler 1979, 252-3). Morning attendances at Anglican churches in Cheshire were regularly limited by the demands of dairy-farming (R.B. Walker 1966, 82-3). Thus did patterns of land-use influence churchgoing. To an extent they continue to do so today. But in the 1850s the claims of the landscape upon a large section of the population were scarcely less remorseless than they had been in the Middle Ages.

Railway England was also Coketown England, where poor urban hygiene and bad sanitation could even affect the plan of a church. In 1872 the Rev Reginald Cayley pointed out that epidemics in cities required reservation of the sacrament, so that communion could be administered to the sick on their death-beds: 'I think that architects when designing churches for large towns, should remember the necessities of the population, and think of such things.'

There had been socio-topographical dreams, like Robert Owen's landscape dotted with Owenite socialist villages; and there would be more, like Ebenezer Howard's vision of a radial garden city, wherein spaces for churches (to be built at denominational expense) would be allotted in the outer ring. Some ideas were on the point of fulfilment: Bourneville, for instance, begun in 1879; Port Sunlight, on the drawing board by 1888; Letchworth garden city, and others.

The later nineteenth century saw a relaxation in attitudes to style and a growth in eclecticism. There was to be fresh experimentation – the boulder-like St Mark's at Brithdir *Gwd* (1896), for instance, or the enjoyable textures of Arts and Crafts buildings like St Michael, Colehill *Do* or St Chad's at Hopwas *St* – and there were to be more revivals. Some of the most magnificent buildings would be built by Dissenters. What, one wonders, would John Wesley have made of the Unitarians' High Pavement chapel in Nottingham (1874–6), or mighty Albion chapel at Ashton-under-Lyne? George Fox had scorned churches as 'steeple-houses'. Presbyterians had rejected the concept of the holy place as idolatrous. John Wesley scoffed at the idea of consecrated ground, which he called 'a popish conceit' (Wesley, *Letters* 8, 57). 'Certainly', wrote Wesley of the site of the City Road chapel, 'that ground is holy as any in England' (*Letters*, 8, 52). The Church of England maintained the theory of the church as a holy place through the eighteenth century, but did so without much conviction. Its commitment was mainly to externals: the steeple as a distinguishing feature, architecture as an ennobling influence, the graveyard as a place apart. By 1800 belief in the intrinsic sanctity of an ecclesiastical site was all but dead. The fact that it exists again today is largely due to the efforts of the ritualists and the Camdenians after 1840. To this extent, therefore, any modern belief that about twenty square miles of England and Wales are in some objective sense 'holy' is largely a reintroduction of the nineteenth century. But that need not diminish our wonder at the relative permanence of a medieval church and the ground that it occupies. Nor should it limit our dreams as we gaze back into the distance of a church's history.

AFTERWORD

Anyone who has never written a book could be forgiven for supposing that published writing represents exactly what its author intended to say. Some authors may achieve such perfection, but I am not of their number. My feeling here at the end of seven years' intermittent labour is an amalgam of frustration and regret. Frustration, because I am well aware of the weaknesses in what stands above; regret, because the opportunity to remedy those deficiencies has gone.

Part-time writing is a selfish activity. Authors who also have regular jobs tend to write in the evenings, at weekends and during holidays: the times that other folk wisely reserve for mending the bicycles of their children, digging the garden, painting the house, entertaining friends, being patient with Jehovah's Witnesses on the doorstep, going on holiday or simply being asleep. Any attempt to be anti-social only part of the time just makes matters worse, for the incubus is in the household that much longer. The completion of this book testifies as much to the fortitude of my wife, the tolerance of my children (two of whom have passed from ages in single figures to adolescence almost without my noticing), and to the patience of its publishers, as to the actual endeavours that lie behind it. Even so, *Churches in the Landscape* is a compromise. It covers less ground than I had hoped, and quite a lot of it only approximates to my original intentions. Its critics may be helped if I point to some of its greater flaws.

Protracted writing has meant that some of the earlier sections have been overtaken by my own further thinking, and by the recent work of others of which it has not been possible to take account. This has led to a certain amount of self-contradiction, which may seem all the more disconcerting for the reason that the chapters were not written in numerical sequence. Built-in obsolescence is the price to be paid for including – as I have rather tended to – too many *ballons d'essai*, and for taking too long about it. I should like, for example, to have read Professor Richard Bradley's essay 'Time regained' before embarking upon Chapter 2, while Dr John Blair's latest contributions on minsters and local churches came just too late for them to cause me to reconsider my own rather wilful views (Bradley 1987; Blair 1987). Meanwhile, almost every trip to the library discloses fresh work on ecclesiastical topography which is not reflected here.

Such regrets are inevitable. A book has to be ended somewhere. But there are other shortcomings which manifested themselves only gradually, as work proceeded. In the main these have to do with the identification and definition of what are – or should have been – the leading themes of the book. The concept of the holy place is one of these. It is mentioned throughout, but my perception of the changes which have occurred in attitudes towards, and beliefs about, holy places only began to clarify properly towards the end. There were other matters, to which I did not give sufficient thought at the outset, which turned out on closer acquaintance to be far more important and interesting than I had anticipated. About half of the book covers the determination of ecclesiastical sites down to the twelfth century. In retrospect that still seems reasonable, because more than half of our parochial sites were selected before 1200. But I did underestimate both the significance and the intrinsic interest of later developments. Only two chapters were allocated to the post-Reformation centuries. I discovered – too late – that this period called for three or four.

Another unwritten chapter would concern the twentieth century. The book breaks off at no very logical point towards the end of the nineteenth century. I am sorry not to have brought the subject up to date. Much has happened. In places like Bristol, Exeter and London, the impact of the Second World War upon churches was considerable. Since 1945 new parishes have been formed to cater for people in conurbations which have expanded across areas that were previously rural. The religiosity of ethnic minorities has created new patterns of worship. Conversely, in the last two decades some 1200 parish churches have been declared redundant. The best of them – so far, about 220 – are cared for intact by an admirable body known as the Redundant Churches Fund. The Fund is financed jointly by Church and State. (One hopes for an extension of this enlightenment into Wales and Scotland, and into the realm of nonconformity, where no equivalent provision yet exists.) Unwanted churches deemed to be of less than national importance have been put to a wide variety of new uses, or, failing this, demolished. These very recent changes are on a scale unparalleled since the losses of the later Middle Ages.

Earlier times are being recalled in other ways. The house-church movement points back, perhaps a little unconvincingly, towards those days in the first century when Christians had no church buildings at all. More dramatic are the changes being forced by tensions between the Church's needs and its resources. Shortage of clerical manpower (exacerbated, some would argue, by the fact that it still is limited to *man*power) coupled with a parochial system which was fashioned largely according to the requirements of the medieval countryside and Victorian towns, are obliging a redeployment of the clergy. The pattern of one incumbent per rural parish has dissolved. In its place are large groups of rural churches being served by itinerant priests. In areas where team ministries operate it seems we are not so very far from the shape of the minster system as it might have existed in the ninth or tenth century. Churchmen may care to give these parallels some thought, for the phase which preceded them was that of conversion, when the English were mostly still pagan. That, too, may soon be recalled, for the unmaking of the parochial system is surely reflecting a slide into popular unbelief.

I have mentioned the English, but what of the Welsh? Or, for that matter, the Scots? At the outset it was my plan to examine ecclesiastical development and settlement throughout southern Britain. In the event, my unfamiliarity with the buildings, sites and sources of Wales caused me to abandon this scheme and stick to what I knew best. Vestiges of my early intentions nevertheless remain, both in the text and the illustrations. I am in no doubt that Wales *ought* to have been included, not least because so many of the supposed contrasts between ecclesiastical development in England and Wales appear on closer acquaintance to dwindle in the face of the similarities. In what significant ways, for instance, did the institutions of the *clas* differ from those of the *mynster*? However this may be, it seemed wise to work within my limitations. Wales received short measure not because I disregarded it, but because it deserved more than I could give.

Other omissions are more excusable. The significance of climate, weather and maintenance in relation to the history of churches could have been explored to greater effect if Chapter 8 had been written after the night of 15/16 October 1987. The Great Storm was a weather event to set beside the most violent of those reported in earlier sources. During following days, colleagues sent news of spires which were felled, roofs which had their lead peeled or sucked away, pinnacles wrenched off, and trees which crashed down upon aisles. An analysis of the long-term consequences for church fabrics in southern England would be revealing. The medieval parishioner had no insurance against such disasters.

For reasons given, *Churches in the Landscape* was a book more exciting in contemplation than in completion. Regret has been tempered by confession. Thus shriven, my farewell lies in the hope that some aspects of our parish churches and their surroundings have been opened up to fresh thought and discussion.

New Year's Day, 1988

NOTES ON THE PLATES

Copyright in all the photographs is reserved to the institutions or individual photographers named, to each of whom the author extends his best thanks for permission to reproduce their work. Plates 18, 25 and 36 are reproduced by permission of the Controller of Her Majesty's Stationery Office.

1   Jewry Wall and church of St Nicholas, Leicester. The church incorporates pre-Conquest fabric, probably of late Saxon date, and has been much modified by later rebuilding. The wall in the foreground is Roman. In 1948 Dr Kathleen Kenyon suggested that the survival of this wall could have been due to its incorporation in an early Anglo-Saxon structure, possibly a church erected in the later seventh or eighth century (Kenyon 1948, 8, 37). More recently attention has been drawn to possibly cognate circumstances in Lincoln, where the first church on the site of St Paul-in-the-Bail was located within the courtyard of the forum (M. J. Jones 1986, 4). The unexplained survival of a large and solitary piece of upstanding masonry close to the heart of Roman Wroxeter *Sa* might also be remembered (*Photo*: Mick Sharp)

2   St Mary, Stanton Drew, Somerset. The nave consists of two aisles side by side: an arrangement characteristic of many churches in south-west England, where the hall church of two or three parallel aisles was a popular theme (cf. Pl. 20). Notice also the asymmetrical position of the tower. The prehistoric monument in the foreground is known locally as The Cove. It is roughly aligned to extreme moonrise, and may have been used for funerary ritual. A complex of megalithic rings stands nearby (Burl 1979, 219). Such a close topographical association between prehistoric monuments and a church is unusual, although if large stones once existed near to churches elsewhere it is possible that they fell victim to scavenging by early medieval builders (*Photo*: Mick Sharp)

3   St John the Baptist, Stanwick, North Yorkshire. The church stands within an area of *c.*750 acres (305 ha) that is enclosed by substantial fortifications of first-

454

century date. Part of this circuit can be seen close to the lower left-hand corner of the photograph. Beyond the church are remains of a smaller and apparently earlier set of defences which enclose a triangular area of about 17 acres (6.8 ha). The church dates mainly from the thirteenth century, but fabric of the twelfth century is visible on close inspection, and the likelihood of earlier ecclesiastical use of the site is indicated by the presence of pre-Conquest sculpture. The sub-circular form of the churchyard is striking. Traces of the arc of an enclosing bank and (internal) ditch are visible west of the church. On the far side of the site this feature has been destroyed by the wanderings of the Mary Wild Beck. It seems that an earlier channel of the beck ran to the north of the churchyard, with the result that here too the original enclosure has been lost. Curvilinear churchyards are uncommon in Yorkshire, although there is another example in the vicinity, at Gilling West (Fig. 33). It is widely assumed that churchyards of this form are extremely old, but this belief has seldom been put to ar-chaeological test, and it is doubtful whether circularity alone can be taken as a sign of great antiquity. In this case, however, there are circumstantial reasons for thinking that the site may have been put to ecclesiastical use before the ninth century. Gilling, a near neighbour of Stanwick, also curvilinear, originated in the mid-seventh century as the site of a religious community. Gilling's first abbot was a man called Trumhere who had been educated and consecrated by the Irish (*HE* iii.24). The physical resemblance between the two sites may be more than coincidental. Further discussion of large curvi-linear enclosures appears in the note on Pl. 10 (*Photo:* A. L. Pacitto)

4 The church of St Paul, Jarrow, Tyne & Wear (*Du*) is visible among trees within a squarish precinct next to oil storage tanks and the rubbish-filled waterway known as Jarrow Slake. Jarrow was the site of a religious communi-ty founded by Benedict Biscop around 680 as a companion house to his slightly earlier monastery at Monkwearmouth. The church of the Jarrow community was consecrated in April 684 or 685. A stone which records this event is preserved in the church. It appears that the seventh-century church survived until 1769, when it was pulled down. A large nineteenth-century nave stands in its place. However, immediately to its east stands a chancel that probably originated as a separate chapel that stood in line with the first church. Some time before the Conquest the two buildings were united by a connecting struc-ture upon which a tower was erected in the eleventh century. The tower is visi-ble, peeping above the trees. The natural boundaries of the seventh-century monastic site remain evident, despite the changed surroundings. After 1856 the river banks were transformed by the Tyne Improvement Commission, which built docks on both banks, including the famous Tyne Dock at South Shields (1859) which has handled more coal exports than any other dock in the world. The Commission also dredged the river and constructed the breakwaters at the river mouth. Such developments are far removed from the days of Bede, who passed almost all his days as a member of the community at Jarrow, where he wrote his *Ecclesiastical History of the English People* (*Photo, and contribution to cap-tion:* Tim Gates)

5 Burry Holms, Glamorgan, lies at the northern end of Rhossili Bay on the Gower peninsula. Like Lindisfarne, Ardwall Isle, Spurn Head in its probable seventh-/eighth-century incarnation, and a number of other places, this is a tidal island, accessible only at low water. Traces of buildings are visible on the sheltered side of the island which faces the mainland. Nearest to the camera

are the interlocking remains of several different buildings erected between the twelfth and fourteenth centuries. Just beyond these are the traces of a twelfth-century church. Excavations in the 1960s disclosed underlying traces of a timber structure, which may relate to the site of a pre-Norman ecclesiastical settlement. The earthwork running across the island to the west is older (RCAHM *Glamorgan* I.3, 14) (*Photo:* Terry James)

6 Llangwyfan, Anglesey. The physical characteristics of this site are comparable to those of Burry Holms in Pl. 5: a small offshore island, with inter-tidal access. But here the church has survived. In origin such sites might be imagined as being inherently unsuited to parochial use, but ideally adapted for occupation by holy men who wished to limit their contacts with the secular world. Whether Llangwyfan harbours traces of an early ecclesiastical settlement beneath its lofty cemetery platform is unknown, but the place must be a candidate for such a background (*Photo:* Mick Sharp)

7 The chapel of St Peter-on-the-Wall, Bradwell, Essex, is seen towards the right-hand margin of the photograph. Former porticus and an eastern apse are outlined upon the ground. The church is believed to stand beside, or even across, the west wall of a Roman fort. The fort was reoccupied by Cedd for monastic purposes in the mid-seventh century. Whether this church belonged to the community of Cedd's day, or was added at a later date, remains uncertain (Rigold 1977, 72–3). Most of the fort has been devoured by the sea, and any monastic remains which may have lain within it have disappeared. Excavations around the east end of the chapel in 1864 are said to have disclosed burials furnished with objects of various kinds, apparently of Middle Saxon date (Chancellor 1877). The marginal location of the church caused it to fall out of use, and for many years it was used as a barn (*Photo:* Royal Commission on the Historical Monuments of England)

8 Breedon-on-the-Hill, Leicestershire. The church of St Mary and St Ardulf perched upon the hill was built for a community of Augustinian canons in the twelfth century. The nave was removed after the Dissolution; what can be seen are the former eastern arm and central tower which were retained for parochial use. The site had been used for ecclesiastical purposes long before the Augustinians inherited it. A *monasterium* was established on the hilltop late in the seventh century, and the present building incorporates Anglo-Saxon sculpture of rare distinction. The monastic occupation in the seventh century was not the first: previously the site had been used as a hillfort. The precipitous profile of the eastern side of the hill has been caused by modern quarrying (*Photo:* Mick Sharp)

9 St Ninian Ninekirks, Cumbria (Westmorland). The church stands within an enclosure of approximately oval form, which in its turn is girdled by a wide loop of the River Eamont, appearing towards the lower and upper margins of the photograph. The church was rebuilt in 1660 under the patronage of Lady Anne Clifford, the unified nave and chancel being characteristic of other churches in this period – though for contrast compare Pl. 38. The church is now cared for by the Redundant Churches Fund and is notable for a suite of contemporary furnishings and fittings. During the repair of a burial vault in 1846 several skeletons were found, one of which was accompanied by an item of metalwork that could date to the eighth century (Bailey 1977). The full significance of this discovery remains unclear, but the site and surroundings of the church assume extra interest when viewed from above, for the church-

yard has a ghostly companion in the form of another enclosure of roughly similar size and shape which is visible intermittently as a mark in growing crops. Traces of irregular features adhering to the edge of this enclosure are too indistinct to permit interpretation, but Fig. 24 and Pl. 10 suggest possibilities (*Photo:* Barri Jones)

10 Llandyfaelog, Dyfed (Carmarthenshire). The church stands within a great enclosure from which the boundaries of fields radiate outwards. The enclosure is watered by a stream which flows past the west end of the church. This layout can possibly be identified as the imprint left by a type of tenure designated variously as *tir corddlan*, *tir corflan*, in the thirteenth century, by which time it was already old. *Tir corddlan* consisted of gardens or allotments under permanent cultivation. Such land has been described as nucleal, because it seems to have been associated with 'the more important ancient settlements which served as focal points for the community' (G. R. J. Jones 1972, 341-2). The term *corddlan* appears to have become associated, if not conceptually conflated, with two other words: *corfflan* 'corpse enclosure', and *corflan*, '*corf* meaning some kind of boundary or defence and the suffix *llan* referring to the area within' (1972, 342). Nucleal land might be associated with secular or ecclesiastical centres, but both (later) written sources and the location of topographical remnants often centre upon the sort of church that belonged to a *clas* – that is, a clerical community of canons under an abbot, or bishop-abbot (1972, 342-3). Such communities could themselves be envisaged as having developed out of earlier monastic groupings, just as the Community of St Cuthbert in the tenth and eleventh centuries is said to have consisted of clerks, described as canons, who lived in their own houses under a head who was called a dean (Barlow 1979, 229-30). Like the successors of English minsters, *clas* churches of the later Middle Ages are frequently of cruciform plan. Dispositions of nucleal land around churches elsewhere (e.g. Eglwys Ail, St Asaph, Llanynys, Llanfilo) have been discussed by Professor Jones (1972; 1981; 1983-4) (*Photo:* Terry James)

11 Odda's Chapel, Deerhurst, Gloucestershire. Now wedded to a house, this late Saxon chapel stands hardly more than a stone's throw from the parish church of St Mary, which embodies extensive fabric of an Anglo-Saxon monastic church. The presence of two religious sites in such close proximity can possibly be traced to a division of lordship which occurred here just before the Norman Conquest. The site illustrated was called Plaistow, and formed the manorial centre of an estate which was given into the control of Westminster Abbey. The nearby priory was administered by St Denis from *c.*1059 until 1419. The house is not older than the sixteenth century, but its site was the scene of the manorial court of the Westminster manor. The chapel may have been consecrated on 12 April 1056. An inscription found locally in 1675 records this date, together with the information that Odda *dux* had built the *aula* 'hall' for the soul of his brother Ælfric, who had died at Deerhurst, and that the *aula* had been dedicated in honour of the Holy Trinity (Okasha 1971, 64). The chapel was later assimilated to the adjoining house, put to domestic use and its earlier function forgotten. When the chapel was recognized in 1885 the fragment of a second inscription was found built into a chimney stack, added in the sixteenth century when the nave was turned into a kitchen. This also records a dedication in honour of the Holy Trinity. It seems likely that both dedications refer to this structure, for which on other grounds a date in the mid-eleventh

century would suit. *Aula* was sometimes used to denote a church in Anglo-Saxon sources, as in the sense of the 'hall of a saint'. The later association between chapel and house may echo the context in which the chapel was founded (*Photo:* Mick Sharp)

12 Itteringham, Norfolk. Marks in growing crops disclose the outlines of at least two former buildings. The apsidal structure on the left is likely to have been a church. The plan is typical of a local church built in the period *c.*1050–1150. A date much after this is improbable, because apses went out of fashion towards the end of the twelfth century. There is a slightly greater chance that the building could be older than the date suggested, as apsidal churches were erected at various places between the seventh and eleventh centuries. The overall impression is nevertheless of a church which was built within two or three generations of the Norman Conquest. No interpretation can be offered for the building(s) to the right of the church, and from the photograph alone we cannot even be sure that the two (or three) structures stood together at the same time. The absence of any visible continuation of the three-sided feature between the church and the larger structure to its right invites speculation that this might have been of composite construction, its absent portion being unseen because the crop has not responded to its former presence. No clear signs of graves are apparent, although indistinct blotches in the crop just west of the buildings might be studied with this possibility in mind. Until this photograph was taken on 16 July 1987 the presence of a church here was unsuspected, making it likely that the church had disappeared before the end of the thirteenth century, by which time references to its existence in written records might have been expected. Itteringham joins a steadily lengthening list of such redundancies, which together point to more fluidity in local provision around the time when the parish system was crystallizing than was once imagined (*Photo:* Derek Edwards/Norfolk Archaeological Unit)

13 Reepham, Norfolk. Churchyards containing more than one church may be found in all the counties of eastern England between the Thames and the Humber. Although never numerous, more existed in the past than is generally realized, and there were some dozens of them in Norfolk. Where one of the churches has gone, the former existence of a pair is not always easy to detect. At Reepham there were actually three churches within the precinct until the sixteenth century. A church which stood in the south-west corner of the churchyard was in ruins at the time of the Reformation and has since disappeared. Each member of the trio served a different parish. The church at the centre of the site is dedicated to St Michael and belongs to the parish of Whitwell. East of it stands the church of St Mary, which is the parish church of Reepham itself. The lost church was used by residents of the parish of Hackford. When founded the churches were probably reasonably spaced, but the site became increasingly overcrowded as they grew. The chancel of St Michael's may have been limited by the need not to encroach upon space which belonged to St Mary's. Similarly, it looks as though the parishioners of St Mary's were unable to build a tower at the west end of their church, and placed it instead next to their south aisle. The photograph is of additional interest for the way in which it reveals the tendency for graves to be aligned with reference to boundaries and paths. Exactly why churches should occur in clumps is not known, but in areas like Norfolk where many churches arose in close proximity it may sometimes have been thought logical to concentrate them on a single

site. At least one case is known where a second church was begun in the later eleventh century because of lack of accommodation in the first. Family interests and the social structure of the region may have played some part, the identities of different groups being given expression through separate foundations, not all of which endured (*Photo:* Derek Edwards/Norfolk Archaeological Unit)

14 St Martin, Cwmyoy, Gwent (Monmouthshire). The church has been contorted by slippage of the ground upon which it was built. Medieval church-builders were usually shrewd in assessing the suitability of sites, but it is necessary to remember that we tend to measure their accomplishments by buildings which have survived. Failure may have been more widespread than is now realized (*Photo:* Mick Sharp)

15 St Michael, Duntisbourne Rous, Gloucestershire. Builders like to work on level ground, but where a flat site is unavailable it is possible to exploit the slope by incorporating extra space within the building. Here the chancel is, in effect, a two-storey building, with a chapel under the chancel floor. This part of the church seems to have been built shortly after the Norman Conquest. The nave must be older (Taylor and Taylor 1965, 221) (*Photo:* Mick Sharp)

16 St Peter, Melverley, Shropshire. Written records make no reference to the existence of this church before the sixteenth century, but their silence does not permit us to assume that the church was then new. The main structure, one of only two completely timber-framed churches in Shropshire, probably dates from the second half of the fifteenth century. The church stands close to the River Vyrnwy, seen here in flood (*Photo:* Mick Sharp)

17 St Michael, Burrow Mump, Somerset. The church is seen atop the conical, natural mound, part of which was once fortified. A rebuilding of the church begun in the eighteenth century was left unfinished. The surrounding landscape has been claimed for agriculture from the Somerset Levels. Artificial cuts between the fields conduct surplus water towards the River Parrett (*Photo:* Royal Commission on the Historical Monuments of England)

18 East Witton, North Yorkshire. This village appears to be a product of co-ordinated planning. Field boundaries set at right-angles to the long central green suggest that the surrounding landscape was laid out at the same time as the village. Some of the fields are very narrow, and possibly correspond with individual crofts of the original layout. Larger fields are the result of amalgamations. The layout existed by 1627, when it appears on a map drawn by William Senior (Beresford and St Joseph 1979, 105–6). How much earlier the plan could be is unknown, but it is possible that the nearby Cistercian abbey of Jervaulx took a hand in its determination. If so, the village is unlikely to have assumed this form before the twelfth century. The church of St John the Evangelist which stands at the far end of the green fits well into the logic of the plan. It is, however, a latecomer, located here in 1809 as part of a pro-gramme of modernization of the village undertaken by the earl of Ailesbury. The former church stood outside the settlement, and was reached by the road which can be seen winding towards the top right-hand corner of the photograph. The site lies just off-picture. The dedication of the old church was to St Martin. The separation of church and village provides a further reason for thinking that the settlement is no older than the twelfth century. By this time the parochial pattern was in existence, and the residents of a new settle-

ment would usually be obliged to make use of a mother church that was already standing (*Photo:* Cambridge University Collection, Crown Copyright)

19 Great Chalfield, Wiltshire. The church of All Saints and the manor house adjoin. Thomas Tropenell acquired the manor during the 1450s, and had either built or begun the present house before his death in 1488. Tropenell also made changes to the church, much of which dates from the thirteenth century. There is a moat. The intimacy between church and house makes this a classic manorial group, but the basis for such a relationship could have been formed four, five or even six hundred years previously (cf. Pls 11, 12, and Figs 62, 73–82) (*Photo:* Mick Sharp)

20 All Saints, Holcombe Rogus, Devon. The parish church and manor house lie close together upon a hill above the present village. Holcombe Court was built *c.*1520 by the Bluett family, which is represented within the church by a family pew, a chapel and monuments. An ornamental lake and landscaped garden are visible within the grounds of the Court. Traces of former settlement and land division appear beyond. A stable block and circular dovecote intervene between Court and church. The individually roofed nave and aisles of the church are well seen from the air, as too is the absence of any marked external differentiation between nave and chancel (*Photo:* Frances Griffith/Devon County Council)

21 Church, ringwork and mound at Earl's Barton, Northamptonshire. The earliest part of the present church is the west tower. When built, perhaps in the late tenth or early eleventh century, the tower may have formed the core of the church, its ground storey being used as a nave. The relationship between the tower and the nearby earthwork is not yet understood. It looks as though the tower could have been peripheral to a ringwork, but from topographical evidence the inclusion of the tower within an enclosure of less regular outline is a possibility that cannot be excluded. The earthwork has often been assumed to date from after the Norman Conquest, but here again facts are lacking. Was the earthwork new, or did it supersede an earlier enclosure with which the tower was already associated? The mound within the earthwork introduces a third area of uncertainty. Although in its present form it appears to be a motte, one wonders if it could be cloaking a feature of greater age. The photograph was taken in 1936 (*Photo:* Allen Collection/Ashmolean Museum, Oxford)

22 Taplow, Buckinghamshire. A large mound stands within the graveyard of the old church, which was replaced by a new building on a different site in the nineteenth century. Taplow Court, rebuilt in the 1850s, is seen nearby. The site overlooks the River Thames. Excavators who penetrated the mound in 1883 found traces of a timber-lined chamber wherein lay a richly furnished burial of the seventh century. The finds are in the British Museum. They point to the funeral of someone of exceptionally high status. Graves containing such levels of wealth are comparatively rare, possibly because the English leaders who were enlarging their dominions at each others' expense were not in a position to engage in such displays until their kingdoms were of sufficient size and prestige to deliver the required resources – a point which was reached in the seventh century, by which time the process of Christianization was under way. Christianity may have caused royal and aristocratic families to divert wealth that might otherwise have gone into the ground to other purposes: the foundation and adornment of monasteries, for example, and the

cultivation of a new kind of burial place. The occurrence of this barrow in a churchyard is therefore a matter of much interest. It may be no more than coincidence, but one could speculate that Taplow relates to a moment in the development of religious mentalities when men still set store by the old way of asserting the status of a deceased leader, and hence to legitimize and reinforce the power of his successor, but when Christian ideas were also coming to be actively pondered. It is possible that a church was established later, and the barrow included within the bounds of its cemetery, as the logical development of an ancestral site – possibly even with some sort of posthumous conversion in mind. Unfettered by facts, the modern imagination runs riot. Nevertheless, a few generations later Mercian kings were being entombed in stone mausolea, not unlike stone barrows, within the grounds of the royal monastery at Repton *Db*, close to a bluff overlooking the River Trent (Biddle 1986, 22). Was that the next stage in the process? (*Photo:* Mick Sharp)

23 Laughton-en-le-Morthen, South Yorkshire (*YW*): church of All Saints and motte-and-bailey castle. The church stands east of the motte. The defensibility of the motte was increased by its position on the crest of a steep scarp. A site with such natural advantages might be thought to have held an appeal to leaders before as well as after the Norman Conquest. There are several indications that this was so. Domesday Book reports that in 1066 Laughton had been the site of a magnate's *aula* 'hall'. This is unlocated, but for reasons explained in Chapter 6 it may very well have lain in the immediate vicinity of the church. Remains of a substantial late Saxon precursor to the present church survive at the north-west corner of the building (see Fig. 73). A bank running east-west through the churchyard nearby may be the remnant of an outer bailey, although the possibility that this might have preceded the Norman fortifications seems not to have been tested (*Photo:* Derrick Riley)

24 Church and ringwork at Culworth, Northamptonshire. The church lies just outside the enclosure (cf. Pls 21, 23, 25). Excavation of a similar ringwork in the nearby village of Sulgrave (Fig. 74) disclosed remains of pre-Conquest buildings, and it seems likely that this was the residence of a local lord in the tenth/eleventh century, before the site was further strengthened (Davison 1977). At Sulgrave, as here at Culworth, the ditch of the ringwork adjoins the churchyard. No excavation has taken place at Culworth, and the history of the site enclosed by the ringwork is not known (*Photo:* Royal Commission on the Historical Monuments of England)

25 Kilpeck, Herefordshire. The parish church of SS Mary and David stands a little to the right of the farm that lies just above the centre of the photograph. The church is of a classic twelfth-century type, consisting of a nave, chancel and eastern apse. The building is adorned with sculpture of a quality that has achieved international renown. Beyond it stands a large motte, which bears fragmentary remains of a later masonry castle. A bailey lies between the motte and the churchyard. As at Culworth (Pl. 24) the bailey ditch formed one side of the cemetery, although here the graveyard has been extended across the ditch into the bailey, and the ditch itself is shrouded by trees and shadow. Other baileys extend to the south and north-west. In the foreground is seen the outline of a massive rectangular enclosure, marked by a ditch and rampart on the right-hand side of the photograph, and emphasized by modern roads which run outside its eastern and southern edges. Enclosed settlements monitored by castles are found at various places in the Welsh borderland (e.g.

Richard's Castle, Caus Castle), and elsewhere; the considerable area involved here is suggestive of an ambition that Kilpeck should become a town. Notice how the church lies on the frontier between the 'private' and 'public' sectors. The site of the church is older than the surrounding layout. The church contains fabric of more than one period. It has been suggested that the builders of the twelfth-century church found the ruins of an earlier one and incorporated a portion of them into their new building (Taylor and Taylor 1965, 350). The twelfth-century *Book of Llandaff* states that some form of religious community existed at Kilpeck long before the Conquest (*Photo:* Cambridge University Collection, Crown Copyright)

26 Castle Rising, Norfolk. The powerful hall-keep was begun by the de Albini family, probably around 1140. Beyond it lie the remains of a church which was engulfed by the making of the castle. As at Kilpeck, the church existed beforehand. But here the church was demolished and its remains incorporated in the rampart of the inner bailey. A new church was built for the villagers in the settlement beyond (*Photo:* Derek Edwards/Norfolk Archaeological Unit)

27 St Catherine's Chapel, Abbotsbury, Dorset. Abbotsbury was the site of a Benedictine monastery. The chapel was built by the abbey in the later fourteenth century. The lofty site is characteristic of the cult of St Catherine, whose body, it was believed, had been miraculously translated to Mount Sinai in the ninth century. The chapel overlooks the sea, and is likely to have been intended also as a beacon or sea-mark. The building is comprehensively vaulted in stone. Outlying chapels stood in the vicinity of monasteries at other places in south-west England (e.g. Malmesbury, Milton Abbas, Glastonbury. They perpetuated a tradition which was ancient. The staircase of terraces on the hillside indicates that at some time in the past the slope was cultivated (*Photo:* Mick Sharp)

28 St Mary, Edlesborough, Buckinghamshire. The church is conspicuous upon a hillock close to the foot of the Chilterns. The south side of the hill has been terraced. (From inspection at close quarters it is not clear whether this is the eroded vestige of early fortification, or represents an attempt to adapt the slope of the churchyard in order to make it more convenient for purposes of burial.) The church embodies contributions made in every century from the twelfth to the sixteenth. Such a site might have been suitable as the eyrie of a local lord in the pre-Conquest period. Although no longer in regular use, St Mary's is cared for by the Redundant Churches Fund (*Photo:* Mick Sharp)

29 Up Waltham, Sussex. Surrounded by delectable downland, this church has been little altered since it was erected in the twelfth century. The windows in the apse were inserted some two hundred years later, but the ghost of at least one of the original windows, now blocked, seems to be discernible behind the rendering. Compare the plan with Pl. 12 (*Photo:* Mick Sharp)

30 St Edmund, Southwold, Suffolk, was rebuilt during the middle years of the fifteenth century. Notice the emphasis upon external decoration, particularly in the flushwork, and the large contribution made by glaziers (*Photo:* Mick Sharp)

31 Birkby, North Yorkshire. The church of St Peter is a survivor from days when it was part of a substantial settlement. The layout of the former village is indistinct, but may have included a green. A moated enclosure, lines of tracks and roads, house plots and abundant traces of medieval and later agriculture are picked out in the low light of a November day. The present church dates

from 1776, when its rebuilding may have been necessitated by neglect brought on by earlier depopulation. The origin of the church site is far older. Pre-Conquest sculpture indicates that it had been selected by the eleventh century, at latest. Today the church is kept company by a farm, and by the high-speed trains that roar past along the railway line between Northallerton and Darlington, seen in the foreground (*Photo:* A. L. Pacitto)

32 Eglwys Gymun, Dyfed (Carmarthen), lies upon a hill about three miles north of Pendine and Carmarthen Bay. The enclosure within which the church stands may be of prehistoric origin. An inscribed memorial stone suggests that the site may have been turned to ecclesiastical use at an early date, perhaps before 700. Around the churchyard are traces of a deserted medieval settlement (*Photo:* Terry James)

33 Argham: a deserted village on the Yorkshire wolds. Shadows and reflections cast by undulations provide a relief map in which traces of house platforms, boundary banks, trackways and enclosures of a former settlement are clearly seen. Argham had a church which existed before 1115. Presentations continued until 1605; the church was entirely defunct by the last quarter of the seventeenth century. Its position has been forgotten, although some remains are said to have been standing until c.1820. Elsewhere in this region, parish churches at shrunken or deserted settlements were extremely tenacious, outlasting depopulation by several centuries and usually surviving down to the present at least as ruins, if not as buildings which have remained in use until the last few years. The rapid disappearance of Argham's church could be connected with the fact that it did not enjoy full parochial status. The church here was a parochial chapel within the older parish of Hunmanby. The concomitant of such institutional inferiority could be financial insecurity, and the abandonment of the village removed the church from map and memory (*Photo:* Cambridge University Collection)

34 Little Hautbois, Coltishall, Norfolk. Medieval Norfolk was crowded with churches. Many of them stood in such close proximity that when the population fell in the later Middle Ages their shares of tithes and bequests fell also, rendering them vulnerable to neglect and, in some cases, extinction. Today more than 100 of Norfolk's churches are in ruins, and at least 90 more have disappeared (see Fig. 99). Little Hautbois seems to be a relatively recent casualty. In 1864 a new church was built on a more convenient site about a quarter of a mile away. Adjustments of this sort were quite common in the nineteenth century, and frequently led to the abandonment of the old churches that were superseded (*Photo:* Derek Edwards/Norfolk Archaeological Unit)

35 Egmere, Norfolk. A flint-built west tower is virtually all that remains of the church of St Edmund, which stands amid the grassy hummocks that trace out the positions of former cottages and features of an abandoned village. Egmere's closure was foreshadowed as early as 1331–2, when the church was being held in plurality with that at Quarles: a common prelude to redundancy. In 1428 there were only ten householders between the two. By 1571 Quarles was in ruins, while between 1553 and 1558 the parson of Egmere complained that his predecessor had demolished most of the church, taken lead from its roof and sold the largest bell. Early in the seventeenth century what was left of the building was turned into a barn (Allison 1955, 147) (*Photo:* Mick Sharp)

36 New Winchelsea, Sussex. The gridiron plan of this town was laid out on the initiative of Edward I (1272–1307) as a replacement for Old Winchelsea, which

had been under attack by the sea for some years and was effectively destroyed by a series of storms in 1287. The layout has value as a kind of high medieval Milton Keynes, and the principles behind its planning are broadly understood. The town occupied about twice the area of the present settlement, its former limits being marked by a fringe of trees. Within, squares and rectangles formed by the rectilinear pattern of intersecting streets were known as quarters. Some of the quarters were allocated for communal use. The marketplace lay in the area now marked by a clump of trees beyond the modern village. At least two quarters were set aside for churches, only one of which, St Thomas, survives. The other was demolished in 1760. The nave of St Thomas's has been removed, leaving the chancel that stands towards the edge of a large quarter close to the centre of the inhabited area. Burgesses were in occupation by 1292, and for fifty years or so the town seems to have flourished. Thereafter Winchelsea entered upon times of increasing economic difficulty, as the estuary of the River Brede became choked with silt and robbed the citizens of their livelihood. The population dwindled. By the end of the sixteenth century New Winchelsea was scarcely more than a village (Beresford and St Joseph 1979, 238–41) (*Photo:* Cambridge University Collection, Crown Copyright)

37 St James, Barton-under-Needwood, Staffordshire. This fine church was built in one main campaign between 1517 and 1533. The patron was John Taylor: a man of humble background who was born at Barton, was educated at royal expense and later rose to high office in the service of Henry VIII. The grandeur of the church belies its early status; St James was a chapel-of-ease to Tatenhill, and remained so until 1881. An older chapel is thought to have existed in the vicinity of the churchyard. Taylor's church is reputed to have been superimposed upon the site of his parents' cottage. He may have intended it as the place for his own burial and chantry. But Taylor died in London, the whereabouts of his grave are not recorded and twelve years after his death chantries were abolished (*Photo:* Mick Sharp)

38 Staunton Harold, Leicestershire. The church of Holy Trinity was begun by Sir Robert Shirley in 1653 and completed in 1665, nine years after Shirley's death in captivity. The thoroughgoing Gothic idiom of the church and associated inscriptions testify to Shirley's Anglican values, which were asserted here in the face of Commonwealth Puritanism. That part of the house which looks towards the church was begun in 1763, but portions of a Jacobean mansion are embedded within later extensions and remodelling (*Photo:* Mick Sharp)

39 Fawsley, Northamptonshire. The church of St Mary is marooned in parkland. It was not always thus; the church had the status of a minster before the Conquest, and in the later Middle Ages a village existed nearby. The present hall, seen on the left of the photograph, was built by Sir Edmund Knightley before his death in 1542, and enlarged in 1867–8. The buildings laid out to a U-shaped plan just to the north are stables. The church is full of Knightley monuments, reflecting its position within their domain (*Photo:* Royal Commission on the Historical Monuments of England)

40 St James, Great Packington, Warwickshire. This remarkable church stands in the grounds of Packington Hall, which were landscaped by Capability Brown in the 1750s. The church was built in 1789–90 by the architect Joseph Bonomi, who was a travelled man. Like many churches associated with estates, St

James's was intended in part as a mausoleum for members of the family of the great house. It has underchambers designed for this purpose, complete with a ramp to facilitate the approach of a hearse (*Photo:* Mick Sharp)

41 St George-in-the-East, London. Built by Nicholas Hawksmoor between 1715 and 1723, this was one of the achievements of the Commission for building new churches which had been established during the reign of Queen Anne. Now overlooked by tawdry high-rise developments, St George's exemplifies eighteenth-century theory that great architecture could have an ennobling effect upon its spectators (*Photo:* Mick Sharp)

42 St Alkmund, Whitchurch, Shropshire. The church was built in 1712–13 following the collapse of its medieval predecessor. It is a fair example of late Stuart native baroque. Notice the minimal chancel: large chancels were unnecessary in this period, when Anglican observances centred more upon the nave, which ideally would be a well-lit auditorium. Although in strict terms the tower had no place in classical schemes, it was generally retained as a traditional and distinguishing Anglican feature. The builder of St Alkmund's was William Smith of Warwick. He may have had a hand in the design; members of the Smith family were also responsible for rebuilding the parish church of Burton-on-Trent *St* (1719–26), which is practically a replica of St Alkmund's (*Photo:* Mick Sharp)

43 Mow Cop lies athwart the boundary between Staffordshire and Cheshire. The folly at the summit was built in 1754. On Sunday 31 May 1807 an assembly of Camp Meeting Methodists was held here. Such meetings contributed to the emergence of Primitive Methodism. The movement enjoyed phenomenal success: a hundred years after the assembly on Mow there were nearly a quarter of a million members. Centenary meetings held here in 1907 and 1910 are said to have been attended by 100,000 people (*Photo:* Mick Sharp)

44 Boyne Hill, Maidenhead, Berkshire. The church of All Saints and associated buildings were designed by George Edmund Street and erected between 1854 and 1858. The complex amounts to a substantial settlement in its own right, with vicarage, school, stabling and other facilities all grouped together, 'the whole forming one organic design' (Goodhart-Rendel 1983, 8). Boyne Hill reflects the influence of Tractarianism, which in origin was a movement concerned with the re-evaluation of Anglican identity and belief, placing stress upon historical continuity with Catholic Christianity. Hand-in-hand with this aim there often went strong social concerns, which could find architectural embodiment in groups of buildings where provision for education, mission, domestic quarters for pastoral staff and, in poor areas, the relief of poverty, were concentrated together (*Photo:* Mick Sharp)

45 Cheltenham, Gloucestershire. Before its expansion as a regal spa, Cheltenham was a modest market town with one parish church. St Mary's was a former minster, and her cruciform layout and central spire remain conspicuous a little to the left of the High Street in the top left-hand quarter of the photograph. Further to the left stands the church of St Matthew (1878–9), distinguished by a lateral steeple that was deprived of its spire very shortly after this photograph was taken on 19 March 1952. Just in front of St Matthew's is the Salem Baptist chapel (1844), with three strongly marked recesses in its façade. In the distance, a little right of centre, stands the church of St Paul. It was built in 1827–31 in a poorer quarter of the town, and stands amid rows of working-class housing. Its architectural idiom is Grecian. In the foreground is another

Baptist chapel, erected in 1853–5 to accommodate a breakaway group from the Salem church (Stell 1986, 75). This chapel is hemmed in by adjacent property, and illustrates the difficulty that dissenters sometimes encountered in securing adequate lateral illumination for buildings on constricted sites (*Photo:* Harold Wingham)

46 St Bartholomew, Ann Street, Brighton, Sussex. Towering above its surroundings, St Bartholomew's was a church that was meant to be seen. It originated as a mission church in a neighbourhood of artisans' housing within the parish of Brighton, and was paid for largely by Arthur Wagner, the incumbent. Work started in 1872 and ceased two years later. A chancel was intended but never built. The architect, Edmund Scott, was a local man (*Photo:* Mick Sharp)

47 All Souls, Haley Hill, stands on the outskirts of Halifax, West Yorkshire. It was designed by Sir George Gilbert Scott and completed in 1859. Funds for its building were provided by Col. Edward Akroyd, who between 1861 and 1868 constructed a planned village nearby for his millworkers. Akroyd himself lived in a mansion on the hillside just beyond the church. It is now a museum. In the foreground stand Dean Clough Mills, then owned by the Crossley family. The Crossleys were Congregationalists. They too experimented with 'model' housing, and financed an outstanding church in Square Road (*Photo:* Mick Sharp)

48 Saltaire, West Yorkshire. Sir Titus Salt's giant textile mill, constructed for the processing of alpaca and mohair, dominates the top right-hand quarter of the photograph. In the foreground run the neat lines of housing which were erected for his workforce in the 1850s and 1860s. Saltaire was furnished with an institute and school, seen side by side a short distance in front of the mill, a park (top left) and a church. Salt was a Congregationalist. His church was built in 1858–9 to the design of Lockwood and Mawson, who were also responsible for the architectural dressing of the mill. The Leeds–Liverpool canal passes behind the mill and can be seen between the church and the park. The railway runs across the photograph on the nearer side of the church and mill (*Photo:* Bob Yarwood/West Yorkshire Archaeology Service)

49 Llangelynin, Gwynedd. A church, and a landscape. The camera looks ENE from a knoll. In the vicinity are seen a walled trackway, the remains of a prehistoric hut circle and several watercourses. There is a holy well in the lower right-hand corner of the churchyard. Much of the settlement of medieval Wales was dispersed. Churches commonly served the scattered populations of districts rather than concentrations of people in particular places. Time – the focus of so many contemporary neuroses – cannot be saved. No church will endure for ever. Yet as places go, those believed to be holy come nearer to a state of permanence than most others (*Photo:* Mick Sharp)

BIBLIOGRAPHY

Aberg, F. A. (ed.) (1978) *Medieval Moated Sites*, CBA Research Report 17. London.

Adams, L. (1979) 'Early Islamic pottery from Flaxengate, Lincoln', *Medieval Archaeol.* 23, 218–19.

—— (1980) 'Chinese pottery from dark age Lincoln', *Lincolnshire Hist. Archaeol.* 15, 89.

Adams, M. and Reeve, J. (1987) 'Excavations at Christ Church Spitalfields 1984–6', *Antiquity* 61, 247–56.

Addleshaw, G. W. O. (1970) *The Beginnings of the Parochial System*, St Anthony's Hall Pub. 3, 3rd edn. York.

—— (1987) *Rectors, Vicars and Patrons in Twelfth- and Early Thirteenth-century Canon Law*, Ecclesiological Soc. London.

Addy, J. (1983) 'Archdeacons' orders for the repair of churches and parsonages', *Churchscape* 3, 27–35.

Airs, M., Rodwell, K. and Turner, H. (1975) 'Wallingford' in K. Rodwell (ed.) (1975), 155–62.

Alcock, L. (1972) *'By South Cadbury is that Camelot . . .'*, *Excavations at Cadbury Castle 1966–70*. London.

Alcuin Godman, P. (ed. and trans.) (1982) *The Bishops, Kings and Saints of York*. Oxford.

Aldsworth, F. G. (1979a) '"The mound" at Church Norton, Selsey, and the site of Wilfrid's church', *Sussex Archaeol. Collect.* 117, 103–7.

—— (1979b) 'Three medieval sites in West Dean Parish', *Sussex Archaeol. Collect.* 117, 109–24.

—— and Garnett, E. D. (1981) 'Excavations on "The mound" at Church Norton, Selsey, in 1911 and 1965', *Sussex Archaeol. Collect.* 119, 217–21.

Allan, J., Henderson, C. and Higham, R. (1984) 'Saxon Exeter' in J. Haslam (ed.) (1984), 385–411.

Alldridge, N. J. (1981) 'Aspects of the topography of early medieval Chester', *J. Chester Archaeol. Soc.* 64, 5–31.

Allerston, P. (1970) 'English village development: findings from the Pickering district of North Yorkshire', *Trans. Inst. Brit. Geographers* 51, 95–109.

Allison, K. J. (1955) 'The lost villages of Norfolk', *Norfolk Archaeol.* 31, 116–62.

Ambler, R. W. (ed.) (1979) *Lincolnshire Returns of the Census of Religious Worship 1851*, Lincoln Rec. Soc., 72.

Ambrose, T. (1979) *Gods and Goddesses of Roman Ancaster*, Lincolnshire Museums Information Sheet (Archaeol. ser.), 8.

Anderson, W. B. (ed.) (1963–5) Sidonius Apollinaris, *Poems and Letters*. London.

Andrews, R. D. (1978) 'St Patrick's Chapel, Heysham, Lancashire', *Bull. CBA Churches Committee* 8, 2.

Anglo-Saxon Chronicle Garmonsway, G. N. (ed. and trans.) (1972) *The Anglo-Saxon Chronicle*, 2nd edn. London.

Anthony, I. E. (ed.) (1968) 'Excavations at Verulam Hills Field, St Albans, 1963–4', *Hertfordshire Archaeol.* 1, 9–50.

Arnold, H. G. (1985) The historical and architectural background, in *Hallelujah! Recording Chapels and Meeting houses*, 6–41. London.

Arnold, T. (ed.) (1882, 1885) *Symeonis monachi opera omnia*, Rolls ser. 75, 2 vols.

Ashdown, J. and Hassall, T. (1975) 'Oxford' in K. Rodwell (ed.) (1975), 133–40.

Aston, Margaret (1968) *The Fifteenth Century: The Prospect of Europe*. London.

Aston, M. (1984) 'The towns of Somerset' in J. Haslam (ed.) (1984), 167–201.

—— (1985) 'Rural settlement in Somerset: some preliminary thoughts', in D. Hooke (ed.) (1985), 81–100.

—— and Leech, R. (1977) *Historic Towns in Somerset*. Bristol.

—— and Rowley, T. (1974) *Landscape Archaeology. An Introduction to Fieldwork Techniques on Post-Roman Landscapes*. Newton Abbot, London.

Atkinson, T. D. (1947) *Local Style in English Architecture*. London.

Avitus Peiper, R. (ed.) (1883) *Monumenta Germaniae Historica Auctores Antiquissimi*, 6, 2.

Ayers, B. (1985) *Excavations within the North-east Bailey of Norwich Castle, 1979*, E. Anglian Archaeol. Rep. no. 28.

Ælfric Thorpe, B. (ed.) (1843–6) *Catholic Homilies*, Ælfric Soc.

—— Skeat, W. W. (ed.) (1881–1900) *Lives of Saints*, Early English Text Soc., 76, 82, 94, 114.

Bacon Matheson, P. E. and Matheson, E. F. (eds) (1964) *Francis Bacon. Selections with Essays by Macaulay and S. R. Gardiner*. Oxford.

Bailey, R. N. (1977) 'A cup-mount from Brougham, Cumbria', *Medieval Archaeol.* 21, 176–80.

—— (1980a) *Viking Age Sculpture in Northern England*. London.

—— (1980b) *The Early Christian Church in Leicester and its Region*, Vaughan Paper no. 25, Leicester University.

—— (1983) 'All Saints Ledsham . . .', *Bull. CBA Churches Committee* 18, 6–8.

Baines, T. (1852) *History of the Commerce and Town of Liverpool*. London.

Baker, N. (1980a) 'Churches, parishes and early medieval topography' in M. Carver (ed.) (1980), 31–7.

—— (1980b) 'The urban churches of Worcester: a survey' in M. Carver (ed.) (1980), 115–24.

Bannister, A. T. (1929, 1930) 'Visitation returns of the diocese of Hereford in 1397', *English Hist. Rev.* 44, 279–89, 444–53; 45, 92–101, 444–63.

Barker, P. (1975) 'Excavations on the site of the baths basilica at Wroxeter 1966–1974: an interim report', *Britannia* 6, 106–17.

—— (1979) 'The latest occupation of the site of the baths basilica at Wroxeter' in P. J. Casey (ed.) *The End of Roman Britain*, BAR 71, 175–81.

Barker, P., Cubberley, A. L., Crowfoot, E. and Radford, C. A. R. (1974) 'Two burials under the refectory of Worcester cathedral', *Medieval Archaeol.* 18, 146–51.

Barley, M. W. (1951) 'Cuckney church and castle', *Trans. Thoroton Soc.* 55, 26–9.

—— (ed.) (1975) *The Plans and Topography of Medieval Towns in England and Wales*, CBA Research Report 14.

—— (ed.) (1977) *European Towns: Their Archaeology and Early History.* London.

—— (1978) 'Castle Howard and the village of Hinderskelfe, North Yorkshire', *Antiq. J.* 58, 358–60.

Barlow, F. (1979) *The English Church 1000–1066. A History of the Later Anglo-Saxon Church.* London.

Bassett, S. R. (1980–1) (1982) 'Medieval Lichfield: a topographical review', *Trans. S. Staffordshire Archaeol. Hist. Soc.* 22, 93–121.

Baughan, P. E. (1969) *The Railways of Wharfedale.* Newton Abbot.

Bede, *Historia Ecclesiastica Gentis Anglorum* Plummer, C. (ed.) (1896) *Venerabilis Bedae Opera Historica*, 2 vols. Colgrave, B. and Mynors, R. A. B. (eds) (1969) *Bede's Ecclesiastical History of the English People.* Oxford.

Bell, M. (ed.) (1933) *Wulfric of Haselbury, by John, Abbot of Ford*, Somerset Rec. Soc., 47.

Bellhouse, R. L. and Richardson, G. G. S. (1982) 'The Trajanic Fort at Kirkbride; the terminus of the Stanegate Frontier', *Trans. Cumberland and Westmoreland Antiq. Archaeol. Soc.* 82, 35–50.

Benson, H. (1956) 'Church orientations and patronal festivals', *Antiq. J.* 36, 205–13.

Beresford, G. (1975) *The Medieval Clay-land Village: Excavations at Goltho and Barton Blount*, Soc. Medieval Archaeol. Monograph ser. no. 6. London.

—— (1981) 'Goltho manor, Lincolnshire: the buildings and their surrounding defences, *c.* 850–1150' in R. Allen Brown (ed.) *Proc. Battle Conference on Anglo-Norman Studies* 4, 13–36.

Beresford, M. W. (1967) *New Towns in the Middle Ages.* London.

—— (1973) 'Isolated and ruined churches as evidence for population contraction' in *Économies et sociétés au moyen âge. Mélanges offerts à Édouard Perroy*, Publications de la Sorbonne, 573–80.

—— and St Joseph, J. K. S. (1979) *Medieval England. An Aerial Survey.* Cambridge.

Betjeman, J. (ed.) (1958) *Collins Guide to English Parish Churches.* London.

Biddle, M. (1975) 'Planned towns before 1066' in M. W. Barley (ed.) (1975), 19–31.

—— (1976) 'Towns', in D. M. Wilson (ed.) (1976), 99–150.

—— (1984) 'London on The Strand', *Popular Archaeol.* July, 23–7.

—— (1986) 'Archaeology, architecture, and the cult of saints in Anglo-Saxon England', in L. A. S. Butler and R. Morris (eds) (1986), 1–31.

—— and Hill, D. (1971) 'Late Saxon planned towns', *Antiq. J.* 51, 70–85.

BIBLIOGRAPHY

—— and Keene, D. J. (1976) 'Lesser churches' in M. Biddle (ed.) *Winchester in the Early Middle Ages: An Edition and Discussion of the Winton Domesday*, Winchester Studies 1, 329–35. Oxford.

—— and Kjølbye-Biddle, B. (1982) 'St Albans abbey', *Bull. CBA Churches Committee* 17, 7–9.

———— (1984) 'St Albans abbey. Archaeology in the cloisters: the first stage 1982–4', *Bull. CBA Churches Committee* 21.

———— (1985) 'Repton 1985', *Bull. CBA Churches Committee* 22, 1–5.

Bidwell, P. T. *et al.* (1979) *The Legionary Bath-house and Basilica and Forum at Exeter, with a Summary Account of the Legionary Fortress*, Exeter Archaeol. Report 1.

Bieler, L. (1963) *The Irish Penitentials*, Scriptores Latini Hiberniae, vol 5. Dublin.

Binding, G. (1975) 'Quellen, Brunnen und Reliquiengräber in Kirchen', *Zeitschrift für Archäologie des Mittelalters*, 3, 37–56.

Binfield, C. (1977) *So Down to Prayers. Studies in English Nonconformity 1780–1920*. London.

Binney, J. E. (transcr.) (1904) *The Accounts of the Wardens of the Parish of Morebath, Devon, 1520–1573*. Exeter.

Birch, W. de Gray (1885–99) *Cartularium Saxonicum*, 3 vols.

Blair, J. (1984) 'Saint Beornwald of Bampton', *Oxoniensia* 49, 47–55.

—— (1985) 'Secular minster churches in Domesday Book' in P. H. Sawyer (ed.) *Domesday Book: A Reassessment*, 104–42. London.

—— (1987) 'Local churches in Domesday Book and before' in J. C. Holt (ed) *Domesday Studies*, 265–78.

Blomqvist, R. (1951) *Lunds historia*, 1. Lund.

—— and Mårtensson, A. W. (1963) *Archaeologia Lundensia: investigationes de antiquitatibus urbis Lundae 2*. Thulegravningen 1961. Kulturhistoriska Museet. Lund.

Boddington, A. (1980) 'A Christian Anglo-Saxon graveyard at Raunds' in P. Rahtz, T. Dickinson and L. Watts (eds) *Anglo-Saxon Cemeteries*, BAR 82, 373–8.

—— (1987) 'Raunds, Northamptonshire: analysis of a country churchyard', *World Archaeol.* 18.3, 411–25.

—— and Cadman, G. *et al.* (1981) 'Raunds: an interim report on excavations 1977–1980' in D. Brown, J. Campbell and S. C. Hawkes (eds) *Anglo-Saxon Studies in Archaeology and History 2*, BAR 92, 103–22.

Bond, C. J. (1985) 'Medieval Oxfordshire villages and their topography: a preliminary discussion', in D. Hooke (ed.) (1985), 101–23.

—— and Hunt, A. M. (eds) (1977) 'Recent archaeological work in Pershore', *Vale of Evesham Hist. Soc. Research Papers* 6, 1–76.

Bonney, D. (1976) 'Early boundaries and estates in Southern England' in P. H. Sawyer (ed.) *Medieval Settlement: Continuity and Change*, 72–82. London.

Bonser, K. J. and Nichols, H. (1960) *Printed Maps and Plans of Leeds, 1711–1900*, Publications of the Thoresby Soc., vol 47. Leeds.

Bonser, W. (1934) 'Survivals of paganism in Anglo-Saxon England', *Birmingham Archaeol. Soc. Trans. and Proc. for 1932* 56, 37–70.

Boon, G. C. (1980) 'Caerleon and the Gwent Levels in early historic times' in F. H. Thompson (ed.) (1980), 24–36.

Borius, R. (ed.) (1965) *Constance de Lyon, vie de saint Germain d'Auxerre*, Sources chrétiennes. Paris.

Bowen, E. G. (1971) 'A menhir at Llandysiliogogo church, Cardiganshire', *Antiquity* 45, 213–15.

Braby, P. (1975, 1976) 'Churchwardens' presentments from the Vale of Evesham, 1660–1717', *Vale of Evesham Hist. Soc. Research Papers* 5, 61–79; 6, 101–16.

Bradley, R. (1987) 'Time regained: the creation of continuity', *J. British Archaeol. Assoc.* 140, 1–17.

Bradshaw, J. T. (1982) 'The Primitive Methodists and the working class: secular education in the Erewash valley coalfield *c.* 1816–*c.* 1850' in *From Mow Cop to Peake, 1807–1932. Essays to commemorate the one hundred and seventy-fifth anniversary of the beginnings of Primitive Methodism*, Wesley Hist. Soc., Yorks. Branch, Occasional Paper 4, 33–45.

Branigan, K. (1971) *Latimer: Belgic, Roman, dark age and early modern farm*. Chesham.

Brenner, R. (1985) 'Agrarian class structure and economic development in pre-industrial Europe' in T. H. Aston and C. H. E. Philps (eds) *The Brenner Debate*, 10–63. Cambridge.

Brett, M. (1975) *The English Church under Henry I*. London.

Brewster, T. M. C. (1972) 'An excavation at Weaverthorpe manor, East Riding, 1960', *Yorkshire Archaeol. J.* 44, 114–33.

Bridbury, A. R. (1973) 'The Black Death', *Econ. Hist. Rev.* 26, 577–92.

—— (1975) *Economic Growth. England in the Later Middle Ages*. Hassocks.

Briggs, A. (1963) *Victorian Cities*. London.

Briggs, C. S. (1979) 'Ysbyty Cynfyn churchyard wall', *Archaeol. Cambrensis* 128, 138–46.

Britton, C. E. (1937) *A Meterological Chronology to AD 1450*, Meteorological Office, Geophysical Memoirs no. 70.

Brodribb, A. C., Hands, A. R. and Walker, D. R. (1971) *Excavations at Shakenoak*, 2. Oxford.

Brooke, C. N. L. (1970) 'The missionary at home: the Church in the towns, 1000–1250', *Studies in Church Hist.* 6, 59–83.

—— (1974) 'The ecclesiastical geography of medieval towns', *Miscellanea Historiae Ecclesiasticae* 5, 15–31. Louvain.

—— (1977a) 'St Albans: the great abbey' in R. Runcie (ed.) *Cathedral and City: St Albans Ancient and Modern*, 43–70.

—— (1977b) 'The medieval town as an ecclesiastical centre' in M. W. Barley (ed.) (1977), 459–73.

—— and Keir, G. (1975) *London 800–1216: The Shaping of a City*. London.

Brooke, R. and Brooke, C. N. L. (1984) *Popular Religion in the Middle Ages: Western Europe, 1000–1300*. London.

Brothwell, D. (1982) 'Linking urban man with his environment' in A. R. Hall and H. Kenward (eds) *Environmental Archaeology in the Urban Context*, CBA Research Report 43, 126–9.

Brown, P. (1971) *The World of Late Antiquity from Marcus Aurelius to Muhammed*. London.

—— (1981) *The Cult of the Saints; Its Rise and Function in Latin Christianity*.

Bryant, R. (1980) 'Excavations at the church of St Mary de Lode, Gloucester', *Bull. CBA Churches Committee* 13, 15–18.

Buckland, P. C. (1975) 'Synanthropy and the death-watch; a discussion', *The Naturalist* 100, 37–42.

——,Dolby, M. J. and Magilton, J. R. (1981) 'Doncaster, South Yorkshire' in J. Schofield *et al.* (eds) (1981), 30–1.

Buckland, T. (1980) 'The reindeer antlers of the Abbots Bromley horn dance: a re-examination', *Lore and Language* 3 (2), Part A, 1–8.

Bullough, D. (1983) 'Burial, community and belief in the early medieval west' in P. Wormald (ed.) with D. Bullough and R. Collins, *Ideal and Reality in Frankish and Anglo-Saxon Society*, 177–201.

Burl, A. (1976) *The Stone Circles of the British Isles*. New Haven, London.

—— (1979) *Prehistoric Avebury*. New Haven, London.

Butler, D. M. (1978) *Quaker Meeting-houses of the Lake Counties*, Friends Hist. Soc. London.

Butler, L. A. S. (1966) 'A fire at Clynnog church', *Trans. Caernarvonshire Hist. Soc.* 1966, 98–106.

—— (1974) 'Leicester's church, Denbigh: an experiment in Puritan worship', *J. British Archaeol. Assoc.* 3 ser., 37, 40–62.

—— (1975) 'Planned towns after 1066' in M. W. Barley (ed.) (1975), 32–47.

—— (1978) 'St Martin's church, Allerton Mauleverer', *Yorkshire Archaeol. J.* 50, 177–88.

—— (1982) 'The labours of the months and "The haunted tanglewood": aspects of late twelfth-century sculpture in Yorkshire' in R. L. Thompson (ed.) *A Medieval Miscellany in Honour of Professor John Le Patourel*, Proc. Leeds Philosophical and Lit. Soc. 18, 79–95.

—— and Morris, R. (eds) (1986) *The Anglo-Saxon Church*, CBA Research Report 60.

Cadman, G. (1981) *Raunds: A Review*.

—— (1983) 'Raunds 1977–1983: an excavation summary', *Medieval Archaeol.* 27, 107–22.

—— and Foard, G. (1984) 'Raunds: manorial and village origins' in M. L. Faull (ed.) (1984), 81–100.

Cam, H. (1944) *Liberties and Communities in Medieval England*. Cambridge.

Cambridge, E. (1984) 'The early church in County Durham', *J. British Archaeol. Assoc.* 137, 65–85.

Campbell, J., (1975) 'Norwich' in *The Atlas of Historic Towns* (general editor M. D. Label), vol. 2.

—— (1979) 'The church in Anglo-Saxon towns', *Studies in Church Hist.* 16, 119–35.

Canterbury Archaeological Trust Topographical maps of Canterbury AD 400, 1050, 1200, 1500, and 1700, 2nd edn., 1982.

Carter, A. (1978) 'The Anglo-Saxon origins of Norwich: the problems and approaches', *Anglo-Saxon England* 7, 175–204.

Carus-Wilson, E. M. (1965) 'The first half-century of the borough of Stratford-upon-Avon', *Econ. Hist. Rev.* 2nd ser., 18, 46–63.

—— and Coleman, O. (1963) *England's Export Trade 1275–1547*. Oxford.

Carver, M. O. H. (ed.) (1980) 'Medieval Worcester: an archaeological framework. Reports, surveys, texts, essays', *Trans. Worcestershire Archaeol. Soc.* 3rd ser., 7.

Cattermole, P. and Cotton, S. (1983) 'Medieval parish church building in Norfolk', *Norfolk Archaeol.* 38, 235–79.

Chadwick, O. (1966) *The Victorian Church.* London.

Chancellor, F. (1877) 'St Peter's-on-the-Wall, Bradwell-juxta-Mare', *Archaeol. J.* 34, 212–18.

Charles, B. G. (1938) *Non-Celtic Place-names in Wales.* London.

Chatfield, M. (1979) *Churches the Victorians Forgot.* Ashbourne.

Chatwin, P. B. (1936) (1940) 'Roman pottery and coins and medieval pottery found at Brinklow', *Birmingham Archaeol. Soc. Trans. and Proc.* 60, 152.

Cheney, C. R. (1941) *English Synodalia of the Thirteenth Century.* London.

Cherry, J. F. and Hodges, R. (1978) 'The dating of *Hamwih*: Saxon Southampton reconsidered', *Antiq. J.* 58, 299–309.

Chew, H. M. and Kellaway, W. (1973) *London Assize of Nuisance 1301–1431: A Calendar*, London Record Soc., 10.

Childs, W. R. (1978) *Anglo-Castilian Trade in the Later Middle Ages.*

Chitty, D. J. (1966) *The Desert a City: An Introduction to Study of Egyptian and Palestinian Monasticism under the Christian Empire.* Oxford.

Choay, F. (1969) *The Modern City: Planning in the Nineteenth Century.* New York.

Christie, H., Olsen, O. and Taylor, H. M. (1979) 'The wooden church of St Andrew at Greensted, Essex', *Antiq. J.* 59, 92–112.

Chron. Abingdon Stevenson, J. (ed.) (1858) *Chronicon Monasterii de Abingdon*, Rolls ser. 2, 2 vols.

Chron. Edward II Stubbs, W. (ed.) (1882, 1883) *Chronicles of the Reigns of Edward I and Edward II*, Rolls ser. 76, vol. 2.

Chron. Knighton Lumby, J. R. (ed.) (1889, 1895) *Chronicon Henrici Knighton, vel Cnitthon, Monachi Lecestrensis*, Rolls ser. 92, 2 vols.

Church Congress (1872) *Authorized Report of the Church Congress held at Leeds, 8–11 October 1872.* Leeds.

Clapham, A. W. (1930) *English Romanesque Architecture before the Conquest.* Oxford.

—— (1934) *English Romanesque Architecture after the Conquest.* Oxford.

—— (1953) 'The survival of Gothic in seventeenth-century England', *Archaeol. J.* Supplement, 106, 4–9.

Clark, K. (1950) *The Gothic Revival: An Essay in the History of Taste.* London.

Clark, W. A. (1937) 'Notes on Midland crypts', *Birmingham Archaeol. Soc. Trans. and Proc.* 61, 31–44.

Clarke, B. F. L. (1962) *Church Builders of the Nineteenth Century. A Study of the Gothic Revival in England*, orig. edn. 1938. London.

—— (1963) *The Building of the Eighteenth-century Church.* London.

Clarke, G. (ed.) (1979) *Pre-Roman and Roman Winchester, Part 2. The Roman Cemetery at Lankhills*, Winchester Studies 3. Oxford.

—— (1982) 'The Roman villa at Woodchester', *Britannia* 13, 197–228.

Clay, C. T. (1939–43) 'The early treasurers of York', *Yorkshire Archaeol. J.* 35, 7–34.

Clover, H. and Gibson, M. (1979) *The Letters of Lanfranc, Archbishop of Canterbury.* Oxford.

Cockayne, O. (ed.) (1866) *Leechdoms, Wortcunning, and Starcraft in Early England*, Rolls ser. 3.

Cole, D. (1980) *The Work of Sir Gilbert Scott.* London.

Cole, R. E. G. (ed) (1913) *Speculum dioeceseos Lincolniensis sub episcopis Gul: Wake et Edm: Gibson, AD 1705–1723*, Part 1, Lincoln Record Soc., 4.

Coleman, B. I. (1980) *The Church of England in the Mid-nineteenth Century. A Social Geography*, Historical Assoc. General ser. 98.

Colgrave, B. (ed. and trans.) (1927) *The Life of Bishop Wilfrid by Eddius Stephanus.*

—— (ed. and trans.) (1940) *Two Lives of Cuthbert.* Cambridge.

—— (ed. and trans.) (1968) *The Earliest Life of Gregory the Great.* Kansas.

—— (ed. and trans.) (1985) *Felix's Life of St Guthlac.* Cambridge.

Collinson, P. (1984) *English Puritanism*, Historical Assoc. General ser. 106.

Colyer, C. and Gilmour, B. (1978) 'St Paul-in-the-Bail, Lincoln', *Current Archaeol.* 63, 102–5.

Constantius, *Vita Germani see* R. Borius (ed.) (1965).

Cook, G. H. (1947) *Mediaeval Chantries and Chantry Chapels.* London.

—— (1955) *The English Mediaeval Parish Church.* London.

Cook, O. (1984) *The English Country House: An Art and a Way of Life.* London.

Cope, G. (1972) 'Theological considerations concerning church buildings, vessels and furnishings' in G. Cope (ed.) *Problem Churches*, Institute for the Study of Worship and Religious Architecture, 6–28.

Coppack, G. (1986) 'St Lawrence's church, Burnham, South Humberside. The excavation of a parochial chapel', *Lincolnshire Hist. Archaeol.* 21, 39–60.

Corke, J. *et al.* (eds.) (1980) *Suffolk Churches. A Pocket Guide*, Suffolk Historic Churches Trust. Lavenham.

Coüasnon, C. (1974) *The Church of the Holy Sepulchre in Jerusalem.* London.

Cox, J. C. (1913) *Cumberland and Westmorland. County Churches.* London.

—— and Ford, L. B. (1941) *The Parish Churches of England*, 3rd edn. London.

Cramp, R. (1984) *Corpus of Anglo-Saxon Stone Sculpture, 1: Durham and Northumberland*, British Academy.

—— and Daniels, R. (1987) 'New finds from the Anglo-Saxon monastery at Hartlepool, Cleveland', *Antiquity* 61, 424–32.

Cra'ster, M. D. (1961) 'St Michael's, Gloucester', *Trans. Bristol Gloucestershire Archaeol. Soc.* 80, 59–74.

Cranage, D. H. S. (1894) *Architectural Account of the Churches of Shropshire.* Wellington.

Crook, J. M. (1981) *William Burges and the High Victorian Dream.* London.

Crossley, F. H. (1921) *English Church Monuments 1150–1550. An Introduction to the Study of Tombs and Effigies of the Mediaeval Period.* London.

—— (1945) *English Church Design 1040–1540.* London.

Crummy, P. (1980) 'The temples of Roman Colchester' in W. J. Rodwell (ed.) (1980), 243–83.

—— (1981) *Aspects of Anglo-Saxon and Norman Colchester*, CBA Research Report 39.

Cunliffe, B. W. (1964) *Winchester Excavations 1949–1960.*

—— (1980) 'The evolution of Romney Marsh: a preliminary statement' in F. H. Thompson (ed.) (1980), 37–55.

—— (1986) *The City of Bath.* Gloucester.

Curl, J. S. (1980) *A Celebration of Death. An introduction to some of the buildings, monuments, and settings of funerary architecture in the western European tradition.* London.

Currie, C. R. J. (1983) 'A Romanesque roof at Odda's chapel, Deerhurst, Gloucestershire?'. *Antiq. J.* 63, 58–63.

Currie, R., Gilbert, A. and Horsley, L. (1977) *Churches and Churchgoers. Patterns of Church Growth in the British Isles since 1700*. Oxford.

Darby, H. C. (1977) *Domesday England*. Cambridge.

—— (1983) *The Changing Fenland*. Cambridge.

—— Glasscock, R. E., Sheail, J. and Versey, G. R. (1979) 'The changing geographical distribution of wealth in England 1086-1334-1525', *J. Hist. Geog.* 5, 247-62.

Davey, N. (1964) 'A pre-Conquest church and baptistery at Potterne, Wilts', *Wiltshire Archaeol. Natur. Hist. Mag.* 59, 116-23.

—— (1976) *Building Stones of England and Wales*. London.

Davidson, A. F. and J. E. (1979-80) 'The deserted medieval village and church at Rhossili, Gower', *Gwent Glamorgan Archaeol. Trust Annual Report 1979-80*, 21-7.

Davies, E. T. (1965) *Religion and the Industrial Revolution in South Wales*. Cardiff.

Davies, W. (1978) *An Early Welsh Microcosm: Studies in the Llandaff Charters*. Royal Hist. Soc. Studies in History ser 9. London.

—— (1979) *The Llandaff Charters*. Aberystwyth.

—— (1982) *Wales in the Early Middle Ages*. Leicester.

Davison, B. K. (1967) 'The origins of the castle in England', *Archaeol. J.* 124, 202-11.

—— (1977) 'Excavations at Sulgrave, Northamptonshire, 1960-76: an interim report', *Archaeol. J.* 134, 105-14.

Dawes, J. D. and Magilton, J. R. (1980) *The Cemetery of St Helen-on-the-Walls, Aldwark*, The Archaeology of York, 12/1. London.

Dawson, D. (1986) 'Handlist of medieval places of worship within the 1373 boundaries of the county of Bristol', *Bull. CBA Churches Committee* 24, 2-15.

Day, M. (1980) 'The Roman period in the parishes' in M. Sparks (ed.) (1980), 5-10.

Dejevsky, N. J. (1977) 'Novgorod: the origins of a Russian town' in M. W. Barley (ed.) (1977), 391-402.

Denton, J. H. (1970) *English Royal Free Chapels 1100-1300. A Constitutional Study*. Manchester.

Dickens, A. G. (1967) 'Secular and religious motivation in the Pilgrimage of Grace', *Studies in Church Hist.* 4, 39-64.

Dickens, B. (1934) *The Place-names of Surrey*, English Place-Name Soc., 11.

Doble, G. H. (1964) *The Saints of Cornwall. Part 3: Saints of the Fal and its Neighbourhood*. Oxford.

Dobson, R. B. (1967) 'The foundation of perpetual chantries by the citizens of medieval York', *Studies in Church Hist.* 4, 22-38.

Dolley, M. (1978) 'The Anglo-Danish and Anglo-Norse coinages of York' in R. A. Hall (ed.) *Viking Age York and the North*, CBA Research Report 27, 26-31.

Downes, K. (1969) *Hawksmoor*. London.

—— (1977) *Vanbrugh*. London.

—— (1982) *The Architecture of Wren*. St Albans, London.

Drew, C. (1954) *Early Parochial Organization in England. The Origins of the Office of Churchwarden*, St Anthony's Hall Pub. 7.

Drinkwater, C. H. (1908) Translation of the Shropshire Domesday in W. Page (ed.) *Victoria County History of Shropshire* 1, 309-49.

Dudding, R. C. (ed. and trans.) (1941) *The First Churchwardens' Book of Louth, 1500-1524*. Oxford.

Dumville, D. N. (1984) 'The chronology of *De Excidio Britanniae*, Book I', in M. Lapidge and D. N. Dumville (eds) *Gildas: New Approaches*, 61-84. Woodbridge.

Dunmore, S. and Carr, R. (1976) *The Late Saxon town of Thetford: An archaeological and historical survey*, E. Anglian Archaeol., 4.

Dunning, R. W. (1975) 'Ilchester: a study in continuity', *Somerset Archaeol. Natur. Hist.* 119, 44-50.

Duprez, A. (1970) *Jésus et les Dieux Guérisseurs*. Paris.

Durham, B. *et al.* (1973) 'A cutting across the Saxon defences at Wallingford, Berkshire, 1971', *Oxoniensia* 37, 82-5.

Dyer, C. C. (1985) 'Power and conflict in the medieval English village', in D. Hooke (ed.) (1985), 27-32.

Dymond, D. P. (1968) 'The Suffolk landscape' in L. Munby (ed.) *E. Anglian Studies*, 17-47.

—— (1985) *The Norfolk Landscape*. London.

Dyson, T. and Schofield, J. (1984) 'Saxon London' in J. Haslam (ed.) (1984), 285-313.

EYC *Early Yorkshire Charters*, 1 (ed. W. Farrer), 1914; 5 (ed. C. T. Clay), 1936.

Edwards, M. (ed.) (1966) *Scarborough 966-1966*. Scarborough.

Ekwall, E. (1966) *The Concise Oxford Dictionary of English Place-names*, 4th edn. Oxford.

Ellison, A. (1980) 'Natives, Romans and Christians on West Hill, Uley: an interim report on the excavation of a ritual complex of the first millennium AD' in W. J. Rodwell (ed.) (1980), 305-28.

—— (1983) *Medieval Villages in South-east Somerset*, Western Archaeol. Trust Survey, no. 6.

Elrington, C. R. (1976) Introduction to Hutton (1783), v-xxv.

Elwes, D. G. C. (1874) 'Bedford Castle', *Assoc. Architect. Socs. Reports Papers* 12.2, 243-60.

English, B. (1979) *The Lords of Holderness 1086-1260. A Study in Feudal Society*. Oxford.

EHD *English Historical Documents*, 1, c. 500-1042 (ed. D. Whitelock), 2nd edn., 1979; 2, 1042-1189 (eds D. C. Douglas and G. W. Greenaway), 1961; 5, 1485-1558 (ed. C. H. Williams), 1967.

Eulogium Historiarum Haydon, F. S. (ed.) (1858-63) *Eulogium Historiarum sive Temporis . . .*, Rolls ser. 9, 3 vols.

Everitt, A. M. (1972) *The pattern of rural dissent: the nineteenth century*. University of Leicester Department of English Local History Occasional Paper, 2 series, No 4.

Everson, P. (1980) 'Thomas "Governor" Pownall and the Roman villa at Glentworth, Lincolnshire', *Lincolnshire Hist. Archaeol.* 15, 9-14.

Farley, M. (1979) 'Burials in Aylesbury and the early history of the town', *Records of Bucks* 21, 116-22.

Faull, M. L. (1975) 'The semantic development of Old English *wealh*', *Leeds Studies in English* 8, 20-44.

—— (ed.) (1984) *Studies in Late Anglo-Saxon Settlement*. Oxford.

—— and Moorhouse, S. (eds) (1981) *West Yorkshire: An Archaeological Survey to AD 1500*. Wakefield.

Fawcett, R. (1980) 'A group of churches by the architect of Great
Walsingham', *Norfolk Archaeol.* 37, 277–94.
—— (1982) 'St Mary at Wiveton in Norfolk, and a group of churches
attributed to its mason', *Antiq. J.* 62, 35–56.
Feine, H. E. (1950) *Kirkliche Rechtsgeschichte, 1, Die Katholische Kirche.* Weimar.
Fernie, E. (1983) *The Architecture of the Anglo-Saxons.* London.
Finberg, H. P. R. (1971) 'The archangel Michael in Britain', *Millénaire
monastique de Mont Saint-Michel* III, 459–68. Paris.
Firby, M. and Lang, J. (1981) 'The pre-Conquest sculpture at Stonegrave',
Yorkshire Archaeol. J. 53, 17–29.
Fletcher, E. G. M. and Meates, G. W. (1969) 'The ruined church of Stone-
by-Faversham', *Antiq. J.* 49, 273–94.
——— (1977) ———: second report, *Antiq. J.* 57, 67–72.
Forster, F. Arnold (1899) *Studies in Church Dedications or England's Patron Saints,*
3 vols.
Foster, C. W. and Longley, T. (eds) (1924) *The Lincolnshire Domesday and the
Lindsey Survey,* Lincoln Rec. Soc., 19.
Fox, A. M. (1952) *Roman Exeter (Isca Dumnoniorum): excavations in the war-damaged
areas 1945-1947.* Manchester.
Franklin, M. J. (1984) 'The identification of minsters in the Midlands', *Anglo-
Norman Studies* 7, 69–88.
—— (1985) 'The assessment of benefices for taxation in 13th century
Buckinghamshire', *Nottingham Medieval. Stud.* 29, 73–97.
Freke, D. (1982) 'An unsuspected pre-Conquest church and cemetery at
Winwick, Cheshire', *Bull. CBA Churches Committee* 16, 7–8.
Frere, S. S. (1972) *Verulamium Excavations,* Soc. Antiqs. Research Report 28.
London.
Galbraith, V. H. (1961) *The Making of Domesday Book.* Oxford.
Galinié, H. (1978) 'Archéologie et topographie historique de Tours – IVème-
XIème siècle', *Zeitschrift für Archäologie des Mittelalters* 6, 33–56.
Gay, J. D. (1971) *The Geography of Religion in England.* London.
Gee, E. (1981) 'Stone from the medieval limestone quarries of south Yorkshire'
in A. Detsicas (ed.) *Collectanea Historica: Essays in Memory of Stuart Rigold,*
247–55. Maidstone.
Gelling, M. (1961) 'Place-names and Anglo-Saxon paganism', *University of
Birmingham Hist. J.* 7, 7–25.
—— (1973) 'Further thoughts on pagan place-names' in F. Sandgren (ed.)
Otium et Negotium: Studies presented to Olof von Feilitzen, 109–28.
Stockholm.
—— (1978) *Signposts to the Past.* London.
—— (1979) *The Early Charters of the Thames Valley.* Leicester.
—— (1981) 'The word "church" in English place-names', *Bull. CBA Churches
Committee* 15, 4–9.
Gem, R. (1975) 'A recession in English architecture during the early eleventh
century, and its effect on the development of the Romanesque style', *J.
British Archaeol. Assoc.* 38, 28–49.
—— (1982) 'The early Romanesque tower of Sompting church, Sussex', *Anglo-
Norman Stud.* 5, 121–8.
—— (1983) 'Towards an iconography of Anglo-Saxon architecture', *J. Warburg
Courtauld Inst.* 46, 1–18.

—— (1986a) 'ABC: how should we periodize Anglo-Saxon architecture?', in L. A. S. Butler and R. Morris (eds) (1986), 146–55.

—— (1986b) 'Lincoln minster: ecclesia pulchra, ecclesia fortis', *Medieval Art and Architecture at Lincoln Cathedral* (= British Archaeol. Assoc. Conference Trans. for 1982), 9–28.

—— (1986c) 'The bishop's chapel at Hereford: the roles of patron and craftsman', in *Art and Patronage in the English Romanesque*, eds S. Macready & F. H. Thompson, Society of Antiquaries Occasional Paper, new series, No 8. London.

Gethyn-Jones, J. E. (1961) *St Mary's Church Kempley and its Paintings.*

Gildas, *De Excidio* Winterbottom, M. (ed. and trans.) (1978) *The Ruin of Britain, and Other Works.*

Gilmour, B. (1979) 'The Anglo-Saxon church at St Paul-in-the-Bail, Lincoln', *Medieval Archaeol.* 23, 214–18.

—— and Stocker, D. A. (1986) *St Mark's Church and Cemetery*, The Archaeol. of Lincoln, 13/1. London.

Glob, P. V. (1969) *The Bog People: Iron-age Man Preserved.* London.

Goodhart-Rendel, H. S. (1983) *George Edmund Street*, Ecclesiol. Soc. London.

Gordon, A. (1980) 'Excavation in the lower church of Glasgow Cathedral', *Glasgow Archaeol. J.* 7, 85–96.

Gracie, H. S. (1963) 'St Peter's church, Frocester', *Trans. Bristol Gloucestershire Archaeol. Soc.* 82, 148–67.

Graham-Campbell, J. (1980) 'The Scandinavian Viking-age burials of England: some problems of interpretation' in P. Rahtz, T. Dickinson and L. Watts (eds) *Anglo-Saxon Cemeteries 1979*, BAR 82, 379–82.

Green, C. J. S. (1977) 'The significance of plaster burials for the recognition of Christian cemeteries' in R. Reece (ed.) *Burial in the Roman World*, CBA Research Report 22, 46–53.

—— (1979) 'Poundbury – a summary of recent excavations at Poundbury, Dorchester'. Dorchester.

Greenoak, F. (1985) *God's Acre. The Flowers and Animals of the Parish Churchyard.* London.

Grierson, P. (1952–4) 'The Canterbury (St Martin's) hoard of Frankish and Anglo-Saxon coin ornaments', *British Numis. J.* 27, 39–51.

Griffiths, R. A. (ed.) (1978) *Boroughs of Mediaeval Wales.* Cardiff.

Grimes, W. F. (1968) *The Excavation of Roman and Medieval London.* London.

Grinsell, L. V. (1976) *Folklore of Prehistoric Sites in Britain.*

—— (1981) 'The later history of Tŷ Illtud', *Archaeol. Cambrensis* 130, 131–9.

Haddan, A. W. and Stubbs, W. (eds) (1869–71) *Councils and Ecclesiastical Documents relating to Great Britain and Ireland*, 3 vols.

Haines, R. M. (1965) *The Administration of the Diocese of Worcester in the First Half of the Fourteenth Century.* London.

Hall, R. A. (1974) 'The pre-Conquest burgh of Derby', *Derbyshire Archaeol. J.* 94, 16–23.

—— and Lang, J. T. (1986) 'St Mary's church, Levisham, North Yorkshire', *Yorkshire Archaeol. J.* 58, 57–83.

Hallam, H. E. (1965) *Settlement and Society: A Study of the Early Agrarian History of South Lincolnshire.* Cambridge.

Hampton, J. N. (1981) 'The evidence of air photography: elementary comparative studies applied to sites at Mount Down, Hants, and near Malmesbury, Wilts', *Antiq. J.* 61, 316-21.

Harmer, F. H. (ed.) (1914) *Select English Historical Documents of the Ninth and Tenth Centuries.* Cambridge.

Harper-Bill, C. (1977) 'A late medieval visitation – the diocese of Norwich in 1499', *Proc. Suffolk Inst. Archaeol. Hist.* 34, 35-47.

Harris, J. (1979) *The Artist and the Country House: A History of Country House and Garden View Painting in Britain 1540-1870.* London.

Harrison, K. (1960) 'The pre-Conquest churches of York: with an appendix on eighth-century Northumbrian annals', *Yorkshire Archaeol. J.* 40, 232-49.

Hart, G. (1965) *A History of Cheltenham.* Leicester.

Harvey, J. H. (1944) *Henry Yevele, c.1320-1400: The Life of an English Architect.* London.

—— (1947) *Gothic England: A Survey of National Culture 1300-1550.* London.

—— (1972) *The Mediaeval Architect.*

—— (1974) *Cathedrals of England and Wales.* London.

—— (1978) *The Perpendicular Style 1330-1485.* London.

—— (1984) with contributions by A. Oswald, *English Mediaeval Architects: A Biographical Dictionary down to 1550,* 2nd edn. Gloucester.

Hase, P. H. (1975) *The Development of the Parish in Hampshire,* unpub. Cambridge Ph.D. thesis.

Haskins, C. H. (1971) *The Renaissance of the Twelfth Century,* orig. edn. 1928. Harvard.

Haslam, J. (ed.) (1984) *Anglo-Saxon Towns in Southern England.* Chichester.

Hassall, M. (1976) 'Britain in the *Notitia*' in R. Goodburn and P. Bartholomew (eds) *Aspects of the Notitia Dignitatum,* BAR S.15, 103-81.

Hassall, T. (1986) 'Archaeology of Oxford city' in G. Briggs, J. Cook and T. Rowley (eds) *The Archaeology of the Oxford Region,* 115-34. Oxford.

Hatcher, J. (1977) *Plague, Population and the English Economy 1348-1530.* Basingstoke, London.

Heanley, R. M. (1922) *The History of Weyhill, Hants and its Ancient Fair.* Winchester.

Heighway, C. M. *et al.* (1978) 'Excavations at Gloucester. Fourth interim report: St Oswald's Priory, Gloucester, 1975-1976', *Antiq. J.* 58, 103-32.

—— (1980a) 'The cemeteries of Roman Gloucester', *Trans. Bristol Gloucestershire Archaeol. Soc.* 98, 57-72.

—— (1980b) 'Excavations at Gloucester. Fifth Interim Report: St Oswald's Priory 1977-8', *Antiq. J.* 60, 207-26.

—— (1984) 'Anglo-Saxon Gloucester to AD 1000' in M. L. Faull (ed.) (1984), 35-54.

Heighway, C. M. and Hill, D. (1978) 'St Oswald's Priory: the history and context of its foundation' in Heighway *et al.* (1978), 118-25.

Hennock, E. P. (1981) 'The Anglo-Catholics and church extension in Victorian Brighton' in M. J. Kitch (ed.) *Studies in Sussex Church History,* 173-88. London.

Henry, F. and Zarnecki, G. (1957) 'Romanesque arches decorated with human and animal heads', *J. British Archaeol. Assoc.* 3rd ser., 20, 1-34.

Herzfeld, G. (ed.) (1900) *An Old English Martyrology,* Early English Text Soc., old ser., 116.

Hewett, C. A. (1980) *English Historic Carpentry.* Chichester.

Hey, D. (1982) 'Saxon churches in south Yorkshire: the historical background' in P. Ryder (1982), 12–15.

Hill, D. H. (1969) 'The Burghal Hidage: the establishment of a text', *Medieval Archaeol.* 13, 84–92.

—— (1981) *An Atlas of Anglo-Saxon England.* Oxford.

Hill, J. W. F. (1948) *Medieval Lincoln.* Cambridge.

Hilling, J. B. (1976) *The Historic Architecture of Wales: An Introduction.* Cardiff.

Hilton, R. H. (1957) 'Winchcombe abbey and the manor of Sherborne' in H. P. R. Finberg (ed.) *Gloucestershire Studies*, 89–113. Leicester.

Hinton, D. A. and Hodges, R. (1977) 'Excavations in Wareham, 1974–5', *Proc. Dorset Natur. Hist. Archaeol. Soc.* 99, 42–83.

Hist. Anglicana Riley, H. T. (ed.) (1863) *Thomae Walsingham, quondam monachi S. Albani, Historia Anglicana*, Rolls ser. 28.1.

HE see under Bede.

Hobson, T. F. (ed.) (1926) *Adderbury 'Rectoria'*, Oxfordshire Record Soc., 8.

Hodges, R. (1980) 'The pottery' in P. Holdsworth (ed.) *Excavations at Melbourne Street, Southampton, 1971–76*, CBA Research Report 33, 40–58.

—— (1982) *Dark Age Economics: The Origins of Towns and Trade, AD 600–1000.* London.

Holden, E. (1980) 'Excavations at Old Erringham, Shoreham, West Sussex: Part II the "Chapel" and ringwork', *Sussex Archaeol. Collect.* 118, 257–97.

Holderness, B. A. (1972) 'Open and close parishes in England', *Agricultural Hist. Rev.* 20, 126–39.

Holdsworth, P. (1976) 'Saxon Southampton; a new review', *Medieval Archaeol.* 20, 26–61.

Hood, A. B. E. (ed. and trans.) (1978) *St Patrick: His Writing and Muirchu's Life.* Chichester.

Hooke, D. (ed.) (1985) *Medieval Villages.* Oxford.

Hope-Taylor, B. (1977) *Yeavering. An Anglo-British Centre of Early Northumbria.* London.

Horne, P. D. and King, A. C. (1980) 'Romano-Celtic temples in continental Europe: a gazetteer of those with known plans' in W. J. Rodwell (ed.) (1980), 369–555.

Hoskins, W. G. (1955) *The Making of the English Landscape.* London.

—— (1960) *Two Thousand Years in Exeter.* Exeter.

Howe, A. (1984) *The Cotton Masters 1830–1860.* Oxford.

Howell, P. (1968) *Victorian Churches.* Feltham, Middlesex.

Howorth, H. H. (1913) *St Augustine of Canterbury.* London.

Huggins, P. J. (1978) 'Excavation of Belgic and Romano-British farm with middle Saxon cemetery and churches at Nazeingbury, Essex, 1975–6', *Essex Archaeol. Hist.* 10, 29–117.

Hughes, K. and Hamlin, A. (1977) *The Modern Traveller to the Early Irish Church.* SPCK.

Hurst, J. G. (1984) 'The Wharram Research Project: results to 1983', *Medieval Archaeol.* 28, 77–111.

Hussey, A. (1917) 'Reculver and Hoath wills', *Archaeol. Cantiana* 32, 141.

—— (ed.) (1936) *Kent Chantries*, Kent Archaeol. Soc., Kent Records, 12.

Hussey, C. (1975), *Introduction* to Stroud (1975), 13–20.

Hutton, W. (1783) *An History of Birmingham*, 2nd edn., republished 1976. Ilkley, West Yorkshire.

BIBLIOGRAPHY

Jacob, W. M. (1979) 'A practice of very hurtful tendency', *Studies in Church History*, 16, 315-26.

James, E. (1977) *The Merovingian Archaeology of South-west Gaul*, BAR Internat. Ser. 25.

James, T. (1980) *Carmarthen: An Archaeological and Topographical Survey*, Carmarthenshire Antiq. Soc. Monograph, ser. 2.

Jenkins, F. (1965) 'St Martin's church at Canterbury: a survey of the earliest structural features', *Medieval Archaeol*, 9, 11-15.

—— (1976) 'Preliminary report on the excavations at the church of St Pancras at Canterbury', *Canterbury Archaeol*. 1975-6, 4-5.

—— (1981) 'The church of All Saints, Shuart in the Isle of Thanet' in A. Detsicas (ed.) *Collectanea Historica: Essays in Memory of Stuart Rigold*, 147-54. Maidstone.

Jenkinson, H. (1926) 'The use of Arabic and Roman numerals in English archives', *Antiq. J.* 6, 263-75.

Johnson, S. (1983) *Burgh Castle, Excavations by Charles Green 1958-61*, E. Anglian Archaeol. Report no. 20.

Jones, A. (1910) *The History of Gruffydd ap Cynan*. Manchester.

Jones, F. (1954) *The Holy Wells of Wales*. Cardiff.

Jones, G. R. J. (1972) '"Tir Corddlan" (Nucleal land)' in H. P. R. Finberg (ed.) *Agrarian History of England and Wales*, I. ii, 340-9.

—— (1981) 'Early customary tenure in Wales and open-field agriculture' in R. T. Rowley (ed.) *Origins of Open-field Agriculture*.

—— (1983-4) 'The ornaments of a kindred in medieval Gwynedd', *Studia Celtica* 18-19, 135-46.

—— (1986) 'Society and settlement in Wales and the Marches 500 BC to AD 1100', *Trans. Caernarvonshire Hist. Soc.* 7-23.

Jones, M. J. (1986) 'Archaeology in Lincoln' in *Medieval Art and Architecture at Lincoln Cathedral* (= British Archaeol. Assoc. Conference Trans. 1982), 1-8.

—— and Wacher, J. S. (1987) 'The Roman period', in J. Schofield and R. Leech (eds) (1987), 27-45.

Jones, M. Lloyd (1984) *Society and Settlement in Wales and the Marches 500 BC to AD 1100*, BAR 121.

Keen, L. (1984) 'The towns of Dorset' in J. Haslam (ed.) (1984) 203-47.

Keene, D. J. (1975) 'Suburban growth', in M. W. Barley (ed.) (1975), 71-82.

—— (1985) 'Introduction to the parish churches of medieval Winchester', *Bull. CBA Churches Committee* 23, 1-9.

Kemp, B. R. (1968) 'The churches of Berkeley Hernesse', *Trans. Bristol Gloucestershire Archaeol. Soc.* 87, 96-110.

—— (1980) 'Monastic possession of parish churches in England in the twelfth century', *J. Eccles. Hist.* 31, no. 2, 133-60.

Kemp, R. (1986) 'St Andrew, York – parish church to Gilbertine priory', *Bull. CBA Churches Committee* 24, 21-4.

Kenny, A. (1985) *Wyclif*. Oxford.

Kent, J. P. C., Tatton-Brown, T. and Welch, M. (1983) 'A Visigothic gold tremissis and a fifth-century firesteel from the Marlowe Theatre site, Canterbury', *Antiq. J.* 63, 371-3.

Kenyon, K. (1948) *Excavations at the Jewry Wall Site, Leicester*, Soc. Antiq. Research Report 15.

Keynes, S. and Lapidge, M. (trans.) (1983) *Alfred the Great. Asser's 'Life of King Alfred' and other contemporary sources.* Harmondsworth.

Knocker, G. M. (1967) 'Excavations at Red Castle, Thetford', *Norfolk Archaeol.* 34, 119–86.

Knoop, D. and Jones, G. P. (1932) 'Masons and apprenticeship in medieval England', *Econ. Hist. Rev.* 3, 346–55.

———— (1938) 'The English medieval quarry', *Econ. Hist. Rev.* 9, 17–37.

Knowles, D. and St Joseph, J. K. S. (1952) *Monastic Sites from the Air.* Cambridge.

Krautheimer, R. (1942) Introduction to an *Iconography of Medieval Architecture, J. Warburg Courtauld Inst.* 5, 1–33.

—— (1965) *Early Christian and Byzantine Architecture.* Harmondsworth.

—— (1980) *Rome: Profile of a City, 312–1303.* Princeton.

Lamb, H. H. (1966) *The Changing Climate.* London.

Lapidge, M. and Herren, M. (ed. and trans.) (1979) *The Prose Works of Aldhelm.* Ipswich.

LDF Russell, N. (trans.) (1981) *The Lives of the Desert Fathers. The Historia Monachorum in Aegypto.* London, Oxford.

Leech, R. (1980) 'Religion and burials in south Somerset and north Dorset' in W. J. Rodwell (ed.) (1980), 329–66.

—— (1981) *Historic Towns in Gloucestershire.* Bristol.

Lehmann-Brockhaus, O. (1955) *Lateinische Schriftquellen zur Kunst in England, Wales and Schottland, vom Jahre 901 bis zum Jahre 1307, I.* Munich.

Levison, W. (1946) *England and the Continent in the Eighth Century.* Oxford.

Lidbetter, H. (1961) *The Friends Meeting House.* York.

Liddle, P. (1982) *Leicestershire Archaeology – The Present State of Knowledge. Volume 2, Anglo-Saxon and Medieval Periods*, Leicestershire Museum Pub. 38.

Lidén, H.-E. (1969) 'From pagan sanctuary to Christian church. The excavation of Maere church in Trøndelag. With comments by Wilhelm Holmquist and Olaf Olsen', *Norwegian Archaeol. Rev.* 2, 3–32.

Lloyd, T. H. (1973) *The Movement of Wool Prices in Medieval England*, Econ. Hist. Rev. Supplement 6.

McCulloch, F. (1981) 'Saints Alban and Amphibalus in the works of Matthew Paris: Dublin Trinity College MS 177', *Speculum* 56, 761–85.

Mackreth, D. F. (1987) 'Roman public buildings' in J. Schofield and R. Leech (eds) (1987), 133–46.

Magilton, J. R. (1980) *The Church of St Helen-on-the-Walls, Aldwark*, Archaeology of York, 10/1. London.

Mahany, C. and Roffe, D. (1982) 'Stamford: the development of an Anglo-Scandinavian borough', *Anglo-Norman Studies* 5, 197–219.

Malmesbury Hamilton, N. E. S. A. (ed.) (1870) *De Gestis Pontificum Anglorum*, Rolls ser. 52.

—— Stubbs, W. (ed.) (1887, 1889) *De Gestis Regis Anglorum*, Rolls ser. 90, 2 vols.

Manby, T. (1985) *Thwing: Excavation and Field Archaeology in East Yorkshire*, Yorkshire Archaeol. Soc. Prehistory Research Section.

—— (1986) *Thwing: Excavation and Field Archaeology in East Yorkshire. The Anglo-Saxon Cemetery*, Yorkshire Archaeol. Soc. Prehistory Research Section.

Mann, J. (1961) 'The administration of Roman Britain', *Antiquity* 35, 316–20.

Markus, R. A. (1963) 'The chronology of the Gregorian mission to England: Bede's narrative and Gregory's correspondence', *J. Eccles. Hist.* 14, 16–30.

—— (1970) 'Gregory the Great and a papal missionary strategy', *Stud. Church Hist.* 6, 29–38.

—— (1974) *Christianity in the Roman World.* London.

Martin, E. A. (1978) 'St Otolph and Hadstock: A reply', *Antiq. J.* 58, 153–9.

Mason, E. (1976) 'The role of the English parishioner, 1100–1500', *J. Eccles. Hist.* 27, 17–29.

Matthew Paris Luard, H. R. (ed.) (1872–83) *Matthaei Parisiensis, monachi Sancti Albani, Chronica Majora,* Rolls ser. 57, 7 vols.

—— Madden, F. (ed.) (1866–9) *Historia Anglorum, sive, ut vulgo dicitur, Historia Minor,* Rolls ser. 44, 3 vols.

Meates, G. W. (1955) *Lullingstone Roman Villa.* London.

—— (1979) *The Roman Villa at Lullingstone, Kent: 1, The Site,* Kent Archaeol. Soc. Monograph ser. 1.

Meyer, I. R. and Huggett, R. J. (1981) *Settlements.* London.

Miller, K., Robinson, J., English, B. and Hall, I. (1982) *Beverley. An Archaeological and Architectural Study,* Royal Commission on the Historical Monuments of England. London.

Mitchell, B. R. and Deane, P. (1962) *Abstract of British Historical Statistics.* Cambridge.

Moorman, J. R. H. (1945) *Church Life in England in the Thirteenth Century.* Cambridge.

Morley, B. (1985) 'The nave roof of the church of St Mary, Kempley, Gloucestershire', *Antiq. J.* 65, 101–11.

Morris, C. (1976) 'Pre-Conquest sculpture of the Tees valley', *Medieval Archaeol.* 20, 140–6.

Morris, J. (1959) 'Anglo-Saxon Surrey', *Surrey Archaeol. Collect.* 56, 132–58.

—— (1973) *The Age of Arthur.* London.

Morris, R. (1983) *The Church in British Archaeology,* CBA Research Report 47.

—— (1986) 'Alcuin, York, and the *alma sophia*' in L. A. S. Butler and R. Morris (eds) (1986), 80–9.

—— (1987) 'Parish churches' in J. Schofield and R. Leech (eds) (1987), 177–91.

—— and Roxan, J. (1980) 'Churches on Roman buildings' in W. J. Rodwell (ed.) (1980), 175–209.

Munby, J. (1984) 'Saxon Chichester and its predecessors' in J. Haslam (ed.) (1984), 315–43.

Nash-Williams, V. E. (1950) *The Early Christian Monuments of Wales.* Cardiff.

—— (1953) 'The forum-and-basilica and public baths of the Roman town of Venta Silurum at Caerwent in Monmouthshire', *Bull. Board Celtic Stud.* 15, 159–67.

Neilsen, E. L. (1965) 'Detaeldste Viborg', *Fra Viborg Amt,* 137–74.

Neville, R. C. (1856) 'Description of a remarkable deposit of Roman antiquities of iron, discovered at Great Chesterford, Essex, in 1854', *Archaeol. J.* 13, 1–13.

Northeast, P. (1980) 'Buildings and benefactors' in J. Corke *et al.* (eds) (1980), 24–8.

Obelkevich, J. (1976) *Religion and Society: South Lindsey 1825–1875.* Oxford.

O'Connor, T. P. (1983) 'Feeding Lincoln in the 11th century – a speculation' in M. Jones (ed.) *Integrating the Subsistence Economy,* BAR Internat. ser. 181.

BIBLIOGRAPHY

Okasha, E. (1971) *Hand-list of Anglo-Saxon Non-runic Inscriptions*. Cambridge.

O'Kelly, M. J. (1958) 'Church Island near Valencia, Co. Kerry', *Proc. Royal Irish Acad.* 59, C2 57-136.

Olsen, O. (1986) 'Is there a relationship between pagan and Christian places of worship in Scandinavia?' in L. A. S. Butler and R. Morris (eds) (1986), 126-30.

Orderic Chibnall, M. (ed.) (1969-80) *The Ecclesiastical History of Orderic Vitalis*, 6 vols. Oxford.

Owen, A. E. B. (1975) 'Medieval salting and the coastline in Cambridgeshire and north-west Norfolk' in K. W. de Brisay and K. A. Evans (eds) *Salt: The Study of an Ancient Industry*, 42-4. Colchester.

—— (1984) 'Salt, sea banks and medieval settlement on the Lindsey coast' in (N. Field and A. White (eds) *A Prospect of Lincolnshire*, 46-9. Lincoln.

—— (1986) 'Mablethorpe St Peter's and the sea', *Lincolnshire Hist. Archaeol.* 21, 61-2.

Owen, D. (1971) *Church and Society in Medieval Lincolnshire*. Lincoln.

—— (1975) 'Medieval chapels in Lincolnshire', *Lincolnshire Hist. Archaeol.* 10, 15-22.

—— (1979) 'Bishop's Lynn: the first century of a new town?', *Anglo-Norman Stud.* 2, 141-53.

Page, W. (ed.) (1894-5) *The certificates of the Commissioners appointed to survey the chantries, guilds, hospitals, etc in the county of York*, Surtees. Soc. 91 and 92.

—— (1915) 'Some remarks on the churches of the Domesday survey', *Archaeologia* 66, 61-102.

Palliser, D. M. (1974) 'The unions of parishes at York, 1547-1586', *Yorkshire Archaeol. J.* 46, 87-102.

—— (1976) *The Staffordshire Landscape*. London.

—— (1979) *Tudor York*. Oxford.

Palmer, W. M. (1940) 'Fifteenth-century visitation records of the deanery of Wisbech', *Proc. Cambridge Antiq. Soc.* 39, 69-75.

Park, D. (1983) 'The wall paintings of the Holy Sepulchre chapel' in *Medieval Art and Architecture at Winchester* (= British Archaeol. Assoc. Conference Trans. for 1980), 38-62.

Parsons, D. (1979) 'St Mary, Ketton, and some other Rutland churches', *Archaeol J.* 136, 118-24.

—— (1983) 'Sites and monuments of the Anglo-Saxon mission in central Germany', *Archaeol. J.* 140, 280-321.

—— (1986) '*Sacrarium*: ablution drains in early medieval churches' in L. A. S. Butler and R. Morris (eds) (1986), 105-20.

Pay, S. (1987) *Hamwic: Southampton's Saxon town*, Southampton City Museum. Horndean.

Pearce, S. (1978) *The Kingdom of Dumnonia; Studies in History and Tradition of South-western Britain AD 350-1150*. Padstow.

—— (ed.) (1982) *The Early Church in Western Britain and Ireland. Studies presented to C. A. R. Radford*. BAR 102.

Perriam, D. (1979) 'An unrecorded Carlisle church, the church of Holy Trinity, Caldergate', *Trans. Cumberland Westmorland Antiq. Archaeol. Soc.* 79, 51-5.

Petch, M. R. (1986 'The Raughton Family Influence on the European Curvilinear Style'. *Yorkshire Archaeol. J.* 58, 37-55.

Petersson, H. B. A. (1969) *Anglo-Saxon Currency, King Edgar's Reform to the Norman Conquest*. Lund.

Pevsner, N. (series ed.) (1951–76) *The Buildings of England*, volumes published by county. Harmondsworth.

Phillips, A. D. (1985) *The Cathedral of Archbishop Thomas of Bayeux. Excavations at York Minster. Volume 2.* RCHME. London.

Platt, C. (1975) 'The evolution of towns: natural growth', in M. W. Barley (ed.) (1975), 48–56.

—— (1981) *The Parish Churches of Medieval England.* London.

—— and Coleman-Smith, R. (1975) *Excavations in Medieval Southampton 1953–1969. Volume 1.* Leicester.

Pocock, M. and Wheeler, H. (1971) 'Excavations at Escomb church, County Durham', *J. British Archaeol. Assoc.* 3rd ser., 34, 11–29.

Port, M. H. (1961) *Six Hundred New Churches. A Study of the Church Building Commission, 1818–1856, and its Church Building Activities.* London.

—— (1986) *The Commissions for Building Fifty New Churches. The Minute Books, 1711–27: A Calendar*, London Record Soc., 23.

Postan, M. M. (1973) *Essays on Medieval Agriculture and General Problems of the Medieval Economy.* Cambridge.

Powell, K. (1980) *The Fall of Zion. Northern Chapel Architecture and its Future.* London.

Proudfoot, L. J. (1983) 'The extension of parish churches in medieval Warwickshire', *J. Hist. Geog.* 9, 231–46.

Pugin, A. W. (1836) *Contrasts: or, a parallel between the noble edifices of the fourteenth and fifteenth centuries, and similar buildings of the present day* ... London.

Purvis, J. S. (1948) *Tudor Parish Documents in the Diocese of York.* Cambridge.

—— (1958) *The Condition of Yorkshire Church Fabrics 1300–1800*, St Anthony's Hall Pub. 14.

Quiney, A. (1979) *John Loughborough Pearson.* New Haven, London.

Radford, C. A. R. 'The Native Ecclesiastical Architecture of Wales (c. 1100–1285): the Study of a Regional Style', in *Culture and Environment. Essays in Honour of Sir Cyril Fox* (eds. I. Foster & L. Alcock), 355–72. London.

—— (1976) 'The church of St Alkmund, Derby', *Derbyshire Archaeol. J.* 96, 26–61.

—— (1978) 'The pre-Conquest boroughs of England', *Proc. Brit. Acad.* 64, 131–53.

Rahtz, P. (1971) 'Excavations on Glastonbury Tor, Somerset, 1964–66', *Archaeol. J.* 127, 1–81.

——, Dickinson, T. and Watts, L. (eds) (1979) *Anglo-Saxon Cemeteries*, BAR 82.

——, and Watts, L. (1979) 'The end of Roman temples in the west of Britain' in P. J. Casey (ed.) *The end of Roman Britain*, BAR 71, 183–210.

Raine, J. (ed.) (1864) *The Priory of Hexham: Its Chronicles, Endowments, and Annals. Volume 1*, Surtees Soc., 44.

Ramm, H. G. (1971) 'The end of Roman York' in R. M. Butler (ed.) (1971) *Soldier and Civilian in Roman Yorkshire*, 179–99.

—— (1976) 'Excavations in the church of St Mary Bishophill Senior, York', *Yorkshire Archaeol. J.* 48, 35–68.

Reddaway, T. F. (1940) *The Rebuilding of London after the Great Fire.* London.

Reg. Antiq. Foster, C. W. and Major, K. (eds) (1931) *The Registrum Antiquissimum of the Cathedral Church of Lincoln*, Lincoln Record Soc., 1, 27.

Reg. Chandler Timmins, T. C. B. (ed.) (1984) *The Register of John Chandler, Dean of Salisbury, 1404-17*, Wiltshire Record Soc., 39.

Reg. Clifford Smith, W. E. L. (ed.) (1976) *The Register of Richard Clifford Bishop of Worcester, 1401-1407. A Calendar*, Pontifical Inst. for Medieval Stud. Toronto.

Reg. Giffard Bund, J. W. Willis (ed.) (1902) *Register of Bishop Godfrey Giffard, 1268-1301*, 2 vols. Oxford.

Reg. Gray Raine, J. (ed.) (1872) *The Register, or Rolls, of Walter Gray*, Surtees Soc., 56.

Reg. Reynolds Wilson, R. A. (ed.) (1927) *The Register of Walter Reynolds, Bishop of Worcester, 1308-1313* Worcester Hist. Soc.

Reg. Sutton Hill, R. M. T. (ed.) (1954, 1958) *The Rolls and Register of Bishop Oliver Sutton 1280-1299*, vols 3 and 4, Lincoln Record Soc., 48, 52.

Renn, D. F. (1973) *Norman Castles in Britain*, 2nd edn. London.

Richmond, H. (1986) 'Outlines of church development in Northamptonshire' in L. A. S. Butler and R. Morris (eds) (1986), 176-87.

Ridout, B. V. (1986) 'The control of dry rot', *Church Building*, summer 1986, 27-8.

Rigold, S. E. (1961) 'The supposed see of Dunwich', *J. British Archaeol. Assoc.* 3rd ser., 24, 55-9.

—— (1972) 'Roman Folkestone reconsidered', *Archaeol. Cantiana* 87, 31-42.

—— (1974) 'Further evidence about the site of "Dommoc"', *J. British Archaeol. Assoc.* 3rd ser., 37, 97-102.

—— (1977) '*Litus Romanum* - the Shore forts as mission stations' in D. E. Johnston (ed.) *The Saxon Shore*, CBA Research Report 18, 70-5.

Riley, H. T. (ed.) (1867-9) *Gesta Abbatum Monasterii Sancti Albani*, Roll ser. 28.4, 3 vols.

Roberts, B. K. (1972) 'Village plans in County Durham: a preliminary statement', *Medieval Archaeol.* 16, 33-56.

Roberts, E. (1972) 'Moulding analysis and architectural research: the late middle ages', *J. Soc. Architect. Historians Great Brit.* 20, 5-13.

Roberts, J. P. with Atkin, M. (1982) 'St Benedict's church', *Excavations in Norwich 1971-1978, Part 1*, East Anglian Archaeol. Rep. no. 15.

Robertson, A. J. (1925) *Laws of the Kings of England from Edmund to Henry I.* Cambridge.

—— (1939) *Anglo-Saxon Charters*. Cambridge.

Rodwell, K. (ed.) (1975) *Historic Towns in Oxfordshire*, Oxfordshire Archaeol. Unit Survey no. 3.

Rodwell, W. J. (1975) 'Milestones, civic territories, and the Antonine Itinerary', *Britannia* 6, 76-101.

—— (1976) 'The archaeological investigation of Hadstock church, Essex', *Antiq. J.* 56, 55-71.

—— (ed.) (1980) *Temples, Churches and Religion in Roman Britain*, BAR 77.

—— (1981) *The Archaeology of the English Church. The Study of Historic Churches and Churchyards.* London.

—— (1984) 'Churches in the Landscape: aspects of topography and planning' in M. L. Faull (ed.) (1984), 1-23.

—— and Rodwell, K. (1977) *Historic Churches - A Wasting Asset*, CBA Research Report 19.

———— (1982) 'St Peter's church, Barton-upon-Humber: excavation and structural study, 1978-81', *Antiq. J.* 62, 283-315.

———— (1986) *Rivenhall: Investigation of a Villa, Church, and Village, 1950-1977*, CBA Research Report 55.

Roffe, D. (1984) 'Pre-Conquest estates and parish boundaries: a discussion with examples from Lincolnshire' in M. L. Faull (ed.) (1984), 115-22.

—— (1986) 'The seventh-century monastery of Stow Green, Lincolnshire', *Lincolnshire Hist. Archaeol.* 21, 31-3.

—— and Mahany, C. (1986) 'Stamford and the Norman Conquest', *Lincolnshire Hist. Archaeol.* 21, 5-9.

Roger of Wendover Hewlett, H. G. (ed.) (1886-9) *The Flowers of History*, Rolls ser. 84, 3 vols.

Rogers, A. (1972) 'Parish boundaries and urban history: two case studies', *J. British Archaeol. Assoc.* ser. 3, 35, 46-64.

Rogerson, A., Dallas, C. *et al.* (1984) *Excavations in Thetford 1948-59 and 1973-80*, East Anglian Archaeol. Report no. 22.

Rollason, D. W. (1978) 'Lists of saints' resting-places in Anglo-Saxon England', *Anglo-Saxon England* 7, 61-94.

—— (1986) 'The shrines of saints in later Anglo-Saxon England: distribution and significance' in L. A. S. Butler and R. Morris (eds) (1986), 32-43.

Roper, M. (1974) 'Wilfrid's landholdings in Northumbria' in D. P. Kirby (ed.) *Saint Wilfrid at Hexham*. Newcastle upon Tyne.

Ross, A. (1967) *Pagan Celtic Britain. Studies in Iconography and Tradition*. London.

Rowley, R. T. (1972) *The Shropshire Landscape*. London.

—— (1978) *Villages in the Landscape*. London.

RCAHMW Royal Commission on the Ancient and Historical Monuments in Wales.

—— (1976) *An Inventory of the Ancient Monuments in Glamorgan*, vol. 1, *Pre-Norman*, Part 2, *The Iron Age and the Roman Occupation*; Part 3, *The Early Christian Period*. Cardiff.

RCHME Royal Commission on the Historical Monuments of England.

—— (1959) *City of Cambridge*, Parts 1 and 2.

—— (1962) *City of York*, vol. 1, *Eburacum. Roman York*.

—— (1972) *City of York*, vol. 2, *The Defences*.

—— (1975) *City of York*, vol. 4, *Outside the City Walls East of the Ouse*.

—— (1981) *City of York*, vol. 5, *The Central Area*.

—— (1975) *County of Dorset*, vol. 5, *East Dorset*.

—— (1929) *London*, vol. 4, *The City*.

—— (1975) *County of Northampton*, vol. 1, *Archaeological Sites in North-east Northamptonshire*.

—— (1979) —— vol. 2, *Archaeological Sites in Central Northamptonshire*.

—— (1981) —— vol. 3, *Archaeological Sites in North-west Northamptonshire*.

—— (1982) —— vol. 4, *Archaeological Sites in South-west Northamptonshire*.

—— (1984) —— vol. 6, *Architectural Monuments in North Northamptonshire*.

—— (1985) —— vol. 5, *Archaeological Sites and Churches in Northampton*.

—— (1987) *Churches of South-east Wiltshire*.

Royle, E. (1983) *The Victorian Church in York*, Borthwick Paper 64.

Ryder, P. (1982) *Saxon Churches in South Yorkshire*, South Yorkshire County Council Archaeol. Monograph 2.

Sala, G. A. (1895) *Brighton as I Have Known It*.

BIBLIOGRAPHY

Salter, H. E. (1936) *Medieval Oxford*, Oxford Hist. Soc. 100.

Salzman, L. F. (1931) *English Trade in the Middle Ages*. Oxford.

—— (1967) *Building in England down to 1540 - A Documentary History*, 2nd edn. Oxford.

Saul, N. (1980) 'The religious sympathies of the gentry in Gloucestershire 1200–1500', *Trans. Bristol Gloucestershire Archaeol. Soc.* 98, 99–109.

Sawyer, P. H. (1965) 'The wealth of England in the eleventh century', *Trans. Roy. Hist. Soc.* 5th ser., 15, 145–64.

—— (1968) *Anglo-Saxon Charters: An Annotated List and Bibliography*. London.

—— (1978) *From Roman Britain to Norman England*. London.

—— (ed.) (1979) *Charters of Burton Abbey*. Oxford.

—— (1981) 'Fairs and markets in early medieval England' in N. Skyum-Nielsen and N. Lund (eds) *Danish Medieval History: New Currents*, 153–68. Copenhagen.

Scarfe, N. (1972) *The Suffolk Landscape*. London.

Scarisbrick, J. J. (1984) *The Reformation and the English People*. Oxford.

Schofield, J. (1984) *The Building of London from the Conquest to the Great Fire*. London.

—— and Palliser, D. (eds), with Harding, C. (1981) *Recent Archaeological Research in English Towns*. London.

—— and Leech, R. (eds) (1987) *Urban Archaeology in Britain*, CBA Research Report 61.

Schofield, R. S. (1965) 'The geographical distribution of wealth in England, 1334–1649', *Econ. Hist. Rev.* 2nd ser., 18, 483–510.

Seals, W. F. (1967) *Methodism in the Otley Circuit 1744–1974*.

Sheppard, J. A. (1976) 'Medieval village planning in northern England', *J. Hist. Geog.* 2, 3–20.

Sheppard, T. (1912) *The Lost Towns of the Yorkshire Coast*. London.

Shoesmith, R. (1980) *Excavations at Castle Green, Hereford*, CBA Research Report 36.

Sidonius Apollinaris *see* W. B. Anderson (ed.) (1963).

Sills, J. (1982) 'St Peter's church, Holton-le-Clay, Lincolnshire', *Lincolnshire Hist. Archaeol.* 17, 29–42.

Silvester, R. J. (1985) 'West Walton: the development of a siltland parish', *Norfolk Archaeol.* 39, 101–17.

Simmons, J. (1959) 'Brooke church, Rutland, with notes on Elizabethan church-building', *Trans. Leicestershire Archaeol. Hist. Soc.* 35, 36–55.

—— (1974) *Leicester Past and Present*, 2 vols. London.

Simpson, W. S. (ed.) (1895) *Visitations of Churches belonging to St Paul's Cathedral in 1297 and 1458*, Camden Soc., new ser., 55.

Smith, D. M. (ed.) (1980) *English Episcopal Acta. I: Lincoln 1067–1185*. London.

Smith, L. T. (ed.) (1907) *The Itinerary of John Leland in or about the Years 1535–1543*, 5 vols. London.

Smith, T. (1870) *English Gilds*, Early English Text Soc., old ser., 40.

Smyth, A. P. (1978) 'The chronology of Northumbrian history in the ninth and tenth centuries' in R. A. Hall (ed.) *Viking Age York and the North*, CBA Research Report 27, 8–10.

Southall, K. H. (1974) *Our Quaker Heritage. Early Meeting Houses*. Friends Home Service Committee. York.

Sparks, M. (ed.) (1980) *The Parish of St Martin and St Paul Canterbury. Historical Essays in Honour of James Hobbs.* Canterbury.

Spufford, M. (1974) *Contrasting Communities: English Villages in the Sixteenth and Seventeenth Centuries.* Cambridge.

Stafford, P. (1985) *The East Midlands in the Early Middle Ages.* Leicester.

Stallard, A. D. (1922) *The Transcript of the Churchwardens' Accounts of the Parish of Tilney All Saints, Norfolk, 1443–1589.* London.

Stancliffe, C. (1983) *St Martin and his Hagiographer: History and Miracle in Sulpicius Severus.* Oxford.

Steane, J. (1985) *The Archaeology of Medieval England and Wales.* London.

Stell, C. F. (1977) 'Nonconformist places of worship', *Bull. CBA Churches Committee* 6, 2–3.

—— (1986) *An Inventory of Nonconformist Chapels and Meeting-houses in Central England,* Royal Commission on the Historical Monuments of England.

—— (1987) 'Chowbent chapel, Atherton', *Archaeol. J.* 144, 32–4.

Stenton, F. M. (1970) *Preparatory to 'Anglo-Saxon England', being the Collected Papers of Frank Merry Stenton.* Oxford.

Stephanus, *Vita Wilfridi see* B. Colgrave (1927).

Stephens, W. R. W. (1879) *The Life and Letters of Walter Farquhar Hook,* 2 vols. London.

Stephenson, W. (1879) 'On the discovery of a well in Beverley Minster', *Yorkshire Archaeol. J.* 5, 126–33.

Stewart, I. (1967) 'The St Martin coins of Lincoln', *Brit. Numis. J.* 36, 46–54.

Storms, G. (1948) *Anglo-Saxon Magic.* The Hague. Nijhoff.

Stroud, D. (1962) *Humphrey Repton.* London.

—— (1975) *Capability Brown,* rev. edn. London.

Stubbs, W. (ed.) (1874), *Memorials of St Dunstan, Archbishop of Canterbury,* Rolls ser. 63.

Stukeley, W. (1776) *Itinerarium Curiosum,* 2nd edn.

Stutz, U. (1938) 'The proprietary church as an element of medieval Germanic ecclesiastical law' in G. Barraclough (trans.) *Medieval Germany 911–1250,* vol. 2, 35–70. Oxford.

Sulpicius Severus *see under Vita Sancti Martini.*

Swanson, H. (1983) *Building Craftsmen in Late Medieval York,* Borthwick Paper 63.

Swire, O. F. (1966) *The Outer Hebrides and their Legends.* London.

Tait, J. (1936) *The Medieval English Borough.* Manchester.

Talbot, C. H. (ed. and trans.) (1981) *The Anglo-Saxon Missionaries in Germany.* London.

Tanner, N. P. (1984) *The Church in Late Medieval Norwich, 1370–1532.* Toronto.

Tate, W. E. (1969) 'The Parish Chest. A study of the records of parochial administration in England. 3rd ed, 93–5. Cambridge University Press.

Tatton-Brown, T. (1978) 'Canterbury', *Current Archaeol.* 62, 78–82.

—— (1980) 'St Martin's church in the 6th and 7th centuries' in M. Sparks (ed.) (1980), 11–18.

—— (1986) 'The topography of Anglo-Saxon London', *Antiquity* 60, 21–8.

Taylor, C. C. (1973) *The Cambridgeshire Landscape.* London.

—— (1974) *Fieldwork in Medieval Archaeology.* London.

—— (1983) *Village and Farmstead. A History of Rural Settlement in England.* London.

Taylor, C. S. (1889) *Analysis of the Domesday Survey of Gloucestershire.* Bristol.

Taylor, H. M. (1968) 'Reculver reconsidered', *Archaeol. J.* 125, 291–6.

BIBLIOGRAPHY

—— (1969) 'The Anglo-Saxon cathedral church at Canterbury', *Archaeol. J.* 126, 101–30.

—— (1973) 'The position of the altar in early Anglo-Saxon churches', *Antiq. J.* 53, 52–8.

—— (1978) *Anglo-Saxon Architecture*, vol. 3. Cambridge.

—— and Taylor, J. (1965) *Anglo-Saxon Architecture*, vols 1 and 2. Cambridge.

—— and Yonge, D. (1981) 'The ruined church at Stone-by-Faversham: a reassessment', *Archaeol. J.* 138, 118–45.

Taylor, N. (1965) 'A Wagnerian high church', *Architectural Rev.* 137, 212–17.

Telford, J. (ed.) (1931) *The Letters of the Rev. John Wesley, A.M.*, 8 vols. London.

Thacker, A. T. (1982) 'Chester and Gloucester: early ecclesiastical organization in two Mercian burhs', *Northern Hist.* 18, 199–211.

Thomas, C. (1971) *The Early Christian Archaeology of North Britain*. Oxford.

—— (1973) *Bede, Archaeology, and the Cult of Relics*. Jarrow Lecture.

—— (1979) 'Saint Patrick and fifth-century Britain: an historical model explored' in P. J. Carey (ed.) *The End of Roman Britain*, BAR 71, 81–101.

—— (1981) *Christianity in Roman Britain to AD 500*. London.

—— (1986) 'Recognizing Christian origins: an archaeological and historical dilemma' in L. A. S. Butler and R. Morris (eds) (1986), 121–5.

Thompson, A. H. (1911a) *The Ground Plan of the English Parish Church*. Cambridge.

—— (1911b) *The Historical Growth of the English Parish Church*. Cambridge.

—— (1917) 'Notes on colleges of secular canons in England', *Archaeol. J.* 2nd ser., 24, 139–99.

—— (1947) *The English Clergy and their Organization in the Later Middle Ages.*

Thompson, F. H. (ed.) (1980) *Archaeology and Coastal Change*, Soc. Antiq. London Occas. Paper, new ser., 1.

Thompson, P. (1971) *William Butterfield*. London.

Thorp, J. (1983) 'St Clement's chapel, Pontefract castle, West Yorkshire', *Bull. CBA Churches Committee* 18, 16–18.

Timmins, T. C. B. (1984) *see under Reg. Chandler.*

Toynbee, J. M. C. (1978) 'Two Romano-British genii', *Britannia* 9, 327–8.

Trowell, F. (1983) 'Speculative housing development in the suburb of Headingley, Leeds, 1838–1914', *Pub. Thoresby Soc.* 59, 50–118.

Trow-Smith, R. (1957) *A History of British Livestock Husbandry to 1700*. London.

Turner, J. M. (1982) 'Primitive Methodism from Mow Cop to Peake's Commentary', *From Mow Cop to Peake, 1807–1932 . . .*, Wesley Hist. Soc., Yorks. Branch, Occasional Paper 4, 1–13.

Usher, H. J. (1978) 'Derbyshire' in *Medieval Village Research Group Twenty-sixth Annual Report*, 6–7.

Vaux, J. E. (1894) *Church Folklore*. London.

Verey, D. (1976a) *Cotswold Churches*. London.

—— (1976b) 'The Perpendicular style on the Cotswolds' in P. McGrath and J. Cannon (eds) *Essays in Bristol and Gloucestershire History*, 127–46.

—— (ed.) (1978) *The Diary of a Cotswold Parson*. Dursley.

—— (ed.) (1981) *Gloucestershire Churches*. Gloucester.

Vince, A. (1984) 'The Aldwych. Saxon London discovered?', *Current Archaeol.* 93, 310–12.

Vita Cuthberti see B. Colgrave (1940).

BIBLIOGRAPHY

Vita Samsonis Fawtier, R. (ed.) (1912) *La Vie de Saint Samson*. Paris.

Vita Sancti Martini Fontaine, J. (ed.) (1967-9) *Vie de Saint Martin: sources chrétiennes*, 133-5. Paris.

Viti Wulfstani Darlington, R. R. (ed.) (1928) *The Vita Wulfstani of William of Malmesbury*, Roy. Hist. Soc. Camden, 3rd ser., 40.

Wade-Martins, P. (1980) *Village Sites in the Launditch Hundred*, E. Anglian Archaeol. Rep., 10.

Walker, D. (1976) 'A register of the churches of the monastery of St Peter's, Gloucester', *An Ecclesiastical Miscellany*, Publications of the Bristol Gloucestershire Archaeol. Soc. Records Section, vol. II, 3-58.

Walker, D. G. (1978) 'Cardiff' in R. A. Griffiths (ed.) (1978), 102-28.

Walker, R. B. (1966) 'Religious changes in Cheshire, 1750-1850', *J. Eccles. Hist.* 17, 77-94.

Ward, B. (1981) *Introduction to LDF*.

Ward, G. (1932) 'The list of Saxon churches in the *Textus Roffensis*', *Archaeol. Cantiana* 44, 39-59.

—— (1933) 'The lists of Saxon churches in the Domesday Monachorum and White Book of St Augustine', *Archaeol. Cantiana* 45, 60-89.

Watts, L. and Rahtz, P. (1985) *Mary-le-Port, Bristol. Excavations 1962-1963*. Bristol.

Watts, M. R. (1978) *The Dissenters*. Oxford.

Weaver, F. W. (ed.) (1901) *Somerset Medieval Wills*, Somerset Rec. Soc. 16.

Webster, G. (1969) 'The future of villa studies' in A. F. L. Rivet (ed.) *The Roman Villa in Britain*, 217-49.

Werner, J. S. (1984) *The Primitive Methodist Connexion. Its Background and Early History*. Wisconsin.

Wesley, John, *Letters see* J. Telford (1931).

West, S. and Plouviez, J. (1976) 'The Roman site at Icklingham', *E. Anglian Archaeol.* 3, 63-126.

West, S. E., Scarfe, N. and Cramp, R. (1984) 'Iken, St Botolph, and the coming of East Anglian Christianity', *Proc. Suffolk Inst. Archaeol. Hist.* 35, 279-301.

Westlake, H. F. (1919) *The Parish Gilds of Mediaeval England*. London.

Whiffen, M. (1948) *Stuart and Georgian Churches*. London.

White, J. F. (1962) *The Cambridge Movement. The Ecclesiologists and the Gothic Revival*. Cambridge.

—— (1964) *Protestant Worship and Church Architecture. Theological and Historical Considerations*. New York, Oxford.

White, W. (1858) *A Month in Yorkshire*. London.

Whitelock, D. (ed. and trans.) (1930) *Anglo-Saxon Wills*. Cambridge.

——, Brett, M. and Brooke, C. N. L. (1981) *Councils and Synods with Other Documents Relating to the English Church, I:* AD 871-1204. Oxford.

Whitwell, J. B. (1970) *Roman Lincolnshire*. Lincoln.

Whyman, J. (ed.) (1985) *The Early Kentish Seaside, 1736-1840*, Kentish Sources, 8.

Wilkinson, J. (1977) *Jerusalem Pilgrims before the Crusades*. Warminster.

Williams, F. (1977) *Pleshey Castle, Essex (XII-XVI century): Excavations in the Bailey, 1959-1963*, BAR 42.

Williams, M. (1970) *The Draining of the Somerset Levels*.

Williams-Jones, K. (1978) 'Caernarvon' in R. A. Griffiths (ed.) (1978), 72-101.

Williamson, T. (1986) 'Parish boundaries and early fields: continuity and discontinuity', *J. Hist. Geog.* 12, 241-8.

Willis, R. (n.d.) *Nonconformist Chapels of York 1693-1840*, York Georgian Soc. Occasional Paper 8.

Wilmot, T. (1986) 'Pontefract, West Yorkshire', *Bull. CBA Churches Committee* 24, 25-6.

Wilson, D. (1985) 'A note on OE *hearg* and *weoh* as place-name elements representing different types of pagan Saxon worship sites', *Anglo-Saxon Studies in Archaeology and History* 4.

Wilson, D. M. (ed.) (1976) *The Archaeology of Anglo-Saxon England*. London.

Wilson, W. D. (1980) 'The work of the Heckington lodge of masons, *1315-1345*', *Lincolnshire Hist. Archaeol.* 15, 21-8.

Wood, A. W. (1981) *A Guide to the Parish Church of Saint James Burton-under-Needwood*.

Wood, I. N. (1979) *Avitus of Vienne*, unpub. D.Phil. thesis, Oxford University.

—— (1981) 'A prelude to Columbanus: the monastic achievement in the Burgundian territories' in H. B. Clarke and M. Brennan (eds) *Columbanus and Merovingian Monasticism*, BAR S 113, 3-32.

—— (1982) 'Roman Britain and Christian literature', *Northern Hist.* 18, 275-8.

—— (1984) 'The end of Roman Britain' in M. Lapidge and D. M. Dumville (eds) *Gildas: New Approaches*. Woodbridge.

—— (1986) 'The audience of architecture in post-Roman Gaul', in L. A. S. Butler and R. Morris (eds) (1986), 74-9.

—— (1987) 'Anglo-Saxon Otley: an archiepiscopal estate and its crosses in a Northumbrian context', *Northern Hist.* 23, 20-38.

Woodger, A. (1984) 'Post-Reformation mixed Gothic in Huntingdonshire church towers and its campanological associations', *Archaeol. J.* 141, 269-308.

Wood-Legh, K. K. (ed.) (1984) *Kentish Visitations of Archbishop William Warham and his Deputies, 1511-1512*, Kent Record Soc., 24.

Woodruffe, C. E. (1917) 'Some early visitation rolls preserved at Canterbury', *Archaeol. Cantiana* 32, 143-80.

Wormald, P. (1978) 'Bede, Beowulf, and the conversion of the Anglo-Saxon aristocracy' in R. T. Farrell (ed.) *Bede and Anglo-Saxon England*, BAR 46, 32-95.

Wren, S. (1750) *Parentalia: or, memoirs of the family of the Wrens ...* Repub. 1965. Farnborough.

Wright, T. (1855) 'Treago, and the large tumulus at St Weonards', *Archaeol. Cambrensis* 3rd ser., 1, 161-74.

Yates, N. (1983) *The Oxford Movement and Anglican Ritualism*, Hist. Assoc. General ser., 105.

Zarnecki, G. (1951) *English Romanesque Sculpture 1066-1140*. London.

—— (1953) *English Romanesque Sculpture 1140-1210*. London.

—— (1966) '1066 and architectural sculpture', *Proc. Brit. Acad.* 52, 87-104.

INDEX

abandonment of churches *and see* disuse of churches, redundancy, 336-9
Abbots Bromley *St*, 69
Abbotsbury *Do*, 266, 462, pl. 27
Aberdaron *Gwd* (*Crn*), 344
Acton Beauchamp *He*, 123, 132-3
Acton Burnell *Sa*, 283
Acton Reynold *Sa*, 447
Acton *Sf*, 424
Adderbury *O*, 310, 351, 352, 353, 354
Aelfric, on necromancy, 61
agriculture in churchyards, 326-7
aisles, 287, 289-95
Akroyden *WY*, 447
Alcuin, on paganism, 59
Aldborough *NY*, 37, 134, 135, 138
Aldbrough *Hu*, 343
Aldington *K*, 326-7
Aidwincle *Np*, 232
Aldworth *Brk*, 78
Algarkirk *Li*, 157, 311
Algarsthorpe *Nf*, 140
Alkham *K*, 326-7
Aller *So*, 240-1, 242, 244
Allerston *NY*, 246
Allerthorpe *Hu*, 135
Allerton Mauleverer *NY* (*YW*), 147
Allerton Park *NY*, 384
Almley *He*, 396
Alne *NY*, 279
Alnmouth *Nb*, 341
Alphamstone *Ex*, 29
Altarnun *Co*, 85-6

altars
  in aisles, 291-2
  burial of, 374
  Roman, 28-9, 72
Alvechurch *Wa*, 157
Alvingham *Li*, 232
Alwinton *Nb*, 239
Amersham *Bu*, 396
Ancaster *Li*, 29, 71-2
Ancroft *Nb*, 252
angels, 370
Ansley *Wa*, 161
Anslow *St*, 161
Antingham *Nf*, 232
Apton *Nf*, 140
archaeology, evidence for dating *and see* name of site, 151, 152
  landscape, 3
architects, 307-8, 407, 409, 412, 414, 415
Argham *Hu* (*YE*), 333-4, 463, pl. 33
Arles, 12-13
Armscote *Wa*, 397
Arnesby *Le*, 395
Ashbrittle *So*, 78
Ashill *Nf*, 80-1
Ashingdon *Ex*, 165
Ashley *Ha*, 261, 264
Aspatria *Cu*, 87
Aspenden Hall *Hrt*, 382
Atcham *Sa*, 28, 381
Aughton *Hu* (*YE*), 250
Avebury *Wi*, 80, 295
Averham *Nt*, 306

Avington *Ha*, 384
Awliscombe *D*, 82
Axminster *D*, 158
Aylesbury *Bu*, 272
Aylesford *K*, 377
Ayot St Lawrence *Hrt*, 385

Badmonden *K*, 161
baileys, churches within *and see* fortifications, military use of churches, mottes, 259, 261
Bakewell *Db*, 154
Bampton *O*, 252, 293
baptisteries, 88
Baptists, 393, 395
Bardney *Li*, 125
Barfreston *K*, 325
Barmby Moor *Hu*, 135
Barnack *Np*, 302
Barnburgh *SY*, 135
Barnwell *Np*, 379
Barrow *Hu* (*Li*), 152, 230
barrows, 40-1, 255-8, 460-1
Barry Island *Glm*, 85
Barton Bendish *Nf*, 149, 152
Barton-under-Needwood *St*, 375, 464, pl. 37
Barton-upon-Humber *Hu* (*Li*), 87, 214, 253-4, 302-3, 317
  burials, 80
Barwick-in-Elmet *WY*, 240
Baschurch *Sa*, 157
Basham *K*, 325
Basing *Ha*, 204
Bassenthwaite *Cu*, 405
Bath *So*, 88
Battlefield *Sa*, 364
Bawtry *SY*, 406
Baydon *Wi*, 325-6
Beaminster *Do*, 158
Bede, 10, 455
  on Albanus, 36
  on Cedd, 115-16
  on *Coludi urbs*, 110
  Ecclesiastical History of the English People, 6, 8-11, 455
  on 8th century monasticism, 121
  on Fursa, 117
  Life of Cuthbert, 106
  on organization of monasteries, 125-8
  on paganism, 58
  on size of monastic sites, 112
Bedminster *So*, 158
Bedmonton *K*, 161
Beercrocombe *So*, 241, 248
bell-frames, 323, 325, 405-6
Benedict Biscop, 94-5, 455
bequests *and see* patronage, wills, 356, 360-4
Berechurch *Ex*, 149
Bergh *Nf*, 140
Bermondsey *Sr*, 378

Bertha, Frankish princess, 23, 25
Berwick *Sx*, 256
Bettwys-y-Crwyn *Sa*, 161
Beverley *Hu* (*YE*), 63, 81, 88, 338, 339, 371, 373
  architect, 307
  parish, 134-5
Bewcastle *Cu* (*We*), 120, 405
Bibury *Gl*, 354
Biddlesden *Bu*, 382
Bifrons *K*, 384
Billingham *Du*, 3
Billingshurst *Sx*, 356
Bilsington *K*, 322
Birdsall *NY* (*YE*), 384
Birkby *NY*, 462-3, pl. 31
Birmingham, 416-20, 445
Bishops Canning *Wi*, 281
Bishops Cleeve *Gl*, 123
Bishopstone *Sx*, 267
Bisley *Gl*, 232, 439
Blackburn *La*, 445
Blackmanstone *K*, 157
Blockley *Wo*, 164
Blyford *Sf*, 140
Blythburgh *Sf*, 370
Boarstall *Bu*, 382
Bodmin *C*, 309
Bolsterstone *SY* (*YW*), 82
Bolton *La*, 425
Boroughbridge *NY*, 28
Bosham *Sx*, 117, 129, 131
Bossall *NY*, 311
Boston *Li*, 171, 219, 338-9
Bowes *NY*, 29
Bradkirk *La*, 149
Bradwell *Ex*, 222, 456
Bradwell-on-Sea *Ex*, 73, 120, pl. 7
Bramber *Sx*, 261, 368
Bramhope *WY*, 394
Brampton *Cu* (*We*), 405
Brancepeth Castle *Du*, 382
Brauncewell *Li*, 334
Breamore *Ha*, 78
Bredon *Wo*, 360-1
Breedon-on-the-Hill *Le*, 111, 132, 456, pl. 8
Bren Tor *D*, 2, 56
Bridekirk *Cu*, 159
bridge-chapels, 368-9
Brighton *Sx*, 389, 441, 443-4, 449, 466, pl. 46
Brightwell *Sf*, 406
Brimpton *Brk*, 28
Brington *Bd*, 406
Briningham *Nf*, 25
Brinklow *Wa*, 255-6
Bristol *Av* (*So*)
  church sites, 210, 211, 368
  parishes, 168
  Redcliffe, 339
  St John the Baptist, 209, 215

Bristol *Av* (*So*) (*contd.*)
St Lawrence, 215
St Mary-le-Port, 208
Brithdir *Gwd*, 450
Brixworth *Np*, 43
Brize Norton *O*, 16
Broad Camden *Gl*, 396
Broadway *So*, 241
Brocklesby Park *Li*, 385
Bromyard *He*, 123
Brook *K*, 252
Brookland *K*, 322
Brough-under-Stainmore *We*, 28
Broughton *St*, 384, 406
Brown, Lancelot 'Capability', 380-1, 386
Buckland *K*, 325
Buckminster *Le*, 158, 385
building development, 48-50
building materials, 28-9, 165, 302, 309-10, 318
building work, time taken, 356-7
Burbage *Wi*, 326
Burford *O*, 366
Burgh on Bain *Li*, 252-3
Burgh Castle *Sf*, 117
Burgh *Sf*, 272
Burgh-by-Sands *Cu*, 252
burhs, 182-3
burials *and see* cadaver tombs, churchyards,
grave covers, gravestones, mausolea,
memorial stones and hazel sticks, 80-1
preservatives, 42-3
within a church, 292
Burmarsh *K*, 322
Burnby *Hu*, 135
Burnham *Li*, 243
Burpham *Sx*, 252
Burrow Mump *So*, 459, pl. 17
Burry Holmes *Glm*, 107, 455-6, pl. 5
Burstall *Sf*, 252-3
Burstow *Sr*, 252-3
Burton Pedwardine *Li*, 274
Burton Stather *Li*, 323
Burton-by-Lincoln *Li*, 25
Burton-on-Trent *St*, 415
Burwell *Li*, 267
Bury St Edmunds *Sf*, 329, 370
Butterwick *Du*, 180
Butterwick *Li*, 180
Bywell *Nb*, 121

cadaver tombs *and see* burials, cemeteries,
churchyards, grave covers, gravestones,
mausolea, memorial stones, 370
Cadbury Congresbury *So*, 84
Cadbury *So*, 272
Caerau *Glm*, 272
Caerinion *Pws* (*Mnt*), 252
Caerleon *Mon*, 38
Caerwent *Mon*, 37, 109
Calne *Wi*, 129

Cambridge Camden Society *see* Camdenians
Camdenians, 434-6, 437, 444
Camerton *Cu*, 405
Canterbury *K*, 17-20
Christ Church, 18, 362
church sites, 19, 216, 217, 220, 222
St Martin, 19, 20-5
St Mary de Castro, 19, 20, 337-8
St Pancras, 19, 20, 25, 73-4
St Peter and St Paul, 17, 18, 19
Capel Aelhairn *Gwd* (*Mrn*), 78
Capel Ddeuno *Cld* (*Dnb*), 87
Capel Fleming *Gwd* (*Crn*), 89
capitals, 310-12, 313, 315
Carlton *Du*, 246
Carlton-in-Lindrick *Nt*, 295, 374
Castle Ashby *Np*, 383
Castle Camps *Ca*, 261
Castle Carrock *Cu*, 405
Castle Hedingham *Ex*, 290
Castle Howard *NY*, 385
Castle Rising *Nf*, 462, pl. 26
castles and churches, 262-4
cathedrals, 275-6
Catterick *Ny*, 131, 134
Cavenham *Sf*, 366-7
Cawood, John, 358
Cawston *Nf*, 329
Caythorpe *Li*, 25
Cedd, 115-16, 118
Cefn Bryn Wells *Glm*, 86
cemeteries *and see* burials cadaver tombs,
churchyards, grave covers, gravestones,
mausolea, memorial stones and dating,
30-1, 153
design of, 423
elevation of, 240, 241
periods of use, 338
positions of, 13-14, 32, 146
size of, 337, 423
cenobitic monasticism, 95-6
Chale Down *IoW*, 266
chancels, 321-3
chantries, 363-6, 371, 374
Chapel St Leonards *Li*, 343
chapels *and see* name of place
additions to churches, 365
bridge sites, 368-9
and muncipal involvement, 367-8
numbers of, 276
Chard *So*, 216
Charlesworth *Db*, 394
Cheadle *St*, 374
Chedworth *Gl*, 354
Cheltenham *Gl*, 123, 440-1, 465-6, pl. 45
Cheristow *D*, 159
Cheriton *D*, 159
Cheriton *Ha*, 159, 268
Cheriton *K*, 159
Cheriton *So*, 159

Chester, 38, 40, 176, 219-20, 306
Chesterfield *Db*, 397
Chichester, 176, 182, 329
  urban development, 195, 197, 201
Chilgrove *Sx*, 333
Chillington *St*, 385
Chippenham *Wi*, 131
Chipping Camden *Gl*, 353
Chipping Norton *O*, 354
Chipping Ongar *Ex*, 317
Chirton *Wi*, 159
Cholesbury *Bu*, 272
Chollerton *Cu*, 29
Chowbent *La*, 394
Christchurch *Ha*, 228-9, 266
Christhall *Ex*, 161
Christianity
  development of, 46-8
  and pagan sites, 70-1
  and paganism, 50-2, 56, 91-2
  and Roman society, 50-1
  St Augustine's mission, 6-8, 12-13
  in Wales, 10
Church Building Act 1818, 428
Church Hanborough *O*, 354
Church Island, Valencia, 107, 108
Church *La*, 159
Church Norton *Sx*, 263
Church Pulverbatch *Sa*, 267
church rate, 403, 405
Church Wilne *Db*, 3
churches
  7th century foundations, 139
  11th century rebuilding, 276
  16-17th century rebuilding, 406-7, 415
  19th century building, 390, 428, 430-4
  20th century, 452
  abandonment of, 336-9
  archaeological evidence for dating, 151, 152
  areas of, 294
  in baileys, 259, 261
  buildings materials, 28-9, 165, 302, 309-10, 318
  burials within, 392
  and castles, 262-4
  chapels as additions, 365
  and class, 438, 439-41, 444
  and clergy, 164
  and climatic variation, 329-31
  on coastlines, 342-4
  consecrations, 150-1
  construction of, 276-7
  dating, 151, 152, 154-62
  definition, 129
  design of, 276-9
  development of buildings, 48-50
  disrepair of, 316-18, 321-3, 403, 405
  disuse, 332-5
  and earthworks, 258-61, 267
  and famine, 331
  fenland, 344-7

  finances of, 284, 358, 360
  as fortified sites, 253, 259, 261
  foundation of, 132-3, 145-8, 171, 173
  gate sites, 214-17
  and geology, 309
  and greens, 246
  history of the study of, 2-3
  and industry, 444-7
  interior layout, 294, 435-6
  and landscaping, 377-81
  lighting of, 296-8
  as lighthouses, 266
  local, 141-3, 162-4
  location of, 205-7, 339-49
  maintenance of, 320-2, 316-18, 323, 403,
    405
  and manorial sites, 248-50, 268
  and markets, 69, 212-13
  military uses, 252
  and monastic sites, 66-8
  and mottes, 250-3, 259
  numbers of, 147-9
  orientation, 208-9
  origins of, 28
  pagan sites, 48-50, 63-76
  Perpendicular, 300, 351-60
  as places, 3-4
  and population, 185, 293, 294, 331-2, 388-9
  and ports, 190-1
  Post-Reformation building, 405-6
  as property, 173, 175
  and railways, 448-9
  reconstruction of, 276-8, 283, 285-7,
    399-400, 402-3
  records of, 147
  redundacy, 332-5
  and Roman building materials, 28-9, 72,
    102, 302
  on Roman sites, 29-39, 41-2, 71, 88, 101,
    102, 272
  Scandinavian parallels, 191-2
  seating, 439-41, 444
  separation from settlement, 240-3, 385-6
  sites of, 209-20, 239-43, 258-9, 264-8,
    381-4, 412, 452
  size of, 289-90, 438-9
  street sites, 210, 212, 214, 412
  town wall sites, 219-20
  in towns, 168-9
  as trade, 150
  trade in, 173, 175
  two storey, 209
  urban, 168-70, 176-9, 219-20, 437
  vandalism, 414, 439
  wealth of, 185, 284
  weather effect on, 329-31, 453
  wooden, 148-9, 319
  'Yorkshire School', 278-9
Churchton *Ch*, 159
churchwardens, 286

churchyards *and see* burials, cadaver tombs,
    grave covers, gravestones, mausolea,
    memorial stones, 143, 420-4
  agriculture in, 326-7
  curvilinear, 455
  elevation of, 240, 241, 421
  landscaping of, 423-4
  as markets, 212-13
  and rising damp, 320
Cilycwm *Dfd (Carm)*, 78
Cirencester *Gl*, 353-4, 366, 381
Clacton-on-Sea *Ex*, 449
Clare *Sf*, 406
clas churches, 457
class and churches, 438, 439-41, 444
Clenchwarton *Nf*, 346
clergy *and see* priests
  behaviour of, 79-80, 105, 325-7, 386-7
  marriage of, 164-5
  pluralism, 386-7, 390
  and proliferation of churches, 164
  qualifications of, 327-8
  wealth of, 444
Cliburn *We*, 28
climate, effects on church buildings, 329-31
Close, Francis, 436, 441
cloth and clothiers, 358-9, 366
Clovelly *D*, 309
Clynnog *Gwd*, 373
coastline change, and church buildings,
    342-4
Coberley *Gl*, 249, 365
Cockfield *Du*, 246
Colchester *Ex*, 40, 193, 196, 207, 415
Colebrook *D*, 365-6
Colehill *Do*, 450
Colkirk *Nf*, 157
Colston Bassett *Nt*, 384
Colthouse *Cu*, 396
Coltishall *Nf*, 463
Coludi urbs, 110
Colwick *Nt*, 384
Colworth *Np*, 461
Combe *O*, 335
Compton Martin *So*, 290-1
Coneysthorpe *NY*, 386
Congregationalists, 393, 395
congregations *and see* parishioners, 289-90,
    449
Conisbrough *SY*, 134-5
Conisholme *Li*, 347, 348
consecrations, 150-1
Conway *Gwd (Crn)*, 421
Cookham *Brk*, 123
Copley *WY*, 447
Coquet Island *Nb*, 109
Corbridge *Nb*, 28, 29, 121, 302
Corfe *Do*, 264
Cotterstock *Np*, 321, 364
Cottingham *NY*, 147

Coventry *WM*, 367
Cowthorpe *NY (YW)*, 335
Crambe *NY*, 302
Crawshawbooth *La*, 397
Crayke *NY*, 111
Cressage *Sa*, 161
Crewkerne *So*, 129
Cricklade *Gl*, 168
Croft *He*, 111, 268
Crondall *Ha*, 424
Croome D'Abitot *Wo*, 383
Crosby *Cu*, 161
Crosby *La*, 161
Crosby *NY*, 161
Crosby *WY*, 161
cross-road sites, 210
crosses, 83-4, 138
Crowhurst *Sr*, 79
crypts, 422
Cuckney *Nt*, 252
Cullompton *D*, 365, 370
Culworth *Np*, 261, pl. 24
Cusop *He*, 78
Cuthbert, 106-7
Cuxton *K*, 42
Cwmyoy *Gnt (Mon)*, 239, 459, pl. 14

Dacre *Cu*, 111
Dalham *Sf*, 406
Dalton-le-Dale *Du*, 153
Damascus, 49
Darley Dale *Db*, 79
dating
  of churches, 151, 152, 154-62
  of cemeteries, 30-1, 153
Deal *K*, 322, 326
dedications *and see* name of Saint, Saints,
    25-7, 53, 145, 157
  coastal sites, 347
  gate sites, 217, 219, 221-2
  hill sites, 265-6
  oldest in England, 25
  and trade connections, 175-6
  wells, 86
Deerhurst *Gl*, 146, 299, 317-18, 457-8, pl. 11
Denbigh *Pws (Dnb)*, 399, 400, 401
Derby, 368
Derwentwater *Cu*, 109
Detling *K*, 322
Dewchurch *He*, 159
Dewsbury *WY*, 120, 134-5, 138
Dexbeer *D*, 161
disrepair, 316-18, 321-3, 403, 405
Dissenters, 392-3, 397-8, 420
disuse of churches *and see* abandonment of
    churches, redundancy, 332-5
Dixton *Mon*, 298
Doddington *Ca*, 321
Dolwyddelan *Gwd*, 373
Domesday Book, 141, 142

Doncaster *SY* (*YW*), 262
Dorchester *Do*, 168
Dowlais *Glm*, 447
Down Ampney *Gl*, 424
Downton-on-the-Rock *He*, 250
Driffield *Hu*, 134, 135, 136, 138
Droitwich *Wo*, 180, 368
dry rot, 318
Dukinfield *La*, 394
Dunchurch *Wa*, 157
Dundon *So*, 241
Dunsby *Li*, 334
Dunsfold *Sr*, 281
Dunsthorpe *Li*, 333
Duntisbourne Rous *Gl*, 239, 459, pl. 15
Dunwich *Sf*, 120, 339
Dursley *Gl*, 354, 406
Dymchurch *K*, 322
Dyrham Park *Gl*, 382

Eardisley *He*, 250
Earl's Barton *Np*, 253, 255, 460, pl. 21
earthworks and church sites, 258-61, 267
Easby *Ny*, 112, 120, 133-5, 138, 145
East Bergholt *Sf*, 357
East Carlton *Np*, 146
East Horndon *E*, 267
East Keal *Li*, 135
East Witton *NY*, 245, 246, 248, 459-60, pl. 18
Eastbridge *K*, 157
Eastchurch *K*, 158
Eastleach *Gl*, 232
Easton *Bd*, 406
Easton Neston *Np*, 447
Eastry *K*, 322
Easton Socon *Bd*, 252
Ebberston *NY*, 246
Ebb's Nook *Nb*, 340
Ebchester *Du*, 120
Eccles *Nf*, 343
Ecclesfield, 134-5
Ecclesiastical History of the English People, 6, 8-11, 455
economics *and see* finance, tithes, Perpendicular period, 351-60
Edenhall *Cu*, 385
Edenham *Li*, 385, 424
Edgeside *La*, 89
Edington *Wi*, 364
Edlesborough *Bu*, 267, 268, 462, pl. 28
Eglingham *Nb*, 25
Egloshayle *Co*, 161
Eglwys Gymun *Dfd* (*Carm*), 463, pl. 32
Egmere *Nf*, 463, pl. 35
Ellingham *Nb*, 25
Elloe *Li*, 348
Elsdon *Nb*, 246
Ely *Ca*, 346
Emstrey *Sa*, 158
English Bicknor *Gl*, 259

Eorcenwold, 43, 44
eremitical monasticism, 95-6
Escomb *Du*, 121, 302
estate churches, 447
estate villages, 447-8
Ettington *Wa*, 384, 396
Euston Park *Sf*, 383
Evesham *Wo*, 329
Ewyas *He*, 325
Exeter *D*, 168-9
  church orientation, 209
  church sites, 215, 368
  dedications, 176
  funerary sculpture, 370
  population, 178
  urban development, 193, 195, 199-200
Eye *Sf*, 264, 356
Eynsham *O*, 173, 354

Fairfield *K*, 322
Fairford *Gl*, 353-4
fairs *and see* markets, 69
famine, effects on church buildings, 331
Fangfoss *Hu*, 135
Farnham *Sr*, 66-7
Fawley *Ha*, 3
Fawsley *Np*, 383, 464, pl. 39
Felixkirk *NY*, 159
Felkirk *SY* (*YW*), 159
Felmersham *Bd*, 283-4, 286
Felmingham *Nf*, 357
fenland, and church building, 344-7
Fenstanton *Ca* (*Hnt*), 395-6
Ferrybridge *WY*, 3
Ferryhill *Du*, 246
Fetcham *Sr*, 28
Ffynnon Angoerion *Pws* (*Mnt*), 85
Ffynnon Beca *Dfd* (*Carm*), 86
Ffynnon Gynhafal *Cld* (*Dnb*), 85
Ffynnon Seiriol *Angl*, 86
finance *and see* economics, tithes
  cathedrals, 275-6
  and industry, 445-6
  parish, 284, 358, 360
Fladbury *Wo*, 123
Fleet *K*, 322
Fleet *Li*, 348
flooding, 340-1, 348
Folkestone *K*, 343
fonts, 29
Forcett *NY*, 384
Forde *Do*, 377-8
Fordwich *K*, 189
Foremark Hall *De*, 384
fortifications *and see* baileys, mottes, 252, 253, 261
Fotheringhay *Np*, 364
Foulsham *Nf*, 356
foundation of churches, 132-3, 145-8, 171, 173
Framlingham *Sf*, 356

fraternities *and see* gilds, 366-8, 376
Freeby *Le*, 395
Frinsted *K*, 63
Frinton-on-Sea *Ex*, 63
frith stools, 63
Fritton *Sf*, 63
Frocester *Gl*, 101
Frome *So*, 356
Fryton *NY*, 63
Fundenhall *Nf*, 140
funeral practices, 61
Fursa, 117

Gainford *Du*, 28, 111
Gargrave *NY*, 232
Gate Burton *Li*, 385
gate sites for churches, 214-17
Gayton-le-Wold *Li*, 87
Gedney *Li*, 346
geology and church siting, 309
Gibside *Du*, 385
Gildas, 98
gilds *and see* fraternities, 213-14, 366-7
Gilling *NY*, 111, 125, 134, 145, 455
Gilmorton *Le*, 250
Gislingham *Sf*, 406
Glastonbury Tor *So*, 56, 111
Glentworth *Li*, 154, 165
Gloucester
  church sites, 204, 205-6, 215
  excavations, 205-6
  parish boundaries, 226
  St Mary de Lode, 34-5
  urban development, 197
Glyntaf *Glm*, 447
Godmanchester *Hu*, 39-40
Godmanstone *Do*, 28
Godshill *IoW*, 267
Goldcliff *Gnt* (*Mon*), 344
Goltho *Li*, 269-71, 334
Goodnestone *K*, 322
Gosberton *Li*, 157
Grainthorpe *Li*, 347
Grantham *Li*, 308, 330, 365
grave-covers *and see* burials, cadaver tombs, cemeteries, churchyards, gravestones, mausolea, memorial stones, 116
gravestones *and see* burials, cadaver tombs, cemeteries, churchyards, gravecovers, mausolea, memorial stones, and dating of foundations, 153-4
Grayingham *Li*, 25
Great Budworth *Ch*, 233
Great Chalfield *Wi*, 248, 460, pl. 19
Great Chesterford *Ex*, 30-1
Great Collington *He*, 332
Great Comberton *Wo*, 403
Great Dunmow *Ex*, 39-40
Great Easton *Le*, 292
Great Fire of London, 407-9

Great Givendale *Hu*, 135
Great Gonerby *Li*, 425
Great Harrowden *Np*, 66, 68
Great Hasely *O*, 292
Great Houghton *WY*, 394
Great Packington *Wa*, 385, 464-5, pl. 40
Great Ponton *Li*, 371
Great Witley *Wo*, 384
Great Yarmouth *Sf*, 338-9, 415
greens and church sites, 246
Greensted *Ex*, 149
Greetwell *Li*, 297
Gregory I, 6, 8, 12, 70
Gretton *Np*, 295
Grimsby *Hu* (*Li*), 358
Grindale *Cu*, 340
Gunton Hall *Nf*, 382
Guthlac, 94, 95
Gutterby *Cu*, 232
Guyhirn *Ca*, 394
gypsum burials, 42-3

Haddiscoe Thorpe *Nf*, 165
Hadleigh *Sf*, 131
Hadstock *Ex*, 293
hagas, 204-5
Hagworthingham *Li*, 323
Haile *Cu*, 29
Hale *Np*, 333
Halesowen *Wo*, 397
Halifax *WY*, 232, 389, 466, pl. 47
Halliford *Mx*, 161
Halliwell *La*, 85
Halstead *Ex*, 306-7
Halstock *D*, 161
Halstock *So*, 101
Haltwhistle *Nb*, 297-8
Hampton *Wo*, 403
Hamwic, 181, 189, 190
Hanbury *Wo*, 111, 123
Hanchurch *St*, 158
Hanslope *Bu*, 147
Harewood *WY*, 385-6
Harling *Nf*, 140
Harris, Howell, 392
Harrogate *NY*, 446-7
Harrow *Mx*, 63
Harrow-on-the-Hill *Mx*, 66
Harrowden *Bd*, 66
Hartlepool *Clv*, 110
Hauxwell *NY*, 306
Haverthwaite *Cu*, 89
Hawkchurch *D*, 157
Hawkinge *K*, 335
Hawksmoor, Nicholas, 385, 412, 414, 415
Hawton *Nt*, 292-3
Hayden Bridge *Cu*, 29
Haydon *Do*, 322
Hayton *Hu*, 135
hazel, 80-1

Healaugh *NY*, 267
Heath *Sa*, 299
heathenism *and see* paganism
   literary references, 58–61
Heckington *Li*, 292–3
Hedon *Hu* (*YE*), 286
Heighington *Du*, 246
Helmdon *Np*, 268
Helmingham *Sf*, 307
Hemingborough *Hy* (*YE*), 370
henges, 72, 83
Hereford, 210, 281
hermits, *and see* holy men, monasticism,
   93–4, 96, 107
Hexham *Nb*, 14, 63, 111–12, 118
Heydon *Nf*, 356
Heysham *La*, 119
Hickleton *SY*, 80
High Hoyland *SY* (*YW*), 267
Hillesden *Bu*, 370
Hinckley *Le*, 68
Hitchin *Hrt*, 135
hof, 74–5
Holcombe Rogus *D*, 460, pl. 20
Holdenby *Np*, 378–9
Holderness *Hu* (*YE*), 342
Holkham *Nf*, 381
Hollym *Hu*, 342
Hollytreeholme *Hu* (*YE*), 78
Holme-by-Newark *Nt*, 370
Holme-on-Spalding-Moor *Hu* (*YE*), 267
Holton-le-Clay *Li*, 154
Holverstone *Sf*, 140
Holwell *O*, 85
holy men *and see* hermits, monasticism, and
   politics, 117–18
Holy Oakes *Le*, 78
Holyhead *Gwd*, 119, 373
Holywell *Hu* (*YE*), 85
Hope All Saints *K*, 157
Hopwas *St*, 450
Horkstow *Li*, 449
horn dances, 69
Hovingham *NY*, 121, 122, 297, 385
Howden *Hu* (*YE*), 134–5, 138, 364
Hubberholme *NY* (*YW*), 375
Huddersfield *WY*, 403, 425
Hugill *Cu*, 89
Hull *Hu* (*YE*), 307, 338–9, 425
Hundleby *Li*, 135
Hunmanby *Hu* (*YE*), 134, 144
Hunsingore *NY*, 267
Hunstanton *Nf*, 343, 449
Huntingdon *Ca*, 173
Hutton Wandesley *Ny* (*YW*), 332
Hythe *K*, 239

Ickham *K*, 322
Icklingham *Sf*, 49
Idle *WY*, 394, 396, 429

Ilchester *So*, 31–3, 336
Ilkley *WY*, 28
Illtud, 98, 100, 115
industry, and churches, 444–7
Ingestre *St*, 384
Inner Farne *Nb*, 106–7
interior church layout, 294, 435–6
Ipswich *Sf*, 169, 173, 181, 189
Irthlingborough *Np*, 334
Isle Abbots *So*, 246
Isle of Thanet *K*, 334
Ismere *Wo*, 121, 123, 132–3
Itteringham *Nf*, 458, pl. 12
Ivychurch *IoW*, 158
Ivychurch *K*, 158

Jarrow *TW* (*Du*), 94, 110, 112, 455, pl. 4
Jerusalem, 48, 90
Jervaulx Abbey *NY*, 248

Keinton Mandeville *So*, 241
Kempley *Gl*, 299
Kenardington *K*, 326–7
Kenchester *He*, 29
Kendal *Cu*, 398
Kenfig *Glm*, 340
Kennington *K*, 78
Kensal Green cemetery *GLo*, 423
Kentchurch *He*, 159
Kensingland *Sf*, 367
Keswick *Nf*, 343
Kidderminster *Wo*, 158, 227
Kilham *Hu*, 134, 135, 138
Kilkhampton *C*, 309
Kilnsea *Hu*, 342
Kilpeck *He*, 261, 264, 461–2, pl. 25
kings *and see* royalty, and holy men, 117–18
King's Lynn *Nf*, 346
King's Stanley *Gl*, 101
Kingston Bagpuize *Brk*, 146
Kingston Seymour *So*, 344
Kingswood *Gl*, 396
Kingweston *So*, 241
Kippax *WY*, 278, 306
Kirby Bellars *Le*, 364
Kirby Hill *NY*, 28, 161, 246
Kirk Deighton *NY* (*YW*), 267, 424
Kirk Hammerton *NY* (*YW*), 149, 267, 277,
   302
Kirkbride *Cu*, 220
Kirkburton *WY*, 376
Kirkby Misperton *NY*, 161
Kirkby Ouseburn *NY* (*YW*), 230, 232, 238
Kirkby Underdale *HU* (*YE*), 72
Kirkbymoorside *NY*, 116, 161
Kirkdale *NY*, 112, 116, 146, 161
Kirkham *NY*, 111, 160
Kirkoswald *Cu*, 87, 405
Kirkstall *WY*, 160
Kirkstead *Li*, 160

Kirkstead *Nf*, 160
Knowle *Cu*, 89
Knowle St Giles *So*, 241
Knowlton *Do*, 57, 72-4, 73

Lacock *Wi*, 377-8
Lambourne *Brk*, 129-30
Lamplugh *Cu*, 159
Lamyatt Beacon *So*, 115
Lancaut *Gl*, III, 159, 322
Lanchester *Du*, 28
Landican *Ch*, 159
landscaping, 377-81
   of churchyards, 423-4
Landwade *Ca*, 339
Lanteglos *Co*, 161
Lastingham *NY*, 115-16, 120, 239
Latimer *Bu*, 104
Laughton-en-le-Morthen *SY* (*YW*), 258-9, 461, pl. 23
Launceston *Co*, 262
Lawford *Ex*, 299-300
Layston *Hrt*, 157
Ledsham *WY*, 121, 295
Leeds *WY*, 134-5, 406, 442
   industrial benefactors, 444
   nonconformist chapels, 425, 446
   parish size, 441
Leicester, 37, 169, 454, pl. 1
Leighton Bromswold *Ca* (*Hnt*), 406
Leominster *He*, 110-11
Leverton *Li*, 348
Levisham *NY*, 246
Lichfield *St*, 56, 118, 215
Lidgate *Sf*, 259
lighthouses, 266
lighting, 296-8
lightning, 329-30
Lilford *Np*, 382
Lincoln
   bridge-chapels, 368
   cathedral, 252
   church sites, 169, 171-3, 175, 223, 335
   funerary sculpture, 370
   population, 178
   St Mark, 152, 154, 224
   St Paul-in-the-Bail, 37
Lindisfarne *Nb*, 110, 124-5
Lingwood *Nf*, 356
Linton *He*, 79
Litchurch *Db*, 158
Little Budworth *Ch*, 373
Little Bytham *Li*, 26
Little Collington *He*, 332
Little Gaddesdon *Hrt*, 385
Little Hautbois *Nf*, 463, pl. 34
Little Hormead *Hrt*, 317
Little Melton *Nf*, 140
Little Oakley *Ex*, 357
Little Ouseburn *NY* (*YW*), III, 297, 383, 385

Little Salkeld *Cu*, 332
Little Wenham *Sf*, 248
Littlebourne *K*, 26
Liverpool, 389, 415-16, 420, 425
Llanarth *Mon*, 382
Llancarfan *Glm*, 100
Llancillo *He*, 159
Llancloudy *He*, 159
Llanddwyn *Angl*, 110
Llandegai *Gwd* (*Crn*), 89
Llandeilo *Dfd* (*Carm*), 86, 154
Llandeilo Fawr *Dfd* (*Carm*), 78
Llandough *Glm*, 100
Llandrillo *Gwd* (*Mrn*), 78
Llandyfaelog *Dfd* (*Carm*), 457, pl. 10
Llandysiliogogo *Dfd* (*Crg*), 82
Llaneilian *Gwd*, 373
Llaneillo *He*, 250
Llanengan *Gwd*, 373
Llanerfyl *Pws* (*Mnt*), 79
Llanfihangel *Glm*, 89
Llanfihangel nant Melan *Pws* (*Rad*), 78
Llanfihangel-yng-Ngwynfa *Pws* (*Mnt*), 56
Llanfyllin *Pws*, 406
Llangelynin *Gwd* (*Mrn*), 78, 466, pl. 49
Llangower *Gwd* (*Mrn*), 78
Llangwunadl *Gwd*, 373
Llangwyfan *Angl*, 110, 456, pl. 6
Llansantffraed-in-Elvel *Pws* (*Rad*), 78
Llantwit Major *Glm*, 100, 116
Llanwnda *Dfd* (*Pmb*), 154
Llanynis *pws* (*Brcn*), 154
local churches, 141-3, 162-4
location of churches, 205-7, 339-49
London
   17th century churches, 407-14
   Aldgate, 378
   All Hallows Honey Lane, 209
   All Saints Margaret Street, 435
   cemeteries, 423
   Christ Church Spitalfields, 422
   church sites, 219
   Great Fire, 407-9
   hagas, 204-5
   Langham Place, 430
   number of churches, 169, 189, 225
   parishes, 411, 413
   population, 178-9, 409, 411
   St Clement Danes, 175-6
   St Clement Eastcheap, 175
   St George-in-the-East, 465, pl. 41
   St Mary Abchurch, 410
   St Mary Colechurch, 209
   St Mary Haggerston, 430
   St Mary Woolnoth, 173
   St Mary Wyndham Place, 430
   St Mary-le-Bow, 281
   St Mildred Bread Street, 410
   St Nicholas Aldred, 173
   St Paul's Cathedral, 176

London (*contd.*)
St Peter Cornhill, 37, 410
St Stephen Coleman Street, 410
Wren churches, 407-10
Long Melford *Sf*, 365
Long Sutton *Li*, 348
Long Sutton *So*, 248
Long Wittenham *Brk*, 369
Longham *Nf*, 243, 248
Longney-on-Severn *Gl*, 79-80
Longnor *He*, 248
Longtown *Cu*, 405
Loose *K*, 78, 322
Loriaco, William de, 360-1
Lostwithiel *Co*, 239
Loudon, John Claudius, 423-4
Loughor *Glm*, 38, 261
Louth *Li*, 358
Lower Peover *Ch*, 373
Lower Poston *Sa*, 79
Ludford Magna *Li*, 332
Ludford Parva *Li*, 334
Ludlow *Sa*, 339, 366, 397
Lullingstone Castle *K*, 382
Lullingstone *K*, 41, 72, 97
Lulworth *Do*, 250, 382
Lyminster *Sx*, 158
Lympne Castle *K*, 382
Lyon, 13

Mablethorpe *Li*, 343
Madresfield *Wo*, 384
Maidenhead *Brk*, 434, 465, pl. 44
Maidstone *K*, 364
maintenance of churches, 316-18, 320-3, 403, 405
Malmesbury *Wi*, iii, 336-7
Malpas *Ch*, 233, 267
manorial sites, 248-50, 268
Mansell Lacy *He*, 250
Maplebeck *Nt*, 25
March *Ca*, 370
Marholm *Np*, 424
Market Harborough *Le*, 338-9
markets, 69, 212-13
Marlingford *Sf*, 140
marriage, of priests, 164-5
Marsh Chapel *Li*, 347
Marshfield *Gl*, 354
Marston Trussell *Np*, 272, 273
Marton *Ch*, 373
Marton-by-Stow *Li*, 154
Masham *NY*, 120, 134
masons, 301-2, 303, 306-7, 310, 351
masses, 363
matrix ecclesia, 226
mausolea *and see* burials, cadaver tombs, cemeteries, churchyards, grave covers, gravestones, memorial stones, 88, 385

Maxey *Ca* (*Li*), 268
Mayfield *Sx*, 149, 209
Meifod *Pws* (*Mnt*), 154
Melbourne *Db*, 56, 281
Mellitus, 6, 69-70
Meiorus, 81
Melrose *Rx*, iii
Melverley *Sa*, 340-1, 373, 459, pl. 16
memorial stones *and see* burials, cadaver tombs, cemeteries, churchyards, grave covers, gravestones, mausolea, 102, 103
Meppershall *Bd*, 261, 264
Mere *Wi*, 365
Merrington *Du*, 252
Mersham *K*, 326-7
Merthyr Mawr *Glm*, 447
Methodists, 425-7
Michaelchurch *He*, 159
Middleham *NY*, 86, 116
Middleton *Du*, 246
Middleton Stoney *O*, 250
Middleton *NY*, 246
Midmer Kirk *Abd*, 82
Mileham *Nf*, 243, 244, 248
Milford *Pws*, 447
military use of churches *and see* baileys, forficiations, mottes, 252
Millington *Hu*, 135
Millom *Cu*, 232
Milton Abbas *Do*, 266, 447
Minster-in-Sheppey *K*, iii
minsters, 116, 202, 204
definitions, 128-30
place-name element, 158
and royalty, 131
Misterton *So*, 241
Mitford *Nb*, 264
moats, 272, 273
Mobberley *Ch*, 373
Moccas *He*, 56, 383
monasteries
8th century, 120-1
benefactors, 113
and land, 113
organization of, 125-8
privacy in, 118
and royal patronage, 124-5
size of, 112-13
monastic sites
choice of, 123
and country houses, 377-8
and early churches, 66-8
hilltop, iii
peninsula, 110
retreats, 118-19
river bounded, 110-11
and Roman sites, 100, 119-20
selection of, 112, 114-15
size of, 112-13
and temples, 115

monasticism *and see* hermits, holy men, 95–7
  in Britain, 97–100, 101–2, 104
  and penitence, 96, 105–6
Monk, J.H., 444
Monk Fryston *NY (YW)*, 302
Monkton *Dfd (Pmb)*, 89
Monyash *Db*, 397
More *Sa*, 249
Morebath *D*, 374–5
Morpeth *Nb*, 368
Morriston *Glm*, 447
mortality rates *and see* population, 376, 420–1
mottes *and see* baileys, fortifications and
  military use of churches, 250–3, 259
Moulton *Li*, 358
Mow Cop, 427, 465, pl. 43
Musselburgh *Lothian*, 425

Nantwich *Ch*, 307
Nately Scures *Ha*, 249
naves, 287–9, 295
Nayland *Sf*, 140
Neath *Glm*, 378
Necromancy, 61
Needham Market *Sf*, 370
Netheravon *Wi*, 326
New Buckenham *Nf*, 262–3
New Winchelsea *Sx*, 198, 343–4, 463–4, pl. 36
Newark *Nt*, 366, 425
Newcastle-under-Lyme *St*, 397
Newport *IoW*, 425
Newstead *Nt*, 377–8
Newton *Sf*, 346
Newton Kyme *NY (WY)*, 382–3
nonconformists, 390, 392–99
  burial grounds, 396–7
  in Cheltenham, 440
  places of worship, 396–7
  sites of chapels, 398–9, 424–5
Nonington *K*, 322
Nonsuch *Sr*, 378
Norbury *Db*, 370
Norham *Nb*, 290
Normanton *Le (Ru)*, 341, 382
North Cadbury *So*, 364
North Marden *Sx*, 249
North Newbald *Hu (YE)*, 281, 307
Northallerton *NY*, 134, 135, 138
Northampton, 210, 290, 414
Northleach *Gl*, 310, 353, 357, 360
Northleigh *O*, 365
Norwell *Nt*, 272, 274
Norwich *Nf*, 174
  chantries, 371
  church numbers, 152, 169, 173, 174, 178, 223, 225, 335
  dedications, 175–6
  place name evidence, 180
  population, 178
Nottingham, 178, 339

Nun Monkton *NY (YW)*, 424
Nuneham Courtney *O*, 386
nuts, 80–1
Nymet *D*, 65
Nympsfield *Gl*, 65
Nympton *D*, 65

oak trees, 76, 78
Offchurch *Wa*, 157
Old Bewick *Nb*, 297
Old Byland *NY*, 149, 245
Old Dissent, 392–5
Old Erringham *Sx*, 261, 262
Old Malton *NY*, 40, 122, 134
Old Romney *K*, 322
Old Sodbury *Gl*, 267
Old Winchelsea *Sx*, 329, 343, 463–4
Oldbury *Gl*, 267, 268
Oldbury *Wo*, 444
Orby *Li*, 307
orientation of churches, 208–9
Ormskirk *La*, 157
ornithomancy, 59, 67–8
Orwell *Ca*, 321
Osmotherly *NY*, 135
Ospringe *K*, 330
Oswald, King of Northumbria, 124–5
Otley *WY*, 84, 121, 138, 448
Overchurch *Ch*, 158
Overstrand *Nf*, 343
Owston Ferry *Li*, 259
Owthorne *Hu*, 343
Oxford, 168, 171, 178, 307
  All Saints, 205, 415
  urban development, 210–14
Oxford Movement, 434
Oxwich *Glm*, 86
Oystermouth *Glm*, 100–1

Pachomius, 95–6
pagan sites, 48–50, 63–76
paganism *and see* heathenism, 57–61
  and conversion to Christianity, 50–2, 56, 91–2
  place name evidence, 63–6
  and re-use of barrows, 256–8
  triviality of, 62
Painswick *Gl*, 423–4
Pakefield *Sf*, 232
Papcastle *Cu*, 161
parishes
  17–18th century creations, 415
  in 19th century, 389–90
  boundaries, 226, 238–9
  finances, 284, 358, 360
  formation of, 207–8, 210, 228–30, 232–3, 237–9
  London, 411, 413
  multi-church, 230, 232
  multi-manorial, 230

parishes (*contd.*)
  origins, 169, 171
  and population, 233, 235
  restructuring, 427-8
  shapes of, 235-9
  size of, 233-7, 437-8, 441, 453
  and topography, 235-7
  and townships, 233
  Yorkshire, 144
parishioners *and see* congregations
  influences of, 285-6
  involvement in church building, 373
parochiae, pre-Conquest Yorkshire, 133-7
parochial allegiance, 229
parochial rights, 226
Patrington *Hu (YE)*, 342
Patrixbourne *K*, 384
patronage *and see* bequests, wills, 124-5, 279, 282-4
Patshull *St*, 383
Peakirk *Np*, 94
Pega, 94
penitentials, 105-6
Penmaen *Glm*, 340
Penmon *Gwd (Angl)*, 87
Pennard *Glm*, 340
Penyland *Glm*, 85
Penynygold *Cld (Fl)*, 79
Perpendicular, 300
  and economy, 351-60
Pickering *NY*, 116, 134, 135, 138
Pirton *Hrt*, 259
Piscinas, 292
Pistyll Golen *Dfd (Carm)*, 85
Pitminster *So*, 158
Pixley *He*, 249
place name evidence
  burh, 252-3
  church elements, 159-61, 232
  and dating of foundations, 154-62
  individuals' names, 157
  'island' elements, 346
  kirkja element, 159-61
  and paganism, 63-6
  position elements, 158
  'priest' element, 161-2
  for reoccupation of Roman towns, 179-81
  'sanctuary' element, 63-5
  'white' churches, 158-9
  for wooden churches, 148-9
Pleshey *Ex*, 261, 265
pluralism, 386-7, 390
Pocklington *Hu*, 134-5, 135-7
politics, and holy men, 117-18
Pontefract *WY*, 230, 264
Ponteland *Nb*, 153
Pontesbury *Sa*, 267
population
  18th century, 420-1
  19th century, 388-9, 421

Birmingham, 420
  and church size, 289-90
  and churches, 185, 293, 294, 331-2, 388-9
  Liverpool, 416, 420
  London, 178-9, 409, 411
  mortality rates, 376, 420-1
  and parish size, 233, 235
Porlock *So*, 365
ports and churches, 190-1
Post-Reformation church building, 405-6
Potterne *Wi*, 230, 281
Presbyterians, 393-4
Prescot *La*, 162
Prestbury *Ch*, 162
Prestbury *Gl*, 162
Presteigne *Rad*, 162
Preston-by-Faversham *K*, 154
Prestwich *La*, 162
Prestwick *Nb*, 162
Prestwold *Le*, 385
priests *and see* clergy, 164-5
Privett *Ha*, 383
property rights, 126-7, 173, 175, 206
Puckington *So*, 248
Pucklechurch *Gl*, 157
Pudlestone *He*, 332
Pugin, A.W.N., 431, 434
purgatory, 362-3, 375

Quakers, 393, 396, 397, 399, 445
Quarr *IoW*, 302
Quarrendon *Bu*, 146, 274
quarries and quarrying, 302, 310, 314-15

Radstone *Np*, 83
railways, 448-9
Raithby Hall *Li*, 395
Ratcliffe *Nt*, 143
Raughton Head *Cu*, 405
Raunds *Np*, 268
  churchyard, 231, 376
  dating, 152
  excavations, 149, 150, 230, 231
Ravenser *Hu (YE)*, 342
Rawdon *WY*, 396
Rawtenstall *La*, 445
Reculver *K*, 120, 341-2, 362
Redbourn *Hrt*, 40-1
redundancy *and see* abandonment of
  churches, disuse of churches, 332-5
Redundant Churches Fund, 452
Reepham *Nf*, 232, 458-9, pl. 13
regenerative view of site continuity, 57
relics, 124
Rendcombe *Gl*, 424
Repton *Db*, 94, 130-1, 256, 257
  excavations, 87, 256
  site, III, 261
retreats, 118-19
Rhossili *Glm*, 340

INDEX

Ribston Hall *NY*, 382
Richard's Castle *He*, 261, 266
Rievaulx *NY*, 380
Rimswell *Hu*, 343
ringworks, 258–61
Ripley *NY* (*YW*), 340
Ripon *NY*, 14, III, 130–1, 134
rising damp, 320
Rising *Nf*, 263
Risley *Db*, 406
Rivenhall *Ex*, 149, 152, 164, 300, 424
  excavations, 164
  Roman site, 102, 104
  windows, 297
Rivington *La*, 267
roads
  and church sites, 239
  and parish development, 237–8
Rochester *K*, 369
Rockingham *Np*, 250, 267
Roman
  altars, 28–9, 72
  buildings materials, 28–9, 72, 102, 302
  statues, 71–2
  society and Christianity, 50–1
  temples, 50
  tombstones, 28
  villas, 29, 100–1, 102
Roman sites, 29–39, 40–2, 71, 88, 232, 272
  influence on parish boundaries, 238
  and parish churches, 101, 102
  reoccupation of, 179–81
Rome, 13–14, 48, 49
Romney *K*, 341
Roos *Hu* (*YE*), 274, 424
Rostherne *Ch*, 373
Rothbury *Nb*, 84
Rotherham *SY* (*YW*), 368
Rothwell *Np*, 395
Roxby *Hu* (*Li*), 232
royalty
  and holy men, 117–18
  and influence on urbanization, 184
  and minsters, 131
  and monasteries, 124–5
Royston *SY* (*YW*), 374
Rudston *Hu* (*YE*), 82–3
Rufford *Nt*, 245
Ryedale *NY*, 144

St Albans *Hrt*, 35–9, 40–1
St Alban(us), 35–6, 40–1
St Amphibalus, 40–1
St Ann, 89–90
St Augustine, 6–8, 12–13, 17, 70
St Botolph, 217, 219, 221
St Bride, 53
St Brigid, 52
St Catherine, 265–6
St Clement, 175

St Dunstan, 149
St Govan's Head *Dfd* (*Pmb*), 87
St Ives *Ca*, 368
St Levan *Co*, 85
St Martin, 15–17, 26, 41, 217
St Michael, 52–6
St Ninian Ninekirks *Cu* (*We*), 68, 456–7, pl. 9
St Olave, 53, 176
St Osyth *Ex*, 378
St Piran *Co*, 340
St Patrick, 98–9
St Trillo's Chapel *Gwd* (*Crn*), 87
St Weonards *He*, 250, 256
St Werburgh, 67
St William, 369
Saffron Walden *Ex*, 381
Saints *and see* dedications and name of saint,
  4, 13–14, 41, 42, 123–4
Salisbury *Wi*, 371
salt, 346–7
Saltaire *WY*, 448, 466, pl. 48
Saltburn *Clv* (*YN*), 449
Saltfleetby *Li*, 347
Samson, 116
Sancreed *Co*, 86
sanctuaries, 63–76
sand encroachment, and church buildings, 340
Sandiacre *Db*, 267, 321
Sandwich *K*, 181, 189
Sarre *K*, 341
Saunderton *Bu*, 261
Sawley *Db*, 365
Saxham *Sf*, 230
Saxton *NY*, 292
Scarborough *NY*, 449
Sceilg Mhichil, 107
Scorborough *Hu* (*YE*), 436
Scredington *Li*, 322
Scrofton *Nt*, 385
Scruton *NY*, 25
sculpture
  8th century, 120–1
  Anglo-Saxon, 153–4, 456
  and dating of foundations, 151, 153–4
  funerary, 369–70
  pre-Conquest, 154, 246, 386
  pre-Danish, 116
  pre-Viking, 137–8
  Roman, 71–2
Seaham *Du*, 121
Seasalter *K*, 341
seating in churches, 439–41, 444
Seavington St Mary *So*, 241
sectional view of site continuity, 57
Selsey *Sx*, 110, 261
Sempringham *Li*, 377
Settle *NY* (*YW*), 397

INDEX

settlement
 abandonment, 333
 formation of, 243-5, 248
 planning of, 244-6, 248
 relocation of, 384, 385-6
 separation of church from, 240-3, 385-6
 shrinkage, 331-2
Shakenoak O, 104
Shalfleet IoW, 252
Sheffield SY (YW), 425
Shelsley Walsh Wo, 366
Sheppey K, 110
Sherborne Do, 336
Sherborne Wa, 383
Sherburn-in-Elmet NY (YW), 134-5, 290
Shillington Bd, 239
Shobdon He, 383
Shugborough St, 385
Silchester Ha, 29, 72
Silkstone SY (YW), 134-5, 321
site continuity, 57
site selection, 209-20, 239-43, 258-9, 264-8,
  381-4, 412, 452
Skeffling Hu, 342
Skegness Li, 343, 449
Skelton NY, 283
Skelton-on-Ure NY, 383
Skidbrooke Li, 348, 424
Skinnand Li, 334
Skipwith Hu (YE), 297
Smeeth K, 326-7
Snaith Hu, 134-5
Snarford Li, 385
Snitterley Nf, 343
Sockburn Du, 111
Somercotes Li, 347
Somerford Wi, 250
soul masses, 369
South Dalton Hu (YE), 435-6
South Elmham Sf, 249
South Hall Green Nf, 243
South Walsham Nf, 232
Southminster Ex, 158
Southport La, 449
Southrop Gl, 249
Southwold Sf, 296, 462, pl. 30
Sparham Nf, 140
spires, Lincolnshire, 280-1
Spofforth NY (YW), 310, 321
springs, 84-91
Spurn Head Hu (YE), 342
Stainburn NY (YW), 297, 298, 299, 449
Staines Mx, 204
Stamford Li, 171, 183, 370
Stanfield Nf, 243
Stanton Drew So, 82, 454, pl. 2
Stanton Holgate Sa, 250
Stanway Gl, 135
Stanwick NY, 145, 454-5, pl. 3
statues, Roman, 71-2

Staunton Harold Le, 382, 406, 464, pl. 38
Staunton-on-Arrow He, 29, 250
Steane Np, 406
Stelling K, 322
Steyning Sx, 131, 258
Stillingfleet Hu (YE), 339
Stisted Ex, 140
Stockwell Dfd (Carm), 85
Stokenchurch Bu, 149
Stokenchurch Mx, 149
Stokesay Sa, 268
stone
 availability, 302, 309-10
 decay of, 318
 types, 309
stone circles, 81-3, 232
Stone-by-Faversham K, 41-2, 73-4
Stonegrave NY, 121, 122, 134
stones, as religious foci, 81-4
Stourbridge Wo, 396
Stowe-Nine-Churches Np, 68
Stowhead Wi, 381
Stratford St Mary Sf, 371
Stratford-upon-Avon Wa, 123
streets, and church sites, 210, 212, 214, 412
Stroud Gl, 425
Studley Royal NY, 383
Sturminster Do, 158
Sudbury Db, 382-3
Sudeley Gl, 354
Sulgrave Np, 259-61
Summerseat La, 445
Surfleet Li, 239, 348
Sutterby Li, 299
Sutton in Holland Li, 146
Sutton-on-Sea Li, 343
Sutton-on-Trent Nt, 365
Swaffham Prior Ca, 232
Swinbrook O, 385
Sydmonton Ha, 382

Tankersely WY, 384
Taplow Bu, 256, 460-1, pl. 22
Tarrant Crawford Do, 101
Tathwell Li, 25
Tattershall Li, 364
Tattingstone Sf, 381
Tavistock D, 306, 366
Taylor, John, 375, 464
temples, 63-76
 as monastic sites, 115
 Romano-Celtic, 50
Terrington St Clement Nf, 346, 348
Thakenham Sx, 396
Theddlethorpe All Saints Li, 346, 347, 348
Therfield Hrt, 261
Thetford Nf, 149, 177, 183, 261-2, 335
 population, 177-8, 335
 sculpture, 154
Thorney Sf, 146, 232, 346

INDEX

Thornton *NY*, 135, 246
Thornton Steward *NY*, 248
Thruscross *NY (YW)*, 340-1
Thundersley *Ex*, 63, 66
Thurlby *Li*, 146
Thwaite *La*, 405
Thwing *Hu*, 74
Tichbourne *Ha*, 267
Tilbrook *Bd (Hnt)*, 406
Tilbury *Ex*, 111
Tilney All Saints *Nf*, 358
Tislea *Ha*, 63
Titchmarsh *Np*, 383
tithes *and see* economics, finance, 210, 233, 235
Tittleshall *Nf*, 248
Tiverton *D*, 365
Tockenham *Wi*, 72
Toddington *Bd*, 213
Todmorden *WY*, 445
Toftrees *Nf*, 357
Topcliffe *NY*, 134
Tormarton *Gl*, 365
Totnes *D*, 264, 306
Totteridge *Hrt*, 78
Tours, 14-15, 16-17
Towcester *Np*, 358
towers, 252, 255, 348, 357, 400
towns
    and churches, 168-70, 176-9, 219-20, 437
    development of, 183-5
    planning of, 447-8, 449
Towthorpe *Hu*, 333-4
Towton *NY (YW)*, 364
Tractarianism, 434-5, 437, 465
trade
    and church dedications, 175-6
    in churches, 173, 175
    of churches, 150
    and royalty, 184
    and urbanisation, 180-1, 184
Tredegar *Gnt*, 447
trees, 76, 78-81, 325, 424
Tremadoc *Gwd (Crn)*, 447
Trimdon *Du*, 246
Trimley *Sf*, 232
Trowse *Nf*, 381
trumpet scallop capitals, 313
Trusthorpe *Li*, 343
Tunstall *La*, 28
Tusmore *O*, 332
Twyford *Mx*, 325
Tydd St Giles *Ca*, 348
Tynemouth *TW*, 110

Uffington *Bk*, 297-8
Uley *Gl*, 57, 115
Ulpha Bridge *Cu*, 396
Up Waltham *Sx*, 277, 462, pl. 29
Upminster *Mx*, 158

Upper Poppleton *NY*, 135
Upper Winchendon *BU*, 269
Upton-on-Severn *Wo*, 397
Uttoxeter *St*, 425

Vanbrugh, Sir John, 412
vandalism, 414, 439
vestments, 374-5
villae regales, 131
villages *see* settlement
villas
    and churches, 29
    and monastic sites, 100-1, 102

Wadenhoe *Np*, 272
Wagner, Arthur, 443
Wakefield *WY*, 368, 430
Walberswick *Sf*, 307
Wallingford *O (Brk)*, 168, 252, 335-6
    population, 178
    urban development, 197-8, 201, 202
Walmsgate *Li*, 334
Walpole St Peter *Nf*, 239
Walpole *Sf*, 396
Walsall *St*, 239
Walton *NY*, 267
Walworth *Du*, 246
Warden *Nb*, 118
Wareham *Do*, 131, 168, 183, 204, 220
Warfield *Sr*, 309-10
Warmfield *SY*, 135
Warmington *Np*, 284, 286
Warminster *Wi*, 158
Warnford *Ha*, 248
Warnham *Sx*, 424
Warram-le-Street *NY (YE)*, 302
Warwick, 365, 414-15
water
    curative powers of, 85-6
    religious significance of, 88
waterleaf capitals, 310-12, 315
Watton *Hu*, 134-5
wealth
    reflected in churches, 185, 284
    of clergy, 444
Wearmouth *TW*, 112, 113
weather, effects on church buildings, 329-31, 453
Weaverthorpe *NY (YE)*, 268-9, 302
Wednesbury *St*, 63, 66
Weedon Bec *Np*, 67-8
Weedon Lois *Np*, 67, 261
Well Hall *Li*, 383
wells, 84-91
Wells *So*, 32-3, 34, 88
Welney *Nf*, 346
Wensley *NY*, 112
Wesley, John, 392, 425-6, 450
West Dean *Sx*, 333
West Dereham *Nf*, 248

West Lynn *Nf*, 341
West Ogwell *D*, 248, 384
West Walton *Nf*, 284, 286, 346, 348
West Wykeham *Li*, 332
Westbury *Wi*, 143
Westminster *GLo (Mx)*, 158
Weston *Nf*, 140
wet rot, 318
Wetheringsett *Sf*, 140
Weyhill *Ha*, 69
Wharram Percy *NY*, 149, 152, 164
Wharram-le-Street *NY (YE)*, 165
Whimpwell *Nf*, 343
Whistley *Brk*, 146
Whitby *NY*, 110
Whitchurch *Ha*, 154
Whitchurch *Sa*, 415, 465, pl. 42
Whitchurch *So*, 158
Whitchurch Canonicorum *Do*, 101, 159, 293
'white' churches, 158–9
Whitefield, George, 392
Whitelackington *So*, 241
Whitkirk *WY*, 158
Whitminster *Gl*, 158
Whitney *He*, 340
Whittlesey *Ca*, 346
Whittlington *So*, 356
Whitwick *Le*, 239
Whyle *He*, 332
Wichendon *Bu*, 201
Wickham *Ex*, 325
Widford *O*, 29
Wigan *La*, 389
Wighill *NY*, 267
Wigmore *He*, 306
Wigton *Cu*, 28
Willesdon *Mx*, 323
Willey *Ha*, 63
Willingale *Ex*, 232
wills *and see* bequests, patronage, 140–1
Wilton *NY*, 246
Wilton *Wi*, 204
Wimborne *Do*, 101, 131
Winchcombe, Richard, 307, 310, 351
Winchcombe *Gl*, 353
Winchester *Ha*
　19th century, 389
　churches, 169, 171, 178, 223, 335
　dedications, 26
　excavations, 205, 206
　methodist chapel, 425
　parishes, 337
　population, 178
　reoccupation, 179
　urban development, 182, 192–3, 194
windows, 296–8, 351
Winford *Ch*, 373
Wingfield *Sf*, 364

Winslow *Bu*, 397
Winterbourne Dauntsey *Do*, 325
Winterbourne *Gl*, 365
Winteringham *Li*, 29
Winwick *M (La)*, 230
Winwick *Np*, 56, 268
Wistanstow *Sa*, 317
Wistow *Le*, 384
Withcall *Li*, 135
Withcote *Le*, 382
Withernsea *Hu*, 342
Woburn Sands *Bu*, 396
Wollaton Hall *Nt*, 384
Wollaton *Nt*, 370
wood, decay of, 318
Woodchester *Gl*, 29, 101, 384
Woodchurch *Ch*, 149
Woodchurch *K*, 149
Woodeaton *O*, 68–9
wooden churches, 148–9, 319
wool, 358–9
wool churches, 357–8
Woolpit *Sf*, 370
Worcester, 209, 210, 219, 223
Worthing *Sx*, 449
Wren, Sir Christopher, 384, 407, 409, 412
Wreningham *Nf*, 140
Wrotham *K*, 239
Wroxeter *Sa*, 29, 129, 204
Wulfric of Haselbury, 291
Wulfstan, 79–80, 143, 145, 164, 165
Wycomb *Bu*, 143
Wye *K*, 66, 68
Wyham *Li*, 306

Yapham *Hu*, 135
Yarkhill *He*, 322
Yarwell *Np*, 321
Yatton *So*, 321
Yeavering *Nb*, 57, 75–6, 83
Yetminster *Do*, 158
Yevele, Henry, 307
yew trees, 78–9
York, 180, 205, 218
　19th century, 389
　bridge-chapels, 369
　chantries, 371
　church sites, 152, 171, 209, 220
　closure of churches, 335, 339
　dedications, 26, 176
　Minster, 88, 171
　parishes, 134–5, 372
　population, 178, 376
　Quakers, 399
　reoccupation, 179
'Yorkshire School' of churches, 278–9
Ysbity Cynfyn *Dfd (Crg)*, 82